G-85

שמש ישׂ

A T.

for the Jews.

...... in the Month Tizri   5586.

...erican Independence

Architect's sketch for Buffalo Jewish Center

FROM ARARAT TO SUBURBIA

FROM ARARAT
TO SUBURBIA

THE HISTORY OF THE JEWISH

COMMUNITY OF BUFFALO

BY

Selig Adler

SAMUEL PAUL CAPEN PROFESSOR OF AMERICAN HISTORY
THE UNIVERSITY OF BUFFALO

AND

Thomas E. Connolly

ASSOCIATE PROFESSOR OF ENGLISH
THE UNIVERSITY OF BUFFALO

THE JEWISH PUBLICATION SOCIETY OF AMERICA

PHILADELPHIA : 1960-5721

Number 12 in the Series

מקדש

לזכר נשמת אבי מורי
יוסף גבריאל בן החבר פינחס אדלר
ולכבוד אמי הורתי (תבדל לחיים)
דבורה בת ארי' זאב
מהם ירשתי חיבתי לתורה ולחכמת ישראל

In devoted memory of my father,
JOSEPH G. ADLER,

and in honor of my mother,
DELLA R. ADLER

Contents

Contents

Preface

Early in 1954, the United Jewish Federation of Buffalo appointed a committee to cooperate with the American Jewish Tercentenary Committee. From this association came the desire to chronicle the story of the local Jewish community, and an Historical Research and Publication Committee was appointed to implement the project.

Its first task was to survey and classify the available sources of historical information. Among those who partook in this preliminary task were: Marvin H. Garfinkel; Mrs. Arthur I. Goldberg; Mrs. Irwin H. Jellinek; Mrs. James Patton; Mrs. Carl Pratter; Dr. Robert H. Stern; Judge Cecil B. Wiener and Isadore Wolk.

After the data was classified, the professional staff began to "mine" it. There was a rough division of labor in which one researcher studied manuscripts, another dealt with secondary sources and scoured newspaper files, and a third tracked down obituaries, census reports, vital statistics, and city directories.* Each week the master bibliography expanded as the researchers and lay volunteers unearthed genealogies recorded in

---

* For a detailed discussion of our methodology, see Selig Adler, "The Buffalo Project: Writing the History of a Medium-Sized Community," in Moshe Davis and Isidore S. Meyer (eds.), *The Writing of American Jewish History* (New York, 1957), 158-169.

precious family Bibles and ancient prayer books, yellow-stained organization minutes, and promising interview leads.

At long last the mound of notes was assembled in rough chronological order corresponding to tentative chapter divisions. Then, epoch by epoch, Dr. Adler absorbed and digested the notes, constructing detailed outlines from which Dr. Connolly wrote the preliminary narrative. The final version was completed after we had both revised the draft from the point of view of historical accuracy and readability. A triple focus on Jewish, American, and globe-wide currents is what we sought, but it was frequently difficult to obtain. With multiple interpretations of Judaism the order of the day, we realized the need for a strict neutrality of emotional tone and intellectual vision. We hoped that the collaboration of a Jewish historian and a non-Jewish student of literature might at once provide the essential knowledge of things Jewish, sound historical craftsmanship, and an objectivity fundamental to the treatment of a complex community. By the extent that we have failed in any one or all of these areas, our human foibles may be measured.

To a veritable host of people we are deeply indebted and offer our sincere thanks. Arthur S. Rosichan, formerly Executive Director of the United Jewish Federation of Buffalo, originated this project and induced the Federation to sponsor it. The present Director, Sydney S. Abzug, read parts of the manuscript, corrected us where we had gone astray, and encouraged us in our labors. His assistant, Sol J. Silverman, was also helpful. Mrs. Reta E. Goldstein, secretary to the Director, patiently, tirelessly, and expertly typed the final two drafts of the manuscript. Her intimate knowledge of local affairs spared us many embarrassing slips. We take this opportunity to express our gratitude to Mrs. Elwood G. Becker, who did some of the preliminary typing. Our indexers, Mrs. Arthur I. Goldberg and Mrs. Israel R. Lederman, went far beyond their specific chore to give this book superlative attention in the final stages of its preparation.

To Dr. Elazar Goelman, we are particularly obligated. In his generous and efficient way, he helped us with the glossary and for five years we took full advantage of his majestic knowledge of things Jewish. This welcome aid was continued by Reuben Resnik, Dr. Goelman's successor in the directorship of the Buffalo Bureau of Jewish Education. David M. Kleinstein provided many practical insights which proved helpful in tracing the evolution of the Jewish Center of Buffalo which he directs. Elias R. Jacobs not only opened to us the files of his paper, the *Buffalo Jewish Review*, but also gave us the benefit of his profound grasp of recent happenings. Judge Samuel J. Harris, whose active participation in community affairs goes back to the turn of the present century, frequently clarified our understanding of facts and trends. For half a decade,

Max M. Yellen has watched the development of this project, and the documents preserved in his letter files have thrown light upon important but forgotten events and organizations. From the imaginative mind of Manus Roizen came many valuable suggestions, including the title to this volume.

Those who assisted with the basic research came early to the task and brought with them a contagious spirit of enthusiasm and dedication. Foremost were Dr. Milton Plesur, Assistant Dean of University College of the University of Buffalo, and Miss Renate Kaufmann, currently on the staff of the Hebrew University in Jerusalem, Israel. Faithfully they "mined" the archival material, and skillfully they extracted many nuggets of information. Later came Ridgway McNallie, head of the Local History Section of the Buffalo and Erie County Public Libraries, who tracked down hundreds of puzzling details and without whose help we would have remained unaware of many points which have embellished our story. In the area of the legal world, Leon I. Schulgasser ferreted out many secrets that lay buried in the bulky tomes that line the shelves of the County Clerk's office.

Professor John T. Horton, Chairman of the Department of History and Government at the University of Buffalo, and author of a distinguished work on the history of this region, was ever ready to probe our problems and to offer constructive suggestions. Dr. Wilbur H. Glover, Director of the Buffalo Historical Society, read the typescript and gave us the benefit of his superb experience. The Librarian of the Society, Miss Alice J. Pickup, guided us through the incomparable local material in her custody and perseveringly hunted for relevant items.

Dr. Jacob R. Marcus, Adolph Ochs Professor of American Jewish History at Hebrew Union College and Director of the American Jewish Archives, read the manuscript in an early stage and his unrivalled mastery of the Jewish story in the United States solved many perplexities. Likewise, we are beholden to our editor, Dr. Solomon Grayzel, who made many fertile suggestions. Help also came from Rabbi Isidore S. Meyer of the American Jewish Historical Society, who furnished us with invaluable photostats.

We were fortunate in receiving friendly cooperation and enlightenment on many details from members of the Buffalo rabbinate. This list includes: Dr. Joseph L. Fink, Rabbi Emeritus of Temple Beth Zion; Rabbi Nathan Gaynor of Temple Sinai; Dr. Martin L. Goldberg, Rabbi of Beth Zion; Dr. Isaac Klein of Temple Emanu-El, and Rabbi Alvin M. Marcus of Ahavas Achim-Lubavitz Synagogue.

The many people who led us to hidden records, who translated material from foreign tongues, and who answered countless queries are listed elsewhere in this volume. All of these favors are gratefully acknowledged, but it is fitting that we make special mention of a few who did so much to ease our task. Mr. and Mrs. Isadore Wolk not only put vital manuscripts in our hands, but also digested and translated many of these Yiddish records for us. Judge Cecil B. Wiener * revealed, in innumerable ways, her unmatched understanding of this community. Custodians of congregational archives displayed stoic patience in guiding us through minute books and storage envelopes. Among those who so helped were Miss Lenny Schnitman and Miss Julia Hanneman, the able Temple secretaries of Beth Zion and Beth El.

Two elder statesmen of Buffalo Jewry were most helpful in counselling us along the way. Sol J. Levy drew upon his wisdom and experience to save us from many errors by reading the manuscript as it progressed. Maurice S. Tabor evaluated several chapters and went behind the surface facts of inanimate minutes to reveal the genuine story of recent happenings.

A host of others contributed to this book in ways that defy detailed ennumeration. Our colleague, Dr. Shia Moser, translated many documents and acted as a walking encyclopædia on Hebraica and Judaica. Moses Von, long-time revered Hebrew teacher in our city, and Rabbi Isaac Furman translated Yiddish minute books. Israel Schoenberg, a retired attorney residing in New York, thumbed the files of Yiddish newspapers to extract pertinent information. Mark Uveeler and Aaron Antonovsky left their desks to locate Buffalo items scattered in the Library of the Yivo Institute for Jewish Research. We were welcomed to the Jewish Division of the New York Public Library by its head, Abraham Berger, who helped uncover useful data. Others in New York City who assisted our 1954 search for Buffalo material included Mrs. Sylvia Landres, Miss Esther Togman, and Mrs. Augusta Shure of the Zionist Library and Archives; Arnold Gurin of the Council of Jewish Federations and Welfare Funds; Miss Miriam Ephraim and Rabbi Philip Goodman of the National Jewish Welfare Board, and Harry J. Alderman and Sydney Kellner of the American Jewish Committee.

Had we relied solely upon cold documents, there would have been many serious gaps in our narrative. Fortunately, we found men and women endowed with keen memories whose recollections provided us with unrecorded details and interesting insights. In addition, some friends of the project prepared briefs on families, institutions, and significant incidents. These kindnesses are listed in our bibliography.

---

* Judge Cecil B. Wiener, who did so much to make this study possible, passed away on September 2, 1960, while the book was in the final stages of production.

Some who rendered valuable assistance are no longer living. Herman Wile, whose rich life spanned almost a full century, gave unstintingly of his time and opened the storehouse of his phenomenal memory in cheerful and pleasant conversation. The visit of Henry Stern to Buffalo provided an opportune moment to solve a mystery that had puzzled experts whom we had consulted. Miss Bertha M. Brock prepared a family chart and made available material in her possession that we otherwise would have ignored. Finally, Miss Martha Morris piloted our way through the maze of documents preserved at Federation headquarters.

Our greatest debt is to our wives, Janet and Mary, who performed many chores throughout the preparation of this book, but whose main contribution was a cheerful willingness to share us with this community study.

To all of these persons we are sincerely grateful, for they have made this history possible. Of course, none of our co-workers bears any responsibility for the interpretation of events here presented or for such errors of fact that may have crept into our discourse.

SELIG ADLER
THOMAS E. CONNOLLY

March, 1960.

ACKNOWLEDGMENTS

We are grateful to the following people who supplied valuable and vital information which so greatly enriched our understanding of the evolution of the modern Jewish community of Buffalo: Louis Ablove; Mrs. Sidney M. Abrams; Mrs. Joseph G. Adler; Howard F. Beir; Mrs. Leo A. Beir; Bernard Berkun; Mrs. Jerry Blanke; Samuel Blinkoff; David Block; Mrs. Harry Blum; Emanuel Boasberg, Jr.; Rabbi and Mrs. Harry J. Brevis; Joseph L. Brock; Mrs. Milton M. Bron; Dr. Theodore T. Bronk; Alfred M. Cohen; Mrs. Henry S. Cohen; Philip Cohen; Pierson L. Cohen; Mrs. Irving I. Crouse; Marvin Davis; Charles Dautch; Judge David Diamond; Nathe Dozoretz; Sam Dozoretz; Miss Elizabeth Dribben; Paul Drozen; Harold B. Ehrlich; Joseph Einach; Victor Einach; Michael F. Ellis; Mrs. Stella Engel; Morton H. Etkin; Mrs. Rhea Fass; Justice Fleischmann; Mrs. Maurice Frey; Jacob Fruchtbaum; Max M. Furer; Arnold B. Gardner; Edwin J. Gerstman; Dr. Louis L. Gitin; Louis A. Goldberg; Stuart J. Goldberg; Mrs. Lawrence Golden; Mrs. Morris Greenberg; Mrs. Melvin Greene; Louis Greenstein; Miss Sophie C. Hadida; Judge Philip Halpern; Mrs. Herbert L. Heymann; Mrs. Harold Hirsch; D. Sloan Hurwitz; Mr. and Mrs. Arnold Jacobowitz; Hyman Kahn; Mrs. Mayme Ruben Kahn; Meyer Kahn; Rabbi Abraham J. Karp, Rochester, N.Y.; Edward H. Kavinoky; Rabbi S. Joshua Kohn, Trenton, N.J.; Mrs. Ernst Levi; Dr. and Mrs.

Hyman L. Levin; Dr. S. Albert Levitan; Martin Lewin; Mrs. John J. Maisel; Sidney B. Maisel; Mrs. Hiram Marcus; Mrs. Jonah D. Margulis; Mrs. Roland May; Milton Milstein; Mrs. Leon H. Miller; Isadore Morrison; Nathan Oppenheimer, Jr.; Mrs. Edward M. Plant; Dr. Victor Reinstein; Benjamin D. Reisman; Bernard Resnikoff, Fairlawn, N.J.; Mrs. T. B. Rieger; Samuel Roberts; Joseph M. Roblin; Miss Anne Rodell; Mrs. Laura Rodell; David Rodenberg; Miss Esther Rogers; Leo J. Rosen; Miss Miriam Rosenau; Miss Dinah R. Rosenblatt; Joseph Rothschild; Joseph Sanes; Alfred M. Saperston; Joseph A. Sapowitch; Samuel Sapowitch; Sanford M. Satuloff; Rabbi Elihu Schagrin, Binghamton, N.Y.; Samuel Schanzer; Arthur E. Schulgasser; Mrs. Harry Schwartz; Randolph J. Seidenberg; Mrs. Ivan Shapiro; Meyer Shapiro; Mrs. Mildred Desbecker Shire; Mrs. Jack Siegel; Dr. Charles Simon; Mrs. D. Bernard Simon; Mrs. Joseph M. Singer; Mr. and Mrs. Morris Singer; Harry Slick; Samuel Slick; Dr. Heyman Smolev; Stanley Snyder; Mrs. Morris Steinhorn; Herman H. Strauss; William Sultz; Harrison G. Swados; Paul Swados; Justice Jacob Tick; Mrs. Robert Tobin; Mrs. Joseph Woldman; Dr. Hiram S. Yellen; and Mrs. Joseph Zisser.

We also wish to acknowledge the cooperation of those who are no longer with us: Daniel W. Barmon; Dr. A. Morris Gilden; Mrs. Bertha Shapiro; and Rudolph Warner.

To those men and women whose favors we inadvertently neglected to recall or record, we extend our apologies and our appreciation.

S.A.
T.E.C.

FROM ARARAT TO SUBURBIA

CHAPTER

ONE

"In the Beginning . . ."

EARLY IN 1814, the city of Buffalo was mentioned for the first time in Jewish history. The Reverend Gershom Mendes Seixas, *hazzan* of the historic Shearith Israel Congregation of New York City, addressed the members of his congregation on behalf of the distressed people of Buffalo. The infant nation was at war again with the country from which she had separated after the long and bitter struggle of the Revolution. The British, in the midst of a harsh winter, burned the village of Buffalo on the night of December 30, 1813. The plight of the people was noticed by the Common Council of New York City which asked that a day be set aside by each religious community so that prayers might be offered for the spiritual sustenance, and contributions made for the material relief, of the victims of the British attack. Reverend Seixas responded to the appeal at a Sabbath service. To his congregation, in name if not entirely in fact Spanish-Portuguese, Seixas spoke rather gingerly about the outbreak of hostilities, for some of the wealthy merchants whom he addressed shared the Federalist conviction that it was "Mr. Madison's war." "They [the ruling powers] have Declared War," said the *hazzan* in an apologetic way, "& it is our bounden Duty to act as true & faithful citizens to support, & preserve the honor—the Dignity—& the Independence of the United States of America! That they may bear equal rank, among the Nations of the Earth." [1]

Seixas gradually warmed to his subject, and he spiced his words, in the fashion of the day, with repetitious biblical allusions about the horrors of war. With appropriate Hebrew quotations, which he translated into English so that his congregants might grasp their meaning, he shifted his attention to the plight of the people of Buffalo. "Witness," he said, "the distressed situation of our fellow citizens, on our frontier settlements, in the northern boundaries of our State." He spoke of the sack of houses, blood-stained villages, destitution, lack of shelter, and then he visualized for the city dwellers the ferocious savages of the frontier. Seixas expanded on the "piercing cold" in Buffalo, "which is much more forcibly felt in those parts, than we can be properly sensible of." He ordered special prayers said each weekday at *Minha,* as well as a prayer for the government which was to be recited in English. He also directed that special offerings be made at *Minha* and that those contributing dedicate their gifts "to the relief of the inhabitants of the Northwestern part of this State who are in trouble and are sorely afflicted." [2]

We have no record of how much money was collected and sent to the people of Buffalo, and consequently it is impossible to measure the material effect of this historic Sabbath sermon. The city of Buffalo had, however, entered the stream of Jewish consciousness.

Meanwhile, a Jew had actually been stationed on the Niagara Frontier during the war. Mordecai Myers, Captain of the Thirteenth United States Pennsylvania Infantry, was, so far as is known, the first of his faith to remain for any length of time in this area. Myers was born in the United States in 1776, in Newport, Rhode Island, which, until the occupation of that city by the British during the Revolutionary War, vied with New York City as the chief center of American Jewish life. With the outbreak of the War of 1812, Myers was launched on a rather full military career during which, if he cannot be said to have distinguished himself, he certainly served well in several responsible assignments. He fought at Sackets Harbor in July 1812, and he began his service on the Niagara Frontier as commander of the cantonment at Williamsville, a small village a few miles northeast of Buffalo, from which place he wrote in a jesting vein to Naphtali Phillips on March 31, 1813: "I find I am Indebted to your politeness for the Naconal Advocate it being marked *Kasher* (kosher) induces me to believe you are one of the Proprietors. Please send it again." [3]

He went on to say that he had been in Buffalo in February 1813, and that he enjoyed his present assignment. He made a point of saying that he was treated with respect by both his equals and his "inferiors." He told Phillips of his assignment. He was in charge of the sick and convalescent of three regiments and, in addition, he conducted the courts-martial. He somewhat apologetically discussed his position as commander

of the small garrison. "I have been for two week and am yeate in command of the Cantonment, the most of our troops being at Buffalo and
Black Rock; a greate man once sayed he would rether be the first in a
small viledge then second in rome." [4] No great speller, Myers, but, if the
reader is appalled by this fact, he is directed to consider the spelling of
the greatest hero of the War of 1812, Andrew Jackson, of whom legend
has it that he attempted to express his approval of an action by writing
that it was "oll korrect."

"Marching to Buffalo so frequently was very severe duty," Myers recalled many years later. "I occupied my quarters only one night after
their completion; the remainder of the time I quartered in a tent either
at Buffalo, or at the Cantonment. I often encamped in the street in Buffalo, there being no quarters to be had." [5]

Myers was present at Fort George on July 8, 1813. Later that year, in
November, he was assigned to recruiting duty at French Mills. In the
ensuing battle nearby at Chrysler's Field, on November 11, 1813, Myers
was seriously wounded. He was eventually removed to New York on
February 24, 1814, and he was subsequently returned to service on
March 25, 1814, in time to fight in a skirmish on June 30, 1814.

After the war, Myers went to New York where he continued his activity in Jewish affairs and became a trustee of Shearith Israel. In New York
City he entered politics and joined the Society of Tammany. Not much is
known of his early interest in politics except that he expressed anti-slavery
sentiments. Myers became very active in the Masons and was elected
Grand Master of New York State, but he would not accept the office. In
later life Myers turned seriously to political activity and served in the
New York legislature as a representative from New York City from 1831
to 1834. He also served several terms as Mayor of Schenectady. He died
in 1871 in his ninety-fifth year.

Mordecai Myers married out of the Jewish faith, and his children were
assimilated into the surrounding community and completely lost their
Jewish identity. To facilitate this assimilation, they added their mother's
maiden name to their father's name and the family became known as
Bailey-Myers. After his military service Mordecai Myers played no major
part in the development of Buffalo. [6]

Far more significant in the course of Jewish history was the appearance
on the Niagara Frontier of the second "Israelite" (as the common appellation then went). A little more than a decade after Mordecai Myers left
the Buffalo area, another Mordecai—Mordecai Manuel Noah—attempted
to establish a homeland for the Jews on Grand Island. This "first American
Zionist" was a widely talented Jack of all trades—politician, soldier, playwright, editor, judge, duelist, and, for a brief period, diplomat. He be-

came rabidly conscious of Jewish nationalism during a serious personal crisis, while on a diplomatic mission in Tunis from which he believed that he was removed because he was a Jew. The Tunis incident fanned into fire the smoldering coals of Judaism in Noah's breast, and he formulated the Grand Island scheme. The year 1825 was memorable for Buffalo: the aging General Lafayette visited the village that year; the Erie Canal was opened and linked Buffalo with the chief American port of entry for immigrants; the three Thayers were hanged for hacking and shooting to death their hard-bitten and ironically named creditor, John Love; and Mordecai Manuel Noah decided to found a haven for the Jews on Grand Island in the Niagara River.

Five years earlier Noah had become interested in the Grand Island location and had petitioned the New York State legislature for the island; but the bill, introduced in 1820, never passed. Noah had read in the papers that the state was about to subdivide the island into farm lots. Without benefit, therefore, of state legislative support, Noah began to set his plan in motion. He persuaded a friend, Samuel Leggett of New York City, to buy 2,555 acres on the island. Part of this land was at the head of the island, and the remainder was at the center, opposite Tonawanda at the point where the Erie Canal met the Niagara River. In his early enthusiasm, Noah was not very much concerned with the problem of acquiring the rest of the island. His plan was not quite as chimerical as it has sometimes been portrayed. He had chosen a spot which might, with suitable management, have developed into a rival of Buffalo and Black Rock. Capital was needed here at the terminus to exploit the opportunities offered by the newly opened Erie Canal. The community that Noah envisioned might very well have grown to a great metropolis, given the impetus of Jewish capital and immigrant brawn.

What sort of man was this visionary, Mordecai Noah? Lewis F. Allen, uncle by marriage to Grover Cleveland, has left an account of him. Allen owned a farm on Grand Island where he was a breeder and improver of cattle. It was through his Grand Island landholdings that Allen became interested in Noah of whom he wrote: "I knew Major Noah well. Physically, he was a man of large muscular frame, rotund, with a benignant face and portly bearing. Although a native of the United States, the lineaments of his race were impressed upon his features. . . . He was a Jew, thorough and accomplished." Noah was a New York Tammany man who, because of this association, had many Gentile friends "who adopted him into their political associations." Allen recounts the tale of Noah, the loyal Jew, imbued with the bumptious optimism of the early nineteenth century, telling a Christian missionary that one day the Gentiles would become Jews rather than vice versa.[7]

At the time of Noah's scheme, Grand Island was a fairly wild place. The island is eight miles long and at its broadest is six miles wide. It is a fertile piece of land; but in 1825, it was heavily wooded. The island had been acquired by New York State in 1815 after a treaty with the Seneca Nation which was concluded in Buffalo on September 12, 1813. Squatters soon invaded the place to strip the forests of their lumber. They were a rowdy lot, and by 1819 the state had to intervene to keep order. Eventually it became a sportsman's paradise, rich in game until the isolation of this Eden of hunters and fishers was destroyed by the bridge which in 1935 was financed by the New Deal to connect the island with the mainland.

Noah began publicizing his plan after the failure of the State Legislature to act on the 1820 bill. In the New York City paper the *National Advocate*, of which he was editor, he urged the Grand Island project. Other newspapers supported the plan. Even during the time that the measure was pending in the legislature, the *Niagara Journal* stated that the plan would help the village and would contribute to local prosperity. As plans for the dedication ceremony were reaching a final stage, the Black Rock *Gazette*, although noting with surprise that so few Jews were interested in the venture, hoped to see the Jewish capitalists, merchants, farmers, and mechanics settle in the area. The local newspapers were no doubt prompted not a little by self-interest.

Finally, in late August 1825, Mordecai Manuel Noah arrived in Buffalo "with his robes of office and insignia of rank securely packed." [8] He had designed the elaborate costume himself. He was accompanied by A. B. Seixas of New York who had, since 1820, helped Noah in his scheme. In the village of 2,500 souls, Noah's only friend was Isaac S. Smith, an acquaintance from his Tunis days. He was ready for the dedication ceremonies that were to climax his dream of the establishment of an American Zion. Unfortunately, natural conditions conspired to frustrate even the dedication ceremony. It was impossible to hold the services on Grand Island for the simple reason that at that time it was too hard to cross the river. Instead, the ceremony was held on September 15, 1825, in Saint Paul's Episcopal Church in Buffalo. It is possible that the rector, Addison Searle, had known Noah during the latter's Tunis mission. Unfortunately, no one had bothered to notify the general public of the change in plans, and crowds consequently lined the shore of the Niagara River. The residents of Tonawanda, believing that the ceremony would take place on Grand Island, awaited Noah with a "supply of cakes and ale, pastries and pies and cold meats to give them [the Jews] a good stomach for their undertaking." [9]

Meanwhile, back at St. Paul's Church, the "Masonic and military" procession had begun. The ceremony was described by an eyewitness, John C. Lord, a young school teacher who was to become a lawyer and still later an outstanding Presbyterian divine; it was a strange mixture of Hebrew and Christian rites. Lewis Allen later commented on the unusual quality of this unique ceremony which he described as "this strange and remarkable proceeding, so novel as that of laying a foundation for a Jewish city, with its imposing rites and formula, its regal pomp and Jewish ceremony, in a Christian Episcopal Church, with the aid of its authorized rector." [10]

After the reading of morning prayers, Mordecai Noah addressed the assembly with what he liked to think of as the "Jewish Declaration of Independence." The speech that he delivered that morning was a rough paraphrase of the "Proclamation to the Jews" which, though dated at Buffalo September 15, 1825, and signed by A. B. Seixas as Secretary *pro tem.*, had actually been sent out to world Jewry sometime earlier. It was a pompous speech. Noah began by noticing that it was a good time to act, for peace then prevailed throughout the world. For the oldest of the nations of the world, he hoped that the projected Grand Island plan would provide a "temporary and provisionary" home. Some historians point to this part of his speech as evidence that he had never really given up the Messianic idea of a return to Palestine. The speaker gathered force, and the pomposity increased: "I have deemed it expedient to reorganize the nation under the direction of the Judges." He actually went so far as to appoint himself a Judge of Israel. He proposed to levy taxes on Jews throughout the world for the support of the community. Each Jew was to be taxed three shekels. He invited, in addition to ordinary Jews, the Karaites (schismatic Jews), Samaritans, black Jews, and even the American Indians, whom he naively accepted as the ten lost tribes of Israel, to join the community. Noah's spread-eagle optimism soon knew no limit. He spoke of expanding to the Pacific; he foresaw a "free and happy country" in which religious differences would be tolerated. He visioned the community that he thought he was founding that day as a lure that would invite capital "into the Western District of this State." "Grand Island," he realistically pointed out, "is surrounded by water power, and is admitted to be an eligible spot for the erection of manufactures." Swept on by his own rhetoric, he called upon Jews to exercise a strict neutrality in the war then raging between the Greeks and the Turks. He even undertook to abolish polygamy in those remote Jewish communities of the eastern world where it still existed. In his peroration, Mordecai Noah recommitted his people to the protection of the Lord: "To Him who shelters and protects the whole family of Mankind, the great omnipotent and omnipresent God, do I commit the destinies of Israel, and pray that he may have you all in his safe and holy keeping." [11]

The Buffalo *Emporium* reported the meeting under the caption "Revival of the Jewish Government." The editor stated that it was important to Christians that "the oldest of nations, from whom every nation and religion have their origin," be revived. After the ceremony, the paper reported, the people adjourned for refreshments to the Eagle Tavern, which stood on Main Street near the corner of Court Street. A grand salute of twenty-four guns climaxed the affair while the band played a medley of patriotic airs.[12]

As part of the ceremony, a cornerstone was brought from Cleveland, and Seth Chapin of Buffalo cut the stone and inscribed it:

ARARAT
A City of Refuge for the Jews
Founded by MORDECAI MANUEL NOAH in the Month TIZRI 5586
Sept. 1825 & in the 50th year of American Independence

After this grand beginning, Mordecai Manuel Noah packed his robes of office and left Buffalo a day or so later, having never, to the best of anyone's knowledge, set foot on Grand Island. The whole idea of a city of refuge was denounced and ridiculed by foreign rabbis and by American Jews. The Buffalo *Emporium* subsequently reported that Grand Rabbi Abraham de Cologna of Paris demanded proof of Noah's authority and mission. He sarcastically called for the prophetic text which consigned a marsh in North America as a spot for the "scattered remains of Israel." [13] Eventually Noah turned to Palestine as a place of refuge for the Jews, settled for a much more modest judgeship in New York City, married a wealthy Jewish woman, and forgot about Grand Island in the Niagara River. He died in 1851.

The cornerstone that was never mounted is all that remains of Noah's grand dream. It is now a prize possession of the Buffalo Historical Society, but it had a strange history and journey before it finally came to rest there. Lewis F. Allen, who came to Buffalo a few years after the dedication ceremony, later recalled that he found the stone "leaning against" the foundation of St. Paul's Church near Pearl Street in Buffalo. He next saw the stone in 1834 on the lawn in front of the home of General Peter B. Porter at Black Rock. Because Noah had asked him to see that the stone was cared for, Allen transported it to Grand Island where he had it installed in a shrine so that it could be seen by passengers on passing vessels. Until 1850, it remained enshrined there, but then it was removed to a farm on Grand Island. Later it appeared at the Canadian resort

"Sheen Water." It was finally taken to the Buffalo Historical Society on January 2, 1866, where it now stands as a memorial to one man's wild and fruitless dream.[14]

In 1825, when Mordecai Manuel Noah's Grand Island venture flared into momentary brilliance, Buffalo was a small town of little more than 2,500 people. To this point in its history, the city, although it was the natural metropolis of the surrounding area, had been very slow in developing. At the close of the Revolution only a few squatters, traders, and Seneca Indians lived at the mouth of Buffalo Creek. The Indian titles to this land were gradually extinguished after 1781, but it was only after another fifty years that the wilderness of western New York was subdued. In 1792-93, Robert Morris sold a tract of 3,300,000 acres west of the Genesee River to the Dutch speculators who formed the Holland Land Company, and a short time later the company acquired a tract of land at the mouth of the Buffalo Creek. The Holland Land Company, composed of four Dutch banking houses that had decided to speculate in the young country, had been formed as a stock company in 1795. In the same year Joseph Ellicott, the real founder of Buffalo, joined the company. Two years later, the general agent of the company appointed Ellicott to survey its lands in western New York, and under Ellicott's administrative leadership headquarters were established at Batavia. Townships were laid out, Indian reservations were established, and religious groups were given land in an effort to stimulate settlement in the area. The few early settlers that straggled in were mostly New England Yankees. On the whole, however, the project got off to a slow start principally because settlers could get free land in the Ohio and Mississippi valleys from the Federal Government and were consequently reluctant to buy it from the Holland Land Company.

Finally, on Ellicott's advice, the company decided to found a village on Buffalo Creek, and Ellicott surveyed the site, laid out streets, and cut the first wagon trail in that part of the state. For the little village that was at first called New Amsterdam, Ellicott devised a plan similar to that used in laying out Washington, D.C.[15]

By 1813, Buffalo had a population of only 500, when the British and Indians wiped it off the map during the War of 1812. They burned the town and left only seven buildings standing. The village had to start all over again and was incorporated in 1816, but very little growth occurred until 1820 when the mouth of Buffalo Creek was deepened to permit lake vessels to enter and deposit their cargoes. This improvement unfortunately was not permanent, for the mouth of the creek filled up again and once more lake boats were unable to land. Buffalo, however, remained an isolated outpost until the indefatigable De Witt Clinton pushed his "big ditch" project through a reluctant legislature.

Prior to the opening of the Erie Canal, the Appalachian Mountains blocked immigration to and trade with the nearer northwest. Clinton realized that the Mohawk River, traversing New York State, offered passage through the mountain barrier. His plans for an east-west canal were delayed by the War of 1812, but he eventually won his argument that a water passageway was feasible and that the escarpment of the Niagara could be conquered by the construction of locks. Work on the canal was begun July 4, 1817, and it was completed about eight years later. It was a great day for Buffalo when Governor Clinton arrived in a bedecked, garlanded canal boat to fill a cask with "Erie water" which he was triumphantly to spill into the sea at New York. The canal had cost about seven million dollars, but it was the magic key that opened the Great Lakes region. Buffalo now became a vital transfer point where passengers and goods left the narrow canal boats for the puffing side-wheelers that churned their way westward. Its future as a great city had been assured.

Seven years later, in 1832, Buffalo was incorporated as a city. Its growth was phenomenal, for by the decennial census of 1840 Buffalo had almost tripled her population within ten years. The boom in lake travel continued and Buffalo's population swelled with the same tide of immigration that developed Cleveland, Detroit, and Chicago.

In time Buffalo overcame several other obstacles to its growth. The harbor was protected with an adequate breakwater that kept Buffalo Creek open during the navigation season and made it possible to construct adequate docking facilities. Now the city speedily overcame its erstwhile rival, Black Rock on the Niagara River, which previously had offered better landing facilities for lake vessels. In 1842, as trade grew, Samuel Dart built in Buffalo the first steam-powered grain elevator in the world. Soon the city was to be known for this type of structure designed to hold the cereals that poured in from the fertile western wheat belt.

As the city grew, the Indians who once straggled along its streets gradually disappeared. The Senecas, once the most warlike tribe of the famous Iroquois Confederacy, had been displaced during the American Revolution and had moved to the vicinity of Buffalo Creek. For fifty years they remained in the neighborhood of the white settlement, hunting squirrels with bow-and-arrow within the village limits of Buffalo. Early white settlers had come to know their chiefs, who bore picturesque names—Cornplanter, Ghastly Darkness and Devil's Ramrod. High in the war councils of the Senecas was Farmer's Brother, so called because on a visit to George Washington the First President described himself as a farmer and welcomed his red-skinned guest as a brother. Contact with the white settlers of western New York had not been beneficial to the Indian character and, after they abandoned the warpath, many of them became idle, lotus-eating loafers or else habitual drunkards. Perhaps the best known of the Seneca chiefs was Red Jacket, who derived his name from the red coat given to him by British soldiers. Red Jacket was an orator and politician rather than a warrior. In his last days he headed a pagan faction of the Senecas who stubbornly refused to yield the autonomy of the tribe. His passing was symbolic for, when he died in 1830, his Christian wife and stepchildren buried him with Christian rites in a mission cemetery despite his wishes for pagan interment. Indian influence on the Niagara Frontier did not long survive Red Jacket. By 1844 the last of the land titles had passed to the conquering whites and the Senecas were hustled off to nearby reservations or shipped westward to the wild country of Kansas. By 1850 the redmen had been replaced in Buffalo by 42,261 busy settlers and within the next decade the population was almost to double.

While Buffalo was growing at a phenomenal rate, the first permanent Jewish settlers were sifting into the city. Both Captain Myers and Major Noah had been birds of passage, transients whom either fate or whimsy had brought to the eastern edge of Lake Erie. They could not be considered settlers in any sense of the word. As far as we know, the first permanent * Jewish resident of Buffalo was Lemuel Flersheim, who came to Buffalo about 1835 to teach German in the public schools. His name appeared in the city directory for the first time in 1840, at which time he was living at Campbell's, a boardinghouse located at the foot of Commercial Street.

About the same time, to the confusion of historians of the period, another Flersheim appeared in Buffalo. The second arrival was Lemuel H. Flersheim and, but for the middle initial *H*, the two might have been permanently fused in history. The directory for 1841 listed a Lemuel H. Flersheim as the owner of a clothing store on Commercial Street at Long Wharf. The same directory also lists a Lemuel Flersheim, teacher of languages, and furnishes a clue to the almost simultaneous appearance of two so similarly named persons in a small frontier town. They both resided in 1841 at the same address on Washington Street near Exchange. One is tempted to guess that the two men were cousins who shared quarters to economize.

---

* Rabbi Samson Falk, author of the earliest account of the origin of Buffalo Jewry, once stated that four Jewish settlers lived in Buffalo for a time before Flersheim arrived. He listed their names as Jacob, Dessauer, Gernsheim, and Fox. See Buffalo *Express,* March 21, 1876.

Apart from the fact that he was born in Frankfort, Germany, where Judaism was strong, not very much is known about this first Jewish settler, Flersheim the teacher. He was more active in Jewish affairs than his cousin, and he was said by Rabbi Falk to have been the first Jew in Buffalo.[16] He disappeared from city directories after the middle 1840s, perhaps because he left the city or possibly because he died young. There is no record of any descendants.

Of Lemuel H. Flersheim, we know a great deal more. He was born in England in 1812, according to the census of 1850. By 1860, however, he had become six years younger, for he listed himself in the census for that year as having been born in 1818. His wife, Maria, presumed to be non-Jewish, also grew younger as the years went by, but did not give herself quite the advantage that her husband took for himself. She was listed in the census of 1850 as having been born in Canada in 1823. In 1860, she clipped two years off her age and became a native-born American: she listed herself as having been born in Vermont in 1825.

As the city of Buffalo progressed, so also did Lemuel H. Flersheim. He was engaged in a wide variety of pursuits: in 1838 he was a jeweler; in 1840 a clothier; an auctioneer in 1847; and by 1850 he was in business with his brother, George B. Flersheim. Together they ran Flersheim Brothers as wholesale dealers in fancy goods. By 1855, he had a fancy-goods store at 187 Main Street, and by 1860 he was prosperous.

As far as we know, Solomon Phillips was the next Jew to arrive in Buffalo. He came to Buffalo in 1837 from Hamburg, Germany, and was first employed as a painter but eventually went into the clothing business. In the early days, he lived on Michigan Street south of Eagle. Later he moved in to live with Barnard Lichtenstein, with whom he made hats and caps. Phillips died in March 1867.

Barnard (or Barnett, as he was sometimes called) Lichtenstein was born in Poland in 1804 and arrived in Buffalo in 1838, a year after Phillips. At first Lichtenstein was employed as a cap and hat maker. In 1840 he was listed as living on Washington Street south of Seneca; two years later he resided at Oak Street near Batavia (later called Broadway). In 1847, when he moved to 32 Main Street, Lichtenstein rented rooms to Jewish boarders, among whom was Solomon Phillips. Another Phillips, Samuel Phillips, a peddler, had been living with Lichtenstein since 1842 and moved with him to the new home. It was a common practice to rent rooms, for many of the Jewish men of the early days were either unmarried or had come West without their families. For Lichtenstein, of course, the boarders supplied a welcome addition to his earnings. By 1850, a Samuel Lichtenstein, presumably a brother, had joined Barnard in Buffalo. Lichtenstein also prospered with the growing city. He married, his wife Eliza having been born in America in 1815; their daughter, Sarah, born in 1841, may be presumed to have been the first Jewish child born in Buffalo. There is an unverified family tradition that Sarah Lichtenstein eventually married a man named Jacob Ehrlich, with whom she lived in Buffalo until her premature death in 1865. By 1860, Lichtenstein, with his wife and two eldest daughters to help him by sewing, owned a thriving clothing store; and in the census of that year he valued his personal property at $4,000. Buffalo was not to be Barnard Lichtenstein's final resting place, however; in 1874, for unknown reasons, he left for Waupun, Wisconsin.

By 1847, Jews had settled in Buffalo in sufficient numbers to constitute a recognizable group. Before the establishment of a congregation, we know that there were services in private homes, presumably on the High Holidays and on *Jahrzeits*.[17] The names of some of these early Jewish residents are known. By 1847, Samuel Altman operated a dry-goods store at 278 Main Street. Joseph E. Strass, born in Bavaria, was living in Buffalo in 1843 and was still living in 1876. Michael W. Noah, who was to play an important part in the early community, was here in 1847.

Two more men with almost identical names cause additional confusion in the early history of the Jews in Buffalo. Both were here as early as 1844; one was born in 1806, the other in 1813. Elias J. Bernheimer was born in Baden, Germany. According to the *Commercial Advertiser* directory of 1850, Elias J. Bernheimer lived at 51 Ellicott Street. By 1860, he had a domestic fancy-goods store and had married a wife, Caroline, who had been born in Bavaria. He eventually owned the first retail clothing store in Buffalo; it was located at Main and Tonawanda Streets.

Elias Bernheimer (without *J*), according to the same source, owned a fancy-store at 362 Main Street in 1850 and resided at 163 Pearl Street. His wife's name was Judith. The men may well have been cousins, because of the Jewish practice of naming children for deceased grandparents. Moreover, the Bernheimers originally (1844) kept a fancy-dry-goods store together at 302 Main Street.

Mark Moritz, another early Jewish resident of Buffalo, was born in the Prussian province of Posen. In 1850, he owned a store at 162 Main Street and resided at 60 Ellicott Street. He left the city in 1876 to live in San Francisco.

All these people are known to have been Jews. But, because of the similarity of Jewish and German names, it is impossible just from looking at the Buffalo city directory of 1840 to know whether Raphael Mayer, a liquor dealer on Main Street; Jacob Myer, a clerk; Judah Bliss, a physician on Seneca Street; Henry Rubins, a tailor on North Division and Elm Streets; Michael Solomon, a laborer; Samuel Wolf, a "ratcatcher," and many others, were Gentiles with names commonly Jewish, or Jews who found it convenient in a society overwhelmingly Gentile to assimilate and disassociate themselves from Jewish society. Many factors would work for the second possibility. One should recall the comparative scarcity of Jewish women on the Niagara Frontier, the common practice of intermarriage, plus the fact that many Jews who came to America were marginal Jews to begin with.[18] Certain it is that many were quickly assimilated. At best the picture is clouded: some Gentile-sounding names belonged to ardent Jews, and an Israel Israels might very well have been a simon-pure Yankee.

These were the first Jews in Buffalo; others were soon to come. The development of the railroads and the completion of the Erie Canal both contributed to the growth of the city by stimulating immigration from older parts of the state and New England. The Canal, of course, had been completed and, shortly after its opening in 1825, canal boats were drawn slowly along the earthen banks by horses that plodded along day and night at an average speed of four miles an hour. Buffalo soon became a natural "jumping off" place for those who were going to the West. Today, the pace of the tow horses seems incredibly slow, for even with around-the-clock travel the boats could average at best only eighty-five miles in twenty-four hours. However, slow as it may seem to men living in the Jet Age, the leisurely canal journey once was the easiest route West for immigrants determined to abandon over-crowded New York City. By 1847, the Buffalo German newspaper *Die Weltbürger* noted that canal boats landing in Buffalo were loaded with German newcomers.[19] By mid-century, the sidewalks of the Queen City were literally packed with the new arrivals and their crudely bundled baggage. As these immigrants were soon to discover, not all of the suffering and hardship involved in building up a new country was confined to the cutting edge of the frontier.

Soon the popularity of canal travel was jeopardized by the coming of the railroads, and immigrants who could afford it went West on the steam cars. The year 1828 had witnessed the first beginnings of railroad transportation in the United States, with the establishment of the Baltimore and Ohio Company. Eight years later the railroad connected Buffalo and Niagara Falls, and then the rails were laid eastward, stretching at first only as far as the nearby village of Attica. But the iron web grew rapidly and by 1842 it was possible to go most of the way from either Boston or New York to Lake Erie by rail. These trips, in the beginning, were painfully slow, and passengers had to make many changes as they were ferried across rivers and routed on a string of local lines that connected the towns en route. Heading westward, most immigrants went up the Hudson to Albany by steamboat or crossed New England to Albany by railroad. The trip to Buffalo could then be completed in seven stages: Albany to Schenectady; Schenectady to Utica; Utica to Syracuse; Syracuse to Auburn; Auburn to Rochester; Rochester to Attica; and thence to Buffalo—a frightening trip to us today, but it meant, in 1842, that Buffalo and the Atlantic seaboard had been joined by a new and speedier method of transportation. Thus the railroads gave the Niagara Frontier as big a boost as the epoch-making construction of the Erie Canal. In 1847, it took twenty-two hours to go by train from Buffalo to the banks of the Hudson at Albany. A decade later there were through connections from Buffalo to New York. This was made possible by the establishment of the first trunk line in the United States, the Erie Railroad. Although the main line of the Erie bypassed Buffalo, the Buffalo and Attica Railroad connected with it at Hornellsville to link the two largest cities of the Empire State. In that same year, 1852, the Buffalo and State Line Railroad was linked to Cleveland. In the following year the New York Central Railroad established through connections with no change from Buffalo to Albany, and by "lightning express" one could travel from New York to Buffalo in fifteen hours! This was pretty good time, for now the same trip takes at least eight and usually nine hours by rail. By the middle of the 1850s, Buffalo's function as a railroad center already foreshadowed its eventual position as the second most important rail junction in the country.[20]

By railroad and by canal the people poured into Buffalo. Some of them remained only long enough to rest and gather supplies before they trekked farther west. Others, however, remained and among those who chose to stay were the founders of the Jewish community. Their motives for selecting this city in which to settle will remain forever buried with them. Today we can merely speculate on the reasons they had for putting down roots.

Most of the early nineteenth-century Jewish immigrants to the United States were either German Jews, including many from the province of Posen and those from German-speaking countries such as Austria and Bohemia, or they were East-European Jews from nearer parts of the Russian-Jewish Pale who had early felt the expanding German enlightenment as it pressed eastward. These early Jewish immigrants were, therefore, naturally attracted to those settlements in the New World in which there already existed strong German-Christian communities.

The Germans had arrived in Buffalo quite early. A market grocer, Samuel Helm, the first German settler in Buffalo, arrived in 1809. A little later John Kuecherer arrived. "Water John," as he came to be known, sold "Erie Water" from house to house to burghers still unacquainted with the convenience of a kitchen faucet. The first brewery was established in 1827 and the first Evangelical Church four years later. A directory was published in 1832, the year of the incorporation of Buffalo as a city, and at that time it carried about seventy German names. The Irish also soon began pouring in, and settled on the south side of the city. Many of the Germans were Roman Catholic as were most of the Irish. The Roman Catholic Diocese of Buffalo was established under Bishop John Timon on April 23, 1847, just a few days before the first synagogue was founded. The German population continued to grow. By 1855, Buffalo, with a total population of 74,000, was almost half German.[21] The Germans at first were not very anxious to assimilate culturally with their non-German Buffalo neighbors. They felt that their own older German culture was much superior to the rough frontier society that they found in the New World, and quite probably the German Jews who joined them in Buffalo shared this feeling. The German population of Buffalo, consequently, built up its own community. By 1850, there were three German newspapers in the city. The Germans formed their own literary societies, musical associations, and soon flexed their political muscles in organizing a political clique. They sought their physical exercise in German Turnvereins. They mingled socially with each other in their beer gardens, playing pinochle and dominoes in their leisure hours. They made and ate good German food—cheeses, pumpernickel bread; and, of course, they brewed and drank German-style beer. All of these factors must have appealed to the kind of Jew who first came to Buffalo, for they were Jews who, in general, looked to Berlin as the intellectual and cultural capital of the world.

The city that these Jews found had grown tremendously since Mordecai Manuel Noah had made his abortive journey to the Niagara Frontier. In 1825, when he arrived, the village was composed of a mere 2,500 people. Twenty-three years later, in 1848, approximately 40,000 people inhabited the city. Thomas B. Cutting, in the preface to the city directory for 1848-49, called the growth "an increase without parallel in the history of cities." Within a quarter of a century Main Street had changed from a rude street lined with stumps and rail fences to an avenue "bedecked with magnificent stores, filled with every variety and delicacy that can please the fancy or tempt the palate." [22] The chief source of all this prosperity was, of course, commerce with the West.

It would be interesting to learn something about the city on the eve of the foundation of the first synagogue in 1847. The main boundaries of the city had been established about a decade earlier: they were North,

High, and Jefferson Streets on the north and east of the city and the Buffalo Creek and the Niagara River on the south and west.

We have the benefit of an outsider's impressions of Buffalo at about this time in the form of a book written by an English author and traveller who toured America in the hard scrabble years following the Panic of 1837. He was James Silk Buckingham (1786-1855) who, after having edited a newspaper in India, returned to England to sit in Parliament. At fifty-one he retired from politics, crossed the rough Atlantic, and set out on a four-year tour of America. Buckingham visited the Niagara Frontier and spent ten days in Buffalo. He recorded that commerce in the Lake Erie port had increased tremendously since 1830 and that within the preceding seven years sail and steam tonnage coming into the city had more than quadrupled. In the same proportion, wrote Buckingham, bushels of wheat shipped into and from Buffalo had increased, while at the same time the local production of flour had multiplied sixfold. The English visitor attributed this boom mostly to the Erie Canal and he predicted that the whole area would continue to grow tremendously because of the easy water passage to the west by way of the Lakes.

When Buckingham visited Buffalo, Main Street was only two miles long; but he noted that it was 120 feet wide and was lined with lawns and railings and was intersected with many attractive little squares. Most of the people of the bustling city, he wrote, were engaged in trade and commerce. Its citizens lived in good comfort; but, in this relatively new settlement, he found "none of the style and fashion so apparent in the equipages and dresses of New York, Philadelphia, and Baltimore." [23] Even among persons of means he noted less pretension and less attention paid to matters of etiquette than in the coastal cities. He was, consequently, not surprised to find a group of Seneca Indians living just outside of Buffalo.

Buckingham paid close attention to the religious life of the community, but, unfortunately for our purposes, he made no mention of the handful of Jews who had already reached the city. Buckingham found many notices of religious revivals, a fact not very surprising, for western New York was often scorched in those days by the intense fire-and-brimstone evangelists of the period. The Britisher was keen enough to sense the tensions in matters religious. With a veteran newspaperman's insight he recorded that the Protestants feared the Catholic penetration, and he recorded that the Catholics were building a new cathedral that would soon put the Protestants to shame.[24]

A gauge to the prosperity of the city was the establishment of a Board of Trade in 1844. It met daily for the purpose of fostering marine commerce. In the following year, the Board of Trade constructed an imposing building, the Merchants' Exchange, which stood, says Professor John T. Horton, "quite literally at the commercial junction of East and West." [25] All the space in the building was taken by tenants before it was dedicated.

The social pulse of the city may be felt from the list of societies and organizations in the city. In 1847, Buffalo had an orphan asylum and a city hospital for the care of the distressed, a "Sacred Music Society" and many churches dedicated to the spiritual welfare of its inhabitants, and for a variety of sacred and profane causes it also boasted a German Young Men's Association, a Temperance and Anti-Slavery Society, a St. Andrew's Society, the Friendly Sons of St. Patrick as well as the Sons of Erin, an I. O. O. F., a Young Men's Association, and the Order of the Rechabites.

The railroad depot stood at Exchange Street where it was to remain until 1929. The city by that time also had a good supply of lighting gas; and, although Samuel Morse had sent the first message by wire only three years earlier, Buffalo in 1847 actually had two telegraph companies operating in the city.

Elbridge G. Spaulding was mayor of Buffalo in 1847, and Bill Hall, at the other end of the political ladder, was the "City Scavenger." The city was politically divided into five wards, and police, constables, and city watchmen guarded the manners, morals, and property of the community composed of 40,521 people.

A good system of private and public schools was developing at this time in Buffalo. The growth of public education was, oddly enough, spurred by the Panic of 1837, for a depression-ridden populace demanded free education for their children. Oliver G. Steele, Buffalo's first effective Superintendent of City Schools, made the system entirely free of tuition fees. It was Steele, too, who kept the schools largely non-sectarian with perhaps only a little Bible-reading each day. Good private schools had actually been established before the public schools were founded and they grew along with the developing public school system. The Buffalo Female Seminary (at present the Buffalo Seminary) was founded in 1851. The first central high school in the area was established in Buffalo the very next year. The natural effect of a good school system is the gradual wearing away of class and ethnic barriers. Professor Horton has commented on this effect of the growth of public education: "In their yards and classrooms the children of the poor and the children of the rich rubbed elbows, scuffled, learnt and played together." [26] Public education contributed greatly to the cultural assimilation of the Jews. As the school system developed, Jews more and more confined their congregational schools solely to the teaching of religion. In turn, of course, this meant that as their religious zeal declined in the secular American environment,

Jews tended to neglect their own schools. They had come to Buffalo at a time when Bishop John J. Hughes of New York was demanding public support for Roman Catholic parochial education; but, although Jews had tried their own parochial education in the old seaboard settlements, they quickly abandoned it, for they seemed irresistibly drawn to the public schools.

This was Buffalo at the time that the first synagogue was established. The fashionable and the wealthy lived at Niagara Square. Millard Fillmore, destined to be President of the United States from 1850 to 1853, lived at Niagara Square. His neighbors were professional men—doctors and lawyers. Throughout Buffalo there were many clusters of pleasant houses; but, as Buckingham pointed out, there was a lack of style. The Irish lived in the first ward in the area of lower Main Street; the Germans in the fourth ward, located east of Main Street between Genesee and Eagle Streets.[27] In the early years there was no distinctly Jewish neighborhood. In general the newly-arrived Jews were poor and lived where they could afford to. Many of them resided in the lower part of town beneath The Terrace on such streets as Deak, Exchange, and Commercial, where Asiatic cholera struck frequently, and particularly hard in 1849. As Horton reports, "It struck hardest below The Terrace, at the Hydraulics and in the wards where the immigrant population dwelt." [28]

In the 1850s, the retail trade was conducted on lower Main Street. The stores usually occupied the front parts of brick houses that were two, three, or four stories high. Merchants did not specialize in their stores, and one was likely to find groceries, dry goods, crockery, glassware, hardware, school books and writing material, drugs, brandy, and rum, all on sale in the same mart.[29]

By 1860, Genesee Street was lined with neat, German homes, with second-story windows filled with bright red geranium plants in the summer sunshine. Horse cars began to carry passengers along the streets in that year. By that time Buffalo had wide and regular streets. They were well lighted at night with 2,700 gas lamps and the city could be proud of its reputation of having some of the best lighted, paved, and watered avenues in the world. There was a fine sewage system, and 400 water hydrants lined the forty-seven miles of paved streets in the city. By the onset of the Civil War, Buffalo was the tenth city in population in the United States.

Meanwhile, as the city advanced and developed, the nation engaged in another war, and another Jewish resident of Buffalo became involved in it. On February 6, 1847, Marcus Flintrowitz enlisted at Buffalo for service in the Mexican War, serving in the First U. S. Artillery Regiment, under the command of Lt. Col. Benjamin K. Pierce. With his regiment he fought at Cerro Gordo on April 18, 1847. Later he was with General Winfield Scott's army as it advanced from Vera Cruz to Mexico City. While in Captain Magruder's company, Flintrowitz lost his left leg by cannon ball at the Battle of Contreras in Mexico.[30] This battle was fought on August 19-20, 1847, when the Americans battled for the heights of Contreras which commanded part of the National Highway to Mexico City. Flintrowitz was discharged from the army in Mexico City on November 28, 1847, on a certificate of pension. He was one of fifty-eight known Jewish veterans of this war and was so proud of his military career that he asked in his will that his tombstone be marked with a record of that service. On the marker in the old Temple Beth Zion cemetery at Pine Hill may be read the legend: "Marcus Flintrowitz a veteran soldier of the Mexican War."

It is not clear when Flintrowitz came to Buffalo. He was born in the ancient Jewish community of Cracow in Galicia, a part of Poland then under Austrian rule. We know what he looked like: at the time of his enlistment he was described as having hazel eyes, brown hair, and a dark complexion. He was a small man, only five feet, five and three-quarter inches tall. When he enlisted, he was a barber, but after the war he made no effort to resume that trade. One wonders if the loss of the leg prompted him to abandon barbering in favor of a trade he could pursue while seated. For whatever reason, shortly after the war he became a cigar maker.

When Flintrowitz married his first wife is not known. On June 17, 1882, when his second wife applied for a widow's pension, Simon and Henry Weil swore before J. E. Ewell, Deputy Clerk of the Superior Court, that they had known the late Marcus Flintrowitz for the past thirty-three years and that his first wife (unnamed) had died of cholera in Buffalo in 1852. Whether or not there were children born of this marriage is unknown. On October 13, 1854, Flintrowitz married Anna Schwartz before Henry B. Burt, Justice of the Peace, in Buffalo. Anna Schwartz Flintrowitz had been born in Pilsen, Bohemia, in 1831. Nothing is known about her life in the United States before she married Marcus Flintrowitz.[31]

Shortly after he returned to Buffalo from the war, on September 30, 1848, Flintrowitz bought property. In 1866, he applied for a pension, received $800 from the United States Government, and with this money bought property at 792 Genesee Street. Here he established the store where he made and sold cigars. Part of the family was still living at that address in 1956. The state census of 1870 valued his assets at $1,000 in real and $300 in personal property.

Marcus Flintrowitz died in Buffalo on April 9, 1882. His widow, then fifty-one years of age, and seven children survived him. The widow

Flintrowitz applied on May 1, 1882, for a pension, and in her application, which she signed with her mark, she named three of those seven surviving children. They were Bertha, David, and Moritz, born in 1867, 1869, and 1874 respectively. One other child was recognized in an unpleasant way in her father's will. When Marcus Flintrowitz died, he left everything to his widow, provided she remain a widow, and in the will he cut off his daughter Rosa "who did not behave herself as a good child ought to do." [32] Evidently Rosa married out of the faith, for her married name was Mathews. Anna Schwartz Flintrowitz died in Buffalo on December 20, 1908. The direct descendants of Marcus Flintrowitz continued to live in Buffalo, the family name over the years having been shortened to Flinter.

These were the first Jews in Buffalo. In the seventy years between the War of 1812 and the death of Marcus Flintrowitz, the city grew and prospered, and along with the city the Jewish community also prospered and grew. Of these early Jewish inhabitants, the three outstanding ones were at some time in their lives military men: Captain Mordecai Myers, Major Mordecai M. Noah, and Private Marcus Flintrowitz. The first two, the officers, were merely passing figures in the parade of people who created and developed the city of Buffalo. The private stayed and put down roots.

CHAPTER

TWO

Roots and Branches

URING THE NINETEENTH CENTURY, Jews poured into America in two main streams. The great bulk of German Jews came from 1820 to 1880. Although some came much earlier, the major part of the Russian or East-European Jewish flood poured into cities on the eastern seaboard after 1880. The German-Jewish infllux had its beginnings in conditions that sprang up in Europe after the defeat of Napoleon in 1815. Although the Jews had escaped from ghettos in Europe and had greatly improved their social position during the time of the French Revolution and the re-gime of Napoleon, a wave of nationalistic reaction broke out with the restoration of peace. This anti-Jewish reaction threatened to return the people of the ghetto to their medieval social position. In the German states, Jews were unpopular first because some of them had financed the French invaders who marched eastward as liberators. Furthermore, the Jews in general had prospered during the long war, and, when their neighbors saw them enjoying their new wealth and their recently acquired liberty, they felt a strong urge to thrust them back where they had been kept until the cry of "Liberty, Equality, Fraternity" sparked the explosion that permitted them to escape from their ghettos. In post-Napoleonic Germany, divided as it then was into petty kingdoms, duchies, and other political subdivisions, the anti-Jewish antagonism grew rapidly. Some of these Graustark-sized monarchies tried to solve their problems by simply banishing Jews entirely.

Conditions in the relatively large kingdom of Bavaria were particularly bad, and consequently the number of Jewish immigrants from that country was exceptionally high during the nineteenth century. Even before the actual defeat of Napoleon, a Bavarian law, promulgated on June 10, 1813, severely limited the occupations open to Jews. The neighboring kingdom of Württemberg soon passed a similar law. After 1815, the laws against Jews were increased in severity. In 1828, in Bavaria, a law was passed that prohibited the sale or exchange of property by Jews unless it had been owned or farmed by the owner for three years. This law often automatically drove the Jews out of business or, if they attempted to evade it, landed them in prison.[1]

The more aggressive and, generally, the younger Jews, many of whom had been born and had grown up in the quarter of a century of ephemeral freedom that the Napoleonic wars had brought, refused to accept the new *apartheid*. They longed instead to continue the economic, social and religious freedoms that they had learned to enjoy. Emigration was the only way out. The German-Jewish emigrants of this period were usually young, unwed, and often possessed only a rudimentary Hebrew education. For the most part, they were the sons (and less frequently the daughters) of poor people: storekeepers in petty towns, horse and cattle traders, and other groups that came from rural rather than urban centers. Generally speaking, the more conservative Jews remained in Europe, whereas some of those that set out for America were casual in the observance of their religion. In a larger sense, however, the majority were devoted to the Jewish tradition and would in time try to Americanize their heritage rather than abandon it. Those who came usually were men willing to make bold changes in religious behavior. Hence, although Reform Judaism was born in Germany, its boldest experiments were to be made on this side of the Atlantic.

The first Jews to reach America sometimes selected a certain city quite arbitrarily, and their enthusiastic letters back to their relatives in Europe set up a chain reaction, as it were; Jew after Jew struggled to escape to the freedom that America seemed to promise. By 1839, at about the time that Jews were beginning to straggle into Buffalo, approximately 15,000 Bavarian Jews were already in the United States.[2] As word drifted back to the old country, reading clubs dedicated to learning more about America sprang up in the little villages in southern Germany. Professor Marcus Lee Hansen, an outstanding authority on the history of American immigration, has suggested that in these hidebound German villages, adventurous Jews received a vicarious pleasure in reading about the success of their brethren elsewhere. Those who could leave were stimulated to action; those who, because of age, infirmity, or poverty, could not leave were able to escape, even if only momentarily, from the gloom of their surroundings when they read of the happiness of their friends or relatives who had found a home in America, the fabulous Land of Gold.[3] Meanwhile, the economic depression that swept through Europe in the 1830s stimulated the emigration of Jew and Gentile alike.

In addition to the economic and social sanctions that prompted emigration, physical violence provided another motive. Groups of young Germans began to flex their muscles and give vent to their nationalistic feelings by physically attacking Jews in the streets of such cities as Bamberg and Frankfort. The medieval cry of "HEP, HEP," was heard once more in the streets. In Baden and Bavaria anti-Jewish sentiment was worse than in other parts of Germany. In the Bavarian Diet it was blatantly said: "The Jews must clear out and go to America." In southern and western Germany especially, the intelligent elders and leaders of Jewish communities began to advise the young to flee to America "to escape endless slavery and oppression." [4]

The first adventurous souls made the trip to America under the most trying conditions imaginable. Gradually, however, a pattern developed. Jews from south and southwestern Germany gathered in the cities of Mainz and Meiningen. From those cities they made their way to the seacoast, to the ports of Rotterdam in Holland, Le Havre in France, and Hamburg on the German coast. En route they stopped, frequently in vain, to buy kosher food. On the sea journey ahead of them and in America many of them would learn how difficult it was to follow the dietary restrictions prescribed by Jewish law. Many of them, too, knowing the lack of religious atmosphere in America, took religious articles with them. Today in Jewish museums in New York City and in Cincinnati, many of these articles are preserved as historic reminders of a stubborn faith that survived, at least, a weary journey to a rugged new country. One can see, for example, a *megillah,* ancient travel-size circumcision sets, and pairs of phylacteries. Toward the middle of the nineteenth century in Germany, many pocket-sized prayer books were printed especially for voyagers about to set out for America. One published in Fürth in 1842 was subtitled, "For the travellers on land and those who cross the sea, for those who set out for the American Country." [5] Many of these books contained special prayers for travellers who braved the stormy Atlantic, then often six-weeks wide.

Other travellers were troubled about different matters. Some tried to bring to the new country a *mohel,* the religious functionary trained to circumcise male infants. Occasionally groups would hire and bring with them a *hazzan-shohet,* a functionary trained to chant the prayers and to slaughter fowl and cattle in the ritual manner.

The stream of voyagers grew stronger. Jews from other areas of western Europe joined the German Jews from Baden in the search for a new homeland. After 1840 a great many Bohemian Jews came to America. Among them, incidentally, was Joseph Brandeis whose son, Louis D. Brandeis, later became the famous Associate Justice of the United States Supreme Court. In 1844, a group of Czech Jews arrived in the United States. Although the Jews actually from Germany never quite accepted the Bohemian, Czech, or Posen Jews as "German" Jews, these people were, in outlook and cultural aspirations, West-European, and they helped to magnify the Germanic overtone of American-Jewish society that so definitely marked the period prior to 1880. Jews from southern Germany usually went to Strasbourg first, then in the French province of Alsace. There they boarded empty cotton wagons for the trip which took them to Paris and then to the seaport of Le Havre where they took ship. Jews from northern and central Germany generally followed the river routes along the Elbe or the Weser to Hamburg and Bremen.[6]

Even though many of them had undergone great hardships in reaching the ports, the most severe part of their journey was yet to come. There were interminable delays in the port cities themselves. In those days there were no regularly scheduled ocean trips. In the 1840s Sir Samuel Cunard began to schedule regular sailings to America, but even then only a few very expensive packet vessels made regularly scheduled crossings. Most of the Jews who came to America in the first half of the nineteenth century made the voyage on small sailing vessels of 300 to 400 tons displacement. "The two months' passage," says Professor Hansen, "gave the Atlantic an opportunity to reveal all its moods." [7] The trip was horrible, especially for the immigrants who usually were in the steerage section of the ship. To get there one descended by a ladder through a hole in the deck. For some this descent marked the last they were to see of sunlight, for the death rate was shocking. Often one-third of the adults died either en route, or within three years after landing in a new land, because they failed to adjust to the strange climate and the hardships of a rugged country. Most of the immigrants left Europe in the spring and arrived in the New World in the midst of the summer heat.[8]

Obviously it was difficult, during such a rough journey, to observe Jewish dietary laws. This fact resulted in the first serious break with tradition for many of these German Jews. Even if one desired to observe and had brought along, somehow or other, a supply of food, the mere act of preparing and eating food was extremely difficult. For example, the steerage passengers had to line up in order to cook their meals at the common stoves. Ultimately, when these people reached America, they experienced no relief from this problem of finding and preparing kosher food. This was especially true of those who left the settled communities and pushed westward.

Despite the hardship of travel, the stream of Jewish travellers to America continued to grow. It was not only the Jews, however, who looked to America as a solution for whatever ailed them in the old country. The immigration figures for all groups climbed amazingly in the years following the War of 1812: from 1820 to 1830 only 151,824 people from all countries came to America. From then on the number of new-comers rose rapidly. From 1830 to 1840 a total of 599,125 new people arrived. In the next decade 1,713,257 more immigrants reached America, and in the 1850s the wave of immigrants crested at 2,598,214 people.[9] By 1847, on the eve of the year of revolutions, 50,000 Jews of Germanic origin were already in the "land of the free."

In 1848, a rash of revolutions broke out all over Europe, and there was a momentary interruption of the immigration procession. For a time, the people hoped that the rule of the tyrant would be relaxed. Especially in the states of Germany, where the revolt threatened to wax strong, the oppressed people hoped that relief had come; but in Bavaria conditions were actually far worse after the uprising than before. In Würzburg, Jewish assemblages were suppressed and discouraged. There a young Jew was fined for accepting the presidency of a charitable institution without prior consent of the city authorities. The march to liberty in the New World began again and with renewed vigor.[10]

Meanwhile, the movement of Jews from eastern Europe had begun. After 1845, the Jews from Russian Poland started to move toward America and freedom. Contrary to his promise that Jews would not be taken into the army until they had been granted equal political and social rights, Czar Nicholas I conscripted many young Jews. To avoid this one-sided draft, many Jews fled from Poland. In addition to the urge to skip military service, many Jews left the Russian Pale for economic reasons, for there the economic restrictions against Jewry that flourished in Germany existed in more severe form. Quite a few of these Jews from Russian Poland, locally called "Hoch-Polish," settled in Buffalo in the early days of the community. The origin of the peculiar nickname "Hoch-Polish" is uncertain. It was, perhaps, a term of contempt coined to distinguish those who came from upper Poland from those from lower Poland or Galicia which went to Austria after the division of Poland.[11] Other eastern Jews came from the province of Suwalki in Lithuania; then as now a Russian captive state. Suwalki was hit hard by famine in the late 1850s, and, although official passports were hard to come by, many Jews managed to evade the law in order to escape over the nearby Russo-Prussian border and make their way to German seaports.

This steady flow of Jews from eastern Europe was much stronger than the earlier historians recognized. "The common opinion prevailing," wrote the late Professor Mark Wischnitzer, "that immigration of greater numbers of eastern European Jews into the United States began with 1870 or even 1881 has to be corrected in the light of recent research." [12] Actually this immigration started before 1850. It was so strong that by 1869 an eastern refugee problem troubled New York City. By 1870, committees in Europe were formed to help those from eastern Europe who wished to migrate. It is consequently not so surprising as it was once supposed to be for the Polish Jews to outnumber the Germans in Buffalo's first congregation. In 1868, a cholera epidemic followed by famine in the *Gubernas* of Kovno and Suwalki accelerated the movement of eastern Europeans. From 1869 to 1880, at least 30,000 East-European Jews migrated to America. Even prior to the tidal wave of the 1880s the East-European Jews formed the majority in many communities, including New York City.[13]

From the very beginning in America there were marked differences between the Polish, or eastern, Jews and those from Germany. The initial causes of the well-known prejudice against Polish Jews were principally social and cultural; later religious differences kept the two groups apart. The first distinguishing mark of the Polish Jew was the Yiddish that he spoke. Although the German Jews until the eighteenth-century Enlightenment had spoken Yiddish too, they had discarded it during and after the French Revolution. When the two groups met in America, the German Jews looked down on their Yiddish-speaking fellow-Americans as uncultured. Furthermore, the Polish Jews, at least along the eastern seaboard, often took jobs that the German Jews had already outgrown. They were, consequently, looked down upon as social inferiors by the others in an age when occupation often determined social station. Apart from occupying jobs on lower social strata, the recently arrived Polish Jews unpleasantly reminded the German Jews of a pre-emancipation status that they wished to forget.[14] Finally, the eastern Europeans did not mix easily into the close-knit clannish communities. Consequently, they established only the flimsiest ties with the already-established Jewish congregations in such cities as New York and Philadelphia. The Civil War produced a further rift between these two groups, for it tended to Americanize the German Jew who then felt that an even greater gap existed between him and the East-European Jew, who tended to remain more isolated from American culture. After 1865, rapid industrialization, the advent of Reform Judaism, and enhanced economic and social position had created a vast gulf between the older generation of Jewish immigrants who were largely German by origin or choice and the newly arrived eastern European "Greenhorns." Not until the second third of the twentieth century was this gulf to be entirely closed.

The country to which these early Jewish immigrants came was rapidly growing. The westward expansion, despite the crudities of living that it imposed upon many who were to suffer greatly in a hostile environment, actually helped many Jews get started in the new country. As the frontiersman drew farther and farther away from the eastern center of supplies, the demand for goods gave rise to a new economic class, the peddlers. At first, pioneers who had been Indian traders catered to the demands of the western frontier-dwellers. Then came the Yankee peddlers, sharp-witted young men who moved out of New England and peddled their way westward until they were forced to return for more goods. The Yankee salesmen with packs or tin trunks strapped on their backs soon became welcome sights in the small hamlets and on the lonely farms in the wilderness. As the roads and canals were built, they penetrated deeper and deeper into the rugged West. These peddlers specialized in shoes, dry goods, tin wear, cloth, clocks, firearms, hats, and salt. They served not only an economic need but they also made a considerable contribution to the social growth of the West.[15] These visits of salesmen were a welcome interruption to the tedium of frontier existence. They brought news as well as badly needed goods to communities cut off from civilization, for the very crude means of communication gave the pioneers very little access to the outside world. The arrival of the ubiquitous peddler, who often was put up for the night by the family he served, was a relief from the monotony of hacking out a living in a stubborn land.

As the frontier moved westward, it became more and more difficult for the peddler alone to serve the people. Regional warehouses or distributing centers sprang up. By 1850, these storehouses had spread throughout the west and the south. They then became the sources from which the peddlers drew their supplies. Gradually these peddlers regularized their rounds and settled down to the routines of custom salesmen. As the years passed the warehouses developed into the modern wholesale houses and jobbers that still dot the cities of the modern West and Midwest.

When the early Jews arrived in America, the peddling business had already been started. Before the Jews could found communities or build synagogues west of the Atlantic seaboard, they had to find some way of simple survival; they had to support themselves and their budding families. Because most of them were poor, with little or no capital at hand, a great many drifted into the only occupation in which they could get a start with modest means. Consequently a disproportionate number of Jews became peddlers. By the 1840s, as Jews stepped ashore, their relatives or *Landsleute* advised them to get a basket and peddle. Most of the early German Jews landed at New York, Philadelphia, and Baltimore, by chance the chief eastern distributing points where peddlers picked up their goods before striking out for the hinterland.[16] In these cities there was a constant demand for peddlers. Farm-to-farm selling was the quickest way to become self-supporting for the poor immigrant, especially for the unskilled who had no craft. Within a few days after landing, an immigrant, with the backing of relatives, could be out on the road with his stock in trade strapped to his back. For a modest investment a family could quickly put cousin Jacob on a pay-as-you-go basis. The common name for the stock that the peddlers carried in the 1840s was "Yankee notions," which in Jewish jargon became "Kuttle Muttle." Sometimes, instead of carrying a selection of articles, the peddlers specialized. In Chicago, one synagogue was familiarly called the "India Rubber Shul" because most of its members dealt in suspenders.[17]

Rabbi Isaac M. Wise, the organizer of Reform Judaism in America, in his description of conditions in America when he arrived in 1846, classified the various kinds of peddlers then operating. First were the basket peddlers whom he declared to be dumb and homeless. A step higher on the peddling ladder were the trunk carriers. These men could at least speak a little broken English. In the "upper middle class" of the peddling hierarchy were the pack carriers. These were the more successful peddlers who, according to Rabbi Wise, often walked the roads with bundles weighing from 100 to 150 pounds on their backs. Many a time the bundle weighed as much as the poor wretch who carried it. The aristocracy of the peddling world contained two groups. The "wagon barons" were those fortunate enough to afford a horse and wagon. Some of them arrived from the old country affluent enough to afford this state; others worked their way slowly up to this lofty position. At the peak of the peddling group were the "jewelry counts." They carried watches and other valuable trinkets in small trunks and catered to a restricted clientele. Ultimately, but really already outside the peddler class, were the "store princes." [18] Many of the German Jews started out as foot peddlers, later acquired a horse and wagon, and eventually settled in some friendly town to open a small store. Out of these modest beginnings emerged some of the greatest department stores in the United States.

Conditions that faced the Jewish immigrant who took to peddling are reflected in the diary kept by Abraham Kohn in the 1840s as he peddled in New England. Kohn, an immigrant from the religious stronghold of Fürth in Bavaria, eventually settled in Chicago, where he was to play an important part in the founding of the Jewish community in that city. At the time that he kept his diary, however, he was a lonely Jewish lad in a strange country. "O misguided fools," he wrote in his diary, generalizing his own hard experiences and including all like himself who had been enticed from a familiar way of life to come to the land of promise, "led astray by avarice and cupidity! You have left your friends and acquaintances, your relatives and your parents, your homeland and your fatherland, your language and your customs, your faith and your religion—only to sell your wares in the wild places of America, in isolated farmhouses and tiny hamlets." He was sensitive, also, to the lot of the wives who had been left behind to live almost as widows while their husbands roamed the countryside. He speaks of the attraction to strange women that tempted these wandering men. He complains of the cold and the hardships of the road.

Although Kohn was more intellectually curious than the average German Jew who found himself in a similar state, and although he was very much attached to his religion, he was nevertheless forced to violate the Sabbath, to peddle on holidays, and to eat *trefa*. For a time he even went to a Christian church on Sunday out of sheer boredom. The Lord alone knows the grief that must have been in his heart as he was forced to peddle on the *Shabbes*. "Better that I be baptized at once," he lamented in his diary, "forswear the God of Israel, and go to Hell." But he survived and kept his faith intact. Where he could, he said his daily prayers, sometimes in open fields, sometimes as he trudged along the road carrying from fifty to eighty pounds of goods in the pack on his back. Sometimes he irrationally lashed out against the country that had received him because his trade kept him on the road over the Sabbath. "This is religious liberty in America," he complained as he bemoaned his forced violation of the Torah, the pentateuchal law.[19]

Peddling affected the life of the Jewish population of Buffalo, and the men of the city were often long absent from their families as they plied their wares along the Niagara Frontier. In fact, one Palestinian messenger, commissioned to collect funds for some institution in the Holy Land, records his frustration at finding that he couldn't collect in Buffalo during the winter because the men were always away. He was forced to wait until Passover to gather his donations from the men who returned for the festival.[20] All in all, however, Jewish peddlers out of Buffalo seemed to have fared rather well. From the census records for 1860 it is possible to trace the personal fortunes of many Jewish peddlers. Of the obvious Jews in the census for 1860, the first is Aaron Bernstein, born in Poland about 1826. Bernstein, whose wife was also born in Poland, declared himself to be worth $500. He lived in a neighborhood predominantly English and German, but there were also some other Jews in the vicinity. Another peddler was Moses Friedman, who was forty-eight years old in 1860 and had an estate of $200. He and his wife and three of his four children had been born in Poland. Among the avant-garde of the East-European Jews in Buffalo was the peddler Louis Gumbinsky who in 1860 was worth $400. Gumbinsky, born in Poland in 1820, fathered many children in Buffalo, one of whom—his daughter Elizabeth—married so young that a few days after her marriage she was seen skipping rope in the streets.[21] Abraham Haas, a German Jew, was listed as worth only $100 in the 1860 census. His daughter Sarah (1853-1918) was one of the first Jewish girls to enter public-school teaching and played an active part in the later life of the Jewish community. David Levi, born in Poland, seems to have been the most successful of the dry-goods peddlers. He listed his assets in 1860 as $700 in real estate and $100 in personal property. Another Levi also seems to have done well at peddling. Isaac Levi, born in Poland, although he listed himself as worth only $100, was able, in those days of cheap labor, to afford the luxury of a domestic servant. The fact that his two children were working may have accounted for his ability to afford household help. The last peddler mentioned in the 1860 census was a third Levi—Moses, born in Prussia about 1836. Though his wife was only seventeen years old in 1860, they already had two children. This Levi was worth $100.

Two things are revealed by an analysis of this 1860 state census. By the time a Buffalo peddler amassed an estate worth about $1,000 he no longer was a peddler. It was a hard type of work and as soon as one could get out of it he did. The second fact revealed by this census is that, at least locally, the German Jews had by that time graduated from the peddling trade. By the time of the Civil War most of the Jewish peddlers in Buffalo had been born in Poland.[22]

The clothing business attracted many Jews in the United States. For some of them it was a natural move, after they had made a success of peddling, to shift to a clothing store. Many other Jews had been engaged in Europe in the second-hand clothing business before coming to the United States. Prior to the Napoleonic Wars very little ready-made clothing existed. The very nature of the styles before 1815—the silks, the satins, the velvets, the ruffles, and the knee breeches—made it almost mandatory that clothing be made to order for each individual. During the Napoleonic Wars, however, the style of men's clothing changed; long pants were introduced, and men's suits roughly resembled the modern business suit. James Monroe, President of the United States from 1817 to 1825, was the last occupant of the White House to wear knee breeches. Naturally, as the clothing became simpler, it was possible to standardize and pre-cut certain garments.

The ready-to-wear clothing business began in America just as the great onrush of German Jews arrived. The Jews, however, did not start the business. It seems to have started in New Bedford, Massachusetts, the center of the whaling fleet. Whalemen who might be at sea for several years required a supply of ready-made clothing to take along with them. Later a demand for ready-made clothing came from the West where there were few women to sew for the men and where the men were too busy with the problems of subduing the wilderness to bother with sewing for themselves.[23] Still, the industry grew slowly. The census for 1830 listed only 3,780 clothiers and 14,988 tailors to meet the needs of 23,000,000 people. Later, New York became the center of the clothing industry, and with the cheap help of the immigrant groups other eastern cities—Philadelphia and Baltimore in particular—also contributed to the growth of the industry. In 1846, Elias Howe invented the sewing machine, and five years later, Isaac Singer perfected it. These contributions spurred great changes in the clothing industry. Soon factories were turning out much more clothing than was produced by piece-work in private homes. By 1860, the clothing industry in the United States employed 120,539 people and earned annually more than $20,000,000.[24]

It was the Civil War, however, that gave the real impetus to large-scale production of clothing. Union army uniforms were produced by the thousands and during the course of the war clothiers learned the secret of sizing. They discovered that amongst every thousand men a certain proportion would fall into each size group. For the individual recruit these early crude statistical calculations may not always have had a striking sartorial effect, but for meeting the necessity of making blue uniforms fast it was a happy solution. By the end of the war manufacturers had expanded their facilities to the point where they could produce clothing rapidly for veterans so anxious to don "civies" that they would not wait for a made-to-order suit. These firms then began to send salesmen out on the road in order to capitalize upon the postwar demand.

Some Jews had entered the clothing business as early as the 1830s. At first they made crude, cheap clothing but they gradually increased the quality of their product as the industry grew. In the early days the work was usually done in the rear of the store from which it was sold with practically all members of the family helping in the business. It was this feature of the trade that proved attractive to energetic immigrants willing to work unbelievably long hours in order to get ahead. Moreover, a small clothing establishment was a perfect arrangement for absorbing the constant flow of friends, relatives, and *Landsleute* coming to these shores. The newcomers could pitch in with the work immediately and, while their "greenness" was rubbing off, they could earn their keep. Furthermore, for an industrious but poor family, the clothing business was attractive, for it was possible in it to make a large profit on a relatively small investment of capital. While the husband was out peddling coats, vests, and pants in the country, many a wife and her children plied the needle at home. These Jewish immigrants, without knowing it, were making a contribution to the spread of social democracy in America. Before the advent of ready-made clothing, one could tell at a glance whether a person was rich or poor. As ready-made clothing became cheaper and more readily obtainable, surface differences between classes were more difficult to discern. By 1880, the men's clothing industry was almost entirely in the hands of German Jews.

In Buffalo, the earliest Jewish clothiers manufactured only for the retail trade and were located either on lower Main Street or from numbers 1 to 10 Commercial Street. They made and sold clothing in the same store. In the infancy of the clothing business complete suits were rarely manufactured. The early tailors made pants, coats, and vests separately and the customer selected the combination that suited his taste, or more likely the ensemble that fitted him. In addition the same tailor often made shirts, collars, and underwear. Many Jews who appear from the records to have been clothing manufacturers were actually merchant tailors who sold at retail in the front of the shop what they and their families made in the living quarters in the rear. Later, as the individual store grew in volume of business, the clothier began to sell to other stores and thereby became involved in wholesale transactions. Although clothing was relatively never as important in Buffalo as it was in Rochester, where in 1850 one-half of the Jews in that city made their living by tailoring, there was a clothing boom in Buffalo.[25] Eventually, however, Buffalo lost out as a clothing center, for it could not compete with the cheaper clothing houses of New York City nor with firms in Rochester that catered to the better trade.[26]

About 1855, the Warner family, destined to be famous throughout the Jewish history of the city, came to Buffalo. The Warners, like the Keisers with whom they intermarried, came from Bisenz (now Bzenec) in Moravia, near the Austrian border. Bisenz was then, as it is now, a small town of only a few thousand inhabitants, but in the nineteenth century it contained a vigorous and well-organized Jewish community. The language spoken there was German, for although it certainly was not in Germany and not even in Austria proper, men of Bisenz considered themselves German in culture and had been influenced relatively early by the Enlightenment as it spread eastward in Europe.

The father of this family was Lasaar Warner, a prosperous wine dealer. His eldest son, Jacob, was born in 1809, and the other three boys, Leopold, Joseph and John, were born in 1817, 1822, and 1827 respectively. We do not know for certain whether all the brothers migrated together. We do know, however, that Joseph came to the United States in 1848, after a month's passage aboard the sailing ship "Isaac Newton." It is possible that he was accompanied by his brothers. By mid-century, at least three of the Warners had settled in Utica, New York.

A few years later they followed the canal route westward to Buffalo and after some experience as furriers set themselves up as wholesale clothiers. Somewhat later they were joined by their oldest brother, Jacob. In the 1860s the family was located at 43-45 Main Street where they maintained a factory and a store. Later, they built an imposing structure, The Warner Block, at the corner of The Terrace and Pearl Street.

Jacob Warner, whose wife was named Rosina, was the father of Edward Warner, who came to Buffalo about 1869 from Raab, Moravia. From the scanty sources available it seems that Edward left Europe after his parents. It was this Edward Warner, however, who was the father of Eugene (1876-1943), a man destined to play so large a part in the later life of Buffalo Jewry.

Prior to the rise to community leadership of Eugene Warner it was his great-uncles who were dominant influences in the Jewish community. The most important of this group from a Jewish point of view was Leopold, whose wife Lena had been born in Austria in 1824. By 1860 the couple had been blessed with eight children, of whom the younger six had been born in America. Leopold and his youngest brother, John, operated the clothing firm of Warner & Brothers, and during part of the life of the concern Joseph and Jacob seem to have been in the business. By the time of the Civil War the firm had a capital investment of $10,000 and the company was producing 1,800 coats, 3,000 pants, 18,000 vests, and 4,000 sets of underwear per year.

Meanwhile, Joseph Warner left the city for a time, but he returned to Buffalo in the 1870s and turned his attention to real estate investments. He and his wife, Charlotte, were the parents of three children. A son, Edward H. Warner (1872-1932), became a prominent Buffalo insurance man and was highly regarded as an expert in the field. A daughter, Mrs. Clara Warner Schwabe, still survived in 1959, residing in Charleston, West Virginia.

Eventually all the Warner brothers save John dropped out of the business. In time the firm originally established by Leopold Warner followed the pattern of so many other Buffalo clothing houses: it flourished for about five decades, but eventually went out of business after the turn of the twentieth century as trade passed into the hands of rival concerns in other cities.[27]

Another early Jewish clothier, Henry Brock, was also destined to father a large and influential Buffalo family. Born in 1818, Brock came to the United States at the age of twenty-six. He first settled in Dunkirk and was so influential in that little city that when he left in 1853 to settle in Buffalo, the community presented him with a Torah and a testimonial that is still a prized possession of the family. Brock was a big, powerful man who was known to thump strangers between the shoulder blades with his gold-headed cane and then to bewilder his victims with the bland remark: "Sorry, I thought you were my friend." High-handed, hot-tempered and somewhat autocratic in demeanor, Henry Brock played a lively part in the business and religious life of the young community. After his son-in-law, Magnus Wiener, came to Buffalo, he was associated with him in the clothing concern of Brock & Wiener, located at 167 Main Street and later at the clothing mart center on Pearl Street. Much of Brock's energy went into communal affairs; in fact, at one time he held office in the Orthodox Beth El after he had helped Beth Zion turn to Reform Judaism. This apparent inconsistency, not unusual in American-Jewish life, did not disturb Brock's remarkable aplomb.[28]

It is not necessary to burden the story with the names of numerous other Buffalo Jewish clothiers whose importance was ephemeral. Several of these men, however, merit individual consideration. Isaac Ellis, one of the early East-European settlers, founded the family of that name that is still important in community affairs. Ellis, like his descendants, was hearty and well-met. A familiar figure on the streets of Buffalo until the 1890s, one finds his name in innumerable clubs and associations, Jewish and non-Jewish. Then there was Emanuel Newman, a clothier, whose two sons became barbers—a strange occupation for Jews at a time when Negroes, rather than Italians, were knights of the scissors.

Although no traces of his family survive in Buffalo, Jonas Gitsky, for many years the stormy petrel of synagogue life, was one of the earliest successful clothing merchants. With his brothers, James N. and Samuel, Jonas Gitsky operated two establishments on lower Main Street. By 1860 the firm had seventy hands working in the shops and was grossing over thirty thousand dollars a year. Because of his personal wealth, which seems to have been considerable for the day, Jonas Gitsky was in a position to dictate to the early Jewish community and apparently he enjoyed the power that he so often used in synagogue meetings. If the early records are trustworthy, there never was a peaceful "shul" meeting when Jonas chose to honor the assemblage with his imposing presence.

The history of an infant community is often at the mercy of an accident. Thus we have sketchy knowledge of another early Buffalo clothier, Daniel Silberberg, because he ordered amulets made to celebrate the births of his sons. It is possible, but not certain, that this Silberberg family was related to the Silberbergs of Niagara Falls who founded the Jewish community in the Cataract City.

In contrast to the Silberbergs who early disappear from the Buffalo records, were the Altmans who have flourished here for over a century. This family reversed a general trend by starting out in Buffalo, moving eastward to Rochester, and then returning during the hard times that followed the Panic of 1857. Stemming originally from Württemberg, Abraham and Julius Altman founded the Buffalo clothing firm of A. Altman & Company.[29] In the sixties they were engaged in wholesale business at 214-216 Main Street and, two decades later, the firm occupied the Altman Block at Seneca and Ellicott. In time, Abraham branched out into banking, but the other Altmans were the largest producers of men's clothing in the city until the business followed the way of so many other Buffalo concerns of its type.

Samuel Desbecker, the last of the important pioneer clothiers to be accounted for, also founded a family that was to become noteworthy in the annals of Buffalo Jewry. We will meet the name many times in narrating the history of the community.

These were the early purveyors of ready-made clothing to the Buffalo market. Some of them rose from the lowly status of peddler to the rank of business tycoon in a relatively brief time. Undoubtedly there were some non-Jews who made or sold clothing, but for reasons already considered, the industry in the city seems largely to have been in Jewish hands. This concentration explains the fact that prior to 1860 a majority of all Buffalo Jews earned their living in clothing establishments. The pattern was not to change until several years after Lincoln had saved the Union.

As these Jewish merchants prospered, they gradually moved away from their places of business to reside in residential districts. By 1860, this tendency had scattered them throughout the first five wards of the city and in wards seven and nine. In typical cases, they moved into neighborhoods that were predominantly German and in other instances Irish. Although they lived in mixed neighborhoods, families anxious for Jewish company tended to settle in clusters and frequently, for the sake of economy, two families shared the same house. As newcomers they penetrated parts of the city then being vacated by older immigrant groups who could then afford to push into more select areas.

A demographic breakdown of ninety clearly identifiable Jewish families in Buffalo in 1860 reveals some pertinent facts. First of all, a slight majority apparently came from countries west of the Russian borderlands. Second, of the people included in the count a startling 44% were minors, but, of course in the days before the prolongation of infancy, children often proved an economic blessing. Like other immigrants of the period, Jews were fecund. Third, the adult females in Buffalo at that time seem to have slightly outnumbered the males. Here there seems to have been no acute shortage of marriageable females as there was in other Jewish communities where immigrants often complained of the lack of wives, and then either intermarried or else sent back to Europe for mates.[30]

A further analysis of the 1860 state census discloses that the clothing and tailoring trades employed at least twenty-one adult Jews, while some of the twelve clerks in the city probably also worked in these industries. Twelve men were listed as peddlers, whereas six had risen to the lofty position of merchants. The balance of the working Jewish population was scattered among various trades: there were two barbers and two day laborers, a cigar maker, a shoemaker, a glazier, a cooper, and a printer. There were also two physicians in the city before the Civil War who were probably Jewish and who may have been related. Joseph S. Goldberger (later shortened to Goldberg) was born in 1816 in Prussia and lived for many years in Holland, the native country of his wife. After he came to Buffalo he practiced in several locations in that part of town which housed the greater number of Jews. The other doctor, Isaac S. Goldberger, had his home and office nearby. Neither doctor seems to have remained long in the city and neither was ever affiliated with any Jewish congregation.

It can be safely said that most of the early Buffalo Jews prospered or appreciably improved their lots in the city. Some of them fared very well. Barnard Lichtenstein, of the earliest pioneers, was modestly wealthy by 1860. Mary Noah, widow of another firstcomer, Michael W. Noah, was among the wealthiest members of the Buffalo Jewish community. The census of 1860 evaluated her property at $15,000 in real estate plus $3,000 in personal property. In this listing, Mrs. Noah stood second only to Lemuel H. Flersheim whose fortune was approximated at $30,000. Flersheim, however, was either an apostate or else had entirely divorced himself from the community, for the existing records fail to show any participation in Jewish social, cultural, or religious life. Generally speaking, by 1860 the most prosperous families were those who had come here first. First come, first served!

CHAPTER

THREE

A Community Emerges

WHEN THE FIRST JEWISH COMMUNITIES began to form in America, the religious customs of the newcomers were often changed by the strange environment into which they were transplanted. In Europe, the *kehillah* and the synagogue reflected the life and needs of the members. By and large, the European-Jewish communities were stable groups with relatively little population fluctuation. Early Jewish *kehillot* in America, however, were in a constant state of flux. New immigrants were always arriving, and the older members, as they prospered or saw greater opportunities elsewhere, often moved on to greener pastures.

In the very earliest communities, of course, Jews instinctively tried to transplant onto American soil the way of life that they had known in Europe. They attempted merely to transport across the Atlantic the same cultural patterns, institutions, and organizations that they had known in the small villages or big cities of the Old World. But the American latitudinarian milieu differed markedly from the strictly controlled environment that they had left. As a result, many modifications of the European stereotype were necessary in America. Inevitably these modifications produced conflicts both in the group and in the individual. Although those who tended to cling most tenaciously to the old order did so in the name of Orthodoxy, the ancient talmudic maxim that said,

"The law of the land is the law to be obeyed," led to a gradual evolvement of an American-Jewish way of life that reflected the new democratic values.[1] The urge to become an integral part of this new world was very strong. In Europe, where Jews had suffered almost incessant persecutions, a tradition of a Jewish *imperium in imperio* had developed, and Jews consequently experienced in their ghettos a total cultural and even a partial civil autonomy that made them unenthusiastic about the State. In America, however, things were different. "Nothing in all history," says Henry Steele Commager, "had ever succeeded like America, and every American knew it." [2] Newcomers embraced the state, its laws and institutions with enthusiasm and even gusto. Professor Hansen has noted of all immigrant groups: "At the threshold of the New World these Europeans faced the unseen with high faith in themselves and in the country they were joining. They were Americans before they landed." [3] This desire for identification and status led to many religious and cultural changes, for the newcomers usually wanted to separate themselves as much as they conveniently could from anything that would differentiate them from other Americans. Furthermore, when they built their synagogues and founded their social organizations they were generally met by indifference rather than by antagonism on the part of the Gentiles, and the very lack of a hostile atmosphere, which might have driven them to a spirited defense of traditional ways, helped to contribute to these Americanizing changes.

In America, a new concept of the nature and role of the rabbi evolved. In eastern Europe, he had been a teacher, a scholar and a judge. In America, as in Germany, he became a Jewish version of a Protestant minister. He had once played an important part in the lives of the members of his congregation but he eventually became, in this country, one who performed functions: he conducted marriages and funerals; he participated in civic ceremonies as the unofficial ambassador of the Jews to the general community. Furthermore, in nineteenth-century America, especially inland from the coastal metropolitan areas, trained and educated rabbis were extremely rare. For many years there were only a handful of fully ordained rabbis in the United States. Buffalo, for example, was without a rabbi trained specifically for his calling until the advent of Rabbi Samson Falk in 1866. Even after that date, traditionalists had to be content until the twentieth century with a functionary who was a combination of cantor, reader, preacher and whatever else he could be induced to do. In addition, unlike the communities of Europe, where the literate and educated Jewish laymen assisted the rabbi, or carried on Jewish life without a professional clergy, American communities had relatively few good lay leaders who were well grounded in Jewish lore. In the land where the gospel of wealth was beginning to be preached, money and not knowledge gradually came to be the deciding factor in the charismatic selection of leadership in the synagogue.

Changes soon became evident in the organization of the synagogue and of the community. In monarchial Europe, democratic participation was unheard of. The *parnas* ruled autocratically. He brooked little interference from the people. In America, however, the *parnas* was soon replaced by the president of the congregation, and a popularly elected board shared with him the responsibility of running the synagogue. Moreover, changes were absorbed from the all-pervading Protestant atmosphere in which the early synagogues existed. The assignment of pews to individual families, and even the sale of pews, although probably practiced to some extent in Germany, was influenced in American synagogues by the similar Protestant practices. A German-Jewish custom that was also followed by some American Protestants was the attempt to force conformity and to enforce attendance through fines (as the Protestants expressed it, to "withdraw the hand of fellowship" from those who were lax).[4] But with the spread of individualism and the lack of public sanction to control private religious behavior in the United States, these fines and other ways of enforcing practice became less and less effective. Eventually, they disappeared entirely.

The American concept of the separation of Church and State made its influence felt in the relationship between the individual and the synagogue. In Europe there had been no such complete division between spiritual and temporal powers. It was difficult, for example, in Germany or in Hungary where the law regulated even Jewish worship, for a Jew to go counter to the synagogue elders. Non-conformity meant at least social ostracism and possibly even coercion from the state authorities. In the United States, however, where conformity was not enforceable, the richer Jews were often the most lax in their observance, and yet the synagogues depended upon their contributions. This "leadership from the periphery," as it was later to be termed, cropped up in America quite early. If the synagogues tried to enforce observance of Jewish law, they lost the patronage of these wealthy members. They soon had to abandon the European practice of attempting to control the religious conduct of their members, for without the state law or the bulk of Jewish opinion to support them they were powerless.

Once in America, the Jewish immigrant invariably faced a reality that caused him, to a greater or lesser extent, to change his ingrained ways of life. If he pushed West to the cutting edge of the frontier, his trials were principally physical. He suffered along with the other settlers the hardships of severe winters and blistering summers. He was exposed to Indian raids and other hazards of the wilderness. He was usually alone, or else was accompanied by only a handful of other Jewish settlers. In the city, his trials were essentially social. He was a member of a socially "out" group whose dress, food habits, social customs and speech temporarily set him apart from his new compatriots. In pre-Civil War days, the Jews, though not persecuted, were certainly out of the main stream of polite society. Socially, at least, they lived as second-class citizens. It did not take these newcomers long to realize that in America money meant power and social status. In their efforts to accumulate money many Jews would work on the Sabbath and thereby break a cardinal precept of their faith. In Europe, fewer temptations of this sort had existed, for the centuries of Sabbath observance had rigidly fixed the habit; the village economy in which most of them lived made allowance for no Saturday work, and to break the Sabbath was to invite loss of social status.

These nineteenth-century Jews, perhaps picking up the influence of the frontier's anti-intellectualism, had no great regard for either secular or religious learning. Even had they been eager for it, the scarcity of Jewish scholars in America would have militated against any serious pursuit of learning among them. Many, of course, had no time for education in their hectic scramble up the social heap toward wealth and recognition.

The paucity of Jewish teachers was, of course, directly related to the scarcity of good ministers, for one of the principal tasks of the minister was to teach. The people as a whole were not deeply interested in religious education. They asked for very little, and they got what they asked for. Furthermore, the average person was more interested in taking advantage of the public schools than in fostering secular education under Jewish sponsorship, for he saw in the public school system an opportunity for his children to become Americanized rapidly. Those Jewish ministers who actually attempted to teach were usually miserably paid, and more often than not they were primarily trained and hired to perform other duties in addition to teaching. They were usually more concerned with their duties as preacher, or cantor, or slaughterer, and as a rule the teaching came off second best. In addition, because of their poor salaries and working conditions, the turnover of teachers was tragically high. A further impediment to the development of a strong parochial system was the fact that there was no set curriculum in these early schools and the subjects that were taught were not oriented to American conditions.

As the burgeoning public school system attracted more and more Jewish children, the problems of even a minimal Jewish education became more complicated. If the Hebrew schools were held on weekdays after public school, the children were usually too tired to absorb the extra instruction. In addition, most of the immigrant groups could not afford to forgo the use of the child either in the home or in the store during these after-school hours. After the Civil War most American congregations tried to conduct Hebrew education on Sunday mornings, but even this compromise was never wholly successful, for the intrusion on the publicly accepted day of rest was resented by many children.

From its earliest days, the members of the Buffalo community faced the problem of a Hebrew education for their offspring. As early as May 7, 1848, the board of the newly formed Synagogue Beth El ordered the minister, Reverend Ansell, to instruct the children in Hebrew on Sundays in the morning hours and after the close of the public schools on Wednesday afternoons. Soon the school was in session three times a week, and a system was worked out whereby parents paid special fees to cover the cost of teaching their children. Apparently the young congregation tried to secure the services of an efficient teacher. In April 1849, the board of Beth El wrote to one of its officers, Mr. H. M. Eder, who chanced to be in New York, and instructed him to look for a teacher. The board indicated to him that it would pay as much as $200 per year, provided the applicant would also agree to collect the synagogue dues. Poor Mr. Eder, who had made the wearisome trip east to buy goods for his store, made the rounds from synagogue to synagogue, and somewhere in the big city he heard of a Mr. Fould who arrived in Buffalo early in the summer of 1849. The following fall a special assessment for the salary of the teacher was laid on the congregation, and thirty-two members pledged amounts varying from five to twenty dollars, payable quarterly in advance, for the cause of Jewish education in Buffalo.[5]

Despite these good beginnings, the school did not run smoothly. Mr. Ansell's forte was not teaching, and he thought of himself primarily as a cantor. Until he left the congregation, he was assisted in conducting the school by Mr. Fould who also acted as sexton, collector and *shohet*, and there is no evidence to indicate which task his employers considered the most important. Hence, Beth El's minute books for the 1850s are filled with complaints about the religious school. In addition to the frequent turnover of ministers, teachers and sextons, each newly-arrived functionary was a law unto himself about method and curriculum. It is known that a man named Marks, who was teaching Buffalo children in December 1856, (besides acting as *hazzan* and *shohet*) used the *siddur* and the Pentateuch to train the children in reading and simple Hebrew writing. It is possible, also, that he taught them some Jewish customs, ceremonies and history.[6] By 1856, the minute books of Beth El contain the first mention of the establishment of what has since become a standard congregational committee, the school committee, to select a teacher and supervise his work.[7] These, good as they were, were but the first feeble steps in the right direction. In the country as a whole, Jewish education was for the most part far from well organized or well conducted in the nineteenth century. In matters of Hebrew culture, the nineteenth century produced a succession of "lost generations."

All these factors contributed to a laxity in religious observance. "As religious practice declined," Dr. Hyman B. Grinstein has noted, "there was no longer a feeling of nearness to God in the intimate acts of daily life, but the ideal of belief in God was not abandoned."[8] Generally speaking, these Jews retained parts of their ancient faith that New World conditions allowed them to preserve. With many, of course, it was merely the outward shell of the religion that remained, and most of them began by shedding inconvenient observances. They wanted to be Jews without the restrictions of the Jewish law. Actually, this informal relinquishment of old practices was the beginning of the Reform movement which crystallized later to adjust the old faith to the conditions of the new environment. Time after time papers such as *The Jewish Messenger* of New York called for a religious revival. "We enjoy every liberty," moralized that paper on April 15, 1858, "we are in possession of every privilege delegated to man; let it teach us to be faithful to God." Again in that same paper, Jews were warned that posterity would deal hard with men who destroyed the underpinnings of Jewish life by desecrating the Sabbath and ignoring the dietary laws. They were warned to beware of "homeopathic doses" in religious observance.

By 1860, there were Orthodox, Reform, and even Conservative (or moderate Reform) synagogues in New York City, and this three-way division spread gradually throughout the other parts of the country, although the term *Conservative* did not come into general use until much later.[9] By this time violation of the Sabbath was more the rule than the exception, and nominal orthodoxy was quite common. Formal adherence but lack of observance and even freethinking outside the synagogue walls were prevalent. Ultimately Reform, which spread rapidly during the Civil War and in the years that followed that conflict, rationalized this laxity by liberalizing the law or else simply ignored it. Usually, the first generation tried to adhere to the law and to tradition as much as circumstances would allow, but they failed to keep or transmit the habit of making only necessary adjustments. As the elders began to forget Europe or deliberately to put it behind them, their children became Americans who cared little for the old traditions but much for the mores and traditions which we call the American way of life.

In these pre-Civil War days, as today, New York City was the metropolitan center of Jewish life in America. Then, as now, Gotham supplied the religious articles and most of the Jewish periodicals. Here was a reservoir of religious functionaries for the hinterland, and from this city transportable kosher food was sent to the rest of the country. In addition, the synagogues of that city set the fashion for Jews elsewhere. Buffalo merchants, for example, who travelled to New York on business trips, often spent spare time visiting New York synagogues, and, on their return, they reported to their own congregations about the services in these synagogues, the changes in ritual observed, and the general conduct of the leading big-city congregations.

New York was also one of the centers of Jewish book publishing and it was to that city that provincial congregations often sent for their prayer books and Bibles. The American-Jewish educational condition necessitated the introduction of English translations of traditional books of Jewish worship. As early as 1766, Isaac Pinto had translated some parts of the *siddur* of the Spanish-Portuguese ritual into English. Solomon Henry Jackson published in 1826 an English translation of the book of daily prayers, and in 1837 he produced the first English translation in America of the *hagaddah*. Isaac Leeser, a learned *hazzan* of Philadelphia, translated the first general prayer book for American-Sephardic Jews in 1837, and in 1848, he translated one for Ashkenazic Jews. He also put a Jewish version of the scriptures into English. A Reform festival prayer book, translated into German, was published in Baltimore in 1856. By the 1860s the firm of L. H. Frank and Sons was importing and publishing a series of Hebrew religious books and soon even carried a line of such titles as *Friday Night* and *The First Book of Jewish Tales* as collateral spiritual reading for Jews.

In the 1850s New York Jewish life spread far. There were in that city of 40,000 Jews kosher boardinghouses, a "painless Jewish dentist," a Jewish daguerreotype parlor, a few kosher boarding schools, and a Hebra Terumath Hakodesh (a Society for the Relief of the Poor in the Holy Land). Jewish firms manufactured and shipped to rural communities kosher smoked meats and sausages as well as *matzot* and kosher cheese. One firm advertised for distribution "prayer shawls of elegant silk Italian patterns." Jewish fraternal and benevolent societies began to appear all over New York in these years, and Jewish meeting halls dotted the city. Simon C. Noot and Co. advertised proudly that it had in its employ a competent *sofer* who could write to order *Sifrei Torah*, phylacteries, etc. on parchment.[10]

A *cause célèbre* in 1858 contributed greatly to the unification of the national Jewish community. Edgar Mortara, an Italian-Jewish boy, had been baptized by a nurse when he was ill, and Church authorities who seized him refused to give him back to his parents. Eventually Mortara became a priest. But in 1859, a Board of Delegates of American Israelites was formed to unify the Jews of America in an attempt to form a national front to meet domestic and foreign Jewish crises. The minute book of Congregation Beth El for November 27, 1860, records that a special meeting was to be called for the purpose of considering letters received from the Reverend Mr. Samuel Isaacs of New York. Isaacs had requested Beth El to appoint delegates to a "Board of All Israelites of America." This early attempt at a national board was partially successful: the Beth El records reveal occasional contacts with the national board; but the Board of Delegates was in the 1870s absorbed by the Union of American Hebrew Congregations, a Reform national group with headquarters in Cincinnati.

The early Jewish national periodicals also served to develop a national community or at least to create a sense of unity among the scattered and isolated Jewish communities. These papers served all the Jews of America as informal communications centers to which they could send inquiries and through which they could exchange ideas, gossip and spiritual tidbits with their brethren throughout the country.

One of the first of these newspapers was *The Asmonean,* founded by Robert Lyon in New York City in 1849. The Reverend Isaac Leeser's *Occident* (founded 1843) of Philadelphia heavily padded the thin news by printing many sermons and a great deal of correspondence. Rabbi Isaac Mayer Wise of Cincinnati, the organizer of the American Reform movement, founded *The (American) Israelite* in 1854. Later on an informal correspondent for Wise's paper resided in Buffalo; and this paper, which often carried local news, was popular among the religiously-progressive German group in Buffalo. The more conservative element at Beth El, however, read *The Jewish Messenger,* founded in New York in 1857 by Reverend Samuel Isaacs. Isaacs does not seem to have had a Buffalo correspondent, but he represented a Western European point of view, liberal in some respects but basically traditional in outlook.

Such were the conditions among American Jewry on the eve and morrow of the founding of the first synagogue in Buffalo. In 1847, the four-story Western Hotel stood in Buffalo at the corner of Pearl Street and The Terrace. It was a popular gathering place where one could watch the bustle of the stagecoaches departing for and arriving from the West. It was here on May 9, 1847, just one year after the onset of the Mexican

War, that a group of twenty-six men met "for the purpose of founding and organizing a Jewish congregation." Almost a quarter of a century had passed since the visionary Noah had flashed across the Buffalo scene. The enterprising peddlers and merchants who gathered at the Western Hotel that spring Sunday afternoon had no wild schemes in mind; they dealt realistically with the problem of establishing a place of worship for the nucleus of Jews in the city. If this gathering lacked the sparkle and glamor that marked Major Noah's strange morning service at St. Paul's Church in 1825, its results were far more lasting, for on that day they founded Congregation Beth El, which has flourished for well over a century.

Among those present at this momentous meeting was a German-Pole, Mark Moritz, who was promptly elected president of the new synagogue. Moritz was a native of Kornuck, province of Posen, and had tarried a few years in New York before pushing west to Buffalo. He apparently served the congregation well, for he was elected once more to the office three years later, and he was remembered years later as an urbane, calm leader and an eloquent speaker. But there was a limit to his patience and, tired of incessant squabbling about petty matters, he resigned his office and subsequently left the congregation. Typical of the restless Jewish business pioneers of the period, he eventually pulled up stakes in Buffalo, headed west, and ultimately settled in the plush, gold-boom city of San Francisco.[11]

The second officer elected at the organization meeting of Beth El was the secretary-treasurer, H. M. Eder, about whom little information has survived. If it was Eder who kept the early minutes of the group, he was well educated, for these books were written in a fine English style. The vice-president was M. B. Katz about whom history is also silent.

Isaac Myer, a clothier and tailor, born in 1804 in Germany; Solomon Phillips; Joseph A. Hill; the two Bernheimers, Elias and Elias J.; S. Altman; Barnard Lichtenstein and Jonas M. Gitsky, the firebrand of the early congregation, were also of this original group.

Of these founding fathers, the most striking perhaps was Michael W. Noah. Noah had been born in Gloucester, England on September 24, 1803, and he may have been, although there is no evidence to support the family claim, a distant relative of Mordecai M. Noah. On March 15, 1844, in New York City, Michael W. Noah married Mrs. Mary Ann Seymour, the widowed mother of a daughter, Amanda M. Seymour. Mrs. Noah had led an interesting and unusual life. She was born Mary Ann Hanna, on the Isle of Wight in 1824, and as a child she had lived in the officers' barracks at Windsor Castle where her father was an officer in Princess Victoria's own regiment. Mary Noah claimed to have played with the future Queen Victoria as a child on the grounds of Windsor Castle. She also maintained that she was related to the Hanna family that later produced the famous American businessman and politician, Mark Hanna. She came to New York and thence to Buffalo by canal boat in the 1830s. Probably their common British origin drew Mr. and Mrs. Noah together.

On her wedding day, Mary Seymour Noah became a convert to Judaism and received the Hebrew name Rebecca. Although after her husband's death the minute books of Beth El cast doubt on her conversion, later entries show that proof was advanced to testify to the validity of a Jewish marriage. Furthermore, to her death in 1895 in Buffalo, and throughout over forty years of widowhood, Mrs. Noah never wavered in her Jewish faith.

Michael Noah was one of the richest Jews in Buffalo before his death in 1853. He seems to have been very generous to the infant congregation and, when he died, a beautiful Hebrew and English inscription was made in a Bible by the spiritual leader of Beth El and the book was presented to the family. Noah lived at 6 Carroll Street and is said to have had the first large retail clothing store in Buffalo. It was called in fine nineteenth-century fashion "The Emporium," and was located at Main and The Terrace.

The Noahs had five children. The first daughter, contrary to usual Jewish custom, was named Mary after her mother. This daughter later married Siegmund Levyn, a tower of strength in the later history of Buffalo Jewry, and some of their descendants are still active today in the Jewish community of Buffalo.

The most interesting of the children was Elkin Joel Noah. Born on October 29, 1851, he died at the age of eighty-one on November 5, 1932. After starting out in the cigar store of his brother-in-law Siegmund Levyn, he eventually went into business for himself. Noah married out of the Jewish faith and had little or nothing to do with Jews during his whole adult life. It is probable that his children scarcely knew their origin. But just before he died, Elkin Noah sent for Rabbi Joseph L. Fink and, when his family had left the two alone, Noah revealed his secret and asked that he be given a Jewish burial. He, too, was buried in the Beth Zion part of Forest Lawn. The story of the Buffalo Noahs points up the fluidity of Jewish life in this period. Michael W. Noah was a conscientious Jew who intermarried but made a pious convert of his wife, yet their son chose to disregard the example of his parents.[12]

One of the first acts of the organization committee was to take up contributions for the maintenance of a *hazzan* and *shohet*. Seventeen members pledged contributions from 25 to 50 cents a week to be paid monthly in advance to the treasurer.

The other problem treated at the organization meeting was to be one that not only plagued the early community but one about which the historical facts are almost hopelessly tangled. At this first meeting a committee was appointed to purchase a burial ground. The problems of this early cemetery purchase are so involved that they demand separate and complete treatment for themselves.

All the nascent Jewish-American communities faced a variety of problems, and the Buffalo group set about, as many others also did, to solve theirs as best they could. Since all Jews at that time were theoretically, if not in reality, traditional, they were concerned from the very start with procuring kosher food. Consequently, their first functionary was the *shohet*. These early *shohetim* were usually poorly trained, for the learned and the pious ordinarily stayed in Europe. Often these early functionaries were, unfortunately, those who failed to make a living in any other way. At first the one synagogue selected and paid the *shohet*, but as ideological rifts spread and as these communities grew and, instead of one, several synagogues served each community, this arrangement broke down. As the synagogues multiplied, so did the *shohetim*. Lest he should find time hanging heavy on his hands, the *shohet* was laden with many other duties. He was usually, in addition to his duties as slaughterer, the teacher, cantor, the keeper of the ritual bath, the reader of the Torah, the celebrant of marriages and funerals, and the preacher of sermons. He might also be asked to serve as sexton and collector of synagogue dues. And many of these men were also trained to circumcise male infants.[13]

In America, the early functionaries merely slaughtered the animals, and the meat was sold through a Gentile shop. In Buffalo, Frank A. Allberger (1825-1877) sold kosher meat in his stalls in the Terrace Square Market near where most Jews then lived in the lower part of town. Allberger's name often appears in the early synagogue records. Later he became interested in politics and served as alderman, Republican mayor of Buffalo (1860-1861), Erie Canal Commissioner and New York Assemblyman. During the Civil War Allberger was prominent in organizing the home guard for local defense of the area.

Ultimately, the sale of kosher meat by a non-Jew produced serious problems, for the Christian butchers were certainly ignorant of and sometimes unconcerned with the niceties of the ritual law concerning the washing of the meat, the proper handling and preparation of it, and other aspects of the Jewish customs. Before the Civil War, Jewish butchers appeared in most cities and large towns where Jews settled in any numbers. In the New World, however, Jewish butchers were much harder to control than in the tightly-knit communities of Europe. With the spread of ideological distinctions, the kosher butcher slipped out from under the domination of the *kehillah* and began to make himself an independent merchant and an American businessman. Among other departures from strict tradition that sprang up in the handling of kosher meat was the growing independence of the butcher who sometimes hired slaughterers who had not been approved by a rabbi.[14]

Another functionary who was required very early in the development of any Jewish community was the *mohel*. Circumcision by a doctor, so common in the twentieth century, was severely frowned upon in the middle of the nineteenth. The *mohel* was carefully trained in his task, and often the *shohet* was also trained to serve as *mohel*. Although Buffalo in August 1847 had a *shohet* and *mohel*, Isaac Moses Slatsky, such was life in mercurial American towns that Slatsky himself was in and out of office many times. Evidently in 1865, Buffalo did not have a *mohel*. *The Jewish Messenger* of New York carried on August 4, 1865, an advertisement of Rev. Levy Rosenblatt of Elmira who offered his services as *mohel* to "Israelites of Rochester, Buffalo and adjacent places." These early American *mohelim* were much travelled individuals, who often ranged through many parts of the country in pursuit of their profession.

On Passover, Jews needed properly prepared *matzot,* and in the early days the procurement of unleavened bread was a problem in Buffalo. Before 1850 the Jews had to buy their *matzot* outside of the city, and in that year, according to the minute books of Beth El, a committee of the congregation was appointed to investigate the possibilities of baking *matzot* in Buffalo. Apparently this committee was not successful, for in 1854, it was still negotiating with an Israel Nussbaum of Albany who offered to supply *matzot* at 9 cents a pound and matzo flour at 10 cents a pound. At that time, from other sources, the people of Buffalo were purchasing *matzot* at 12½ cents a pound and the flour at 14 cents a pound.

Another article necessary to Jewish ritual had to be sought out and imported by the young Buffalo community. For use on Succot of 1864, the Beth El community paid fifteen dollars for two *ethrogim.* By 1865, Beth El hired a man who tended the *hadas* tree "which stands at Colman's hot-pot-garden." [15]

One of the most troublesome problems facing a young community was the purchase of a suitable cemetery site. The history of how the Buffalo community met this problem is extremely involved. In the average community one of the first acts was to buy a piece of land for this purpose. We do not know what was done in Buffalo before 1847, when the organization committee appointed a subcommittee to purchase land. If there were Jewish deaths, possibly the remains were taken to a nearby

city, but, since embalming was not permitted under Jewish law, that
course was probably not usually followed. Perhaps those who died before
1847 were simply buried in some corner of a Christian cemetery. There is
no evidence to throw light on this problem.

The Jewish law to which these immigrants gave technical adherence
is very strict about the preparation of the dead for burial. No community
could get along without a *Hevra Kadisha* to prepare the dead for burial.
No one in the town is allowed to work in case of a death unless an organized group is available to take proper care of the remains. Even to
this day in America, Jews, no matter how far they have strayed from the
traditional paths of their ancestry, tend to pay closer attention to certain
rituals for the dead than to other facets of the law. European Jewish
practice had been to bury people in order of death and often, moreover,
to inter men and women in different parts of the cemetery. There was no
such thing as family plots, for there was to be no distinction, family or
social, after death. In America, however, this practice began to change.
In the 1840s the newly-organized Reform congregation, Temple Emanu-
El of New York City, sold family plots. Thereafter, many cemeteries in
America had two rows, one for general burial without distinction and the
other, at extra cost, for family burial plots. Probably the earlier Jewish
cemeteries in Buffalo followed the old-country practice, but by the 1860s
family plots were the rule in most cemeteries. Ultimately, cemeteries became, and still are, a prime source of revenue for synagogues. A man
might avoid paying his synagogue dues all his adult life, but when it came
to burial, few families wanted to risk burial outside of an established
Jewish cemetery. The late Louis Wirth once remarked of the sustained
Jewish interest in observance of burial rituals: "The profound interest in
burial seems to be explained finally in terms of those innumerable strong
ties of sentiment that bind the individual to the tribal organization."
Men live, according to Wirth, "in their memories of the past and their
dreams of the future." [16]

Before Buffalo Jewry made its first move to found a cemetery, several
burial places had already been established for the non-Jewish community. The first burials in the city of Buffalo date from about 1804. A city
cemetery was subsequently established on Church Street. The first privately owned cemetery was set aside in 1830, and in 1832, another cemetery was established on North Street east of Michigan Avenue. This
cemetery had a special section set aside for Roman Catholics, and it is
possible, although we do not know surely, that some Jews may have been
buried there.[17]

Few cities in the United States made sufficient initial allowance for
urban growth. Hence, as population increased and more room was

needed for business fronts and residences, the dead had to make room for the living and remains in older downtown cemeteries often were removed to new plots beyond the city limits. This situation was made manifest to Buffalo Jews just about the time that they were looking for a burial ground of their own, for remains in the city cemetery on Church Street were re-interred in Forest Lawn, several miles to the north of the then settled area of Buffalo. It is reasonable to suppose that this long-considered step on the part of their Christian neighbors played a part in the selection of a cemetery far enough removed from the civic center to seem safe, at the time, from future encroachment.

The story of Buffalo's first Jewish cemeteries is intertwined with the personal lives of two aforementioned men, Elias and Elias J. Bernheimer. The first to act was Elias Bernheimer who, a few weeks after the founding of Beth El, bought for $800 a piece of land that lay one mile south of the city and was located in an area now bounded by Fillmore Avenue, Gibson and Sycamore Streets.[18] Evidently Bernheimer was acting in his capacity as a trustee of the congregation, for he deeded the land to Beth El promptly after the synagogue was incorporated. There is no hint in the local records that Elias Bernheimer was motivated by a personal tragedy in his immediate family. He was a man in his early forties, his wife was almost twenty years younger, and their family seems to have been steadily increasing.

There is, however, a strong tradition in the Buffalo community, dating from the first annals of Rabbi Samson Falk, that the death of a Mrs. Elias Bernheimer led to the purchase of a cemetery. This tradition is so strong and venerable that it seems foolhardy to refute it. Evidently tradition recalled the death of the first wife of Elias J. Bernheimer, the cousin of the first purchaser of cemetery land, who, in 1850, bought cemetery land adjacent to the Beth El ground and subsequently deeded it to the Jacobsohn Society of which he was a leading member. If we read between the lines of surviving evidence, one of two conclusions seems plausible. Possibly Mrs. Elias J. Bernheimer died in 1847 and Cousin Elias acted for the grief-stricken young husband in tending to legal matters. Or, perhaps Mrs. Bernheimer died after the acquisition of the Beth El cemetery but, for some reason, was buried in land not included in the original purchase. This would explain why her husband, even after his re-marriage, should have wanted to buy the additional land to make certain that his wife's last resting place would form part of a Jewish cemetery. Belonging to the rival Jacobsohn Society rather than to Congregation Beth El, he may have used the 1850 purchase to start another cemetery.[19]

Thus for reasons that will probably forever be shrouded in mystery, Buffalo by 1850 had two Jewish cemeteries lying adjacent to one another in what is now the Fillmore-Broadway area. We know much more about the Beth El land than that of the Jacobsohn Society, for the synagogue's early minute books reveal the difficulties in supervising a cemetery so far away in a day of horse and buggy transportation. The land had to be drained after each winter's snows had melted, tree stumps had to be removed as new graves were needed, and rail fences were built and re-built only to be collected as firewood by conscienceless trespassers. To help defray the upkeep, Beth El leased some of the land to Richard Heonbuckle. This illiterate farmer, whose descendants still dot the countryside around Buffalo, promised in return for a nominal rent to keep the burial place fenced in, to construct gravel walks, and to ward off would-be pillagers with his gun.[20]

Beth El soon discovered, like so many other congregations that were to come after it, that American Jews loosen their purse-strings more willingly to house the dead than to support a faith for the living. Because the circumstances varied in each case, different rates for burial services early became commonplace. There was a tendency to take advantage of affluent strangers from nearby small communities, although due consideration was usually shown to all who pleaded "reduced circumstances." When the well-to-do Michael Noah died in 1853, the trustees held a special meeting to arrange for his obsequies, and his estate was charged the princely sum of twenty-five dollars.[21] But there were few Noahs to bury and most of the time Beth El had to be satisfied with a more modest fee.

Although the intention, in 1850, was to maintain two adjoining cemeteries, in reality, there was no partition between them and most of the interments were made on the Beth El side of the land. On July 19, 1861, as the Union army was advancing on Bull Run, Buffalo Jews were told that they could no longer use either cemetery. The order probably came from the municipal authorities who, for reasons not entirely clear, wished to keep the land for other purposes. For many years thereafter, Buffalo Jews, in time-honored fashion, obeyed the Jewish edict not to disturb the rest of the departed. But the time came when removal was a lesser evil than toleration of the vandalism that plagued the abandoned cemeteries. Eventually, the German Jews who had formed Temple Beth Zion removed most of the remains of their relatives from the old Jacobsohn Cemetery to the Beth Zion plots on Pine Ridge Road. Here the visitor may still read a plaque that tells some of the pathos associated with this long-forgotten episode: "Erected in memory of the remains removed from the JACOB-SOHN CEMETERY in the month of April, 1893, by the congregation Temple Beth Zion." Nearby, in Pine Hill Cemetery of Beth El, a similar marker states: "In memory of the Unknown Dead who have been brought here from the Old Beth El Cemetery Fillmore and Stanislaus Streets."[22]

The secrets of the pioneers that this study has been unable to recover lie buried with these men and women.

If, by some magic, these early Buffalo Jews could be interrogated, speculation concerning the origin and dissolution of the Jacobsohn Society (sometimes Anglicized to Jacobson) would not be necessary. From the sparse documents that remain, however, all that we can deduce is that five months after the establishment of Congregation Beth El, a group of young Jews founded the Jacobsohn Society for mutual benefit. Organized on October 3, 1847, it may have been named in honor of Israel Jacobsohn, a layman who founded Reform Judaism in Germany during the Napoleonic Era. There is no evidence to support this hypothesis, but no other feasible explanation of the name is forthcoming, except the possibility that these men thought of themselves collectively, in traditional fashion, as the sons of the patriarch Jacob. The future history of the group could be used to support either contention, for although many of its members eventually brought Reform Judaism to Buffalo, there is not an iota of evidence to suggest that they were originally impelled by a desire to modernize Jewish worship.

Organizations similar to the Jacobsohn Society were to be found in almost all American-Jewish communities of the 1850s, for they were formed to meet some very urgent needs. Most of their members lived from day to day, dependent for their bread on their weekly earnings. Sickness or accident left them living a hand-to-mouth existence without funds and often without friends or relatives able or willing to assist them. Furthermore, in a relatively raw part of the country where hospitals, doctors, and nurses were rare, death was near at hand always; the now-controllable respiratory and infectious diseases cut down many hardy men and women, to say nothing of the shockingly high toll of children that they claimed. The Jacobsohn Society was founded in an effort to do something about these conditions. Its main objectives were to aid men in financial distress and to be of help in severe illness. Thus its members took upon themselves the obligation of "watching with their sick co-religionists in their dying hours, and reciting the religious profession that they might expire in the faith of their fathers." [23] The Jacobsohn Society served still another purpose. Jews had learned during the Middle Ages to avoid resorting to the secular courts in disputes among themselves. In Europe each town had its *Beth Din* in which rabbis were the judges and before whom disputes among Jews were aired. To this day these informal courts still arbitrate disputes among Jews in such cities as Baltimore and New York, where tradition is strong. The Buffalo immigrants arrived with the memory of these courts of Europe and were reluctant to make public their

grievances against each other. Consequently, the constitution of the Jacobsohn Society required that its members bring disputes arising from verbal
injury, and those touching upon honor and reputation, to the board of
the Society for arbitration. It was an age of violent quarrelling and bickering among Jews who had many differences both of national origins and
ideology to iron out, and an organization like the Jacobsohn Society did
what it could to ease the stresses and tensions arising from these quarrels.
The constitution provided not only for arbitration of disputes, but also
established a set of fines for such offenses as proven slander or attempts
to injure or do bodily harm to another. This type of institution was by
no means peculiar to Buffalo. In 1851, Syracuse had three such societies,
all with aims similar to the Jacobsohn Society of Buffalo.[24]

The leaders of this Society were mostly young Germans or German-
Poles. The first president was Louis Dahlman (1820-1889), a dry-goods
merchant who was born in Alsace, then a French province. Shortly after
the founding of the Society, Louis Dahlman is known to have been the
owner of Dahlman Co. at 276 Main Street and a boarder at 27 Pearl
Street. Later, he was a member of the firm of Dahlman, Giershofer &
Spiegel. Dahlman prospered: by the time of his marriage in 1860 he was
worth $8,000 of which $7,500 was in real property, and he and his wife
were able to afford the luxury of a domestic servant. He was later an
important figure in real estate. Eventually, in 1872, Dahlman became a
member of Beth Zion. Other founders of the Jacobsohn Society included
Henry Zinsheimer (or Sinsheimer), a cigar maker; Moritz Weil; Emanuel
Strauss, a clerk who had been born in Bavaria; Joseph Mayer, who
worked for Dahlman; Samuel Held, a peddler; Abraham and Joseph E.
Strass, clothiers, and two of three brothers who came to Buffalo from
Bavaria; and Samuel Desbecker.

Desbecker, who lived on into the twentieth century and established an
important Buffalo family, was born in 1826 in Sulzburg, Baden, and the
story of his success in Buffalo led to a sizable immigration to Buffalo
from that German Grand Duchy, particularly from Ihringen, Baden.
From that area came the Wile family of clothing fame, their distant relatives the Weils, the Blocks who went into banking and the jewelry business, the Geismar family, and others. Desbecker came to the United
States in 1847 by sailing ship and came to Buffalo in 1848. He was the
father of five sons: David, Nathan, Daniel, Joseph, and Louis. Daniel,
a one-time pharmacist, and Louis, an attorney, were graduates of Cornell
University. Desbecker lived in Buffalo until his death on January 21,
1916, except for short periods during which he lived in New Orleans, and
in Hamilton, Ontario.

Desbecker was a wholesale clothier who, for many years, was manager and president of Desbecker, Weil and Co. He was a well-known figure in town and was evidently a "joiner." He became a Mason in 1850 and was later prominent in that organization. He retired from business in 1886 at the age of sixty, but he remained active in social affairs of the city. In his old age he was affectionately called by the nickname *Mein Neshama,* because he so frequently used this expression which means, "Oh, my soul!" So well known was he that in 1906 his eightieth-birthday celebration at the Colonial Club on Lafayette Avenue was a major social event.[25]

It was not until April 21, 1851, that the Jacobsohn Society was incorporated under the New York State law of 1848, "An act for the incorporation of benevolent, charitable, scientific, and missionary societies." The purposes stated in this act of incorporation were to receive, collect, accumulate funds through assessments and voluntary gifts and to help members, their widows, and their orphans defray funeral expenses and to take care of other misfortunes among members. At the time of its incorporation, the Society also asked for power to hold real estate and to own a burying ground. At this time Isaac Drucker, a cigar maker at 11 Gray Street, was listed as president and H. Zinsheimer was vice-president. They, together with three other members, served as the board of trustees for the organization. The articles of incorporation stated that the Society was to continue until two-thirds of the members should vote to disband.[26] The articles were realistic, for soon internal dissension killed an organization founded in fraternity.

After the dissolution of the Jacobsohn Society, its place was taken by the Hebrew Benevolent Society of the City of Buffalo, for there was no diminution of the need for financial and physical help for the poorer immigrants of the city. The Benevolent Society was incorporated on April 14, 1854, with the stated objectives of nursing and watching over the sick and burying the dead with the proper religious rites. Its original directors were A. Samuel Bennett, Abraham Jacobs, Isaac Ellis, Mark Nelson, and Nathan Boasberg.[27] Boasberg, who fathered a prominent Buffalo family, was born in Amsterdam, Holland, in 1827 and came to Buffalo about 1846. He, too, lived on into the twentieth century, dying in Buffalo on September 6, 1910. Boasberg married Rachel Van Baalen, also of Dutch-Jewish descent, in February 1848. Nathan Boasberg was said to be of Sephardic descent and a graduate of Leyden University. He served in the Dutch navy and arrived in New York aboard a Dutch man-of-war. An uncle persuaded him "to stay" in America, and he came to Buffalo on an Erie Canal packet boat. He was naturalized in Buffalo on April 8, 1854. He was a charter member of Beth El and the last of the founders to die. He was the secretary of Beth El in 1856, but in 1869 he joined Beth Zion where most of his descendants have since worshipped.

Boasberg, who was always proud of his Dutch ancestry, was in the clothing business for many years, but was never very successful at it. His various addresses throw some light on the shifts of the Jewish population of Buffalo during the second half of the nineteenth century. In the early 1850s he lived at 229 Carroll Street; in 1858, he lived at 5 Commercial Street where he also conducted a business; by 1865 he had moved to 173 Swan Street; by 1884 he had moved to the old West Side of Buffalo and lived at 294 Carolina Street; three years later in 1887 he was still on the West Side at 165 Prospect Avenue; in 1895 he was pushing north but still on the West Side of the city and resided at 290 Ashland Avenue. Boasberg's movements during an unusually long life are typical of the pattern of shifting Jewish neighborhoods in Buffalo.[28]

A third charitable group of this early period was organized on October 25, 1861. The Young Men's Hebrew Benevolent Association of Buffalo was established "to bestow aid and comfort to all Israelites passing through the City of Buffalo who may be in need." The eight trustees, mostly young men, represented a cross section of the Jewish community. They were Leon Goldsmith, Isaac Alexander, Louis M. Brock, Henry Hyman, Suchman Marks, David Richwald, Gustave Silberberg, and Samuel Gensler.[29]

One of the pressing problems that faced the committee that had established Beth El, was to find a permanent place of worship for the new congregation. Until 1847, Buffalo Jewry had no formal meeting house for worship. They met, probably for *Jahrzeits* and for important holidays, in the parlors of private homes, often in the home of Abraham Jacobs on Deak Street, but there were no regularly scheduled services. A few weeks before the committee met to found Beth El, the first public Jewish religious services were held in Buffalo. To celebrate Passover, a group, through voluntary contributions, rented Concert Hall (later called Townsend Hall), which then stood at the southwest corner of Main and Swan Streets. It was there that they conducted Passover services in April 1847. The first regular place of worship, rented in the spring of 1848, was the Hoyt Building at the northeast corner of Main and Eagle Streets (at 292 Main Street). This building, which at that time served as the Company D Armory, was still standing as late as 1911. Beth El used the top floor beginning in the spring of 1848. At about that time there were twenty-four Jewish families in Buffalo, according to *The Occident* which also announced that the congregation had a cantor who also served as *shohet*.[30]

This first "minister," who was a cantor as well as a *shohet*, was Isaac Moses Slatsky. His birthplace is unknown, but his nickname "Itzig" implies that he was an East-European who had become accustomed to the western style of prayer. Slatsky was born sometime between 1791 and 1795. His wife, Leah, was born in Holland in 1785.

Whenever Slatsky was in office there was trouble in the Beth El congregation. He was removed from office sometime in the end of 1849 or early in 1850, but he was restored as *shohet* on February 3, 1850. He was sent, however, to Rochester to qualify before Rabbi Mordecai Tuska. By the end of that year he was squabbling again. On December 8, 1850, he threatened to use the law against the congregation unless they "desist from their unjust course pursued towards him as a citizen and clergyman." [31] By the following spring, however, he was back in office again. On April 2, 1851, he was reinstated as *hazzan, shohet, Ba'al Koreh,* and *mohel* at the annual salary of $200. In all probability Slatsky was Buffalo's first *mohel;* at least he acted in that capacity, although his qualifications in this as in other offices were frequently questioned. He was still doing part-time work for Beth El as late as 1860 when he was the one who "watched the dead," that is, sat up with the corpse according to Jewish law.

Falk tells an amusing incident involving Slatsky that occurred during the very early days while the congregation was still located in the Hoyt Building. "It was on a Day of Atonement that Rev. Mr. Slatsky stood in the synagogue the whole day, as the custom was, in his white linen robe and white cap, with a white girdle about his loins. Toward dusk he again began to officiate. The congregation could no longer read without lights; but it being strictly forbidden to the Israelites of the orthodox school to kindle a light or touch a candlestick on such a day, they sent for some non-Israelite to light their hall. They happened to procure a tall Negro. He, on entering the synagogue, seeing Mr. Slatsky with his pallid face and his long white beard, in full keeping with his white attire . . . was seized with terror—ran out as quickly as he could—and reaching the stairs, fell headlong down the whole flight, causing quite a sensation by his precipitate exit." [32]

Slatsky eventually left the Beth El congregation. He spent the last ten years of his life in the Buffalo General Hospital, where the Hebrew Union Benevolent Association provided for his care. After his death, on December 16, 1875, he was buried in the old Beth Zion cemetery.

After the Beth El organizational meeting in May 1847, no meeting was formally called until April 23, 1848, a Sunday and one of the intermediate days of Passover. (It was a European custom for congregations to call meetings during the workdays of the Passover week.) The Beth El group met to consider the adoption of a constitution and by-laws drawn up by a committee that had studied similar documents of the

Baltimore Hebrew Congregation. The Buffalo set, though modelled on the Baltimore documents, was modified to meet local conditions. This committee was composed of Elias Bernheimer, J. M. Gitsky, Joseph A. Hill, Mark Moritz and Mone Fridenberg. At this time Fridenberg was a merchant at 126 Main Street and he resided at 32 Exchange Street. He was then forty years old and the father of a large family. He had been born in Poland—his wife, Elizabeth, in France. He was a newcomer to Buffalo, having lived many years in Pennsylvania, but quickly became involved in the activities of the congregation. The Fridenberg family was quite important in early Buffalo history. In 1849, his son Samuel Fridenberg, was one of the first Jewish boys to be registered in the public schools of Buffalo. He attended Public School Number 7. A relative, Solomon Fridenberg, charitably assisted a Palestinian messenger who came to collect in Buffalo in February 1850. He called a meeting at his home and the list of donors, fortunately preserved, shows that six members of the family contributed. There were probably three brothers in the family, Mone, Solomon and Julius, although the records are by no means clear.[33]

The constitution and by-laws of Beth El were adopted at this meeting, and elections were held at the same time. Abraham Jacobs from Hanover, in Germany, was elected president to succeed Mark Moritz. This was the Jacobs who lived on Deak Street and in whose home, tradition states, some of the earliest services were held. Elias Bernheimer was chosen vice-president, and J. M. Gitsky, Mone Fridenberg and Joseph A. Hill were elected trustees. Alexander Grunewald, an importer with a store at Main and Hanover Streets, took the notes for the meeting. This meeting took place during one of the many times that Isaac M. Slatsky was out of favor with the congregation, and a young man named Rev. A. Ansell was elected *hazzan-shohet-mohel*. Ansell's salary was later fixed at $250 per year. In addition to his other duties, Ansell taught the children on Sunday mornings from 9:00 to 12:00, and on Wednesday afternoons from 4:00 to 7:00. Later he acted as secretary for the congregation, and he evidently wrote a good English hand. The Board of Trustees for Beth El met next on May 7, 1848, at the house of the president who lived, as the Teutonic-minded secretary recorded, on "Bearl" Street. At that meeting they agreed to the establishment of four classes of members: $25, $15, $10, and $5 per annum. Of the thirty Jewish families in Buffalo at that time, twenty-five members were listed that day. An application for a charter was filed on June 13, 1848, on which date the official name "Synagogue Beth El" was chosen. A local judge granted the request for incorporation on June 19, 1848, and the name "Synagogue Beth El" was formally adopted. The group met the next month and declared themselves a legally chartered congregation "and in all respects well organized by a place of worship and a burial ground giving its members the sacred benefit of worshipping Almighty God in Holy Conclave." The members were called upon to cooperate with the board and to support the congregation.[34]

Beth El, like so many other early synagogues, faced the problem of church discipline, and it tried to settle the problem by adopting a system of fines. The records show that on September 10, 1848, Joseph A. Hill, one of the trustees, was fined one dollar for non-attendance, and during Hanukkah, 1848, the synagogue tried to force attendance at an evening service through fines. Some of the members who lived outside of Buffalo, although subject to all dues and assessments, were declared exempt from fines for failure to attend synagogue. The fine system failed because the free American atmosphere discouraged this type of discipline, and because many of the members were too poor to pay fines. Consequently, as a mark of defeat, on April 24, 1849, the congregation voted to cancel all outstanding fines. Even in the traditional funeral collections, when a box was passed among the mourners with the cry in Hebrew "Charity staves off Death," next to nothing was collected. On one occasion only $2.66 was collected in this manner.[35] One early source of revenue was the operation of the cemetery; this was an area that no one could avoid. One other source of income peculiar to the American scene was the sale of seats to members. In 1848, men were charged three dollars, and women one dollar, for seats for the High Holiday services, then still held in the armory in the Hoyt Building.

Beth El planned carefully for its 1847 High Holiday services. Reverend Ansell was to chant the principal part of the prayers—read the Torah, blow the *shofar*—and the demoted, but probably not chastened, Mr. Slatsky was to assist by leading both the early morning devotions and the *Minha* service on Yom Kippur. Other meticulous preparations were made. The honor of being called to the reading of the Law (*Aliyah*) was to be extended only to members of the congregation. Minor honors, such as the opening and closing of the Ark, were, in the European manner, to be auctioned off. In sharp contrast to the laxity later shown by East-European Orthodox synagogues in matters of decorum, it was "ordered that notice be written up in and declared in Synagogue for the strictest decorum and conduct." [36] Offerings by men called to the reading of the Torah were closely regulated, and steps were taken to make sure that no one would leave his seat during the services. It was evident that Beth El was anxious to make its first High Holiday services both solemn and impressive.

Within two years of its founding, Beth El took the first steps to acquire a permanent location. On January 18, 1849, the younger of the brace of Bernheimers, Elias J., moved that the congregation purchase a piece of property centrally located on downtown Pearl Street. The lot measured 40 feet by 79 feet and was situated 50 feet removed from Pearl Street in the block bounded by Main, Pearl and Eagle, with no frontage on any street save for an eight-foot alleyway that led to an exit on Pearl Street. On this land stood an old tree-shaded schoolhouse that could easily be converted into a synagogue. The site of the first Jewish house of worship in Buffalo was approximately that of the present building of the S. S. Kresge Company that now fronts on 388-390 Main Street. In 1849, the old schoolhouse lay directly behind the American Hotel, which burned sixteen years later.[37]

One can only speculate why the congregation chose this site. It seems, however, sensible to believe that here was an opportunity to secure a good bargain in the form of a readily convertible building. The location was good, for it was within easy walking distance of lower Main Street where most Buffalo Jews both lived and conducted their businesses. Possibly the seclusion of the schoolhouse from the noise and bustle of the horse-drawn traffic on Main Street was an additional attraction, for a courtyard location offered an attractive privacy. In Europe, Jews had formed the habit of locating synagogues away from the prying eyes of their neighbors, and to some Beth El members the new site might have reminded them of the *shul* in their native towns. To be sure, the lot offered little opportunity for physical expansion, but, in 1849, the men who made the purchase probably thought that there would be more than ample space in the 150 seats that would be provided.

On February 18, 1849, the congregation voted to ratify Bernheimer's option of $2,000 for the land and building, and title was transferred about five weeks later. Bela D. Coe of Buffalo was given a mortgage for the entire purchase price. In the Spring, a printed appeal for help in acquiring a new synagogue was sent to all existing Jewish congregations in the United States. At that time this method of raising funds was common, and Mark Moritz, then travelling through the state, was able to raise $183 in New York, Utica and Rochester. On April 24th a building committee was appointed to supervise the changes necessary to convert the schoolhouse into a synagogue. A ladies' group, established as early as July 15, 1849, also helped to raise funds. The conversion was planned by the architect T. Abrahams. Among other things, this committee was directed to put in new "privies" and bookshelves. A "trustee's chamber" was to be provided and living quarters in the basement for the minister. The people were justifiably proud of their new place of worship, and the minute books show that they tried to improve and beautify their "pretty little synagogue." On July 8, 1849, they voted to install a system of gaslights at a cost not to exceed $150, and by August 12, 1849, seats in the Pearl Street synagogue were assigned to members by lot. It was decided that each member was to pay $50 for a seat, by installments if necessary, and that reductions in price for the seats would be made for the "incapacitated." Each man was to pay at least $10 in annual dues, payable quarterly.

On April 1, 1850, Mone Fridenberg bought two pews on the ground floor and one in the Ladies' Gallery "to be used for the purposes only of religious worship, according to the Law of Moses, and for no other purpose or use whatever." Fridenberg agreed to pay $50 in ten yearly installments with interest on the unpaid balance. One year later he paid the first installment of $5 with interest of $3.15! On August 16, 1858, the debt was transferred to his brother, Julius Fridenberg, on the death of Mone; and poor Julius was still paying interest in 1861! In America a new attitude toward synagogue seats arose. Unlike European Jews who highly prized the front seats, American Jews, according to the records of Beth El, had to be urged to occupy these seats. Apparently they seemed to prefer the seats at the rear of the synagogue. Perhaps there they found it easier to slip out unobtrusively before the conclusion of services.

Meanwhile, although the conversion and occupancy of the new synagogue moved along fairly smoothly, other matters occupied the community. The dispensation of kosher meat continued to be a problem. No one could slaughter kosher without the "sufferage of the congregation," and the Gentile butcher, Allberger, not only was closely supervised, but was also assessed for his monopoly of selling to Jewish patrons. He paid the congregation one dollar for every ox slaughtered, one "shilling" for every lamb, and eighteen cents for every calf. The Rev. Mr. Ansell was paid by his patrons much more modestly for the less difficult task of killing fowl. He was paid three cents each for geese and turkeys, two cents for ducks and other fowl, and one cent for pigeons. Early in 1849, Allberger ended the piece-rate payment and agreed to pay the congregation a flat sum of $125 for a six-months' exclusive franchise to dispense kosher meat and was given an option to continue for the next six months at the same rate. He didn't seem to please, for a formal charge was placed against him early in 1850. It was hard to control the distribution of kosher meat; and we find that in 1850, Samuel Lichtenstein tried unsuccessfully to get permission to buy meat at a butcher shop other than Allberger's. In the late 1850s, Beth El's Gentile butchers were James and John Farthing, who succeeded Allberger after he lost or gave up the franchise. The Farthings didn't last, for they insulted the *shohet* and failed to provide fresh meat on Fridays. The congregation was understandably annoyed.[38]

Another problem faced by the young congregation was the construction of a *mikvah*. The first mention of a ritual bath appears in the minutes for August 26, 1849, when Fould, the sexton, was authorized to charge women 25 cents for the use of the bath, and brides were to pay one dollar. This *mikvah* must have existed before they acquired the Pearl Street property, for another one was installed in the newly acquired edifice. It was apparently used quite regularly. In 1853, the congregation paid Thompson and McFarland $455.55 to improve it, but by 1856 it again was in need of repair and "new machines for the bathing place" were installed.

The congregation continued to have difficulty securing a good minister. The minute books for June 10, 1849, record "a desultory conversation" about the services of the Rev. Ansell. He was accused of intemperance and discharged, and the congregation advertised in *The Occident* for a replacement to serve as *hazzen-shohet,* who could teach the children and who must be able to read and write English. His salary was to be $300 a year plus quarters in the basement of the new synagogue. Only two replies were received to this advertisement. Morris Switzer was appointed sexton in December 1850, but the office was not continously filled. Meanwhile the ever-present Slatsky had been filling in and did so until April 1850, when Gershon Landsberg was named minister. But by the end of that year Landsberg was replaced by a Mr. Marcusson, who in turn left in April 1851. Of course, Slatsky then came back in again.

The minute books of this period show that the community was pestered with all sorts of trouble, some of it serious, some of it verging on the absurd. The one-time vice-president, M. B. Katz, fell behind in his dues and owed the congregation $22.82, and to force him to pay, the congregation impounded his *Sefer Torah* that he had evidently lent to the congregation. On July 9, 1849, Mone Fridenberg forced open the door of the Ladies' Gallery and took back his friend's *Sefer Torah,* evidently for worship elsewhere. Fridenberg was fined, and the dispute was settled when Fridenberg paid off Mr. Katz's arrears. The founders of the community were not all great men nor clear-eyed visionaries. They had their human intermingling of foibles and follies.

On October 14, 1849, after a spirited election, Joseph Lessler was elected president of Beth El. Lessler, only thirty-one years old at the time of his election, had been born in Prussia as was his wife Betsy. He had been in the United States for only about three or four years at the time of his election, but he already was prospering as a clothier at South Division and Oak Streets. In the late 1850s he seems to have been a fairly successful land speculator and by the seventies he had pushed north on Delaware to Delevan Avenue. Lessler finally left Beth El and, after a period of indifference, joined Beth Zion in 1869. It is not known when he died; but at the end of his life he seems to have been estranged even from Reform Judaism.

Also elected that same day, as secretary at a salary of $25 a year, was William Sylvester. He wrote a precise, idiomatic and beautiful English and was evidently either native born or British. Proof positive is lacking, but the assumption is that he was Jewish despite his Anglo-Saxon name. Unfortunately nothing more is known about him; historians of the community assume that he left Buffalo in the 1850s.

On July 26, 1850, the new Beth El synagogue was ready for consecration. It was a Friday evening and the event, as far as we know, marked the first rabbinical sermon in Buffalo. Elaborate and ambitious plans had been drawn to make the consecration a gala occasion. Mark Moritz, the chairman of the arrangements committee, in a fine gesture, invited his fellow Buffalonian Millard Fillmore, then President of the United States, having assumed office on the death of Zachary Taylor only a few days before. Mr. Fillmore understandably did not attend the consecration. Governor Hamilton Fish of New York also could not come; but he sent his regrets and "a liberal donation" to the congregation.[39]

A crowd that exceeded the seating capacity passed through the entrance to the synagogue on which was inscribed "This is the Gate of the Eternal—The righteous enter it." The committee, wearing badges, saw that they were seated properly and saw also that no boys under thirteen nor girls under twelve were admitted. The next day the Buffalo *Commercial Advertiser* commented on the large number of non-Jews who witnessed "this novel dedication."

For the occasion a rabbi was brought from New York to Buffalo. The Reverend Samuel M. Isaacs (1804-1878) of the "Gates of Prayer" (Sha'arei Tefillah) Synagogue, was the celebrant and orator for the consecration. And for the following Saturday services a special cantor was brought in. The committee sent out of the city for an extra Torah, complete with silver vestments. Isaacs, a pro-Orthodox partisan who later became editor of the traditional *Jewish Messenger,* chanted the Hebrew prayers and delivered the sermon in English.

Although no special effort was made to raise funds at this consecration, the congregation was in a generous mood and a total of $560 was collected. It was, to speak conservatively, a highly successful day.[40]

Unfortunately, after this day of triumph, Beth El was to experience hard times for a full half decade. Perhaps the spark of enthusiasm over the acquisition of the new building cooled. Surely the congregation was weakened by the secession of some members. The treasury fell dangerously low. It was reported that members would not pay their assessments. The wealthy members had to lend money to the congregation. On January 14, 1851, not six months after the consecration, the board of trustees warned the members that they would not maintain the synagogue without increased cooperation.

The first hint that there might be dissension of a more serious nature than the usual bickering that went on in most newly formed immigrant groups came on January 7, 1849. The Beth El minute books state that a resolution was passed "that in the event of a deviation taking place in the Congregation among its members that the deed be recorded of said Burial Grounds in the name and title of the Hebrew Congregation Beth El." The entry continues, "And it was further resolved that should they divide into two separate congregations that no less than ten members shall constitute a congregation—and if either of the two aforementioned Congregations secede themselves again from each other, they shall not be entitled to any portion of the Burial Ground. And they must adhere in every manner and shape follow up to the Strictest Letter of the Constitutional Laws—and further it is required that every member shall sign his name to this Resolution."

Very clearly trouble was anticipated and this resolution was an effort to avoid a legal tangle over the ownership of the cemetery land. The resolution was carried by nine votes to four at a general meeting, and only nine members signed it. Presumably the four who voted against the measure would not put their names to it.

A year later, on January 20, 1850, at the first meeting of the congregation in the still unfinished Pearl Street synagogue, the air was blue with talk of secession. At this time the entire country was buzzing with talk of possible secession of the Southern States and Henry Clay was formulating the compromise measures of 1850 that temporarily postponed the disruption of the Federal union. The Buffalo congregation was therefore in the height of fashion. On the motion of J. M. Gitsky, it was voted that secessionists would get no part of the cemetery "even if one member should remain of this original Congregational Society, he alone, in Name of Synagogue Bethel of Buffalo, shall have the right and title to the above named Burial Ground." [41] This entry is typical of the tone of the minutes of the meetings that took place during this stormy time. The records are studded with such entries as "the meeting broke up in confusion." Tempers flared, insults were freely exchanged. Once the president threatened to sell Beth El to get rid of certain members with whom he was unwilling to associate.

According to Rabbi Falk, the basis of all this discord was a squabble over ritual. This question of *minhag* plagued every American city. In the old country there was relatively little trouble over variations in ritual, for certain areas followed one ritual and one would usually have to travel about to observe serious variants. In America, however, Jews from all over Europe might be thrown together in the same synagogue. The people, quite naturally, wanted to pray as they had in the Old World, and it was hard to get a compromise ritual. It was especially difficult to get the Germans and the Poles to agree on a common *minhag*. The result, in almost all cities, was a plethora of synagogues and a general weakening of the *kehillah*.

In Buffalo at this time the Polish Jews were in control of the synagogue and, though the minute books are silent about the exact cause of the rift, it appears that the Germans were the malcontents. It is quite possible that some German newcomers to Buffalo tried to force the adoption of their own ritual. At the meeting on January 20, 1850, Henry (or Heinz) Zinsheimer, the German-born cigar maker and leader of the revolt, left the meeting "after using some very improper language." Elias J. Bernheimer, who had played such an important role in founding the congregation, was only with difficulty discouraged from resigning. Later on he was to become the president of the new congregation Beth Zion. Within three months, Joseph Lessler, also a German, resigned as president of Beth El, and several of their *Landsleute* also threatened to quit the organization.

There were other causes for the unrest. Henry Zinsheimer, Isaac Drucker and Louis Rindskopf, all Germans and all cigar makers, were in arrears in their synagogue dues. All three were also "fire-eating" secessionists, to use the language of the day. Whether they withheld their dues to try to force their views on the group, or whether they actually could not afford to pay, is anyone's guess. When Zinsheimer was "subpoenaed" before the board, he contemptuously refused to appear.[42]

The presence of Jonas Gitsky did not make matters easier for the moderates who were trying to patch up the quarrel. Evidently Gitsky was fanning the flames of controversy in the hope that he would emerge from the conflagration as the strong man of the congregation. Tactless, stubborn and given to the use of offensive speech, Gitsky refused to follow the example then being set by Clay and Webster in the Senate and he made no compromises to prevent secession. When Gitsky got entirely out of hand, he was fined ten dollars for misconduct and, when he refused to pay, the board deprived him of his privileges as treasurer. Amidst all this disorder and bickering the counsel of cooler heads could not prevail.

As the year 1850 drew to a close, the German element withdrew from Beth El and organized a new congregation. It is evident that there were many causes for the split. Probably, in 1847, the Germans had joined the Polish majority in Beth El unwillingly, and now they left of their own accord. At this time most Jewish communities in the United States were dominated by German Jews, and Zinsheimer and his friends were determined that Buffalo should not be an exception to the general rule. Undoubtedly quarrels over control of the cemetery contributed to the secession, for only three weeks after the split, Elias J. Bernheimer bought the land that was to become the burial ground of the Jacobsohn Society. It is tempting to argue that the Germans that constituted this Society, possibly named for the first Reform Jew, were liberal in spirit and were in revolt against some hide-bound Orthodox practices in Beth El. There is, however, no evidence to support this theory and it is refuted by the fact that the group established a new congregation that did not deviate, for thirteen years, from traditional Judaism. The quarrel seems chiefly to have come from a clash of personalities, differences in national origins, and a desire to pray according to the German *minhag.*

The secessionists met on November 14 and 27, 1850, to organize the Orthodox congregation Beth Zion. Originally the group was small, including only eleven members. The leaders chosen were Elias J. Bernheimer, president; Albert Strass, a clothier, vice-president; Moritz Weil, secretary; while Isaac Drucker, David Kurtz, and Jacob Strauss became trustees. Apart from Bernheimer we know very little about these men. We do know that Kurtz, a grocer, was born in 1816 in Baden and that before coming to Buffalo he had lived in Ohio. Most of the others do not appear in the city directory and this fact seems to support Falk's contention that newly-arrived German malcontents sparked the breakup at Beth El.[43]

The ubiquitous Mr. Isaac Moses Slatsky, who was then in one of his many periods of estrangement from Beth El, appeared as the first minister of Beth Zion. He was hired to serve from December 1, 1850, to May 1, 1851, at the rate of $5 per month. This fee was ultimately raised to $100 per annum. Slatsky was not hired without some reservations, for it was specified that he was not to teach. His duties were limited to preaching, chanting the prayers, and reading from the Torah. He was also to provide the kosher meat. He chanted the first service on a bitter cold Friday evening, December 6, 1850, the Sabbath of Hanukkah. The service was held in the parlor of Henry Zinsheimer's house at 55 Oak Street. This was the first place of worship for Congregation Beth Zion, and Zinsheimer was paid 50 cents a month for the use of his parlor for services and for necessary congregational business meetings. Poor Slatsky evidently couldn't please the new congregation any more than he could please the old. Three weeks after he was hired, he was fired. He was succeeded January 6, 1851, by Daniel Shire, a German, who later founded a famous Buffalo family. Slatsky packed his bags and went back to Beth El.[44]

Very little is known of these early years of Beth Zion, for the minute books, if they were kept at all, have not been found. Scattered bits of evidence survive; hearsay evidence contributes something to the story; but for the most part the history of that period of Beth Zion's existence is cloudy.

There was an early alliance with the declining Jacobsohn Society which, it will be recalled, was composed mostly of young German Jews. An agreement was drawn up between Beth Zion and the Society that allowed non-members of the Society to be buried in the Jacobsohn cemetery on payment of an initiation fee and a premium of 12½ cents a month for life. On November 18, 1857, the Jacobsohn Society finally deeded its cemetery to Beth Zion.[45]

The early Beth Zion services were strictly Orthodox and followed the German ritual. A surviving prayer book shows that after 1860 they used an English translation of a *siddur* published by L. H. Frank and Co., of New York.[46]

On January 19, 1851, a group of the Germans met to decide on a petition for incorporation. Bernheimer and Albert Strass handled the incorporation proceedings. They were assisted by Emanuel Van Baalen, a Dutch-born auctioneer, related by marriage to Nathan Boasberg. A fourth member of this group was Henry Cone, a Bavarian dry-goods dealer.

During the first fifteen years of its existence, Beth Zion moved many times, and at one time they even petitioned Beth El for the use of the Pearl Street synagogue. The petition was, of course, denied. In 1851, Beth Zion worshipped at the corner of Ellicott and Clinton Streets. In 1854, their minister was the Rev. Joseph Fry and the president of the congregation was Victor Burger, the owner of a shoe shop at 169 Washington Street.[47]

In 1864, the original Beth Zion was still in existence and was then worshipping in a house located on the corner of South Division and Elm Streets. Their last minister was Dr. Isaac N. Cohen during whose incumbency the old Orthodox Beth Zion merged with the newly-founded Reform group that was to bear the same name. This development, so important for the future history of Buffalo Jewry, will be told in the following chapter.

To return to events in the early 1850s, once the split between the Germans and the Poles had actually taken place, relations between the two groups began to improve. *The Occident* reported in September 1851: "We learned to our regret that the people [of Buffalo] are divided into two congregations; still, there seems to exist a perfect good understanding between the two bodies." The editor, in a diplomatic effort to gloss over the fiery disputes that had led to the breakup, went on to state that there were so many Israelites in Buffalo "that it may perhaps be practicable to maintain two respectable congregations." [48] The two congregations, however, gradually settled down to a peaceable co-existence, and we find that ultimately Beth El recognized the *kashrut* of meat slaughtered by Congregation Beth Zion. In 1860, relations were so amicable that there was talk, at least, of staggering services so that the same minister could read the Torah in both synagogues at different times.[49]

The early days of Beth Zion are shrouded in mystery, and it is not until they began keeping records in 1863 that we know very much about their history. Falk, who arrived in Buffalo in 1866, knew something of the history of the congregation. "Beth Zion," he said, "struggled on, without any sign of prosperity." That this infant congregation was also split by internal strife is attested to by Falk who spoke of great discord "arising from their peculiar notions, which none were willing to relinquish for the sake of peace, or to favor others." [50] Thus it was with so many of these young Jewish communities. Cut off socially from free and complete intercourse with the greater communities in which they existed, these immigrants rubbed against each other far more than was good for the peace of the community. They were generally overworked and poor; their recreational facilities were almost non-existent. Whatever pent up energy and desperation induced by social boredom was in them burst forth into heated arguments in congregational meetings. Much of the bickering recorded in all of these early synagogues must have acted as an emotional catharsis for these high-strung people.

Not all of the Germans left Beth El at this time, of course. Lessler, for example, returned and was elected president once more in 1853. Nathan Boasberg remained until the late 1860s as did the Warners, Keisers and Altmans. Until the founding of the Reform Beth Zion in 1864, Beth El was the stronger of the two congregations, and this fact attracted some newly arrived Germans and held others. Many of the ministers of Beth El continued to be German; and, despite the Polish ritual, as late as the 1880s the ministers were required to speak German and English, and *not* Yiddish. This fact is significant, for it reveals the sense of inferiority under which the Polish Jews in this country labored prior to the present century.

After the secession of Beth Zion in 1850, Beth El or the "Polish Congregation" as it was soon called, had some years of stormy weather and hard times. Internal dissension continued and, in addition, the congregation suffered from financial difficulties. By 1852, the financial condition became so bad that Beth El was in danger of losing its synagogue. The mortgage on the Pearl Street synagogue was held by a Lawrence Myers of New York City. As the payments fell behind, Myers threatened to foreclose and the board of trustees was forced to appeal to the members on February 15, 1852, for contributions to prevent the synagogue from being sold at auction.

From this point on, the minute books for the next few years are scanty and poorly kept. It was almost as though the heart had gone out of the congregation. They do record an important meeting on February 13, 1853. This meeting was called for the purpose of re-organizing the congregation and re-examining and publishing the by-laws.[51] It is interesting to notice that this meeting marks somewhat of a step back toward the European traditions and habits. Those who master-minded the meeting were obviously seeking to re-establish order in the conduct of synagogue affairs and to restore the peace and maintain it. The by-laws called for the appointment of a *parnas,* the European term now temporarily replacing the American term *president.* They also asked for a minister who was cantor, *shohet,* and sexton, and re-emphasized the requirement that all prayers should be in Hebrew and should follow the "Polish *minhag.*" Another movement backward was the re-establishment of a system of fines. This time, the by-laws emphasized that the fines *must* be paid.

Article 29 of the by-laws was a strong effort to enforce attendance at the synagogue by a return to the fine system. At the same time, however, this article contains a compromise that indicates that many or most of the members were forced to work on the Sabbath. Accordingly, the board of trustees was allowed to summon "some of the members or seat holders" to attend on the Sabbath and it went on to state that "he who shall neglect coming shall be fined fifty cents when in the city." It had already proved impossible to maintain a strict fine system whereby the member was fined automatically if he missed a Sabbath service. The 1853 version compromised with the American scene since only those who refused to answer the summons were fined and not all those who missed the services. This pragmatic arrangement evidently permitted members to take turns at working and praying on the Sabbath.

A regular system of synagogue financing was established through the rental of seats, offerings made at the reading of the Torah, donations and subscriptions by the wealthier members, and special assessments to be made at the discretion of the board.

Apparently the re-organized Beth El decided to be much more cautious about the members it accepted, for the new by-laws were careful to state that new members must be acceptable to the congregation. Specifically excluded from membership, to conform with New York State law, were the "unmoral, irreligious, impious" members of the community. Prospective members were required to apply to the secretary a week before the meeting at which they would be voted on. Furthermore they were required to have attended synagogue services for the previous six months, during which time they paid dues and "complied with the usages and customs." If an applicant was found unable to fulfill one or all of the requirements, he was to be declared an *orah* (guest) and be denied the right to vote. In addition to these requirements, the applicant was required to be eighteen years old, or married if younger.

An example of the organizational tightening was the provision that at the annual meeting, to be held on one of the intermediate days of Passover, the trustees would be elected by the congregation and the trustees in turn would elect the *parnas* from their own midst.

Marriage laws were clarified and strengthened at this meeting in 1853. The by-laws now required that members must be married by the minister of Beth El or else be granted permission by the trustees to marry elsewhere. In addition, the minister was forbidden to marry or to bury anyone without consent of the majority of the board of trustees. It is apparent that in this age of transient ministers, mobile congregations, and general confusion, the laymen of the congregation were attempting to maintain and uphold the Jewish marriage laws. They were trying to prevent marriages without valid Jewish divorce, to prevent marriages that might be legal in the eyes of the civil law but illegal or incestuous according to the law of the Torah. The by-laws provided that if a member were defiant in seeking an unlawful marriage, he might suffer a fine of as much as $100 and be deprived of his rights in the congregation. Greater strictness was essential, for there was bound to be considerable laxness in an immigrant community as fluid as was Buffalo, located at a railroad hub that linked the East with the West. Strong barriers were therefore erected to prevent intermarriage and to regulate conversions. The new synagogue laws provided for the impeachment of any lay officer who made conversions himself (technically possible) or who "will allow such to be done." To prevent members from seeking marriage in another congregation and to insure that the marriage fee would go to the rightful Beth El minister, members who married in other congregations were to be fined $10 to $50 and were to be suspended until the fine was paid.[52]

Before strict control was lost, the congregation very strenuously upheld the Jewish marriage laws. For example, in October 1855, a member requested permission to marry a widow who, though originally born Jewish, had been married to a non-Jew. The case was presented to the board of trustees. To support his request the applicant submitted a letter from a prominent liberal New York rabbi, Leo Merzbacher, who sanctioned it. In his letter, however, Merzbacher, although he gave sanction, invited the opinion of the Beth El minister as well. The latter concurred in permitting the marriage.[53]

Other matters received attention at this meeting. Probably still smarting from some of the things said during the split between Beth El and Beth Zion, the congregation Beth El now provided punishments for insults to synagogue officers and for disorderly conduct. The machinery for a trial of these trouble-makers was set up and members could be fined up to $25. Men who carried their arguments outside of the congregation and prosecuted the congregation in the civil courts were to be expelled.

A sign, perhaps, of a growing desire for social respectability was the new requirement that those who attend the synagogue must wear hats, rather than caps, if they wish to be called to the Torah.

In the midst of these efforts to establish and maintain order in the synagogue, the members present at this meeting took time to consider the needy. The new by-laws provide for charity for the wayfarers of whom there were probably many passing through the cross-roads of Buffalo in those days. The *parnas* was permitted to give up to one dollar to a needy traveller; but any larger sum could be given only by the trustees, and they were limited to $10 for any one person or cause.

These by-laws of 1853 were signed by twenty-two members, and afterward, Joseph Lessler, who had returned to the Beth El fold for the time, was elected president and Louis Blumgarden was appointed minister.

Although this meeting of February 13, 1853, set out with the best of intentions to establish perpetual peace and harmony in Beth El, it failed for a variety of reasons. The minute books show continued quarrelling. Jonas M. Gitsky, the rich clothier, who probably felt that for his generosity he was entitled to run the congregation, continued to be a troublemaker. Evidently the rigid rules for admission to membership were too strict to enforce, for by August of that year the laws were relaxed to admit to membership in the congregation "any Israelite subscribing for a seat in the Synagogue and a resident of the city for six months and of the age of twenty-one years." [54] Eventually this was to be the standard for most American synagogues as they reached the point where they accepted almost anyone as a member.

Beth El continued the disheartening search for capable ministers. The turnover rate was high and the minutes speak disgustedly of "much useless discussion." Isaac Leeser, *hazzan* of the Spanish-Portuguese Congregation Mikveh Israel of Philadelphia passed through Buffalo on a visit to Cleveland in 1855. On his return to Philadelphia, he wrote in his periodical, *The Occident,* of the need for intelligent ministers and of the difficulty that well-meaning lay officers experienced in controlling the restless members of their congregations. Leeser listed the things that militated against the procurement of good ministers: poor salaries and precariousness of tenure. The profession, he said, attracted only a few able men and these were unavailable to hinterland congregations.[55] Buffalo knew this last fact only too well.

At this time there was constant quarrelling between President Lessler and Gitsky who had opposed Lessler when the latter was elected in July 1854.

At the beginning of the year 1854, Beth El had received a sudden, fortunate gift which, paradoxically, was to become the cause of yet another rift. On January 9, 1854, a wealthy Jewish bachelor, Judah Touro, died in New Orleans. Item 52 of his will, dated only three days before his death, stated: " I give and bequeath to the Hebrew Congregation, 'Beth El,' of Buffalo, New York, Three Thousand Dollars." [56] Beth El was listed as a beneficiary along with all firmly established American synagogues then in existence.

The Touro bequest seemed to be a godsend, coming as it did at a time of great trouble for the congregation. The bequest is first mentioned in the minute book for March 13, 1854. The congregation sent a delegation to attend the final rites for Touro at Newport. It also appointed a "fit and proper person to say the *Kaddish*" for the traditional eleven months and decreed that Touro's soul be remembered in special prayers on festivals for a year: these prayers were to be said, "for the Soul of the departed and much lamented friend of mankind." It was further decreed that the synagogue burn a light for one year in memory of Touro and on all of his subsequent *Jahrzeits*. The board of trustees formally requested "that as long as this Congregation shall exist all future generations shall adopt the same custom," a request that has been faithfully obeyed for over one hundred years. The resolution adopted that day was placed in a frame in the vestry of the synagogue and published in *The Asmonean* and *The Occident* and a copy was sent to Touro's executors. Suitable marble tablets were inscribed in Hebrew and in English and placed on the walls of Beth El where they may be still seen today.[57] The Touro bequest so inspirited the optimistic officers of Beth El that they spoke of the "final Settlement of a Perpetual Harmony & Peace" that they now saw descending on the congregation, and they looked forward hopefully to an "everlasting Peace never again to be Shaken." [58] These are strong terms and they indicate the extent and seriousness of the internal strife that had torn the tiny congregation since its founding.

These pious statements reveal, however, a basic lack of understanding of the human elements involved in the congregation's troubles. Things went from bad to worse. Some months after the receipt of the bequest, Lessler resigned as president and Gitsky, who won out in the struggle for power, was restored to his favorite position as treasurer. Meetings became stormier than ever before, and the minutes degenerated into a confused mass of notes. At times two sets of minutes were recorded; perhaps the rival factions kept separate notes. In addition, Beth El was once more plagued by ministerial troubles, and usually had to import a *hazzan* for the fall Holidays.

The volcano erupted again on May 26, 1856, and the cause of the eruption was the disposition of the Touro bequest. Just what use each faction wished to make of the money is not clear; all that is certain is that a brawl ensued that almost destroyed Beth El. The old board of trustees not only resigned, but also boycotted meetings to prevent the selection of their successors. After two weeks of confusion and alarm the minute book states revealingly: "The majority of members tired of such unlawful proceedings called out for two successive Sabbaths [in synagogue] for a meeting." [59]

This assembly was duly held on May 26th, and Barnard (or Barnet) Jacobs, S. Bennet, and Jonas Gitsky constituted the nucleus of the new board. Probably to buttress their future actions with legal backing, they delivered the records of their election "to the county clerk's office for recording." But the previous officers, led by Alexander Grunewald, refused to surrender the synagogue's cash reserves. A month later the new officers turned to legal means to force Grunewald and his associates to turn over the funds. At the same time it was necessary for the congregation to dismiss the minister "as the corporation under present circumstances are not able to support a chasan [*hazzan*]." [60] The whole mess was not settled until April 4, 1858, when the congregation made a settlement with Abraham Altman, a clothier who held the funds. He had had $2,147 originally, but he returned only $1,958.57 of the Touro legacy. The congregation finally made use of what was left of the $3,000 of the original Touro bequest. In 1858, $1,570.57 of this money was used to pay off the outstanding mortgage on the Pearl Street property. [61]

The year 1858 marks not only the final settlement of the Touro legacy, but also the establishment of the Buffalo YMHA. In America the various functions of the synagogue were being gradually dispersed. In Europe the synaguogue had been a house of prayer, a school, and a social club. In America, secular-minded Jews went outside the synagogue to satisfy their social needs. This movement gradually weakened the synagogue in America, for it left prayer as its most important function, and in this country comparatively few Jews seemed anxious to pray more than on Rosh Hashana and Yom Kippur. When European Jews came to America they discovered many non-Jewish social organizations, especially among the Germans. In New York City, in the 1840s, Jews began to form literary societies that gradually developed into the "Young Men's Hebrew Literary Association" and eventually into the YMHA. The Jewish "Y" was not a direct result of the parallel YMCA movement, for both "Ys" appeared almost simultaneously. After 1851, YMHAs spread rapidly throughout the United States, although the first real "Y" in the modern sense was founded in Baltimore in 1854.[62] In Buffalo, the Jews were possibly inspired by the German Young Men's Association that had been founded in 1841. It had a program of arts, sciences, literature and study of the German language. Perhaps some Jews were even members of this association.

On Friday evening, October 8, 1858, a group of young Buffalo Jews met with the objective of mutual improvement "in Hebrew and general culture." They also pledged themselves to engage in useful debates, perhaps influenced by the famous Lincoln-Douglas debates, then a current topic of conversation. The first president of the Buffalo "Y" was Simon Bergman (1831-1888), a naturalized American citizen who had been born in Saxe-Weimar. Bergman, a small man about five feet tall with side whiskers, seems to have been a joiner, for in later years he was an influential Ben B'rith.[63] Bergman was married to Adelheid Marcus, sister of Leopold Marcus. The vice-president was Louis Gitsky, clothier and probably a brother of the Beth El fire-eater, Jonas M. Gitsky. Aaron Levy was treasurer and another Gitsky brother, Joseph, was secretary. The programs of the "Y" in those early days included lectures, debates, dramatics and social evenings.[64]

About this time another flood of Jewish immigrants hit Buffalo. Jewish life in the semi-frontier regions was never able to stabilize in the nineteenth century, because the ever-increasing tide of westward-moving immigrants always brought new people and new problems. This immigration was to Jewish life what the frontier was to American life in general. Sometimes the congregations, like the outlaw towns in the Wild West, had to pay a premium for their growth in the disorderly conduct and disrupting influence of some of the newcomers. The sharp but short-lived Panic of 1857 sent many Jews to Buffalo, and they brought their troubles with them.[65] By this time national immigration figures were climbing steadily. During the period, 1850-1860, over two and one-half

million people landed on American shores, and Buffalo got its share of
them. Often strangers, unable to return home for the High Holidays, had
to be accommodated during this fall season of intensified Judaism. On
Sunday, September 13, 1860, the Pearl Street synagogue was kept open
all morning for the sale of seats to non-members and out-of-towners. Forty-
nine seats were rented that day for the sum of $117. In depending upon
the Rosh Hashana rush for synagogue support, Beth El, by 1860, had
come more to resemble an East-European immigrant *shul* of the future
than the orderly congregation that its 1847 founders had in mind.

The deterioration of the services was in large part caused by the parade
of ministers who came to Buffalo, tarried awhile, and then were sent away
or else left for greener pastures. Nathan Boasberg, secretary of Beth El
during this stormy period, complained of the itinerant *hazzanim* who
"disturb the peace of this congregation every year." [66] A certain stability,
however, came in 1862 with the election of Israel Warrensky, the first
Beth El minister who remained long enough to have a permanent influence
on the Jewish community. With Warrensky's arrival the congregation
sought to ward off drastic reform by moderate changes in the service
and by making serious efforts to restore order during the chanting of the
prayers. [67] The seed-time of Buffalo's first congregation was over, and
its members strove to recapture the original sense of dignity that they
had lost during hard struggle for survival.

CHAPTER

———◆◆———

FOUR

War, Prosperity, and Reform

THE CIVIL WAR brought many changes to the hitherto sleepy town of Buffalo. The city geared itself for an upsurge in business as its men marched off to join the blue-clad ranks. Most of the 20,000 men from Erie County who enlisted fought in infantry regiments. Some joined the 44th Infantry, the Ellsworth Regiment, named in honor of a national hero killed in the early days of the war. Almost all members of the 21st and 49th New York Volunteers were from Erie County. The 100th Infantry Regiment was built up by the Buffalo Board of Trade, and the 116th was recruited by the Mayor's Military Committee. Buffalo and Erie County were well involved in the four-year strife. In the crucial summer of 1862, out of a total population of 141,971, Erie County enlistments had reached 3,406. The midsummer draft of 1863, the first resort to general conscription, drew relatively few men from western New York. The registration figures show that in the first class, ages twenty to forty-five and unmarried, there were 56,671 eligible men.[1] Of these, only a small number were actually drafted. In the nation as a whole the draft produced in conscripts or substitutes only about six per cent of the Federal forces. In general, the draft was a failure and its loose provisions encouraged widespread evasion.[2]

In the Buffalo area many committees were formed to meet the problems of the Civil War, and it is fair to assume that Jews participated in some of these activities. Committees were organized to raise funds for the support of the families of volunteers, such as The Union Defense Committee, and The Committee of Twenty. Eventually the care of the Union Army wounded was taken over by the forerunner of the modern Red Cross, the United States Sanitary Commission. In Buffalo, a local group to aid the wounded was started and later affiliated with the national organization. The Civil War equivalent of the USO of World War II, known as Soldier's Rest, was opened opposite the New York Central railroad station in Buffalo, then and for decades thereafter located on Exchange Street.[3]

According to the custom of the day, a great central Fair was held in 1864, at St. James Hall on Main and East Eagle Streets, to raise money for war relief, and there is reason to believe that Buffalo Jewry participated in this municipal event. By and large, Buffalo's Jews were staunch Unionists, and if any bore secret sympathy for the Confederacy, there is no record of their disloyalty. In 1863, the newly formed Hebrew Union Benevolent Society sent $150 to the General Aid Society for the Army, one of the local relief groups, with the apology "that our limited number of members and the short period of our existence, precludes the sending of a larger amount."

The enlistment records of the Civil War challenge the resourcefulness of anyone interested in tracing the activities of a particular group. Among the regular army, the militia units, the volunteer companies, and the conscriptees, the maze of records is often hopelessly tangled or obscure. Taking only those names that are indisputably Jewish, we can reconstruct the war records of about twenty Jews who either came from Buffalo or settled here in the years after Appomattox.

Outstanding among these men was Leopold Marcus (1831-1905). He was born in the city of Posen, and before coming to the United States had been in the dry-goods business in Germany. With his mother, Rosalie, he came to America in 1850 and was naturalized in Buffalo in 1854, although he lived in Dunkirk at the time. On June 3, 1860, Marcus married Amelia E. Levey of New Orleans who died in 1885. Marcus enlisted from Dunkirk on September 23, 1861, just as the fall festival season was drawing to a close. He entered the Union Army as a First Lieutenant of D Company, 68th New York National Guard. This regiment later became the 72nd New York and Marcus served in H Company.

On the battlefield Marcus was promoted to captain by brevet by the "foolish and glorious" Daniel E. Sickles, then commander of the Excelsior Brigade of the Army of the Potomac. In the Peninsular Campaign at the battle of Williamsburg, under General George B. McClellan, Marcus was wounded on May 5, 1862. He suffered a "gunshot wound over collar bone." According to family tradition, Louis M. Brock went to the field hospital and brought his uncle back to Buffalo. The wound itself was not serious enough to warrant his discharge, but his war record also reveals that he suffered from a gastric ailment and weakness of the lungs. He was honorably discharged on July 7, 1862, not quite one year after his enlistment.[4]

Leopold Marcus remained in Buffalo, residing at 393 Michigan Avenue. At first, he was a clerk in a wholesale clothing house, but in 1873, as owner of the firm, L. Marcus & Co., he manufactured clothing on Exchange Street. In 1878, in conjunction with his son Marvin, he conducted his business on Washington Street. Later, the elder Marcus became an insurance agent, but was probably not prosperous, for in his later years he applied for a federal pension claiming "age, rheumatism and an inability to work." [5] Marcus was proud of his war record and was active in the affairs of the Bidwell-Wilkeson Post of the Grand Army of the Republic in Buffalo. He was instrumental in bringing Reform Judaism to Buffalo and took an active interest in Beth Zion affairs and those of other Jewish organizations of his generation.[6]

Abraham Oppenheimer (1841-1916), another Jew from the western New York area, served as a captain in the Union Army. Born in Hesse-Darmstadt, he settled with his family in Nunda, New York, a small community southeast of Letchworth State Park. Before the war he operated the Rochester Clothing Store in Nunda but moved to Buffalo subsequent to his marriage to Adelle Hofeller whose family was living in the larger city. In Buffalo, this one-time clothier established Oppenheimer & Company (later the Oppenheimer Corporation, dealing in industrial chemicals), a firm that has, since the 1870s, been important in the economic life of the city. Abe Oppenheimer was a "grand master of the free and accepted Masons in the State of New York." He was an unostentatious, quiet, bearded man who was president of Beth Zion for seven years.[7]

Three members of Jewish families that had already made an impact upon the Buffalo community served in the war. Henry Van Baalen, son of the auctioneer Emanuel Van Baalen and related by marriage to Nathan Boasberg, enlisted at Buffalo on September 2, 1861, as a private in E Company, 49th Regiment, commanded by the Buffalo hero, Colonel Daniel D. Bidwell. Van Baalen was killed in action on May 5, 1864, at the very beginning of the Battle of the Wilderness. Max Rosenau, half-brother of Sol Rosenau, who was so closely connected with the founding of Temple Beth Zion, enlisted in Buffalo on August 14, 1862. He was honorably discharged a year later on August 15, 1863, from the Naval

Hospital Ship "Red Rover." William Noah, son of Michael W. Noah who had been influential in the founding of the Beth El congregation, enlisted in the navy and was assigned to the gunboat "Essex" then stationed at Cairo, Illinois. Noah returned to Buffalo sick at the age of nineteen, became a fireman, but later left Buffalo and was never heard of again.[8]

Sketchy information is available about other Jews from less well-known families. Nathan Levi, who had recently arrived in Buffalo, enlisted in the Union Navy on January 1, 1865, for three years. Levi had been born in England in 1846, the son of Louis Levi of Poland. He served aboard a United States man-of-war as an ordinary seaman. Philip Silverberg, a peddler born in Poland in 1837 and as yet unnaturalized, enlisted in the 12th New York Cavalry on September 2, 1863. Silverberg who, as the father of a child, was not subject to the draft, was evidently sick with rheumatism for most of his period of service. Simon Jacobs, German-born, served as a private in D Company, 99th Pennsylvania Infantry, from 1862 until 1865. After the war he settled in Buffalo and entered the women's millinery business. He died in Buffalo in 1903. George Rosenberg (1839-1889) enlisted in Rochester and served in the hospital corps. Tradition holds that he was captured at the first battle of Bull Run and was subsequently imprisoned at Libby Prison. A daughter, Hattie, was the first wife of the well known Buffalonian, Daniel W. Barmon, and another daughter, Theresa, was later prominent in Buffalo life. In the 100th New York Volunteers, recruited by the Buffalo Board of Trade, were three Jews: Jacob Friedman, Joseph Sinsheimer and Henry S. Goodman. Isaac Weinberg enlisted in F Company of the 49th New York Volunteers, in Buffalo, on August 22, 1861, and was discharged at Newport News, Virginia, for disability, on October 19, 1862. W. G. Lehman of F Company, 116th New York Volunteers, was probably a Jew, as was Lieutenant Lewis Samuels of the 62nd New York Volunteers. Samuels died in 1870 and was interred in Buffalo.[9]

One blot appears on the record of Buffalo Jewry in the Civil War. Isadore Goldberg, a school teacher who had been born in Germany in 1829, enlisted in the 49th New York Volunteers for three years on September 7, 1862. At the time, he was married and had four children and certainly didn't have to go. He was wounded at the beginning of Grant's mighty push on May 5, 1864, and he deserted both the army and his family on June 9, 1864, and was never heard of again.[10]

Nathan Dutch, a glazier who came to Buffalo in 1850, was forty-three years old when he enlisted on June 17, 1861, in the 36th New York Volunteers. He re-enlisted three years later as a private in the 179th New York Volunteers. He died in Buffalo on December 24, 1895, and the male line has since disappeared, although he still has direct descendants in the city through a daughter, Fannie, who married Isaac Isaacs.[11]

Of all the Jewish veterans of the Civil War, Edward Emanuel Josef was the most famous in Buffalo. Josef had been born in London on May 1, 1835. He arrived in the United States at the age of twelve and started out in this country as a copy boy for the Philadelphia *Evening Bulletin;* later he was apprenticed to a silversmith. At the time of his enlistment he was operating a truck farm near Camden, New Jersey, with his brother. Josef enlisted in E Company, 4th Infantry Regiment of the First New Jersey Brigade and served under Brigadier General Theodore Runyan. Josef's war record was very good. He fought in fourteen battles and was twice wounded. At Ball's Bluff, Virginia (October 21, 1861) he was shot in the head, and later at Falls Church, Virginia, he was wounded in the leg. After his recovery from his wounds he went on to serve long and well in the Union Army, and he was finally discharged at Baltimore in 1865. During his military career Josef served with Oliver Wendell Holmes, Jr., who later became Associate Justice of the United States Supreme Court.

After the Civil War, E. E. Josef returned to his parents in Philadelphia; but then he became a wanderer for a time. He drifted to California, then back to St. Louis, and finally his meanderings led him to Buffalo about 1869. Josef had a clever and inventive mind, and he held patents on thirty devices, one of which was a new design for an egg crate. For many years Josef had no connection with Jewish life in the city, and he married out of the faith. In his nineties he re-identified himself with the Jewish community after he had outlived all his relatives. He was taken to the Rosa Coplon Jewish Old Folks Home.

During his final years, Josef became a great hero and the pride of all the veterans groups in Buffalo. He lived on vigorously and was said to be the last surviving Union veteran in Erie County. He was treasured by the Bidwell-Wilkeson Post 9 of the G.A.R., and whenever he appeared he was received with a standing ovation. At these times he fascinated his listeners with tales, which lost nothing in the telling, of his conversations with Lincoln, Grant and Oliver Wendell Holmes. On his hundredth birthday in 1935, the Jewish War Veterans (which Josef joined at the age of ninety-seven after walking from his home at 1388 Jefferson Avenue to the post headquarters at 277 Linwood Avenue) and other groups of old soldiers turned out in force for a huge celebration. A cake of 100 pounds and decorated with 100 candles dominated the table.

When he died, on April 18, 1936, E. E. Josef was given a hero's rites; he was buried in Beth El Cemetery in the Jewish War Veterans plot with full military honors. Every veterans' post in Buffalo was represented as the old hero was laid to rest.[12]

On the home front the Civil War brought prosperity to Buffalo in general and as the city prospered so did the Jews of the city. "While statesmen deliberated, politicians disputed and armies fought," writes Professor Horton, "Buffalo grew rich at an unprecedented rate." There are several reasons why the Queen City thrived during these years. Unlike many other cities, Buffalo had before the war relatively little trade with the South. Consequently she did not suffer the initial setback at the loss of business that other cities endured. On the other hand, as King Cotton was deposed in the financial realm, King Wheat took its place as the chief American export, and Buffalo became a booming center in the wheat trade. With New Orleans deep in Confederate territory, the port of Buffalo became a major point of transfer for goods that once had reached the Atlantic seaboard by way of the Mississippi and the Gulf. In addition, the city enjoyed a great bonanza in ship building, and her foundries and engine shops were busy with wartime trade. Furthermore, during the war the northern railroads were strengthened and consolidated and, since Buffalo was already a rail center, the city prospered and became even more important in this respect than before Fort Sumter. The engine and car shops in the city were busy turning out rolling stock for these burgeoning northern railroads. For some unknown reason Buffalo did not participate heavily in the clothing boom in Civil War uniforms, but there was a parallel development in civilian apparel that enriched many of the Jews of Buffalo. As the city profited from expansion, its Jewish citizens did not gain directly from the increased output of heavy industry, but many of them improved their positions indirectly as their neighbors had more money to spend on the soft goods that the Jewish merchants vended.[13]

An indication of the tremendous prosperity that came to some Buffalo Jews may be had by a glance at the statements of income at that time. The newspapers published this information in order to keep the people from cheating on the wartime income taxes.*

Among Buffalo Jews the highest income was reported by Abraham Altman who reported $8,732 for the year 1863. His brother and partner, Jacob, reported $4,721. The fortune of the Altman family came through ready-made clothing. Some estimate of their wealth can be gained from the knowledge that when their store, at 38-40 Pearl Street, burned in 1866, the stock was valued at $225,000 but unfortunately insured at only

---

* All figures listed are exclusive of the standard $600 personal exemption and of the other exemptions for rent, state and local taxes.

$160,000.[14] The clothing business was so attractive during the war that we find many of the influential Jews of the period drawn to it.

H. Perry Smith, a county historian of later days, implied that only Jews were important in Buffalo in the retail clothing business that flourished during and after the war.[15] The prosperity of the Buffalo clothiers, however, proved ephemeral and the local firms lost out eventually to competition from Rochester, New York and Chicago. Elsewhere clothing manufacturers seemed to realize that the newly-discharged soldier would want to shed his army blue as speedily as possible for ready-made civilian clothing and they anticipated the new market by sending salesmen on the road. In Buffalo they seem to have been less energetic, possibly because they had made few uniforms during the war and were therefore not spurred on to greater sales activity by the prospect of cancellation of orders.

Although the retail clothing trade occupied most of the Jewish men of Buffalo in the 1860s, a sprinkling turned to selling dry goods, millinery, and fancy goods. The shop salesman was now becoming a commonplace and many Jews were employed as clerks in retail stores. There was, significantly, in the boom years which preceded the Panic of 1873, a sharp decline in the number of Jewish peddlers.

Outside of the clothing trade, one Buffalo Jew was significantly prosperous. Henry Cone (1824-1900) had a retail dry-goods store on Main Street and later a wholesale business on West Seneca Street. He was also an original trustee of the Third National Bank. In 1851 Cone came to Buffalo, where he married Elizabeth Exstein. During the war he prospered and one year listed his income as $6,099. Although he spent his last years in Boston, his body was returned to Buffalo for burial.[16]

Jews were active during the war not only in business; they were also making social progress. The founding of the Hebrew Union Benevolent Association produced two rather important effects. According to Rabbi Falk, the Association was organized on July 15, 1863, at the home of Samuel Kohn on Batavia Street (now Broadway). In all likelihood, the new organization was a wartime successor to the Hebrew Benevolent Society of the City of Buffalo of the previous decade. Although the Association ultimately served the community's charitable interests, the immediate purpose of the organization meeting seems startling to modern readers. It was called, Rabbi Falk relates, "for the purpose of raising funds to buy substitutes for every Israelite who might be drafted into the army of the United States." [17] Although this statement seems shocking to a reader who remembers the role of the modern draft dating from 1917, one must view this action in the light of the Civil War *Zeitgeist*. In the first place, the Civil War draft law permitted men to buy substitutes or to avoid service by paying a flat sum. At the time there was a distinct stigma attached to being drafted, and one of the intended effects of the passage of the conscription act was to spur enlistments. A young lawyer named Grover Cleveland, among other prominent Buffalonians, bought a substitute for himself.

According to Falk, Jewish patriotism ran so high that, instead of raising funds to buy substitutes, the young men tried at this meeting to raise a company of Jewish volunteers. A list of thirty-two names was drawn up as a protest to the stated purpose of the meeting, and of these men "nine actually enlisted in different regiments." Although there were occasional attempts to raise such purely Jewish units, many Jews throughout the country opposed this practice because they felt that it was a brand of *apartheid*.[18]

Instead of furnishing substitutes, the meeting of 1863 founded a benevolent society. The Hebrew Union Benevolent Association did some creditable work as a charity organization during the war, but it is historically far more significant for its contribution to the local spread of Reform Judaism.

The men who formed this association were in general progressive and more Americanized than many other Jews in the area. Most of them were young Germans. A comparison of groups is revealing; the minute books of the traditional congregation Beth El, although very full and complete for the Civil War years, make not the slightest mention directly or indirectly of the conflict. But the Hebrew Union Benevolent Association drew up a resolution of sympathy when President Lincoln was assassinated, and ordered its meeting hall draped in black for thirty days. During the funeral services in Washington, the members of the Association participated in a simultaneous service in Buffalo. There is some reason to believe that the president of the Association, Louis Michaels, entrained for Washington for the occasion. A week later, when, for a few hours, Lincoln's body lay in state on The Terrace, in the vicinity of which so many Jews lived, the Hebrew Union Benevolent Association joined other groups in the local obsequies. Many Jewish children long cherished the memory of being taken by their parents to view the remains of the martyred hero of the Civil War.[19]

It was during the war years that Reform Judaism spread rapidly in the United States. Liberal Judaism had, of course, begun in Germany. It is therefore not surprising that the German Jews who migrated to these shores were generally the leaders of Reform here, although the first domestic impulse for ritual changes came in Charleston, South Carolina, in 1824. It arose in the ancient Sephardic Congregation Beth Elohim, but soon lost momentum. It was revived elsewhere in the 1830s by a group of German Jews, most of whom were progressive and advocated change. But the really effective beginning of Reform in this country did not come until the next decade. Rabbi Leo Merzbacher, once an Orthodox rabbi, joined the "Cultus Society" which founded Temple Emanu-El, in New York City in 1845. As the Reform movement grew, Temple Emanu-El came to be known simply and importantly as "The Temple." At first changes came slowly, for the original intention was merely to omit seemingly obsolete prayers and to introduce a choir and instrumental music into the synagogue. By 1848, when Temple Emanu-El moved to Chrystie Street in New York, German hymns were introduced. In 1850, the *aliyot* were dropped; that is, individuals were no longer called up to the reading of the Torah. With the next move of Emanu-El came another change, the introduction of family pews or mixed seating. In 1855, the first move was made to modernize the prayer book. Rabbi Merzbacher edited a version of the traditional *siddur,* called *Seder Tefillah,* in which he introduced moderate reforms of the Hebrew prayers, but he included only a few German prayers. By the mid 1850s, the second day of *Yom Tov,* which existed by talmudical rather than biblical edict, was dropped. The next reform to be introduced involved sitting with uncovered heads in the synagogue.[20]

Rabbi Merzbacher's Reform prayer book was the first to have wide influence. He had set out to shorten the service, to eliminate repetition of certain prayers, and to remove portions of the liturgy that seemed to him no longer fitting, such as mention of the ritual of animal sacrifice once performed by priests in the Temple at Jerusalem. Rabbi Samuel Adler, who succeeded Merzbacher, revised the prayer book further in the direction of Reform. Whereas Merzbacher did not like prayers in the vernacular, Adler did. He went further than Merzbacher in minimizing references to a personal Messiah and to the resurrection of the dead. The Merzbacher-Adler position occupied the middle ground between that of the radical reformer Rabbi David Einhorn then in Baltimore, and that of Rabbi Isaac M. Wise, the conservative reformer of Cincinnati.

There were other reasons for reform. Some American rabbis, in attempting to halt the stampede toward religious laxity and outright indifference to things Jewish, thought that by yielding minor concessions they might retain in their congregations some of the extremists and bring others back. And thus, these men, though they would not have initiated serious modifications on their own, often yielded to them in the hope of avoiding something worse, the loss of their young people altogether.

Much of the impulse toward Reform came from the women. During the Jacksonian period the cause of women's rights was given impetus. The younger Jewish women, especially the wives and daughters of those more Americanized men who favored change on other grounds, supported and urged it in rebellion against the segregation of the Ladies' Balcony. These women also resented the indifference of traditional Judaism at that time toward female education, and they advocated confirmation for both sexes.

Still another motive for Reform was the immigrant's natural desire to blend into the American atmosphere. Perhaps unwittingly he hoped to improve his social status by making his synagogue as much like the Protestant churches that surrounded him as possible. "He sought to remain Jewish," one able historian has noted, "but he proclaimed himself a new type of Jew. A reform of Jewish ritual carried to him the imputation of enlightenment, of progress, of true Americanization." [21]

Another very real contribution to the advance of liberalism was the existing laxity of religious practice. Some Jews in America assimilated and severed completely the ties with their faith. Others, as they prospered, especially during the Civil War years, wanted the kind of Judaism that would sanction in theory the relaxation of the Jewish law that had already taken place in practice. This motive, combined with the social-status motive, made them desire a type of religion that would draw the line between themselves and the newer, unpolished immigrants. They wanted the kind of service that would sharply distinguish them from their newly arrived ultra-Jewish neighbors. They wanted a religion, in fine, that would let them emphasize their Americanism rather than their Europeanism. Rabbi Wise's *Israelite* expressed the feeling of this group: "Americanize the synagogue, render it rational and intelligible, give everybody a chance to understand you, and you remove a thousand prejudices from our religion and our race." [22] The desire to conform, to be a part, to be American is clearly evident here. *The Occident,* conservative organ of Isaac Leeser, took a far less optimistic view of this trend: "There is a spirit of innovation abroad which threatens to level everything to the ground." [23]

Rabbi Wise repeatedly issued rallying cries in his Reform periodical, *The Israelite,* which seems to have been widely circulated in Buffalo. At times he stressed the confusion in traditional synagogues, complaining that, "anybody can preach—a London *Shamesh,* a New York comedian, a German *Shohet.*" [24] Again, considering the Orthodox situation in Rochester, he bemoaned the fact that the people had no rabbi, no choir, no uniform *minhag,* no official *shohet.* He said that the people were almost ashamed to call themselves Israelites and were greatly in need of a decent service and the "sublime words of a good minister, the refreshing tunes of a fine choir." [25] At another time he prayed, after a visit to Syracuse, that the community be "redeemed from the iron grasp of orthodoxy." "Behold!" he thundered to the traditionalists of that city, "Ye champions of darkness, this is your work. Compare Syracuse to Albany or Cincinnati, to Louisville or Chicago, . . . and see the difference of light and darkness in the system." [26]

At Albany, Wise visited his old congregation, Anshe Emeth, and observed the simple, sublime service. "The minister facing the Congregation reads the prayers in a solemn tone without any sort of song," he reported. "All singing is done by the choir . . . A singing minister looks funny, as foolish almost as a singing orator . . . All singing must be done by the choir." [27]

And so, given impetus by the spirit of change engendered by the war, Reform began to sweep through the country. It is interesting to note that the questions that were aired in the liberal periodicals of a century ago are the same questions that still vex many traditional American synagogues. Should the sexes be segregated? Should the cantor or minister face the Ark or the congregation? Should the full portion of the Torah be read each week so as to complete the Pentateuch each year, or should Jews return to the ancient system of reading it over a three-year cycle? Are mixed choirs and organ music permissible in Jewish services? These questions bothered some Jews of 1860 just as they do their descendants of today.

In the 1860s, however, a certain restlessness had taken hold on the soil of America. "The Civil War," Professor Hansen notes, "changed the ideals of the foreign group and substituted a new leadership." [28] As the boys of immigrants marched off to war, their parents turned their eyes away from things European and began to concentrate on things American. Foreign languages, folkways, and religious customs were superheated in the crucible of nationalism made red hot by the fires of war, and they lost their identifying forms as they melted into the basic Americanism of the land.

It was in this period of flux that Reform came to Buffalo. We know relatively little of what actually happened, for the records are scarce. It was a time of great religious confusion, a dark period in local Jewish history brightened only here and there by occasional rays of light. We do know enough, however, to recognize that the confusion and instability led to dissatisfaction with the status quo, and to the desire for change.

A few short-lived congregations appeared and disappeared in Buffalo from 1860 to 1863. These ephemeral groups denoted trouble in the older congregations, tension between nationalities, disputes over ritual, and

friction between the older, Americanized Jews and the new, still Europeanized immigrants. A Palestinian messenger, Abraham Nissan Ashkenazi, reported that a Congregation Shearith Israel had been founded in
Buffalo in May 1861.[29] The membership was very small, but, like so many
other new congregations, this one thought very early about securing a
burial ground. On July 19, 1861, the day that burials ceased at the old
cemeteries, Shearith Israel United Congregation purchased land on Pine
Ridge Road from George and Maria Freund. The congregation did not
last, however, and by 1862 it was in financial difficulty if not already out
of existence.[30]

Other evidence of quarrelling and unrest, some of it bordering on the
absurd, is reflected in Rabbi Wise's *Israelite*. Beth El's newly arrived
minister, Rev. H. Lowenthal, established a kosher boardinghouse at 118
Pearl Street and advertised that "he offers all kinds of accommodations
to travellers." The reformists, of course, opposed the old system in which
a minister was forced to make a living by these undignified outside activities. Shortly after his arrival in Buffalo from the rebel outpost of Macon,
Georgia, Lowenthal became involved in an embarrassing squabble. The
Rev. Israel Hochwald of Toronto, probably a competitor, criticized
Lowenthal's work as *mohel*. In retaliation, a protest drawn up by the
Buffalo clothing magnate Abraham Altman and seven other friends of
Lowenthal charged that Hochwald was "no more than an impostor, being
no priest in the Jewish Church." The following month *The Israelite* carried the charge of Joseph E. Strass, Wise's Buffalo correspondent, that
his name had been used against Hochwald without his consent. Thus it
was that quarrels great and small fragmented the community.[31]

Meanwhile, Beth Zion was also shaken by unrest. Rabbi Falk, writing
about these times, stated, "Those Israelites of Buffalo who favored liberal
ideas, felt the weight of responsibility for the fact that they were not
worthily represented before the Christian community." Young Louis M.
Brock wrote that the liberal Buffalo Jews had a strong desire "to see the
elevation of their fellow co-religionists to the same standard as that
occupied by those in Cincinnati and New York." [32]

The first actual step toward Reform in Buffalo came in 1863. As the
High Holidays approached, a group of liberals wrote to Rabbi Isaac M.
Wise in Cincinnati and requested him to send a minister to Buffalo. In-
cluded in this group were Jacob Altman, Henry Brock, Henry Cone,
Henry Friend, Marcus Wall, and Leopold Marcus just recently returned
from the war. One of the principal men in this group was Siegmund
Levyn, and another was Leopold Keiser.

Levyn was born on January 23, 1837, in Berlin, and he came with his
mother Bertha to America in 1847. A few years later he moved to Buffalo

where he attended public school. Levyn, who was a strong individualist, caught the gold fever of the 1850s and joined the California prospectors. Evidently he was not successful, for he returned to Buffalo and settled into the cigar business. He prospered in tobacco; and eventually in the 1870s he engaged, not only in the retail trade at Main near Eagle Street, but also in the wholesale cigar business. His trade was sufficiently large for him to make frequent trips to Cuba for the raw materials.

On May 10, 1860, Siegmund Levyn married Mary Catherine Noah (1845-1899), the eldest daughter of Michael W. Noah and the first child of Mrs. Noah's second marriage. The fact that they were married on Lag baOmer (one of the few days between Passover and Shavuot on which marriages are allowed), indicates that even the liberal-minded Jews of Levyn's circle were at that time still observing Orthodox practice in some respects. The Levyns were moderately wealthy, and they entertained in fine style at their home at 333 Pearl Street. They always kept open house on Friday evenings.

At the age of twenty-seven, Levyn was the first president of Temple Beth Zion. He has been described as a gentleman of the old school. A short man, he stood only five feet five and a half inches. Nevertheless, he was a dynamic leader with a good speaking and singing voice. He was swarthy, with a high forehead, dark brown eyes, black hair and a bushy mustache. Socially, as well as in business, Levyn was energetic. He was a great joiner. He was active, as we have already seen, in the Hebrew Union Benevolent Association; later, he was to become a charter member of the Jewish Orphan Asylum Association of Western New York. His interests reached outside of the city of Buffalo, for he was a governor of the Home for Aged Jews in Yonkers and of the Hebrew Union College in Cincinnati. He was a charter member of Montefiore Lodge of B'nai B'rith and, at the convention in 1872, was appointed a "Grand Nasa Ab" by the District Grand Lodge No. 1. He travelled widely as spokesman for various Jewish groups of Buffalo, and he was known as a man of tact and good judgment. Many times he served as the local delegate to national conventions. In addition to these Jewish activities, Siegmund Levyn was active in non-Jewish societies. He belonged to the Exempt Firemen's Association, the Independent and Liberal clubs, and to the Liedertafel and Orpheus singing societies. Within and without the Jewish community he was an important and energetic force in Buffalo society.

Although his son Bertram married out of the faith, Levyn had many Jewish descendants. His daughter Minnie married Joseph Desbecker who lived in Buffalo until his death in 1937. Another daughter, Rosalie, married Mark Rafalsky of New York City, and a third daughter, Fanny, was the first wife of Theodore Hofeller. Siegmund Levyn died in Buffalo on December 15, 1900.[33]

Leopold Keiser (1826-1912) was another important member of the founding group of Beth Zion. Keiser, who had been born in Bisenz, Moravia, was a staunch friend and admirer of Isaac M. Wise. The evidence seems to indicate that Keiser had been a teacher in Europe, and this fact may account for his lifelong interest in Jewish education. Although Leopold Keiser appears never to have prospered as a clothing dealer, his son August, whose mother died at his birth, was eminently successful in the wholesale tobacco business. To mark his own seventieth birthday in 1928, August Keiser contributed $10,000 to the Hebrew Union College Endowment Fund to be earmarked as "The Leopold Keiser Fund." [34] Closely associated with Leopold Keiser was his *Landsman* from Bisenz and future *mehuttan*, Leopold Warner (1817-1900). For many years the history of Temple Beth Zion was to be influenced by these two Leopolds of Moravian origin.

After these liberal protagonists sent the previously mentioned letter to Rabbi Wise, they took steps to implement their plans. Lower Kremlin Hall, located on Main Street between Niagara and Eagle, was obtained for the organization meeting, held on Sunday, September 7, 1863, just a week before Rosh Hashana. Keiser presided while Louis M. Brock, then a youth of nineteen, kept the minutes. This lad seems to have been the mouthpiece of his father, Henry Brock, who may have been reluctant to take the leadership because, at the time, he still held high office in Congregation Beth El. It was the younger Brock therefore who read to the meeting a current article by Rabbi Wise in which the principles of Reform Judaism were outlined. Those interested in forming a new synagogue were asked to attach their names to the minutes, and twenty-two men of those present signed the book. Siegmund Levyn, Henry Brock and Jacob Altman were named to make immediate arrangements for High Holiday services. Another group was appointed to make arrangements for the establishment of a permanent organization.[35]

A good deal of the work of the latter committee was done by Solomon Rosenau (1833-1923) who was to be active in Beth Zion's affairs for almost sixty years. Rosenau, born in Disbeck, Bavaria, had come to Buffalo just before the Civil War. He enjoyed an ephemeral prosperity as a young man, but his millinery store burned down in 1865 and he seems never to have recouped his losses. Perhaps to compensate for this lack of business success, he devoted most of his time to organizational affairs. It was Rosenau who kept Beth Zion's books for forty-one years without an assistant, and his scrawling hand, difficult to read at best, did not improve with the years. Destined to outlive his entire generation, this old man was a familiar sight in the vicinity of his North Pearl Street home until the "jazz age" of the 1920s.[36]

After the success of this first meeting another was called to prepare for Rosh Hashana. At this second meeting Siegmund Levyn presided, and a committee, composed of Levyn, Leopold Marcus, and Siegmund Hofeller, was directed to draft rules and regulations for the congregation. This second meeting seemed to be greatly concerned with insuring decorum during the coming services and appointed ushers to maintain order. By this time the Reform group had mustered forty-six members.[37]

The first Reform services in Buffalo were observed in Lower Kremlin Hall on Monday and Tuesday, September 14-15, 1863, the two days of Rosh Hashana. For the ceremony, Siegmund Levyn had borrowed an Ark of the Law from Beth El. The services were conducted by Rabbi Isaac Schoenbrun of Cincinnati, a kindly elderly gentleman whose picture still hangs in Temple Beth Zion. He was assisted by Leopold Keiser, who chanted part of the services "with much emphasis and elegant delivery." [38] Siegmund Levyn had trained the volunteer choir.

The first Reform sermon preached in Buffalo was on the subject of Sabbath observance! So effective was Rabbi Schoenbrun's message that a group promised thereafter to close their places of business on the Sabbath and holidays. The local press noted that the services in Lower Kremlin Hall were performed after the manner of the "reformed Jewish church." Rabbi Wise was, of course, pleased with the news, and he noted that the Buffalo group was "fully imbued with the spirit of religious reform now pervading among many of the more enlightened people of our faith." [39]

Of these, the first Reform Jewish services held in Buffalo, Rabbi Falk says, "It was an entire novelty to many Israelites in this city, to see a Divine service conducted with such essential deviation from the old Ritual:—a modern service, enhanced in interest by choir singing, and edifying through the preaching of the word of God in a known tongue."

The connection between the Hebrew Union Benevolent Association and the early Reform movement in Buffalo becomes evident from a comparison of the names of the members and the officers of both groups. The first of the members of the Association to sign the sympathy resolution for Lincoln's death was the Rev. Dr. Isaac N. Cohen, first permanent rabbi of the new Beth Zion. Siegmund Levyn, who was also president of the Association, became the first president of the Temple. Leopold Marcus was vice-president of the Association. Louis M. Brock, the secretary of the Association, also acted as secretary of the first meeting to launch the Reform movement in Buffalo. Finally, there is evidence that the meeting to form a "Temporary Reform Congregation" was held on September 27, 1863, at the meeting hall of the Hebrew Union Benevolent Association.[40]

Collaterally with the foundation of the men's organization, a ladies' charity group was formed, probably to help sick and needy women. There is evidence that this women's group also was influential in the Reform movement. As the women met for the purpose of charity work, they had ample opportunity to work for the desegregation of the sexes in the synagoguge and for female equality in the services. Whatever the manner of their getting started, the ladies most influential in the movement were also part of the women's charity organization. The files of *The Israelite* reveal the connection between the Ladies Benevolent Association and religious change. In an article for October 2, 1863, that paper reported that while Rabbi Schoenbrun was in Buffalo conducting the Reform service of 1863, he encouraged the ladies to form the "Hebrew Ladies' Benevolent Society." The paper listed the principal members of the Society—Mrs. Simon Bergman, Mrs. David Rosenau, and Mrs. Joseph E. Strass, all ardent reformers.

Consequently, one is inclined to believe that the Hebrew Union Benevolent Association and its affiliate, the Hebrew Ladies' Benevolent Society, evolved into a Reform group that eventually took over and converted the old Beth Zion congregation into a Reform Temple.

After Rabbi Schoenbrun left Buffalo, the women, who had presented him with a gold-headed cane, did much to keep the spirit of change alive, and Rabbi Wise speaks fondly of *Die treuen Schwestern,* Mrs. Frederica Strass (wife of Joseph E. Strass), Mrs. Sarah Abraham (wife of Abraham Abraham), and Mrs. I. Cassell.

In the following spring, *The Israelite,* in speaking of a great Purim Ball arranged by the Ladies' Hebrew Benevolent Society, reported: "Although the Israelites of Buffalo are far behind other Jewish congregations in occupying a respectable position in the religious world, or in cherishing and maintaining religious institutions; still, of late, a more progressive spirit is prevailing among the more enlightened." The ladies, it was reported, raised $400 for the Reform cause at this ball.[41] One source of funds was the sale of an oil painting donated by Magnus Wiener of Dunkirk. Wiener, who had been born in Posen in 1832, was naturalized in Buffalo and moved here in 1866. He was the father of Judge Cecil B. Wiener.

In 1864, several meetings were held to solidify the ranks of the liberal group and to organize a permanent congregation. On the eve of the Day of Atonement, a meeting was called by Joseph E. Strass. Leopold

Keiser presided and it was agreed to form "The Congregation of Temple Beth Zion." At this meeting the proper education of the children was stressed as the main objective of the new congregation. A few days later, during one of the intermediate days of Succot (October 18, 1864), Dr. Isaac N. Cohen (1820-1895) of the old Beth Zion was appointed rabbi of the new congregation at the impressive salary of $2,000. Evidently the new group was determined to see to it that its minister was paid a sufficient salary to preclude his working at ignominious part-time jobs to support himself.

At a subsequent meeting, the members declared that divine worship be "celebrated according to the rites of the Reformed Temple Church." The trustees elected at that time were Siegmund Levyn, Siegmund Hofeller, Jacob Altman, Sol Rosenau, Henry Cone, Leopold Keiser, Leopold Marcus, Solomon Biesenthal and Joseph E. Strass. At this meeting the first steps toward incorporation were taken, and a committee was appointed to lease, buy, or build a synagogue. Despite the appointment one month earlier of Dr. Cohen, this committee was also empowered to engage a minister for one year. At the meeting it was also decided that no member was to subscribe less than $25 for the synagogue fund.

The connection between the Hebrew Union Benevolent Association and the Reform movement has already been pointed out. It is clear from Falk's account that the insurgents, most of whom had at one time been associated with the Beth Zion Orthodox congregation, sought union with that group. "Old Beth Zion," wrote Falk, "lacking numerical strength, was satisfied that it could sustain itself no longer, yet its members insisted on retaining their name Beth Zion for the new union and this was agreed upon." The last president of Congregation Beth Zion was Aaron Aarons, who went over to the new Temple. A further connection between the new and the old Beth Zion is the fact that the new group, in addition to the rabbi of the old synagogue, also took its Ark, scrolls of the Torah, and part of its cemetery land.[42]

The first rabbi of Temple Beth Zion had been a doctor of medicine before drifting into the rabbinate.* He preached in both English and

---

* Much needed information on Cohen came to light too late to be incorporated into the body of this book. W. Gunther Plaut's *The Jews in Minnesota* (New York, 1959, p. 73 ff.) uncovers the full story of Temple Beth Zion's first rabbi because his final twenty years were spent in Minnesota. Cohen was born in Mecklenburg, Prussia. Known as the "Doctor-Rabbi," he had received an M.D. in Berlin in 1852 and had also been formally trained for the rabbinate. Dr. Cohen came to Buffalo from a pulpit in Albany, in which city he had married Jane Rice, a union that was eventually blessed with nine children. Dr. Plaut's meticulous research, a pointed commentary on the need for cross-indexes in the field of local American-Jewish history, explains Cohen's short tenure in Buffalo. A man given to unconventional clerical behavior, he was much at home at the card table. Moreover, his mercurial temper

German and taught the children Hebrew and the principles of their religion. Cohen was instrumental in uniting the two groups and forming Temple Beth Zion. Unfortunately the only physical description of him that has survived is that found in the recollections of a Gentile lady of Buffalo, Frances Metcalf Wolcott. She wrote many, many years after his death, and her account seems to be more a description of something out of the *Arabian Nights* than that of a German rabbi and doctor: "His rich flowing black robe, silken well-kept beard, and a cap, marked him as a Sephardim [sic] Jew of royal or sacerdotal tribe. His two stately daughters of Oriental beauty seemed to me of the same blood as Rebecca in *Ivanhoe*. It was whispered that in the family of Cohen should come the Second Messiah. Socially, in that era, the Jew had no place in Buffalo."[43]

When one compares the acquisition of the Beth El synagogue in 1850 with the acquisition of the Beth Zion synagogue fourteen years later, an estimation can be made of the prosperity that the Civil War brought to Buffalo Jewry. By the end of 1864, Temple Beth Zion had bought the thirty-two-year-old Methodist-Episcopal Church on Niagara Street from William G. Fargo for $13,000. The down payment was $7,000 and the congregation spent another $5,000 to remodel the church and install an organ.[44] It was said that Fargo, who had been Democratic mayor of Buffalo during the war and connected with Wells-Fargo & Co., sold the church property to the synagogue at half its true value. The church, which Beth Zion occupied until 1889, when it was razed for the erection of a Masonic Temple, was Gothic, and it was predicted that after remodelling "it will equal if not exceed any similar edifice in the United States for beauty and finish." This equality of status, of course, was exactly what the group sought. The new synagogue would truly become part of the American scene, for it was located on the very site of the first church built in the city.

The merger of the new and old congregations in all likelihood did not come about smoothly. Time has buried the evidence that a die-hard segment of the old Beth Zion refused to go along with Reform and continued a shadow-like existence for a decade after the Temple was established. We do know that there was a great deal of agitation at the time. Louis M. Brock wrote to *The Israelite* that there had been repeated attempts before 1863 to bring Reform to Buffalo "but all in vain." He said that until 1863, "orthodoxical prejudice" continued strong "but whose

---

hardly suited him to provide the type of dignified leadership demanded by the Buffalo Reform group. Cohen retired from the rabbinate and, until his death in 1895, practiced medicine in Minneapolis. Previously, he had served Temple Mount Zion in nearby St. Paul.

baneful influence we have at last succeeded in removing, thus allowing the tender sprout to feel the strength engendering effects of intelligence and progress." [45] Falk recalled that the whole controversy severely "agitated the Jewish community."

In 1863, a new congregation, Anshe Emes Beth Zion, came into being. It was evidently composed of a group of the Orthodox members of the Congregation Beth Zion who rejected the new departure. This group evidently felt that it was preserving the true way of worship for the title of their organization means "Men of Truth." It was composed of Henry Wertheimer, Simon Weil, Joseph Goldberg, Aaron Weil, William Southeimer, and the still nominally Orthodox Elias J. Bernheimer who had been an important figure in the founding of two other congregations.

Because of this split among the members of Beth Zion, it was necessary to divide the cemetery lands. The legal proceedings involved offer proof positive that, not only did the traditionalists continue to maintain a congregation which they asserted was the "true" Beth Zion, but that they even bought additional cemetery land. The group, however, soon fell apart and its final act came in 1874 when Anshe Emes Beth Zion turned over its property on Pine Ridge Road to the Temple, certifying that the congregation had ceased to hold services and that practically all of its members had joined the Reform group.[46]

In the meantime the reconstruction of the Niagara Street Temple of Beth Zion had been completed and the building was dedicated on Friday, May 26, 1865. It was a fine spring day and there was joy in the hearts of many Buffalonians, for each train arriving at Exchange Street station brought additional bronzed veterans home from the war. Riding in a car filled with these blue-clad men, Rabbi Isaac M. Wise arrived in Buffalo from Cincinnati to officiate at the dedication services of the new Temple. Among additional guests were Mayor Fargo, members of the Common Council, a State senator and other non-Jewish dignitaries. The dedication procession started from the vestry punctually at three in the afternoon with "trustees of the church, church officers, invited rabbis, and presidents of congregations, with the building committee and architects." They marched into the Temple carrying the scrolls of the Torah and mounted the *bimah* which was draped in crimson damask and surrounded by potted evergreen trees. Siegmund Levyn led a volunteer choir, made up of members and their daughters, which was accompanied by Professor Charles G. Gegenhard at the organ. The choir first sang "Blessed be he that cometh in the name of the Lord," and then chanted the *Mah Tovu* prayer in Hebrew to the music of the famous European composer, Solomon Sulzer.

At this point in the ceremonies Samuel Desbecker's young daughter,

Amelia, presented Mr. Levyn, the president, with an ornate key to the Temple. Then the *Sifrei Torah* were placed in the Ark while "seven young ladies beautifully arrayed in white took part in these ceremonies, forming a most pleasant feature. Then the choir sang Psalm 150."

After an address in German and English by the Reverend Doctor I. N. Cohen, Leopold Marcus sang a solo, "Bow down thine ear," which was followed by a rendition by Miss Hannah Exstein.

Rabbi Wise, then a vigorous forty-six, preached the principal sermon in English. He reminded his audience that the preservation of the great truths proclaimed by Judaism was worth more than all the sufferings of the Jewish people throughout the ages. He was a masterful speaker and the *Commercial Advertiser* reported: "The address was unwritten and apparently given without previous preparation, but was such as to stamp the reverend gentleman as an eloquent divine and ripe scholar." [47]

After Rabbi Wise's sermon, Solomon's prayer at the dedication of the First Temple at Jerusalem was read in English. Following these ceremonies came the usual Sabbath eve services. Rabbi Wise preached again the following morning and once more on Sunday.

The new Temple Beth Zion resembled in several ways Temple Emanu-El of New York, the Temple that most Buffalo Reform Jews had seen. The Ark was modeled after that of the New York synagogue and the congregants used the Merzbacher-Adler prayer book. However, in 1865, some vestiges of Orthodoxy still remained in Beth Zion. Most members still kept two days of Rosh Hashana. On February 17, 1865, they advertised for a *hazzan-shohet*. Moreover, they still had a cantor and still were concerned about kosher meat. But they now had a Temple that was praised by their non-Jewish neighbors. The Buffalo *Courier* spoke with admiration of the personal sacrifice of the members in making the Temple possible and added that "a neater place of worship the city does not boast of." [48]

Meanwhile, during these years of religious upheaval, Beth El remained traditionally oriented, primarily because of the addition to its membership of newly arrived immigrants stemming from parts of Europe that thus far had been untouched by liberal currents. To understand Beth El's history during this period of ritual revolution it is necessary to recount the story of its newer members who, in the 1860s, replenished the congregation's strength just at a time when its more liberal elements were attracted to the new Temple Beth Zion.

During the earlier years of the Civil War, immigration to these shores had almost ceased, for not many people were anxious to come to a country torn asunder by fratricidal war. However, as the Union victory became apparent after Gettysburg and Vicksburg, the flood of immigrants began to flow once more. In the period between 1860 and 1870, despite the interruption of the early years of the war, 2,314,824 immigrants came to America, only about 284,000 less than in the preceding decade.[49] For several reasons, additional eastern European immigrants, who would naturally gravitate toward Beth El, came to the United States in the 1860s. Suwalki, a province in Lithuania near the Prussian border, was badly hit by economic depression and cholera in the 1860s and sent many of its people to America and some came to Buffalo. In 1863, Poland rose up against the rule of Czar Alexander II, and the results of that abortive rebellion uprooted additional Jews. The Central Polish Committee in the United States of America, ironically forgetting the ingrained anti-Semitism of many of its supporters, appealed for help "to the Poles of the Mosaic Persuasion" in America and reminded them that it was the Czar who taxed them, who snatched their children for his armies, and who expelled them from their villages. Either in callousness or in stupidity, they told the Jews of America, "In all our attempts to free ourselves from tyrannic oppression, we regarded you as equals." [50]

When some of these Jewish "stepchildren of the Czar" arrived in Buffalo, Beth El was affected. As the Jewish population increased, it became less necessary for Jews from different parts of Europe to cling to one another in mutual society. Consequently, in the 1860s the cleavage between the Germans and the Poles became more noticeable. In this period there were enough German Jews in Buffalo to allow them to carry on as a social and religious unit by themselves. They began to ape the seaboard Jewish society where the older group, usually German, looked down upon the green newcomers even as the Spanish-Portuguese colonials or their children had once looked down on them. Buffalo's Jewish families that had already achieved a measure of economic and social stability resented these immigrants, because they saw them as blocking their own acquisition of status in American society and because the newcomers were rapidly forming a Jewish stereotype in Gentile eyes.

The Beth El minute books of the period reveal the impact of the stepped-up East-European immigration. One now finds, for the first time, such familiar names as Lichtenstein, Grodzinsky, Barnetsky, Brumberg, and Salinsky. Yiddish expressions and nicknames became increasingly common. Moreover, the minutes themselves became sloppy and often illegible—a far cry from the meticulous notes of William Sylvester. Some of the newcomers whose remarks were recorded seem to have been hardly literate in any language, but talk at meetings they could and did.

Amongst the group that began to worship at Beth El in the 1860s were the founders of some distinguished families. Isaac Gumbinsky came from Suwalki and his wife, Rebecca, from Vishtinetz, a Lithuanian village the inhabitants of which seemed drawn to Buffalo. Near Vishtinetz was Volkovisk, a town that was also early affected by the exodus to America. From Volkovisk came Harris Cohen, whose children included the late Mrs. Alexander Bohne, Frank L., and Etta Cohen; also Mrs. Leo A. Beir and Dr. J. Y. Cohen. From the same hamlet stemmed the family of David Lawrence (b. 1888), the nationally syndicated columnist. Lawrence began his career on the Buffalo *Express* and rose to national fame during the presidency of Woodrow Wilson who had recognized Lawrence's ability during the latter's student days at Princeton.

The forebears of Judge Samuel J. Harris also belonged to this second wave of Jewish immigrants to Buffalo. The judge's maternal grandfather was Abraham Brown, a glazier from Warsaw, who came here prior to the Civil War. Solomon Joel Harris (1835-1920) arrived just before the tide turned at Gettysburg. Five years later he married Rachel Adeline Brown when she was but sixteen. At that time Isaac Ellis (1824-1901), another founder of a well-known Buffalo Jewish family, had already been here for over a decade.

More influential in Beth El affairs than the previously mentioned families, were the Hymans who provided sorely needed leadership for the struggling synagogue. Barnard (or Bonney) Hyman (1810-1875) and his brother Nicholas (1812-1905) arrived from Poland a decade before Lincoln's first election precipitated the War between the States. With the brothers came their mother, Amelia, born in 1786 and destined to live in Buffalo until the ripe old age of eighty-four. While not strictly Orthodox, the Hymans fought revolutionary changes at Beth El and guided its affairs during the years of crisis that followed the establishment of Temple Beth Zion. The Hyman brothers were pioneer retail clothiers and their store, located a few steps from the foot of Main Street, was the place where Beth El leaders were wont to gather on Sundays to discuss congregational matters.[51]

While Beth El's Polish membership was increasing proportionately, a good many Germans remained with the congregation. Amazingly enough, these men were not only the occasional German immigrant who liked a more traditional service, but also some leaders of Reform. Among those who retained their Beth El affiliation longer than might have been expected were Joseph Lessler, Leopold Warner, Nathan Boasberg, and even the firebrand Henry Brock who was responsible for Beth El's "new marble baths," or renovated *mikvah*.[52] It is difficult, in the absence of concrete evidence, to explain their reluctance to leave Beth El. Possibly they stayed as long as any hope remained of making radical modifications in the older synagogue's liturgy; or perhaps they felt a sense of obligation towards a congregation in which they had held high office. Certain it is, however, that the defection of the liberally-minded from Beth El to Beth Zion did not come on any one day or even year. It was a gradual movement, extending over many decades, and its net result was to leave Beth El in the hands of men distinctly unwilling to follow the leadership of the New York or Cincinnati reformers.

Nevertheless, Beth El slowly but surely evolved from a strictly Orthodox synagogue to one which today we would label right-wing Conservative. Bold changes were avoided but, as early as 1865, the religious habits of its members were lax enough to cause some recently-arrived traditionalists to found a *shul* of their own. By the 1860s, attendance at Beth El had already become largely a High Holiday affair. It is significant that now members were no longer fined for failure to attend synagogue *services,* but for failure to attend congregational *meetings.* By 1863, it was difficult for Beth El to gather a *minyan,* even on the Sabbath. For instance, the traditionally-minded Nicholas Hyman kept his store open on Saturday, walking down Main Street to his business after the conclusion of the morning services. But there were not enough men willing to make even this partial sacrifice and, on October 8, 1863, Beth El resolved that five members be notified to attend services each week. *Minyan* by rotation was thereby insured. But Buffalo was a little bit better off than some of the synagogues in New York City where, during the busy war years, some of the leading synagogues had to hire a *minyan* in order to make certain of Sabbath services.

At the same time that there was this laxity in attendance on Sabbath, many ultra-Orthodox practices continued at Beth El. We know that in the 1860s some men still sat up and learned Torah the whole night on the first night of Shavuot and on the eve of Hosha'ana Rabba. Thus, as in so many synagogues of later times, zealous pietists, free-thinking conformers, and the majority of the indifferent banded together.

On April 18, 1862, an event took place at Beth El that was to have far-reaching effects. On that day Israel Warrensky was elected minister of the congregation. Warrensky was the first minister of Beth El to remain for an extended period. A colorful figure, he was born as Israel Brodie in Vilna in 1812. Before coming to America with his wife Esther (b. 1813), Brodie had served in several places in Europe—Berlin, Paris, London. The Chief Rabbi in London sent him to Cork, Ireland, and this tour of duty left a deep mark on his family. Before Israel Brodie came to the United States he had read widely in American history, and he became fascinated with the life of the revolutionary patriot Israel Warren.

Thereupon, Israel Brodie changed his name to Israel Warren. When Warren was hired in New York by Barnard Hyman, his name was changed once again, for Hyman thought that the name Warren did not sound Jewish enough.[53] Hence, the thrice-named Warrensky arrived to be minister at Beth El. Hyman, evidently seeking some degree of permanency, insisted on a three-year contract, at $300 per year, plus a residence in the basement of the synagogue. It took two meetings to get the appointment through.

Warrensky presented an impressive appearance. He was fair, with a platinum beard and noble features. He was descended from a long line of rabbis and had previously served in Quincy, Illinois, and in the first Russo-Jewish synagogue in the country, Beth Hamedrosh Hagadol of New York. He was a progressive who had been influenced by the secular enlightenment that was then penetrating the Russian ghetto. Correspondingly, he seems to have been rather lax in religious practice, for in 1864 Beth El ordered him to be at the synagogue punctually at 6:00 p.m. on Friday evenings, 8:00 a.m. on Saturday mornings, and at 5:00 p.m. daily for afternoon services. He was also repeatedly warned to be more careful in supervising the slaughtering.[54]

His Irish past caught up with Warrensky in May 1866 when a group of Fenians (Irish-American revolutionaries who hoped to force England to free Ireland by raids on British-controlled territory) came to Buffalo and launched an attack on Canada. About 1,500 Fenians, led by John O'Neill who had been a captain in the Union Army, crossed from Black Rock to Canada. At Limestone Ridge, on June 2, 1866, three miles from Ridgeway near the junction of Garrison and Ridge Roads, they met the "Queen's Own" regiment from Toronto. The Canadians fell back to Port Colborne and the Fenians took Fort Erie to await reinforcements. The reinforcements were prevented by the U.S.S. "Michigan," which captured a few hundred of the retreating Irishmen. Tradition in the Warrensky family states that his son Samuel, who had been born in 1849 in Russia, joined the Fenians and was captured by the Canadians. He was later released. Samuel married a Roman Catholic, and this branch of the family resumed the name Warren.

Warrensky, who mildly prospered in the job to the extent that he declared himself worth $3,000 in real property and $500 in personal property in 1870, remained at Beth El until his death in 1876. Apparently he performed his services satisfactorily in spite of the warnings to be on time, and he even took sufficient interest in the maintenance of the buildings to complain of the poor state of the *mikvah*. At the same time there was a definite attempt, perhaps prompted by the coming of Reform to

Buffalo, to present a more dignified service at Beth El, and Harris Goldman, born in 1828 in Russia, was made *Shomer ha-Petah* (guardian of the
door) to preserve order at the services. Warrensky himself enjoyed the
fruits of the war prosperity, for his salary was raised during these years,
first by $50 a year and then by $100. Beth El, during these flush years,
was able to employ, in addition to Warrensky, a sexton and a secretary
(J. Cassel) who was also a collector.[55]

It seems that in the early years, every time Beth El began to enjoy
some measure of prosperity or peace, disaster struck. So it was again in
1865. On Wednesday, January 25th of that year, fire broke out in the
American Hotel on Main Street (at the site later occupied by Adam
Meldrum & Anderson Co.) and spread rapidly to other locations. Beth
El stood directly behind the American Hotel, and when the wall of the
hotel collapsed it damaged the Beth El synagogue. Warrensky's living
quarters were made uninhabitable. So bad was the fire that three volunteer firemen were killed in the blaze, and the damage to property was
made even worse by a severe storm that followed the fire. Several Jewish
merchants were also seriously set back by this fire. It wiped out the
Rosenau Brothers' fancy-goods and millinery store which was lightly
insured for only $25,000. Bernheimer's Block, which consisted of a bakery,
a drug store and other stores, was damaged to the extent of $10,000. M.
Spiegel's clothing business and Hochstetter and Strauss' dry-goods store
were destroyed.[56] At emergency meetings on February 5th and 6th, the
Beth El congregation discussed the sale of the synagogue, for they feared
that if it could be repaired, the rebuilding of the American Hotel would
so block light and air from the eastern wall of the synagogue that a
skylight would have to be installed. A committee was appointed to investigate the possibility of selling the building. Money was collected
for Warrensky who had been made homeless. Eventually, however, the
congregation decided to repair the building, although complete rehabilitation was delayed until after Passover. On April 16, 1865, the day after
Lincoln's death and Hol Hamoed Pesach, the members advanced money
for the rebuilding of the synagogue. One of the most generous was
Leopold Warner, who was then already a member of Temple Beth Zion
but still a trustee of Beth El. A master-builder repaired the damaged
synagogue for $708.[57]

When, for whatever unknown reason, burials in the old cemeteries
stopped, Beth El was left in need of a new burial place. On September
30, 1862, a motion was made at a meeting of the Board of Trustees that
new land be bought and that all the dead be removed from the old
cemetery and buried in the new. It was also moved that a "fine wall"
be placed around the new cemetery and that each family would have

its own plot. These motions were carried by the Board and were to be laid before the congregation. No definite action to buy the land seems to have been taken at that time, for the next year, there was still talk of the need for a "proper" cemetery, and a committee reported that it had found some good sandy land three miles out of town at White Corners Road, but no move was made to buy it. It must have been during that same year, 1863, that two and a half acres of land were purchased on Pine Ridge Road from George and Maria Freund who supplied all the other Jewish congregations of that day with burial space. It is not known for certain where Beth El buried between July 19, 1861 and 1863, when they acquired the Pine Ridge Cemetery. Perhaps some burials were made in the Shearith Israel United Cemetery which lay near the new Beth El land.[58]

In 1864, probably for financial reasons, Beth El petitioned the court for permission to sell five acres of the old cemetery which was in what is now the Fillmore-Broadway region. After permission was granted, Beth El decided to sell one and a half acres of the unused part of the old cemetery.[59] A prime mover in this cemetery land transaction was Beth El's president, Henry Brock, one of the great instigators of Reform. Double membership in several types of synagogue was evidently fairly common then as it is now. A noble intention to build a "fine wall" seems, like many noble intentions, to have been neglected, for we read in the minute books for October 31, 1864, that some members were agitating for the construction of a fence around the Pine Ridge Cemetery before the frost came, for, as they argued, if it were built after the onset of winter, it would be more expensive.

By 1865, with the founding of a third permanent congregation, Buffalo showed the beginnings of the pattern that was to develop throughout the United States. Temple Beth Zion was a Reform congregation; Beth El, though nominally Orthodox, was drifting toward what later would be termed Conservative; B'rith Sholem Synagogue, the newly established congregation, was a European-style *shul*.

The prime mover in founding the new synagogue was Harris Greenberg who held High Holiday services in his general store located at the corner of Jefferson and Seneca Streets, possibly as early as 1864. Tradition states that many of the worshippers were clerks in Greenberg's store. Greenberg was born in Russia in 1824 and lived for a time in England where one of his children was born. He was evidently prosperous, for his wife in 1860 declared that *she* owned $5,000 in real property. The Palestinian messenger, Abraham Nissan Ashkenazi, records his generosity. Ashkenazi was collecting in Buffalo in 1861-62, and Harris Greenberg's group donated $10.25, whereas the entire Beth El congregation gave only $25.[60]

There is reason to believe that this new Chevra B'rith Sholem Synagogue (later the Pine Street Shul) grew out of the Mutual Benefit Society founded by East-European newcomers in 1864. If so, its origin resembles that of Beth Zion.[61]

Greenberg was helped in founding the new group by the Grodzinsky family, another group from Volkovisk, Lithuania. Max Grodzinsky's sister, Harriet, was married to Harris Greenberg. She had urged her brother to come to Buffalo, where he established himself as a tailor and then sent back to Europe for his family. In 1860, Max Grodzinsky was a widower with six children. This was a family of fine singing voices, and Max's son Moses, who came to Buffalo in 1864 at the age of twelve, often helped his father chant the services in Greenberg's store. For a time, this synagogue met in Greenberg's store every Saturday morning for services. The congregation was made up mainly of peddlers and other newcomers.[62]

On February 1, 1866, the synagogue was incorporated under the name of Chevra (Society) B'rith Sholem, with the stated objective of helping sick and bereaved families. In addition to Grodzinsky and Greenberg, the other important founders of this congregation were Samuel Bernstein, Abraham Lewis, Abraham Aaron, Isaac Mendelsohn, William Weber, Nathan Alpern, and Abraham F. Cohen. Harris Greenberg left Buffalo about 1870 and after that the B'rith Sholem congregation fell on hard times. By 1870 the congregation worshipped on the second floor above William Weber's hoop-skirt store on Main Street between Eagle and North Division Streets. Early in the 1870s it moved to 169 Elm Street near Broadway where it worshipped above a grocery store operated by a member. On August 24, 1873, B'rith Sholem dedicated a frame synagogue, probably a converted house, on Elm Street between Broadway and Clinton. Louis Gumbinsky was then the president, and the minister was a Reverend Jacobsohn. The members supported the synagogue by a system of weekly contributions.[63]

Another Palestinian messenger, Nathan Neta Natkin, visited B'rith Sholem in 1876 and reported collections from many of the worshippers. His list is a prime source of information about the men who kept Orthodox Judaism alive in Buffalo at that time. The donors included Harris Einach, Moses Cohen, Harris Cohen, Jacob Garliner, Isaac and Moses Grodzinsky, Littman Abba (Louis) Gumbinsky, Isaac Kloneck, Joseph Saperston, Meyer Lichtenstein, and Israel I. Friedlander (d. 1925). Also on this list was Nicholas Hyman, one of the powers in Beth El at this time, but his name is here listed probably only as a donor rather than as a member of B'rith Sholem. Two other contributors were Jacob H. Mayerberg and his son-in-law, Louis W. Rubenstein.[64]

Also a member of B'rith Sholem and active in the 1880s was Joseph Saperston, the father of Willard and grandfather of Howard T., Alfred M., and Irving L. W. Saperston, of legal and real estate fame. Saperston came to Buffalo in 1862. Abraham Rabolinsky (the family name has been shortened to Roblin), Max Grodzinsky, Louis Gumbinsky, and Jacob Garliner, grandfather of Judge Jacob Tick, were also active at this time. Another old member was a colorful figure, Harris Einach, who, because of his learning and ability to preach lay sermons, was nicknamed the *Maggid*.

An old-timer, speaking of B'rith Sholem, once said that "Perhaps no other synagogue in Buffalo so completely typified the house of worship of European Jewry." Like its European prototype, it was a community in itself. There was not a breath of Reform or Americanization to be found in the synagogue. In 1884, because it emphasized education, twenty-six children were enrolled in its school. The synagogue had its own *Hevra Kadisha* (burial society), *Hevra Mishnayes* (Talmud class), and *Hevra Tehillim* (association for reciting the Psalms daily).

In keeping with its origin as a mutual benevolent society, the congregation always emphasized humane, informal charity. The recipients were unknown except to the president and the secretary. Many a peddler and small merchant was indebted to the secret helping hand of this unique society.[65]

In 1875, Beth Zion exchanged the rear part of its Pine Ridge Road cemetery with Congregation Beth Israel which in turn seems to have been swallowed up by B'rith Sholem.[66] To this day, the Pine Street Shul's cemetery is situated behind the old Beth Zion cemetery on Pine Ridge Road. Perhaps it is symbolic of the amalgamated community of our time that the fence that once separated the two cemeteries is now gone.

While Beth El was constantly, if slowly, turning to a mild liberalism during the nineteenth century, B'rith Sholem carried the burning torch of uncompromising Orthodoxy.

CHAPTER

FIVE

The Gilded Age

THE LAST QUARTER of the nineteenth century has been called the "Plush Age," or the "Brown Decades" (because of the brownstone houses that the newly rich liked to build), but perhaps the "Gilded Age" best describes this period. The name is derived from the title of a satirical book about the times written by Mark Twain in collaboration with Charles Dudley Warner. It was an age of unexpected and unprecedented prosperity. Karl Marx once described war as "the locomotive of history," and the American Civil War had been just that: it speeded up the Industrial Revolution by decades. Furthermore, during the war years, big business gained such economic advantages as a truly protective tariff, a national banking system, and a law which enabled businessmen to import contract labor. A subservient Congress allowed the masters of capital to make, as Vernon L. Parrington termed it, a "great barbecue" of the vast resources of the West. This was an age of monopoly during which industry and wealth were consolidated in the hands of relatively few men. It was the day of the millionaire exploiter of natural resources, the financial juggler, the cattle baron, the steel and textile tycoons, and the railroad magnate.

As great personal fortunes were accumulated, a new class emerged in America, and the ostentatious display of wealth by the very wealthy

set the social tone for the rest of the country. It was fashionable to over-
eat and overdress. Gingerbread architecture and overdecorated living
rooms were characteristics of this era of the potted palm. Too much attention to the "society page" and to the "social season" resulted in a veneer of
artificial, overdecorous manners. The rich displayed their wealth at fancy
balls, musical evenings, and lawn fetes at which iced champagne and
lawn tennis competed for the attention of those in attendance. Meanwhile
the masses of laborers and immigrants huddled together in cold-water
tenements and worked in sweatshops in the big cities. While America
was being industrialized, thousands of Americans left the farms for the
factories and the uprooted left Europe for America. Many years of gruel-
ling hardships were in store for the masses. But each member of this
moving mass of humanity hoped that he, like the ferryman Cornelius
Vanderbilt or the drover Daniel Drew, would strike it rich; and the only
way up the ladder was to cease to be an employee and to become an
employer.

In cities like Buffalo, a rather farcical system of double imitation went
on during the Gilded Age. The upper-middle-class Gentiles imitated the
social maneuvers of the tycoons of New York and Chicago. They tried
on their own scale to set their standards by those of Mrs. William Astor
of New York whose drawing room, because of its capacity, gave rise to
the term "The 400," or they tried to copy in Buffalo perspective the ele-
gance of Mrs. Potter Palmer who ruled Chicago society from her mansion on the Lake Shore Drive. In turn, Buffalo Jews at times mimicked the
affluent local Gentiles. In the disordered scramble to achieve social
status, they pushed into the areas of comfortable and fashionable homes
on the better streets; if they could afford it, they hired a Negro butler;
they played such fashionable games as polo; they formed their own
exclusive clubs and fraternal lodges; they established reading groups to
discuss Shakespeare and Robert Browning, probably more for effect than
to promote culture.

In their own community Jews at this time were also divided into the
haves and the have-nots. There was a right and a wrong side of the
Jewish railroad tracks in Buffalo, and Jews exhibited the same over-
anxiety to cross the tracks that their Gentile neighbors throughout
America were exhibiting. In Jewish society, German birth or psychological
affiliation with the western European group helped one to cross the track;
but again, as in the rest of America, the main key to acceptance was
wealth. It is essential, therefore, to begin this phase of the study of the
Jews of Buffalo with an examination of their economic status at this
crucial period in history.

Most Jews had prospered during the Civil War, and now they settled down to a period of leisurely social expansion and development, unwittingly awaiting the onrush of the East-European hordes that would come after 1881. Since their social development was a direct result of the economic status that had been achieved during the war years, it is important to glance at the various occupations in which Jews were then engaged. The best source of information on this subject is the original book in which were recorded applications for membership in the Montefiore Lodge No. 70 of B'nai B'rith which fortunately still survives. The entries in this book made in 1866 show a cross section of the Jewish community, although it should be borne in mind that this will be a sampling of the more affluent members of that community, for B'nai B'rith tended to be rather exclusive and selective.

By far the greatest number of applicants (forty-six) listed themselves as merchants. The term *merchant* is, of course, broad and can include anything from the keeper of the corner grocery store to the owner of a large firm. Since only two men listed themselves as clothiers, it is safe to assume that many of the merchants were clothiers or merchant tailors.

One man listed himself as a banker.[1] Abraham Altman, who we have already noted, started out in the clothing business, helped found the Third National Bank. Altman at the end of the war was vice-president of the bank; and, in 1869, he became its president. Altman was the one Jew to pierce the social barrier (he was president of the Buffalo Club in 1880), and the Altman family has been among the Buffalo gentry ever since. Abe Altman lived at 184 Delaware Avenue, then a fashionable area, and later moved to a mansion at the present site of the Jewish Center at Delaware and Summer. His wife, whose maiden name was Clara Abrams, was socially ambitious and, perhaps in an attempt to advance a notch on the social ladder, late in life turned Episcopalian. Mr. Altman, however, was interested in Reform Judaism and gave $1,000, probably the largest single gift, for the purchase of the Niagara Street property for Beth Zion.

A local tradition states that Altman met and gave some assistance to the notorious Jay Gould while the latter was a surveyor, and that Gould later lent Altman the money to invest in the founding of the Third National Bank. This bank, unlike other American banks of the period, was not owned and run by old Yankee families. Rather, it was run by immigrants, some of whom seem to have been German Jews. Altman served as its president for a dozen years.

Altman, in addition to his banking and clothing interests, engaged, according to records in the County Clerk's office, in many real estate dealings throughout the city. In 1881, broken in spirit by the accidental death of his son David in a fall from a horse while playing polo in Delaware Park two years before, Abraham Altman resigned from the bank. This seems to have been the turning point in his career, for his fortunes declined from then until his death. Despite his former high social and economic position, he died almost penniless. In his last days he sold tailor's trimmings and worked for the clothing firm of Levey & Co., although he still lived in his palatial Delaware Avenue home.[2]

At this time there was one Jewish optician in Buffalo. He was William Adolph, born in Prussia and naturalized in Buffalo in 1857. Adolph conducted his business in 1866 in the Franklin House. He was far from wealthy and in the 1870s was constantly in need of financial help from his "co-religionists."

Although there were probably several Jewish doctors in Buffalo by this time, only one that we know of chose to identify himself as Jewish. Dr. Edward Treusch, a relative of the well-known Warner family, was born in 1824. In Buffalo he practiced first at 27 Pearl Street and, in 1866, he owned a "German apothecary" at 101 Genesee Street between Oak and Elm Streets. It was not unusual in those days for a physician also to be a pharmacist. Treusch's residence in Buffalo seems to have been only for a short period. Whether he moved away or died is not known.

Cigar-making seems to have been especially attractive to Jews in the period after 1865. The Mexican War veteran, Marcus Flintrowitz, was still in this business at 792 Genesee Street, the property which he bought with the government money paid for the loss of his leg. Isaac Pollack made "segars" at 152 Pine Street; and, as we have seen, Siegmund Levyn in 1870 had a retail tobacco store at 389 Main Street. One of the best known of the tobacco companies was that of the brothers Samuel and Jonas Dismon. The latter was Grover Cleveland's favorite cigar-maker and supplied Cleveland with smokes while he was governor of New York. Cigar-making was a popular immigrant business because a man could enter it with almost no capital and very little equipment. All he needed was a small room, a board, a knife and a supply of tobacco leaves. After making his stock, he could then simply go out and peddle it.

The clothing trade, as has been generally noted in previous chapters, attracted many Jews during and immediately after the Civil War. It seems apropriate here to review in detail the firms that engaged in this business and the men who controlled them.

The first generation of Jews in America to enter the clothing trade were usually merchant tailors. Their children either jobbed clothing out of wholesale houses or else manufactured it on a large or small scale. After 1865, the travelling salesman or drummer appeared and roamed the countryside. Unlike his economic ancestor, the peddler, the travelling salesman did not carry his stock on his back. He visited the country general stores with his sample case and orderbook, and was prepared to supply the men of America (and later the women) with ready-made clothing.

> Gay are the boys
> The Knights of the grip;
> A wink for the girls,
> For the bell boy a tip.[3]

This was the trade song of the fraternity of salesmen. As trade increased and the country got used to the fact that lower prices and wider varieties of clothing were available in ready-made wear than could be secured through their home-town tailors, more and more people were supplied with clothing by travelling salesmen—most of them German Jews. "After the Civil War," writes Professor Oscar Handlin, "the tribe of drummers increased rapidly, establishing a network of distribution by which shopkeepers in the remotest hamlets were brought into contact with the great urban markets. The Jewish drummer became a familiar figure, nattily dressed, blowing in and out of town with a style." [4] By 1888, about sixty Jewish drummers worked out of Buffalo and sold Buffalo-made clothing as far west as San Francisco.

Gradually, in Buffalo as elsewhere, clothing manufacture became less of a family affair; the work was done by division of labor in factories. In 1877, about thirty-four Jewish clothiers lived in Buffalo. Of course, many of these probably were still not much more than merchant tailors, but there were at least five wholesale clothing firms and fifteen retail clothing firms owned and operated by Jews. In addition, nine men listed themselves as tailors and one listed himself as a cutter.

Some of the more prominent clothing firms have already been briefly mentioned. Warner Brothers & Klein was capitalized at $100,000 in 1870 and employed 150 people. At that time the firm produced annually a stock of pants, coats, vests and shirts worth $160,000. The firm's first business site was at 41-43 Main Street. Later it moved to Exchange Street; and still later it was located at Pearl and Swan Streets. By 1884, this firm employed 1,000 people.[5]

Altman and Company has already been identified as an important Buffalo clothing firm dating from 1854. Jacob Altman, brother of Abraham, had the distinction of fathering the first Jewish child born in Rochester, his daughter Bertha, later Mrs. David Rosenau. He had been bron in 1814 in Württemberg. In 1870, Jacob Altman was worth $30,000 in real property and $25,000 in personal property. Besides his daughter Bertha (who survived until 1921), Altman had three sons: Isaac, Julius J., and Henry. The boys were at first associated with their father in business, as was his son-in-law David Rosenau. Jacob Altman, like his brother Abe, was very much interested in Reform and was the first man to enter Beth Zion hatless, thereby giving impetus to this liberal innovation in Buffalo.[6] He was a trustee of Beth Zion from 1864 until his death, at which time the trustee room at Beth Zion was draped in black for thirty days. He was a quiet, unostentatious man who placed service to his community above personal glory. He died in Buffalo on November 11, 1881. Altman and Company was the largest of its kind in Buffalo in 1887. The company, located at 68-72 Seneca Street in a five-story building, then employed 1,500 people and conducted a million-dollar business annually.

Jacob's son-in-law, David Rosenau, half-brother of Sol Rosenau, was born in Bavaria in 1840. He started in business in Buffalo as a liquor dealer, but after his marriage he joined his father-in-law in the clothing business. Rosenau was also very active in Beth Zion affairs. He died in Buffalo in 1905.

Very prominent in community affairs was Aaron Aarons who had a clothing store at 35 Exchange Street. Aarons was born in Holland in 1805 and first settled in Massachusetts after his arrival in the United States. Aarons was the last president of the old Orthodox Beth Zion, and so important was he in the affairs of the new Reform congregation that his funeral, in 1871, was held from the Temple, then as now, a somewhat unusual practice in Jewish life. He was very active in B'nai B'rith, and at his death Montefiore Lodge asked the members to attend his funeral en masse, and his picture was placed in the Lodge rooms. Aarons was a very charitable man who busied himself with the sick and distressed of all races and religions. He was also very influential outside of the Jewish community. He was an active Mason and one of the original "Union Continentals," a Civil War home-guard group of middle-aged respected citizens, headed by former President Fillmore. At the time of his death he was sergeant-at-arms of the Buffalo Common Council. Aarons, the father of a large family, died on April 16, 1871, and was survived by his widow, Bianca Rachel, who lived until 1908.[7]

Brock and Wiener was another clothing firm in Buffalo at this time. Henry Brock and his in-laws, the Wieners, started their clothing business in 1865, and the firm grew to employ 250 people before it closed its doors in the 1880s.

The Hofellers, another family that became very prominent in Jewish affairs, was likewise engaged in the clothing trade in the 1860s and 1870s. The Hofellers, like so many other Buffalo Jews, were "Badenzers." They came from the small village of Eichstetten in Baden where their father kept a kosher boardinghouse. Siegmund Hofeller (1828-1875) was the eldest of the three brothers. He owned a boys' clothing store on Washington Street and was moderately successful in business. Lehman Hofeller (1830-1886), who operated the Queen City Clothing House on Main Street, once proudly advertised: "My goods are manufactured under my own supervision . . . ; my prices are surprisingly low." Another brother, Nathan (1832-1872), worked for Brock & Wiener. Theodore Hofeller, later to become so important in Buffalo Jewish affairs, was a younger relative who came here as a lad. A Hofeller family prayer book, printed in 1802, found its way into the possession of one of the authors of the present study. It had been sent from Germany to the Buffalo Hofellers by their father and contains a warm, affectionate inscription in which the parent expressed his regrets at not being able to send his sons any other gift.[8]

Another of the older clothing firms was that of Desbecker, Weill & Co. The founder was Samuel Desbecker and his partners were his son Benjamin, and Louis and Alphonse Weill. Both of the Weills married daughters of the elder Desbecker. This firm was located in a seven-story building at 41 Pearl Street, in the late 1880s, and employed about 1,500 sewing women alone. They made "dollar pants" as well as good clothes. In the next decade, as Desbecker Brothers at 347-51 Main Street, they seem to have abandoned manufacture of clothing to concentrate completely on retail sales.

The largest clothing company in Buffalo today dates from 1877. It is that of M. Wile and Company. The Wile family, destined to play a vital part in the history of the city of Buffalo, came from the village of Ihringen, Baden. Isaac Wile, who came in 1867, was the first of the family to arrive. He had heard of Buffalo from the pioneer Samuel Desbecker, a distant relative who had written back about the city. When his brother Mayer arrived in 1869, Isaac was a cattle dealer, a trade which most of the Ihringen Jews had followed in Germany. Mayer Wile (1849-1928), departed from tradition, however, and went into the jewelry business. At first he peddled jewelry in a cart drawn by his horse Fannie. Then he went into business as Block and Wile. By 1880, M. Wile & Co. began as a clothing firm at 187 Washington Street. Mayer Wile had married Lena Strauss in 1874. For many years he was prominent in Beth Zion and later served it as president. A third brother, Herman, born in 1864, survived until 1958. In 1890, the firm, then known as Wile Bros., was located at 37-39 Pearl Street. Later the firm moved to its present site on Goodell Street. The three brothers, Isaac, Mayer and Herman, were then temporarily together, and they employed about 250 people in the six-story building and had six salesmen covering the whole country.

Somehow, M. Wile & Co. managed to survive all the troubles that beset the other Buffalo clothing firms, and it eventually became the largest house in Buffalo. Mayer Wile had no sons, and after his death the business was carried on by his sons-in-law, Sigmund Bock, born in Buffalo (1875-1943), the German-born Ben Hirsch, and the American-born Ben Gunzberg (1875-1953).[9]

Three other Jewish-owned clothing firms sprang up at this time. Leopold Marcus & Son (dating from 1873) were in the wholesale clothing business at 84 Pearl Street in 1888. They specialized in boys', children's and youth's clothing. In 1884, a branch of the Exstein family started to manufacture clothing as Exstein & Co., and in the 1890s the firm of Levin Michaels was doing a brisk business in wholesale clothing. All of these concerns were of ephemeral importance. The growth of the clothing trade in Buffalo can be indicated by the available statistics. In 1858, there were only twelve wholesale clothiers in Buffalo. Thirty years later the industry had multiplied many times: one thousand firms, employing five thousand people, were making or jobbing clothes to the amount of over fourteen million dollars a year. Pearl Street became the headquarters of this industry, and in 1888 the Buffalo *Express* called the clothing trades in Buffalo "a Jewish monopoly." [10]

Some Jews in the 1870s were in the women's wear trade. Nearly all the hoop skirt and corset, and related women's wear businesses listed in 1870 seem to have been in Jewish hands. N. Alpern conducted a hoop skirt business at 325 Main Street in that year, and Abraham Binnard had already been established in the same business nearby on Main Street.

One of the most important men in this trade was Abraham F. Cohen (1843-1900). He was the son of Avram haCohen Fike and Frimet Aaron of Dubreen, a town on the German-Polish border. His name was changed by error when he arrived in the United States at an early age. When the interpreter asked his name, he became confused and told him that he was of the priestly tribe of Cohen, and, because the interpreter didn't understand the significance of the title, Cohen he was till he died.

Abraham Cohen was first in business in Elmira, before coming to Buffalo during the Civil War. By 1870, he owned a hoop skirt store at 477 Main Street and produced 2,800 dozen skirts a year. He married Bertha Rosenthal, whom he had known in Dubreen, and they had ten children. A. F. Cohen was a gifted man. He served Beth El for a long time, was said to have been a brilliant speaker, and was the first Jewish member of the DeMolay Lodge of the Masons. He was also very active in Jewish fraternal circles. Religiously inclined, Abraham F. Cohen was president of Beth El in the 1870s and gave the congregation vigorous leadership.[11]

The Barmon family, very well known in Buffalo, established Barmon Bros. Inc., which for many years has been a nationally known dress concern. The first member of the Barmon family to arrive in Buffalo was Jacob Barmon who came in the late 1850s. His nephew, Abraham M. Barmon (1844-1924), born in Lipno, Poland, came to the United States in 1869 after a two months' voyage in a sailing vessel. Abe began his business career by peddling in the vicinity of Detroit. He married Rachel, the daughter of Nicholas Hyman prominent at Beth El. After a period in a small Michigan town, Barmon came to Buffalo in 1874. He bought a millinery and dry-goods store and, for a time, jobbed boys' clothing. Then he turned to the manufacture of women's house dresses. In 1877, Mrs. Barmon made these wrappers in the back of the store at 136 East Seneca, while her husband peddled them. About the turn of the century, the business was greatly expanded primarily because of the efforts of Abraham's two sons, Daniel Webster and Marcus Barmon. Both of these men were originally trained as lawyers, but they chose to enter the family business. Marcus died in 1936, and Daniel, a Spanish-American War veteran, died in 1955. The business has been carried on by their descendants.[12]

Associated with the Barmons for many years was the Buffalo-born Aaron Brown (1855-1928), grandfather of Harold B. Ehrlich and who, like A. M. Barmon, married a daughter of Nicholas Hyman.

The prominent Hiram Exstein, in 1870 specialized in "Gents Furnishing Goods" at 194 Washington Street. The firm Hiram Exstein & Co. was founded in Buffalo in 1867, and in the first year the business grossed $100,000. By 1880, this firm was jobbing men's clothing and had six travelling salesmen. Its annual trade amounted to $400,000. Hiram, born in Oswego, New York, in 1844, was the son of Henry Exstein who had been born in Saxony in 1813. Henry Exstein came to Buffalo in 1864 after his retirement and lived until 1882. He was the father-in-law of both Henry Cone and Louis M. Brock.

In the 1870s and 1880s, clothing, though still dominant as a trade in which Jews engaged, underwent a gradual local decline. In these years there were few Jewish professional men. There were no Jewish lawyers, and what doctors there were in Buffalo had been trained in Europe. Jews were almost entirely absent from the heavy industries of the region that brought so much wealth to non-Jews. Quite a few Jews, however, were interested in real estate. Rabbi Falk estimated in 1876 that about 100 to 120 of them owned residential or business property. He called special attention to the Michael family, but these soon dropped out of Jewish life. Here and there a Jewish distiller or saloon keeper could be found in those years. In 1870, E. Altman owned a saloon at 48 Exchange Street; and Samuel Aaron, a Polish-born Jew, kept a tavern and boardinghouse in a mixed American and Irish neighborhood. A Jewish telegrapher, a

Jewish printer's "devil" and a handful of Jewish glaziers lived in Buffalo. Harry Warner was a baker, and Emanuel Newman and A. H. Aaron kept boardinghouses. There were two Jewish music teachers in Buffalo in 1877: the Austrian-born Emanuel Fleischmann and his wife, the parents of the famous lawyer, Simon Fleischmann, taught music at their home at 462 Ellicott Street. There were a handful of Jewish laborers at this time; a distinct Jewish proletariat was to be formed only with the East-European tide of the 1880s. Peddling was still, as before the war, the occupation mainly of the newly arrived, but with the rapid growth of transportation systems and the rise of mail-order houses, house-to-house selling was becoming less attractive. Some of the German immigrants continued the Old World practice of trading in cattle.

These were the occupations of the Jews in the America of Ulysses S. Grant. For the most part, Buffalo Jews had prospered greatly during and immediately after the Civil War. They were now prepared to settle into a fairly well-defined community pattern which in turn would soon be disrupted by a tidal wave of new immigrants.

A discussion of this community pattern is in order, for it was markedly different from the kind of Jewish urban society that developed in the United States after the disruption of the Russian Pale. The earlier society was only relatively more homogeneous than the sharply cloven community of later years. By 1865, as a result of the consolidation of German-Jewish society and the advent of Reform, almost all American cities had already developed two Jewish communities, one of which was German and the other East-European. Buffalo was no exception to the general rule. The legend that American Jewry was once overwhelmingly German is not founded on fact. For many reasons a very large number of East-Europeans came to the United States long before the pogroms began in earnest. Even under the "tolerant" Czar Alexander II (1855-1881), there were persecutions of Jews. In 1869, American Jews appealed to President Grant to assuage the plight of their oppressed Russian co-religionists. As early as 1870, the Hebrew Immigrants' Aid Society of the City of New York was formed to help eastern European Jews, and throughout the decade that followed persistent efforts were made to induce the new arrivals to become farmers in the United States rather than to congregate in eastern cities. Even prior to the tragic events of the early 1880s that forced hundreds of thousands to flee, The Independent United Hebrew Association had been formed in New York to aid refugees from the Russian Pale.[13]

Rabbi Falk estimated that in 1876 there were 1,500 Jews in Buffalo. Population figures gathered a little later show that of the 250 Jewish families in Buffalo, eighty-one were Reform and therefore were to be psychologically identified with the Germans even if they were not all actually German; 169 of these families were listed as Orthodox and largely non-German. Thus, it seems clear that in Buffalo at least, even before the mass of Russian Jews arrived, the eastern Europeans outnumbered their western brethren by at least two to one.[14]

Although throughout the nation the German Jews looked with disfavor upon the eastern Jews, the social gap between the two groups never seemed quite so great in Buffalo as it was in some other cities. *The Jewish Messenger* of New York, for instance, reflecting a pro-western bias, complained of the lack of refinement in the new immigrants and called upon the German Jews to Americanize them. "Is it not better," asked the paper, "that they should be taught and refined in the synagogue than in the penitentiary?" [15] In Buffalo, however, the two communities often co-operated. Although most of the contacts between the two groups came through business dealings, the fraternal orders in a measure helped bring them together. Those East-European families that were fairly well Americanized seem to have been welcomed in B'nai B'rith. Barnard and Nathan Hyman, both active in Beth El, belonged, as did Samuel Cohen, a Pole. Isaac Grodzinsky became a member, and Abraham F. Cohen was actually elected president of the Montefiore Lodge. And even the kosher butcher Abraham Rabolinsky was admitted to B'nai B'rith in 1882 (he signed his application card in Yiddish). There were several reasons for this lack of ardent hostility in Buffalo. In the first place, too many East-Europeans arrived in Buffalo in the very earliest days and were, by the Civil War, too well established and too well Americanized to tolerate wholesale discrimination. Finally, Buffalo was never as heavily German-Jewish as Baltimore and Cincinnati, for example. From the point of view of mere numbers, the German-Jewish group in Buffalo was forced, before long, to welcome some outsiders, especially eligible bachelors.

In matters pertaining to general Jewish interests, all elements in the community usually were interested and cooperative. In 1872, B'nai B'rith took up the cause of helping the Roumanian Jews in answer to an appeal by the United States consul in Bucharest, Benjamin F. Peixotto. A one time Grand Master of B'nai B'rith, Peixotto came to Buffalo in 1877 and was entertained at the Standard Club, where he raised $100 for Roumanian Jews. At various times, B'nai B'rith sent money to needy Jews elsewhere, once to Jews of Boston thrown out of work by a fire, and once to help start a Jewish cemetery at Columbus, Mississippi. Occasionally money was sent to Jews in need in the South during the harsh days of Reconstruction.[16]

It should not be thought, however, that all was sweetness and light between the German and non-German communities in Buffalo. The local correspondent to *The (American) Israelite* complained, in 1879, of the cliques that controlled Beth Zion. The Temple, he charged, had become "an outward show." The leaders gave support of only a monetary nature. "Their hearts, their minds," he asserted, "appear to be wrapt in the cares of business, or in their home life, or in their lodges, or in their particular social circles." He argued that the leaders of the Temple, unlike leaders of the Buffalo churches, did not care if the congregation was composed of only seventy-five members, so long as it was kept exclusive.[17]

While there was a clear-cut division in Buffalo Jewry even prior to the Great Folk Migration of the late nineteenth century, the gap between the earlier groups of settlers was partially bridged by the development of an indigenous American-Jewish social structure. The backbone of this new social order was composed of the various fraternal societies that spread west and south from the seaboard metropolitan centers. Most important of these organizations was, of course, B'nai B'rith.

B'nai B'rith was founded and flourished in an age when people, especially immigrants, were recreationally starved. Lodge night in the period before the telephone, movies, radio and television, was a great social moment in a week filled with drabness and hard work. Furthermore, the lodges served a utilitarian as well as a social function, for they were also mutual benevolent societies. They cared for the sick, conducted health and life insurance operations and, as such, like the early Jacobsohn Society, were of special benefit to recent settlers. For the secular minded, the lodge took the place of the synagogue as a social meeting house.

B'nai B'rith, dating from 1843, was greatly influenced by the Masonic order. Its founders had probably belonged either to this or to other similar non-Jewish fraternal orders. B'nai B'rith began as a select group and maintained its exclusiveness for many years. Julius Bien, a German immigrant of the 1848 era, who served for thirty-five years as national president of the organization, said that the order was "based on the teachings of Judaism," and that it "would banish from its deliberations all doctrinal and dogmatic discussions and, by the practice of moral and benevolent precepts, bring about union and harmony." [18] In a day of endless religious bickering and controversy, B'nai B'rith tried to keep out of the fight over Reform, although in the early days its members were much more closely allied to the liberal than to the traditionalist group. In 1883, when the national Reform movement tried to enlist the help of B'nai B'rith in raising funds, it received a stinging rebuff. The mission of B'nai B'rith, the Cincinnati theologians were told, was to unite not to divide Jews.[19]

The fraternal order spread from New York to Cincinnati, to Baltimore, to Philadelphia, and finally B'nai B'rith reached Buffalo in 1866. In the fashion of the day, it used elaborate rituals, passwords and degrees of membership based on Jewish historical occurrences. At first the officers were given Jewish titles: The Grand Master was called the Grand *Sar;* the Scribe or Secretary was the Grand *Mazkir;* the Council was initially the Grand *Zekenim.* Originally it was a secret society, but gradually the secrecy was lessened; and in the twentieth century it lost all sense of mystery and membership was opened to all Jews of good character. Part of the reason for the survival of B'nai B'rith at a time when so many other fraternal societies faded from sight was the ability of the leaders to respond to changing conditions in the American environment; the organization abandoned old programs as their objectives became obsolete, and tried to meet new needs as they arose.

Nationally, B'nai B'rith enjoyed a great growth during the Civil War, partly because of increased prosperity and partly because of the desire of Jews to establish themselves socially. Many members were recruited from the ephemeral literary societies of the day. Libraries and reading rooms established in the lodges assuaged the intellectual curiosity of young Jews absorbed in the popular cult of self-improvement.

On Monday, February 19, 1866, Montefiore Lodge of Buffalo was formally consecrated and important figures in B'nai B'rith came here for the occasion. Joseph Sulzberger attended; Dr. M. Mayer of New York was there; as was L. Loewenthal of Zerubabel Lodge in Rochester. These men stayed in Buffalo for several days, and at a grand banquet on February 21st, conferred degrees on certain of the new members of the Buffalo lodge. The first president of the Buffalo branch was the Civil War veteran Leopold Marcus, and Louis M. Brock was vice-president. Although the founders piously hoped that Montefiore Lodge would unite all Buffalo Jews on common grounds, it was for many years a type of informal appendage to Beth Zion, even though, as has been observed, some Jews of East-European origin were accepted. Of the nineteen members who joined on February 19, 1866, sixteen were German Jews.[20]

The surviving minutes of Montefiore Lodge date from 1870. By that time, Rabbi Falk was president, and Louis Brock was once again vice-president. The lodge kept quarters, Montefiore Hall, at 13 Court Street and met on Mondays. The fact that initiation dues were $30 indicates that a measure of indirect discrimination was shown against the poorer immigrants. In 1872, the lodge signed a five-year lease on its hall on Court Street, at a yearly rental of $120. Apparently the members liked music, for they owned an organ, and sometimes lent it to Beth Zion. On occasion, too, the lodge let Beth Zion borrow its elaborate Menorah.

The lodge often helped its members out of financial difficulties. In 1871, for instance, it gave or lent one member $394. Other lodges supplied $190 of this total; private subscriptions supplied $62; one donor gave $42; and the balance of $100 was donated by the lodge itself.[21] Sometimes sick brethren were subsidized; on other occasions they were forced to enter hospitals or homes for the infirm. If a member were confined to his home with sickness, the president appointed a "night watch" to help with the nursing.

Montefiore Lodge had its disciplinary problems and attempted to fine members for non-attendance, but without much success. It also kept a "black book" in which the names of suspended members were kept as well as the names of those members that had been "black-balled." This book was circulated to other lodges.[22]

One important function of B'nai B'rith in Buffalo involved participation in funerals. The lodge paid for someone to sit up with the corpse according to Jewish custom, and appointed official pallbearers and a marshall. It hired two sleighs during the winter to be at the disposal of the family for the funeral. When funerals were conducted on Sundays or on non-working days, the members met at the lodge and marched in a group to the house of mourning. When Brother Joseph Lowenberg of New York died in Buffalo in 1875, the lodge as a group accompanied the remains to the Exchange Street station. B'nai B'rith even went to the extent of erecting a gravestone for Brother William Adolph, the optician, "who died in distress." [23]

Unlike the informal modern B'nai B'rith meetings, the lodge meetings of the Victorian Age were full of pomp and ceremony. The minute book solemnly records that, "Solomon Brown presented himself for the 1st degree. Secretary and Assistant Monitor retired to the anteroom with Question Book. The necessary questions being answered, he was admitted into the mysteries of the 1st degree in due form." [24] Most of the members, however, did not bother to study or work to achieve the higher degrees, and they were excluded as a result from certain parts of the meetings. The minutes record at various times: "The president brought the Lodge into the 1st degree," and "The president closed the Lodge in the 3rd degree."

In the 1870s, Montefiore Lodge was still engaged in mutual insurance. Thus it was assessed each time a member in any other lodge in the district died. Gradually, however, most members chose to insure themselves through private companies, and by the 1890s the lodge did away with the compulsory endowment of new members. At that time it was struggling to pay the death payments of its older members whose mortality rate was rising rapidly. As private insurance became more popular in America, more and more Jews were attracted to it and the care of widows and orphans became less pressing on the benevolent societies. By 1892, Grand Lodge No. 1 stated that the Order would work for the heritage of the Jew in America and noted at the same time that endowments and sick benefits had sunk into insignificance. Some of these early endowments, however, were still due as late as 1911.[25]

From 1878 until 1901, the membership in B'nai B'rith in Buffalo shrank from ninety-eight to about fifty. With World War I and the infusion of new blood as the East-Europeans were welcomed *en masse*, it revived again. Following the Russian influx in the 1880s, B'nai B'rith, along with some *ad hoc* organizations, tried unsuccessfully to keep the new immigrants from congregating in New York City. A national "American Committee" sought to Americanize them, and it was joined in this attempt to help the Czar's "stepchildren" by a Central Russian Refugee Committee. Well has it been said that in the nineteenth century B'nai B'rith tried to make Americans out of Jews, and in the twentieth century it has tried to make Jews out of Americans. By 1914, District Grand Lodge No. 1, to which Buffalo belonged, showed the new trend by stressing Jewish Holidays and by reminding member lodges that B'nai B'rith stood, not only for spread-eagle patriotism and over-generous philanthropy, but also for Judaism.[26]

One of the leading men in the lodge in the early period was Rudolph W. Wolffsohn who served as president in 1876. Wolffsohn, brother-in-law of Leopold Marcus, was a close friend of Thomas C. Platt, later New York State G.O.P. boss, and it is believed that this friendship was responsible for his appointment in 1881 as consul at Mannheim, Germany. Wolffsohn had been born in Germany and came to Buffalo in 1873. He was a recognized gourmet, which fact may account for his large size. In the tradition of fat men, Wolffsohn was a man of delightful humor and given to composing songs for weddings, birthdays, and other festive occasions.[27]

Apart from B'nai B'rith, Buffalo had a scattering of other fraternal societies during the last quarter of the nineteenth century, many of which lasted only a brief period. Because no minutes survive, we know almost nothing about their activities. The most important of these ephemeral societies were Kesher Shel Barzel (Chain of Iron), the Independent Order of the Free Sons of Israel, the Independent Order of B'rith Abraham, and the Free Sons of Benjamin.

Kesher Shel Barzel was founded in 1860 and had two lodges in Buffalo by 1876, both meeting in Montefiore Hall which was rented from B'nai B'rith. The last national convention of this order was held in 1890, and the order was formally disbanded thirteen years later. We know from indirect evidence that the local Queen City Lodge had sixty-two members in 1900, that it met on the first Sunday of each month, and that it attracted the affluent and well established.

The Independent Order of the Free Sons of Israel was founded in 1849 by some German Jews who, it is believed, withdrew from B'nai B'rith. The ritual of this lodge consisted of regalia, degrees and passwords similar to those of the parent organization. Its motto was *Freundschaft, Liebe und Wahrheit* (Friendship, Love, and Truth). A Buffalo chapter of this order existed at least as early as 1873 and later a second lodge was formed. At the turn of the century both lodges boasted a combined total of ninety-six members.

The original Independent Order of B'rith Abraham was founded in 1849. This lodge, toward the end of the century, seemed to cater to the newer immigrants in Buffalo. Its real growth in Buffalo dates from the turn of the century when it was reorganized.

The Free Sons of Benjamin was founded in 1879 to do among the eastern Europeans what B'nai B'rith and the other fraternal orders had done among the German Jews who, until about 1880, dominated almost all social groups. In Buffalo, many of the later immigrants became interested in lodges because the East Side synagogues could not unite the various factions in the Jewish community, whereas the lodges could. Moreover, membership in an order gave the newcomer the feeling of belonging that he had had in his small European village but which he had lost in the strange environment of America. The Free Sons of Benjamin spread rapidly and within a few years, 120 lodges had been established in the eastern United States. The group was in Buffalo before the turn of the century, where the Queen City Lodge met every second Sunday with seventy-four members.[28]

While the men had their lodge meetings to get them out of the house one or two nights a month, the ladies were not sitting in a corner mending socks. They, too, formed clubs and had their own secret signs and passwords. There was, for example, in the Buffalo of the Grant Era, a Sisters of Rebecca Lodge No. 12 that met once a month in Montefiore Hall; plus a True Sisters Society, which was a sickness and benefit lodge.[29] Housewives found it a relief to get away from the drudgery of their everyday chores. The late Victorian period saw a steady advance in the position of women, caused, to a certain extent, by a lessening of household drudgery with the introduction of prepared cereals and canned foods, together with improved household facilities. Furthermore, members of well-established Jewish groups, following the general American pattern, began to limit their families several generations before modern birth control was practiced by the European-bred groups.

These fraternal organizations served a good purpose. They gave the

American Jew both security in a strange and often hostile society and a welcome relief from an often barren existence. In addition to these functions, however, they introduced the immigrant to American social customs, for their clubs were not much different from those frequented by their non-Jewish neighbors.

During this period of organizational growth, the Hebrew "Y" was revived and, like B'nai B'rith and other fraternal groups, fulfilled some of the functions that had once been monopolized by the synagogue. The local "Y", like many others throughout the country, was destined to lead a very shaky existence, primarily because the scattered chapters lacked a formal national organization to guide them. In the spring of 1880, twelve persons met in Buffalo to re-establish the Young Men's Hebrew Association, in an effort to draw the Jewish community together. "Not that there is any discord here," wrote a contemporary observer, "but there is a sort of coldness that exists between different circles that must and will be thawed out." [30] Buffalo correspondents to the national Jewish magazines of the day complained of the clans and cliques in Jewish circles, and Rabbi Falk preached against this anti-social attitude from his pulpit. One source writes about the Friday night services at Beth Zion: "One man shuns his neighbor, neglecting even to exchange friendly greetings." This snobbery, it was stated, was even taught to their children by parents. "There are not many clans. There are only two or three. But these few are felt in everything. Every enterprise is *headed* by one or the other, rarely by all." [31] It was, therefore, apparently in an effort to break up these coteries and to inspire a feeling of friendship and brotherhood that some members of Beth Zion became interested in revitalizing the "Y".

On Tuesday, November 9, 1880, the new "Y" dedicated its rooms in the German Insurance Company Building, a new, imposing structure that stood on Main Street at Lafayette Square until it was demolished in 1957. Rabbi Falk spoke; Simon and Bianca Fleischmann played a duet; Sam Weil sang a tenor solo; and young Nathaniel S. Rosenau—in an age when such a thing was considered pleasurable—declaimed.[32]

The "Y" soon launched a full program of entertainment. There were musical evenings, declamation contests, instrumental and vocal solos, nights devoted to the reading of German poetry and sometimes to learned papers. Most of the intellectual diet was of a secular nature, and the "Y" seemed to specialize in scheduling balls to coincide with important Jewish Holidays. Even the Reform newpaper, *The (American) Israelite*, criticized the Buffalo "Y" of the 1880s as being too non-Jewish in its program.

On April 3, 1882, the club was incorporated as The Young Men's Hebrew Association of Buffalo, and its objectives were listed as "literary pursuits, the maintenance of a library and reading room, and social entertainment." Its nine trustees were all Beth Zion men. At that time there were ninety-six members, and the library contained 326 books. On April 27th, the new quarters were dedicated with a grand dress ball. The attendance was small, and from Cincinnati Rabbi Wise snorted: "There should have been none at all. What has a fancy dress ball to do with a Hebrew Association?" [33]

The Buffalo "Y" petered out, however, probably because it offered only secular activities that could be more profitably engaged in elsewhere. Undoubtedly a contributing factor to its decline was the fact that directly or indirectly it excluded the "green" eastern European newcomers. Significantly, the Buffalo "Y" succeeded only after the German and non-German halves of the split community "benefited from the accrued experience of living together." [34] In the 1880s, the "Y" failed to accomplish the purpose for which it had been revived. The Buffalo Jewish community continued to be riven for many years.

No account of the emergence of a nineteenth-century Jewish society would be complete without some consideration of the American social pattern which set the standard for immigrant groups. Despite the democratic political orientation of the country, social elitism was the rule of the day. Each city had a closely-knit group of "first families" who clustered together in selected neighborhoods, who attended fashionable churches, and who spent their leisure hours in exclusive informal circles and organizations. Unable, for the most part, to penetrate into this closed group, newcomers created a fashionable society of their own which was designed to differentiate them from their co-religionists or *Landsleute* who had not yet started to climb the ladder of success.

To move into a better section of town was usually the first step toward social advancement, for it meant physical separation from sordid surroundings and foreign-speaking neighbors. Buffalo Jews who had gained economically during the business boom of the 1860s began to move out of the bustling lower Main Street area and to penetrate into purely residential neighborhoods. A few of the most successful families, such as the Altmans and the Lesslers, were able to afford residences on Delaware Avenue. Then popularly referred to as "The Avenue," this fashionable boulevard was the center of Buffalo society, where the elite of the city engaged in their favorite pastime of racing. "Fast driving on this avenue is licensed by city authority," writes a contemporary, "and racing down its gentle incline is much in vogue." [35] "The Avenue" resembled a Currier-and-Ives stereotype, especially in the snowy winter months when the whitened road formed a marked color contrast to the black sleighs that raced above its frosted surface.

Many of the older Jewish families, however, settled on streets that paralleled Delaware, such as Franklin or Pearl, or streets that crossed it, like Tupper and Allen. Still others penetrated east of Main to such streets as Scott, Swan, Exchange, North and South Division, Michigan, Carroll, Clinton, Eagle and Elm. But this section of the city was already showing signs of deterioration by the time of Appomattox, and the general push was in a more northwesternly direction. Meanwhile, the foundations of a distinctly Jewish neighborhood that was later to center about William Street had already been laid. In the 1870s, some newly-arrived eastern European Jews moved into this general area, the avant-garde of the thousands who were to come in the following decades. Countless Buffalo Jews were to be educated at School 32, on Cedar Street between William and Clinton, under the supervision of Principal N. G. ("No Good" in student parlance) Benedict who was to become a familiar figure to several generations of Jewish parents. Some Jewish families, however, still remained in the lower part of town, below The Terrace, where they could be close to their business establishments. This area, however, was very unruly and at night one took his life in his hands to venture out on the street among the brawling lake sailors marooned in Buffalo during the long winter.

As the city recovered from the Panic of 1873, the push uptown was renewed. In 1877, Louis M. Brock moved from Eagle Street to 255 North Street, where he built a home at a cost of $14,000. His brother-in-law and partner, Magnus Wiener, built a home next door. North Street was then the outer limit of the city, and almost no buildings existed beyond that point. In the Grant Era, Richmond Avenue, which by 1890 was a beautiful wide street paved with asphalt, had only a few rude planks for sidewalks. Until the advent of the electric trolley in 1890, most Buffalonians were forced to remain in the center of the city, within walking distance or travel by horse-car to their places of business; and as late as 1900, many wealthy Jews were still living within a half-mile radius of Tupper and Franklin Streets. Generally speaking, the newly arrived East-European Jews spread eastward from Main Street toward Jefferson, whereas the older German group moved northward and westward, first into Franklin and Tupper Streets and then spilled over into the lower West Side. It is obvious from a study of the census of 1870 that, although there were yet no purely Jewish neighborhoods, the beginnings of such clusters were there. Until the following decade, however, the Jews tended to form little islands in otherwise Irish or German streets.

Even before Samuel Ward McAllister coined or popularized the expression "The 400," each city in the United States had already a *recherché* group called "Society." Professor Horton describes the society of Buffalo in the Gilded Age as a "charmed and exclusive circle which fascinated shop girls and housewives then as Hollywood does now." [36] This was the élite of the upper middle class. They bloomed in a world of security, confidence in business, rosy optimism and faith in human progress. German-Jewish society of the age has been described as "intense, closely knit, and characterized by Old World *gemütlichkeit*." [37] In the 1880s, Blue Books and Social Registers began to appear throughout the country, and the principal key that unlocked the gate to this distinguished circle was made of gold. Unlike the social stratification of Europe, however, the American social structure was more flexible; and even if the wealth were acquired relatively recently, it was possible to enter the set. Of course, it was easier to be admitted if one were an Anglo-Saxon Protestant instead of a European Jew; but as the self-styled Israelites of the day made money, improved their manners and bought fine houses, an occasional family made the grade. Generally, however, Jews like other immigrants created their own "Society," and obviously those who had been in America longest were the ones who formed this group, for the newcomers were too poor and too bound by European village customs to aspire to such a position. The German Jews, therefore, created a parallel exclusive set which, like its Gentile prototype, was based on wealth and on nationality in the sense that it was reserved for German Jews or those whom they chose to regard as "adopted" Germans. If the wealthy Gentiles gave charity balls and lived in castle-like houses on Delaware Avenue with equipages and coachmen in livery, this was exactly what the wealthy Jews, starved for recognition and social status after a thousand years of pariah-like existence, wanted to do. This "cult of the arrived" had its own fairs, balls, débuts, amateur theatricals and musical evenings. Art, in the fashion of the age, was cultivated not for the sake of art but because it was the thing to do. Huge family and community picnics were held on Grand Island, and boats, sometimes with a scow in tow to carry the food and equipment, were chartered to transport the guests to the site. The Chapter House on fashionable Johnson Place, built in 1884, attracted many wealthy German-Jewish people, and it soon became the scene of many upper-class Jewish social affairs.

In the Gentile world, the last quarter of the nineteenth century was a day of clubs, for slow transportation prompted many people to remain close to the city. In every city of any size during this age, Jewish clubs appeared bearing such names as Phoenix, Standard, Harmony, Progress, Eureka and Apollo—all good, solid, Victorian names. In the 1870s, the Standard Club was established in Buffalo as an informal offshoot of Beth Zion. Its membership was completely Jewish, but the program was often not even remotely Jewish in character or in subject. For example, in April 1879, the club presented with great success an operetta called "The Crimson Scarf." In December of that year, the group held a social at the Orpheus Club, probably because their own quarters were too small to accommodate the crowd. On New Year's Day, 1880, an afternoon children's ball was followed in the evening by a young folks' social. Jewish custom was not completely ignored by the Standard Club, however, for they followed the European practice of holding a ball at Purim time. On February 29, 1880, the young ladies of the Standard Club conducted a Leap Year Social for the young men. These were only some of the activities of one of several Jewish clubs of Buffalo which followed one another seriatim.[38]

Marriages were perhaps the most important social events of the time, for, if marriages gave wealthy men the opportunity lavishly to entertain their families and their friends, they also gave them the chance to impress the outside world. Upper-class Jewish weddings were frequently elaborate affairs, with many out-of-town guests and parties that lasted until dawn. The 1886 marriage of Marvin M. Marcus to Adelaide Louise Rosenau, the daughter of Mr. and Mrs. David Rosenau, was an impressive event, the description of which has survived. The ceremony was preceded by a musical, literary and dramatic evening at the Chapter House, an echo of the old German *Polterabend*. The next day the wedding was performed at 6:00 p.m. at Temple Beth Zion. The bridal chorus from *Lohengrin* boomed from the organ as the bride marched down the aisle to be married with two rings that had been worn by her grandmother and the grandmother of the groom. The wedding was followed by a reception at the Rosenau home, at 320 Franklin Street. There, 160 guests, some from New York, Boston, Cincinnati, New Orleans and Rochester, partook of the elaborate wedding supper and danced to the orchestra. The gifts filled two rooms of the house. The Rosenau residence with its "long drawing-room with its heavy draperies of mouse plush" was so large that the young couple were to live in a private apartment in one section of it.[39]

Another splendid wedding was that of Carrie Block to Nathan Desbecker, on May 25, 1886. This ceremony was also performed at Beth Zion, but the reception was held at the Chapter House. On June 1, 1887, the wedding of Mr. and Mrs. Joseph Desbecker included a bridal quadrille. In all these weddings there were elaborate, specially written song sheets, usually in German. Often the song writer was the portly, good-natured Rudolph Wolffsohn, who delighted in writing humorous musical compositions. In one case he wrote a parody of a letter from Mrs. Grover Cleveland, who had been a Buffalo girl, Frances Folsom. "Und sage ich Dir in Grover's und meinem namen," wrote Wolffsohn, and then went on humorously to make jokes with the rest of the letter. Hebraic idioms, still used in the homes, found their way into many of these songs: *brocheh* for blessing; *mishpocheh* for family; and *kallah* for bride. Some of these wedding songs poked fun at the Yiddish-speaking Jews:

> All the Yüden will be there:
> Chaim Saft and Mosche Baer;
> And the Goyim they will stare,
> When they see us shastening.[40]

The peak seems to have been reached in the wedding of Abraham J. Elias (1862-1933), a prominent lumber dealer, to Pearl Spiegel (1870-1947), on January 22, 1890. Elias was later politically close to Norman Mack, editor of the Buffalo *Times* and nationally prominent in upper-level strategy in the Democratic Party. Because the present Beth Zion Temple was then being built on Delaware Avenue, the wedding was held at the Central Presbyterian Church. The family went to great expense to import the floral decorations from New York City, but felt perfectly satisfied with the results. The Buffalo *Express,* after declaring the wedding the most brilliant ever held at the Central Presbyterian Church, stated, "Never in this city has there been a finer display of decorations than were used at the church and the hotel." [41]

In addition to the weddings, there were coming-out parties for young ladies and twenty-first birthday parties for the young men of the better families. The Society of Concord, as the Reform Temple in Syracuse is called, held an annual ball in the 1880s and the Rochester and Buffalo élite attended; the young ladies, in the best fashion of the day, being escorted by a male near-relative.

This was a period when most Germans were proud of their Old World heritage; and Jews, especially Reform Jews, shared this pride in German *kultur.* When Ismar S. Ellison, editor of several German newspapers in Buffalo, published his work on the Germans of Buffalo, *Geschichte der Deutschen in Buffalo und Erie County, N. Y.,* he failed to distinguish the Jews from the Germans. Most likely the Jews and non-Jews mingled to an extent perhaps even greater than they do today. They probably met in the Harugari lodges and in the Turnverein, both of which dated from mid-century. These groups shared the Teutonic heritage of a love of

regular exercise in the form of calisthenics and organized games. There
is also evidence that some Jews were active in a social order called
Sprudel's and in the Pumpernickel Club. Scrapbooks that have survived
reveal that many non-Jewish guests were invited to graduation parties,
social "at homes" and masquerade balls.

All these clubs, large homes, elaborate weddings, coming-out parties
and other social events reflect the increasing prosperity, increasing acculturation, and increasing secularization in which the social rather than
the religious motif was dominant. These activities, especially those in
which Jews deliberately sought to imitate and court polite Gentile society, also meant sharper and sharper cleavages between the German
group of older residents and the newcomers who clung to the Jewish
customs and mores of the European *shtetl*.

This was the age when the Industrial Revolution brought riches
to some Americans and poverty and exploitation to many others. The industrial upheaval and the constant flow of immigrants provided the occasion and need for help for less fortunate Jews who did not, as yet, share
the good business fortune that befell so many of the pre-Civil War families. The German Jews, great organizers, with a marked talent for systematizing philanthropy, eagerly responded to the call of the poor. In
time, this charitable impulse became so strong that it out-stripped the
interest in religion and in many instances seems to have all but replaced it.

The Hebrew Union Benevolent Society continued to be active until
the turn of the century. Before the great onrush of the immigrants, however, its budget was small and it seldom spent over $1,500 for relief for
the poor of Buffalo and to assist transient Jews who wandered into
the city.[42] The Ladies' Hebrew Benevolent Society, which also dated
from the war days, continued to share the burden of relief, spending about
a third as much as the men's group. About 1883 the older organization
seems to have been replaced by the Ladies' Hebrew Charity Association.
These two groups were the principal Jewish charitable organizations
of the city until, early in the twentieth century, they were gathered up
into the Federated Jewish Charities of Buffalo.[43]

For a time after the advent of Reform, some members of Beth Zion
continued to maintain traditional congregational societies such as the
Chevra Bikur Cholim. This society, in time-honored fashion, also prepared
the dead for burial. In 1872, the group dissolved, probably because by
then visitation of the sick was usually performed by the rabbi. At the
time of its dissolution, the Chevra presented the congregation with its
tools and utensils used in preparing the dead for burial. For a time, a

Hevra Kadisha took over these functions, but later Reform Jews began to bury their dead in the manner of the country. For many years, Leopold Keiser was interested in this phase of humanitarian and traditional Jewish work.[44]

One persistently troublesome charitable concern during this period was the care, supervision and education of orphans. At a time when adequate insurance was extremely rare, when the adult death rate from diseases now easily curable was high, it seemed mandatory that some sort of home be established for the care of Jewish orphans. There were, of course, several non-Jewish orphanages in the city of Buffalo at this time; but there was need for an institution that would keep Jewish children Jewish. They could get along without a Jewish hospital, but there was a genuine basis for the wide-spread fear that children raised in a Protestant or non-sectarian atmosphere might stray from their ancestral faith.

The problem of placing an orphan rose rather early in the life of the Buffalo community. In 1867, Beth Zion tried to have young Emanuel N. Carr admitted to the New York Jewish Orphan Asylum, but the question never came to a decision, for, while red tape was being tangled and untangled, the boy was adopted locally.[45] In 1877, simultaneous movements started in Syracuse, Rochester and Buffalo to found a Jewish home for orphans. Delegates from the three cities met centrally in February 1879 at Temple Berith Kodesh in Rochester. Albany and Troy refused to join in the effort. Rabbi Falk and Siegmund Levyn spoke for Buffalo, which city presented the most pressing problem, for there was immediate need to care for two orphaned sisters. Temporary quarters were found for them in Rochester, but the 1879 meeting did not fully solve the problem of orphans in general. Four more years were to be spent in haggling and discussion before the three cities were ready to take clear and definite steps to establish some permanent home.[46]

Agreement among the three cities was not accomplished without the impediment of other attempts to solve the problem. In 1878, a Young Folks' Hebrew Orphan Asylum Association appeared in Buffalo and raised funds by performing comedy shows. A Gentlemen's Hebrew Orphan Asylum Association was established in Buffalo the following year. This group attempted to raise money by a raffle of property on Main Street. Leopold and John Warner, the clothiers, donated a piece of property which was said to be worth $10,000. They stipulated that an additional sum must be raised to match their gift. Nothing came of the offer, for Rochester and Syracuse demurred.[47]

The merger with the other two cities came about at a meeting apparently held in Buffalo on May 25, 1881, at which time a constitution satisfactory to the local group was drawn up. The decision to locate the home in Rochester, midway between Syracuse and Buffalo, was reached in Buffalo the following year, and a committee of seven was appointed to search for a suitable site.

In 1883, the Jewish Orphan Asylum of Western New York was finally established. By the following year, 500 subscribers in Buffalo, Rochester, and Syracuse had raised a capital fund of $45,000. In December 1884, the home on St. Paul Street, Rochester, was opened under strong Reform influence. This fact, unfortunately, caused the Orthodox in all three cities to remain quite indifferent or even hostile to the project. The Asylum later built a school and a hospital, and, although in its entire history it never had a population of more than thirty-five to forty orphans, it was maintained for many years. The three cities felt that it could not be discontinued because of the public reaction to such a move as well as a feeling of pride of accomplishment and a sincere charitable interest. Consequently, by 1900 the home had an annual income of almost $11,000.[48]

An improved plant was started on Genesee Street in Rochester in 1909, and the new home was completed in 1915, at a cost of $100,000. Unfortunately, this new building came just at a time when the Genesee Home, as it was later called, was suffering from the triple factors of having even fewer orphans than ever, the opening of a rival institution in Rochester under Orthodox auspices, and a growing trend away from asylum care to the placing of children in foster homes. Furthermore, for some years Buffalo had been dissatisfied with the Rochester home, and in 1910, had almost set up its own orphanage. As late as World War I, some local Jewish children were placed in the non-Jewish Buffalo Orphan Asylum and there is evidence that some of these children tended to turn toward Christianity.[49]

In 1925, thirty children were in the Genesee Home, but no new Rochester orphans had been admitted for three years. Nevertheless, Buffalo, as the largest of the three cities and with the greatest number of wards to care for, continued to contribute the greatest share of the income to the home. During these years a Buffalo Jewish Orphan Asylum Association with its own local officers buttressed the work of the Rochester people.

The Genesee Home of Rochester became a constituent member of the Buffalo Jewish Federation for Social Service in 1926; but even that did not help, for two years later it closed its doors.[50] A few Buffalo children returned and were placed in foster homes under the supervision of a child placement worker of the Buffalo Jewish Federation. When it closed, the Rochester orphanage had an endowment of $175,000, and its physical plant was evaluated at more than $100,000. At long last, in 1949, the assets were divided among the three cities, and Buffalo received $93,000 out

of a total of about $300,000. The money was placed in the custody of the
Foundation for Jewish Philanthropies and was used for the purchase of
Camp Centerland in Elma, New York, to provide for a Jewish day camp
for Buffalo children.

As the Buffalo Jewish community matured and became more
Americanized, the German Jews extended their charitable interests beyond
purely Jewish charities and began to concern themselves more widely
with communal affairs. Most striking of the activities that attracted attention of certain Jewish groups was the unique Buffalo social experiment, the
Charity Organization Society that was founded in the late 1870s. For the
first time in the history of the United States, a city attempted to cut
through the chaos of charity groups and face up to the problems of the
needy and distressed sensibly and systematically. It was said of the Charity Organization Society: "The eyes of all parts of the country are turned
toward Buffalo; for here, first in the country, was established systematic
and scientific charity on a broad and comprehensive basis." [51] Buffalo became the model for the entire nation. By 1882, nineteen similar organizations were scattered throughout the United States, all in essence based
on the Buffalo plan.

Prior to this reform, the local treatment of charity cases was completely
chaotic. The successive panics of 1837, 1857 and 1873 had confounded
confusion, and the community had in these periods of acute economic distress never quite worked out a sensible system of aiding the under-
privileged. On December 11, 1877, under the guidance of the Reverend
S. Humphreys Gurteen, then Assistant Rector of St. Paul's Episcopal
Church, a group was formed to establish the Charity Organization Society.
Humphreys Gurteen had come from London, where he had been familiar
with the London Charity Organization Society, and he was shocked with
the lack of order discoverable in the philanthropic activity in Buffalo.
Alms giving was completely indiscriminate; one scarcely made the attempt to distinguish real from feigned need. Various organizations overlapped in their functions, and the consequent waste could not be avoided.
Because the help of the needy was considered a charitable obligation
rather than a social good, the kind of aid offered in those days tended
to encourage indolence rather than self-support. These were to be the
same problems that faced the Jews of Buffalo a generation later, when
they came to federate their own charities. Gurteen set about to remedy,
if possible, this planless situation and, to prepare himself for the task,
he returned to England to study the London system more closely. On
the night of December 11, 1877, Gurteen, with a nucleus of young men,
mostly under thirty, who had long been pressing for some such action,

federated sixty relief societies in the city of Buffalo. Later the number grew to ninety-one.

With the motto "Not alms, but a Friend," to guide it, the Charity Organization Society was formally incorporated with the objectives of systematizing and organizing charity groups to reduce and prevent pauperism and "to promote . . . social and sanitary reforms and habits of thrift and self-dependence among the poorer classes." The first president was the noted ironmonger and banker, Pascal Paoli Pratt.[52]

Jews were quick to join in the task of establishing the COS. Abraham Altman, in all probability one of the organizers, served on the first board of trustees and as treasurer of the Society in 1879. Also on the first board and serving as its vice-chairman was Louis M. Brock. Siegmund Levyn was active in its founding and represented Temple Beth Zion on the District Committee. After the turn of the century, the famous lawyer Moses Shire became a trustee, and the attorney Simon Fleischmann and Rabbi Israel Aaron of Beth Zion served on its Council.

Initially, the Charity Organization Society—a coordinating, not a disbursing agency—investigated all relief applications for member societies and even for the Overseer of the Poor. Partly because of this activity and partly because of a business recovery, the percentage of population on relief in Buffalo in the five years after its organization dropped from 10% to 2.6%. In the beginning only the investigators were paid a salary. The first paid executive was young Nathaniel S. Rosenau, son of Sol Rosenau, only twenty-two years old when he began his career with the Society. He served first as secretary and later as secretary-treasurer. Eventually he established a national reputation in social work, as a result of his participation in various conventions. He resigned from the Buffalo Society in 1893 to go to New York City, where he became secretary of the United Hebrew Charities of New York, and died six years later at the early age of thirty-nine. As secretary of the Charity Organization Society, Rosenau always insisted that material aid to the needy is less important than education and stimulation toward self-reliance.[53]

Siegmund Levyn, Louis M. Brock, and Joseph B. Block were particularly active in the Charity Organization Society. These men worked hard to urge their fellow Jews to make a liberal yearly contribution to the Society. The minute books of Beth Zion show an active interest in the federated Society (COS), and the congregation formed one branch of the Society and was represented on the central board. Somewhat later, the Temple accepted responsibility for relief in District 103, in which area lay the Jewish settlement along William Street.[54]

Side by side with their husbands, Jewish women were also active in this non-Jewish relief organization. They functioned mainly through the

Fitch Crèche, located at 159 Swan Street corner of Michigan. Fitch Crèche was established in the early eighties as a result of an endowment by the wealthy New Yorker, Benjamin Fitch, who had settled in Buffalo in 1832.[55] Modelled on the London Day Nursery, it was at first a place for working mothers to leave their children during the working day, and it was also a place where they could learn the latest and best methods of child care. It eventually developed into a sort of settlement house and training school for nursemaids. Ladies from Beth Zion often participated directly in the work of the Charity Organization Society as volunteer visitors not only in District 103, to which they would ordinarily have been assigned, but also in other sections of the city.

All this experience in the establishment and operation of the COS was of great benefit to the Jewish community of Buffalo. In the first place, the Hebrew Board of Charities and Temple Beth Zion directly benefitted by using the Society as a charity clearing house and investigating agency. There is no doubt, however, that Buffalo Jewry also learned a great deal about the problems and pitfalls inherent in federating various charitable groups. This knowledge they would put to good use when the Buffalo Jewish charities were united in 1903. One finds many similarities between the methods of the Charity Organization Society and those of the Jewish Federated Charities of later days. They both used a Penny Savings Fund, penny banks, and similar systems of "Friendly Visitors." Later, local Jews learned principles of vocational education, medical care, the operation of a dispensary for the poor and a day nursery, all from the Society. The tuberculosis dispensaries also show similarities. The Society pioneered budgetary guides for measuring adequacy of relief, and it, like the later Jewish Federation, accompanied relief with social therapy. They shared the same emphasis on sound family life, the struggle against slums and filth, and the fight against fire hazards. They were both concerned with prevention of disease among children, the building of playgrounds, and child guidance. The Charity Organization Society had a Fresh Air Mission as early as 1888, and this too served to inspire the later Jewish Fresh Air Camp. It seems safe to say that the Jews of Buffalo learned much about social welfare work from the Charity Organization Society.

As the first generation of Jews became acclimated to the United States and as they reared a generation who thought of themselves as Americans, other communal activities attracted their attention. During the Civil War, this process of acculturation was speeded up because of the partriotism engendered by the conflict and because of the prosperity that brought the leisure in which to enjoy outside interests. Beth Zion was particularly involved in these non-Jewish community activities, since the very basis of classical Reform was the belief that Judaism was largely another religious sect and as such should fit into the general pattern of the society in which it exists.

In 1867, for instance, a special committee of Beth Zion collected $132 to be used for the relief of "southern sufferers" who were at that time enduring the rigors of Radical Reconstruction.[56] This generosity toward the South is not surprising among Reform Jews, for Rabbi Isaac M. Wise reflected empathy for the South in his paper *The (American) Israelite* which was read by many of his Buffalo admirers.

Other appeals from outside the city also met with favorable responses. In 1870, Rev. Mr. Atkinson spoke at the Temple on behalf of the Gettysburg Orphan Asylum, and a collection was taken up for its relief. The congregation donated $152 for "Persian sufferers," sent money to the victims of yellow fever in the southwest, and even tried to interest Beth El in this venture. The board of trustees acted in 1875 on a petition from the Buffalo Board of Trade to help "Kansas sufferers," but shortly thereafter they tabled a petition from London asking for help for poor Jews of the Holy Land.[57]

As the hundredth anniversary of the independence of the United States approached, Jews, appreciative of all the benefits gained in this country, enthusiastically joined in the celebration. On January 10, 1875, Beth Zion appointed a committee to raise funds by subscription for a centennial monument. This group affiliated with the national Israelite Centennial Monuments Committee, and it tried to interest other congregations and fraternal orders in Buffalo in the project. Special centennial services were ordered by the Beth Zion trustees for Monday evening, July 3, 1876.

In many American cities Jews built their own hospitals, but locally Jews became interested in and supported Buffalo General Hospital, which had been founded in 1858. As early as 1871 Beth Zion became affiliated with the Protestant Ladies' Hospital Association. Each year the congregation gave a liberal donation to this group, and Mrs. Abraham Altman once served as its vice-president.

B'nai B'rith early shared this interest in community affairs, as the following extract from the minute book for December 25, 1876, shows. "The Bro. President left the chair to address the meeting and appealing to the sense of charity of the brethren as Israelites and to set an example to other secret organizations in the city on behalf of the distressed people without differences as to religion, *moved* to donate and hand over to the Poor-master of this city $50 out of the Lodge fund for distribution of bread among the needy." This long-winded motion was carried unanimously.

So far we have been considering some special occasions when European-born Jews, acclimated to the country, participated in the general life of the community. Their children widened this trend and made genuine contributions to the culture, politics and professional life of late nineteenth-century America. Some younger Buffalo Jews entered the world of entertainment and even achieved national fame. Adele Boasberg, daughter of the Dutch-born Nathan Boasberg, went on the stage under the name of Judith Berolde, playing parts with such famous actors of the day as William Gillette and E. H. Sothern. Her last Buffalo appearance was at Shea's Theater in 1902. She married Edward Marshall, manager of the American Press Association and lived in New York for her few remaining years.

Andrew Andrews was an actor and stage manager of the Eagle Street Theater. His original name was Isaacs, and he had been born, probably a Sephardic Jew, in Jamaica. He also conducted a school of landscape painting with society ladies as his chief pupils.[58] Josephine Bonne, daughter of Dr. Edward Treusch, achieved some national attention by writing a German-style cook book: *Continental Recipes.*

One Buffalo Jew entered the fantastic world of circus and carnival life. Joseph M. Roblin, son of Abraham Rabolinsky, a pioneer kosher butcher in the city, was a midget who was discovered and engaged about 1880 by the owner of Bunnell's Museum on Eagle Street. Roblin also played at the Wonderland Show in the Arcade, then located where the Brisbane Building stands at present. Later, Roblin added magic to his act and toured the West and Canada in vaudeville. Eventually, he joined Ringling Brothers and stayed with the circus until he retired at the age of sixty-three to return to Buffalo and the family metal business where he was still active thirty years later. In Boston, during his circus career, Roblin was jocularly challenged to a fight by the heavyweight champion John L. Sullivan, and he accepted provided Sullivan could make the weight—fifty-five pounds.[59]

In sharp contrast to Irish and German immigrants, the earlier American Jews usually avoided active participation in politics. Of course, some men like Rudolph Wolffsohn did actively participate, but most were uninterested. On the whole, until the days of Franklin D. Roosevelt, Jews tended to be Republicans rather than Democrats. But some Buffalonians such as Moses Shire the attorney, Joseph B. Mayer the traction magnate, and Abraham J. Elias the lumber merchant were active Cleveland Democrats. The Buffalo Republican Club, on the other hand, had many prominent

Jewish members. Henry Altman was once president of the club and a life member. Louis W. Marcus, lawyer, surrogate and judge; Frederick Ullman, lawyer and real estate tycoon; the Exsteins; the Marcuses; Rudolph Wolffsohn; and Edward Jellinek were all G.O.P. enthusiasts. Perhaps many young lawyers interested in politics affiliated Republican at this time in hopes of advancing their careers, for this party was the usual winner in local elections. There were several additional reasons for this tendency toward G.O.P. affiliation among Jews. Many German Jews had made their fortunes during the Civil War, and they often identified their material success with the cause of the Union which the Republican Party had preserved. Furthermore, with the exception of some importers, they, as business people, liked the Republican protective tariff. Moreover, Jews had little affinity for the kind of monetary inflation advocated by Bryan and the Democrats in 1896.

As a group, however, Jews had no particular political program in those pre-Zionist days, and they generally resented any political advice from their rabbis. Under the caption "Grant and the Israelites," *The Jewish Messenger* severely criticized a rabbi who had preached a political sermon: "Israelites are too intelligent and too self-asserting to be driven or led by their ministers, especially in matters that have no connection with religion." The paper went on to state that the people should exercise their suffrage as Americans, not as Jews.[60] It was not until the 1930s that many Buffalo Jews changed their Republican affiliation, although at the end of the nineteenth century many of them were already friendly with the local Democratic Party boss, William Francis ("Blue-Eyed Billie") Sheehan.

If in the early days in America there was relatively little anti-Semitism, it was beginning to rear its ugly head in Buffalo in the post-Civil War period. *The (American) Israelite* of March 17, 1882, carried a message from G. W. Cutter, a local Unitarian minister, who spoke of being criticized for his defense of Jews. "Even among Protestants," he wrote, "and in enlightened Buffalo, the spirit of persecution is shown in common talk of the people and the disposition to socially ostracize the race." The Reverend M. Rabe, pastor of the Third German Baptist Church, accused Buffalo Jews of being "a people without religious moorings, largely freethinkers." Possibly Rabe formed his erroneous judgment partly on the knowledge that Julius Brock (1829-1878), a Posen-born foreman at Altman Brothers, was a founder and active member of the Buffalo Freethinkers' Association and also active in Socialistic labor associations. The Rochester *Daily Democrat* in 1866 reported that an article was stolen from "a Jew store," and *The (American) Israelite* complained: "They never use the word Jew to qualify anything great, magnanimous or sublime." In the following year, a number of fire insurance companies refused to insure property owned by Jews, and in retaliation many Jews cancelled their existing policies with these firms.[61]

Despite these sporadic outbursts, both Jewish and Christian Germans were interested in common social activities and the two groups met in such associations as the Buffalo Orpheus Club where they attended concerts, recitals and balls. Other music groups attracted both Jew and Gentile. There were the Liedertafel and the Saengerbund. The Elmwood Music Hall, demolished in the 1930s, originated in a meeting of the North American Saengerbund in Buffalo in 1883. At this twenty-third *Saengerfest*, Simon Fleischmann, Ismar S. Ellison, Nathaniel S. Rosenau, Magnus Wiener and Hiram Exstein all participated. The Buffalo Liedertafel, in 1882, had 460 members with a fair sprinkling of German-Jewish names, such as Brock, Desbecker, Exstein, Hofeller, Rosenau and Weill, represented on the list.

Freemasonry attracted many Buffalo Jews, and some of them were members of volunteer fire companies. Perhaps because of their desire to achieve status, they expended more energy on joining than did the average non-Jew. Rabbi Falk was aware of a certain danger in this social aggressiveness: "The praiseworthy aspiration of Israelites to associate with the better class of society," he noted, "may sporadically revive the old prejudice in malicious and narrow-minded individuals." However, a true child of his age, Falk piously trusted in the general enlightenment of the times to dissipate such prejudice.[62]

While their parents were mingling with Gentiles in social and charitable associations, Jewish children were, through the public school system, fraternizing with non-Jews and absorbing Americanism. Some Jewish children went to high school, although by far the greater number in the 1880s terminated their education at the end of the eighth grade. The one high school in Buffalo, till the very end of the nineteenth century, was old Central, which had opened its doors in 1854. Central High School was famous for its faculty of unusually competent and erudite teachers. In the 1870s the principal was Ray T. Spencer, dubbed "Rat-Tail Spencer" by his pupils. He was succeeded by Henry P. Emerson, who later became Superintendent of Education in Buffalo. Some members of the faculty were: Miss Ripley who taught English, Miss Eastman, Composition, Mr. Pitt, Chemistry, Mr. Linden, Physical Geometry, and Mr. Schmidt, German.[63] In 1876, Rabbi Falk commented on the unusually good work done by the Jewish children. It is not surprising that Jewish children in that age should do well in a public school system. They were starved for secular education; they were the only immigrant group that didn't have to learn to learn, for they belonged to the "People of the Book." In addition, as a

minority group, they tended to over-compensate in school for the handicaps of such a situation; and perhaps unconsciously they worked hard at
their secular studies and neglected their Hebrew because they sensed that
their parents prized the former knowledge more than the latter.

Although most Jewish children went to public schools, a few children
of wealthy families attended private schools. Adelaide Rosenau, daughter
of David Rosenau, was graduated from the Buffalo Female Academy in
1883, and Carrie Block was also graduated from the same seminary.
Louis W. Wiener, who later entered Harvard, attended the Buffalo Classical School from 1880 to 1881; Hiram C. Marcus was at this school from
1881 to 1883.

It was at the beginning of this post-war period of economic pros-
perity and struggle for middle-class respectability that Rabbi Samson
Falk came to Buffalo, where he was to remain for twenty years and leave
an indelible mark on the city. Samson Falk was born on February 7,
1827, in Höchburg, Württemberg. He studied at the State University of
Württemberg and was probably ordained in Germany. He came to the
United States in 1853, serving as a rabbi in Albany and later in Milwaukee.
His wife, Doris, was born in Mecklenburg-Schwerin in 1836. When the
Falks arrived in Buffalo from Milwaukee in 1866, they had two children;
a third child was born shortly after their arrival. Pauline Falk, born in
1862, later married Julius Altman, and was said to have been a very
beautiful woman. Of the two sons, Isadore H. was born in 1864 and his
brother Eugene L. Falk was born in Buffalo two years later.

Rabbi Falk was the first real Reform rabbi in Buffalo (though not the
first rabbi of Temple Beth Zion, who was Dr. I. N. Cohen). Falk was the
first Jewish clergyman in Buffalo with enough *savoir faire* and western
secular education to represent the Jews before the general population
and make an impression. He helped tremendously to strengthen the tenuous social ties between the Jews and their Christian neighbors.
Furthermore, his gentle manner and the evident tolerance he bore for East-
Europeans, combined with his moderate Reform outlook, served to bridge
the gap between the two halves of the divided Jewish community. The
attitudes of Rabbi Falk, plus the fact that the eastern Jews were in Buffalo
in the 1840s, contributed to the comparatively early infiltration of these
easterners into the Reform movement and the consequent weakening of
the traditional congregations that they abandoned. The evidence is clear
that, in a time when many Reform rabbis, especially those of German
birth or ancestry, often either patronized or ignored the Russian Jews,
Falk busied himself, during the migrations of the eighties, in finding jobs

for the immigrants and seeing that they had sustenance until they could become self-supporting.[64]

Because Falk was the first rabbi in Buffalo to be given a secure livelihood with tenure, he was able to achieve a social status that permitted him to become a spokesman for Buffalo Jewry. He was elected for three years, in 1866, at an annual salary of $1,800. In 1869, he was re-elected for an additional three years. At that time he had been offered a pulpit in Pittsburgh at a larger salary, but he chose to remain in Buffalo. He was so popular at that time, that the board of trustees offered to raise extra money for his salary by private subscription and a special tax. By 1872, his salary had been raised to $3,000, and he was granted yearly vacations "for recreation and rest." He was elected for ten years in 1876 and for ten more in 1886. When he became sick in that year, he was given a leave of absence and a purse was raised to send him south for his health. Unlike the fly-by-night rabbis that had preceded him, Falk brought dignity and prestige to the pulpit in Buffalo.

Falk was socially graceful and a very good mixer. He was a one-time president of the local lodge of B'nai B'rith and later served as its secretary. He was active in the Grand Lodge and temporarily held the office of Grand Nasa Ab. He was known to be interested in the cause of Irish home rule and at his death the Irish Land League paid him tribute. He was also a councillor of the Buffalo Historical Society and it was before this group that he read his oft-cited paper, "A History of the Israelites in Buffalo."

Falk, who incidentally was the only one to apply when Beth Zion advertised for a rabbi in 1865, began his functions in Buffalo with the performance of a wedding between Hannah Exstein and the rising young Louis M. Brock. This wedding was celebrated on January 16, 1866, actually before he took up permanent residence in Buffalo. A contemporary survivor states that Falk was only a fair preacher. His forte was human kindness and a sincere interest in his congregants. He was more fluent in German than in English, but he did, in accordance with the constitution of Beth Zion, preach in both languages.

Very often the degree of Reform or the amount of Jewish content in liberal synagogues was determined by the attitudes of the rabbi, and it is interesting to find out just where Falk stood. On March 1, 1867, he wrote to the Buffalo *Express* to protest against the policy of that paper in using the term "Jew" in connection with the reporting of criminal cases. The letter reveals that, like other nineteenth-century German Jews, Falk was *not* a Jewish nationalist. It shows further that he considered moral laws more binding than specific religious practices of ritual. It reveals, finally, that he looked upon Judaism as a religion and not as a civilization or nationality. He wrote:

> Since the destruction of the 2nd temple the Jews have ceased to form a nation of their own. Since then their language is defunct, and all their laws referring to the occupation of Palestine by the Jewish nation have lost their obligatory legality, and only those laws of a specific religious, or moral and human nature, remain intact & binding up to this day. Their adherents, the Jews, ever since became parts of the respective nations among whom they lived, and more so in modern times, when advancing civilization improved the political condition of the Jews & placed their civil rights on an equal footing with all other citizens. Since the Jew is a Frenchman in France, a German in Germany, an Englishman in Great Britain, & an American in the United States, consequently the term Jew simply denotes a member of a religious community which still professes the Mosaic law & doctrines.

After this preamble, he went on to state that the term "Jew" should be used only with reference to religion and not in other circumstances. He argued in vain, for the *Express* replied that "so far as the *Express* is concerned, the expression complained of is not used in any intentionally abusive sense, but simply as a very common and natural distinction of race."

Rabbi Falk believed in unilinear human progress and was therefore typical of the early American Reform Jews who were prime optimists because they found prosperity and tolerance in nineteenth-century America. Like his colleagues, he stressed prophetic Judaism and, although he minimized the ritual of rabbinic Judaism, he never scoffed at it. He stressed the universality of religion, saying in his sermon on Shavuot, 1869, "God also loves other nations." Again like other reformers, Falk believed in the "mission of Israel"; he repeatedly said that God had dispersed the Jews throughout the world so that they might become His witnesses.[65]

It should be emphasized, however, that Falk was not a religious radical. He made changes, it is true, but he made them slowly. Inevitably, however, the congregation which was more traditional than liberal when he came to it, was a fairly typical Reform congregation twenty years later. It is interesting to compare Falk with his contemporary, the Rochester radical Rabbi Max Landsberg. In the early days of Falk, Beth Zion used the Merzbacher-Adler *Seder Tefillah* prayer book. Landsberg managed, by compiling his own prayer book, to remove practically all Hebrew from the service. Landsberg seems also to have encouraged intermarriage, and he eventually agreed to, even if he did not lead, the movement for

Sunday services. Perhaps the proximity of Landsberg's radicalism, criticized even in Reform circles, helped to keep Buffalo more moderate.

The minute books of Beth Zion reveal that each minor change that Rabbi Falk recommended had to be voted on. For example, the board passed the recommendation that each mourner say *Kaddish* in his own pew instead of coming up before the Ark in a group. In August 1867, however, Falk was voted down on a suggestion for the removal of the *Musaf* service (consisting mainly of prayers for the restoration of the Temple at Jerusalem). Services began in traditional fashion at sunset for the High Holidays in 1868, and in time-honored fashion, additional readers were appointed to chant each of the separate Yom Kippur Day services.

The first mention of a Ritual Committee, set up perhaps to accelerate Reform, comes in the constitution of 1868. The members were Sol Rosenau, Leopold Keiser and Leopold Marcus. The essential conservative bent of the congregation can be seen by the fact that, when this committee was set up, it was instructed to order the congregation to pray with covered heads.[66] Changes came slowly and Falk did not try to force any issue that met with determined opposition. In 1878, the covered-head issue produced a crisis. Some complained that the president and vice-president of the congregation did not wear hats at the reading of the Torah. Majority and minority reports were submitted in the best American tradition, and the decision was reached that from that date forward the wearing of hats would be optional. Another important change had already come by 1867, when Beth Zion dropped the second day of the festivals. For many years, despite the fact that boys and girls were confirmed on Shavuot, the boys celebrated their traditional *Bar Mitzvah* at thirteen. Dropped probably in the 1880s, this ceremony was restored toward the middle of the twentieth century.[67]

An anonymous letter published in *The (American) Israelite* of June 28, 1867, throws light on the kind of congregation that Falk faced in his first year in Buffalo and reveals how he was received by the congregants. The writer of this letter began by complaining that, when Rabbi Isaac M. Wise travelled east from Cincinnati, he failed to visit Beth Zion. In an accusatory and hurt tone, the correspondent scolded Wise for this neglect of the Temple "at whose birth you stood as Godfather." The writer then went on to complain that Beth Zion could not attract new Jewish settlers to Buffalo because it was handicapped by the "great illiberality both in mind and pocket of many of the old settlers." The only ray of light or redeeming feature that this man could see in Beth Zion was "Dr. Falk." Falk caught the imaginative sentimentality of his congregation. It was reported that there was not a dry eye in the congregation when Falk blessed three fatherless children at confirmation on Shavuot. Falk brought harmony and better synagogue attendance on that day as he confirmed seven boys and six girls before a good crowd that included a large number of Gentiles. The correspondent took evident pride in Falk's ability to attract Christians to witness the ceremony. Falk so won over his congregation that later that night congregants called at his residence to bring him "many handsome presents." [68]

For the first ten years of his residence in Buffalo, Rabbi Falk lived in Ward 4; but on May 22, 1876, he bought a home at W. Tupper and Franklin Streets, where he lived until his death on December 24, 1886.

Rabbi Samson Falk's funeral drew many people. So great was the demand for space that the cards distributed for his obsequies were marked, "Good until 2:30 p.m.," and if the space was not by then occupied it was given to one of the other waiting mourners. Young Nathaniel S. Rosenau was in charge of the ushers, who were ordered to report, dressed in black Prince Albert suits and formal gloves, at the side door of the Temple at 11:45 a.m. The funeral was attended by fellow clergymen and lay representatives, not only of all the Jewish congregations, but of most of the Christian churches as well.

The chief speaker was the Rev. Dr. Max Landsberg of Temple Berith Kodesh in Rochester. Landsberg, a universalist in outlook, stressed his favorite theme in eulogizing his colleague: "His fair name . . . has succeeded in breaking through the barriers of sect and form and creed . . . It is the most beautiful testimony to his value as a man that at his funeral this Temple foreshadows to us the glorious time announced by the ancient prophets when 'there will be but one shepherd and one flock' and 'when the house of the universal Father will be the house of prayer for all nations.' Over the casket of our friend the hand of fellowship is extended by those who adhere to the most various creeds, recognizing that in religious deed we are all one and inseparable."

Rabbi Lippman Mayer of Pittsburgh also spoke, as did Rev. Ferdinand C. Iglehart and Rev. G. W. Cutter of Buffalo. The latter, pastor of the Unitarian Church of Our Father, spoke of the religious discussions he had often had with Rabbi Falk and of the latter's delight in discovering the essential agreement between them, both in their belief in the one God and in their emphasis on religious morality.

The board of trustees of Beth Zion, which had voted $500 for his funeral, served as honorary pallbearers, and the Temple was draped in black for thirty days. A plaque in his honor was placed in the Temple; and in memory of the beloved rabbi, Beth Zion established the Samson Falk Ward in the Buffalo General Hospital.[69] In Forest Lawn Cemetery a tall shaft, towering over other markers, stands over the grave of Rabbi Samson Falk, and at its base is inscribed: "In the sincerity of our love and esteem this monument erected by scholars and friends to one of the noblest most honorable and self-sacrificing men. God rest his soul."

From 1866 to 1886, the period during which Rabbi Falk was spiritual leader of Temple Beth Zion, Reform Judaism gradually developed in the congregation. The pattern that presents itself to the historian who attempts to reconstruct what happened is that usually there was little record of initial changes. It would not be until long after a reform had become a *fait accompli* that the minute book recorded it, and then it was mentioned only as an established precedent when some other problem had arisen and was being debated. Many of the reforms came about when functionaries either died in office or left and no action was taken to replace them. Some congregations dropped their cantors in this manner. At the same time, there was often some focal point of conflict, and a serious battle would result over a single radical innovation. Sometimes these reforms, that marked a turning point in the history of a congregation, came over the wearing of hats, sometimes over the use of an organ, sometimes over the adoption of a revised prayer book.[70] It was a period of great optimism, and the people looked forward to a time of world peace and local prosperity, and in this spirit Reform services became things of great dignity and éclat. The depth of this optimism is evident in Rabbi Isaac M. Wise's belief that Reform Judaism was so reasonable that eventually it would take hold in Christian circles! *The (American) Israelite* for June 11, 1875, described Shavuot in Cincinnati. The Temple was gaily decorated and filled with people. "Choirs, cantors and organists did their best, rendering classical music in a most happy style." After the services, the people filled the streets, well-dressed, comfortable, prosperous. "All Cincinnati is in motion, the promenades are alive with smiling countenances, black eyes, blazing gems, silk, broadcloths, etc., as though the golden age had suddenly come back upon us." Indoors, too, one feels this optimistic security. "All parlors are in the Holyday garb, plenty of wine, fruits and cakes, ice creams and lemonades, gala times everywhere."

There was no national pattern in the spread of Reform. Each congregation moved at its own pace. At first services were held three times daily at Beth Zion, but this practice was soon abandoned. At a time when circumcision was denounced by some German radicals, Article XIX of the constitution of Beth Zion excluded all uncircumcised boys "from all privileges that those enjoy who are educated according to our faith and laws." Intermarriage was not encouraged, and for many years Beth Zion insisted on prior conversion of the non-Jewish party before a marriage would be preformed.[71] At the same time, a certain relaxation of attitude is discernable in the provision of Article XIX of the Beth Zion constitution, which permitted those not wed according to Mosaic Law to obtain seats by consent of the board of trustees. For many years Beth Zion continued a traditional practice of holding a *minyan* in the house of mourners. At least until 1869, the congregation tried to encourage observance of the dietary laws. Daniel Shire, who was appointed *shohet* and collector in 1866, was still slaughtering in 1869, at which time meat was dispensed through a Mr. Farthing who paid the congregation $18 per month for the monopoly. The evidence is inconclusive, but the observance of the dietary laws probably dwindled rapidly after 1871 when Shire retired as *shohet* and was not replaced. Until at least 1879, however, Beth Zion was still baking *matzot* for the congregation locally. *The (American) Israelite* on May 16, 1879, carried a letter from "L. W. Jr." of Buffalo. He reported: "Our *Matzos* was[sic] a success, and those who sent to New York and received the pasteboard of that city are forgiven. Their repentance was, at least, a practical one." The congregation tried to have the children excused from attending school on Jewish Holidays without "demerits for absence." They even went so far as to take the question before the Common Council. The minor festival of Purim was still observed by Beth Zion with special services as late as 1881, and it was not until the next year that uncovering the head was made compulsory.[72]

For many years after 1865, Beth Zion had the sexton it inherited from the parent Orthodox congregation. He was Samuel Weil, father of the later well-known Dr. Abram Lincoln Weil and Walter Weil.[73] Samuel Weil (1828-1895), a distant relative of the Wiles of clothing fame, was born in Ihringen. He came to Buffalo in the late 1850s and married the native-born Sarah Newman. Weil supplemented his meager income as sexton in many ways. He sold clothing to sailors, and in the seventies was also custodian of Montefiore Hall of B'nai B'rith, where he was designated as "Brother Janitor."

The first organist in Beth Zion was a Christian, "Professor" Charles G. Degenhard, who was paid $25 a month. Degenhard died in 1867 and, on August 6, 1871, he was replaced by another non-Jew Joseph Mishka, who played the organ and directed the choir at Beth Zion for over forty years, until his death in 1911. Mishka, born in Bohemia on May 6, 1846, came to Buffalo at the age of nine. Before entering on his long service with Beth Zion, Mishka served as organist for a number of Protestant churches. Ultimately he both directed and led the Temple choir. For twenty-four years Mishka led the famous Buffalo singing group, the Liedertafel, and he also was supervisor of music in the Buffalo Public Schools. Mishka is said to have mastered the Hebrew pronunciation. He was a one-time Roman Catholic who, having no religious affiliation of his own, seemed to have been attracted to Judaism although he never became a convert.

When he died, his picture was hung in the trustees' room and his family donated his music collection to Beth Zion.[74]

Originally, the choir of Beth Zion was a volunteer group under the leadership of Siegmund Levyn. In 1870, it was composed of Matilda Wiener (later Mrs. Edward Warner), Matilda Brock (later Mrs. Ismar S. Ellison), Fanny Biesenthal, Louis M. Brock, Magnus Wiener, Siegmund Levyn, Daniel Shire, Leopold Marcus, and Henry Cone. It was not until 1878 that Beth Zion hired, for $150 a year, an alto soloist who may have been a Gentile.

Matilda Wiener, born in Heinzheim on the Neckar, May 25, 1850, lived in Buffalo until July 16, 1929. She was the daughter of David and Fannie Wiener, and came to Buffalo as a child in 1854. Beth Zion expressed its appreciation of her services by a present and a series of resolutions, on the occasion of her marriage, saying "that we have no means at our command, which can adequately reward such sacrifices, as she has brought for our congregation, or for such services she has so disinterestedly tendered it." Not exactly idiomatic English, that, but the sentiment is good. Her husband, Edward Warner (1849-1926), whom she married on January 2, 1875, was born in Raab, Moravia. This son of Leopold Warner's brother, Jacob, came to Buffalo in 1861. The Edward Warners raised an important family, and many of their descendants are still prominent in Jewish affairs in Buffalo.[75]

After 1870, the minute books of Beth Zion show that the congregation was following the typical Reform pattern of the day. The entries reflect less concern with ritual and a growing interest in secular social and charitable ventures. Beth Zion was becoming more and more a close-knit German-Jewish social group, a "cult of the arrived." Jewish groups in general from this time on tended to replace interest in the synagogue as a place of worship with charity, welfare and social clubs. There was so much to do and only twenty-four hours in each day.

The groups that were formed during this period reflect this attitude. The Ladies' Sewing Society, "to furnish wearing apparel for the destitute," was established in 1874 by Mrs. William Friedman, wife of the owner of a large dry-goods store. The Daughters of Israel seems to have been another such club composed mainly of Beth Zion women. Of these groups, the one known as *Die Gemütliche*, whose motto was *Nichts für Ungut*, lasted longest and seems to have been the most important. It was founded about 1873 by Mrs. Henry Brock and was composed of a group of Beth Zion women who met regularly for charitable purposes. Among other things, the members of this Wednesday afternoon group sewed and gave away trousseaux to impoverished brides, and confirmation suits and dresses to poor boys and girls. The ladies owned a silver charity box with the names of deceased members inscribed thereon.[76]

There was a great deal of interest in music at this time and the records reveal that a Concert Committee was appointed in 1869 and, seven years later, a concert produced with the sale of the old Temple organ the sum of $1,689. Purim balls were held, and the congregation appointed a group known as "Managers of the Social Parties." One such "social party" was held on October 26, 1884, to celebrate the hundredth birthday of the eminent English Jew and humanitarian Sir Moses Montefiore. These were days of lawn tennis, gay social gatherings and happy parties.

Throughout this period the German language persisted with remarkable strength at Beth Zion. There is good evidence that, when Rabbi Falk came to Buffalo, both German and Hebrew were taught in the congregational school. In some measure, this was a way of using the synagogue to perpetuate the German culture that its members loved. There was in that day a fairly firm belief that Reform could not thrive outside of a German atmosphere. These Temple members showed a skill in keeping the synagogue household in order. Unlike most of the other nineteenth-century synagogues, Beth Zion meetings were not marked by disorder sometimes verging on anarchy. A formal "Constitution of Temple Beth Zion" was adopted in 1868, and according to its provisions the Temple was governed by a board of nine trustees, three of whom were elected every three years. The officers of the Temple were then chosen by the board. Two regular meetings were scheduled each year in the months of Nisan and Elul (approximately April and September). A very detailed set of by-laws contained the duties of the president (who in the early days gave the rabbi permission to marry and bury members), and outlined the duties of the minister. The latter, in turn, was directed to officiate at weddings "in his official costume" and was instructed to announce the marriage banns on Saturday before service. He was given the task of writing out Hebrew epitaphs for deceased members, and he kept the records of births, marriages and deaths.

Beth Zion at this time was a small, homogeneous group, given to intermarriage between families within the congregation. The congregation grew very slowly. A few German Jews who resided in such nearby towns as Dunkirk, or Lockport, were married at Beth Zion and buried in its cemetery. Such new members as were added were either children of members of the congregation who reached maturity, or late German-Jewish immigrants who settled in Buffalo after the Civil War. Meyer Geismer was one of the latter group. He had been born in Ihringen in 1842 and after the Civil War came to Buffalo, where he was a very successful cattle dealer, like his ancestors in Baden. Geismer met and married Matilda, the daughter of a fellow drover, Emanuel Straus, of

Bavaria. Eventually Geismer abandoned his ancestral occupation and entered the clothing business at 48-50 Pearl Street. He has achieved the distinction of having his name carved in stone on that building, which still stands. His daughter, Carrie (d.1955), married the contractor Isadore H. Falk, son of Rabbi Falk.

Until 1900, no great eagerness to get new members is discernable, and applications were automatically tabled for thirty days. Occasionally some of the older East-European families in Buffalo drifted into Beth Zion, to replace some members who either moved to other cities or returned to Europe. In 1880, Beth Zion had seventy-two members, and ninety-two children were enrolled in the religious school. The concern of these times was for exclusiveness, not size.

An important arrival was Louis Weill, who was born in Alsace-Lorraine on October 18, 1850, and came to Buffalo in 1869. At his death in 1943, he was the oldest member of Beth Zion. He was active at first in the jewelry business and in banking and clothing, but he is principally known for his real estate interests. On January 22, 1873, he married Amelia, daughter of Samuel Desbecker. Amelia was the girl who carried the key when Beth Zion dedicated its Niagara Street Temple, and it was her daughter (later Mrs. Jacob G. Rosenberg of Rochester) who carried the key when the present Delaware Avenue Temple was dedicated in 1890.[77]

Another new arrival was Henry Weill, Louis's older brother. Henry was a well-educated Alsatian who arrived in America in 1867. After his marriage to Fanny Shire in 1870, he became involved in Buffalo affairs. He helped organize the Metropolitan Bank and was very active at the turn of the century in real estate.

Another family new to Buffalo at this time was that of Louis Jellinek of Austria, who came to Buffalo at least as early as 1870. Because his daughter Josephine and her fiancé, Louis E. Warner, died before their marriage, a plaque to their memory was hung in Beth Zion.

Closely connected with the affairs of Beth Zion during this period, and progenitor of well-known descendants, was Daniel Shire. Although Shire (1826-1891) came to Buffalo and began to work for the original Beth Zion early in 1851, the important part of his relationship with the congregation began in 1864, when he returned to Buffalo from a six-year stay in Hamilton, Ontario. Shire was born in Gemünden, Bavaria, and it was in Germany that he was trained as a religious functionary. He was *shohet, hazzan,* teacher of Hebrew, and sounder of the *shofar* on Rosh Hashana. It was natural for Shire to come to Buffalo, for his sister had married the influential Samuel Desbecker. After his return from his sojourn in Canada, Shire was associated with Beth Zion as ritual slaughterer, collector and teacher. He was the principal teacher in those days and also sang in the choir. He gave up some of his functions in 1871, but continued to teach in the congregational school for nineteen additional years. The evidence indicates that Shire was not a very effective teacher, but he was a likeable person, a fine fisherman and a congenial companion. His association with Beth Zion remained fairly close, for in 1886 he was ordered, in the absence of the rabbi, not to chant (evidently it was hard for him to shed his traditional practices) but to read, in the Reform fashion, portions from the Bible. The trustees obviously had some reservations about his taking over in the absence of the rabbi, for he was also ordered to "abstain from delivering any sermons or prayers." Shire, who married Yetta Weil, knew sufficient Hebrew to write an ode in that language to Sir Moses Montefiore.

In the early days, Shire rented rooms to boarders in his home at Ellicott near Eagle Street, and ultimately his house became a Mecca for newly arrived German Jews, many of whom were cattle dealers. It was not an uncommon sight to see a few sheep and other livestock cropping the grass in Shire's back yard. If he was competent enough in the sacred tongue to teach Hebrew to the children, this talent was offset by an amazing deficiency in English. One of his entries in the minute books of B'nai B'rith reads "No further business before the Lodge, she was closed in Harmony." [78]

Certain members of the Shire family were destined to become very wealthy and influential. The most distinguished was Moses Shire, one of the greatest local lawyers of his day.

Long before the death of Daniel Shire who, as we have seen, formed a link with Beth Zion's Orthodox days, the congregation moved into the mainstream of the liberal movement. In 1873, the synagogue hailed the formation of the Union of American Hebrew Congregations with headquarters at Cincinnati. Rabbi Falk who had studied for the rabbinate in Germany before Isaac Mayer Wise established his Hebrew Union College, naturally threw in his lot with the new seminary. There, he subsequently became an examiner in Hebrew. Beth Zion of Buffalo is said to have been the first congregation from an Atlantic seaboard state to affiliate with the national group. To raise the necessary funds for the U.A.H.C., each member of the congregation was assessed one dollar. The first national council of the Union of American Hebrew Congregations was held in Cleveland in July 1874. Rabbi Falk and Siegmund Levyn, with L. M. Brock and Henry Brock as alternates, paid their own way to the meeting as delegates of Beth Zion, for the congregation felt unable to meet their travel expenses. [79]

The second annual council of this group was held at McArthur's Hall in Buffalo on July 13-15, 1875. Seventy congregations sent about 100 delegates, and Rabbi Wise himself came to Buffalo. Beth Zion went all out to make this meeting a huge social success. Montefiore Lodge of B'nai B'rith invited all its members "to a summer night's festival to be given in honor of the delegates." Music was furnished by Kehr's "full cornet band." The delegates were the ladies' guests at luncheon at Zeigle's Hall on Main Street near Virginia, where they were presented with floral bouquets and later were driven about the city on sight-seeing tours. The ladies of Beth Zion were especially successful in their efforts to make the meeting a social success. *The (American) Israelite,* on July 30, 1875, said gratefully: "The ladies of Buffalo have evinced an extraordinary interest in the Council, not only by paying distinguishing attention to the august body in magnificent evening entertainments, but also by their steady presence in the hall." There is no question that the meeting was a huge social success.

In matters of business, too, it was successful. After Rabbi Falk opened the meeting with a prayer, Leopold Keiser was elected temporary chairman. After the invocation, Henry Brock, president of Beth Zion, welcomed the delegates to Buffalo and was promptly elected national vice-president of the group. At this meeting, the final steps were taken for establishing the Hebrew Union College, which opened its doors in the fall of that year. The delegates discussed the need for a rabbinical school, and some complained that since many congregations refused to affiliate with the national group, only $40,000 of the $160,000 needed to open the college had been raised. Of this amount, $35,000 had come from Cincinnati. Mr. Siegmund Levyn was appointed on a committee of correspondence designed to spark the campaign to endow the contemplated school.[80]

While the congregation was engaged in matters of national scope and importance, certain local problems continued to press for attention. Foremost among these was the ever-present problem of Jewish education. What made the proper religious instruction of children particularly difficult was actually a complex of causes, the same throughout the United States, in Orthodox as well as in Reform congregations. In the first place, all communities faced a shortage of teachers. Such instructors as were available were often failures in life. Some of them had been trained for other work in which they could not earn a livelihood, others were greenhorns who more often than not failed to establish rapport with American children. The turnover, under these circumstances, was exceedingly high. Salaries in general were very low and, if an opportunity was offered the average teacher to improve his income in some other field, he usually grasped it. In addition, among the various synagogues, even within one grouping such as Orthodox or Reform, there was no agreement on aims, no established curriculum, no adequate texts. Neither enough money nor enough energy was invested for the purpose of settling the problem by ambitious businessmen whose energies were drained by long, hard hours of work. Furthermore, the competition from secular public schools often proved too much for the synagogue school. In the get-rich-quick atmosphere of the day, parents really valued the public schools as a means of accomplishing the end of social status, and the children sensed this fact all too well. It was a vicious circle, for the generations that were born and matured in America during these years were far too often unlearned in Jewish culture and in turn did not value Jewish education.

At Beth Zion, although the original constitution paid a great deal of attention to education, the situation was not much better than in other parts of the country. The constitution set up a School Committee which was directed to inspect the school monthly and report to the board. In the beginning, the Beth Zion school was quite traditional, for the students used as a text the traditional *siddur* that was printed at Rödelheim near Frankfort, and they used the Pentateuch in Hebrew.[81]

In 1867, Beth Zion's school was in session for eleven months each year, and students paid tuition of $40 a year. Daniel Shire was assistant teacher, the term "teacher" apparently being reserved for the rabbi. In addition to his teaching duties, Shire, as we have seen, served several other functions. By 1869, things were not going well and, probably for this reason, Rabbi Falk took charge of preparing the confirmation class on Wednesday afternoons. The School Committee was told that the parents were not satisfied, that the school was poorly managed, and "that the children make no progress." [82] By 1870, the school had to depend upon "Voluntary Assistant Teachers," but they didn't seem to help the situation. Later, schoolroom facilities at the Temple were enlarged and Adolph Duschak was hired to teach. Duschak, a Hungarian, born in 1842 in Pressburg (now Bratislava), was educated at the University of Vienna. He came to the United States in 1867, when he was twenty-five years old. He taught school at Williamsville and at the East Aurora Academy before moving to Public School 9 in Buffalo, where he was principal for thirty-six years. Subsequently, Duschak became an active member of the First Unitarian Church in Buffalo.

By 1880, Beth Zion school had ninety-eight students who were taught by the minister and two assistants. In this year, the Temple was faced with the problem of educating children not affiliated with the congregation. It was then voted that twenty such students would be allowed to enroll provided their parents worshipped at Beth Zion even though they could not afford membership.

Young Isaac Weil was at this time preparing for confirmation and he carefully kept a notebook based on his instruction in Beth Zion school. This notebook, which fortunately has been preserved, gives us an insight into the curriculum of the eighties. In the non-Jewish fashion of the day, a catechism was used to instruct the children. The theology seems to have been unimpaired by contemporary biblical criticism or Darwinian scientific scepticism. Direct revelation of the Torah at Mount Sinai was taught, and a positive assertion of the immortality of the human soul was made. Personal repentance was stressed. The customs and ceremonies, even in regard to the observance of Holidays, were quite traditional except for the observance of the second day. Sigmund Hecht's *Epitome of Post-Biblical History* was the text used. Hecht, a Reform rabbi of Montgomery, Alabama, filled his book with the glowing optimism and faith in progress so typical of the false dawn of the Victorian Era and assumed that, except for darkest Russia, Jewish conditions were good and were going to be better.[83]

No attempt at a national organization to guide Hebrew schools was made until 1886, when the Sabbath School Union (Reform) was organized to develop a uniform pattern, and not until after World War I did the Cincinnati group create a commission on Jewish education to solve the problems common to all schools. In the early days, the American Jewish religious schools paid far too much attention to subject matter and formalized discipline and far too little attention to the psychological needs of the student. The average school, according to one authority, was "moralistic, theological and catechetical in its approach." [84] The curriculum was deadly. Hebrew was taught, in those pre-Zionist days, as a dead language. The Bible and other subjects were presented with no effort to relate them significantly to current American life. There was altogether too much emphasis on rote memory.

In 1890, the Beth Zion School Committee began keeping minutes, and we can derive some information about the school from them. A School Fund advanced the money for books, and the students paid 25 cents every three months. Prizes and medals were given to induce the students to study, and in 1891 Walter Jellinek and Rachel Bock were nominated to receive them. According to the old custom, the board still examined the children every June, but this practice would soon fall into disuse as younger men took charge and discovered that they did not know enough themselves to question the children. The school was then in session from 9:00 to 10:30 a.m. on Saturday and from 9:00 to 12:00 on Sunday, and it was taught by volunteers who knew scarcely more than their pupils. In 1890, Leopold Warner, in memory of his son Louis E. and his deceased fiancée Josephine Jellinek, donated $1,000, the interest of which was to be used to purchase books for needy scholars. The teaching situation had improved a bit, for later we find instruction by Rabbi Aaron, assisted by Leopold Keiser who seems to have been a religious-school teacher in Europe. In 1893, Miss Sarah Haas, an experienced public school teacher who was affiliated with Beth Zion until her death, was appointed assistant teacher at Beth Zion at $125 a year, and the Rev. Schlager had replaced Keiser as teacher.

The first full information that we have is for the year 1895. At that time the curriculum included Hebrew reading, translations of certain prayers into English, biblical and post-biblical Jewish history, some study of the Psalter and the Book of Proverbs, and "moral lessons." On Sunday, the rabbi held services for the children after class and delivered a sermonette. The school term ran from September to June, and an attempt was made to set certain standards that the children would have to meet before confirmation, but the tendency was to look on confirmation as a purely religious ceremony and one that was rarely if ever denied merely because the child did not know enough.[85]

Another public school teacher soon joined Miss Haas. Rachel M. Marks (1869-1954) taught Hebrew and Bible history from 1895 until 1913, and was later principal of the Beth Zion school for eight years. It was Miss Marks who introduced the system of hiring trained and paid teachers. These new instructors were, at least in the early days, usually well trained in secular subjects and almost invariably deficient in Hebrew knowledge, but their hiring marked a step in the right direction. For some time, so few Jewish books suitable as school texts were published that Miss Marks was forced to use in her classes leaflets of the Unitarian Association and material from the (Protestant) Bible Study Publishing Company of Boston.

Rachel Marks was graduated from Central High School in Buffalo, took extension courses at home, and studied at three universities. At first Miss Marks gave private German lessons in Buffalo, and then she taught English and German at Public School 9. Finally she moved to Technical High School, and in 1910 she was made head of the Department of Modern Languages which post she retained until her retirement twenty-two years later. Her grave in Forest Lawn carries the following inscription:

> When I am Forgotten as I Shall Be
> And Lie in the Dull Marble
> Say I taught Thee.

By the turn of the century the school still seemed to be suffering from many of the same problems it had faced throughout the final quarter of the century. Good teachers were hard to come by, salaries were low, texts were scarce, and children of non-members continued to clamor for admittance. In the nineteenth century, some problems seemed never to get solved.

One of these persistent problems was the cemetery. It has already been noted that Beth Zion had a cemetery on Pine Ridge Road; but in this period the congregation began to show interest in acquiring land in the new cemetery, Forest Lawn.

Erastus Granger, appointed by President Thomas Jefferson first post-master of Buffalo, owned the land that was eventually to become Forest Lawn Cemetery. The site had been part of the vast domain of the Six Nations, and arrowheads and artifacts are still occasionally found there. The Christian part of the cemetery dates from 1849, when eighty acres of the land were purchased from the heirs of Granger. This land was improved, and soon became the most fashionable Protestant burial ground in the city. It is said to be one of the most beautiful cemeteries in the country, with variegated foliage, knolls, hills and dales, and with picturesque Scajaquada Creek winding through its trees. Because the cemetery was made up of almost equal parts of forest and lawn, it was given the name Forest Lawn. "Forest Lawn," says one person who remembers the seventies, "had good roads, and there shy lovers proposed to willing maidens."

Jewish interest in Forest Lawn dates from December 18, 1870, when it was first mentioned in the Beth Zion minute book. Rabbi Falk seems to have urged the members to take action when he addressed the congregation about the cemetery situation first in English and then, on request, in German. On May 11, 1871, a committee was appointed to investigate the possibility of purchasing from the Forest Lawn Association part of the new section adjoining Chaplin Street with an option to buy the entire section. The committee reported it as "a project which is entirely beyond the reach of our Congregation." [86] Apparently the plan to buy land was dropped. At any event, the minute book is silent on the subject from that time on, and representatives of Forest Lawn Cemetery state that no land was ever sold to Beth Zion. Sometime later, section FF was merely reserved for Beth Zion, and much later section Z was added. Meanwhile, private families began to buy land in Forest Lawn, and the first Jewish burial was held in 1879, when David DeVeaux Altman, killed in a polo accident, was interred there.[87]

While Beth Zion was meeting the problems that arose during the Gilded Age, solving some and adjusting to others, Beth El also found itself in a period of expansion and change. Like congregations elsewhere which resisted drastic changes, Beth El had to contend with the Reform wave of the sixties, the Americanizing and secularizing effects of the Civil War, and the constant influx of immigrants who clustered around newly founded, more traditional synagogues. In addition, Beth El faced a problem of competing with the affluent and socially more secure Beth Zion. The Orthodox synagogues were at a disadvantage in the sense that they did not have any national cohesiveness; they did not have any central group to direct them. As one historian of the period remarks, the traditionalists suffered from the "lack of a movement on the national level to counterbalance Reform." [88] The liberal groups organized on a national level in the 1870s, but the more conservative synagogues were not united until the twentieth century.

Although, for over sixty years, the ritual did not change at Beth El, attendance at worship grew smaller and smaller as violation of the Sabbath was accepted as the norm. Even those who came to synagogue on Saturday generally kept their businesses open and returned to work in them after the conclusion of the services. Eventually even this partial observance of the Jewish day of rest almost ceased. Before long, men began to quip that the principal difference between Reform and Orthodox Jews was that the former group *didn't keep* one day of *Yom Tov* and the latter *didn't keep* two days! The direct result of this was, of course, diminished congregational participation; but a further result was that the more pious immigrants either avoided Beth El because of the irreligiousness of its members, or else founded synagogues based on the Sabbath observance of its members. Consequently, after 1865, Beth El faced stiff competition from both the right and left.

The parade of functionaries at Beth El continued, and in November 1868, the following typical advertisement appeared in *The Jewish Messenger:*

"Notice—Election for Shochet & Chasan, orthodox, will take place on the first Sunday in January next, at the rooms of the Congregation 'Bethel,' Buffalo, N. Y. All applications, accompanying good references, will be received until then. No travelling expenses allowed. Address James Binnard, Pres., 466 Main Street, Buffalo, N. Y."

This instability in the Beth El congregation was so marked that when, in 1870, the famous biographer, James Parton, published his well-known article "Our Israelitish Brethren" in the *Atlantic Monthly,* he put in, as illustration, an advertisement for a *shohet* and *hazzan* for Beth El.[89] During his period of tenure, Israel Warrensky was constantly in need of as-

sistants. And the turnover in presidents after the resignation of Henry
Brock in 1865 (probably to devote all his time to Beth Zion) was just as
rapid as that of teachers and assistants. Apparently the congregation was
searching in vain for someone with the ability, time and energy to give
effective leadership.

In that memorable spring when Lee surrendered to Grant at Appomattox, there was much talk of rebuilding the synagogue, which had been
damaged by fire the previous winter. The congregation finally decided on
only temporary repairs to prevent collapse of the existing structure. As
a result of the fire, the synagogue was constantly plagued by legal actions,
counter actions, and legal fees. Of the $1,200 received from insurance,
a considerable portion was deducted for counsel fees. In desperation, the
board tried to induce a man named Stevenson to buy the synagogue in
1868. They asked $8,000 for the property, but the attempted sale failed.
Soon it was clear that Beth El would have to move. The light was in fact
cut off by the erection of a wall on another piece of property, and the
traffic in mid-town was becoming so noisy and congested that it interrupted services.

Then, Abraham F. Cohen, a vigorous leader, became president and
pushed the project of the building of a new synagogue. On October 9,
1873, the congregation bought property on 71 Elm Street for $3,450. The
lot, 46 feet wide and 110 feet deep, was on the east side of Elm Street
about 100 feet north of North Division Street. A building committee
composed of A. F. Cohen, Henry Brown, and M. B. Friedman was appointed. Under the direction of the architects Porter and Watkins, a
company of masons began to build a brick building. Much of the car-
pentry work was done by a master carpenter named John Higham.
Meanwhile, the Pearl Street synagogue was sold to the Jewish firm of
Dahlman, Giershofer, Spiegel & Co. Louis Dahlman, who owned the adjoining building, began acquiring property shortly after his arrival in
Buffalo in the 1840s, and eventually he and his partners owned a great
deal of real estate in the business district.

The red brick, Romanesque, stone-trimmed building cost approximately
$9,400. Part of the money for the new building was raised by the sale of
seats in the new Elm Street synagogue. They sold, depending on location, for $125 to $75, and everyone who had owned a seat in the old
synagogue was credited with $25 toward the purchase of one in the new.
To the money derived from the sale of the Pearl Street synagogue, the
Ladies' Auxiliary added receipts from picnics and other social events, and
soon all but $4,738 of the land and building costs had been paid for by
the congregation which then consisted of forty-six heads of families.

The brick, slate-roofed building was 40 feet wide and 75 feet long. It contained a vestry room, a large vestibule, and cellar living quarters for the minister. Apparently, however, the building committee had learned very little from the congregation's experience on Pearl Street, for the minister soon complained that his quarters were dark and gloomy. There was also a *mikvah,* which the Buffalo *Commercial Advertiser* called, in ignorance, a "baptistry," and the ladies' galleries fringed the synagogue auditorium on three sides. Schoolrooms to accommodate several hundred pupils were also included, and the synagogue would seat 500 people.[90]

The Elm Street synagogue was dedicated on Rosh Hodesh Elul, a Friday evening, August 14, 1874. The choir of Beth Zion under the leadership of Joseph Mishka sang, and Rabbi Falk delivered the chief sermon at the dedication. The minister of Beth El, the Reverend Philip Bernstein (1845-1890), presided. Bernstein had been born in Berlin, and he was a talented linguist and musician. He and his wife, who had also been born in Germany, gave the congregation the Teutonic touch that it seemed to like.[91]

Henry Brown, chairman of the building committee, presented the keys to President Cohen, which two young girls, Augusta Hyman and Jennie Brown, carried on a plush cushion. Henry Brown had been born in Prussia in 1837, and was in the ready-made clothing business at about this time. Added to the original building committee were Joseph Warner, and Abram D. Davis (1851-1904), a merchant who served as its secretary.[92]

As often happens with congregations, the new building seems to have given the congregation a new lease on life. Unfortunately the minute books are lost for much of this period, and accurate information about this critical time in the life of the synagogue is lacking. When light goes on again in the history of Beth El, we find that a new group, mostly East Europeans, has taken over control. Influential in Beth El in the closing decades of the century was Joseph Saperston, who served many terms as president. Saperston had been born in Stalopoener, East Prussia, in 1838 and lived for a time in England, where his son Willard was born, before the family came to America in 1864. At first Saperston owned a retail clothing store, but he later shifted his interest to real estate; and he retired in 1886 to live on his rentals. During his long career as an officer of Beth El he ruled the congregation with a strong hand and by his inflexibility sent a number of families to other congregations.

Jacob H. Cohen, who became president of Beth El in 1882 and lived in Buffalo until 1922, was very active in almost every Jewish organization. He had left Poland in 1869 and gone to London, where he lived until 1872 at which time he came to Buffalo. Originally a tailor, later, in 1874, he and his brother Samuel started a retail hat-and-men's-furnishing store on Main Street. Three years later, Cohen celebrated St. Valentine's

Day by marrying Sarah Jacobs, and the next year he joined Beth El. Here he was one of the leading liberals, and it was during his incumbency as president that one of the significant reforms of the period was introduced. In the eighties, men and women were permitted to sit together during the Friday evening services, and this marked a distinct step toward what was later to be called Conservative Judaism.[93]

The new building did not, of course, solve all problems. The line, before 1885, between Reform and American-style Orthodox, was by no means clearly marked. For example, at first Beth El decided to support the new Hebrew Union College at Cincinnati, but soon did a complete about face and withdrew its support. Before long, the congregation bogged down into its old habitual bickering. The congregation lost the momentum gained by the move to new quarters, and once more Beth El was in the doldrums.

By 1877, the old routine of trying to replace the minister occupied the congregation. It is significant that now they advertised for a minister who could preach both in English and German, for they were probably still trying to catch up with the Germans of Beth Zion, despite the fact that the great majority of their own congregation spoke not German but Yiddish. Part of the trouble arose from the depression-ridden years of the seventies. They were forced to resort to all sorts of means to raise funds and, as times got worse, members paid toward the building debt of the congregation in installments of 50 and 25 cents. No doubt because of the constant influx of immigrants, the problem of decorum during the services continued to bother the more serious and sedate members. Probably more than any other cause, this lack of proper dignity in the services eventually drove many of the second generation into the arms of Beth Zion.

As a generation of Buffalo-bred young men and women grew up, there were more purely social occasions in Beth El, although they never came near equalling the éclat of similar events at Beth Zion. A series of dances was held; and eventually an annual ball was held at McArthur's Hall, beginning in 1878. A summer excursion aboard the S.S. "Arundel" was followed by an even more elaborate excursion aboard the same vessel in 1880, at which time wine, beer, pop and ice cream were brought along, and apparently under this stimulation, the participants spent so generously that the excursion netted $108.04 toward easing the synagogue's financial situation.[94]

Beth El, in those years, clung to many customs that a number of congregations were abandoning. Each year before Passover, the congregation arranged with local bakers for *matzot*. This practice continued into the eighties, with the secretary supervising the baking. The *matzot* were

sold to the congregants at 11 cents a pound. Another practice still retained at Beth El was the erection of a *succah* in the yard of the synagogue on the festival of Succot. In 1878, Beth El spent $1.98 for grapes,
60 cents for apples, 90 cents for cakes, and a whopping $7 on brandy for
"spiritual" refreshment in the *succah!* [95]

During those years, there was, however, a sincere attempt to make the
synagogue more attractive in order to hold the younger people. Beth El
began to tussle with a persistent problem: how could the service be made
more meaningful than the East-European Orthodox rendition, and yet
how could they, at the same time, avoid reforms that would seriously
violate Jewish custom and practice? In 1879, the congregation appointed
a ritual committee "for the purpose of dictating to the Minister before
the service or ceremony to be given." The first act of this ritual committee was to decide that men would no longer be called to the Torah
on Saturdays and Holidays by their Hebrew names, but that tickets would
be distributed before the reading of the Torah to designate those to be
honored at the services. Although this very minor change carried, there
was a reaction by the old-timers and the ritual committee was dismissed.
This pattern of behavior would repeat itself time and time again as part
of a persisting attempt to introduce reforms that would enhance the dignity of the service.

In 1881, a new Ritual Committee recommended that synagogue honors
be no longer auctioned off in the European fashion. They also urged that
certain *piyyutim* be deleted on some festivals. These two reforms were
accepted by the congregation, but other suggested minor changes were
not accepted. At the same time, a far-reaching new step was taken. The
congregation voted that the rabbi confirm girls as well as boys on Shavuot.
This indicated that Beth El had already accepted, by 1881, the Reform
practice of confirmation. But, at the same time, they were not yet ready
to allow men and women to sit together, although they would soon permit this on Friday evenings.

In the late nineteenth century, Beth El, like Beth Zion, faced the difficult problem of Hebrew education for the children. The Pearl Street
synagogue never had adequate space for a school, and in 1866, in order
to provide suitable quarters, the card room of the synagogue was converted into a classroom.[96] Then began the task of searching for a teacher,
a task not made any easier by the fact that they wanted the teacher also
to be a *porcher* who could prepare meat in the ritual manner by removing certain veins. Conditions, however, remained unsatisfactory, and a
committee was appointed to build a school house in the yard of the
synagogue. Either the committee failed to act or it was merely appointed
without the necessary funds, for nothing ever came of this plan. A decade

later, a School Committee was designated, with the president of the congregation as chairman. This committee established a tuition plan by which a single child would pay $18 a year and two children in the same family $30 each year. Provision was made for teaching the children of non-members, and indigent children were to be taught free. The school lists reveal that many children left the school. Apparently the boys were simply not interested and quit promptly after *Bar Mitzvah*. But some progress was made in modernizing Jewish education, and by the end of the century Beth El's school printed report cards and taught Hebrew reading, Hebrew translation, religion and Jewish history.[97]

The story of the defection of Reverend Bernard Cohen is an appropriate conclusion to the account of Buffalo Jewry during the late Victorian years, for it throws much light on the religious controversies that occupied the attention of men during this age. Bernard Cohen, in a sense, is a symbol of the religious quarrels of the time.

Cohen was born on July 2, 1842, in Melawa, near Warsaw, Poland. He came to the United States about 1860, having met his future wife, Yetta Aronberg, aboard ship. They were married in New York, where Cohen served the Chrystie Street synagogue. Later he served in several smaller eastern cities until chance brought him to Beth El in 1879.

In many ways Cohen was superior to the peripatetic preachers of his time. He was a handsome, meticulously groomed gentleman, well mannered and likeable. From all accounts, he must have been, at least in his younger years, an inspiring teacher and rabbi. In all probability he was the first minister at Beth El who could preach a good English sermon. This fact, of course, made him popular with the younger elements in the congregation. His rendition of the service was also superior, for he pronounced his Hebrew correctly and was well versed in the best cantorial music of the day.

Nevertheless Mr. Cohen's troubles in Buffalo were to become a legend in the community. Despite his Polish origin, he had been deeply influenced by the German Reform theologians and he was sincerely convinced that Beth El must fall in line with the liberal tendencies of the day. Cohen was probably encouraged to suggest changes by his president, Emil Bernstein, a German, who had long urged certain reforms on his fellow members at Beth El.

The trouble started soon after Reverend Cohen's arrival, when he asked permission to perform marriages during the traditional midsummer period of mourning for the destruction of the Temple at Jerusalem. In the controversy that ensued over the request, some old-timers resigned, but the minister won a temporary victory and was re-elected at a salary of $1,100 a year. Then the Ritual Committee, spurred on by Cohen, pressed for additional innovations. In addition to confirming girls in

1881, Cohen was permitted to officiate in the synagogue proper at the marriage of a member to a non-Jewess, whom he had previously converted. But the real crisis came in the spring of 1882 when Cohen delivered a sermon on the last day of Passover. The following Sunday, he was ordered to "lecture in a more orthodox method and less radical than heretofore." Matters became more strained, and Cohen resigned when Emil Bernstein's motion to introduce mixed seating was tabled. A committee tried unsuccessfully to have him reconsider his decision, but he said that "it was impossible for him to tarry here longer." [98]

Bernard Cohen after his resignation went to Grand Rapids and then to Chicago to serve as minister in those cities. In the meantime at Beth El the parade of ministers continued. Some of them lasted only a few months. After Cohen's departure the traditionalists seem to have resumed control, for in answer to a candidate's inquiry, they replied that the congregation was "strictly orthodox."

Solomon J. Kohn was one of the rabbis who lasted only six months at Beth El. He served here in 1889. Kohn graduated from Yale after he left Buffalo, became a lawyer in Louisville and later apparently studied medicine.

After Kohn left, Beth El sent an invitation to Bernard Cohen to return, in spite of his latitudinarian views. In 1889, therefore, he came back and remained until March 1, 1895, when he suddenly left to become assistant teacher, sexton and collector at Beth Zion. We know none of the details of this second quarrel, but it can be assumed that Cohen left once more because of religious differences that could not be compromised. At Beth Zion, Cohen was first employed at a salary of $75 a month, probably through the influence of Julius Altman.[99] In 1902, he was permitted to officiate in Temple on certain occasions and became a sort of assistant rabbi. Ten years later, his salary was $1,200 a year and shortly thereafter, on his golden wedding anniversary, he was given a purse of $350 by the congregation. He retired from his duties as collector in 1917, but he retained his function as assistant rabbi until his death in 1926. Cohen was not very happy at Beth Zion while Rabbi Aaron was there, but after 1912, under Rabbis Kopald and Fink, he was treated with dignity and respect. Rabbi Fink would invite Cohen to give the benediction at services, and this honor greatly pleased the old man.

As the Gilded Age drew to a close, Buffalo could look back on an era of general prosperity and progress. The city had emerged from the Civil War in much better general economic and social health than before the war. The pioneer spirit of Buffalo Jewry had yielded to a period of settling in; and when the great numbers from eastern Europe reached the city they found the older generation of Jews already firmly established. A new chapter of American-Jewish history was in the making.

CHAPTER

——◦◦◦——

SIX

The New Exodus

"THE MOST STIRRING historical event in the life of American Jewry was the coming of the East-European Jews to the United States." So writes the contemporary historian Maxwell Whiteman, and, in a sense, his remarks are an understatement, for he need not have confined himself to the impact on American Jewry. The movement of the Jews to the United States during the third of a century that followed 1881, constituted the greatest population shift in Jewish history since the Exodus from Egypt. This hegira, *en masse*, marks an axial turn in American-Jewish history, for the vast majority of the present Jewish population in America stems from this influx. Ultimately, these hordes drowned out the Germanic overtones, and the East-European synagogue ritual, foods, mores, folklore, and even the Yiddish that they spoke, became the American standard. So thoroughly did this tide engulf the country that many American Jews today tend to be purblind to the fact that variant forms of Judaism did and do exist elsewhere. Of the two and three-quarter million Jews who came to America since the first Jew arrived in 1654, 90% to 95% arrived after 1880.[1]

The Russian pogroms were the primary cause of this mass migration, but these persecutions were planned by the czarist government to distract public attention from internal problems. As the Industrial Revolution moved across Europe and upset the old economic order, the peasants were crowded off their lands by the advent of large-scale farming. Some of them replaced Jews who for centuries had made their livings as middlemen, innkeepers and artisans. "In the east," writes Oscar Handlin, "as the peasants were displaced, the Jews, who lived by dealing with them, became superfluous." This economic upheaval was all the more disastrous, for it came at a time when the Russian-Jewish population was to increase threefold within a hundred years.[2]

Some Jews who lived in the cities improved their financial status in the reshuffling, but the majority in the villages were pressed in the jaws of a vise. Most of Russia's Jews, however, were huddled in the Pale in Lithuania, Poland and the Ukraine, and were prevented by imperial edict from pushing their way into the cities where they could find new job opportunities. The economic causes of the Great Migration are illustrated by the fact that the percentage of Jews who pulled up roots to go to America was just as large in the Austro-Hungary of the Hapsburgs, where there were no pogroms, as it was in the unhappy Russia of the Romanovs.[3] Nevertheless, the movement out of eastern Europe was greatly accelerated by the decision of the czarist government to step up political persecution in the hope that the Jews could be made the scapegoats for evils that a reactionary regime was unwilling to correct. Political oppression was nothing new to the Jews of the Pale, but unlike former times when only the few could flee, the nineteenth-century revolution in communications offered a way of escape for the many. Railroads could now carry tens of thousands of the hounded to ocean ports, where express liners with ample steerage space could speed them to New York.

The assassination of Czar Alexander II, in March, 1881, set the new anti-Jewish policy in motion. Alexander, who enjoyed the reputation of being a "good" Czar, was blown to pieces by nihilist bombs; and his successor, Alexander III, under the influence of his tutor Konstantin Pobiedonostzev, siezed upon the fact that some Jews were involved in radical movements to instigate the pogroms. Pobiedonostzev proclaimed that the new regime would force one-third of the Jews to emigrate, one third to be lost in the surrounding population, while the remainder would die out.[4]

The riots began at Elizabethgrad (now Kirovo) on April 15, 1881. By summer, 4,000 refugees crowded into Brody, near the Russian border in the Galician part of Austro-Hungary. Soon there were 24,000 terror-stricken refugees crammed into this border city. A French-Jewish organization, dating from 1860, the Alliance Israélite Universelle, began the work of rescue and arranged to get these hounded Jews safely to Hamburg. Then, for a brief period, Russia opened her western border, as an encouragement for the Jews to leave. However, in short order came the

Russian May Laws of 1882, that increased restrictions on Jews and over-crowded the Pale by forcing those outside to return. Then, new pogroms were started and the large-scale emigration to the United States began in earnest; 25,619 came in the years 1881-1882. A decade later, there were anti-Jewish riots in southern Russia in the provinces of Poltava, Ekaterinoslav, Kiev, Kherson and Odessa. Some victims went to other parts of Russia and other parts of Europe, some formed the avant-garde of the Palestinian migration, and many went to the United States.[5]

These refugees arrived in the New World at Castle Garden in New York harbor, a "vast, domed shed," where they received perfunctory medical examinations and slept their first sleep of freedom on bare floors and wooden benches. By fall of 1881, hundreds of Jews were arriving daily in quaint costumes and speaking only Yiddish. Eventually, to ac-commodate the crowds, barracks were built on Ward's Island in the harbor. Soon, the newly formed Hebrew Emigrant Aid Society met the boats, fed and clothed the needy, employed some, and cared for others temporarily on Ward's Island. During the twelve years ending in 1893, the American Jewish population doubled.[6]

The East-European Jews who came after 1880, unlike the earlier im-migrants, frequently did not brave the ocean for reasons of personal am-bition. Many of the later arrivals had been pushed out and came to America for security or in desperation. Many of them were Orthodox and they tended to part with their traditional ways more slowly than had their more Westernized predecessors. The earlier arrivals almost all left voluntarily for a less Jewish atmosphere; but now, American Orthodoxy, which was almost defunct in 1880, was revitalized.

On their part, the newcomers were suspicious of the American Jews who tried to help them. In the Russian Pale, charity had been dispensed as a religious commandment. Here, they were baffled by and resented the forms, questionnaires, red tape and formality that was involved in New World charity. Most of them came from lands where all Jews spoke Yiddish, and they could not understand how American Jews could be Jews without speaking the "mother-tongue."

Had these masses of immigrants all been homogeneous, their absorp-tion into the older Jewish communities would have been difficult enough, but they came from Latvia, Lithuania, Poland, parts of Austro-Hungary, Rumania, the Ukraine and other areas of eastern Europe. And they came with their prejudices intact; and when they got to America they added new prejudices. All these factors led to a multiplication of synagogues, religious functionaries and social organizations. Each group wanted to re-create in America as far as possible the *shtetl* or European village environment. Each group preferred to cluster among its own *Landsleute* or countrymen, and to socialize and pray with them if possible.

Some were Hasidim, the followers of a sect of Jews founded in the eighteenth century by Reb Israel Ba'al Shem Tov. By 1800, Reb Israel's disciples had almost completely won over to the new movement the Jews of the southern provinces of Russia and Galicia, and had made strong inroads into Poland. The Hasidim emphasized that God could be served, not only with the cold rationalism of the talmudical scholars, but also with a warm mysticism based upon meaningful prayer and the joyful practice of religious precepts. The opponents of this new dispensation, called the Mitnagdim, resisted its advance in the north, especially in Lithuania, Latvia and certain sections of Poland. Both groups maintained a different liturgy, separate folkways, and contrary outlooks upon tradi-tional Judaism, and both sects were strongly represented in Buffalo. Al-though actual statistics are not available, it seems probable that a ma-jority of Buffalo's newer Jewish immigrants were Hasidim. They were earthy men, who had lived their lives close to their native soil; and on the whole they were more unlearned and less sophisticated than the Lith-uanian Mitnagdim who had preceded them to the shores of Lake Erie. By and large, the Hasidim had been less touched by the secularism that so marked the Haskalah, as the nineteenth-century eastern European Jewish Enlightenment was called.

A European journal stated that in 1887 there were about 1,500 Jews in Buffalo. This source described the tensions that existed between the Russian newcomers and, not only the Germans of Beth Zion, but also the old East-European families of Beth El. Relations were also strained be-tween the newcomers and the Lithuanian Jews who dominated B'rith Sholem, then on Elm Street but later to move to Pine Street. According to this correspondent, the Russian newcomers hated the Lithuanian Jews "with the extremest hate," and maintained their own synagogues even though there was no lack of room in the older Orthodox synagogues. In-deed, it was said that the Russian Jews disliked the "Litvaks" so much that they contemplated starting a "Jewish street" of their own in Buffalo or else wished to move outside the city in order to establish a new com-munity of their own, but these plans seem to have remained in the realm of pipe dreams.[7]

By 1880, the Haskalah had penetrated the Russian-Jewish Pale and had produced many Maskilim. These Maskilim were loyal Jews who had, however, a secular rather than a religious outlook on life. When these "enlightened ones" came to Buffalo they contributed their part to the interminable disputes that shook the ghetto on William Street.

Many were the stresses and strains among the Jews of the period in

Buffalo that threatened community solidarity. Some were ardent Hebraists who, in the spirit of the East-European Enlightenment, wanted to make Hebrew a vital and living language. On the other hand, some of the enlightened were devout Yiddishists. Some were radicals or labor unionists; others were devoted to *laissez faire* and believed that such a philosophy was the best system for the individual Jew. Some were devout observers; others were agnostics or even militant atheists. These newer immigrants, unlike the earlier ones, were not torn between Orthodoxy and Reform, but rather between Orthodoxy and such non-religious movements as Marxian Socialism, Jewish secular nationalism and, later, Labor Zionism. All these factors led to countless issues, ideologies and a multiplication of Jewish institutions not only in Buffalo but throughout the country. The strifes of this period were intense and bitter, and the Jews of America lived in a "community of communities." [8]

For these more recent arrivals, acclimation to the American environment was much more difficult than it had been for their forerunners. These newcomers received a frigid welcome from the non-Jews and often indeed from their "co-religionists." They came expecting to find fresh air in a land of promise and freedom. Instead they were crammed into slums and had the freedom to risk life and limb shoving a pushcart through city streets. Some worked their lives away in lightless and almost airless sweatshops. Often their days were made bitter by the slurs and sometimes even the physical assault of street rowdies. In spite of all these hardships and adversities, however, their rise was phenomenal. As outsiders, they were less bound by habit and by convention, and they often took great economic risks that sometimes paid off. Their European culture gave them a sense of contrast that was intellectually stimulating. They brought with them a habit of learning and a respect for knowledge so typical of Jewish life that made them eager to learn new ways and practices. They consequently easily transformed their hunger for Jewish learning to a hunger for secular knowledge and were the first group of the newer immigrants to break into American colleges and the professions.[9]

It was not long, therefore, before the effects of this irresistible pull toward Americanization began to make their appearance in the minute books of the newer synagogues. These records were kept in Yiddish, the only language that most of them knew; but by the 1890s interesting Anglicisms begin to creep in. One finds the following English words in the minute books of the time: *petition, meetink, President, members, appointed, committee, ballot, suspended, excuse, majority, resignt, outsiders, debates,* and *rotation.* These English words are significant, for in eastern Europe there were no democratic forms in synagogue government. In America, the environment demanded self-government in the synagogue;

but the symbols of democracy, the words used to express it, had to be in the vernacular because they did not exist in Yiddish. Thus, the synagogue was a means of acculturation as well as a means of preserving Old World culture.

In general, fewer Jews returned to their homelands than other national groups, who often came to America just to strike it rich. A European source reports an exception to this rule. In the depression year 1894, several thousand newly arrived Jews from Poland petitioned the mayor of Buffalo for funds to return to Europe, "for they already loathe the country of liberty that makes the soul of its inhabitants hunger and does not provide them with the bread that is their portion." [10] There is no way of verifying this source, and the report may have been exaggerated. In general, the institutions of the post-1881 immigrants tended to be more significantly Jewish because, unlike their German predecessors, they were not diluted by attachment to any other national culture. The East-Europeans, by and large, had never been Poles or Russians in the way that the German Jews were German. These men and women who had come from the Russian Pale were simply Jewish.

The reception offered to these immigrants was frequently lamentable. The quarter of a million American Jews of 1880 were unfortunately often indifferent and frequently hostile to these strangers. The United States was so far from the refugee city of Brody that it was almost impossible to grasp the full horror of the Russian nightmare. What a man does not understand rarely prompts his sympathy. The older American Jews registered many complaints. In 1881 they protested to the London Board of Guardians that they were sending to America only the "utterly helpless." The older German Jews did not want to be overwhelmed by people whom they considered to be "not ripe for the enjoyment of liberty and equal rights." Some felt that the newcomers were ungrateful: the more that was done for them, the more they expected.[11] Even *The Jewish Messenger,* although it eventually changed its tone, initially took a hostile attitude and stated that it did not want to become "Russianized."

In 1889, the United Jewish Charities of Rochester wrote to London to express its reaction to the new immigrants. "They are a bane to the country and a curse to the Jews." Harsh words, but they express well the tenor of the times. The Rochester group concluded that "all who mean well for the Jewish name should prevent them as much as possibile from coming here." [12] The new arrivals threatened the status of the older Jewish population which felt that their progress in breaking down social barriers might be jeopardized by the onrush of the uncouth. They reasoned that the Gentiles would identify all Jews with the obviously crude newcomers. One relatively minor example might suffice to illustrate the ways in which the established and newly arrived Jewish groups clashed. Many of the older Jewish families rested, like the remainder of America, on Sunday. The new immigrants observed, at least for a time, the historic Jewish Sabbath and worked on Sunday. When they were caught breaking local ordinances and arrested and fined, Reform Jews felt that they were besmirching the good name of the Jew.

One must be careful, however, to avoid the conclusion that everyone in America was against the Russian Jews when they arrived. One who raised his voice strongly in their behalf was the communal leader and diplomat Benjamin F. Peixotto, who denounced those who said, "Send them back, let them stay at home; we don't want them here." [13] Nor was he alone in trying to help these poor people. Some did their very best to aid their stricken brethren, but their best was often not very effective and not always well coordinated. The Hebrew Emigrant Aid Society of the early eighties, though well intentioned, operated with a pitifully small budget, and its leaders were often devoid of genuine understanding of the needs, attitudes and sufferings of the refugees. Later, this organization was replaced by the Jewish Protective Emigrant Aid Society which was formed in New York in 1885. When, in the following decade, another wave of persecution broke out in Russia, the Jewish Alliance of America was formed in Philadelphia. This organization was devoted to the persistent but unsuccessful attempt to disperse Jewish immigrants throughout America. [14]

Although the Jews of America held mass meetings to protest the czarist actions, they were pitifully divided when it came to practical moves to make the lot easier for the uprooted. [15] Jews were divided between Orthodox and Reform, between Easterners and Midwesterners, between those in the big cities and those in the rural communities. Spectacular individual acts of charity, such as the gift of $10,000 for refugee relief by Jacob H. Schiff, failed to offset the inadequacy of the general attitude. Differences in life habits, cultural backgrounds, attitudes toward Judaism, and the widely varying social and economic backgrounds, all tended to isolate the newcomers physically into separate neighborhoods. The older German Jews disliked the growth of an American ghetto because they thought that on this side of the water society should be uniform, not, like "Neapolitan Ice Cream" with nationalities in unassimilated bands sectioning the cities. [16] They resented the Old World flavor of the new arrivals; they feared the radicals among them; they thought the Yiddish that they spoke was pure jargon. By 1880, many of the German Jews in America had developed a "Mayflower Complex." Professor John Higham, a gifted non-Jewish historian, states: "Many German-American Jews, appalled at the outlandish looks and ways of the newcomers, feared that their own reputation was suffering from the popular habit of judging all Jews as alike. Perhaps it did. Certainly the new immigration accentuated the aura of foreignness that still clung to American images of the Jew. Moreover, this mass migration involved Jews prominently in the multiple ethnic conflicts that arose along with the increasing volume and diversity of the whole immigrant influx." [17]

Originally, in the dispensation of Jewish charity, it was often quite difficult to distinguish between the giver and the receiver. But with the coming of the Russians, the equivalent of a permanent tax was placed on the older groups, and ironically the only claim that the Russian Jew had to help was, as one cynic put it, "a tenuous tie of emotional appeal and an incidental negation in religious belief." [18] The Russians soon became a burden, and relief was given in a patronizing form which the recipients did not relish. The old splits which divided many Jewish communities now looked like minor rifts in comparison to the new cleavage.

What was Buffalo like in the last years of the nineteenth century? Why did it attract so many of the later Jewish immigrants? Prior to the eighties, Buffalo had often been described as a "sleepy community." But after recovery from the depression touched off by the Panic of 1873, the growth of the city, according to a chronicler of the times, "is the story of an awakening; the unfolding of mighty limbs and a re-energizing of great ambitions." [19] This reawakening came slowly and just at the time when the Jewish population of the city was being greatly augmented by the coming of the Russian Jews. From the Civil War to 1880, with the exception of Chicago, most of the Great Lakes cities languished. Of Buffalo, which fared no better than the other inland northern ports, it was often said that it was ready for the undertaker. In the closing decades of the century, however, Buffalo became a city known for its heavy industry and vital rail connections.[20]

This change in the very nature of the city came almost as a direct result of the changes that were taking place in the great Midwest area. As the American heartland developed, lake traffic in coal and grain increased. Buffalo, the Queen City of the Lakes, became a natural exchange point. Grain boats discharged the newly prominent hard winter wheat in Buffalo and picked up coal for the West. After Western wheat, came the Lake Superior lumber and ultimately the opening of the Mesabi iron mines in Minnesota which contributed to the establishment of the steel industry at the eastern head of Lake Erie.[21]

While lake traffic was making its contribution to the growth of Buffalo, the railroads also began to develop to their fullest capacity. Water passage did not establish a continuous connection with the West, for the lakes were closed by ice for many months of the year. The real connection with the West came by rail in 1882, when the New York Central consolidated its westward lines. Buffalo, assuming an imperial position, became one of the greatest rail hubs in the United States, with tracks running east, west, north and south. As the railroads concentrated in Buffalo in ever greater strength, the coal and oil of nearby Pennsylvania became readily available to the burgeoning industries of the city.

Meanwhile, Buffalo's blast furnaces had begun to belch their smoke. Soon thereafter came factories that produced heavy industrial machinery, railroad cars and car wheels, iron pipe, girders for bridges, and boilers. In those days, Buffalo beer was famous throughout the country. Oil refineries, flour mills, chemical plants, meat packing houses, bicycle and engine shops, all sprang into existence. Added to this, the prospect of cheap electric power from Niagara Falls seemed to guarantee that Buffalo would become one of the chief manufacturing cities in the United States. No wonder that people spoke glowingly of their "electric age." [22]

One of the immediate results of all this increased industrial activity was a phenomenal increase in size. During the 1880s the population in Buffalo increased 65%, or three times as fast as New York, Boston, or Philadelphia. The rate of increase in Buffalo was exceeded among large cities only by that of Chicago.[23]

Despite all this industrialization, however, Buffalo remained a beautiful city. The houses were well set back from the streets and the trees, which had been carefully planted as the city expanded physically, arched gracefully overhead. The park system, one of the best at the time among American cities, had been designed by Frederick Law Olmstead, the famous landscape designer of Central Park. Buffalo then covered forty-two square miles and was physically large for its population. For the incoming immigrants, there was relatively less overcrowding here than elsewhere. Then, as now, Buffalo was a city of individual homes rather than large apartments, a city of homes for "poor and humble artisans as well as for the wealthy." Although real estate prices had risen by the end of the century, Buffalo could claim to have proportionately more homes owned by workingmen than any other city.[24] It was a characteristic of Jews that they liked to own their homes as soon as practical after arrival in the city.

In those other-world days, prices were cheap in Buffalo because labor was slow in organizing in this rather conservative community. Although this fact permitted some of the immigrants to purchase goods somewhat more cheaply than elsewhere, in the long run this lack of unionization did not work for the advantage of the newcomer who so often had to eke out a living behind bleak factory walls.

The Jews, of course, were only one of many new immigrant groups that arrived in Buffalo during this period. About 1872, Father John Pitass, a Polish priest, came to Buffalo and engineered the migration of many of his countrymen to the city. Buffalo soon had a Polish weekly newspaper. The editor was liberal and generally sympathetic to Jews, but he was hindered by prevalent prejudice from expressing this friendship freely. The *Gazetta Polska*, a contemporary Chicago Polish newspaper, was violently anti-Semitic and exerted some influence on Buffalo.[25] Jews, especially the new immigrants, often knew Polish and understood these people. Despite the surviving animosities from Europe and the complete lack of social intercourse, they often traded with their former countrymen and many Jews prospered in the Polish section of the city.

As the nineteenth century drew peacefully to an end, the Italians and the Hungarians began pushing into Buffalo. At this time the city had a somewhat colorful foreign flavor as a result of the new influx and the persisting Germanic culture of some of its older inhabitants. The Hungarians came in still greater force after 1905, and they settled along River Road and in the Riverside and Black Rock areas. They followed the steel mills and formed distinctly Magyar neighborhoods. By the outbreak of World War I, the Slavs were the most numerous of the immigrant groups in Buffalo, and thousands of them huddled in houses that were built in the shadows of the Lackawanna steel plants.[26]

As the first wave of Russian refugees reached these shores, Buffalo Jews began to take steps to prepare for the onslaught. A local non-Jewish historian estimates that, by 1882, hundreds of new arrivals from the Russian terror had already reached the city.[27] Because Buffalo was the most convenient western rail-head from New York City, many of the newly arrived Jews made it their exchange point for the next stage of their journey. A good number of these weary travellers undoubtedly chose to remain in Buffalo either from preference or from necessity.

Shortly after news of the pogroms reached these shores, Montefiore Lodge #70 appointed a committee to confer with representatives of other local fraternal orders to adopt a citywide plan for assisting "our Russian co-religionists." To help the work of its committee, the Lodge voted a special assessment and later sent contributions to the Jewish Protective Emigrant Aid Society in New York.[28]

On May 28, 1882, Louis M. Brock presided over a meeting at Beth Zion and, in calling the crowd to order, stated that the object of the meeting was not to denounce the Czar but to help his victims. Among those who spoke that evening were Rabbi Falk, who was to show great sensitivity in dealing with the problems of the refugees, and Father Patrick L. Cronin, who for thirty years was editor of the Buffalo *Catholic Union and Times*. Father Cronin was interested in Hebraic lore and often spoke before

Jewish groups. At this meeting a Russian Refugee Relief Committee was appointed, and this group during the ensuing year dispensed $2,800, far more than the amount usually required to meet the entire needs of local Jewish charity. Siegmund Levyn went to New York City to confer with authorities there about relief problems. At this first meeting more than $1,000 was raised by private subscription, and the special committee was ordered to raise additional funds.[29] Louis M. Brock recalled twenty years later that this committee alone had helped 1,500 Jewish refugees.

Soon, immigrants began to arrive in Buffalo daily and many changed trains here on their way to Brockton, New York, where the British philanthropist and Judeophile, Lawrence Oliphant, had founded a community for the Czar's victims. In 1882, there were about ten Russian-Jewish families at Oliphant's place. He supplied them with kosher food, housing, farm equipment and even a Torah. This project of Oliphant was one of many intended to lure immigrants out of the congested seaboard cities and on to the farms; but like most of the others this one, too, was ephemeral.

In Buffalo, some travellers en route to Oliphant's haven were fed and cared for over Shavuot (May 24-25, 1882). "They appeared to be a very intelligent group," wrote an observer, "and will no doubt make good citizens." [30]

The reaction to the Russian Jews was, unfortunately, not all favorable in Buffalo. A local correspondent to *The (American) Israelite* reported that the Russian Refugee Relief Committee had been formed and described the steps that were being taken to care for the "Russians." They were housed in a building leased by the Buffalo committee, where they remained until jobs and living quarters were found for them. Strict rules for cleanliness were maintained and a Committee of Ladies saw that the rules were enforced. Each person was given two sets of clothing. The reporter insisted that Buffalo could not absorb any more penniless Jews, for some recent arrivals had taxed the capacity of the house. The correspondent stated that, although some of the refugees had a trade, the rest were unskilled and were consequently forced to peddle, "which is rarely anything but a cloak for wandering mendicancy." This anonymous reporter had undoubtedly forgotten that many of his own German forebears had received their start in America through peddling. His antagonism toward the most recent arrivals is fully revealed as he continues: "As a class much can not be said for those Russians who have found their way to this city. Many of them are indolent and unclean in their habits, dissatisfied with what they get, and frequently insubordinate—a city like Buffalo is no place for the refugees. They should be settled in the West." [31] Clearly another case of "Let George do it."

Nine years later, three families arrived in Buffalo via Montreal because the port of New York had been closed to paupers. Superintendent of the Poor, Adam Rehm, refused to care for them because they were aliens, and the city almshouse turned them away for the same reason. The local Federal authorities wanted to deport them if they could not furnish bonds to guarantee that they would not become public charges. Finally, they were rescued by the energetic Siegmund Levyn who managed to delay their deportation until he could attend a meeting of the Baron de Hirsch Commission in New York to get the necessary bonds to permit them to stay in Buffalo. To meet the problems of the new stream of homeless persons, Temple Beth Zion called a city-wide meeting on November 9, 1891, in order to form a local committee to work with the New York Jewish groups in handling the new immigrants.[32]

The immediate problem facing the new arrivals was to find work. Many of the East Europeans had been needle workers in their homelands; many became "Columbus" tailors after they arrived, for here they could be absorbed relatively easily as a result of the ready-to-wear clothing boom of the day. Some of the older Jewish clothing firms farmed out their work to immigrants who bought sewing machines and toiled in their homes on piece work to earn a scant living. Others worked in the factories, where the women sewed while the men were employed as cutters or pressers. The millinery trades saw a similar influx of Jewish labor. In time, some of these erstwhile workers established retail millinery stores and even factories.[33]

Some of the newcomers collected and peddled waste materials. This type of work offered opportunity to an immigrant with little or no capital and permitted him to control, to a great extent, the hours that he worked.[34] Many of the Orthodox found it attractive because work could be suspended on the Sabbath without serious monetary loss. Other new immigrants, arriving at a time when the American proletariat was growing, became glaziers, shoemakers, or factory workers. But not for long: they were soon attracted to more congenial occupations. It has truly been said of the American Jew who did manual work "that he was neither the son of a laborer nor the father of a laborer."

Gradually, however, the occupational distribution became more normalized as the extreme concentrations of Jews in the clothing trades and in peddling lessened. By 1895, Buffalo even had two Jewish policemen and one Jewish fireman, although it was rare in those days for Jews to be attracted to that type of civil service. In the mid-nineties, of the seventeen wholesale clothing firms listed in the *Buffalo Business Directory*, fourteen were Jewish; and of the eighty-eight retail clothing firms, at least thirty-four (and perhaps a dozen more) were Jewish.[35] As families grew, these business enterprises multiplied, with cousins and former employees often setting up for themselves. Gradually the professions attracted Jews; but before there was any strong move in that direction, they moved toward white-collar businesses, like insurance and real estate.

Twenty years after the Russian wave started, a newspaper reporter found Buffalo Jews still heavily represented in the manufacture and sale of clothing and in retail dry goods, and becoming increasingly important in the wholesale jewelry trade. They were very strong in the junk and scrap metal business; and many, many of them were "manufacturers' agents," or salesmen. This latter occupation had become almost a Jewish vocation. At the beginning of the twentieth century not many Jews operated drug stores, cleaning establishments, or grocery stores, trades which they were later to enter. Livestock, produce, lumber, grain and flour, appliances, seem also to have had little attraction for them. And, as we might well suspect, almost none were engaged in heavy industry.

Above all other areas of endeavor, the real estate boom that accompanied the industrial expansion of Buffalo benefited the Jews most. "Years ago," a newspaper observed in 1889, "it was an exceptional thing for an American Jew to own land. Times have changed. The wealthy Jew of today invests his surplus money in real estate." [36]

For some years after the Civil War, real estate was not a good investment in Buffalo, for property was cheap and there seemed little likelihood of a rise in values. In 1880, land on Delaware Avenue near Lafayette sold for $8 to $10 a front foot; a decade later, the same land sold for $100 to $115 a front foot. On the West Side, where the Jews were beginning to acquire property, land went up in the same ten-year period from $5 to $52 a front foot. Assessed valuation of land in Buffalo rose in this period 83%, while real estate transfers doubled. [37]

One of those who became wealthy through this boom was Frederick Ullman (1864-1939), a German immigrant who came to Buffalo when he was very young. His father, David Ullman, who had been a grain contractor in the Rhineland, followed one of his sons to America and a year later sent for the rest of his family. As Fred Ullman put it years later, "America was the Mecca that attracted every ambitious youth." The family followed the eldest brother, Emanuel, who had moved from Erie to Buffalo, and they settled here in the early seventies. The youngest of the children, the well known Dr. Julius Ullman, was born in Buffalo.

Fred Ullman was graduated from Central High School in 1882, and at the graduation ceremonies, held at St. James Hall at Main and East Eagle

Streets, he read an essay entitled, "An Outlook on Life at Graduation." For a time he read law with the firm of Osgoodby, Titus and Simons, but he went to New York to continue his studies. He was greeted at New York University with the song, "Hey, Solomon Levi, tra la la la," but, as he realized, it was not a vicious form of anti-Semitism. Later, at Columbia University Law School, he was a fellow student of the future Chief Justice Charles Evans Hughes. Ullman passed the New York State Bar and practiced in Buffalo; but the law never occupied much of his attention. He stated later that he gave up many opportunities to practice law to help his brother, Louis, the "blind lawyer."

Fred Ullman turned to investments in real estate to make a living, and his law practice was incidental to his career. About 1888, he was one of the directors and promoters of the Black Rock Land Company, the first land investment company in Buffalo. In his autobiography, Ullman later described his real estate speculations during the plush eighties: "With the aid of other people's money, I bought and syndicated vacant lands on Pine Hill Road, on both sides of Genesee Street between the City line and Pine Hill Road, on Delavan Avenue . . . on Military Road, on the River Road and, toward the close of the boom, on Ward Road in North Tonawanda." He stated that all of these purchases were paid off except the Ward Road land. Ullman Street in the Riverside section was named for him.

Ullman was also a local pioneer in the motion picture business. Along with Herman Wile and Jacob Rosokoff, he entered the moving picture business in the heyday of the nickelodeons. Ullman owned the Harmonia Theater on Genesee Street, the Edisonia Theater on Brayton and Utica Streets, and helped establish many other well known motion picture houses, among them the Elmwood and the Allendale. But, said Ullman in his memoirs, changes in motion picture equipment that he failed to judge properly "consumed my capital and eventually smashed my earning power." In 1929, he was almost entirely ruined. "Fate," he said with romantic emotion, "leveled its shafts against me and unerringly found the victim." [38]

Another Buffalo Jew who became interested in the new motion picture business was Jacob Rosing (1870-1946), who came to Buffalo as a young man. He early became interested in motion pictures, and eventually became vice-president of the Monument Theater Corporation which built the Lafayette Theater. Five years later, in 1926, he held similar office in the Greater Rochester Properties, Inc., which financed Loew's, then the largest theater in Rochester. He and his associates later formed the Erie Amusement Corporation and built the Roosevelt Theater at 887 Broadway. With Max Katz he organized a real estate firm that financed one of the first groups of business buildings on Delaware Avenue in Kenmore.[39]

Henry Weill (1847-1924) was another of the later immigrants who found his fortune in real estate. He had been born in Alsace when it still belonged to France, and had received an unusually good French education. He worked for a time in his native province, but he came to New York in 1867 and to Buffalo six months later. At first he peddled cloth to country tailors; later he became one of the first local Jews to enter the jewelry business in which he was associated with his brothers, Louis, Alphonse and Lazare, whom he helped bring to the United States.

In the late eighties he helped open up the North Buffalo section, which curiously enough today houses the bulk of Buffalo Jewry. In 1871 he married Fanny Shire, the daughter of Daniel Shire, long-time sexton-teacher of Beth Zion. He was very active in Beth Zion, of which he was president when the Deleware Avenue Temple was dedicated.[40]

The tobacco business attracted other famous Jewish families during the last two decades of the nineteenth century. Locally, the Seidenbergs were important in this field. This family came to the United States from Baden in 1855. They settled first at Hoboken, New Jersey, where Samuel Seidenberg (1837-1924) claimed to have been the first man to think of making Havana cigars in Key West, Florida. Samuel Seidenberg came to Buffalo late in life, in 1906. He was an "ethical culturist," a charter member of Felix Adler's band; but his son reversed this radical trend and returned to Reform Judaism.

Rudolph J. Seidenberg (1867-1931) brought the family tobacco business to Buffalo in 1895, after having served here as an agent of the firm. Known as the R. J. Seidenberg Co., the firm branched out from Buffalo and established tobacco stores in Syracuse, Jamestown, Cleveland, Detroit and Worcester.[41]

The firm of Keiser and Boasberg was also important in the wholesale tobacco business. This concern had been established in 1889 by August Keiser, son of Leopold Keiser, and Emanuel Boasberg, son of Nathan Boasberg. These two Buffalo-born Jews, who survived until 1937, built up a native leaf-tobacco business that developed into one of the largest independent tobacco houses in the United States. Located in later years on Elm Street, they advertised themselves as "selling agents of the Keiser & Boasberg Plantation, Inc., South Windsor, Connecticut, growers of shade tobacco."

Another success story of the period occurred in the rise of Joseph B. Mayer, who amassed a fortune in Buffalo and then retired to New York City where he died shortly after Pearl Harbor at the ripe old age of 102. Like so many other Buffalo German Jews, Mayer had been born in Ihringen, Baden. He was one of the first of his generation to see the possibilities of the wholesale jewelry business and, in partnership with a *Landsman* from Ihringen, Joseph B. Block, he jobbed jewelry to small-town retail stores. The great bulk of Mayer's fortune, however, came from other enterprises. In a day when inter-urban trolleys knit the cities of the country together, he was president of a line that paralleled the southern shore of the lake as far westward as Erie, Pennsylvania.[42]

Mayer was soon followed in the jewelry business by a number of other Buffalo Jews who made the city known for this type of enterprise. Isaac Boasberg (1852-1920) was a diamond broker who claimed friendship with Grover Cleveland through a common concern with the fortunes of the local Democratic party. Gustave J. Weil (1864-1930), in the fashion of the day, also left clothing for jewelry, and built up the important Electric City Box Company. His son, Don Weil, started the Buffalo Jewelry Case Company, and Harry H. Weil, who was no kinsman, joined this firm. For a time, Buffalo became a national center of the jewelry box industry, and the Warner Jewelry Case Company was established by a branch of this important local family. Perhaps the most important of these jewelry firms was the Queen City Ring Company, founded by a branch of the Block family. From this original firm sprang many branches, for, following the pattern laid down in the clothing trades, young relatives would join the parent firm and, after they had learned the trade, would leave to establish their own companies. In the twentieth century, as automobiles rather than rings became symbols of status, many of these concerns underwent a relative decline, but the ephemeral importance of the industry left its mark on the economic history of the city.

In the case of Joseph B. Block (1851-1927), success in the jewelry business led to banking enterprise. As we have already noted, Abraham Altman had invaded this field early, and Block was to become the second outstanding Jewish banker of Buffalo. Born in Ihringen, he received a good education in Germany and France before emigrating to the United States. Block was attracted to Buffalo by the other immigrants from Baden, and he arrived here at the age of twenty. He first entered the wholesale jewelry business, but soon drifted to real estate, for the county clerk's records reveal that he acquired considerable holdings in the early eighties. It was in this field that he probably built up his fortune.

Block founded the Citizens Bank of Buffalo in 1890 at William and Spencer Streets. It is said that his success in banking could partially be attributed to the fact that, with a bank on William Street, he enjoyed the confidence and the respect of the newer Jews who huddled in this neighborhood. Block's bank was the first on the East Side, and he remained as president until it merged with the Black Rock Bank to become the Citizens Commercial Trust Company. In 1923, it merged with the Marine Trust Company as its William Street branch. Block became a member of the board of directors of the Marine Trust Company. He was also a member of the Buffalo Board of Trade and a treasurer of the Buffalo Clearing House. He was very active in civic and Jewish affairs. He lived in a grand house at 905 Delaware Avenue and at that time was said to be the only Jew in Buffalo to have a home on that fashionable boulevard. Block Street in Buffalo was named for this business pioneer.

It was a far cry from Ihringen when Mr. Block found himself a dinner guest, along with Henry Weill, at the Ellicott Club to celebrate the harnessing of the electric power of the Niagara on January 12, 1897. Among the non-Jewish guests were President Grover Cleveland, Mark Hanna, John D. Rockefeller, and J. P. Morgan.[43]

While Block's banking activities were somewhat exceptional for Jews of his generation, many of his contemporaries were branching out into lines of endeavor that marked the business optimism of McKinley's America. Among them was Rabbi Falk's eldest son, Isadore H. (1865-1942), who joined the Klondike gold rush of 1897, drilled oil in Oklahoma, and returned to Buffalo to found a contracting firm that built bridges and highways in New York and neighboring Pennsylvania. Eli David Hofeller (1867-1918) participated in the revolution that gave the city decent sidewalks, and his "Crescent" pavements dotted the streets of Buffalo. Late in life, Hofeller used part of his wealth to establish the foundation that bears his name, and it was through his generosity that the Jewish Fresh Air Camp leased land at a dollar a year on the lake shore near Angola. Eventually this site housed Camp Lakeland, a Jewish project that was to bring summer relaxation to an ever growing number of children.[44]

Frank L. Cohen (1868-1949) was perhaps the best known local Jewish contractor. Cohen was born in Buffalo, the son of Harris and Rachel Cohen. As a young man he entered the business world in the employ of Hasselback Lumber Company. He eventually became a road builder with offices in the Prudential Building. The F. L. Cohen Co. built roads in New York, Delaware, Pennsylvania and Ohio. His company constructed the Delavan Avenue sewage system, the Scajaquada Creek flood control system, and it laid part of Clinton Street and Transit Road.[45]

The foundations of the present W. Bergman Co. were laid by Wolf Bergman (1862-1948). Bergman, born on Elk Street in Buffalo, was one of the early graduates of Bryant & Stratton Business Institute. In 1890, together with his brother Sol, Bergman went into the hardware and wholesale supply business. Later, Sol left the firm to found the Bergman Tool

Manufacturing Company, destined for long existence at 1573 Niagara Street. Wolf Bergman later expanded into electrical appliances and automotive supplies, and the business was later conducted by his son-in-law, Sol J. Levy.[46]

Jacob G. Joseph (1861-1931) was another important Jewish entrepreneur of his time. Born in Philadelphia, he had been in the iron and steel industry in Vincennes, Indiana. After his arrival in Buffalo, at the age of forty, he was one of the few Jews in "hard industry." He was connected with Inland Steel and at the time of his death was president of Buffalo Steel Co., Tonawanda, and a director of the Marine Trust Company.[47]

In Buffalo, as elsewhere, the Jewish concentration was more in lighter than in heavier metal construction. On occasion, the European background of particular immigrants led to unusual business undertakings. Abraham S. Ruslander (1841-1932) came from a family of coppersmiths. After an interesting and varied career which included farming near Verona, New York, and manufacturing torpedo shells for Pennsylvania oil drillers, Ruslander arrived in Buffalo in the 1890s and engaged in the hardware business and tinsmithing. Through the enterprise of one of his sons, Levi (1878-1958), this small business, later known as Ruslander & Sons, became one of the largest producers of kitchen equipment in the region.[48]

The majority, however, retained the Jewish preference for softer goods. Among the local firms that grew to national reputation were the Rugby Knitting Mills, founded by Siegfried Levi (1877-1941) and his brothers, Ernst and David. The Niagara Apparel Company, which started out as an overall concern, was founded in 1895 by Morris and Wolf Pincus, and in time developed from part-time operation in the rear of an art-goods shop into one of the country's largest manufacturers of men's and boys' sportswear and slacks.

The large Buffalo store, Victor & Company, was established during this period of Buffalo history by Henry Nathan and Arthur Victor. Henry Nathan (1875-1931) was born in Toledo. At the time of his death (he was killed in an accident while visiting France), he was president of Victor's. His widow, Mrs. Gertrude Nathan, later became nationally prominent in Temple Sisterhood affairs. Arthur Victor (1875-1927) was born in Cincinnati, and he was very active in the Buffalo Jewish community. This great businessman was a wise and generous philanthropist, and his children, Arthur, Jr., Robert L. and Charles J. Victor, have remained active in community life.[49]

These were some of Buffalo's Jewish citizens who found a measure of success in business in the period of disruption and unrest that followed the tidal-wave immigration of East-European Jews.[50] While they were forging ahead in store, office and shop, others were slowly penetrating the professions. Frederick Ullman, who received his law degree with honor, has already been mentioned, but he never actually engaged in the practice of law as his sole profession. His brother, Louis Ullman, the "blind lawyer," did. Louis was older than Fred, and had been born in Germany where he lost his sight as a result of scarlet fever. After his arrival in the United States, Louis Ullman was started on a musical education in Boston. He attended the Institute for the Blind at Batavia, New York, and learned to use the method of reading known as the New York Point System, which was somewhat different from Braille. He decided, however, to turn to the law for his livelihood, and paid readers helped him in his work, as did his brother Frederick. Louis was graduated from the Buffalo Law School (later affiliated with the University of Buffalo). For a time, he and his brother Fred were associated as partners, with Fred taking all of the trial work. In 1894, Louis Ullman was appointed U. S. Commissioner, an office that brought him a certain amount of fame in an age when Jews seldom were selected for political honors.[51]

The legal profession in Erie County became increasingly popular with the establishment of the Buffalo Law School in 1887. Hitherto, an enterprising student had either to make the proper connections so as to "read law" in some local office, or else go out of town for professional training. Now it was easier and less expensive to become a lawyer, and the calling early became attractive to Jewish boys.

Among the first to attend the local law school was Willard W. Saperston. He was the son of Joseph Saperston and was born in Leeds, England, on March 18, 1863, and died in Buffalo in 1955. Willard was educated in the Buffalo public schools and after school went out West to work as a telegrapher and stenographer. He returned to Buffalo with this experience and in 1881 was one of three managers of the new and tiny Buffalo telephone exchange. He always cherished his memories of telegraphy and the early telephone, and he appeared on a television program at the age of ninety-one to celebrate the seventy-fifth anniversary of Bell's invention. He went out West again in 1890 with the Southern Pacific Railroad, but he returned to Buffalo to study law in the offices of Quinby, Meads and Rebadow. He later attended the University of Buffalo Law School and was graduated with honors. Saperston, dapper, handsome, a good singer and interested in music, started out as a criminal lawyer. In later years, he turned from criminal cases to the practice of corporation and commercial law and laid the foundation for the present firm of Saperston, McNaughton and Saperston. Mr. Saperston was active in Beth Zion, was once president of the Jewish Orphan Asylum of Western New York and headed, until late in his life, many fund-raising campaigns. He was connected with the East Side Jews through his father, and, as one of the earliest Jewish lawyers, he conducted much of the business for the synagogues in that area.[52]

At the turn of the present century, Moses Shire (1857-1913) was one of the most successful lawyers in Buffalo. He had been born in Hamilton, Ontario, before his father, Daniel, returned to Buffalo for his long service with Beth Zion. After reading law in the offices of Judge Beckwith, Shire was admitted to the bar at the age of twenty-one, and he then became a clerk of the Superior Court at a time when it was unusual for a Jew to receive even such a picayune political plum. Subsequently, he joined Edward L. Jellinek (1868-1943) to found the firm of Shire and Jellinek. Jellinek had been born in Vienna and came to Buffalo as an infant. Following his graduation from Harvard, he studied law under Moses Shire (nine years his senior) and Shire's ephemeral partner, Mr. Van Peyma. Soon, Jellinek became managing clerk of this busy office, passed the bar and became a partner.

Shire and Jellinek was one of the most widely known law firms in the state and specialized in fire insurance adjustment. Shire himself was an expert in this field and his exploits are still legend. It was said that insurance companies so feared him that they preferred to make out-of-court settlements rather than to try cases against him.

Shire's phenomenal rise in the city was the result of certain other factors. He bought a great deal of real estate at a time when values were rising. In addition, his firm represented several big brewing concerns in Buffalo, and he took some of his fees in stock which ultimately became very valuable. When he married Helena Waterman (1870-1954), he benefited by the Waterman fortune which had been accrued through Canadian oil stocks.

As a successful lawyer, Shire was influential in the councils of the Democratic party. When the local ring of "Blue-Eyed Billie" [William F.] Sheehan was breaking up, Shire successfully defended several men charged with election fraud. He was also active in the Municipal League, the Wanakah Club, the Country Club, the Lawyers' Club, and at one time was director of the Erie County Bar Association and later its president.[53]

Even better known, perhaps, than Moses Shire, was Louis W. Marcus (1863-1923), the first Jew in this area to ascend the judicial bench. Marcus, the son of the Civil War veteran Leopold Marcus, was graduated from Central High School and the Williams Academy. At Cornell University he was a member of Delta Kappa in a day before the establishment of Jewish fraternities. Here he received the LL.B. in 1889, and in that same year he married Ray Dahlman, the daughter of Louis Dahlman

whom the reader may recall as one of Buffalo's earliest and most successful Jews.

Louis Marcus became a member of the law firm of Swift, Weaver and
Marcus. His real love, however, was politics, and in 1895 he was elected
Surrogate of Erie County. He received national notice for his election
(on the Republican ticket), for he was very young for such a post and,
in addition, for a Jew to win in politics in those days still was headline
news for the national Anglo-Jewish papers. He was re-elected to his office,
but before his term expired, Governor Frank W. Higgins appointed him
to the Supreme Court, Eighth Judicial District. He won the election to
that post the following year and maintained his seat until his death,
eighteen years later. Judge Marcus was a man of great charm and
oratorical power, although it is said that he could use blunt, top-sergeant
language when he wanted to make a point emphatic. Unlike his father,
Louis Marcus took little interest in organized Jewish life, although he
was an avid student of the Bible and of the early history of his people.[54]

While Judge Marcus was receiving Republican political rewards, Louis
E. Desbecker (1871-1932) was rising within local Democratic ranks.
Youngest son of the patriarchal Samuel Desbecker, Louis went to Harvard
where he was graduated with high honors. He then attended New York
Law School and was admitted to the bar in 1894. Desbecker rapidly became one of the most able of the younger men of the Buffalo bar. An
ardent Democrat, he was defeated in his attempt to gain election as
councilman. In 1905, however, he was elected Corporation Counsel of
Buffalo, the first Jew to occupy that position here. He served four years
in this position under Mayor J. N. Adam. Later, he was a member of the
School Board, from 1917 to 1924. He was a delegate to the National
Democratic Convention in San Francisco in 1920 when Cox and Roosevelt were nominated. Governor Alfred E. Smith appointed him vice-
president of the Home Rule Commission which helped to decentralize
the state government. Desbecker belonged to a group called "The Old
Guard Democracy." A bachelor, he lived from 1901 until his death at the
Buffalo Club.[55]

Of all the Jewish attorneys in Buffalo in this period, the one who really
became a legend during his lifetime was Simon Fleischmann. Whereas
Moses Shire became famous for his work for his clients, Fleischmann was
a lawyer's lawyer. He had been born in Iowa City, Iowa, on September
11, 1859, and lived in New York, Meadville, Pennsylvania, and Dunkirk
before coming to Buffalo at the age of twelve.

Simon Fleischmann attended School 13 and Central High School. He
never attended a university, but he read law first with William C. Bryant
and then with William H. Gurney. In 1881, he was in the law firm of

Cleveland, Bissell and Sicard, of which Grover Cleveland was senior partner. Cleveland liked this bright boy and pushed him ahead. He was admitted to the bar in 1882, and two years later opened his own office, specializing in civil cases. A popular, sharp-witted, original thinker, he was a great counsellor to other trial lawyers. An indefatigable researcher, he often took cases that seemed almost hopeless. In later years he did little but appeal work and enjoyed helping younger members of his profession. In one of the many stories told about him, the courtroom is said to have shaken with laughter when he told a judge: "My opponent's speech reminds me of the hoop skirts that women used to wear during the Civil War. It covers everything and touches nothing."

Simon Fleischmann in the course of his lifetime enjoyed almost every honor his profession could bring. From 1901 to 1903 he was a member of the Buffalo Board of Councilmen, then the upper house of the City Council, and was once president of that body. He was elected president of the Erie County Bar Association in 1903 to succeed Moses Shire and was an active and a powerful influence in the American Bar Association.[56]

Apart from his legal practice, Simon Fleischmann, together with his sister Bianca (1862-1955), achieved fame in the realm of music. Emanuel Fleischmann (1836-1903), their Bavarian-born father, long-time secretary of B'nai B'rith and a music teacher, passed his artistic heritage on to his children. The Fleischmann home at 190 Edward Street was a music center in the city. Simon, who played the violin and the cornet, when he was eighteen appeared with his younger sister in a concert at St. James Hall. They were known as "the Fleischmann Children" and were introduced as musical prodigies. Simon mastered the organ and, at an early age, was organist in several churches in Buffalo. Bianca often appeared as accompanist for the Liedertafel, Orpheus, Saengerbund and other musical organizations. She began to write music when she was eight years old and some of her works were translated into German. When she left Buffalo in 1940, she donated her musical collection to the Grosvenor Library where it is now housed. She always claimed that she learned whatever she knew, especially about the organ and harmony, from her brother Simon.[57]

Although, as we have seen, an occasional Jewish physician wandered into Buffalo in the 1860s, it was only a generation later that Jews began to penetrate the profession of Hippocrates in any numbers. The growth of the University of Buffalo, of course, greatly helped local youths. The University of Buffalo is one of those rare institutions of higher learning in the United States that started out, in 1846, as a medical school. The beginnings of the School of Pharmacy came in 1886; the School of

Dentistry was founded in 1887. Five years later, the University's building of a new medical school on High Street gave a great boost to the study of medicine in Buffalo. This proliferation of schools made it easier for local Jewish lads to enter the learned professions. Meanwhile, as the University of Buffalo School of Medicine was growing, there were several Jewish doctors in Buffalo who had been trained in Europe. Of these, Marcel Hartwig, born in Austria in 1851, was the most successful. His original name was Hartwig Marcus, but by some freak in the process of his growing up, it was changed to Marcel Hartwig. He took his M.D. at the University of Berlin and at that time received a prize for his work in chemistry. He came to Buffalo in the late seventies because his uncle Leopold Marcus lived here.

Hartwig was a general practitioner and is remembered as a clever doctor. He had a scientific mind and he pioneered, without ever receiving credit for it, in the wiring of the patella. He also conducted research on kidney diseases in children. In an age when doctors generally were the products of a liberal education, he knew a great deal about chemistry and engineering and was able to use eight languages; at seventy, he started to study Spanish. Dr. Hartwig was the first president of the Maimonides Club (organized 1914) made up of Jewish doctors of Buffalo and its environs. His closest friends were Moses Shire, Judge Marcus, Ismar S. Ellison, and Rudolph Wolffsohn. In their card club he was known as "The Professor."

Although Marcel Hartwig's associations were Jewish and he was the earliest local medical examiner for B'nai B'rith, he was not a synagogue Jew. He retired to California about 1920, but continued to practice until his death.[58]

Another active member of the early Jewish medical circle was Ludwig Schroeter of Lodz, Poland, where he had been one of the early revolutionaries against the Czar. He fled Russia and studied medicine at Berne, Switzerland. There he married a fellow medical student, Celina Margulies, who gave up her medical career after her marriage. He came to New York in 1889, and after six months he decided to settle in Buffalo because of its large Polish population whose language he spoke. When he and his wife arrived here in mid-winter, they got off the train at the snow-banked station in East Buffalo. After she surveyed the scene for a few moments, his wife turned to Schroeter and said, "Now, we *are* in Siberia."

For many years, Dr. Schroeter practiced medicine in the Polish district of the city at 798 Fillmore Avenue, and later on Franklin Street. He was a good obstetrician and taught obstetrics at the University of Buffalo, but he engaged in general practice as well. A great idealist, Dr. Schroeter was a visionary who believed in the ultimate victory of Socialism. He was not a religionist, but always stoutly defended the good name of the Jew. At fifty-two, he developed a brain tumor and was operated on by the great Dr. Harvey Cushing at Johns Hopkins. The operation was not a success and there was no hope; nevertheless, Mrs. Schroeter insisted on taking her husband to specialists in Berlin. On the way, they stopped off at the Isle of Capri to visit the exiled writer, Maxim Gorky. Dr. Schroeter had lunch with Gorky and died three hour later, attended only by some friendly nuns on the island.[59]

All the other Jewish doctors of this period were trained, as far as we know, in the United States, and all but one of them at the University of Buffalo. Probably the earliest local graduate was Charles Weil (1859-1921), who received his M.D. at the University of Buffalo in 1882, and later became post-mortem examiner for Erie County.[60]

Bernard Cohen (1866-1941), who was graduated from Niagara University Medical School at the age of twenty, seems to be the next local boy to have entered medical practice. Dr. Cohen interned at Fitch Hospital and did post-graduate studies in New York, Baltimore and Boston. He was one of the first Jewish doctors to set up an office on the West Side, and practiced for many years at Elmwood and Lafayette Avenues.[61]

The well known Goldberg brothers also were trained locally. Sigmund Goldberg (1854-1929), was born in Germany and was brought to the United States in 1860. He received his M.D. at the University of Buffalo and practiced medicine in Buffalo all his life; he eventually became chief of staff of the old Memorial Hospital. He was long a familiar sight on the old East Side as he pedaled his bicycle along its streets, his medical bag strapped to the handle-bars.[62]

Jacob Goldberg (1863-1933), younger brother to Sigmund, combined politics with a medical career. Jacob helped his mother support the family and worked his way through medical school by making cigars. He was proud of the fact that he always held a union card, and this, of course, helped him up the political ladder. He also received his M.D. from the University of Buffalo and did post-graduate work in ear, nose and throat diseases. It is a safe guess that he was the first Jew in this area to specialize in otolaryngology.

Dr. Goldberg's interest in politics came early; and in his twenties he was elected, as a Democrat, to the State Legislature where he served three terms. In his first election, in 1884, he defeated John H. Hazel for a seat in the second assembly district. As federal district judge, Hazel later became famous as the man who administered the oath of office to Theodore Roosevelt after President McKinley was assassinated.

In addition to his service in Albany, Goldberg was active in local politics. He served as chairman of the Board of School Examiners (since 1916 the Board of Education), and he was one of the organizers of the Public School Athletic League. As vice-president of the Boy Scouts, he helped bring Sir Robert Baden-Powell to Buffalo to further this youth movement. He was a one-time member of the State Board of Health, served as sanitary inspector for the state and, in 1906, became consultant from western New York and western Pennsylvania to the United States Pension Bureau. Dr. Goldberg was a great fraternal man and rose to become supreme commander of the Knights of Joseph. One of the first Jews to engage in various uplift organizations and to espouse the cause of the Negro, he urged the introduction of sex education at a time when the subject was taboo. After his death, the Buffalo City Council had a memorial engraved in which his work as a physician and public figure was recorded.[63]

Among the first Buffalo born and trained Jewish physicians to emerge as a major medical figure in the city was Dr. Julius Ullman (1872-1953), the youngest member of that gifted family. After his graduation from the local medical school at the age of twenty-one, Dr. Ullman interned and did post-graduate work in neighboring Rochester. Shortly after his return to his native city, he volunteered for service in the Spanish-American war and was stationed at Chickamauga, Tennessee. During the course of over a half-century of medical practice, Dr. Ullman helped found the City Hospital (now the Meyer Memorial Hospital) and served as president of the Buffalo Academy of Medicine.[64]

The next of the Buffalo-trained doctors was, perhaps, the most colorful. Abram Lincoln Weil (1876-1942) was the son of the long-time sexton of Beth Zion. He took his M.D. from the University of Buffalo in 1898 and then in the following year received his Ph.G. from the School of Pharmacy. After graduate work at Columbia University and study of obstetrics in Vienna, he returned to Buffalo. This generous bachelor had a large practice and became known in his home and office at 6 Maple Street as a ministering angel to the poverty-stricken Russian Jews. No one will ever know the extent of his charity, but it is estimated that he was paid for only a small percentage of his work. "I have a very interesting practice," Dr. Weil once said, "the poor and the poorer." He often left money or paid coal or electric bills for his patients. When the ambulance came to take Dr. Weil to the hospital in his last illness, he kept it waiting while he treated a patient for a broken arm.[65]

Some of the more far-seeing young immigrants soon saw the possibilities of a medical career. The bearded Nathan Kavinoky, a well-known East Side doctor, had been born in Grodno, Russia. He married a Rein-

stein, of the family of medical and labor fame, and like his wife's relatives, Dr. Kavinoky was an economic radical. He was the official physician
of the Arbeiter Ring until he left Buffalo for California in the early years
of the present century.

More important locally was his brother, Dr. Samuel Kavinoky (1874-
1943). Samuel, also born in Grodno, came to Buffalo in 1896. He was first
graduated from the University of Buffalo School of Pharmacy, and for
over four decades the almost legendary "Dr. Kavinoky's Drug Store" at
1059 Broadway was an institution among the Gentile Poles of Buffalo.
While operating this drug store, Kavinoky went to the Medical School
at the University of Buffalo and received his M.D. in 1905. A few years
later, he went to Germany for further study and returned to Buffalo to
combine obstetrics with his general practice. Most of his patients were
poor; some paid and some did not. He never bothered much about keeping the accounts of the hundreds of Polish families for whom he cared.[66]

As a promising profession for an ambitious lad, dentistry developed
somewhat later than medicine. It is therefore not surprising to discover
that Jewish penetration into this field was initially retarded. Probably the
first Jewish dentist in the city was Dr. Richard Kessel, who opened his
office on West Huron Street shortly before 1890. Destined to be much
better known to the East Side clientele was Dr. Jacob H. Brown (d.1945),
who entered the profession via the back door. The son of an immigrant
tailor, Brown was in his early teens an apprentice helper to a dentist and
then, in some mysterious fashion and with the help of friendly professors,
he got through the Dental School at the University of Buffalo. While still
a student, he bought a hand drill and attended patients for twenty-five
or fifty cents a visit. In 1898, he began to practice in a bedroom of his
father's house on Superior Street. A short time afterwards, he opened an
office on William Street at Jefferson and remained in practice there for
many years until he moved his office to the Polish section of the city.[67]

As these ambitious young Jews were entering the respected professions, the refugees from the Russian Pale, then thronging into the city,
were settling down to establish distinctly Jewish neighborhoods. We have
seen already that originally Buffalo Jews tended to live scattered among
the Gentiles in certain parts of the city. Shortly after the Civil War, however, a gradual residential shift set in which brought many Jewish families east of Main in the direction of William Street. In the early eighties,
when the German Jews were looking for housing for the eastern Europeans, they placed a number of families on William Street, east of Jefferson, near the point where William Street intersects Madison and
Monroe. This had originally been a German neighborhood, and it is pos-

sible that as the Jews moved in the older residents moved out. This part of town proved attractive to immigrants, for many of its houses already contained store fronts for the new businesses that they wanted to start. Furthermore, it was a location in which there was a large reservoir of customers. It was then, to middle William Street that the new arrivals flocked, and soon the older Jewish residents were calling the area "Castle Garden" because of the number of refugees there who had so recently passed through Castle Garden at the New York port of entry.[68]

At the time of the maximum Jewish immigration, the newcomers crowded together in this neighborhood. Eventually they pushed west on William Street to Michigan and spread north and south on the streets that intersected William. Rentals were cheap amidst this generally depreciated property, and the disdain of older settlers caused the immigrants to band together to seek security in each other's company. Many consciously sought to locate where Yiddish was spoken and understood, where the synagogues were located, where kosher butcher shops, bakeries and food shops could serve their needs, and where they could purchase out-of-town Yiddish papers. Furthermore, the nearer East Side was in walking distance of most places of employment, and the nickels saved in carfare were significant. Many newcomers made a living by trading with and servicing other Jews as tailors, carpenters and so forth, and it was economically wise to settle in the ghetto.[69] This phenomenon was to be seen in every American city. New York had its Delancey Street; Chicago its Maxwell Street; Rochester its Joseph Avenue; and Baltimore its Exeter Street. In Buffalo, the Jewish section grew steadily until it reached its full development about 1914, and then it slowly disintegrated because of certain economic and social forces accelerated by World War I.

As Buffalo's first distinctly Jewish neighborhood developed, it brought into being its own shops and business institutions. One of its features in later years was Rosenblatt's Bakery. Joseph Rosenblatt (1854-1934) arrived in Buffalo from Vishtinetz, Lithuania. To prepare himself for business, he went to New York to learn the baking trade. After he returned to Buffalo, he first baked *matzot* on Clinton Street. Later, he opened his well-known bakery at 268 William Street where Jews met as they picked bagel, honey-cake and *hallah* out of the bins in the store window.

Almost as soon as Rosenblatt began baking in Buffalo, Joseph N. Cohen (1863-1933) went into the same business. He claimed to have brought with him from Warsaw a secret recipe that had been in his family for 300 years, and he began to bake pumpernickel on Monroe Street shortly after his arrival. Later, he shifted his location to 18 Strauss Street and here his son, Albert, made "Cohen's rye bread" a household word in Buffalo.[70]

By the turn of the century, kosher butcher shops throughout the area had multiplied rapidly. There were Jewish barber shops in the neighborhood, a bicycle shop operated by Levi Ruslander at 136 William Street, and a number of Jewish shoe repair shops. Shoemaking was quite a Jewish business before the Jews were forced out of it by the Italian competition and a growing disinclination for this type of work.

William Street also had its own milkman, Casper Munter. Munter (1859-1929), who had his own herd of cows, started a milk business in 1886. "Casper the milkman" was a pillar of Beth El when it worshipped on Elm Street, and he strongly opposed its removal uptown to Richmond Avenue.[71]

Broadly speaking, William Street was a half-way house between the culture of the eastern European village and the mainstream of American life. It was a state of mind as well as a physical settlement, and as such was comparable to the Chinatowns, Little Polands and Little Sicilies that once dotted the country's cities. Here it was possible for the "green" immigrant to live in two worlds, for he could retain in part his customary habits and surroundings, and at the same time he could catch a glimpse of the other world that lay outside. Usually it was his children who first discovered the joys and sorrows of life in Grover Cleveland's America.

The great vehicle of acculturation for these children was the public school system. Here they mingled with schoolmates of other nationalities and religions, here they first heard the ugly words "sheeny" and "kike"; here they discovered that there were no Yiddish equivalents for "first base" and "home run." The schools that they entered were often overcrowded, poorly lighted and badly ventilated. The teachers were poorly paid, sometimes inadequately prepared for their profession and, as likely as not, bored their students by teaching by rote from obsolete textbooks. But for these children from Yiddish-speaking homes, these schools were nevertheless a very important factor in their Americanization. By the hundreds they crowded into School 31 at Emslie near William, and School 32 at Cedar near Clinton.[72]

Just as the earliest German immigrants founded their own social groups for gregarious purposes, mutual aid and benefit, so later did the Russian Jews. As early as 1886, the Ladies' Hebrew Association, Inc., which combined some of the older groups with the new, was formed. "The object of this society," reads the certificate of incorporation, "shall be to mutually benefit each other by caring for its members and ministering to their wants in case of sickness and to meet in social gatherings at fixed times." [73] It is not certain how long this group stayed in existence, but it was still functioning as late as 1919. Other ephemeral groups were the quaintly named Benevolent Boot and Shoe Club, the Ladies of Loyalty, and a Lady Dreyfus Lodge.

Much more permanent was the Manhattan Social and Benefit Society, which was founded in 1895 and met originally at Stendt's Hall on Seneca Street. The chief organizer was Harris Levy (father of the late Dr. Jesse Levy); he was joined in this project by Simon Selling, a salesman who lived on Eagle Street, and Nathan Neubauer. In later years, Justice Samuel J. Harris was twice president of the Society. It was organized as a charitable group designed to help younger members get started in life. It seems originally to have been a group made up of second generation people or those who came here at an early age. In 1925, when this organization celebrated its thirtieth anniversary, it was, with about 800 members, still a vital force in the community.[74]

The East Buffalo Social Club also dated from the 1890s. This group, which resembled the Manhattan Society in many ways, dissolved after fifty years of activity because the older members had died and their Americanized children were not interested in carrying on the work that had lured their forebears.[75]

The only one of these groups to survive to 1960 is the Buffalo Hebrew Social Club, founded fifty years earlier. It proved less ephemeral because, in addition to holding various social functions, it established a credit union and so continued to serve a useful function.[76]

All of these social and benevolent groups testify to the loneliness of the poor immigrants before an efficiently operated Jewish welfare system and Federal Social Security (which did not come until 1935) could take care of them.

A fraternal society of East-European Jews organized in 1887 was of more lasting importance. The Independent Order of B'rith Abraham played a part in the lives of the new immigrants similar to that played by organizations like B'nai B'rith and Kesher Shel Barzel in the lives of the older German group. B'rith Abraham had been founded in Philadelphia, and by the time it reached Buffalo, the organization already had over 56,000 members scattered in 302 lodges throughout the country. Consisting almost exclusively of newer immigrants and their children, it grew by 1915 to 700 lodges with 220,000 members. Later known by the shortened name of B'rith Abraham, it was the first Jewish order openly to espouse the cause of Zionism.

Erie County Lodge #300 began on April 13, 1902, as a result of a decision by the local McKinley Club to affiliate itself with the national order. The watchword of the club was "Unity, Liberty, and Justice." B'rith Abraham went out of its way, unlike some of the earlier Jewish fraternal groups, to make the newer immigrants welcome, to make them feel that all Jews were brothers, and to aid them in times of sickness, distress and loneliness. Unlike other such organizations that segregated their womenfolk, B'rith Abraham pioneered in husband-and-wife combination memberships. In 1905, the Buffalo lodge even had a woman president, Rose Adelman. An insurance plan and provision for cemetery plots were added in 1913. In its heyday Erie County Lodge was one of the largest in the order, and boasted of 500 members.[77]

As the number of Jews in Buffalo increased, it naturally followed that the number of synagogues should multiply. Several factors, however, contributed to the proliferation of synagogues to the point where the community soon became "over-churched." Ironically, as the religious fervor died in the newcomers and they went less and less frequently to synagogue, they built more and more houses of worship. One wit has called this paradoxical quirk the "edifice complex." Differences in national origins, liturgy, social and economic backgrounds contributed to this multiplication of synagogues. Originally, there was a distinct tendency to found *Landsleute* synagogues; groups of individuals from the same country, and even from the same town in Europe, would gather and some of them even named their congregations after their place of origin.

In 1881, on the eve of the Great Migration, there were only three synagogues in Buffalo: Beth Zion was Reform; B'rith Sholem was Orthodox; Beth El, nominally Orthodox, was then tending toward what later would be called Conservative. Very few, if any, of the Russian Jews went directly to Beth Zion. To these traditionalists, the Reform services were almost as unfamiliar and strange as any church worship would have been. Neither would they have been particularly welcome at Beth El at that time. Some of them, however, immediately joined the older *shuls* and these synagogues gained strength from the new influx.

Newcomers from Lithuania and other Mitnagdim were attracted to B'rith Sholem, then located on Elm Street. This congregation, founded in 1865, was re-incorporated on January 3, 1882. At that time, Marx Harris was president and Samuel Brumberg (d.1898), who occasionally expressed heretical thoughts but was an outward conformist, was vice-president. Harris had been born in Lithuania in 1843 and went to England when he was twenty to escape the revolution that was then raging in Poland. He came to Buffalo during the Civil War and lived on to the New Deal era, the last of his generation to survive.[78] In 1893, B'rith Sholem, having gained strength from the new arrivals, sold their Elm Street property and bought land on Pine Street near William. There they built their new Pine Street Shul, a building that was used continuously for sixty-five years.

Settled in their new location, B'rith Sholem adopted a constitution in which there were many safeguards against radical change. A contemporary observer noted the deep traditionalism of this group and its reluctance to depart "from the opinion of their forbears." [79] The constitution provided that all congregational affairs be conducted in Yiddish, and further stated that this language could not be abandoned as long as ten members opposed the move. B'rith Sholem, which had grown out of a benefit society, still maintained some mutual benefits in 1894, for the constitution of that year provided that to become a member one had to be in good health and had to receive an affirmative vote of two-thirds "white balls." The initiation fee was then one dollar and dues were three dollars a quarter.

Many of the provisions of the constitution were similar to those of the early Beth El, and they illustrate the tendency of the strictly Orthodox congregation, made up principally of poor people, to retain European synagogue customs, mores and controls. There was a provision for furnishing "night watches" for the sick. These volunteer nurses were assigned from the congregation by the president, and they were required to pay penalties for not attending to their assigned duties. They were directed to report on the patient's condition each morning to the president. At the death of a member, a special meeting of the congregation was to be called, and members were fined for not attending the funeral of a congregant. There were even fines for telling "outsiders" what happened at meetings. To enforce Jewish marriage laws, the cantor was forbidden to officiate at a marriage without a paper of consent from the congregation and the document had to bear the seal of the synagogue.[80]

The leading lights of B'rith Sholem at this time were Samuel Apenheim, the president for twenty years, Joseph Saperston, Abraham Rabolinsky, Louis Simonsky, Jacob Fass, Joseph Mendelsohn, Louis Gumbinsky, Samuel Altman, Israel Starsky and M. J. Elfendeim. From 1890 to 1914, the rabbi of the Pine Street Shul, Simon Paltrovich (1843-1926), was a familiar and picturesque figure on the East Side, and for many years he was the best known Orthodox rabbi in Buffalo.[81]

"*Hazzan* Singer" was another famous functionary of the Pine Street Shul. Joshua H. Singer (1848-1925) was born in Ponivez, province of Kovno. Harry Singer, as he was often called, began as a cantor in Kreutzberg, Russia, where he served for twenty years before coming to the United States. In the 1890s we find him first as *hazzan* and preacher at Beth Jacob, and then at B'rith Sholem for the balance of his active career. *Hazzan* Singer knew not only the classical East-European chants, but had studied the western cantors, Sulzer, Lewandowski and others, and he thus was able to combine the old with the new. He was also an excellent choirmaster, and his choir contained many East Side boys later destined to make their mark in the Jewish community. In addition to his synagogue functions, Singer kept a religious-articles store in the heart of the William Street district. In his spare time, he wrote two books in Hebrew, *Zekhoron Basefer* and *Mishneh Zekhoron;* one was published in Vilna and the other in Jerusalem. About 1920, he retired from the cantorate and continued to operate his book store at 169 William Street. This store soon became a Mecca for local scholars and Jewish savants who passed through the city. The store was bought by Rev. Isaac Manch, father of Dr. Joseph Manch, Superintendent of Schools in Buffalo, and this quaint store remained an East Side landmark until the middle of the present century.[82]

Shortly after the close of World War I, B'rith Sholem brought an outstanding talmudical scholar to Buffalo. Rabbi Nissen Markel (1877-1947) came from the Polish-Lithuanian Jewish stronghold of Grayevo where, in true Old World style, he had engaged in business rather than the active rabbinate. But the fires of war had left their mark upon Poland, and Rabbi Markel came with his family to join a brother who lived in Buffalo. By chance, he preached a funeral sermon there, and he was promptly elected rabbi of B'rith Sholem. Unfortunately, Rabbi Markel soon developed a chronic disease that virtually incapacitated this gentle and erudite man for the last twenty years of his life.

During Rabbi Markel's long illness, the Pine Street Shul continued to be a strong force in the Orthodox community as long as the neighborhood retained any semblance of its former vitality. The leadership, in part, came from the picturesque Philip (Pinky) Goldstein (1876-1937) who was dubbed "the Mayor of William Street." Goldstein, a keen politician, owned a secondhand clothing and jewelry store in the vicinity, and the community's attention was focused upon him when his personal friend, Mayor Frank X. Schwab, presented him the key to the city.

On the eve of World War II, B'rith Sholem still retained 125 members and operated on an annual budget of $4,000. A *Hevra Tehillim* which, in addition to reciting Psalms daily, operated as a free loan society, and a *Hevra Kadisha* that was the pride of downtown Jewry, still flourished. The decline of the synagogue was temporarily delayed by the establishment, under the leadership of Max M. Yellen, of the B'rith Sholem Credit Union. For many years thereafter, a loyal group of members tried to keep the synagogue's doors open; but removals from the neighborhood finally frustrated their efforts.

For some reason that will remain locked in history, a faction split away from B'rith Sholem about 1880 and founded a rival congregation,

Beth Jacob. Since both groups were largely Lithuanian, and both were strictly Orthodox, and both were made up not of newcomers but of old-timers, the cause of the split remains a mystery. The best assumption that can be made is that a deeply rooted personality clash must have brought the division about. The new congregation began with a meeting held shortly before the Day of Atonement, October 2, 1881.

The leaders in founding the new synagogue were Jacob H. Mayerberg (grandfather of the well known Rabbi Samuel S. Mayerberg [b.1892] of Kansas City), after whom the new congregation was named, and his son-in-law, Louis W. Rubenstein (1849-1898). On November 20, 1881, Beth Jacob met to file papers of incorporation. Among other of the leaders besides Mayerberg and Rubenstein, were Joseph Saperston, who had joined many synagogues in the course of his long life, A.S. Cohen, Simon Harris, Simon Cohen and David Friedlander.[83] For a time at least, the congregation prayed at the home of Jacob Mayerberg, 34 Bennett Street. By 1884, there were thirty-five members and the minister was the Reverend Raphael Josephson.

By the end of the decade, thanks to the constant influx of new members, Beth Jacob was ready to erect a synagogue. On Sunday, June 30, 1889, the New Moon of Tammuz, the cornerstone was laid for the building at the corner of Clinton and Walnut Streets. Despite the strictly Orthodox nature of the synagogue, Rabbi Israel Aaron of Beth Zion prayed and spoke in English for the benefit of those who could not understand the principal Yiddish oration. The Clinton Street Shul, as the new synagogue was familiarly called, cost about $10,000. It was rushed to completion in those days of cheap labor, and was dedicated on Sunday, September 22, 1889, just four days before Rosh Hashana. At the dedication, the rabbi of Beth El spoke in English and the rabbi of Beth Jacob, Reverend M.G. Levensohn, spoke in Yiddish. Solomon's prayer for the dedication of the Temple in Jerusalem was read.[84]

Closely associated with the history of Beth Jacob about the turn of the century was Rabbi Israel M. Fineberg (1850-1915). A tall, thin man with a chin beard, he had been ordained in Europe at the famous rabbinical seminary at Volozhin and had served as rabbi in Bialostok. He was said to have been a first-rate talmudist and one of the best prepared rabbis of his type to come to Buffalo. For a time at least, he served both the Pine and Clinton Streets Shuls, but Beth Jacob was his favorite and there he usually preached and prayed. The regard in which he was held can be estimated by the imposing mausoleum that was erected over his grave by this congregation. His wife, Miriam (or Marian), lived on until her eighties. For years she was an impressive figure in the city and known simply as *the Rebbitzin.*

For many decades, Beth Jacob, like the Pine Street Shul, was an outstanding example of a superior Orthodox synagogue. Its Lithuanian Jews were good, charitable people and intellectually curious. They gave liberally to all good causes and sent money regularly to *Yeshivot* abroad. A contemporary Buffalonian, Yehuda ha-Cohen Vistinazky, reported to a European Hebrew paper that hardly a day passed without a collection for one worthy cause or another. He described the congregation of Beth Jacob as the most distinguished parishioners in Buffalo. He spoke of their regular study of the Talmud in the synagogue and of their fine business reputations. Most of them, he said, had graduated from peddling "from door to door and from courtyard to courtyard." [85]

In the early years of the present century, Beth Jacob was the most powerful, strictly Orthodox synagogue in Buffalo. Its roster of members reads like a "Who's Who" of the East Side: Sapowitch, Rosenblatt, Diamond, Rubenstein, Grossman, Ravnitsky, Becker, and many other names familiar to old-time Buffalonians.

Morris Diamond meticulously kept the Beth Jacob minute books for the thirteen years that followed 1916. His accounts reveal the steady decline of the once proud and powerful congregation. Soon there was trouble in getting a daily *minyan*, for each week vans rolled uptown from William Street, moving another family to the West Side. Nevertheless, Beth Jacob cherished its tradition of having distinguished cantors render the services and, as late as 1920, paid an unusually high salary to its *hazzan*. A decade later, however, the synagogue could not make ends meet, and had to petition former members for support.[86] Eventually, in the 1940s, after a long death struggle, the Clinton Street Shul finally closed its doors. The red-brick structure stood vacant for almost two decades, as the legatees were unwilling to use any loophole of Jewish law in order to dispose of the property. At long last its prayer-saturated crumbling walls were purchased by the city to make way for a new park, and another East Side landmark passed from the scene.

To return once more to 1880s, while the Lithuanian immigrants were being comfortably absorbed by B'rith Sholem or Beth Jacob, the Russian Hasidim felt the need of a synagogue of their own. In addition to the desire to band together in order to preserve their own *minhag*, these self-sufficient men from southern Russia wanted to be their own leaders and had little desire to submit to the haughty "Litvaks" who controlled the older congregations. A plethora of synagogues resulted; some of them lasted; others sprang up only to wither. Yehudah ha-Cohen Vistinazky, the rabbi correspondent to the Hebrew journal *Ha-Maggid he-Hadash*, observed with alarm the proliferation of synagogues in Buffalo at this time. He pleaded for unity among the Orthodox of the city and pointed to the high price the people were paying for their failure to stay together. Keenly he observed that disunity was often caused by personal ambition, for "as the synagogues multiply, the presidents multiply, every one of whom finds great satisfaction in this 'Vocation,' until they come to say to themselves: 'If I had come to America only to be President for one hour, *dayenu;* it would have been sufficient'." [87]

The first permanent synagogue established by the newcomers of the eighties was also the first hasidic *shul* in Buffalo. B'rith Israel, although in existence earlier, was incorporated on February 13, 1887. Its nickname, the *Russiche Shul* (the Russian synagogue), indicated that it was created as a place of worship for the hasidic Russian immigrants who could not get along with the Lithuanian Mitnagdim. When B'rith Israel was founded, it was located at 160 Lutheran Alley. Among the original trustees were Henry Pasman, who later operated a delicatessen shop on William Street, Moses Reisman, a journeyman tailor from Bessarabia and father of the attorney and B'nai B'rith leader Benjamin D. Reisman, Simon Harris, and Max Mittleman, a Seneca Street clothier. All of these men had come to Buffalo from the southern provinces of Russia.

Obviously in search of a suitable site for a synagogue, the congregation owned two parcels of land, one on Mortimer Street and another on Hickory Street. But the Panic of 1893 interrupted their building plans. Membership fell off and the minute book reported that "the few remaining ones are out of employment and unable to continue the payment of interest." [88] By 1898, with economic recovery, they were able to build a synagogue on the east side of Hickory Street near William. Soon B'rith Israel had as "rabbi," Jacob Abramowitz, its own *Hevra Kadisha,* and its own *Hachnosat Orhim.* As the population shifted from the East Side, the power in these synagogues also shifted. By 1905, the president of B'rith Israel was a worldly scrap-iron dealer, Louis Sukernek, Sr. Also active was the long-time secretary, Morris Smolev, and a bearded old-timer, Harris Schlossman.

In 1912, B'rith Israel sold the original synagogue to a new congregation, Anshe Emes, and built a few doors to the south at 177-179 Hickory Street. To construct this new synagogue (with a seating capacity of 800), the congregation borrowed $15,000. In this rather gaudy structure, a remnant of the congregation worshipped until World War II completed the Jewish depopulation of the East Side. [89] At this time, the great majority of the sons and grandsons of the founders of B'rith Israel were already members of Beth Zion or of the Conservative synagogues. After the sale of the Hickory Street synagogue, B'rith Israel moved to 1119 Hertel Avenue, to a converted store. In 1947, the congregation consolidated with Anshe Emes under the name Congregation B'rith Israel-Anshe Emes.[90] Together, they subsequently erected a new synagogue on the south side of Hertel, between Commonwealth and Traymore Avenues.

The second permanent house of worship founded by the post-1880 immigrants was the Anshe Lubavitz congregation. The group was probably formed some years before, but was not incorporated until 1890. It was in one sense another *Landsleute* outfit; but it also was a minor religious sect that grew out of a dynasty of hasidic rabbis that settled in the town of Lubavitz in White Russia. There are devoted followers of this sect all over the world, including many in Buffalo. Although hasidic, they have their own individual ritual.

The five original trustees of Anshe Lubavitz were Louis Bernstein, Israel Slater, Peter Rakin, Z. Dickman and Israel Barkun. At first the congregation worshipped at a house on Pratt Street near William. Their strong leader for many years was Jacob Rosokoff (1858-1940), a jeweler and pioneer in the motion picture industry in Buffalo. He came to Buffalo in 1890 and for twenty-seven years was president of the Lubavitz Shul. There is a story about a member of this congregation named Schiller who, at his citizenship examination, when asked, "Who is President?" answered, "Jacob Rosokoff!" "The President," who was a very religious man and attended services daily, moved his business to Lackawanna where, during the Panic of 1907, he conducted his own bread line, giving away as many as 200 loaves a day to unemployed laborers. Rosokoff, together with his sons, opened a penny arcade in 1904, at 1021 Broadway, and then converted it into a nickelodeon. In Lackawanna, he opened one of the earliest movie houses on Ridge Road.[91]

In 1911, Anshe Lubavitz erected a synagogue at 115 Pratt Street that was said to have cost $30,000 and which seated 650 people. The congregation fluctuated, for in 1917 they could manage a budget of only $700; but six years later there were 140 members and the organization was spending $5,000 a year. For many years the cantor and good friend of this *shul* was Mendel Loeb Gilden (1869-1937) who had been born in the Witebsk province, Russia, where he was trained as *hazzan, mohel,* and *shohet.* Gilden came to Buffalo in 1902, and served the Lubavitz Shul on and off for many years until he moved uptown.

After Reverend Gilden left the East Side, Cantor Perez Freedman officiated at Anshe Lubavitz from 1923 until the synagogue closed its doors on Pratt Street. A businessman with a fine voice and choir training in Europe, *Hazzan* Freedman became a downtown favorite and long retained his devoted followers.

Anshe Lubavitz remained on the East Side until the 1940s; but, as its members moved elsewhere, the congregation slowly declined. The Pratt

Street building was sold for $30,000, strangely enough the sum it was supposed to have cost.[92] The group then united with Congregation Ahavas Achim (the Fillmore Avenue Shul) and in 1950, the merged groups built on Tacoma Avenue near Colvin. It is known as the Ahavas Achim Lubavitz Synagogue. Both congregations in one jump skipped all the intervening Jewish neighborhoods and moved directly to North Buffalo where, by 1950, the majority of the city's Jews had congregated.

In the height of the Jewish concentration in the William Street area, there had been two synagogues on Hickory Street. In addition to B'rith Israel, there was the "little Hickory Street Shul." This was the Anshe Emes outfit that originally worshipped on Mortimer Street near Peckham. Its leaders were Jacob Rosenfield, Barney Berman (later to be first president of Temple Emanu-El), and Harris Rosenblitt. The members of this congregation were Hasidim, but either for personal reasons or because of the individual ambitions of some members, they could not get along with the Russiche Shul group. When Anshe Emes purchased the old B'rith Israel synagogue in 1912, it was a small group with a meagre annual budget of only $400. It seems to have been constantly hard pressed, for they borrowed many times from banks and affluent Jews to keep the synagogue in repair. The president from 1910 until 1918 was Morris Simon in whose memory a plaque was placed near the cornerstone of the present synagogue.

In the 1920s, Morris Bergman (1878-1954), a tall, lean gentleman and, strangely enough for an Orthodox Jew, somewhat of a labor leader, took charge of the affairs of the little congregation. He virtually ran it single-handedly until he moved to the Hertel area at the time of World War II, when he helped re-establish the congregation in new quarters. He was serving his eleventh term as president in 1932 and continued in power until his death twenty-two years later.[93] By that time the congregation had sold the Hickory Street property and had joined, as we have seen, the B'rith Israel congregation on Hertel Avenue.

Rabbi Abraham M. Franklin (1861-1932) was, for many years, the rabbi of Anshe Emes. He came from Vilna, where he prepared for the rabbinate under the great scholar Isaac Elhanan Spektor (1817-1896). In Buffalo, Rabbi Franklin served a number of congregations before settling down at the "little Hickory Street Shul." He claimed to be, and was often called, the "Chief Rabbi" of Buffalo, although here, as in other American cities, the title was inevitably disputed. It is strange that he should have settled with Anshe Emes, for he was a Mitnagid and a "Litvak," whereas his congregation was hasidic and Russian.[94]

Meanwhile, other permanent synagogues had been founded at this time. What was to become known as the Jefferson Avenue Shul was incorporated on March 21, 1892, as Ahavas Sholem. The president at the time of incorporation (the members had begun worshipping together two years earlier) was Joseph Harris. The vice-president was Hyman Gaba; the secretary, Louis Kaplan; and the treasurer was Hyman Joseph. Louis Dautch (1870-1937), later important in Beth El, was a pioneer member of this congregation. Born in Riga, Mr. Dautch had a *Yeshiva* training in Europe and arrived in Buffalo newly married in 1893. A hardware merchant on Seneca Street, for many years he lent his talent in blowing the *shofar* on Rosh Hashana and reading the Torah, first at various East Side congregations, and later at Beth El on Richmond Avenue and in the chapel at the Rosa Coplon Jewish Old Folks Home which Mrs. Dautch helped to found.[95] The early minutes of this group, for the nineties, reveal that it suffered the usual troubles. In 1895, they tried to enforce discipline and decorum by the use of fines and threatened expulsion; but the system failed here as elsewhere.[96]

In this synagogue, however, there was more demand from the congregants for mild reforms than one finds in the other Orthodox synagogues of the day. In 1896, the minutes reveal, there was a motion to eliminate the priestly blessing by those Jews *(Kohanim)* who claimed descent from Aaron. It was defeated at first, but eventually adopted. Several other actions indicate that a progressive element demanded some changes in ritual. A motion was made to omit some of the less important prayers at service, a sharp distinction from the other East Side synagogues where such questions were never raised. Other evidence of less intense Orthodoxy is the fact that, while other East Side synagogues had no difficulty in getting a daily *minyan,* Jefferson Avenue early had to resort to fines to secure one.[97] The congregation sponsored dances and opened a Sunday school—both unusual innovations for downtown synagogues of the day. Old-timers say that Ahavas Sholem was, in its prime, the "stylish *shul*" on the East Side. The president and trustees appeared in cutaway coats and silk hats on Saturdays and festivals. A wealthier and more Americanized element seems to have been drawn to this synagogue which at one time was said to have over 600 worshippers on the High Holidays.

In 1903, under the presidency of David Wagner, Ahavas Sholem constructed a new synagogue on the site of its temporary quarters, on Jefferson, a few doors north of the William Street intersection. In this new building, which cost $28,000, the congregation showed a hardy vitality that kept it alive after all other downtown synagogues had been forced to abandon regular services.[98] In 1957, this venerable synagogue found itself in the local headlines, for the Jewish Lord Mayor of Dublin visited Buffalo, and the Jefferson Avenue Shul was spruced up in honor of Robert Briscoe.

The last important synagogue to be founded on the East Side proper (exclusive of the Broadway-Fillmore district) was Anshe Sokolovka. In the province of Kiev, in southern Russia, was the village of Sokolovka which furnished the Buffalo congregation with its name. Because Sokolovka was a village *(dorf)* and not a town *(shtetl)*, Jews were not permitted to live there. Across the river from Sokolovka, however, were the estates of a nobleman who, many years ago, saw an opportunity to derive an income by renting land to Jews. In order to do so, he founded the town of Ustingrad, named in honor of his wife Justina. In this town, the Jews of this area concentrated, and it was from there that so many of them came to Buffalo. The migration seems to have followed the pattern of other wanderings. One man settled here and was successful. He was then able to influence and aid others in coming here also. One of the pioneers from this area was Abraham Criden, a junk dealer who came to Buffalo about 1903. He in turn brought some of his relatives and friends. Then pogroms of the Russo-Japanese War period sent as many as 200 families to Buffalo from this same place. After one massacre, Samuel Abba Cohen helped many to come to Buffalo, and at one time the Sokolovka group collected money to send Leo Lieberman over there to help a hundred families to emigrate. Many prominent Buffalo families stemmed from this small town: they include those of Victor Wagner, past president of the United Jewish Federation of Buffalo, Hyman Kahn, the Abloves, the Dozoretzes, the Carrels, the Chernoffs, the Rovners, the Rekoons, and many others. About 1910, *Hazzan* Elia Berkun (1870-1943), a picturesque, bearded functionary, arrived to serve the congregation. When the synagogue was incorporated in 1915, Joseph Berleant was president, and Nathan Gelman, a well known real estate broker, also played an important part in the early history of the group.[99]

Anshe Sokolovka purchased some land and a house on Spring Street south of Broadway. In 1917, the building was remodelled and the congregation worshipped at that spot until 1945, when the property was sold. Sam Dozoretz (b.1884) seems to have been the person chiefly responsible for establishing this synagogue. Born in Sokolovka, Dozoretz came to Buffalo in 1908 and was interested both in synagogue matters and in the Farband, a Labor Zionist group. When the synagogue was sold after many years of use, the money was kept for a while intact, but was later increased to $4,000 and, on Dozoretz's insistence, was sent to Israel for some worthy purpose.[100]

Although all the new synagogues that were established in the four decades following 1880 were Orthodox, there was no strength in division, and traditionalism in the city of Buffalo failed to exert the influence or play the role in the community that its numbers actually warranted. The Orthodox engaged little in community life; they spent their strength in constructing buildings, establishing cemeteries, and in petty quarrelling among themselves. They failed, because of this dissension, to furnish the kind of education for their children that would have overcome the obstacles of America and that would have transmitted their ancient heritage to their children. The result was that most of the traditional synagogues of the day became feeders for the more liberal congregations.

Hence, in the 1890s, there were actually three segments of Buffalo Jewry: the Orthodox, consisting of the new immigrants, together with some older inhabitants, who worshipped at the Pine, Clinton, Hickory and Jefferson Avenue Shuls; the old German group and their associates at Beth Zion; and the more liberal traditionalists who were already tending toward Conservatism. This group was made up of the original Polish families of Beth El and some new immigrants who had begun the climb up the social ladder almost as soon as they arrived.

Beth El is a classic example of a Conservative synagogue that had evolved before the term to describe it had come into common use, and before a nationally organized middle-of-the-road movement existed. It is regrettable that, because the minute books for twenty vital years have been lost, we know less than we would like to know about this interesting time of transition. We do know, however, that in 1895 Beth El elected Rabbi David H. Wittenberg. This man, who had trained for the rabbinate in New York, was more Americanized than his predecessors. He organized a Bible class for adults and, at their Sunday meetings, attempted to answer the questions about the conflict then raging between science and religion that the intellectually curious raised.[101]

Wittenberg was still rabbi when Beth El celebrated its golden anniversary. The main celebration was held on Sunday, August 29, 1897, at which time H. Meyer was cantor, Jacob H. Cohen was president, and Joseph Saperston was vice-president. At the afternoon synagogue service, the pulpit was decorated with American flags as a "symbol of the loyalty of the Jews." President Cohen spoke of the history of the congregation, and Secretary Simon Selling read the minutes of the first meeting of May 9, 1847. He then read the minutes of a meeting held fifty years later to the day. Rabbi Wittenberg delivered a stirring address in which he stressed the point of view of moderately liberal Judaism. The service was followed by a banquet at Golden Hall, that well known East Side meeting place, on Clinton and Oak Streets. Other speakers of the day included Mayor Edgar B. Jewett and Rabbi Joseph H. Hertz of Syracuse.[102] (Rabbi Hertz was the first graduate of the Jewish Theological Seminary of America and later became Chief Rabbi of the British Empire.)

On its fiftieth anniversary, the nucleus of Beth El, popularly known as the "Hoch Polish Shul," still consisted of its early families: the Barmons, Grodzinskys, Desmons, Hymans and Gumbinskys. An occasional German, such as Samuel May, who would not move to Reform, was also to be found in the congregation. There were then about eighty members in the synagogue, slightly less than the membership of Beth Zion and even less than congregations of some of the newer *shuls*. The members do not seem to have been strikingly successful, for the monthly dues of $2 reflect the relative poverty of the members. One or two professional men, like Dr. Jacob Brown, a pioneer Jewish dentist in Buffalo, and Dr. Ferdinand Simon, popularly called "the herb doctor," were to be found among the worshippers. Most members still lived on the East Side; but already the more affluent were pushing uptown toward the lower West Side, an area bounded by West Ferry on the north, Allen on the south, Delaware on the east, and Niagara on the west. For real growth, however, Beth El had to await the present century when the crystallization of the Conservative movement supplied it with national backing. Furthermore, early in the twentieth century it moved to its new quarters on Richmond Avenue where it was able to attract many new congregants by erecting the first synagogue in Buffalo that was thoroughly modern, yet not Reform.

While the hordes poured into the city, the older community of German Jews lived in splendid isolation from the inhabitants of William Street. This was an age of social registers and clubs, and some Jews who had made good financially crossed the tracks and entered society. The Buffalo "Blue Book" of 1898 listed among those "who formally entertained and are entertained" the following established Jewish families: the Fleischmanns, Keisers, Marcuses, Shires, Ullmans, Warners, Altmans, Desbeckers, Falks, Rabbi and Mrs. Aaron, and the banker, Joseph B. Block. Six years later, Dan's *Buffalo Blue Book* had added the names of Berthold Block, a relatively new immigrant from Ihringen, the Boasbergs, Exsteins, Saperstons, Wiles, and Levis; but still there were no names in this register that can be definitely identified as belonging to the newer group of East Europeans.

The older families at this period took part in various civic functions and belonged to distinctly non-Jewish organizations. The list of members of the German Young Men's Association for the nineties includes the names of Rabbi Aaron, the Rosenaus, Jellineks, Warners, the Altmans, Blocks, Marcuses, and other members of the German-Jewish community.

The Liberal Club listed quite a few Jewish members, including the magnate Joseph B. Mayer, the Hofellers, the Oppenheimers, and others. This group, in the spirit of the day, fought for civic reform. Another uplift group, the Civil Service Reform Association of Buffalo, contained a generous sprinkling of Jews. The Jews followed the then fashionable practice of the élite in promoting reform. In addition, they quite naturally joined various businessmen's associations.

Politically, the established Jews were making slow but steady progress upwards. They began to be appointed as clerks in various city and county offices; they were represented on the Board of School Examiners after it was established in 1892; some actually obtained more significant political plums, such as appointment as Commissioner of Parks or as members of the City Civil Service Commission. Three fraternal orders seem to have attracted Jews in this period. Many of them were Masons. Although as we have seen, Jews were Masons from the earliest days in Buffalo and were active in various lodges, Perseverance Lodge #948, which dates from 1917, was almost entirely Jewish in composition. Attached to it as a women's auxiliary was Perseverance Chapter #702, Order of the Eastern Star. Of Mrs. Mildred Desbecker Shire, a member of this latter group, it has been said that she had "the unique distinction of having as Masons her father, grandfather and great grandfathers—both maternal and paternal." [103] Because the leadership of the Odd Fellows was in German hands, the Jews were attracted to that organization, but they were especially drawn towards the Knights of Pythias. Jonathan-David Lodge of this order was unmistakably Jewish, and contained the names of some communal leaders who rose to high rank within the state hierarchy of the organization.

Relations between Jews and Gentiles were fairly cordial at this time in Buffalo, although in other parts of the country the lines of social discrimination were becoming more sharply drawn. Professor John Higham states of the country as a whole:

> . . . the unusual ambition and competitive drive for which the Jews were widely admired were not an unmixed blessing. . . . These incentives propelled them upward in American society with amazing rapidity at a time when a general scramble for social prestige was dislocating the American status system. The rise of social discriminations against Jews, beginning in the 1870's, cannot be understood apart from the involvement of a good many Jewish *nouveaux riches* in the hectic social competition of the Gilded Age.[104]

Whatever may have been the conditions in the rest of the country, the evidence indicates that in Buffalo, at least, Jewish-Christian relations were good during this pleasant period of human existence. St. Paul's Episcopal Cathedral had burned on May 10, 1888. After the castastrophe, Beth Zion, mindful of the role played by St. Paul's long before, when Mordecai M. Noah dedicated his Grand Island haven for the Jews, permitted the Episcopal congregation to worship at the Temple on Sundays for more than a year with only a token charge for gaslight. A plaque expressing the gratitude of the Protestant group was placed on the wall of Temple Beth Zion.

Once again, in 1894, Beth Zion extended similar hospitality to the Delaware Avenue Baptist Church for a period of four months. Through James F. Chord, the church asked permission to give Beth Zion a plaque "which shall continue as long as it abides, to silently, but surely keep in memory and testify, as did the twelve stones which Joshua took—and set up for a memorial." [105]

Almost all the references in the local press at this time were favorable to the Jews; some of them were even saccharine and sentimental and studded with platitudes about the thrift, industry and lack of criminality among the Jews, "a pacific and law-abiding class." At least one, however, was not laudatory. A Buffalo minister reported to the *Missionary Review* that the Jews were more powerful than ever before and soon would control "all the seats of justice." He pointed out that in Germany they had already gained control of the banks, and in Rome, the newspapers. This correspondent complained that the Jews no longer believed in the Messiah and did not observe the Sabbath. At the same time, however, he did not despair of their eventual conversion to Christianity.[106]

Despite an occasional note of opposition, however, the *fin de siècle* atmosphere in Buffalo was tolerant and pleasant. Of the Jews of this period who penetrated polite society, the most outstanding couple were Mr. and Mrs. Henry Altman. Henry Altman (1854-1911) was the first local Jewish boy to graduate from an American college. At Cornell University, he had been a "Greek Letter Man," a member of Alpha Delta Phi Fraternity. He was president of the Class of 1873, and later headed the Cornell Alumni Association. After his graduation, he was associated with his father, Jacob Altman, in the clothing business, and after Altman and Company went out of business, he first studied law and then established himself in the insurance business.

Early in his career, Henry Altman began a very active public and social life in Buffalo. He served as trustee of the Buffalo Public Library, and was a member of the original Board of School Examiners, and eventually served as its chairman. He was three times chairman of the Buffalo Republican League and active in the American Protective Tariff League. In the club life of the city, Altman was unmatched by any other Jew of his era. He is said to have been the "father of the University Club idea," and presided at the organization meeting. In addition, he was a member of the Buffalo Athletic Club and served on its executive committee; he was also a director of the City Club of Buffalo, which could boast that Grover Cleveland had been on its first board. He belonged to the Buffalo Club, the Ellicott Club, and moved in certain even more exclusive circles.[107]

Even more spectacular than her husband was Mrs. Altman (1860-1936), for her career came in an age before complete female emancipation. Educated in Europe, Miss Sadie Strauss grew into a versatile, witty, tactful, eloquent and charming woman and served for a time on the staff of the Baltimore *American*. She was first married to George W. Rayner, brother of Isidor Rayner later to sit in the United States Senate from Maryland. After the death of her husband, she met Henry Altman in Europe where she married him. She plunged into the social, political and literary life of Buffalo like a whirlwind. She became president of the City Federation of Women's Clubs. She organized a home for newsboys and bootblacks that later became the Children's Aid Society. She was active in bringing about the installation of nurses and public health centers in the public schools, and she campaigned for women's rights. It was Sadie Altman who induced conservative Buffalo to appoint the first policewoman and the first female probation officer. In World War I, she was the only woman on the Buffalo draft board, and, because of her valuable work in five Liberty Loan drives, she was sent to Washington as an official representative for the dedication of the tomb of the Unknown Soldier.

Mrs. Altman was a talented painter and writer. Active in the Scribblers Club, she was associate editor of the *History of Buffalo and Erie County in the World War*, and she wrote lyrics for the Manuscript Club of New York City. In the 1920s, she was a pioneer radio speaker. Belonging to the Cosmopolitan and the Twentieth Century Clubs among others, she was described as a "brilliant clubwoman" who often travelled out of Buffalo to present papers on various subjects.[108]

The older German group of Jewish residents of the day made it a habit to keep to themselves socially. The men had their card and social clubs, the most prominent of which for a time was the Phoenix Club. This club was opened on May 20, 1890, with Louis M. Brock as its president and Henry Weill as vice-president. After its organization, the club first met in the Tracy Mansion, at Court and Franklin Streets, the site of the present Walbridge Building. The membership was almost exclusively identical with that of Beth Zion; the Brocks, Warners, Desbeckers, Boasbergs, Falks, Ullmans, Jellineks, Marcuses, and Shires. In 1893, a Gentile said of this club: "It exhibits a hospitality towards the families of members unusual among organizations of [its] kind." The club sold its house at 352 Franklin Street (the present site of the Tudor Arms Hotel) in 1901, and some time thereafter the Phoenix Club was replaced by the Apollo Club. This group, started by the same men that had been the core of the Phoenix Club, was a very exclusive poker club. It began apparently at the old location, but later moved uptown. Another organization, less exclusive than the Apollo, was the Progress Club which was devoted to Sunday poker and pinochle. A mixed group, made up of young men and women, the Friends Club was established in 1895 and its activities were almost exclusively bowling and whist.[109]

While the men had their clubs for recreation and relaxation, their wives and daughters organized themselves for philanthropic and social purposes. In the gay nineties, the National Council of Jewish Women opened a branch in Buffalo that attracted many women of the élite. The national group, the oldest Jewish women's group in the country, developed out of the Jewish Women's Congress at the Parliament of Religions which convened at the Chicago World's Fair of 1893. The National Council of Jewish Women did much to protect working women and girls of the immigrant group who found themselves in a strange country pretty much at the mercy of the street-corner rowdies who preyed on their ignorance and fears. They gave advice and help to underprivileged groups to help them establish more sanitary and efficient methods of housekeeping and child care. Part of the early success of the organization came because of the results of the Panic of 1893 and because its growth coincided with years of heavy immigration and the increasing employment of women. The National Council of Jewish Women was, furthermore, the only organization of its day that permitted participation by all Jewish women regardless of social station or religious ideology. This group helped sponsor Sabbath schools for immigrants, fought against white slavery and child labor, and extended a helping hand to the deaf and the blind. It was, moreover, responsible for circulating the famous pamphlet *What Every Emigrant Should Know.*

The Buffalo Section of the National Council of Jewish Women was founded on December 27, 1895, with Miss Cecil B. Wiener as president. It grew rapidly and within five years had 150 members. Besides Miss Wiener, other women who were active in the early days were Miss Elizabeth Hirschfield and Miss Rachel R. Marks, high-school teachers, Mrs. Israel Aaron, for a time the president of the local group, and Mrs. Julius Altman. The monthly meetings were held in the assembly hall of Beth Zion and were open to the public. The original chapter dissolved sometime before World War I, because its work overlapped that of a local group, the Sisterhood of Zion. At its peak, however, the Buffalo Section of the National Council of Jewish Women conducted groups that studied Russian culture (including the reasons for the czarist pogroms), Jane Addams' social work at Hull House in Chicago, Jewish medieval history, and facts about the Talmud. For five years Miss Marks led a Women's Bible Class. The section often brought both Jewish and non-Jewish volunteer lecturers to its meetings.[110]

Meanwhile, shortly after the first inroads of new immigrants, Rabbi Falk of Beth Zion died. In 1887, Rabbi Israel Aaron was appointed to replace him and he served Beth Zion for exactly a quarter of a century. Israel Aaron had been born in Lancaster, Pennsylvania, on November 20, 1859, the son of Moses Aaron and Zelta Greenbaum Aaron. His father, an officer in the army of the Grand Duke of Hesse-Darmstadt, had come to the United States in 1850. He seems to have had a good Jewish education, for although he was a layman he served as rabbi in Lancaster. He died when Israel was six years old, but he had already designated his son for the ministry.[111]

Israel Aaron, after his graduation in 1875 from Lancaster High School, attended the Hebrew Union College in Cincinnati, where he was a member of the first graduating class. Simultaneously with his studies at Hebrew Union College, Aaron attended the University of Cincinnati, was ordained in 1883, and four years later was awarded the degree of Doctor of Divinity by Hebrew Union College. The other members of that pioneer class of H.U.C. were the famous rabbis Henry Berkowitz and Joseph Krauskopf, both of Philadelphia, and David Philipson of Cincinnati. This quartet of the first American-trained Reform rabbis remained close friends throughout their careers.

Just prior to his ordination, Aaron became rabbi of Temple Achduth ve-Sholom in Fort Wayne, Indiana, and there he married Miss Emma Falk. According to report, Louis Weill met Rabbi Aaron while he was travelling in Fort Wayne and brought him to the attention of the Buffalo leaders. Rabbi Aaron applied for the position at Beth Zion in January 1887, and preached trial sermons in German and English. The next month, Rabbi Aaron accepted the offer of Beth Zion at the then attractive salary of $3,000 and signed a five-year contract. He preached his first regular sermon in Buffalo on May 1, 1887.[112]

Dr. Aaron was a genial, cheery man, the life of any gathering. He was handsome, with deep, soulful eyes, possessed great charm of manner, and was said to have been "genial to a degree." Although he was a rather dull preacher, he was a good extemporaneous speaker. He lectured extensively on circuit outside of Buffalo and, in 1897, was invited to speak at Hamilton, Ontario, for the Diamond Jubilee Celebration of Queen Victoria. He was a great mixer, and he early assumed the role of "ambassador to the Gentiles." In 1897, when the G.A.R. held its encampment in Buffalo, the veterans marched from Lafayette Square to Beth Zion to hold a memorial service in the Temple. The choir sang "Tenting on the Old Camp Ground," and Rabbi Aaron spoke on patriotism and the service of the Grand Army of the Republic.[113]

Rabbi Aaron was very active in the uplift and political reform movements of his day. He was a member of the Buffalo Good Government Club and served on its executive board. He was also a moving spirit in the Referendum League, a local branch of a statewide movement to advance democratic reform.

There is good evidence to imply that the congregation became slightly estranged from Dr. Aaron about halfway through his service with them. About 1901 there was a move to re-elect the rabbi and reader by a secret ballot, a move which is evidence of dissent and the desire to protect the names of the malcontents. At the same time, in a period of normal prosperity, his salary was reduced and he was re-elected for only two years. In the following year, although the congregation took an antagonistic position by requiring a two-thirds vote for the election of the rabbi, the difference seems partially to have been patched up, for his salary cut was restored.[114] In later years, Rabbi Aaron and Herman Wile, who served for over forty years as president of Beth Zion, engaged in dispute. Part of the reason for the estrangement was Rabbi Aaron's "Kitchen Cabinet," headed by his good friend and neighbor, Daniel Desbecker. Mr. Wile resented this attempt to bypass the Temple officers. When the rabbi tried to dispense with summer services, the board of trustees sided with Mr. Wile to force the rabbi to continue devotions during the vacation season. No doubt there was a personality clash between the easy-going rabbi and his energetic president, who was anxious for his congregation to grow to a position of prominence in Buffalo. One of the interesting results of this conflict was the purchase by Wile of *haggadahs* for the whole Temple, and on Monday evening, April 5, 1909, the first congregational *seder* was held at the Apollo Club with 107 in attendance. Henceforth, the congregational *seder* became an annual affair.[115]

We fortunately have concrete evidence of the philosophy of Judaism embraced by Dr. Aaron in the form of a sermon and an article that he wrote. He preached the sermon in 1889, and in it he expressed a universalistic outlook that later was to make him a profound anti-Zionist. In this message, Rabbi Aaron said that Judaism expected no Messiah, but that "there will be a final union, a thorough amalgamation of all men is the hope of Israel." When men cooperate and come together, he preached, the Messiah will have indeed come. Imbued with the optimism of his generation, he looked forward to the coming of a "crowning age of love." [116] Unlike some of his Reform contemporaries, however, he was not an assimilationist. In 1896, he denied that he favored religious integration, but wanted Jews to retain their faith and to fight for full religious toleration for all creeds. If the Jews assimilated, he argued, they would all become "beggars at other shrines." [117]

Despite the fact that Rabbi Israel Aaron has gone down in men's memories as an extreme exponent of Reform, the one article that he wrote does not support this reputation. In this essay, he said that as a boy he attended a traditional synagogue that had a religious fervency that Temples lost in "the stirring reformatory period." He deplored the lack of congregational participation in worship. He felt that the choir and organ had usurped their position and that "the religious melodies which once rose freely from the throats of congregants in all parts of the building, now float in artistic procession from some curtained corner of the temple." He called for a revival of traditional Jewish music as part of the "singer's subjective being." He even asked for the reintroduction of some traditional prayers with pleasant tunes.[118] At the same time, however, some of the currently-used "pleasant tunes" were a bit odd. Siegmund Levyn wrote a protest against the singing of part of the Confirmation Service to the music of "Ave Maria," but Rabbi Aaron was apparently not impressed, for the protest was merely read and filed.[119] Taken together, the facts do not make Rabbi Aaron a traditionalist, but they do indicate that he occupied more of a middle-of-the-road position than some of his bolder contemporaries.

Under Rabbi Aaron, who was somewhat less traditional than his European-born predecessor, certain changes took place at Beth Zion. As late as 1893, Beth Zion still retained a cantor, Reverend Schlager, who chanted part of the service and still held sundown services on the eve of the festival of Succot.

In 1897, Rabbi Aaron urged that the congregation hold Sunday morning services to replace the principal Friday evening service. This question agitated Beth Zion for a decade, but Rabbi Aaron never seems to have been successful in bringing about this reform. At times, he came close to getting his wish, but the congregation apparently laid down conditions that he found unacceptable (probably to add Sunday services to regular Friday night and Saturday services). The Ritual Committee later ruled that Sunday services were to begin on January 1, 1910, but one does not know if they ever began, and it is sensible to doubt that they ever did.[120] Although this dispute about Sunday services occupied the congregants and the rabbi, the synagogue long clung to certain traditional practices.

For example, as late as 1903, *Kol Nidre* at Beth Zion began at sundown.

As he approached his fiftieth birthday, Rabbi Aaron seemed to be in great difficulties. There had been constant complaints about poor attendance at services. In the years before the advent of the automobile, but not before the push to more remote parts of the city began, congregants in more distant areas often found it difficult or impossible to attend Temple. In the face of the small congregation, Rabbi Aaron did not want to lecture on Friday nights. The Ritual Committee, once more supported by Herman Wile, insisted that he preach. Mr. Wile answered his plea that the attendance was too small to warrant a lecture with the ultimatum: "You write the sermons, and I will get the people there." [121]

As relations became increasingly strained, Beth Zion talked, perhaps to prod Dr. Aaron to greater efforts, of the appointment of an assistant rabbi. It is possible that at this time the rabbi's health had already begun to fail. The minutes of this period reveal that the congregation directed him when to preach, forced him to take a larger part in the religious school, and urged him to participate more actively in teaching the children.[122]

Despite the differences between the rabbi and his people, the congregation planned a gala celebration to honor Rabbi Israel Aaron on the occasion of his silver anniversary with Beth Zion. Joseph B. Block was chairman of arrangements and Leo Tabor (father of Maurice S. Tabor) was chairman of music. The celebration was scheduled to take place on May 1, 1912, but on the actual date of the anniversary Rabbi Aaron was ill and could not attend. It was held, therefore, ten days later and Israel Aaron had the pleasure of hearing his good friend and schoolmate, Rabbi David S. Philipson of Cincinnati, preach the sermon. Rabbi Aaron, however, was too ill to attend the reception in his honor at the Apollo Club. On May 15, 1912, he died at the early age of fifty-two.

Dr. Aaron was buried from the Temple two days later. In the black-draped synagogue, 2,000 people were crowded. Fifty carriages, twenty automobiles, and twelve taxicabs accompanied the hearse to the Beth Zion section of Forest Lawn Cemetery. Rabbi Philipson returned from Cincinnati to preach the funeral sermon. All the surviving ex-presidents of Temple Beth Zion acted as honorary pallbearers, and the board of trustees were the active bearers. Rabbi Philipson returned later that memorable spring to conduct confirmation services.[123]

Rabbi Aaron's incumbency coincided with the great exodus from the Russian Pale. The new immigration introduced into American Jewry a new avocation—settlement work. It became a national movement that within a generation had established some seventy-five Jewish neighborhood centers and settlement houses for the relief of the miseries of the immigrant groups. In general, similar Christian organizations preceded the Jewish relief houses. These were motivated by the reform impulse of the Populist-Progressive era to arouse the American conscience against the social evils and human exploitation of the Gilded Age.[124] For example, in Buffalo the Remington Gospel Settlement catered to Italian immigrants, while Westminister House served mostly Germans, as did also Neighborhood House; and Watson House offered assistance to both Irish and German working people; Memorial Chapel at Cedar and William Streets was a mission of the Lafayette Presbyterian Church; and Welcome Hall at 404 Seneca Street served a mixed clientele.

Jewish settlement work proved to be only a passing phase. Several factors served to bring an end to the movement; but in Buffalo it died a slow death. Usually, as soon as a Jewish immigrant became established, he left the depressed areas of the cities and moved to a more fashionable location. Furthermore, unlike other immigrant groups, the Jews were more motivated to educate themselves, and thus earlier than other groups moved themselves out of the hardship class.

The whole settlement movement coincided with the emancipation of women who were afforded hitherto unknown leisure by the advent of prepared foods and cereals and better household equipment. In this new-found time, the women turned to self-education and the rendering of aid to others. Consequently, the settlement movement was largely a women's movement. It was spurred by the establishment in 1889, by Rabbi Gustav Gottheil of the Sisterhood of Personal Service at Temple Emanu-El in New York. This group was widely and quickly imitated throughout the country. The first Jewish settlement house for immigrants was opened in Chicago in 1888. Buffalo was not, therefore, far behind when it entered this work shortly thereafter. In 1891, Rabbi Aaron urged the organization of the Sisterhood of Zion, and it proved to be the most lasting work of his ministry. These ladies naturally turned to the most pressing problem of the day, help for the Jewish immigrants, a problem made more urgent by the hard times that soon set in. The Sisterhood of Zion listed as its objectives: 1) "to promote good fellowship and social culture among its members," and 2) "to further works of charity, philanthropy and education among poor and unfortunate Jews." [125]

The Sisterhood was established on Sunday, April 16, 1891. In a meeting held at Temple Beth Zion, the rabbi instructed the women in their obligation to improve, Americanize and elevate the children of the Russian Jews. He spoke of the lack of knowledge of the English language among the children of the ghetto and described how they retained the Old World ideas of their parents. He urged that the best way to improve conditions would be to build up the confidence of the immigrants in the women who would do the relief work. He called upon his audience to advise the immigrants, to give them a chance to associate with other Jews, and to inspire them with American patriotism.

Elected to office at this meeting were Mrs. Alphonse Weill, president; Mrs. Israel Aaron, first vice-president; Mrs. Louis M. Brock, second vice-president; Mrs. Benjamin Desbecker, secretary; and Mrs. Abram L. Warner, treasurer. Mrs. Marcus Spiegel, who was to serve twenty-five years as president of the Sisterhood, was hailed by a contemporary as "a born, not made philanthropist, who instinctively knows how to lighten the burden of others." Although she was interested in many types of charity, Mrs. Spiegel's favorite project was the Sisterhood of Zion.[126]

The new organization promptly rented a house at 26 Walnut Street in the heart of the immigrant neighborhood. There, despite the mistrust of many Orthodox parents, they conducted a school for children who could not speak English. The teacher was Miss Theresa Rosenberg, daughter of a Civil War veteran who later settled in Buffalo. During the early days she conducted "Americanization" classes, teaching the adult immigrants at night and during the day helping their children.

The Sisterhood moved to larger quarters in 1892. Their house at 452 Spring Street was already being called Zion House, and by the next year there were eighty volunteer workers. Soon, the women stocked their headquarters with 300 books, 3 rugs, 3 stoves, 6 school desks, 36 chairs, pictures, mirrors, a desk, a sofa, kindergarten equipment, blackboards and slates, and a sewing machine. In 1896, the Sisterhood raised money by a fair and built a house at 456 Jefferson Avenue (near Peckham), for they had outgrown their old quarters. The new house was bright and cheerful and included accommodations for bathing, to promote cleanliness among the "clients." In 1898, the group brought the famous English Jew, Israel Zangwill, to Beth Zion to lecture. The proceeds of this lecture went to support Zion House, as did a sum of money left by a non-Jew, Max Wahle. At the turn of the century, there were 280 members of the Sisterhood and its auxiliary organization, the Daughters of the Star. In addition to the classes taught by volunteers, there were a boys' club for children eight to twelve years, a sewing school, and a Sunday school which was necessary because the neighborhood synagogues then often neglected Jewish education. There was by this time a resident worker on the premises. Miss Krombach, a young and enthusiastic professional social worker, had been trained in New York City. She laid plans for music and dancing classes; she brought a branch of the public library to Zion House and set up a playground for the children. A Working Girls' Club had been already established, the first of many such groups at Zion House.[127]

A report for 1903 shows that at Zion House there was daily teaching. A kindergarten was in operation, and darning, mending and dressmaking classes aided immigrant women in their housekeeping, as did the cooking class. The House had a library and, in the spirit of Benjamin Franklin, a "penny provident bank." A mother's club rounded out the functions that kept almost fifty volunteer workers adequately occupied.[128] By 1907, Zion House had become the headquarters for the Federated Jewish Charities, the Sisterhood of Zion having been one of the original constituent units of this new organization. Volunteers visited the homes, teaching cleanliness and child guidance. They helped the immigrants get jobs and worked out family problems and mended broken homes. There was a "house mother" and a "resident worker," and the alliance with the public school system was so close that the kindergarten of School 41 at Broadway and Spring Street met at Zion House.[129]

The Ladies' Sewing and Aid Society arose from the same conditions that motivated the organization of the Sisterhood of Zion. This group, led by such ladies as Mrs. A. L. Warner, Miss Miriam Bergman and Mrs. Isidore Loeser, purchased material, helped the Jewish poor to knit stockings, and made underwear and other articles of clothing. With the formation of the Federation in 1902, this group became the Committee on Sewing and Distribution. It became defunct with the decline of the immigrant problem.

After the first influx of immigrants from eastern Europe had arrived and settled down in Buffalo, Beth Zion began to take action to move to the site so long to be occupied by that congregation. Since Appomattox, the Temple had worshipped on Niagara Square in a reconverted church. In 1886, a motion was passed by the board to sell the Niagara Street Temple. This property, exclusive of the furniture, gas fixtures and organ, was subsequently sold to the Masonic Hall Associates for $33,500; and in the fall of 1888, a committee, composed of Leopold Warner, Sol Rosenau, Siegmund Levyn, Leopold Marcus and W. Wolf, was appointed to select a site for the new Temple. Later that year a building committee (Siegmund Levyn, Sol Rosenau, Marcus Wall, Leopold Warner, Henry Weill, Magnus Wiener, Julius Altman, Edward R. Warner and Joseph B. Block) was appointed.[130] The following year, because they were forced to vacate the Temple, the congregation worshipped first at the Unitarian Church of Our Father on Delaware Avenue; but apparently the rent was too high, for they negotiated for the use of the Central Presbyterian Church at Pearl and Genesee Streets and used its sanctuary until the dedication of the new Temple.[131]

On May 22, 1889, just a few years before the American economy was to slump into one of its periodic depressions, the congregation purchased a lot at 599 Delaware Avenue from Charles Cushman for $27,500. At that time Delaware Avenue was one of the most picturesque residential streets in Buffalo. It was lined with oak and maple trees, and the mansions of substantial brick stood well back from the street. The new location was excellent. It was not too far from the downtown area, and yet it was near where many Jews lived in the fast-growing West Side. The plans for the new Temple were received from the architect, Edward A. Kent, in July 1889. The building was to cost about $50,000 in addition to to cost of the land.

The cornerstone of the new Temple was laid on October 29, 1889, and the congregation accepted the gift of a perpetual light from its patriarchal vice-president, Leopold Warner. On Sunday, September 7, 1890, pews were auctioned to the highest bidders to finance the new structure. The sale was conducted by Henry Weill who was then president. At this time Beth Zion had 112 members who bought, so a newspaper reported, the amazing total of $60,000 worth of pews. The choicest benches brought as much as $1,000 each.[132]

The building, which has been considerably changed in the course of seventy years, was constructed according to no definite type of synagogue architecture because none existed at the time. To avoid marked resemblance to Christian churches, the architects tried to make the synagogue look oriental, thereby hoping, no doubt, to give it a Jewish look. Consequently, Beth Zion was built with a large central Byzantine dome. The Buffalo *Courier* called it a "bit of Constantinople designed in Buffalo," and the *Evening News* reported: ". . . it is low in proportion and wanders in an oriental way along the west side of the dome." The cautious architects lighted the Temple with both gas and electricity, evidently deeming that electricity was not yet to be trusted. Behind the sanctuary, schoolrooms were cleverly designed so that they could be combined to seat 400 people. A Directors' Room was also included in which the Temple was to preserve portraits of its distinguished members, officers and staff.

On Friday, September 12, 1890, just three days before Rosh Hashana, the new Temple was dedicated. Rabbi Aaron, Mayor Charles F. Bishop and the revered Rabbi Isaac M. Wise, who had dedicated the Niagara Street Temple, spoke. At the Temple service, every seat was filled. Miss Bianca Fleischmann played the organ. Siegmund Levyn was, appropriately, the first to enter the new Temple. Rabbi Aaron paused on the steps to pray: "Open unto me the gates of righteousness that I may enter into them and praise the Eternal." Blanche Weill, whose mother (Amelia Desbecker) had performed a similar function at the dedication of the Niagara Street Temple a quarter of a century earlier, carried a pillow of flowers on which rested a big brass key to the Temple. The officers entered carrying two *Sifrei Torah* on their arms, and the other synagogue dignitaries followed. The choir, led by Joseph Mischka, sang "This is the gate of the Lord, the righteous shall enter therein."

Rabbi Louis Grossman of Detroit offered the dedicatory prayer and followed it by a short speech. Blanche Weill presented the key to the venerable Leopold Keiser, who spoke of the history of the Temple and of Rabbi Falk of blessed memory. He said that the Temple would be open to all who wished to pray to the God of all mankind. The choir then sang a Hebrew hymn. When Rabbi Aaron said in Hebrew, "God has said, 'Let there be light,'" a current of electricity illuminated the impressive central chandelier. Old Leopold Warner then advanced and lighted the *Ner Tamid* that he had donated.

The *Sifrei Torah* were placed in the Ark while a psalm was recited, and then the rabbi spoke. He lauded "the broader vision of this era," and he hoped that Jew and Gentile alike would pray in the Temple. He reminded the congregation of the mission of the Jews to edify the world and stated that he viewed the new Temple as a testimonial to that mission. While he spiced his words with generous quotations, he preached that the mission of the Jews would not be fulfilled as long as anyone believed that salvation was connected with dogma. He denounced the "Heaven-ignoring and defying systems of Socialism." He then dedicated the Temple, and afterward the choir sang a special hymn to the melody of "America." Rabbi Wise, the graying dean of Reform Judaism, then seventy-one years old, reminisced on the dedication of the Niagara Street Temple and thanked God that he had lived to open the doors of another House of God. The ceremonies of the day were followed by the regular Sabbath-eve service. After the final benediction, 150 guests gathered for a banquet at the Phoenix Club with the witty Siegmund Levyn acting as toastmaster.[133]

In the decade between the dedication of the Delaware Avenue Temple and the end of the century, Beth Zion seems to have been in the doldrums. Although some of the newer immigrants, who had succeeded financially, joined, nothing was done seriously to encourage growth. The whole spirit of the congregation was that of a closed corporation. At the same time, immigration from Hohenzollern Germany had virtually ceased and the natural increase of the original families was not sufficient to keep Beth Zion vibrant and expanding. For real growth, the Temple had to await the present century when new blood would be recruited from the sturdy sons and daughters of the East Side masses.

Progress and Poverty

THE DECADE AND A HALF that separated the Spanish-American War of 1898 from the onset of World War I has generally been called the Progressive Era. During these years of world peace and general prosperity, the American conscience revolted against the abuses of the Gilded Age. Reform was in the air, for men of good will were confident that they could, in Bessemer-like fashion, blow out the impurities that marked the old social and economic order. By and large it was a middle-class revolt against the corrupt alliance of the moguls of Big Business and the bosses of Big Politics. On the grass roots level this uprising took the form of countless uplift and reform societies.

There was, however, another aspect to the American picture. In sharp contrast to the bold confidence and sweet smell of cleanliness that was on the side of progress and improvement, apathy and despair ruled the souls of the unwashed and the poor so many of whom had just arrived from depressed areas of the Old World. This contrast was especially marked in Jewish communities where the older settlers shared the uptown optimism of the American bourgeoisie, while the recent arrivals wallowed in the slough of their downtown slums. But so all-pervading was the belief in progress that some of it spilled over into the camp of the under-privileged. Among Jews of the East Side this hope for the salvation of mankind was sometimes translated into enthusiasm for the cause of Zion rebuilt. After twenty years of the Russian nightmare, prescient Jews all over the world were searching for new answers to the old questions of persecution and displacement.

The Zionist movement came to America in full force shortly after the first of the Russian pogroms, although flashes of Zionist spirit had appeared earlier, such as in the visions of Mordecai M. Noah. As a direct result of the new persecutions, the concept of Zionism stirred the Russian Pale, so that as one group went westward toward the United States, another but smaller band headed eastward to reclaim the Holy Land. Consequently, the idea of a Jewish state was imported to these shores by immigrants who soon formed pre-Herzlian Zionist groups in the cities in which they settled. In the early eighties, a group called the "Hovevei Zion" was formed in New York City under the leadership of Dr. Joseph I. Bluestone. This group and several similar organizations appeared on this side of the water almost as soon as they did in Russia. The spirit of Zionism quickened, and, as part of the movement, Hebrew-speaking clubs sprang up all over the country, for the revival of Hebrew as a spoken tongue was part and parcel of the Jewish national renaissance.

In 1895, Dr. Theodor Herzl published his seminal book, *Der Judenstaat,* and two years later the First Zionist Congress was held at Basle. A non-Jewish contemporary correctly described this program of 1897 as "a combination and collection of movements, arising spontaneously and independently of each other in a half-dozen countries, and developing under diverse local side aims and purposes, having an agreement only in the one object, that of effecting a return of the people of Israel to Palestine." [1]

Soon, the Federation of American Zionists was formed in New York City, with Professor Richard J. H. Gottheil as president and Rabbi Stephen S. Wise as vice-president. Within two years, about fifty-two Zionist Societies were organized in the United States, and they generally affiliated with the Federation of American Zionists. During this period, Israel Wolf, a representative of a New York Jewish newspaper, travelled the country to help organize these groups, many of which were, of course, ephemeral. [2]

Meanwhile, the Knights of Zion had been formed in Chicago. It was from this group, and not from the New York Federation, that the first effective Zionist message was carried to Buffalo. The most important nationalist of the Chicago school was Leon Zolotkoff, a Yiddish-newspaper man who had travelled extensively. The Knights resembled the fraternal type of organization then so popular in America, for Zolotkoff hoped to use fraternal bonds to arouse interest in Zionism. The order grew rapidly, each branch being called a "Gate" and each unit having both an English

and a Yiddish "orator." Zolotkoff's plan was to bring order out of chaos at
a time when so many cities had budding Zionist groups with separate
memberships, undefined dues and uncertain programs.[3] In time, the
Knights of Zion, which waxed strong in the West, came to rival the Federation of American Zionists; but it was eventually absorbed into the
larger movement.

There was a pre-Herzlian group of Zionists in Buffalo, but it amounted
to little or nothing until interest in the movement was sparked by Leon
H. Miller's arrival here in 1903. Miller had been born on June 15, 1880,
in Upina, Lithuania, and prior to his departure for America had been
steeped in Jewish learning in various talmudical academies including the
famous *Yeshiva* at Telshe. He was an avid scholar and a powerful Yiddish
orator. As a young lad he had been fired by the Hebraic translation of
Herzl's *Judenstaat,* and even in the Old World he had worked for the
cause of Zion rebuilt. He came to these shores at the age of twenty-one,
a thin bespectacled youth, but burning with zeal and possessed of a
tongue that could spread that zeal. He went first to Marshfield, Wisconsin, where his father resided, and it was there that he joined the
Knights of Zion.[4] In 1901, Zolotkoff appointed him "official organizer and
travelling speaker for the Order of the Knights of Zion for the Middle
Western States." Audiences in many cities, from Waco, Texas, to St. Paul,
Minnesota, were held spellbound by his impassioned pleading for the
restoration of the ancient Homeland. Despite his own liberal approach
to religion, he was able to reach the Orthodox masses, who had heretofore been either indifferent or actually hostile to Zionism. In Chatta-
nooga, Tennessee, he was acclaimed the best speaker that had ever
addressed the Jewish community of that city. At New Orleans, in 1902,
he was described as a "tall, pale young man. . . . He wore a long black
coat, and four-in-hand scarf, gold eyeglasses . . . long hair, black cap." [5]
During his widespread travels for the Knights of Zion, he utilized the
Kishineff pogrom of 1903 to gather supporters for the nationalist cause.
Favoring action rather than polemics, he repeatedly pointed out that to
argue with Russia was useless. The only effective thing to do, he maintained, was to buy land in Palestine from the Sultan and settle pioneers
thereon.

In August 1903, Leon Miller came to Buffalo where he was ultimately
destined to spend the rest of his life. Mutual friends had given him the
names of Harris W. Holender who had already been organizing the Buffalo Zionists, and Harry Gintzler, a local printer who wrote a column for
a conservative Yiddish daily. Harris W. Holender had been born in
Augustov, Russia, in 1860, and had come to Buffalo when he was thirty.
He was a gentle soul, known for great kindness and integrity. At his death

in 1926, his funeral was said to have been one of the largest that the Buffalo Jewish community had ever witnessed. Leon Miller organized the Sons and Daughters of Zion out of the nucleus of the Hevra Hovevei Zion which Holender had nurtured. Its first president was Sundel J. Holender, son of Harris. Leon Miller soon married Ada G. Holender (b.1881), a daughter of the family, and became a permanent resident of Buffalo. The extent to which the Zionist movement had taken hold in Buffalo can be judged by the fact that, by June 1904, Buffalo sent a delegation of about fifty people in a special railroad car to the Cleveland convention of the Federation of American Zionists.[6]

The Sons and Daughters of Zion met in the Talmud Torah which was the unofficial headquarters of the group. There they held debates and listened to visiting Zionist thinkers from other parts of the country. Among the important members of the group were Miss Martha Morris, the future psychiatrist Dr. Hyman L. Levin, Charles Blumenthal, then principal of the Talmud Torah, Miss Anna P. Abramson and William Singerman. This group was purist: it rejected the plan of the territorialists, which urged acceptance of the British offer of Uganda (Kenya) in South Africa as a place of refuge for Jews and, under the leadership of Miller, they demanded the Holy Land as a future homeland. In the meantime, the original group, Hevra Hovevei Zion, continued an independent existence, and in 1905, perhaps as a result of some misunderstanding with the Knights of Zion, Leon Miller became president of this older group.[7]

In time, all segments of Zionist thought were represented in the city. The first of the special interest groups to organize locally was Poale Zion (Workers of Zion), whose goal combined peaceful socialism with Jewish nationalism. Organized in Europe, Poale Zion was brought to these shores by Dov Borochov and Joseph Barondess. Here they met stout opposition, for the pure Socialists criticized them for their Zionism, while the undeviating Jewish nationalists looked askance at their economic radicalism.

A branch of Poale Zion was founded in Buffalo in 1905, and it too met in the Talmud Torah. Among the early members were Israel Luskin, later a high school mathematics teacher, a Dr. Saltzman who soon moved to Los Angeles, J. B. Zackheim, a druggist, and Moshe (Morris) Gubenko. The activities of the group centered around the reading of papers and literary discussions. Sholem Aleichem, the famous Yiddish writer, was brought to Buffalo by them for his first visit to the city. In true proletarian style, the Poale Zion hymn was sung at each meeting.[8]

It is appropriate here, before we reach the full development of American Zionism, to take a general estimate of the climate in which the first seeds of the movement were planted. Originally, Zionism stood as a very real barrier, among so many others, between Jews of Russian and German extraction. With the exception of the ultra-Orthodox, the East Europeans almost entirely supported the idea of statehood, and equally unanimously the German Jews, with some very noteworthy exceptions, opposed the plan. In Buffalo, not a single member (as far as we know) of the older Reform community was a pioneer Zionist.

Liberal Judaism in America, it will be recalled, was initially made up almost exclusively of the older German Jews and similarly oriented groups. The Cincinnati reformers regarded themselves as different from other Americans only in religion, not in nationality. As a result, when the flame of Zionism began to burn, some members of this more Americanized group regarded the growth of Jewish nationalism as a threat to their own positions in America. All of them wanted to help the persecuted Jew who came to America on a philanthropic basis; many resisted and resented, however, any organized political activity that would call attention to a world-wide Jewish problem. They are not, of course, to be condemned out of hand for taking the position they did; many factors contributed to their stand. They did not, first of all, understand nineteenth-century European nationalism that so influenced Zionism; they were oblivious to the "ties of birth, of membership in a folk community, of loyalty to . . . language," that formed part of the East-European Jewish tradition.[9] They were, in fact, Americans who were assimilated to the extent that they rejected those parts of the Jewish heritage that differentiated it from other religious denominations. Furthermore, because they understood only the religious facet of Judaism, they failed to see that, in eastern Europe, Judaism had also been a way of life. Nor did they fully comprehend the extent of the Russian persecution that made so many of their "co-religionists" hail Herzl's plan for a "total solution" to the Jewish problem. In this respect, Liberal Judaism badly underestimated the new European anti-Semitism that, since 1870, had assumed the complexion of persecution on the basis of race rather than religion. They were too American, and in a larger sense, too isolationist to grasp what German or French anti-Semitism (for instance in the *cause célèbre* of Dreyfus) really portended for the dawning twentieth century.

Forgetting that the Jewish prophets had been nationalists as well as universalists, some Reform Jews tended to emphasize the catholic aspects of Judaism. Viewing political Zionism with suspicion, many American Jews of 1900 feared that they would be accused of a dual loyalty if they espoused the concept of a Jewish state, for Zionism seemed to negate the almost religious love that these men had for their adopted land. Herzl's blueprint seemed to them to threaten the Americanization of all Jews here, a goal that they held close to their hearts. This universalist feeling found expression as late as 1917, when the Central Conference of American Rabbis reaffirmed that "the essence of Israel as a priest people consists in its religious consciousness, and in the sense of consecration to God and service in the world, and not in any political or racial national consciousness." [10]

Gradually the opposition of the German Jews toward Zionism waned. They themselves were actually inundated in the flood of East Europeans, and in due time they lost their leverage on the community. The subsequent closing of America as a haven to the persecuted made Zionism a necessity. This, plus the 1917 Balfour Declaration, the Hitlerian tragedy and the eventual emergence of Israel combined to all but wipe out antagonism to Zionism.

While the fires of Zionism were being fanned into flame, the rest of the United States was itself involved in a nationalistic frenzy that finally erupted in the Spanish-American War of 1898. All told, it is estimated that from 2,500 to 4,000 Jews served in this brief conflict and in the Philippine uprising that followed it, and, as they did in all previous wars, Buffalo Jews answered the call to duty. It has been observed, and probably correctly, that throughout the country Jews wished to see Spain humbled, for they had never forgotten the 1492 expulsion at the hands of Ferdinand and Isabella.[11]

In Buffalo, the 65th Regiment, under Colonel Samuel M. Welch, left for the war. The 13th United States Infantry, regarded as a local outfit, entrained from Fort Porter and was destined for active service first in Cuba and later in the Far East.[12]

Eight known Jews from Buffalo served in this war. David Rodenberg (b.1880) enlisted at the age of eighteen. He joined the 202nd New York Volunteer Infantry and sailed from Savannah, Georgia, for the scene of action in Cuba. Samuel C. Dutch, grandson of Nathan Dutch who served in the Civil War, was in the hospital corps. Charles G. Hyman was a private in the 65th Infantry, while his brother, Daniel, commanded a company in the 27th Infantry. Dr. Julius Ullman was Assistant Surgeon at Chickamauga, Georgia. Joseph Cohen, later a podiatrist, served in the 202nd New York Volunteers, in which unit Solomon Feldman also served. Daniel W. Barmon enlisted in the National Guard (later absorbed in the 74th Regiment), following his graduation from Cornell University Law School. In Cuba, Mr. Barmon rose to a corporal's rank before being mustered out in April 1899.

At home, the Buffalo section of the National Council of Jewish Women engaged in relief work, and at least one Jew (Abram L. Warner) served on the eleven-man Executive Committee of the General Aid Committee appointed by Mayor Conrad Diehl.[13]

Apart from these relatively minor activities, the hundred-day conflict did not disturb the even temper of the times. The great bulk of Buffalo Jews, then crowded into the William Street area of the city, were largely untouched by events of the electric spring of 1898. They were in effect isolated by their own social and economic problems, and thus were almost oblivious to America's emergence as a world power.

In the first decade and a half of the new century, the Jewish population of the East Side increased almost sixfold. During the same period, the total population of the United States increased by 8,795,386 compared to an increase of 3,687,564 recorded by the decennial census of 1900. One scholar has stated that, whereas in the century following the downfall of Napoleon four immigrants arrived in America for every native-born American, 1,000 additional Jews arrived for each native-born American Jew. Another way of pointing up the problem is to observe that the total number of Jews that reached America after 1815 was greater than the total Jewish population of the world in George Washington's day.[14]

One cause for the torrential Jewish immigration of the day was the new pogroms that occurred under Czar Nicholas II. The most celebrated of these massacres, but by no means the only one, was that at the town of Kishineff in Bessarabia on Easter Sunday, April 19, 1903, which happened to coincide with the last day of Passover.

To instigate the riots, the rumor of a ritual murder story was spread; and, although there were thousands of soldiers present who could easily have prevented trouble, they made no attempt to interfere with the mob. In fact, the local chief of police actually incited the rioters. In the course of two days, forty-seven Jews were killed, ninety-two were seriously injured, and over 500 received minor injuries. Many Jewish homes were destroyed, several thousand families were left without shelter, hundreds of stores were plundered, and the property damage was estimated at 2,500,000 gold rubles. The pogrom had been organized by czarist officials in order to draw public attention away from the venality that marked a decadent regime.

Immediately throughout the United States protest meetings were held to express indignation and outrage. In Buffalo, Rabbi Abraham M. Franklin called a mass meeting at the Pine Street Shul, on Sunday, May 17, 1903. The chairman of this gathering was the energetic young Orthodox attorney Emil Rubenstein, then only twenty-two years old. While Rabbi Franklin addressed the excited audience in Yiddish and *Hazzan*

Singer chanted the traditional prayer for the dead, the women in the galleries moaned and wept.[15]

Rabbi Israel Aaron of Beth Zion, who knew no Yiddish, spoke in English. He took a strange position, remarking that weeping was useless, but he let his anti-Zionism seep out in his speech. "There is a refuge for the downtrodden," he said, "America, the land of freedom, of honest hearts, of noble minds, this magnificent country filled with men whose hearts rise to heaven day after day. We must make America a place of refuge for our downtrodden brethren, make it a place where Jews will act so, live so, labor so, that they will lift their heads in honor and be above reproach and criticism. *The highest ambition of a Jew,* and no other man can have a higher ambition, *is to become an American citizen.*" [16] *

Police Justice Thomas Murphy brought the meeting back to its basic purpose. He extended sympathy to the Jewish people and said that America would always help the oppressed. Next, Attorney David Ruslander, Chairman Rubenstein's brother-in-law, spoke in behalf of a petition to President Theodore Roosevelt which asked him to intercede with the Czar. This step was strongly opposed by Rabbi Aaron, who argued that it would do more harm than good and that the United States had no right to interfere with the internal affairs of Russia.[17]

Because of this opposition, a second meeting had to be held, although the first gathering did produce a Kishineff Relief Committee. This second meeting was held on May 24th at Jefferson Hall to arrange for the petition to President Roosevelt and another to the United States consul at St. Petersburg.

About 200 people came out for the occasion. Robert Steiner, editor of the *Arbeiter Zeitung,* spoke in German and Dr. Ludwig Schroeter, the Fillmore Avenue Jewish physician, addressed the gathering in English. The Protestant minister, Dr. O. P. Gifford, delivered the strongest speech in favor of the proposed petition. To Rabbi Aaron's almost incomprehensible opposition he said, "Bah, for this talk that we can't protest against these outrages." But the aging Louis M. Brock, who voiced Beth Zion sentiments, still protested. Brock suggested practical help for the victims rather than petitions; but he was not permitted to speak a second time. Later he charged that he had been silenced by the Socialists who dominated the meeting. However, the petitions finally were approved and were duly forwarded to the proper authorities.[18]

The sporadic pogroms that continued for several years after Kishineff were not the sole cause of the huge Jewish immigration of the

---

* Italics added

Theodore Roosevelt Era. The Russo-Japanese War of 1904-05 precipitated an economic and political crisis that uprooted additional inhabitants of the Pale. Furthermore, many Jews came here to avoid unwelcome
service in the army of Czar Nicholas II. Prior to the abortive Russian
Revolution of October 1905, many of the Jewish intelligentsia remained
in Russia in the hope that conditions there would improve. However,
after the failure of that revolt, a new group set sail for America. Some
were learned and pious, others were disillusioned revolutionaries, and
many were dedicated Zionists. Another factor in increasing the rate of
immigration was the drastic lowering of steamship fares. This, joined
with the fact that by 1905 many of the first wave of East Europeans were
in a position to send for their relatives and friends in the old country,
also boosted the number who landed at Ellis Island. In Berlin, the Hilfs-
verein der Deutschen Juden was organized to help the uprooted escape
from the Romanov tyranny. To keep the stream moving, this organization
established hostels at rail junction points so that few fell by the wayside
but were assured of a night's rest on their way to the German seaports.
The Hebrew Immigrant Aid Society, organized in 1902 through the influence of the Independent Order of B'rith Abraham, received the wan-
derers on this side of the water and facilitated their entry into their new
homeland. HIAS, as it was familiarly called, helped the Jewish immigrants to gain lawful entry, and once here, it gave them immediate aid
in the form of dockside service, saw them to their destination, enabled
them to find relatives or friends in strange cities, and later helped them
find employment and take out citizenship papers. Five other organizations beside HIAS also helped settle the new wave: the United Hebrew
Charities of New York, the National Council of Jewish Women, the Baron
de Hirsch Fund, the Clara de Hirsch Fund, and the Industrial Removal
Office.[19]

Of these groups, the Industrial Removal Office was perhaps the most
successful. Organized in 1901 by the Jewish Agricultural Society (which
had been created by the Baron de Hirsch Fund), it labored valiantly to
ship refugees out of congested New York City. The immigrant in New
York was given a ticket to some inland city, one week's board, and tools
so that he could establish himself as a mechanic. Working in the hinterland, IRO kept in touch with its clients through local agencies and its
own travelling agents. The newly Federated Jewish Charities of Buffalo
joined IRO in 1904, and within one year 125 new arrivals were sent to
the Queen City. Although immigrants frequently claimed relatives in
Buffalo, the records of the Federation reveal that less than half of these
new arrivals were supported by their kinsmen. Thus, the burden of support fell largely on the entire community. Although, all in all, IRO han-

dled about 100,000 cases, there was a great psychological opposition to dispersion among the immigrants, and the overwhelming majority chose to remain in eastern seaboard cities. Nevertheless, a great many fresh Jewish immigrants came to Buffalo in the early years of the present century. And most of these arrivals were drawn as though by a magnet to the William Street settlement where they added to the clutter and confusion of that already crowded neighborhood.[20]

From the youngster on the street to the aged patriarch in the home, Jews of the William Street ghetto now faced almost insurmountable problems. There were many, many children in its overcrowded houses and they had no place to release their boisterous spirits. Buffalo then had no public playgrounds; but the situation was somewhat eased when Public School No. 31 on Emslie Street provided a convenient one in 1900. Principal Herman DeGroat, a progressive educator, opened his schoolyard for recreation before classes, at the noon period and on Wednesday afternoons. In addition to promoting health and organized play, Dr. De-Groat hoped to stop dice games, street fights and other acts of juvenile hoodlumism. Soon, the Society for Beautifying Buffalo formed a Playground Committee, with Moses Shire, the well-known lawyer, as a member. Such facilities gradually increased, but the lack of sufficient recreational areas long remained a pressing municipal problem.[21]

In this atmosphere in which there were no decent play outlets for children, many youngsters got into trouble; but worst of all, ordinary cleavages between parents and children widened dangerously. Often a stern, worried, sadly muddled and over-worked father tried to reconcile Jewish tradition with the American slum milieu. Even the mothers, who were generally more understanding and more persuasive with the young ones, tried, it is said, "to heal the unhealable." There were great temptations to vice in the form of poolrooms and street gangs that infested the neighborhood, and even the best families did not offer the rising generation sufficient attractions to cause them to stay close to the fireside. Miss Cecil B. Wiener of the Buffalo Federation remarked in 1910: "When, for reasons known to all, they are compelled to seek their recreations in the saloons, poolrooms and streets, we can only wonder that so few go wrong." She noted to the credit of Jewish girls under such circumstances, that of twenty-two cases of juvenile delinquency handled by the Federation that year, not one was a girl.[22] Some of the boys, however, were so wild that they had to be committed to Father Baker's. One can imagine the double worry for an Orthodox parent: not only to have a delinquent for a son, but to have him sent to a Christian reform school!

In addition to difficult social conditions, the William Street community faced unfortunate economic conditions. In the first place, the average family size among Jews was about twice that of other Americans.[23] Immigrants ordinarily had as many children as the Lord sent them, for birth control was then largely unknown and the very concept was frowned upon in Orthodox circles. Furthermore, Jewish families of this period tended to be swollen because they often included aged parents and elderly relatives. The migration of the day was by and large a family affair and, in the new country, the elders were often unable to find any employment or else were incapable of adjusting to America. They consequently fell back for support on sons and daughters already overburdened with a large brood of children.

A second cause for economic embarrassment was religion. Most of the William Street inhabitants were genuinely Orthodox, or else tended to be more rigid in observance than some of the earlier arrivals. A fair proportion of them, two generations ago, refused to work on Saturday or on the Holidays. As a result of this observance, many Jews peddled junk, for in that type of employment they could suspend their activities on the Sabbath without too great financial hardship. But in other trades, the suspension of work two days a week opened the observant Jew to too much competition. In addition to these obstacles, Jews were particularly vulnerable to the persistent recessions of the American business cycle. In the Panic of 1907-08, for instance, peddlers, hucksters and small market dealers were hit especially hard because their customers were laid off and could not buy. Even the Buffalo weather conspired to make life hard for peddlers, and in snowy winters junk men earned as little as two or three dollars a week.

In those days, large corporations and department stores, seldom employed Jews. Unlike the peasant Slav immigrants, Jews were not inured to hard labor, for they often arrived from Russia with inferior physiques. Moreover, a great many of the newcomers came here proficient in no particular trade. They therefore had to be absorbed in the economy as factory workers, store clerks, peddlers, or as day workers. An unskilled laborer usually earned from $8 to $11 a week, and on this wage he was sometimes obliged to support as many as eight dependents. All too often, however, there was not enough work to go around even at this Scrooge-like pay. Furthermore, many of the arrivals were misfits. In small Russian towns, Jewish men often studied while their wives worked to support the families. Many who had led this cloistered life in the old country could not adjust to the American way of life and became charges of their families or of the community.[24]

Accidents and sickness forced many a family into impossible economic straits. The tuberculosis rate, although somewhat lower among Jews than among similar groups, was still shockingly high. Mothers were worn out by the age of forty from constant childbearing, and often they were widowed by natural death or accident and left to support a large family. Industrial machinery was dangerous and there were, until 1913, no binding industrial compensation laws in New York State. To cite a specific case, David Feldman, of 17 Watson Street, was killed by a falling beam, and he left a wife and seven children ranging in age from one year to twelve. There was no compensation, for the corporations seemed habitually to win such lawsuits. This particular family was helped by an Aid Society that met at Star Hall, Broadway and Pratt Street, for the purpose of taking up a collection.[25] Soon, such cases were to be handled by the Federation; but pending its formation, a widow and her children had to depend upon the charity and thoughtfulness of neighbors who were usually in only a slightly better condition than the recipients of their largesse.

Those old-fashioned winters were bitter, and it was a problem to get coal to keep the family warm. Miss Wiener once wrote in desperation: "Such a winter as this, experienced by many, should add thousands to the ranks of the socialist and even the anarchist." [26] Much of the relief was devoted to meeting on-the-spot emergencies; the death of a peddler's horse was a major catastrophe, and a funeral was a stark tragedy. When some Jewish girls complained that they could not live on $4 a week, their employers slyly suggested that they get "a friend." "If tenement house regulations were properly enforced," it was observed, "if factory and labor laws were not wherever possible evaded . . . then we could do away to a large extent with Charity and Relief." [27] Year after year, Miss Wiener reported the sordid facts: "Dark, damp rooms, in unsanitary surroundings; bad environment, through the supplementing of income by the keeping of boarders; lack of delicacy, lack of privacy, wrecked nerves, by constant worry and overcrowding, loss of health by underfeeding, malnutrition. . . . Oh, for a place where some of these little ones might be taken for three or four times a year for building up and strengthening." [28]

Not a pleasant picture, indeed! And the wonder is that out of all this economic misery so little crime actually arose; for most of these people, in spite of their adversity, fought their way upward and established decent, respectable families who later became the backbone of the Jewish community.

One of the persistent, non-economic problems of the William Street neighborhood was the nuisance of missionaries. Jews, themselves not members of a proselytizing religion, never could understand missionaries and always, even the heterodox, resented them. Probably the first of these settlements was the Buffalo Hebrew Mission, at 280 Hickory Street, which was conducted by the Buffalo Baptist Union. These evangelists worked from house to house and emphasized things that would attract children, going even so far, it was said, as to lure with lollipops. The people whom they sought to convert detested their methods, for among other things, they held Friday night services to make their missions more attractive. They were not discouraged with only an occasional convert, and they once claimed to have converted two Jewish women who, they said, had to conceal their new religion for fear of being ostracized. By 1923, the Mission was spending over $6,000 a year. Four years later, the Kuell Memorial Hall of the Hebrew Christian Mission was dedicated at the Hickory Street site of the old Buffalo Hebrew Mission.[29]

More important than these direct-pressure groups was a type of concealed influence that existed despite the work of the Sisterhood of Zion. The underprivileged children of the area were constantly visiting Christian-sponsored settlement houses and play classes. At 155 Cedar Street, stood the Memorial Chapel Social Center. Erected in 1887, this building was a project of the Lafayette Avenue Presbyterian Church and was originally intended to function as a Sunday school. In time, however, it became a settlement house, and many recreation-starved Jewish children drifted there for scouting, music, domestic arts and even for a Daily Vacation Bible School. English classes were three-quarters Jewish, and seven groups organized for children were said to be entirely so. Although there was no direct, or even subtle, attempt to convert these children, Jewish leaders were concerned, for at one time hundreds of Jewish children were in one way or another affected by this settlement house.[30]

With the tidal wave migration of the pre-war era, came certain family problems, and Buffalo shared with the rest of the country in one of the most serious of these problems—wife and family desertion. In 1910, Henry Weill, president of the Federated Jewish Charities of Buffalo, said what everyone knew to be true: "Wife desertion is anything but an uncommon occurrence." [31] Because of the European habit of early marriage, the young husband, lacking funds for all, often came to America first, intending to send for his dependents as soon as he had earned the passage money. Either for romantic or economic reasons, some of these husbands forgot their Old World vows and married anew in a strange country. The situation was pathetic, for, according to Orthodox law, the man must tender the wife a religious divorce; it cannot be granted by anyone else. Accordingly, women stranded in Europe were doubly handicapped, for even if they did not want them back, they had to locate their husbands in order to secure a Jewish divorce if they were to mend their lives through a new marriage. One Jewish newspaper of the day, the *Jewish Daily For-*

ward, printed a "gallery of missing husbands" to help locate these philanderers.[32]

The desertion problem was, fortunately, only a temporary aberration caused by the mass exodus, for Jews, generally speaking, were not prone to desert their loved ones. Against those who did desert, however, action was vigorous, and by 1915 there were no more local cases of missing husbands.[33]

Such were some of the conditions that faced the newer immigrants in Buffalo in the Edwardian Age. Uptown, there existed the older community of Jews who had already fought their way through their own peculiar problems and who now formed an established and stable society. But the total Jewish community of the time was divided in a sense that the young people of today can scarcely imagine. As a step toward bridging the gap between East Side and West Side, there came into being the organization that is now known as the United Jewish Federation of Buffalo, Inc.* It all began with the consolidation, in 1903, of the old German philanthropic societies; and gradually, as the community matured and as the old stocks mingled with the new, almost all non-synagogue functions in Buffalo were united under the leadership of a single organization.

This tendency toward consolidation was by no means peculiar to Buffalo. Throughout the country similar movements rose indigenously in almost every major city. Gradually cities began to combine their charities in an effort to avoid duplication of effort. The Federation of Jewish Charities in Boston, however, was the first attempt made to cut across boundaries and establish a community-wide organization in order to avoid duplication in charity fund raising. Four years later, in 1899, the National Conference of Jewish Charities of the United States was founded. Its objective was national cooperation in handling inter-city transient charity cases, desertion, and an attempt to cut down the tuberculosis rate among Jews. Simultaneously, there was a parallel movement all over the United States towards greater consolidation in industry and finance. The Jewish efforts reflected, therefore, the general American picture.[34] Of these Jewish combinations, C. Bezalel Sherman, of the Labor-Zionist Organization of America, has remarked: "By one of the ironic twists with which Jewish history is replete, German Jews who denied the Amer-

---

* Since its founding, this organization has been known by many names. From 1903 to 1918, it was called the Federated Jewish Charities of Buffalo. From 1919 until 1949, it was known as the Jewish Federation for Social Service. Unofficially in 1948 and officially in 1949, this group merged with the United Jewish Fund of Buffalo, Inc., an emergency overseas relief organization, under the name of the United Jewish Federation of Buffalo, Inc.

ican-Jewish community a secular *raison d'être* also supplied the most important architects and builders of Jewish institutional life outside the synagogue. They failed to draw the logical conclusions from the fact that Jewish religion, even if interpreted in broadest universalist terms, accentuated Jewish distinctiveness." [35]

Locally, there was already in existence a Hebrew Board of Charities, probably an extension of the old Hebrew Benevolent Association of Civil War days. This was a union of Men's and Women's Benevolent Societies with a membership drawn principally from the Beth Zion group. Leopold Keiser was president; Rabbi Aaron was vice-president; and Leopold Rothschild, a wholesale liquor dealer, was secretary. The board met twice a month at 49 Chapin Block and lay workers, since there were no professionals, did the chores. By the turn of the century, this organization included the Sisterhood of Zion and a Ladies' Sewing Society. Since it operated on a budget of only $2,000 a year, obviously much relief was handled by other, non-affiliated groups.[36]

As the old century gave way to the new, the leaders of Buffalo Jewry began to talk about the advantages of consolidation. They were rapidly tiring of endless fairs, lotteries, raffles and subscriptions, often for the same cause, and they had taken notice of the success of the local Charity Organization Society. Moreover, needs were multiplying rapidly as poor Jews poured into the city. Finally the 1903 Kishineff pogrom provided the last motive for organization of the non-synagogue activities of the city, for renewed czarist terror promised to send even more exiles and voluntary immigrants to these shores. A mass meeting was held at which tentative plans for union were drawn up. A resolution was drafted which condemned the inefficiency of too many organizations doing the same thing and upheld the need of unity to draw more financial support. It was resolved to create the Federated Jewish Charities of Buffalo.[37]

Several people had already begun preliminary investigations which anticipated public action. Young Eugene Warner, who had written a bachelor's thesis at Harvard on charity federation, joined with Miss Cecil B. Wiener to perform the necessary preliminary leg work. Mrs. Marcus Spiegel, president of the Sisterhood of Zion, hearing of the attempt to federate in Cincinnati, sent for the plans already drawn up in the Ohio city. She studied this draft and then discussed it with other groups in Buffalo. By September 1903, after months of meetings by the delegates representing constituent organizations, a constitution and by-laws were ready.[38]

The beginnings of federation in Buffalo were modest but effective. Four organizations, all with strong Beth Zion ties, were the first to come in: the Men's Hebrew Benevolent Society, the Women's Hebrew Benevolent

Society, the Ladies' Sewing and Aid Society, and the Sisterhood of Zion. The purpose of the Federation was "to secure the harmonious action of the different Jewish charities of Buffalo, to provide means for furthering the educational and charitable work of its members and for such purposes as will tend to raise the poor beyond the need of relief." Membership was limited to those Jewish groups with benevolent, industrial, or educational objectives, and each constituent society retained its individual autonomy. A Board of Governors, composed of representatives from each group, was established, and officers were duly elected. Membership dues were set at $10 a year, and all money collected was to be placed in a joint fund from which allocations were to be made to the constituent groups. In order to prevent duplication of effort and encroachment upon the central office, units were required to have special permission before making any attempt at fund raising or accepting legacies or gifts.

Headquarters for the Federation were set up at Zion House, 456 Jefferson Avenue. Early committees included Executive, Finance, Relief, Education, Removal Work, Law, and Maternity. These, in turn, were made up from the constituent society most interested in the particular aspect of the work to be performed by each committee. Thus, the men's division helped in fund raising, administration and relief, whereas the women's division volunteers were known as "Friendly Visitors" to the poor. The Ladies' Sewing and Aid Society distributed clothing, and the Sisterhood of Zion extended recreational and educational assistance to the teeming East Side.[39]

The first president of the Federation was Julius L. Saperston, (1865-1909), or "J. L." as he was affectionately known. After spending some time with his brother Willard in California, Julius returned to spend his last twenty years in Buffalo. Before becoming president of the Federation, Saperston had headed the Men's Hebrew Benevolent Society. As president, he was very active, even to the extent of visiting the poor himself and maintaining a bench at his clothing store (at Main and Seneca) where he could talk to his "clients" of the Federation. Although he specialized in the manufacture of pants and uniforms, he made countless coats for the children of the poor. This good man hated the word *investigation,* for he thought the term had no place in a charity that sprang from the heart.[40]

At first, only several hundred out of a Jewish population of 10,000 became Federation subscribers. The organization was very weak: its treasury was empty and it had no home of its own. Like the states and the federal government in the early days of the republic, there were differences of opinion concerning the amount of autonomy still to be retained by the individual societies that made up the new union. "What money they had," it was later recalled, "had been gathered in the main from bazaars, suppers, entertainment, and this method of revenue the new [Federation] constitution forbade." [41]

The Federation originally relied on its Finance Committee to raise funds; but it soon turned to an annual appeal on the eve of Yom Kippur. This *Kol Nidre* appeal, however, was effective mainly in Beth Zion, with little coming in from other synagogues, partly because of latent suspicion and hostility and partly because of poverty.

Growth continued to be slow. The Board of Governors was fearful of new ventures lest opposition diminish the number of subscribers. Its activities were considered by its critics to be too parochial, too greatly limited to the interests and outlook of Beth Zion (members of the Federation out of long habit spoke of the rabbi of Beth Zion as "our rabbi"). There was still rivalry among constituent societies, despite the fact that members of one group were sometimes members of another. Gifts were small; the largest in 1905 was that of the contractor, Eli D. Hofeller, who donated $200.[42] But despite these obstacles, some progress was made, for in that same year the Young Men's Hebrew Benevolent Society and the Young Ladies' Hebrew Benevolent Society were merged and admitted to the Federation. There was still no paid staff; and in the following year the Buffalo Federation could raise only $8,741, of which almost one-third came from a single benefit performance. Expenditures in the same year exceeded income; and it became apparent that, to avoid raising money in other ways, the Federation would need at least $9,000 a year in subscriptions.[43]

It was not scarcity of funds, however, that presented the greatest obstacle to the growth of the Federation; it was the attitude of the downtown masses that slowed, like a great counterweight, the progress toward union. Undoubtedly, the majority of the East-European Jews looked askance at the Federation in these early years. Part of their opposition arose, of course, from the fact that those most active in the Federation were of the Reform persuasion. Partly, too, they opposed the organization because it was controlled and run by the Germans, and these "Deutchuks" were most often the bosses in the establishments that hired and fired the East Siders. Besides, many of these people disliked unity on general principles. They knew to their sorrow that, in Europe, the police state produced what unity there was. Now these new immigrants relished the freedom—almost anarchy—of America. Why should they desire to reestablish even Jewish communal tyranny? It took them some time to realize that liberty always has to be reconciled with order, so that any government or community may survive.

Furthermore, these newcomers had their own organizations that had been established to meet their own immediate needs. The rather loose and careless structure of these groups reflected the eastern European outlook and cultural tradition. Principal among these organizations was the Jewish Aid Society. Charles Polakoff of Beth El, Harry Harriton, Sundel J. Holender and Henrietta I. Tucker, later a well known New York social worker, were the chief functionaries of this relief-giving society. As early as 1906, there was a move by President Saperston to federate as many of the East Side societies as possible, but the talks proved abortive. Sundel J. Holender (1883-1929) later emerged as the principal spokesman for the Jewish Aid Society. This short, compact, affable man did much to knit the community. He was loved by all and was known as "Sunny," a name that fitted him well. Born in Augustov, Russia, he had come to Buffalo at the age of nine and worked his way through the local Law School. Holender was a natural leader and a great interpreter of differing values, and he often lectured effectively before Jewish organizations. Through his marriage to Estelle Weil, of a German Reform family, he was able to see both sides of the cultural picture. Widely admired, idealistic rather than materialistic, Sundel Holender led a devoted life as a public servant to all the Jewish causes of the city of Buffalo. His premature death deprived the community of one of its most resourceful leaders.[44]

In 1909, the Jewish Aid Society was in financial trouble, and Federation leaders sat down once more with members of the Society in an effort to iron out common problems. A merger of sorts was effected, and the following members of the Jewish Aid Society were subsequently appointed to the Federation Board of Relief: Miss Henrietta I. Tucker, Solomon Morrison, Mrs. Saul Rubenstein, Mrs. Wolf Pincus, Isaac Hoenig and Charles Polakoff.[45] The Jewish Aid Society continued as a separate constituent agency of the Federation for many decades until it was absorbed into the Jewish Family Welfare Society of the Federation.[46]

Even with the absorption of the Jewish Aid Society, the victory for consolidation was only partial. The Buffalo Jewish Mothers Club, the Gemilut Hasadim, the Jewish Fresh Air Camp, the Old Folk's Home, the Hachnosat Orhim, remained outside for many years, some until the 1950s. Despite these holdouts, however, the merger with the Jewish Aid Society was a landmark, for from that time on the Federation was indeed a combination of all Jews, not just of uptown organizations. Even the Beth Zion overtones of the Federation gradually gave way. In 1910, only four of thirty-five members of the Board of Governors really represented the newer immigrants. Five years later, however, the following spokesmen for non-German Jews sat on its Board: Rabbi Max Drob of Beth El, Harry Harriton, David Ruslander, J. L. Davis, Isador Setel, Sundel J. Holender, Isaac S. Given, Samuel Cristall and Samuel Liebeskind.

Of this group, Isaac Given (1872-1941) had an especially outstanding career. Born in New York, he later moved to Chicago where he grew up. He was the brother-in-law of Louis L. Berger, founder of the only large Jewish-owned downtown department store in Buffalo, L. L. Berger, Inc. Given had been in business with his brother-in-law in Toledo, Ohio, and together they came to Buffalo in 1905. Given soon demonstrated his leadership abilities on both the business and community levels.[47]

The Federation was now in fairly good financial condition and raised more money than it thought necesary to expend for relief and education in any one year. In 1911, with $30,700 on hand for building purposes, it was formally incorporated, so that it could acquire property and receive bequests. These anticipated gifts were not long in coming.[48]

Meanwhile, the professional staff of the Federated Charities had begun to develop. In the nineteenth century, as a direct inheritance from the Puritan tradition, there was fairly general belief in the American ethic: if one would but work hard, fear God and pursue good habits, these would almost invariably lead to personal success. Conversely, if a man failed, it was his own fault or his destiny: he either had bad habits or else he was lazy or dissolute. By contrast, as poverty gradually came to be considered a social rather than a moral disorder, social work came to be professionalized case work. Although thorough-going professionalism did not come into full practice until many years later, there were early tendencies in this direction. As the Jewish relief problem became greater and more complex, voluntary lay aid proved to be insufficient to meet the situation. In time, the modern idea evolved that lay people should set the policies for large-scale organizations like the Federation, but that professional social workers should carry out the programs.

In the days when the Federation was a novelty, volunteer "Friendly Visitors" furnished by the Women's Division worked on a case-by-case basis. They were trained for their duties by the local Charity Organization Society in special classes which met on West Tupper Street. But this system soon broke down for a complex of reasons: the press of family and social affairs withdrew many from the ranks of volunteers, although some, like Mrs. Emil Pollak, were very faithful to their charitable tasks. It was, furthermore, difficult to control or supervise lay volunteers, and sometimes they lacked understanding of the people they were striving to help.

In an effort to set up a more closely knit organization, Mrs. Emily L. S. Elkus was appointed Superintendent of the Federated Jewish Charities in 1905. This lady, then a young widow and the daughter of Samuel Seidenberg, assumed when she was less than thirty years old, the responsibilities of directing volunteers, keeping the Federation records, and running the central office. Nevertheless, the tradition of lay workers who still thought that charity workers need only be dominated by altruism continued strong. Mrs. Elkus soon found that she had responsibility without adequate authority. Not only did the board make policy, but it insisted on interfering in actual cases. All this confounded confusion, and Mrs. Elkus resigned after less than two years of service.[49]

A turning point in the Federation's history came when, in 1908, Miss Cecil B. Wiener succeeded Mrs. Elkus. Daughter of the pioneer settler Magnus Wiener, Miss Wiener was a native of the city she was to serve so long. She was first educated by private tutors, and then she attended Central High School. Following her graduation from the University of Buffalo Law School, she practiced for five years with the celebrated firm of Shire and Jellinek. Later, she opened her own office and for a time enjoyed the distinction of being one of two women members of the Erie County Bar Association.

Perhaps more than any other individual, Miss Wiener was responsible for the growth of the Federation. She knew both the East Side and the West Side: in a word, she knew Buffalo Jewry. Rabbi Kopald called her "the Jane Addams of Buffalo," and to some of the immigrants on the East Side she was the "*Stadt Mutter*" ("City Mother"). She early realized that to deal with immigrants one must understand them and their frame of reference, and she set out to comprehend these things. She had been secretary of the Federation, but in 1908 she became General Manager. Interested in social work on a city, state and even a nation-wide basis, Miss Wiener over the course of the years amassed a wealth of knowledge about such fields as desertion, tuberculosis, housing, playgrounds and settlement work.

As General Manager, Miss Wiener ran the Relief Department and also some recreational activities. She was not only an employee of the Federation, but she also served as a member of its Board of Governors, and it is sometimes difficult to differentiate between her duties as a policy maker and as an executive. In 1940, she became Executive Director of the Federation and served in that capacity until the first professional director, Arthur S. Rosichan, arrived five years later, at which time Miss Wiener retired after a lifetime devoted to the Federation.

This vibrant woman could not expend all her energies in the great tasks she performed for the Federation. At various times she was treasurer of the Professional Women's Club, member of the Political Equality Club, member and chairman of the Municipal Civil Service Commission, active on the Social Welfare Board, and a crusader for women's suffrage. She was president and director of the Buffalo Chapter of the American Association of Social Workers, a member of the committee that organized the Child Welfare Board of Buffalo, a member of the Buffalo Federation of Settlement and Social Workers Club. As if all these accomplishments were not enough, this indefatigable lady successfully campaigned for election on the Democratic ticket. She served as First Judge of Children's Court from 1933 to 1938, during which time, just to keep her finger on the pulse of Jewish activities, she became president of the Jewish Family Welfare Society, a unit of the Federation. She thus became the first woman in the Niagara Frontier area to be elevated to the judicial bench. In 1959, the Inter-Club Council of Western New York named Judge Wiener "Woman of the Year." [50]

During the earlier part of her Federation career, Miss Wiener had two able lieutenants who also served as Buffalo agents of the Industrial Removal Office. The first of these men, Dr. Isaac Sernoffsky, was a graduate of the local medical school and later specialized in ophthalmology. He has been well described as a "keen and original thinker, with profound convictions, outspoken in his view, socially minded and trustworthy." [51] When Dr. Sernoffsky left for Vienna to pursue post-graduate study, he was succeeded by Harry L. Lurie. One of the most skillful social workers in the Jewish field, Mr. Lurie did an outstanding job in Buffalo until wartime conditions forced the IRO to close its local office. His departure was a great loss to the Federation, for he was to rise to national prominence in his chosen profession. [52]

In those tranquil years before the Kaiser War, much of the work of the Federation was devoted to relief among the immigrants in the William Street area. One major obstacle to full community effort was the difference in attitude between the old-timers and the Americanized Jews toward charity. The former looked upon charity as a *mitzvah*, an exercise of personal piety. Consequently, they gave freely to any itinerant *schnorrer*, even though the recipient might prove unworthy, because it "was still a *mitzvah* that entered into the reckonings of the world to come." The latter, on the other hand, influenced by the then popular doctrines of Andrew Carnegie and his "Gospel of Wealth," viewed charity through American eyes as an instrument of reform and amelioration. Hence, they wanted to methodize philanthropy; they sought to eliminate the chaos of a multiplicity of relief organizations; they tried to dispense alms in such a way that the recipient would be urged to develop confidence and to become a good, self-supporting citizen of his adopted land.

One of the early aims of the Federation was to prevent Jews from becoming public charges. Statistics testify to the efficacy of the Federation in accomplishing this worthy purpose. [53] Such unquestioned success was the result of a great deal of work and expenditure, for each year the

Federation budget for relief grew larger and larger. Transients who flocked into the rail hub of Buffalo were processed and either temporarily aided or directed toward employment and permanent homes. By 1910, for instance, the Federation handled 419 applications for aid, and administered 103 actual cases. Money was advanced for the purchase of coal, to pay gas bills, to supply shoes and clothing, and even for burials.[54] For the impoverished immigrant, municipal licenses were major problems. At the turn of the century a pushcart license cost $10 per year, a one-horse vehicle permit cost $25, and even a handwagon license cost $2 a year. Although these sums seem bagatelles today, they were serious obstacles for impoverished men, and many of them tried, because of circumstances, to circumvent the law. One problem led to another, and the Federation had to help those who ran afoul of the law by dodging the payment of these fees.[55]

In summing up the problems that the Federation had to face in its first decade, Miss Wiener reported: "None of our people are creatures of light or joy when they come to us; if we could weave the fabric of their lives into a tapestry visualized for you, you would shut your eyes, and never would you wish to see again the endless misery, unhappiness, sickness, grief, misfortune, wrong, death and evil portrayed in warp and woof of every shade of gray and black." To face the growing demands upon her time and energy, Miss Wiener said that she needed the patience of Job, the wisdom of Solomon and the diplomacy of Machiavelli.[56]

In addition to the actual dispensation of charity, the Federation devoted itself to educational work among the new immigrants. Initially, a Sunday school was established at Zion House. Such a school was necessary, for Orthodox synagogues of the day were not equipped to give the children of the neighborhood adequate religious instruction. The first superintendent was Louis E. Desbecker, the lawyer and political figure. He was succeeded by another attorney, Morris E. Greenberg, who, in turn, was followed by a businessman, Charles Pollak.[57]

By 1909, the school had 297 registered students with an average Sunday attendance of about 120. The next year, the school got a new lease on life when Samuel J. Harris, later Supreme Court Justice of the Eighth New York Judicial District, succeeded Mr. Pollak as principal. Mr. Harris found five grades in which Hebrew, biblical history, and religion were taught. Hitherto, there had been many complaints from the sponsors of the school because of low registration, and from the parents of the pupils because of its strong Reform emphasis. Mr. Harris, learned and devout in matters Jewish, did much to satisfy the critics of his school. He established eight grades, took vigorous steps to increase attendance and to enrich the curriculum and thereby made the subject matter more interesting than it had been. Assisted by Miss Rebecca Brezen who came from a traditional background, he introduced visual aids, provided suitable maps for teaching biblical lore, and furnished his teachers with up-to-date texts and other suitable materials. School picnics and meaningful celebrations of Jewish holidays now graced the annual program.[58]

In the early days of Harris's superintendency, the children ranged from six to fourteen years of age. On the whole, they were drawn from the Orthodox *shuls* located nearby, with the Jefferson Avenue Synagogue having the largest representation. Most of the pupils probably received additional Hebrew instruction at a synagogue *heder* or at the Talmud Torah, for the Zion House Sunday School remained an English-speaking school that Americanized as well as Judaized.

By 1913, the Zion House school was so crowded that some of the classes were held at the conveniently located Jefferson Avenue Shul. The next year, however, the new Jewish Community Building was opened at 456 Jefferson Avenue, and there was a resultant increase in registration. Enrollment climbed to 700 and the school was renamed The Jewish Community Religious School. A good kindergarten had already been established under the direction of Miss Florence Oppenheimer. In the best progressive tradition of the day, a PTA was established, and plans were laid for a student self-governing council. At the dedication of the new Jewish Community House, Mrs. Moses Shire announced a gift of $1,000, the interest of which was to be used for an annual "Moses Shire Memorial Prize" to the outstanding student of the school.[59] As a move to appease lingering traditionalist opposition, a Hebrew School was opened under the direction of a trained pedagogue, Sidney Marcus. However, the emphasis on St. Valentine's Day and other non-Jewish celebrations must have caused some misgivings among Orthodox parents, some of whom were very obdurate and looked on the school as a step toward conversion, if not to Christianity, certainly to Reform Judaism.[60]

At the same time that Buffalo Jewry was enhancing its system of religious education, it, like other cities in the land, was actively engaged in an intensive Americanization program for the immigrants. Today, no longer faced with a torrent of foreigners, reflective Americans believe in cultural pluralism, that is, that each national or racial group has certain values to give to the United States which, in the interest of all, ought to be preserved. But in the Progressive Era there was a genuine fear of being overwhelmed by alien cultures, and most men reasoned that the best safeguard against such a possibility was a speedy acclimation of the newcomers.

In certain Jewish circles, this fear was strengthened by another dread. The German Jews felt that the more rapid the process of Americanization of the newly arrived Russians, the less would be the danger that these strangers would engender anti-Semitism. Oscar Handlin has noted that the German Jews shared the prevalent notion that the "essential forms of American culture were already fixed, and that it was the task of the immigrant simply to assimilate those forms." Hence, the "Mayflower Jews" demanded, not only "an appreciation of the institutions of this country," but also "absolute forgetfulness of all obligations or connections with other countries because of descent or birth." [61] Naturally the new immigrants who had a cherished Jewish culture of their own refused to acquiesce in this program. Tensions increased between the two groups when the East Side citizens felt that the advances were aimed against their traditional way of life. Frequently, the patronizing air of would-be benefactors was met with resentment and even hostility.

In Buffalo, part of the urge toward Americanization was a result of the backwardness of the public schools. In the final two decades of the nineteenth century, although the population more than doubled itself, few new plants were added, while those schools already in existence were sadly inadequate. Adjustable desks were lacking; ventilation was inadequate; fire hazards existed, especially in the annexes; all schools were overcrowded.[62] For the Jewish immigrants in the East Side "New Jerusalem," elementary school conditions were especially bad. Although most of these children did not go on to high school, there was a fair sprinkling of Jewish matriculation in the several secondary schools.

As part of the Americanization program, civics courses were introduced both to the public schools and to private classes for the immigrants. The reforms of the Populist-Progressive Age sought to destroy the tacit alliance between Big Business and corrupt politics. The study of civics at this time thus became part of the program to restore control of the government to the people. Furthermore, since the great political machines in the cities were supported largely by immigrant votes, it was felt that to give the newcomer a good understanding of American government might help to break the power of the bosses. Not only were the would-be citizens introduced to the intricacies of democratic statecraft, but they were also oriented to the current pattern of the American dream; thrift, hard work and the equation of cleanliness with godliness.

By 1908, Miss Theresa Rosenberg was conducting English classes with about a dozen students in attendance. She also taught citizenship to students who were sometimes so poorly clad that they dared not venture out on cold nights. Gradually Zion House was converted to a social center where, in addition to English and citizenship, sports and calisthenics were taught, good clean recreation was provided, and sound reading habits were inculcated through the provision of good books, "thus enabling the foreigner to become one of us." [63] The Sisterhood of Zion later employed two English instructors who taught classes the year round, and sponsored a Citizens Club which met at the settlement house.

Not all citizenship education was under Jewish auspices, of course. Because of the high percentage of foreign born in the city, Buffalo's leadership in this movement was recognized even before the term *Americanization* had been coined. The modern night school system is said to have started there in Public School No. 31 in the heart of the Jewish district. By 1914, thousands were studying English and the principles of American government in night schools. Seven years later, Buffalo had more "lighted schoolhouses" than any other city in the Empire State including metropolitan New York. These evening sessions, which served about 18,000 students, were designed to be social centers where old and new Americans could meet, for there were always some native-born men and women who wished to enhance their meager learning.[64]

In the meantime, Independence Day of 1915 was celebrated by a "Newly Naturalized Citizens' Committee," on which Emanuel Boasberg, Joseph B. Block and Louis E. Desbecker were active. In that same year, an attempt was made to organize a "Jewish Citizens' League" with meetings at the Talmud Torah and the Jewish Community Building, but the group proved to be ephemeral. A Civic Education Association was in operation with Dr. Isaac Sernoffsky, who had long been associated with immigrant problems, as one of the directors. As part of the 1917 war effort, Mayor Louis P. Fuhrmann named a City Commission on Americanization with Rabbi Louis J. Kopald of Beth Zion as chairman. In the postwar decade, to celebrate their golden wedding anniversary, the Edward and Matilda Warner Fund for Promoting Americanism was founded, and for a full generation this fund financed declamation contests on American themes at the Jewish Community Building. As immigration declined and formal oratory went out of fashion, the contests were abandoned.

From all this education in patriotism, happy results were not always forthcoming. One of the saddest aspects of this period was the growing hostility between Jewish parents and their children. Dr. Sernoffsky commented on the widening breach between Old World parents who "retain some or most of their inculcated characteristics from abroad," and their offspring. The oldsters often found "solace in the synagogue," but the children of the new generation were foot-loose and fancy-free. "The interests of one," he said bluntly, "cease to be the interests of the other and both suffer." [65] Often youngsters who had become

Americanized came to despise their parents because they were foreigners. This was a great factor in loosening the Jewish ties of a generation whose own children were to reverse the trend because by the time they matured they took their American nationality for granted and did not look down upon the synagogue as an alien importation. Meanwhile, however, a disproportionate number of the second generation turned to economic radicalism as a sort of substitute value system for organized religion.

It was during this trying period of cultural adjustment that the Talmud Torah (Buffalo Hebrew School) was founded. Until the public school system was well established in the first half of the nineteenth century, Jews in cities larger than Buffalo often maintained day schools which combined secular and religious education. After this type of school disappeared, three variants of purely religious education developed. The first was the congregational school, similar to those of Beth El and Beth Zion in Buffalo, which were conducted primarily for the children of members. Another type was the private *heder,* a Hebrew school usually operated by one individual. In Buffalo one of these *hedarim* was conducted by Rabbi Aaron Joseph Bloch (1861-1935). Rabbi Bloch, a great talmudical scholar and saintly in character, was born in Volkovisk, Lithuania. He came to Buffalo in 1889 and started a private *heder* on Clinton Street. Although Rabbi Bloch's methodology would today be considered almost hopelessly antiquated, many middle-aged Jews of Buffalo owe their present knowledge to the solid biblical foundation that they received in his *heder.* Almost too unworldly to handle American children, Rabbi Bloch nevertheless remained somewhat active until he retired in the 1920s.[66]

A more progressive private *heder* was that of Morris Diamond (1860-1944). Diamond was educated in Lomza, a famous European seat of Jewish learning. Before crossing the ocean, he spent some time in Dublin, Ireland, where he learned fluent English. He arrived in Buffalo in 1889 at which time he established his own *heder.* Later he taught at the Talmud Torah which he helped to found, as well as in many synagogues. An outward conformist in religion, he was much influenced by modern Jewish writers who reflected the influences of the East-European Haskalah. Although he was a life-long scholar of the prophetic parts of the Bible and knew the old exegesis, he was acquainted with and influenced by modern Bible criticism. Many Buffalo men received a sound Hebrew education from this gifted teacher.[67]

The third type of Hebrew school to emerge was the Talmud Torah, or communal school. The idea of a community school with a strong emphasis on Hebrew was tried out in New York and Chicago and gradually spread to the hinterland. These schools were set up by public-spirited citizens to compensate for the deficient congregational schools of the day. Although they often bore the stigma of being charitable institutions, these schools were usually forward-looking and their curricula frequently showed the influence of the eastern European *Heder Metukkan* (progressive type of Hebrew school). Imbued with the spirit of Jewish nationalism, they early began to stress Hebrew as a living language.

By 1891 there was local agitation for the establishment of a free Hebrew school open to all. The Orthodox *shuls* just could not handle the situation. Hence, poorer parents, unable to afford private instruction, were confronted with the choice of sending their children to Zion House, which stressed Reform, or else letting them grow up ignorant of their religious heritage. On May 9, 1897 (fifty years to the day after Beth El had been founded), a meeting was held to moot the possibility of setting up a Talmud Torah. A committee was appointed and quarters were rented from the Jefferson Avenue Shul. Instruction seems to have continued there until the committee purchased for $8,000 from the trustees of the Buffalo Police Pension Fund an old fire house at 323 Hickory Street near Broadway. To convert the L-shaped building to a school an additional $5,000 was spent.[68] This Talmud Torah building became a real "lighted schoolhouse," with its lamps burning almost every night in the week, for it housed various Zionist groups, the Gemilut Hasadim, and many other organizations of the newer immigrants. The first non-synagogical edifice of the Orthodox Jews, it served, in its day, as an embryonic Jewish Center.

The Buffalo Hebrew School was incorporated "to provide an education for children of Jewish birth of the City of Buffalo, New York, to charge tuition fees for same; also to admit and teach children without any fee." The first president and one of the prime movers in founding the school was Harry Harriton, who had come to Buffalo in 1884 from the famous Orthodox stronghold of Berditchev, in the Ukraine. Harriton's Buffalo Jewish interests were very broad. A pioneer Buffalo Zionist and charter member of many worthy institutions of his day, he was one of the men who helped bring the East Side charities into the Federation, and for fifteen years he served on its Board of Governors.[69]

The Talmud Torah opened its doors on Hickory Street late in 1904. Within two years, there were 287 students, four teachers and nine classes. Boys paid tuition of one dollar a month; and girls, for some strange reason, paid one dollar and a half a month; and the poor were admitted free. The principal was Charles Blumenthal who had been brought here from Toledo. School was in session six days a week from 3:15 until 8:00 p.m. Younger students attended for one hour and older students for two hours a day, and classes continued for most of the summer.[70]

In 1909, the principal was Rabbi Abraham Geller who had received a Ph.D. from the University of Breslau and had studied at New York University and Columbia. By that time there were 400 students and also a Sunday school, conducted by Miss Henrietta I. Tucker assisted by seven teachers, which probably operated to offset the attraction of Zion House. The Buffalo *Express* called it with pardonable exaggeration "the finest institution in Western New York." Although the daily curriculum had a strong Hebraic emphasis, there were classes in Yiddish for those whose parents demanded it. To accommodate children in the Fillmore Avenue neighborhood that was then growing, a branch was opened in that vicinity. Relations with all Orthodox synagogues were said to be excellent, for the Talmud Torah spared the expense of running individual congregational schools.[71]

In the stirring years of the Wilson Era, the Talmud Torah had two teachers who were destined to become nationally famous. Ephraim E. Lisitzky, born in 1885 in Minsk, was to become the celebrated Hebrew poet of New Orleans. The other scholar was Hillel Bavli (b. 1893)—then known as Price—who received a B.S. degree from Canisius College while in Buffalo. He left the city for the Jewish Theological Seminary in New York where he became one of its distinguished professors.

Following World War I, Israel Swados (1862-1936) emerged as the virtual dictator of the school. Born in Kovno, he had received a good education and had taught in some of the more progressive Lithuanian Hebrew schools. Swados came to Buffalo early in the century and, for a time, was a teacher at old Beth El on Elm Street. He was a great fund raiser and if, because of his imperious manner, he was the terror of the teachers, he got the proper results.[72] Operating expenses at the time were about $12,000 a year, and although there was a paid staff, much of the work was still done by volunteers. Soon the school began branching out into post-high school education open to qualified students.

In the 1920s, the school ran into financial difficulties. The building by that time was old and in need of repair. A general appeal was made to provide modern quarters, but it failed in its ultimate goal. It was pointed out during this 1923 drive that the institution stood opposite "those snatchers of souls," the Hebrew Christian Mission. During that year, 275 pupils filled eight classes and were taught by four teachers. The Sunday school provided for 250 students and was conducted by ten teachers. Despite this healthy registration, the school was beset by money troubles until the Federation began generously to subsidize it about 1925.[73]

Eighteen years later, the school moved from Hickory Street, when that property was sold, and after a short time on Monroe Street, it moved to 206 North Park Avenue, where it now functions under its devoted principal, Samuel Israeli.

Another institution that dates from the first decade of the century is the Jewish Fresh Air Camp. In the beginning, a few haggard Jewish children were sent to the Fresh Air Mission of the Charity Organization Society at Cradle Beach near Angola. As time went on, the Federation, through its constituent organization, the Young Ladies' Hebrew Benevolent Association, became increasingly aware of the summer needs of East Side youngsters.[74] Initially there were many difficulties involved in sending children away from the city. Kosher food was a problem and parents did not want their young ones to spend their vacation weeks in a non-Jewish atmosphere. Hence, for several years, a separate Jewish camp was maintained on the Canadian shore of Lake Erie. Finally, in 1908, the Young Ladies' Hebrew Benevolent Association leased an abandoned hospital at Athol Springs on the American side of the lake, and here was established the Jewish Fresh Air Camp. Although this organization maintained a separate existence for twenty-eight years. Federation authorities always selected the children who most needed summer camp. Later, thanks to the establishment of the Eli D. Hofeller Fund, thirteen acres of land were purchased near Angola and this property was leased to the Jewish Fresh Air Camp for ninety-nine years.[75]

For a long time this camp was operated as a charity, staffed by volunteers who went to Angola in turns to give the children proper supervision. Frequently, Jewish teachers on summer leave contributed their time and skill. By 1920, they were caring for about three hundred youngsters, with girls going out for the first part of the summer and boys for the final month of the season. A fortnight prior to Labor Day, wearied mothers, together with their infants, were sent to Angola for a rest.

Although the camp was of great service to the under-privileged, occasional voices protested its summer programs of scout lore, bird hunts, basket-weaving, dramatics and sport contests. Was there no room, some asked, for Jewish content? Time, however, was to remedy this defect. In an effort to eliminate one more independent appeal for funds, the Jewish Fresh Air Camp was taken over by the Federation in 1936. In the decade that followed, the need for a charity camp gradually disappeared while the demand for a pay-as-you-go setup mounted. By 1947, there was Camp Lakeland, a community camp on the Angola site, designed to service children drawn from all segments of Buffalo Jewry. Under the new name, group activities enriched with Jewish content were emphasized as well as the sports and hobbies so dear to the hearts of American boys and girls.[76]

During the colorful days of President Theodore Roosevelt, Buffalo Jewry split over the desirability of a Jewish "Y". From the 1850s, as we have seen, there had been sporadic but persistent efforts to establish such an institution in Buffalo. In parts of the country, however, the movement flourished and in the hectic days of the maximum Jewish immigration it might have accomplished much had it not been impeded by several factors. Unfortunately, some of its leaders had patronizing airs and looked down at the new immigrants whom they nevertheless earnestly tried to help. Another obstacle to establishing the Jewish "Y" on a firm basis was competition from similar Christian organizations. These latter groups always seemed to have better musical evenings, better dances, better reading rooms and better facilities in general than the Jewish groups. Finally, the Panic of 1893 killed the national group, the United YMHA of America.[77]

When the "Y" movement caught new breath with business recovery, it interested itself in the Americanization of immigrants, and thus enjoyed a new *raison d'être*. The German Jews no longer needed its services, and in city after city branches fell into the hands of second generation eastern Europeans. For these people, the institution filled a genuine need which derived from the lack of dynamic religious leadership and good social institutions. The new "Y" of this period often served as a place of refuge for foot-loose adolescents, for its clubhouse offered cultural outlets not to be found in the downtown synagogues and other immigrant organizations.

Locally, the "Y" was beset by special obstacles that were to hamper its growth until the eve of Pearl Harbor. We know little of the group that met in a Walnut Street house in the 1890s, but certain it is that this "Y" was not a direct continuation of the older organization of the previous decade. From the scattered records that remain, it is apparent that both its officers and members were recruited from the younger members of the East Side social circle.

As the old century ended, the Buffalo "Y" placed increasing emphasis on the popular cult of self-improvement. Its members sponsored a Literary Club, promoted oratorical contests, arranged musical evenings, presented dramatic productions and engaged in athletic contests. For instance, to celebrate Hanukkah, 1900, the "Y" presented a farce entitled *That Rascal Pat*, and a dance at Morgan Hall. At their meetings local rabbis were invited to speak on Jewish problems.[78] The president at that time was a young attorney, David Ruslander (1873-1940). As a boy, Ruslander had worked on a farm and went only as far as the third grade in a country school. After his family moved to Buffalo, David went to North Clarendon, Pennsylvania, to become a tailor. Later, when he decided to enter professional life, he came to Buffalo and entered the law firm of Walter G. Smith and Aaron Fybush. Despite his lack of formal schooling, he completed a two-year course at the University of Buffalo in one year, and was admitted to the bar. For nineteen years, he taught the law of wills at the University of Buffalo, and for years he was a national figure in B'nai B'rith. In 1913, Ruslander was among the 100 outstanding members of B'nai B'rith who constituted the first Executive Committee of the Anti-Defamation League.

It is not certain whether or not this "Y" of Spanish-American War days had an uninterrupted existence. At any event, in 1915 it re-organized for another start with an appeal for new members. By this time the group was meeting in the newly built Temple Centre of Beth Zion.[79] This appeal, which brought in among others the rising young attorney Israel Rumizen, was not the solution to the problem, for the group never quite succeeded in its purpose. Jack Yellen, speaking shortly after the Armistice, called the "Y" a shadow. He went on to say: "Sectional jealousies and differences have fostered the establishment of small organizations among the Jewish youth of this city, based on narrow social and economic lines." [80] Actually what Yellen was charging was the simple fact that some Federation leaders opposed the whole idea, and were fostering a rival organization at the Jewish Community Building. Although the "Y" had 800 members at the time, it could not support a building and the Federation would not back one. By 1920, the East Side youth had fought for almost a generation without avail for the establishment of a recreational center. In that year, Jack Yellen, David Diamond, and Samuel B. Darlich bravely set out to get several thousand new members. Bitterly they charged that "Buffalo Jews, living east and west of Main Street have been thus rending each other and keeping aloof from one another from time immemorial." The "Y" ironically was dedicated to a unity that some did not want. "Men of Buffalo," went the rallying cry, "you are either with us or against us." [81] All of this is another way of saying that, despite the cohesive influences of World War I, the old cleavages persisted until the Great Depression and the Nazi terror finally welded the community together.

Meanwhile, with the energetic David Diamond as president, the men's and women's "Y" groups temporarily united in a gigantic drive for expansion. Much work was done by the secretary, Harry A. Freedman, for many years a probation officer, but the effort failed, and the Jewish Young Men's Association (the same as the YMHA) withdrew from the Jewish Community Building and, simultaneously, membership in the women's branch dwindled.[82] The Jewish Young Women's Association, with no home of its own, became inactive and was not revived until the 1930s.

As a result of the failure of the Jewish "Y" to achieve its major goal, many Jews joined the YMCA.[83] Samuel Leff, the field secretary for the Jewish Welfare Board, tried in vain to drive these facts home to the local officials of the Federation in 1924. He stressed with prescience what the pending close of immigration would do to the old settlement philosophy so dear to the hearts of certain Buffalo Jews. But the Federation wanted to enlarge its Jefferson Avenue plant, and all that it would promise was to back a "new Jewish Center building as soon as a more organized demand for such a center is expressed." [84] Hence, the Buffalo "Y", facing competition from the newly formed Young Men's Club of the Jewish Community Building, was almost moribund. But a few hardy souls led by Samuel B. Darlich, David Diamond, Jack Yellen, Edwin J. Gerstman and Harry A. Freedman, kept the center idea alive. Boldly they proclaimed, "we do not intend to QUIT until our mission is accomplished." They had struggled, they said, for a score of years, and they vowed to continue the good fight.[85] But the group carried on in vain, and by 1930, only a corporal's guard of active members retained serious hope in the future of the movement. The final victory of these hardy souls, however, belongs to the chronicle of the Jewish Center of Buffalo and must be reserved for a later chapter.

While educational and recreational problems were being argued, the national labor movement was gathering strength, with Jews often playing leading parts. Jewish interest in unionization, which reached its apex half a century ago, was entirely a product of the post-1881 immigration, for the earlier arrivals had never formed a distinct Jewish proletariat. A fair percentage of the newcomers, however, were skilled workers and these men naturally turned to collective organization. Furthermore, many of them had been villagers in Europe, but here they became urbanized and it was the cities that spawned strong labor organizations. The Jewish labor movement, however, unlike other examples of unionism, built from the top down, with the leaders organizing the workers. Jewish workers had the advantage of a tiny but dynamic coterie of commanders who had been trained in the Russian Bund (the Jewish Social Democratic Party in eastern Europe) or, like Samuel Gompers, had been oriented to the English type of unionism. With the notable exception of Gompers, Jewish labor leaders generally regarded unionism as an instrument in the fight against the capitalist system. The United Hebrew Trades, dating from 1888, was a pioneer attempt to organize the Jewish proletariat. Here and in similar organizations, the more revolutionary-minded leaders eventually lost out to more conventional men who, like Gompers of the AFL, were willing to co-exist with capitalism.[86]

The Jewish labor movement was particularly cursed with division. Two contradictory trends must always be kept in mind. One part of the group was militantly assimilationist and viewed participation in purely Jewish organizations as a betrayal of Socialism. On the other hand, another segment cherished a modern secular form of Yiddish culture and wanted to use their unions to obtain for the workingman a place in Jewish affairs. As the Jewish labor movement began to take shape during the decade that preceded Sarajevo, it branched into three paths:

1. The predominantly Jewish unions, principally in the needle trades;
2. The Workmen's Circle (Arbeiter Ring); and,
3. The Socialist groups under the leadership of Abraham Cahan, long-time editor of the *Jewish Daily Forward*.[87]

Adherents of the first group were not active on the local scene, although some unions did have, as we shall see, many Jewish members. More interesting in the history of Buffalo, however, is the Jewish participation in the remaining two segments, both of which stood politically left of normative unionism. The sordid conditions of the William Street ghetto, where laborers eked out a bare existence, afforded the radicals their opportunity to establish a limited but effective influence. Immigrant Jews, it should be recalled, had a double adjustment to make, from Europe to America and simultaneously from a village to a city environment. Many were forced to do manual labor since that was the only way in which they could be absorbed into the burgeoning American economy of the day. As laborers, however, they were exposed to the taunts and prejudices of the Irish and German foremen who did not like cheap labor in general and Jews in particular. It is therefore not surprising that many were attracted to Socialism as the promised answer to all their problems. Although the total number of Jewish revolutionaries is said to have been small, there sprang up all sorts of Jewish radicals: Socialists of one variety or another, about five varieties of anarchists ranging from peaceful to violent, dogmatic Comtian positivists, and pipe-dreaming Utopian reformers. Even before the Communist-Socialist split of 1919, various schools of Marxian Socialists fought bitter internecine wars. It was natural that men so imbued with a sense of mission should use unionism to preach social and economic revolution and that they should use Yiddish as the medium of their propaganda. At first, the earliest Jewish radicals opposed purely Jewish unions, for such a concept ran contrary to their assimilationist philosophy. Later, however, for opportunistic reasons, they reversed themselves and fostered Jewish unions. One contributing factor to this *volte-face* was the anti-Semitism then rampant in many of the older unions. In time, labor unionism became a great factor in Americanizing the Jewish immigrant. It helped prevent a demoralization that otherwise would have come with sweatshop and tenement conditions; it gave its adherents a sense of belonging; it taught them the values of discussion and provided them with practice in ballotting and democratic procedure which they did not know in Europe.[88]

In the Buffalo of the 1890s, an organization of radical Jews seems to have been headed by Albert Goldman, a packer who lived at 386 Hickory Street. This group was affiliated with the left-wing Socialist Labor Party and had a score of active members. These earnest men, who were called "comrades," banded together under the motto, "Let there be light." Soon, this particular section of the Socialist Labor Party became non-partisan in an effort to stop the quarrelling and bickering that marked the incessant debates over the respective merits of anarchism and Socialism. To promote ideological neutrality, the group redesignated itself the Social Democratic Club, and its new emphasis was to be upon recent scientific advances with lectures by "Comrades" Weinstein and Reinstein. Goldman was elected secretary of the reorganized group, with Boris Reinstein (1866-1946) corresponding secretary, and Morris Cohn, librarian.[89] Reinstein had been born in Rostov-on-Don. He came to the United States about 1891 and, after a brief period as a homesteader in the Dakotas, headed east and was graduated as a pharmacist from the University of Buffalo. Anna Mogelova (1866-1948), his non-Jewish wife, had been born into the Russian nobility. She was a physician who practiced gynecology in Buffalo until her death in 1948. Both were Socialists, but they became increasingly inactive in their later years.[90] Back in 1893, however, the young firebrand, Abe Cahan, future author of *The Rise of David Levinsky*, came to Buffalo to address the Social Democratic Club, and "Comrade" Reinstein went to Chicago to represent Buffalo at the Socialist Congress held in conjunction with the World's Fair. In order to move closer to the heart of the Jewish section, the club rented Schwetzer Hall on Broadway at Mortimer Street. There they met every Sunday evening, sponsoring classes in English, disseminating the Socialist point of view, and urging that the Jewish problem be settled along Marxian lines, that is, amalgamation into the general proletariat who would, when they came to power, erase all racial and nationalist lines.

The following year, Abe Cahan returned to Buffalo, this time to address the group on "Unionism and Socialism." Other speakers lectured on topics congenial to the society, such as "Why the Jew Should be an Internationalist," and "Socialism as Messiah." Active in the club at this time was Nathan Sussman of 429 William Street, through whom brochures on Socialism were obtained from a source in Brooklyn.[91]

Meanwhile, the foundations of the Arbeiter Ring had been laid in New York City. A group of workers banded together to unite "by a ring of friendship every worker in the land, and with many links unite the workers of every land." The members of this alliance soon split into two camps. On one side, stood the unabashed assimilationists who thought that all creeds, nationalities and races would soon be drowned in the sea of Socialism. On the other, stood the Yiddish culturalists who wanted to preserve a non-religious, non-Zionist culture in the Diaspora by promoting Yiddish. Eventually this second group came to dominate the organization.[92]

In 1900, the national Jewish workingmen's group was re-organized, and at that time it officially became the Arbeiter Ring or Workmen's Circle. An organization devoted to spreading the social gospel to the worker, it also included, as did other fraternal orders, sick and death benefits. An Educational Committee was set up, and later the Arbeiter Ring opened a tuberculosis sanatorium at Liberty, New York, which lasted for forty-four years.

The Arbeiter Ring in Buffalo dates from June 21, 1903, when fifteen men met and elected Sol Kissin secretary. Following a later "mass meeting" at 1112 Broadway, the group decided to affiliate with the New York outfit and became Arbeiter Ring Branch #29. Here, as elsewhere, all varieties of leftists flocked to the new organization, and though there were many ideological differences, members were in general agreement on three points: (1) they were inclined toward the new Socialist Party of Eugene V. Debs that had been organized in 1900; (2) they wanted a mutual benefit society in addition to adherence to long run Socialist aims; (3) and most of them, at least in the beginning, leaned toward assimilation.

The local group stressed self-improvement and education. Schwartzmeyer's Hall at Sycamore and Broadway was rented for lectures in English and Yiddish, with the first address given by the clothing merchant Louis Slotkin who spoke on the subject of "Socialism and Religion." Many non-Jewish Socialists spoke to the group. The members were strongly influenced by the social theories advanced by Abe Cahan in his *Jewish Daily Forward*. Although they expelled members who voted either Republican or Democratic, they made a religion of democratic procedures in their meetings, with referendums on every imaginable subject.[93]

The Workmen's Circle soon set up its own "Socialist Library." Located at William Street near Monroe, the library was open from nine in the morning until late at night and was entirely independent of the Buffalo Public Library or any Jewish group. In the reading room, since there were almost no funds, were shelved books donated or lent by individuals. The periodical room kept files of leading Russian, American and Yiddish papers. A small theater group, led by one Mme. Labul, was formed and met at the library every Tuesday evening. This group was very fond of Yiddish drama as well as the works of Ibsen, Gorky and Tolstoy. Sometimes they even brought New York Yiddish plays to Buffalo. Each member was taxed to maintain the Jewish Socialist Agitation Bureau and the library distributed the effusions of Eugene V. Debs who was brought to Buffalo for a lecture.[94]

More Jewishly conscious than other Arbeiter Ring members, were the Diaspora nationalists, glorifiers of the Yiddish language, who were led by Chaim Zhitlowsky (1865-1943). He, as director of education for the Arbeiter Ring, was really the father of the *Folk Shule* idea, and after World War I, began working on a national scale, training teachers and publishing texts in Yiddish. Zhitlowsky, like the famous Jewish historian Simon Dubnow, held that the struggle for survival and not religion had kept the Jewish people alive. He was, therefore, anti-Zionist and argued for an active Jewish group here in the United States that would preserve its particular identity through the medium of a Yiddish folk culture.[95]

Before Zhitlowsky's ideas led to the establishment of a *Folk Shule* in Buffalo along non-Zionist lines, the Poale Zion had already entered the field of elementary education. In one form or another, a Labor Zionist Yiddish school existed in Buffalo from World War I until its doors were closed by the Great Depression. Then, in 1937, the local Arbeiter Ring established a school to purvey its own philosophy to the younger generation. The school, which lingered until Korean War days, was the last secularist, non-Hebraic educational institution in the city.

Long before, however, the arrival of the post-1905 immigrants had greatly strengthened the Arbeiter Ring. Some of the new members were European Bundists, some were assimilationists, some were Labor Zionists, and others were extra-territorialist Nationalists who advocated the establishment of a homeland somewhere outside of Palestine.[96] But in so limited a circle as Buffalo, these splinter groups could not survive independently, and they therefore found a common, but often uneasy meeting ground in the Arbeiter Ring. Gradually the Buffalo branch became more intellectually flexible, going so far in 1909 as to raise money to mourn the death of the Yiddish playwright and reformer, Jacob Gordin, despite the fact that he had been an outspoken opponent of Abe Cahan.

The local minute books reveal that ideological tempers often ran high. Civil war broke out between the moderate followers of Cahan and the extremists who read and absorbed *Der Arbeiter*, an organ that spread the doctrines of the "creative" Marxist, Daniel De Leon. Despite the fact that the conservatives dominated in New York, the more radical group in Buffalo generally outvoted the Cahan "conservatives" (who later evolved into peaceful Socialists). This confllict ended in a truce, with the emphasis shifted from politics and economics to cultural and educational affairs. After 1917, the outright Communists (the old De Leon group) tried to take over the national organization as well as the locals, but they gradually lost out and by 1930 the struggle was over, with the Socialists in firm control.[97]

In the interim, the local Arbeiter Ring met a crisis by forming a co-operative. In 1910, at a time when bread was in fact rather than in fancy the "staff of life," Buffalo Jewish bakeries raised their prices. Branch #29 had observed the cooperative movement in other cities of the United States and decided to apply the lesson they had learned by forming a cooperative bakery. The project was led by Jacob Miller, Jacob Morrison, Sam Brody, Benjamin Porent (a former Polish underground anti-Russian revolutionary) and that old stalwart, Sol Kissin. The cooperative functioned for about two and a half years, and it forced the commercial bakers to lower their prices. Eventually, because it was badly managed by amateurs, the workers' bakery was forced out of business.

Then the unexpected happened. The commercial bakeries, motivated by a desire for revenge on those who had bought the co-op bread, closed down their shops for a time. When Jewish women rose in violent protest and stormed the bakeries, a public scandal threatened. Representatives of the Workmen's Circle approached the East Side communal leader, Harry Harriton, and Ephraim Lisitzky, the principal of the Talmud Torah. The bakers were summoned to a *Beth Din,* and as a result of the trial, Harry Block, leader of the bakers, was fined $50 to be donated to the Jewish victims of World War I. As a result of this action, the bakeries opened their doors again at the regular prices, and the incident was peacefully settled.[98]

At about this same time, the Buffalo needle trades were organized as a result of a strike. Of all related trades here, including the cap makers and the men's tailors, the highest Jewish concentration was in the production of women's garments. Most of this manufacturing was done, prior to 1914, in small shops with store fronts for the sale of the product. Usually the employers and employees were Jewish, although there was a sprinkling of Poles, Hungarians and Italians in this business. Even these non-Jews, so heavily did the Jews dominate the industry here, picked up the language of their fellow-workers and it was not an uncommon thing to hear an Italian crooning a Yiddish ditty. The hours of work were unbelievably long, from 8:00 a.m. until 7:00 p.m. The pay was very low, with no overtime, except perhaps with an extra quarter in the $3.00 weekly pay from a generous employer during the rush periods that preceded every holiday.

In addition, there was always the garment industry's "fifth season"—the slack season when there was no work and, of course, no pay.

Consequently, when a professional organizer came to Buffalo from New York City to unite the workers in the garment industry, he was enthusiastically received. This unionizer secured a job as tailor to support himself while he propagandized for a strike, for he refused to accept money from the union. Thus he won the respect of both sides and formed a satisfactory local. A strike followed; but it was soon settled, for the bosses, many of whom remembered their own bleak days at the sewing machine, were ready to negotiate with the newly formed union.[99]

Not all of the activities of the Jewish proletariat were concerned with political or labor agitation. In 1917, the Arbeiter Ring purchased its own cemetery land. Because many of the members were religiously unaffiliated and they ordinarily did not want to be buried in Christian cemeteries, this organization in practically every city in which it existed bought burial ground. The Workmen's Circle joined with the Anshe Emes Congregation (the little Hickory Street Shul) in the cemetery venture, for they both were poverty-stricken organizations.[100]

In addition to the radical labor organizations, many other non-synagogue groups sprang up in Buffalo during the high noon of the William Street area. All of them were established to serve a need or to fulfill some purpose. But even when these needs had been eliminated, there was a tendency for the organizations to linger on. At the turn of the century, duplication in social organizations was the order of the day in American-Jewish communities, then so divided by place of origin and conflicting ideologies.

No one is quite certain of the founding date of the Hachnosat Orhim, a sheltering home for transients. We do know that Henry Tasman, a member of B'rith Israel, was active in the late 1890s in this home, as was Isaac Singerman. For many years, a short gray-bearded man named Eli Abramson was secretary, and Max Swerdloff and Max Fagin were ardent supporters of the project. Fagin (1880-1945), a barrel and bottle manufacturer, was long a prominent participant in all Orthodox ventures.

The Home of Shelter was located for many years at the rear of the Talmud Torah. There wayfarers were sheltered and fed while they paused to rest on their way to a new home or a new job. The Home was usually run by the janitor of the Talmud Torah, the first of these being Abraham Chasin whose wife, Alice, later opened the well-known delicatessen at 942 Elmwood Avenue. Some of these transients were professional *schnorrers* and others were *meshulahim*, solicitors for rabbinical academies all over the world. The worthy project was supported for years by donations, sustaining memberships, bazaars and appeals in synagogues.

An early president of the Home of Shelter was Joseph M. Kronman (1871-1933). Kronman, who is said to have spoken seven languages, found an outlet for this talent in his business. With Henry Land, father of Professor Adelle H. Land, he operated a steamship ticket agency and thereby helped many immigrants send for their friends and relatives. By 1920, partially as a result of Kronman's efforts, the Home was caring for about 200 men a year, providing them with a night's lodging, a bath and two meals. Not only were transients housed and fed, but would-be settlers were cared for until they could get located and find permanent jobs. In later years, the Home was known as the Buffalo Hebrew Sheltering Home, Inc.; and in the Eisenhower decade it was still functioning at 491 Hickory Street where it moved after the Talmud Torah left the vicinity.[101]

Much more vigorous and active than the Hachnosat Orhim was the Hebrew Benevolent Loan Association. During the years of heavy immigration, the need of an organization to grant loans speedily and without interest was great. Many small tradesmen, who could not get credit from the banks and who did not want charity, looked to this Gemilut Hasadim for financial assistance.

The Hebrew Benevolent Loan Association was founded in 1897 at the home of Saul Rubenstein. Mr. Rubenstein (1859-1949) was born in Kalet, Suwalki Province, and in 1880 followed his brother, Louis W. Rubenstein, to Buffalo. The younger Rubenstein, Saul, was a big, strong, bearded, earthy man who had a zest for living that marked his personality until he was almost ninety. He was engaged in many businesses, among them operation of an agency on William Street that sold steamship tickets to immigrants who wished to bring over their families. He prided himself on the fact that he was a *hazzan,* and he performed free of charge in this capacity all his life. An inveterate joker and seller of all sorts of tickets for benefits, he was once sitting in a car parked in a no-parking zone when a policeman came up to give him a ticket. Instead, he sold the policeman a ticket to a benefit!

Other founders of the Loan Association were Morris Balber, Harry Harriton, Aaron Cohen, Morris Pincus, Enoch Schulgasser, Isaac Feldberg and Moses Shapiro. Also active was Henry Land (1873-1913) who was one of the very rare Jews who had attended a university in Poland. A reliable source says that the real inspiration came from Morris Diamond who raised $700 as an initial loan fund.

The Loan Association, which was incorporated in 1899, was necessary to offset the pawnbrokers and loan sharks who plagued the East Side with usurious rates of interest. Especially important during recurrent business recessions, it was anxious even in good times to lend money for specific purposes: to help a peddler replace a horse that had died, or to pay for a funeral. It especially liked to help indigents become self-supporting. "The aim is solid citizenry not charity," said its brochure.[102]

For many years the headquarters of the Hebrew Benevolent Loan Association were at the Talmud Torah. It began by lending up to $25 without interest and later doubled the limit. Most business was conducted in the evenings and on Sunday mornings, the office being staffed by volunteer workers who checked on the applicant and his endorsers.

By the early 1920s, the Loan Association was helping about 125 persons a year and lending out about $10,000. Its income was derived not from interest but from a modest membership dues, donations, picnics and raffles. In order to grant loans to all worthy applicants, it was often necessary for the Association to borrow from banks and individuals. During the Great Depression, the Gemilut Hasadim kept many Jewish families from becoming public charges. During that debt-ridden decade, with a capital fund of about $32,000, it at times had more than twice that amount out on loan. Often the men would meet on Sunday mornings to approve loans, and then on Monday the officers would privately approach generous-minded individuals for money without interest, a practice that it always followed when the Association was temporarily embarrassed for funds. Even during hard times, few loans (less than 5%) had to be made good by endorsers.[103]

In 1947, the Gemilut Hasadim celebrated its golden anniversary by honoring its first president, Saul Rubenstein. At that time, Meyer Shapiro was serving as president of the Association, and Alex Yenoff was vice-president. The Association took the occasion to promise that there would be no more service fees and that all future income would come from dues and donations.

After the Talmud Torah moved to North Buffalo, the organization had several homes before settling down at the Jewish Center. In later years, its board was composed of forty members, three of whom were at headquarters every Sunday in rotation. One of its greatest benefactors and the Association attorney for many years, Maurice Yellen, worked for one dollar a year and put in countless hours at headquarters. The Hebrew Benevolent Loan Association well fulfilled the biblical precept: "If thou loan money to my people . . . thou shalt not lay upon him [them] interest. . . ."[104]

Another method of catering to the financial needs of the individual that found popularity with Buffalo Jews was the credit union. In time, virtually every synagogue except the very old ones established such facilities. In addition, many loan associations were independent of the synagogues, especially the *Landsleute* groups that combined credit with sick and death benefits and recreational activities. These clusters, made up of people from the same places of origin, seem to have had their start in what have been called the *Landsmanschaften* (Mutual Benefit) Societies. Devoted to relief and aid for their members, for decades they helped friends and kinsfolk in the old country, perpetuated memories and culture of the homeland, and relieved the monotonous existence of hard working immigrants by providing social outlets.

To the first generation and perhaps to their children, the *Landsleute* groups were of vital importance, but to the youngsters born in America they had relatively little appeal. Some of these associations lingered on, slowly fading into non-existence. Others that adjusted to the changing needs of the people survived longer. One way of adjusting to the needs of a newer day was to convert a social organization that had outlived its usefulness into a credit union. The First Warsawer Lodge Credit Union dates from 1913. The East Buffalo Credit Union, organized in 1927, later affiliated with the Ahavas Achim-Lubavitz Synagogue. There was also a Roumbespod Unterstitzung Verein, originally designed to help *Landsleute* in Roumania, Bessarabia and Podolice. (In 1954, it was still in existence but functioned as the Roumbespod Credit Union.) [105]

Other organizations were formed, some of which lasted and some of which did not. In 1903, there was the Roumanian Verein; in 1913, Buffalo inhabitants from Sokolovka formed the Ustingrader Unterstitzung Verein; and two years later, came the Hungarian Social and Benevolent Association. There were also a Minsker Verein and a First Austrian and Galician Association of Buffalo. In the 1930s, this group merged with the Liberty Social and Beneficial Club. Charles Etkin (1892-1959), one of two Jewish undertakers in Buffalo, was president of the first group which had its own cemetery on Pine Ridge Road. It is not, perhaps, accidental that the other Jewish undertaker, Nathan Mesnekoff, chose to be a member of the latter organization, the Liberty Social and Beneficial Club. Somewhat belatedly, the combined organization changed its name to the Mount Carmel Lodge of Buffalo, Inc., despite the fact that a ladies' group already had pre-empted that name. *Landsleute* ties were obviously going out of fashion. [106]

Meanwhile, in order to meet the needs of the immigrants crowded in the William Street area, other social institutions flourished. There was the Zuleika Grotto of the Mystic Order of Veiled Prophets of the Enchanted Realm. Some East Side Jews even joined the Improved Order of Red Men and the Wahcandah Tribe. Some groups were purely Jewish, as was the Buffalo Hebrew Social Club, organized in 1910. Another was the Hebrew Progressive Club of Buffalo, founded "to cultivate the minds of the members to the expediency of adopting the motto of Fraternity."

The members pledged themselves to pursue "Liberty and Justice," and to avoid discriminating between "sect, class or nation as the highest aspiration of life." [107]

Jews have always been concerned with cemeteries, and one of these newly-formed groups was still another burial society. The Holy Order of the Living (not to be confused with the credit union of the same name) was founded in 1909, acquired its own cemetery, and has long operated as the most active Orthodox institution of its kind in the city. Until World War I, however, the perennial problem of interments continued to vex the community. There was, in those days, no Jewish undertaker in Buffalo, and although most East Side Jews patronized Louis Becker on High Street,* the more affluent used E. L. Brady who had established his business in 1882 on Franklin Street.[108] For the staunchly traditional, however, the preparation of the body for burial still remained in the hands of volunteer groups. In Europe, the washing of the body and the shrouding of it had been performed by a volunteer *Hevra Kadisha*. In America, where men were busier and less inclined to help in these matters, burial societies came into being. Often they were attached to congregations; but some were not.

One such society, the Chevra Kadisha Anshe Lubavitz, was founded in 1910. Although attached to the Pratt Street Shul, it was in effect separated from the synagogue, for it had its own officers and trustees. The strictest precautions were taken that Jewish law would be preserved even if the family should insist upon such violations as burial in ornate coffins. All active functionaries of the society were required to be Sabbath observers, and on the 15th day of Kislev the society conducted the age-old traditional fast to beseech the dead that had been prepared for burial in the past year for forgiveness if the members had been negligent in their duty. This fast was broken jointly by the members of the society in the evening after a day of special prayers. The original minutes end with the following expression of quaint piety: "He [God] will banish death forever and remove tears from all faces from all the earth—the Lord has spoken it" (Isa. 25.8).[109]

During the years of tidal Jewish immigration, over three-quarters of Buffalo Jewry lived in the William Street area, and by 1909 it was estimated that ten thousand had come to the city within the previous twenty years. The neighborhood in which they settled centered on William Street, and it was bordered by Michigan, Eagle Street, Jefferson Avenue

---

* Mr Becker had in custody a special hearse, decorated with a Star of David, which was used only for Jewish funerals. This vehicle had been purchased by several Jewish burial societies in the city.

and Broadway. On the fringes of this district, there lived Germans, Italians, Irish, Negroes and Poles. Many of the shops displayed Yiddish signs; and, since Jews brought with them a fondness for delicatessen, there prevailed throughout its streets a mixed smell of sausages of every description, pickled foods and smoked meats. Loaves of bread in bakery windows were braided, for these twisted loaves decorated the tables on the Sabbath and festivals. There was plenty of imported tea available, one of the most popular brands being "Wissotzky tea direct from Russia." William Street itself was the business hub of the ghetto. Its shops were generally small, and only a few of them imitated the glitter and display of the downtown stores. Some pawnshops and second-hand stores with dark interiors and sombre occupants recalled the pictures of the ghettos of Europe. A step below one could see the rag peddlers in wagons or behind handcarts who emerged from the neighborhood and scattered all over the city. A continuous procession of vehicles driven by Jewish provision dealers clogged the congested thoroughfare. The many kosher butcher and fish shops were busiest on Fridays and on the eves of the Holidays. On the sidewalk, bearded men ground horse-radish, and nearby bakery windows displayed huge mounds of rye bread, pumpernickel and bagels.

A contemporary account describes the Jewish section of the day: "With the spring and summer the people fairly live on the corners and doorsteps, crowd the little balconies of their tenements, and, with the inevitable dash of bright color somewhere about their dress, they give picturesqueness and life to the dingy background of cellarways and broken fire escapes." [110] The William Street area of that period was, in miniature, every bit as picturesque as the Lower East Side of New York City. It was most interesting, said an observer, to stroll along William Street on a Saturday evening at nightfall, after "the apathy of the Sabbath" was over. Crowded as the Buffalo East Side was, however, it did not develop the sordid tenement house so typical of New York City. There were a few cold-water flats, but most of the Buffalo families lived in separate houses on tree-lined, grass-edged streets. Only with increasing numbers and poverty did the real over-crowding begin. Most of the Buffalo immigrants began by renting, but they generally tried to purchase a home as soon as possible. Usually such houses were made up of a kitchen, dining room and parlor on the first floor and three or four bedrooms on the second.[111] But, as the ghetto became more and more congested, and the homes began to be occupied by several families, cottages were built in the back yards. Unlike New York, where the expansion was forced to go upward, Buffalo had sufficient room for horizontal expansion.

The United States Immigration Commission surveyed the Jewish section of the city in 1911, and it considered the heart of the "Hebrew district" to be Mortimer Street between William and Broadway. But even here, less than half of the householders were "Russian Hebrews," the remainder consisted of Germans and other foreign-born Gentiles. The Commission did not find the housing conditions too bad in Buffalo, and it conceded that, of all recent immigrants in Buffalo, the Jews had the highest degree of literacy. A high incidence of boarders and lodgers was, however, noted amongst them. The yearly wage for adult males was estimated at $468, and the average family income in the area was said to be only $753.[112]

As the stream of immigrants continued, the ghetto deteriorated rapidly. A competent authority predicted on the eve of World War I that it would soon become a "typical American slum." It could not expand to the west to relieve the over-crowding because "at its upper extreme a large portion of the restricted section dips down and interlocks, holding in check, as it were, its growth in that direction." The front lawns and back yards of the district were disappearing, and the ordinary lot now held several two-family houses, frequently filled with boarders who cut down the living space in each house. The sanitation just reached the minimum standards set by the Buffalo Health Department, and tuberculosis was on the increase as a result of these conditions. "The street life mingles freely with the half-world of vice and crime," noted an observer.[113] Professor John T. Horton has aptly described the times: "The municipality was corrupt. Every one knew it who lived there. Some knew it who lived in other places." Despite the law, saloons were open on Sundays, and only a feint was made at controlling open and unabashed solicitation by well-known prostitutes.[114]

Mortimer, a street that intersected William, was perhaps the most unmistakably Jewish place in the city. Here stood the *mikvah*, and associated with it was a Russian and Turkish bath. "There the tired and dispirited went for a relaxing session to come out glowing and invigorated with a bottle of deep red pop and a corned-beef sandwich." A brawny Jew named Grossman kept a smithy a few doors away; and there before the admiring eyes of children he shod the horses that pulled their fathers' junk wagons. On this street was a Jewish grocery store, Bergman's kosher butcher shop, a *shohet* who slaughtered fowl in his yard, and a family that kept a goat. A man named Mamat kept a dry-goods store there; Isadore Posner sold paint and wallpaper; and the Brody family operated a variety store.

About 1910, Alderman Charles Willert persuaded the city to raze the houses that stood in the area bounded by Mortimer, Spring and Hollister Streets; and there Willert Park was built. Here it was that old Jews sunned themselves while their grandchildren played ball in summer and ice skated in the winter. Many young Jews smoked their first cigar, or on their day off took their first date for a stroll in this park. Boys exchanged tattered Horatio Alger, Nick Carter and Tom Swift books, played cops and robbers, made "scooties" out of roller skates and a soap box, and even made bicycles from parts sought out in the junk yards that abounded in the neighborhood.[115]

At Clinton and Michigan stood Golden Hall, owned by a well-known ghetto character, Rose Goldstein; and here it was that people gathered for weddings, *Bar Mitzvahs,* and other gala occasions. A Yiddish theater was located on William Street, where the "Jewish King Lear" was acted out in Yiddish. This was a very popular play with dispirited parents, for it dealt with the meaningful theme of ungrateful children.

At 12 Spruce Street, Harry Wiener, a one-time waiter at the old Iroquois Hotel, conducted a kosher catering service; and he rented silverware, china, glass and candelabras. In the downtown area, Samuel Altman (1868-1936) established Altman's Buffet, and like many other tavern keepers, was in politics as the G.O.P. committeeman from his ward. Altman subsequently sold out to Paddy Lavin and retired to Los Angeles, where he was among the first to start a Buffalo colony.[116] Samuel Altman was an older brother in a prominent Buffalo family which included Morris Altman, a vigorous community leader, and Harry Altman, of Town and Glen Casino fame.

Isaac Rosen cared for the insurance needs of the people. Born in Russia in 1867, and orphaned early in life, he began at the age of twelve to earn his own way. Soon after his arrival in Buffalo, he entered the insurance business as a representative of the Prudential Life Insurance Company. Rosen introduced these new immigrants to the American type of life insurance, prospered in his work and eventually became superintendent of his area.[117]

The Jewish neighborhood had its own physicians. The more affluent sent for Dr. Hartwig, or Dr. Schroeter, and some even called Dr. Ullman. The poor depended on Dr. Horwitz and Dr. Nathan Kavinoky, or else patronized the public dispensaries. There was also the commanding figure of Dr. Ferdinand Simon. Born in Lithuania, he was said to have graduated from medical school there and to have been apprenticed to a Lithuanian doctor at Kaunas (Kovno). He came to the United States in 1879 and received another medical diploma from a college in Cincinnati. Bearded and formal in appearance, Dr. Simon seemed severe, but he was in his private life quite gay in his manner; and for many years he was a powerful force at Beth El. Dr. Simon, who practiced mainly on Poles and Irish, was said to have had an intuitive flair for diagnosis.[118]

Buffalo Jews of the period read Abraham Cahan's moderately radical,

PROGRESS AND POVERTY   [259

non-religious newspaper, the *Jewish Daily Forward,* as well as *Der Tog*
and the Orthodox *Der Morgen-Journal.* The *Tageblatt (Jewish Daily
News)* was also published at this time. It seems likely, also, that Joseph
Fybush locally published a weekly, the *Jewish Advance,* in the early
1890s; but it proved ephemeral.[119]

In the pre-1914 outpouring from eastern Europe were many old
folks who were no longer able to work and who had no relatives to contribute to their support. The situation was further complicated by the
overcrowding of the homes and the doubling of families. Rooms in which
aged parents once could live were no longer available to them. In addition, the advances in medical knowledge were steadily extending life
expectancy. With the Jewish sick and aged scattered throughout Gentile
institutions, mental depression and bitter disillusionment abounded. The
need for a Jewish home for the aged became increasingly apparent with
the advent of the new century.

On June 13, 1909, a meeting was held at the Talmud Torah to discuss
the problem. Some of the men present suggested a temporary arrangement
that would care for elderly parents who formed part of the heavy immigration of the day, but Mrs. Saul Rubenstein insisted on a larger plan.
She had, she said, the names of fifty women who were eager to pay dues
to an organization that would provide a permanent home for the old
folks. In general, the ladies took the initiative and won out over the more
cautious men who urged further investigation. The slate of officers reflected this victory: for Mrs. Benjamin Kadetsky was chosen president;
Mrs. B. Feldberg, vice-president; Miss Rose Abrahamson, secretary; and
Mrs. L. Goldsmith, treasurer.[120]

Many "founders" have been named for the home, but it is impossible
to recapture the entire story. It seems safe to say, however, that the
project languished for a while after this 1909 meeting, but that new enthusiasm was ignited the following spring at a gathering at the East Side
home of Mrs. Pauline Agranove. At this meeting, Mrs. Simon Kahn, destined to be active in the project for half a century, entered the picture.
Other hard working pioneers in the venture were Mrs. Catherine Rubenstein, Mrs. Rosa Coplon, Mrs. Louis Dautch, Mrs. Elizabeth Goldman and
Mrs. Louis Maisel.

In the meantime, a similar move was under way in uptown Buffalo,
and for several years two groups were trying to accomplish the same
purpose. On September 3, 1912, the rival organizations united as "The
Daughters of Israel Jewish Old Folks Home," and the downtown women
subsequently relinquished the property that they had acquired on West
Bennett Street. The leaders of the reconstituted group were Mrs. Sarah

Rivo, Mrs. Bertha Gilden, Mrs. Isaac Smith, Mrs. Sarah Schaffer, Mrs. Bessie H. Bear, Mrs. Bessie H. Wagner, Mrs. Dora Chafetz and Mrs. Kahn. Although most of the impetus came from the newer immigrants, Joseph B. Block, Mrs. Herbert Guggenheim, Miss Sara Haas and Adolph Winters, all of Beth Zion, also helped.[121]

In 1915, the Daughters raised enough money to buy property at 210 Porter Avenue, and it was repaired and remodelled to house about thirty people. The next year, upon approval by the State Board of Charities, the home was incorporated. At that time, Isaac S. Given, Mrs. Mary Pincus and Mrs. Alexander W. Bohne (1864-1945), who was to be president of the home for six years, lent particularly valuable assistance.[122]

Mrs. Rosa Coplon (Mrs. Samuel Coplon), who had been so helpful in founding the home and in helping it in its early years, died in 1920. Four children survived, two of whom, Joseph and David H., were enterprising furniture merchants on Main Street. In 1922, Joseph, David H. and Philip Coplon gave a surprise gift to the home in memory of their mother, for it had been her favorite charity. This, together with proceeds from the sale of the Porter Avenue property, was used for the purchase of the George Walbridge Miller home at 310 West North Street. After being remodelled to accommodate thirty-two residents, it was dedicated on May 25, 1924. The new home contained a sun parlor, a garden and grounds for strolling, a Venetian fountain, and a chapel located in a room over an arch that spanned the driveway. At the dedication ceremonies, Sundel J. Holender opened the services, and Reverend Bernard Cohen of Beth Zion read the invocation. The daughters of David H. and Joseph Coplon presented the keys of the home to the president, Mrs. Alexander W. Bohne. The memorial prayer for the dead was chanted by the Reverend Bernard Schachtel, cantor of Beth El, and other rabbis and prominent laymen addressed the gathering. The name of the home was officially changed to the Rosa Coplon Jewish Old Folks Home,* and eighteen oldsters moved in immediately.[123]

An annex was built the next year to increase the number of residents that could be cared for. From the first, physicians gave freely of their time, especially Drs. Bernard Cohen, Abram L. Weil, Hiram Yellen, Edgar Beck, I. Sernoffsky, A. M. Gilden and Harry Chernoff, to mention only a few of the many who generously devoted themselves to this cause. Until his death in 1952, Emil Rubenstein lent his service as attorney. Mrs. Joseph Coplon (1878-1951) was also very active in the project for many years.

Two years later, a great membership drive, the first of many, was con-

---

* In 1958 the name of the institution was changed to "The Rosa Coplon Jewish Home and Infirmary."

ducted. Mrs. Wolf Pincus was chairman of the drive which brought in 467 new members. In that year, the State Department of Charities went out of its way to praise the work of the institution.[124]

Another landmark was reached in 1928, when Simon Perlman (1885-1958) was brought from Rochester to serve as superintendent. With the assistance of his wife, Gertrude, whose mother, Mrs. Sarah Rivo, had been one of the founders, Perlman was able to be of great help to the aged with whom he could converse in Yiddish. Mr. Perlman, who served until he retired in 1949, also conducted chapel services daily and on the Sabbath.

Then came the depression, and problems multiplied here as elsewhere. In 1931, Nathan Rovner guided the fund-raising campaign, but the theme was now no longer expansion. Now it was merely "keep the doors open." A little later, with Gilbert M. Finkelstein as General Chairman, the home began a drive for $10,000 with the slogan: "Shall the Doors Stay Open?" [125] There was at this time a great need for expanding the facilities to include a sick bay, for the number of residents had reached over seventy and all but four of them required constant medical care. Work was begun on the construction of a sick bay in 1937. Morris Altman, who already had done so much for the institution, was then president, while Joseph Coplon headed the Building Committee. In the fall of that year the cornerstone was laid for the new addition which was dedicated to Mrs. Max Grossman who, with her husband, had helped the home in countless ways. The following year, the three-story annex was completed at a cost of $22,000.[126]

The home continued as an independent institution during the trying war years when the drain of overseas relief hampered so many local institutions. Each year there was a special campaign to meet immediate needs. Finally, after years of intermittent negotiations, the home joined the Federation alliance in 1956. Meanwhile, because almost half of the residents were in the crowded sick bay, an expansion of facilities for the chronically ill had necessitated action. Built at the cost of $700,000, a new infirmary containing three floors and fifty-four beds had been dedicated in 1954. By that time, Samuel Roberts had replaced Mr. Perlman as executive director, and Dr. Theodore C. Krauss, a skilled geriatrician, had been appointed medical director.

As time passed, changing economic and social conditions raised new problems for those concerned with the care of the aged. Steady advances in medical science, that preserved the health of the "golden agers," accompanied by the blessings of social security and general prosperity, made an increasing number of oldsters shy away from institutional care. Hence, while the space for sturdy old folks proved more than adequate, it seemed almost impossible to provide sufficient beds for those less fortunate in matters of health. This trend is highlighted by the fact that within less than five years after its erection, the new infirmary had to be enlarged.

It was during the formative years of the home that that famous East Side landmark, the Jewish Community Building, was erected. Buffalo, like most American-Jewish communities, experienced a building boom as the consolidation of local resources provided the funds for physical expansion. Many new edifices of pre-1914 days were patterned after the Jewish Educational Alliance building in New York City, opened in 1889 to Americanize, "humanize" and westernize the immigrant. The Alliance conducted courses in English, civics, domestic science and manual trades and, in the fashion of the day, popularized physical education. It became the prototype for the country and its program was duplicated in many cities.

Originally the tendency in these institutions was to serve only the underprivileged, and only gradually did they evolve into genuine community centers. Initially, they were maintained by the socially élite who rode downtown in their carriages in order to supervise rather than to participate in activities. Since these turn-of-the-century community houses often served as local relief headquarters, it was only slowly that they lost their settlement house stigma.[127] In Buffalo, the Jewish Community Building served as the transition between Zion House, which had the single aim of charity, and the Jewish Center with a program designed for the entire population.

On the eve of World War I, Zion House was in sore need of increased facilities. The youth of the East Side needed a place to keep them off the streets, a place where they could be trained in what the Jewish leaders of the day deemed most important—cleanliness and athletics for the boys, cleanliness and domestic science for the girls, and good reading habits for all. Members of the Sisterhood of Zion, intimately acquainted with the situation, were the first to press for expansion. Mrs. Jacob G. Joseph, whose husband was to head the building committee, was then president of the Sisterhood, and she provided many of the arguments for expansion. After a brief campaign, the ladies won their case, and the Federation granted permission for a building campaign.[128]

One of the first acts of the committee was to purchase a lot at 406 Jefferson Avenue near William Street, and the property on Mortimer Street just to the rear of the selected site. This private dwelling was remodelled to provide administrative offices for the Federation and to serve as an annex to the main building. Said to be the largest building of its kind at that time between New York and Chicago, the three-story new structure was 80 feet wide and 100 feet long. It was reported to cost $40,000 and the nucleus of this sum was raised by a special subscription campaign.

Construction took a full year and, finally, March 1-8, 1914, was declared dedication week. On Sunday evening there was a banquet, and the days that followed witnessed a series of receptions, inspections and entertainments.[129]

In addition to their praiseworthy work in creating enthusiasm for this Community Building, the Jewish women of Buffalo came to the fore in other fields during the colorful decade that preceded the 1914 Armageddon. It was an age that marked the rising importance of women. We have already noted Mrs. Henry Altman's phenomenal career. Another important Jewish woman of this time was Mrs. Felix Kessel. Born in Buffalo in 1863 as Sara Hirshfield, Mrs. Kessel wrote for the old Buffalo *Express*. When she applied for the job on that paper, her only qualifications were that she had attended Old Central, where she was chosen to read a graduation essay. Nevertheless, her column "The Rocking Chair," spread her fame in the city. During her active career she interviewed many of the great and near-great who came to Buffalo. Among others whom she met and described to her readers were Presidents McKinley and Theodore Roosevelt, the actors John Drew, Joseph Jefferson, E. H. Sothern, and the feminist Susan B. Anthony. Most of her interviews were conducted at the old Park Club where, on a dilapidated divan brought from her home, she interrogated her visitors. Some of Mrs. Kessel's newspaper articles were syndicated and she also wrote on occasion for dramatic magazines outside of the city. She helped organize the Women's Press Club of Buffalo, and she was responsible for the formation of The Scribblers, a writers' club. In addition to her journalistic efforts, Mrs. Kessel gave public lectures and held a salon in her Auburn Avenue home where she held forth as an expert on current problems. Together with her sister, Elizabeth Hirshfield, Mrs. Kessel lent a stout hand to the women's suffrage movement.[130]

In the life of the city by far the most important area which Buffalo Jews penetrated relatively early was the teaching profession. Partly because they formed the avant-garde of the "New Immigration," and partly because of their age-old intellectual curiosity, Jewish girls were attracted to the classroom long before other recent arrivals such as the Poles or the Italians. On the other hand, very few, if any, Jewish men were drawn to teaching in the early days, for public school salaries in 1900 began at about $400 a year. Teaching, however, was a fine vocation for a young girl, for prior to 1898, a good high school record made one eligible for the competitive examination open to candidates for elementary school positions. Moreover, training was free at the State Normal School and here an ambitious girl had an excellent opportunity to acquire professional status.

As early as 1870, Lizzie Levin was a seventh grade teacher at School No. 31. We know nothing about her except that her name strongly suggests a Jewish origin. In the following decade, Hattie Given entered the public school system; Margaret Boasberg joined the faculty of School No. 1; and Cecelia Levy (Mrs. Isaac Boasberg) taught German at School No. 25. The stream of Jewish teachers increased as the old century neared its end. Miss Sarah Rubenstein (1878-1926) spent her entire adult life at School No. 32, teaching the Jewish children who then lived in the immediate vicinity. Among her colleagues on its faculty were Miss Mollie Cohen and Miss Bertha M. Brock (1872-1958), who later became assistant principal of old 32. The Buffalo *Courier-Express*, January 3, 1960, carried a feature article on the career of another early Buffalo Jewish teacher, Miss Sophie C. Hadida (b.1874). Born in Lapeer, Michigan, Miss Hadida came to Buffalo at the age of seven. She graduated from Central High School and began teaching grade school in 1898 at School No. 48. Fifteen years later, after further training in Boston, she returned to teach music in the Buffalo schools. Still occasionally active in tutoring at the ripe age of 86, Miss Hadida is the author of a book on etiquette and several books and articles on the English language.

Three-quarters of a century ago, high school teaching was a limited field, and large-scale Jewish penetration here was retarded. Among the first to break the barrier were Fannie Zenner and Elizabeth Hirshfield. Miss Zenner (1871-1943), Buffalo born and bred, began her teaching career in 1890 under the supervision of the famous Dr. Frank S. Fosdick, then principal of Central High School Annex. When he was chosen to head the newly erected Masten Park High School, Miss Zenner joined his first faculty. At one time or another she taught Latin, mathematics, history and English.[131]

More prominent in public affairs was Miss Elizabeth Hirshfield (1862-1909). This sister of Mrs. Felix Kessel once wrote a pamphlet for the Buffalo Political Equality Club called "Concerning Women Suffrage." In it she declared that she had been brought up in a home in which there was "pure democracy" and for this reason she had become an advocate of equal suffrage early in life. The obstructions to full equality between the sexes, she vehemently said, "were constructed by man and by man alone!" Elizabeth, whose brother Marcus was the second Jewish Buffalo boy to go to college, was herself college bred. Miss Hirshfield taught first at Central High School and later at Lafayette High. A tablet to her memory decorates the walls of the latter school.[132]

Frequently, primary school teachers of those days did post-graduate work in the hope of obtaining a high school appointment. Among those who accomplished this purpose was Etta Cohen (1880-1931). Starting her teaching career at No. 32, Miss Cohen did extension work at the University of Buffalo and rose to the headship of the English department of Fosdick-Masten High School.[133]

In later years, Jewish teachers became commonplace. The Great Depression increased the number of Jewish high school teachers by driving into the profession young men who preferred its small but steady salary to the greater risks of other professions. Because they lived in two cultures, American and Jewish, many Jews were blessed with a keen perspective that helped make them outstanding teachers.

Among the better known Jewish educators of the city, Mrs. Anna Bear Brevis enjoyed an unusually full career. She began as a teacher in 1920 and nine years later became the first Jewish public school principal in the city, heading School No. 41. The daughter of Moses Bear, long-time secretary of Anshe Lubavitz Synagogue, this future wife of Rabbi Harry J. Brevis was brought to Buffalo from Russia as a child. Soon after she began teaching, she developed a method of teaching reading that gained for her city-wide recognition. In 1949, Mrs. Brevis published a series of articles in the *Reconstructionist Magazine* entitled "A Public School Principal Looks at Jewish Education." The ideas that she advanced won wide acceptance among Jewish educators of a progressive bent. As a result, Mrs. Brevis was invited to lead the Judaism-in-the-Home movement which became a permanent part of the educational program of the National Women's League of the United Synagogue of America. Furthermore, her creative "Holiday Institutes" have influenced both Reform and Orthodox circles.[134]

Another contemporary who advanced in the public school system was Abraham Axlerod (1906-1958), who became principal of Lafayette High School. He died there while attending to his duties. Louis T. Masson, for many years head of Beth Zion's religious school, was, like Mr. Axlerod, a science teacher who later was appointed assistant principal of Kensington High School. Dr. Louis L. Gitin, who succeeded Mr. Masson in the Beth Zion position, became in time Assistant Superintendent of Schools.

By all odds the most remarkable climb up the ladder of the Buffalo public school system was that of Dr. Joseph Manch. Dr. Manch, who had been born in Lomza, Russia, came as an infant with his parents to the United States. His father, Reverend Isaac Manch (b.1882) was a religious functionary at Niagara Falls who came to Buffalo to take over *Hazzan* Singer's famous Jewish Book Store on William Street. It was probably in this strong intellectual center that the younger Manch developed his love of learning. In 1928, he entered the University of Buffalo where he subsequently received three degrees. His M.A. thesis on "Swift and Women," published in the *University of Buffalo Studies,* earned well-merited praise. Dr. Manch taught English in various high schools in Buffalo, was a leader in the Buffalo Federation of Teachers and in 1946 was brought into school administration. He rose steadily in guidance and counselling and through his efforts at arresting juvenile delinquency attracted nation-wide attention. He became Associate Superintendent of Education, and in 1957, when Superintendent Parmer L. Ewing resigned, Dr. Manch was the outstanding candidate for the position. He thus became one of the very few Jews in the country to reach such a high post in public education.

While Buffalo and its Jewish citizens were advancing steadily, the oldest synagogue in the city was preparing itself for its own growth and reform. Beth El, already a venerable congregation, was almost moribund in 1900. The old Elm Street neighborhood, to which Beth El had moved a quarter of a century before, suffered a gradual decline. The records reveal that slowly the original Beth El folk migrated to the lower West Side of Buffalo.[135] The German Beth Zion families had already made the change, and now many others were following the trail that led from the East Side. This first group had settled, as we have noted, on such streets as Franklin, Tupper, Edward and North Pearl. Because Beth El members moved a generation later, they skipped the intermediate district and settled farther uptown.

We know relatively little about the Beth El of those days, for the minute books have been lost. We do know that Simon Selling (1843-1916) served as secretary in the 1890s, that that old stalwart Abraham F. Cohen, was still president in 1900, and that the secretary was Samuel May. The treasurer was Dr. Ferdinand Simon, the picturesque East Sider. But the congregation was almost defunct with only fifty members left.[136] Something had to be done, and obviously that something was to find a new location and to make the synagogue service more attractive.

To move was not an insurmountable problem; but to become Conservative, before there was even a word to describe what you became, was quite a trick. In many American cities new neighborhoods gave rise to congregations that were established as, or eventually became, Conservative. But in Buffalo a nominally Orthodox congregation, that for a generation had been drifting toward liberalism, pulled up its roots and replanted itself as a Conservative congregation—all with foreknowledge of what it was doing.

Nationally, a middle-of-the-road movement got under way in 1883, when a rightist segment broke away from the Reform group and established headquarters in the camp of the opposition, Cincinnati. Two years later, the split was widened when the Central Conference of American Rabbis adopted an outspokenly radical platform at its 1885 Pittsburgh meeting. Basically two reasons prompted the splinter group. Those who left disliked extreme Reform, and some local interests in New York and Philadelphia had long resented the mid-western leadership.

These original Conservatives were nominally Orthodox, but they were much more Americanized and liberal than their recently arrived East-European contemporaries. In 1887, they founded the Jewish Theological Seminary of America in New York City. This seat of learning was greatly strengthened in 1902 when Dr. Solomon Schechter (1850-1915) was brought from Cambridge University in England to direct and re-vitalize it. Initially, the Conservatives avoided theological controversies and, in the established American way, emphasized utilitarian reforms. Historical Judaism was stressed: although the Conservatives never abjured the revelation at Sinai, the sanction for their beliefs came more from the historical development of faith. These points appealed to the leading members of Beth El, for this congregation had long adhered to tradition and had avoided outright Reform. Yet it had drifted from Orthodoxy. The intermediate position in American Judaism had a magnetic appeal for these people.

While Beth El was going through the process of shifting from Orthodoxy to Conservatism, the first native-born rabbi in Buffalo history was associated with the synagogue. He was Rabbi Marvin Nathan (b.1879), who stemmed from one of Beth El's oldest families. He must have ministered to the congregation before he was fully ordained, for he was the rabbi of the Philadelphia Congregation Beth Israel for the quarter of a century immediately following his graduation from the Jewish Theological Seminary.

Before and after Rabbi Nathan's brief stay, Beth El endured a parade of rabbis and other functionaries that reminds one of the early days on Pearl Street.[137] One of the best remembered was Reverend Isaac Slick (1867-1924), who was *hazzan* toward the very end of the congregation's downtown existence. A staunch traditionalist, Mr. Slick preferred East Side Orthodoxy and he remained in the vicinity to chant the prayers at other synagogues then still untouched by modern innovations.[138]

It was during Cantor Slick's incumbency at Beth El that some progressive leaders proposed to sell the synagogue, thus forcing on the more lethargic a move to the West Side. Charles Polakoff, then emerging as Beth El's man of the future, more than any other person was responsible for the switch to Conservatism, and it was he who engineered the move uptown. Polakoff (1866-1940) had come to Buffalo at the age of nineteen and began his business career as a wholesale coal and ice dealer. He eventually moved into real estate and insurance, and for twenty-five years was president of the Charles Polakoff Agency, Inc. One of the more exceptional young immigrants of his day, Polakoff achieved business success early and then turned to help his own East Side Jews by trying to incorporate them into the older community. His first wife, whom he married in 1892, was Lillian Gumbinsky (1872-1921), the daughter of Isaac Gumbinsky, and this union brought him into one of the oldest non-German families of Buffalo.

Mr. Polakoff's entire career demonstrates leadership: leadership in business, in the movement to federate Jewish charities, in the establishment of the Rosa Coplon Old Folks Home, even in helping Cornell University students to build a temple near the Ithaca campus. Of all these activities, however, his pet project was Beth El. Elected a trustee in 1903, Polakoff consolidated his power and became president in 1909, an office that he held almost continuously for twenty-nine years, until he was retired as Honorary President.[139]

In the year of Mr. Polakoff's rise to power, 1909, Beth El had only forty-one members, some of whom wanted to move the synagogue and some of whom refused to budge. During the drawn-out debate, former members of the congregation who were already living uptown organized to build in the new neighborhood; but they indicated their readiness to rejoin if Beth El would take the initiative in providing a West Side house of worship. "We had neither minister nor cantor," Polakoff said of those days. "[We] were exercising the strictest economy, and still our income was not sufficient to pay necessary expenses." [140] Less than a month after he took office, following a victory over the Old Guardists, Polakoff called a meeting of Beth El people who had moved into the West Side. Meeting at Orient Hall on West Ferry Street, they decided to select a site for a temple that was to be moderately Reform. (The term *Conservative* was still not in common use.) Prior to this meeting, the Beth El group had privately voted to build a new temple.[141] Soon a strong joint committee was named and it was empowered to select a proper location.

A spurt in membership now began and it ultimately increased the roster by forty-eight new names. Among them were Louis Sukernek, Sr., a wealthy scrap-iron dealer, Isaac S. Given, the prosperous Main Street merchant, Emil Rubenstein, the rising young lawyer, David Ruslander, a prominent attorney, and Jacob L. Davis, West Side merchant and future politician. On July 25, 1909, the committee decided to locate on Richmond Avenue. Tradition has it that one Saturday morning after services, a group of men setting out from Elm Street went for a walk. Heading in a northwesterly direction, they are said to have arrived in forty minutes time before the empty lot on Richmond Avenue that was subsequently purchased. If there is anything to the legend, it shows that the younger men were trying to appease those who might choose to remain on the East Side and who might still walk to the new Beth El.[142]

The next step was the appointment of a building committee. Charles Polakoff served as chairman, Marcus Barmon as secretary, and I. S. Given as treasurer.[143] One of the most forceful men in the group, Marcus Barmon (1875-1936), was the grandson of Nicholas Hyman who had been so active in Pearl Street days. Not long after he assisted in the move of Beth El to the West Side, Barmon left the congregation for Beth Zion.[144]

Charles Polakoff turned the first earth at the ground-breaking ceremony on March 23, 1910. The cornerstone was laid on July 24, 1910, at an impressive ceremony at which J. L. Davis presided. Rabbi Harry C. Harris of New York gave the opening prayer, and Rabbis Pizer W. Jacobs of Jacksonville, Florida, and Marvin Nathan of Philadelphia, spoke. Frank L. Cohen presented the ceremonial box to be placed in the cornerstone and Marcus Barmon read the list of contributors. The building, designed by H. Osgood Holland, and to be constructed by Charles H. Everitt, was expected to cost $100,000.[145]

Now that it was going to have a new home, Beth El was faced with a problem that sometimes can inspirit and unite a congregation—raising funds. The Ladies' Auxiliary was re-organized and became very active. This group helped conduct a colorful and elaborate Grand Fair at the German-American Hall on March 7-12, 1910, for the benefit of the new building.[146]

While the congregation was studying the blueprint for the Richmond Avenue Temple, the Elm Street synagogue was sold and the last service was held there on the eighth day of Passover, May 1, 1910. Spurred on by these plans for the future, many additional members joined during the ensuing months. Even outsiders became excited by the prospect of a West Side synagogue, and Grace Carew Sheldon serialized a full history of Beth El in the Buffalo *Times*.[147]

In the meantime, the die-hards, led by Casper Munter and Meyer Lichtenstein, tried to block the contemplated move. These men did not want to give up their accustomed place of worship and, with good reason, they feared the talk of Reform that filled the air. They chose, however, to base their case on legal grounds and demanded guarantees of their cemetery rights. For a time, a serious lawsuit threatened, but it was averted through a series of successful negotiations.[148]

When the Richmond Avenue structure was completed, it contained one of the most beautiful synagogue interiors in the United States. The synagogue auditorium could seat 770 and the gallery 160. The domed ceiling stood forty feet high, and to the rear of the sanctuary were schoolrooms, a small auditorium, a daily chapel, a kitchen and the trustees' room later converted into a library. The congregation began to worship in the new building on Shavuot, June 2-3, 1911, several months before it was formally dedicated. Prior to that time, the uptown group had gathered for worship at the home of the patriarchal Joseph Saperston on West Avenue.

The imposing synagogue was dedicated on Sunday afternoon, September 11, 1911. After the usual preludes and hymns the *Sifrei Torah* were solemnly carried in and Helen Barmon, daughter of Marcus Barmon (later Mrs. John F. Desbecker), presented the golden keys to J. L. Davis, chairman of the Dedication Committee. After the Perpetual Lamp was lit, Rabbi Aaron of Beth Zion delivered an address. Then Julius Singer rendered a violin solo and the *Minha* prayers were chanted by Cantor Samuel Arluck. Sol Ginsberg, President of the Federated Jewish Charities, and Herman Wile, President of Beth Zion, spoke words of greeting. Rabbi Jacob Henry Landau, the new rabbi of Beth El, then preached the dedication sermon.[149]

In many ways Beth El became a new synagogue after the move to Richmond Avenue. After sixty-four years of existence, it took the first real step away from Orthodoxy when it adopted such reforms as mixed seating and anticipated the use of an organ by providing place in the plans for one. A mark of the change was the fact that a fresh set of synagogue officials, led by Rabbi Landau, assumed control of the synagogue.

Jacob H. Landau was a London-trained rabbi who had lived in many countries before crossing the Atlantic. This erudite man had taught Hebrew at Cardiff University in Wales, and classics and ancient history at the University of St. Andrews in Scotland. After he left the British Isles, he served very successfully for thirteen years at the "great synagogue" in Sydney, Australia. A typically modern rabbi who wore his clerical garb well, he managed somehow to combine a high-church air with a liberal theology. He was probably too much of an intellectual for his Buffalo congregation, for he left after two years. Meanwhile, he had built up the religious school to an enrollment of 176, established a library, and published his own manual for Sabbath services. But he was too liberal, too ministerial, and too formally British for the old-timers who were the most conscientious temple-goers.[150]

Cantor Samuel Arluck was eventually succeeded in his post by Bernard Schachtel (1886-1931) who was *hazzan* at Beth El for seventeen years. Born in Poland, Schachtel studied music in Berlin and at the London Conservatory and sang for a while with the London Opera Company.

He was thus able to combine his East-European background with a western way of presenting services. He even jokingly called himself an Englishman and spoke with a slight British accent. An extremely affable and well-liked man, Schachtel was a leader in the local cantors' association, chaplain of B'nai B'rith, and honorary life member of the Buffalo Consistory. As a teacher at Beth El, he had an easy way with children who appreciated his informality.[151]

Another of the new group was destined to become a fixture at Beth El. It was the sexton, Zachariah Gross (1866-1946), who served from 1911 to 1945. The last of the original Richmond Avenue synagogue officials was Samuel S. Luskin (1881-1959) who was born in Horka, Mohilev Province, White Russia. Trained as both a Hebrew teacher and musician, Luskin prepared over a thousand Buffalo boys for *Bar Mitzvah,* and taught or guided countless other youngsters. With the late Cantor Harry Hart Kaufman, he composed and published *Manginot Beth El,* a liturgical service. In addition, he wrote many religious compositions that were widely used throughout the country. A self-taught musician, he learned to play the violin, French horn, trumpet, flute and piano. Samuel Luskin was the real father of the Jewish Choral Society that was organized in 1929. In 1956, Beth El publicly celebrated the seventy-fifth birthday of this devoted choirmaster and teacher.

The first impulse of the reconstituted Beth El was toward serious reform; but after Rabbi Landau left, a traditionalist reaction set in. Meanwhile, there had been talk of reading only a portion of the Torah each week and of adopting the moderately Reform Jastrow prayer book which Polakoff urged as "the most acceptable to the younger generation, and the least repugnant to the older generation." [152] One check to this reformist trend was the fact that the congregation was getting into serious financial difficulties. It cost about $8,000 a year to maintain the temple, and business conditions were so bad in the early Wilson Era that Polakoff had to appease the traditionalists in order to gain their support. It was evident that the elaborate new temple could not be maintained without the support of all in the neighborhood, and it was estimated that a membership of at least several hundred was required to meet the budget. It was time to close ranks on the vexing question of synagogue ritual.

A sign of the new departure was the appointment of a strong traditionalist, Max Drob (1887-1959), who was elected rabbi in 1913 to replace Rabbi Landau. Rabbi Drob was a native of Melawa, Poland, which town also chanced to be the birthplace of the Reverend Bernard Cohen of Beth Zion. Drob came to this country at an early age and spent his childhood in Pittsburgh. He was valedictorian of his class at the Jewish Theological Seminary, where he was graduated with highest honors.

When Max Drob arrived in Buffalo, Beth El was in very serious trouble. The enthusiasm engendered by the building program had cooled; membership had dropped to sixty-eight; the congregation was heavily in debt to the contractors; and the city was threatening to sell the temple at auction for non-payment of taxes.[153] Rabbi Drob brought back the rightists, and he persuaded the temple to affiliate itself with the United Synagogue of America, the official national group of the Conservative movement.

Then began the task of rebuilding. Rabbi Drob was energetic enough to guide the congregation in setting up the choir, reducing the mortgage, stabilizing the ritual along traditional lines, and expanding and beautifying the cemetery. By 1915, when prosperity had returned to both Beth El and the country, Rabbi Drob was re-elected for a term of five years. In that year, Beth El was so well known that a group from Rochester, anxious to found a Conservative synagogue, came to inspect the Richmond Avenue Temple to see what a modern synagogue was like. Before long, the financial situation was reported to be "excellent." [154]

On the eve of American intervention in the first war against Germany, the social pulse at Beth El began to quicken. On May 2, 1915, the congregation celebrated the fifth anniversary of the Richmond Avenue Temple. Dr. Solomon Schechter, the venerable scholar and president of the Jewish Theological Seminary of America, spoke at a banquet at which there was a gay reunion of old and new members. There was a Committee on the Gymnasium; and in the next year Boy Scout Troop 106 was organized.

In marked contrast to their apathy on Elm Street, the young people now began to take an active part in synagogue affairs. A Young Men's Club was established and it began rehearsals for a musical called *On With the Dance,* produced in the spring of 1916. The next year the club presented *Very Good Peggy* at the Majestic Theater. Some of the songs in the play were "When Those Sweet Hawaiian Babies Roll Their Eyes," and "Good Bye Dear Old Bachelor Days." Much of the production and management was under the direction of Bertram Krohn, and Frank E. Freedman was in charge of the publicity. The song writer Jack Yellen helped, and Samuel Luskin was in charge of orchestration.[155]

In these final days of a carefree age, while the men were engaged in putting on musical comedies, the ladies were busy with strawberry festivals, Dutch suppers, balls and Hanukkah banquets. Beth El, at long last, seemed to be revitalized.

The other major synagogue in Buffalo, Beth Zion, had been a sleepy place under the leisurely leadership of Rabbi Israel Aaron. The synagogue was too Reform to attract even the more liberal of the eastern

European immigrants, and very few Germans had come to the city in recent years. When, however, Herman Wile (1864-1958) became president, life at Beth Zion became far less unhurried. According to our lights, this congregation, destined in time to care for over 1,500 families, grew partly as a result of inexorable historical forces, and partly as the result of Wile's Herculean efforts. He had not been in office one year before he realized that members were so indifferent to Judaism that they had even lost interest in the religious education of their children. He took vigorous steps to wipe out the all-pervading nonchalance.

This patriarch of Buffalo Jewry hailed from Ihringen, the little Baden village that sent so many of its *Yehudim* to the Niagara Frontier. Herman followed his older brothers to the New World and, after business experience elsewhere, joined them in the Buffalo of Grover Cleveland. For twenty-seven years Herman Wile ran his own clothing factory, located at Ellicott and Carroll Streets. This establishment was closed on the Sabbath and on Jewish Holidays, for Wile always took the precepts of Reform Judaism seriously. For much of his long career, Wile was associated with the famous clothing firm founded by his brother Mayer, and he was still travelling for it in the 1940s, some sixty-five years after his first business trip in America.[156]

Herman Wile joined Beth Zion in 1893 and, because he was one of the late German arrivals, he was closer to European traditional Judaism than most other members of the synagogue. Five years later, he was elected to the board, where he became active immediately. In those days, the president, Abraham Oppenheimer, displayed even less energetic leadership than did Rabbi Aaron. Mr. Wile began his long years of service as president of Beth Zion in 1902, and all in all served intermittently for thirty-six years in that capacity.[157] When, at long last, he retired in 1948 from active leadership, a bronze plaque was placed in the temple in his honor, and he was given a gold membership card, a silver cup, and a leather-bound volume of the proceedings in his honor.

The Wile years coincided with the eastern European influx into Beth Zion and this new blood helped speed the return to a more normative type of Judaism. Probably such a moderate rightist reaction would have occurred even without Herman Wile, for it happened elsewhere as a new generation of Reform rabbis, stemming from traditional homes, filled the ranks of the CCAR. But Wile, in contrast to most Germans of his genre, accelerated the change. He welcomed families of Russian extraction into the temple family, often persuading them to join. Another of his interests was the re-introduction of Hebrew instruction into the school curriculum. In many ways this sturdy man participated in Jewish affairs outside of his own synagogue. For ten years he was the oldest active member of the Executive Board of the Union of American Hebrew Congregations, and he gave the National Jewish Hospital at Denver fifty-seven years of dedicated service. Genuinely devoted to the furthering of Jewish education, Wile was the real founder of the local Bureau of Jewish Education which he headed, in a lay capacity, until he was eighty. No one in the city did more than he to bridge the old gulf between East Side and West Side. Partly through his efforts Buffalo became one of the first cities in the country to boast of a truly consolidated community.[158]

In the meantime, in the first six years of Wile's presidency of Beth Zion, membership rose from 112 to 171, and the budget almost doubled. Most of the newcomers were members of older Polish families who had become thoroughly Americanized, new immigrants who had made money quickly, or some genuine liberals among the Russians who rebelled against Orthodoxy. Consequently, even before that year of destiny, 1914, Beth Zion was on its way to becoming representative of all elements in the then still widely divided community.

As we have seen, Rabbi Aaron died in 1912, a few days after he celebrated his silver anniversary as rabbi of Beth Zion. A Pulpit Committee was appointed to fill the vacancy, but for the coming High Holidays, Rabbi Julian Morgenstern (b.1881), the famous Amos scholar and later long-time president of Hebrew Union College, came to Buffalo. A permanent successor was subsequently found in Rabbi Louis J. Kopald (1885-1931).

Louis J. Kopald was born in Cracow (Galicia), Austria-Hungary, and was brought to America as an infant. At the early age of sixteen, he entered the University of Cincinnati and simultaneously matriculated at Hebrew Union College. Ordained in 1909, his first pulpit was in Stockton, California.

Rabbi Kopald came to the attention of Beth Zion during the summer of 1912 while he was visiting the Reform congregation at nearby Niagara Falls. Accounts of his charming manner and winning personality were transferred to Wile by some close friends who worshipped in the neighboring congregation. Rabbi Kopald was interviewed by Buffalo leaders and then returned West for the High Holidays. He was elected rabbi of Beth Zion the following January.

A talented musician, a Beau Brummell with an ever genial smile, and a man blessed with a radiant personality, Kopald swept the congregation off its feet. "No man so young," said one who knew him well, "ever made as deep an impression on the city of Buffalo as did he." One of the functions of a modern rabbi is to serve as a messenger of good will to the general community, and in this role Rabbi Kopald excelled. A real civic leader, he was active in the Buffalo Symphony Orchestra, the Red Cross, the Syrian and Armenian Relief Committee, among countless other interests. His talents for organization and philanthropic work were recognized by his election as president of the New York State Conference on Charities and Correction. He served on the newly re-organized Board of Education in Buffalo for a year; but he was forced to resign because of the demands of his parish work. An eloquent speaker, he was in constant demand at public functions and, during World War I, he lectured at the University of Nebraska on Jewish themes.

Rabbi Kopald came east at a time when necessity demanded that Beth Zion attract the second generation non-German Jews; and this he did. In marked contrast to his rather formal ministerial predecessor, Rabbi Kopald had a light touch and knew how to handle delicate situations with ease. Whereas Dr. Aaron had been very anti-Zionist at a time when the spirit of Herzl was making steady progress, Rabbi Kopald at least understood Jewish nationalism and to some extent cooperated with it. Rabbi Kopald once said that the rehabilitation of Palestine was an unbreakable bond among all Jews, but, he went on to say, "This is not Zionism. This is not a mere political hope. In that, as you may well know, I have no interest." He wished instead to emphasize Jewish humanitarianism by making Palestine a place where "less fortunate Jews may go." Instead of opposing Zionism outright, Rabbi Kopald straddled the issue. On one occasion, he denied that he was a Zionist, but he added that, "It is true that in these latter years, my heart is turning toward Palestine, the land of my fathers." He spoke of a "Zion above Zionism," and of "The Jewish People above Zion." [159]

His relations with other rabbis in the city were good, and he also got along splendidly with Christian ministers. For example, in 1921, Rabbi Kopald arranged what he later called an unprecedented joint service with the Lafayette Presbyterian Church at Lafayette and Elmwood Avenues. He and the Reverend Murray S. Howland spoke and the church choir rendered some parts of the Jewish ritual. A few years earlier he had spoken before the First Congregationalist Church on the subject, "Is One Church for Everybody Desirable?" In this talk he took a middle course between the crusading Reform rabbis who tended to be quite universalist and their latter day successors who were prone to be far more traditional in spirit.[160]

Unquestionably, Rabbi Kopald breathed new life into Temple Beth Zion. He organized the Men's Temple Club. Unlike Dr. Aaron who disliked preaching and had to be urged to do so, Rabbi Kopald spoke at both the late Friday night and Saturday morning services during the regular season. Not only did he speak, but the congregants enjoyed his sermons! Moreover, he introduced a reception and refreshments after the Friday night service, and this spurred attendance. He also revived many practices that had fallen into disuse, such as candle lighting and *Kiddush* at home before the customary Sabbath eve meal. Furthermore, Rabbi Kopald stimulated interest by bringing many Jewish and non-Jewish dignitaries to Beth Zion.[161]

In 1920, at the Hotel Gibson in Cincinnati, Rabbi Kopald married Elsa Rheinstrom of that city. An accomplished pianist, Mrs. Kopald promised to add much to the cultural life of the congregation. Rabbi Kopald reached the height of his meteoric career at this time; but then he developed cancer; a tragedy that saddened a later period of Beth Zion's history.[162]

To return to the happier days of Rabbi Kopald's ministry, Beth Zion in 1915 engaged in a gala threefold festival. Simultaneously, the congregation celebrated the twenty-fifth anniversary of the dedication of the Delaware Avenue Temple, the *supposed* fiftieth anniversary of the founding of the congregation, and the dedication of a new Temple Centre.[163]

For a decade, the temple school had been crowded for space, and the pupils complained of bad ventilation. As membership increased, classroom facilities became even more inadequate, and there was talk of partitioning the assembly hall to provide more desks. Anticipating the ultimate need for expansion, some additional land was purchased in 1908 at the rear of the temple. Five years later, Herman Wile strongly urged the expansion of facilities. At a special meeting, a building committee, led by August Keiser and Adolph Spangenthal, was appointed. They borrowed $45,000, and after using part of this sum to pay off the existing mortgage on the Delaware Avenue Temple, applied the remainder to construction of the new wing which eventually cost almost as much as the original building. The Ladies' Temple Society, guided by Rabbi Aaron's gracious widow, furnished the Centre.

The annex was added to the rear and the right side of the old building. Three stories high, it contained a spacious auditorium, a stage and dressing rooms, a gymnasium, a basement kitchen and dining room, a ladies' room, a new vestry room for the directors, a study for the rabbi and a temple office.[164]

From Friday, September 24th, until Monday, September 27, 1915, a massive celebration took place, which thousands attended. An Historical Committee led by Eugene Warner prepared a souvenir history of the temple. On Friday evening, Rabbi Moses Gries of Cleveland spoke, and Rabbi Kopald delivered the sermon. President Herman Wile greeted the audience, while the patriarchal Sol Rosenau, still secretary at eighty-two, spoke as a founding father of the Reform Beth Zion.

On the following morning there was a special children's service, and that evening the Young Men's Temple Club presented a vaudeville show which was followed by a dance. The festivities were concluded on Monday night at a banquet. The principal address was delivered by Mrs. Abram Simon, president of the National Federation of Temple Sisterhoods, and wife of a prominent Washington rabbi.[165]

As America prepared to join the "war to end wars," Buffalo Jewry could look back with satisfaction upon a period during which its development kept pace with the increased tempo of the times. During the Progressive Era, the Buffalo Jewish community reflected in miniature happenings throughout the land. Under the impact of an unprecedented number of immigrants, the two extremes of prosperity and pauperism had existed side by side. While the well-to-do uptown families enjoyed a relaxed and comfortable existence, the downtown masses sweated and toiled in poverty. However, ere the peace of 1914 was broken by the fateful pistol shots of Sarajevo, even those who had begun at the bottom of the ladder had advanced a rung or two on the climb upward. Then came four ghastly years that were to alter the entire course of modern history.

War, Prosperity, and Unity

WHEN THE WAR of 1914 broke out in Europe, American Jews, like the rest of their countrymen, wanted to stay out of this foreign conflict. Although virtually all Jews wanted the United States to remain neutral, at first there was a slight pro-German tendency, for the Kaiser's soldiers were fighting the anti-Semitic Russia of the Czars. However, as the German atrocities were publicized, American-Jewish feeling became increasingly pro-Ally. With the exception of some anti-war Socialists who dogmatically regarded all wars as the supreme curse of capitalism, Jews gradually turned against the Central Powers and ultimately their ardor reached the super-patriotic fervor of the general population. It is estimated that about a quarter of a million Jews participated in the American war effort, and about 10,000 of these men were commissioned officers. Some 3,500 of the total number made the supreme sacrifice; another 12,000 were wounded; and over a thousand of them were cited for valor.

Shortly after the United States intervened in the war, Congress passed a general conscription act. Under its terms, 170,763 men of military age were registered in Erie County. Buffalo alone contributed over 20,000 soldiers to the war. The first men drafted left the city on September 3, 1917, for Camp Dix, New Jersey, while many in the months to come entrained for Camp Upton, Long Island. The 77th Division contained the

278

famous Lost Battalion and the ranks of this heroic group included one Buffalo unit.[1]

Unlike the Civil War, which involved relatively few Jewish lads from the small Buffalo community, this later conflict drew so many that it is impossible to mention the names of all who fought. For the most part, history can only list those who we know were lost in action, were wounded, were cited for valor, or others who later became community leaders.

Jerome Michel, was drafted and sent overseas after six weeks of basic training. In April 1918, his unit arrived in France attached to the 305th Machine Gun Battalion of the 77th Division. After a respite, the outfit moved forward in an attempt to break the Hindenburg Line. At Chateau-Thierry on the night of September 8th, Corporal Michel's unit prepared to attack and he joined Sergeant Milton H. Petzold's squad. They met machine-gun fire, and the men were separated as Petzold moved off to try to destroy a German machine-gun nest. Michel was wounded and was removed to the first-aid station. He died of his wounds, and after the war, his body was returned and re-interred in the Beth Zion section of Forest Lawn Cemetery.[2]

The names of many additional Jewish youths from Buffalo appear on the casualty lists. Sam Apstein of the 302nd Engineers was killed in action after being cited for valor. Private Henry Bernstein died of wounds on October 21, 1918, and Private Fred Bohne also fell in battle. Among those listed as either killed, lost in action, or dead of natural causes while in service, were Benjamin Cohen, Harry Ginsburg, Maurice Rosen, David Weintraub and Morris Shochet. Private Benjamin Swerdloff died of influenza complications at Camp Upton in 1918. One week before the Armistice, Corporal Arthur B. Finkelstein fell in the blood-stained ground near Verdun.[3]

One Buffalo soldier was captured by the Germans. Sergeant David L. Ullman, son of the blind lawyer Louis Ullman, was reported missing in action, but finally a message came through to his family. "Dear Ones:" he wrote, "I am held prisoner here. The news of my demise is much exaggerated. Love, David." Ullman was subsequently released in time to serve as field observer and interpreter at the Versailles Peace Conference. Buffalo heard from him once more when, in 1959, he was appointed to high judicial office in Philadelphia.[4]

The "Sergeant York" of Buffalo was Lester Bergman (1889-1958). Bergman was the first local man to enlist in the Marine Corps in World War I. Wounded five times, he was awarded the Distinguished Service Cross and the Croix de Guerre. At the battle of Belleau Wood, where he received one of his wounds, he participated in the capture of a Maxim gun, 23 machine-guns, and 170 Germans who were making a flank attack on a trench occupied by American troops.[5]

Two other local Jewish boys were also known to have served in the Marine Corps. Drs. Reuben Cohen and Benjamin Harris, both podiatrists, enlisted on the same day and were immediately appointed to the rank of sergeant. Dr. Cohen, who was assigned to the Navy sick bay at Parris Island to care for Marines, was said to have ministered to 70,000 pairs of sore feet during his enlistment.

Two men who later became prominent in the Jewish affairs of the city were in service during the war. Maurice S. Tabor (b.1894) enlisted as a private, became a first lieutenant at Camp Upton, and subsequently was promoted to major and served in the Adjutant General's office in San Francisco. Hyman Kahn, who settled in Buffalo after the war, a founder and oft-times president of Temple Emanu-El, enlisted at Milton, Massachusetts. After his training at Camp Upton, Kahn was with the Ordnance Department at Camp Hancock, Georgia. There he was a victim of influenza and so missed going to France. Later, in Buffalo, he commanded Post 25 of the Jewish War Veterans.

Several members of the familiar older Jewish families also were in the war. Clarence S. Desbecker was a sergeant in the 501st Engineers and spent eighteen months overseas. Richard W. Desbecker, who later married Rabbi Kopald's sister, Hanna, served in this country. The Hofeller family was represented by Robert Hofeller, who was with the Headquarters Regiment of the First Army in France, and Sigmar Hofeller, who was at Langley Field, Virginia. Nathan Oppenheimer, Jr., whose grandfather Abraham Oppenheimer had served in the Civil War, was a private assigned to a French battery, and the attorney, Adrian Block, was an officer. William J. Brock (1897-1952), who later became a famous trial lawyer, served in the Navy.

Henry Altman, later an attorney, also represented one of the oldest Jewish families. He enlisted on April 7, 1917, one day after the United States declared war, in Troop I, New York Cavalry of the National Guard. (This unit later became the 102nd French Mortar Battery as part of the 27th Division). Altman fought in many battles in the Meuse-Argonne, St. Mihiel, and Verdun sectors. On October 19, 1918, he was decorated for gallantry in action and exceptional devotion to duty. He was discharged as a sergeant on February 4, 1919, and rose to become Commander of the American Legion in Erie County.

Other representatives of well known families were Israel G. Holender (1885-1944) and Edgar N. Block. Holender, the brother of Sundel J. Holender, served in the Judge Advocate's Office in France. Block was a captain in the 309th Infantry of the 78th Division, having been graduated as a "ninety-day wonder" from the Madison Barracks Officer Training School. During the assault against the St. Mihiel salient of the Hindenburg Line, Captain Block was seriously wounded.[6] Captain Alex Jokl (1883-1945) was also graduated from Madison Barracks, but he was kept stateside, training rookies at Ft. McArthur, Texas.

Harry J. Rubenstein (1887-1954) was in the Marine Corps long before the war started. After his discharge, he returned to Buffalo where he joined the 74th Regiment of the National Guard. During the Mexican Border campaign, he served under General John J. Pershing in the futile attempt to capture the bandit Pancho Villa. Following American entry into the European war, Rubenstein was sent to Camp Wadsworth, Spartansburg, South Carolina. He mentions in a letter of March 17, 1918, that he went to the camp hospital to visit another Buffalonian, "young Ray Morrison." "The poor kid," Rubenstein wrote his sister, "was sure enough tickled to death and it did my heart good to see the happy expression on his face."

On the way to France, Rubenstein's convoy sank three attacking submarines. They landed at Brest on May 30, 1918, and "Fesh" Rubenstein and the others were taken in box cars to Mayelles where they were temporarily assigned to the British Army. Later with the 27th Division, Rubenstein's assignment was to the battalion transport train that carried food and men to the trenches. "The flashes," he wrote from *somewhere in France,* "light the sky up for miles but you get so used to it that you pay no attention to it."

The 27th Division, under the command of Major General John F. O'Ryan, attacked the Hindenburg Line from September 27th to October 1st in the last weeks of the war. Rubenstein's unit went over the top on September 29th. The LaSalle River was crossed and the enemy was forced to retreat beyond the Canal de la Sombre. Rubenstein recorded that his unit that day "took 6,000 yards of the hardest country on the Western front." "We have to follow the fast retreating Hun," he said, "and he is some runner." To celebrate the Armistice when it came, he "and a couple of friends went down to a nearby town and got keyed up."[7]

Many more Jews from Buffalo than have here been named actively participated in the armed services. A plaque in the library of Temple Beth Zion carries the names of fifty-one men from that congregation alone who served. By 1917, the Jewish community of Buffalo had grown to such large proportions that it is impossible within the confines of a single volume to record all the names and events of those stirring years.

On the home front, the patriotic war fever in America went so far that the study of German in schools in many parts of the country was suspended, and a New York City rabbi, Joseph Silverman of Temple Emanu-El, tried to persuade local clergymen to refuse to perform the marriage ceremony for slackers. German measles were renamed "liberty" measles; sauerkraut became "liberty cabbage"; and even the poor dachs-hund was called the "liberty pup." The Jews of Buffalo were swept up in this chauvinism along with the rest of the country. At Beth Zion on August 10, 1917, the board solemnly voted that "no Peace Society flag or any other flag or emblem of any association or society" except "the flag of the United States of America," be displayed in or about the Temple without the express permission of the board.[8]

In a more constructive fashion, however, the bulk of Buffalo Jewry participated in Liberty Loan drives and other war work. When the United War Work Campaign was organized in 1918, Rabbi Kopald was one of its vice-chairmen and gave up his vacation that summer to do religious work at Camp Mills and Fort Dix. Ladies' groups at Beth El sent pack-ages to sick soldiers at Fort Dix as well as food for Passover. They knitted sweaters and socks, rolled bandages for the Red Cross, and prepared jams, cakes, and canned fruit for the soldiers. The Temple Centre at Beth Zion was used by Medical Advisory Board #43, which met three times a week to process draftees, and Beth El voted to erect a plaque to honor men in the service even before any American soldier had fallen in battle.[9]

Psychologically, the nineteenth century ended with World War I, rather than in 1900, for it was not until that time that the transition came from the old peaceful order to the present age of never-ending crises and constant uncertainty. The year 1914 was also a great turning point in Jewish history, for it marked the end of the world leadership of European Jewry. Just as America marched onto the stage of history as a prime power, so also did the American-Jewish community emerge as the most powerful and the richest in the Diaspora. As the war spread on the east-ern front to devastate the heartland of European Jewry, Americans had to take over problems of leadership and relief, for Germany's once rich and proud Jews were now powerless to help. American Jews, who keenly felt the sufferings of their brethren overseas, were moved to action by such leaders as Jacob H. Schiff, Louis Marshall, and Louis D. Brandeis. Furthermore, the Zionist movement, which had been given a gigantic fillip by the Balfour Declaration of 1917, helped to turn the attention of American Jews outward from their own concerns to the cause of national redemption. Finally, these events coincided with a shift in power in the United States in which the more complacent German Jews yielded power to the new East-European groups whose interests were more intimately allied to those of their kinsmen from whom they had been so recently separated.

The war had other effects: it greatly weakened Jewish Socialism in America because it divorced the Socialists from their cohorts in the Old World, and it knit the Jewish communities in America into united groups that in the "Hang-the-Kaiser" spirit of the day knew neither the old divisions nor the old affinities. The most notable effect of the war, however, was the plethora of Jewish national organizations that it spawned. The Joint Distribution Committee, the American Jewish Congress and the Jewish Welfare Board all stem from this turbulent period. Of these organizations, the Joint Distribution Committee was the one most actively involved in relief work.

J.D.C. was organized in New York on November 27, 1914, with the famous banker, Felix M. Warburg, as chairman. Its purpose was to serve as a single agency to disperse war relief funds for many miscellaneous groups that formed to meet the emergency.

Although its first national drive for funds was begun late in 1915, it was not until two years later that the Joint Distribution Committee organized local drives, and it was then that Buffalo joined forces with the national group for its first overseas relief appeal. At the beginning, the local leaders attempted no high-pressure tactics, but simply used the synagogue mailing lists to reach contributors. Shortly thereafter, however, the Buffalo Federation began annual drives for Jewish War Relief.

For the duration, the Federation pushed local relief problems into the background and concentrated on war work. The Community Building at 406 Jefferson Avenue was opened to Jewish soldiers and sailors stationed in the Buffalo area, but more important than this type of local service, the Federation turned its attention abroad. "With an enlarged horizon we are concerned with the terrible distress existing in the war-stricken countries," said President Theodore Hofeller in expressing the general sentiment. By 1918, the Federation had raised the remarkable sum of $100,000 for Jewish War Relief.[10]

The unsettled conditions that followed the Armistice increased the need for American dollars. In Bolshevist Russia, as Lenin's program systematically destroyed the middle man, thousands of Jews actually starved to death. In the newly formed succession states of Poland, Lithuania, Latvia, Roumania and Hungary, anti-Semitism and persecution increased the misery of many unfortunate Jews trapped in those lands. For example, in 1919, in at least 150 Polish communities, atrocities against the Jews were perpetrated, and in the Ukraine, the Communists and White Russians between them slaughtered about 30,000 in almost four hundred different towns. In other countries, such as Roumania and Hungary, Jews were denied equality. Thus, in addition to rendering relief, the emergency organizations had to fight for civil liberties for hapless Jews in a half-dozen states of Central Europe.[11]

In a dramatic manner, the people of Buffalo were made aware of conditions in Europe with the murder, in 1920, of one of their own sons, Rabbi Hyman Bernard Cantor. The son of Isaac Cantor and the brother of the late Professor Nathaniel Cantor of the University of Buffalo, Hyman was born in 1892 and ordained at Hebrew Union College in 1916. He was associated with Rabbi Stephen S. Wise in the Free Synagogue of New York. Early in 1920, together with the distinguished scholar Professor Israel Friedlander of the Jewish Theological Seminary of America, Rabbi Cantor left America for J.D.C. relief work in eastern Europe.

On July 7, 1920, both men were murdered by bandits at Yarlomince, Ukraine, after a severe struggle in which they vainly fought for their lives. The motive was apparently robbery, for they are reported to have been carrying a large sum in United States currency. It was a foolhardy thing for them to have journeyed into the Ukraine, for they had been warned in Warsaw of the danger on the highways, but they went ahead anyway, impelled by a sense of duty.

Rabbi Cantor's body was returned to Buffalo for burial, and on September 7, 1920, a city-wide memorial service for him was held at Beth Zion, where he had frequently spoken and where he had strong ties with Herman Wile who had encouraged him to enter the rabbinate. His charming fiancée, Irene Abramowitz, who came to Buffalo to be with his mother, spoke at this meeting. The incident aroused the entire city to the plight of the Jew in post-war Europe.[12]

Several years later, Eugene Warner, was appointed state chairman of the American Jewish Relief Drive. Mr. Warner established headquarters at the Hotel Iroquois and thus brought the city into the international movement in a very real way. The local group, the Buffalo Jewish Relief Committee for Sufferers from the War, held its initial meeting early in 1922, with Theodore Hofeller presiding. In addition to his role as state chairman, Eugene Warner led the Buffalo campaign, assisted by Samuel J. Harris.

The quota for Buffalo was $150,000 out of a state total of $5,000,000 and a national goal of $14,000,000. With the motto "We Save Them or They Die," a highly organized drive was conducted that, in the language of the day, "went over the top." The experience gained during the wartime Liberty Loan drives was put to good use. At a great victory dinner, "Dean" Warner, dressed in academic costume, presented diplomas to the workers. All elements in the community had united to make the appeal a success and three thousand individuals had made contributions.[13]

By the mid-twenties, American Jewry could look back with pride on its accomplishments in disarrayed Europe. About four million hungry children had been fed; one million tons of clothing had been sent abroad, and over $63,000,000 had been distributed in the early days of the war alone. By 1924, however, J.D.C. had been largely replaced by the American Jewish Relief Committee. The older group continued to function, but its efforts in recent years have been mainly devoted to providing subsistence to depressed areas of the Diaspora, aiding the exodus of Jews from centers of oppression to Israel and the free world, and in maintaining special social service institutions in the Jewish state.

The American Jewish Relief Committee owed its origin to Louis Marshall who called together the heads of some three dozen national organizations to form a new group.[14] In 1925, a meeting was called at Philadelphia to raise an additional $15,000,000 for overseas relief. Because the war had by that time faded from vivid memory, the national leaders wanted to tighten up and expand their organization. They proposed to campaign in a hundred cities for the principal purpose of assisting Russian Jews.

This proposal to devote money largely to the assistance of Russian Jews touched off much Zionist opposition. The Zionists demanded parity, that is, that at least half of the dollars leaving America be earmarked for Palestine. Carl Sherman, ex-Attorney General of New York and brother-in-law of the local Zionist leader Louis Goldring, led the fight to prevent the major share of the money from going to the Soviet Union. He correctly argued that it would not only be dangerous, but absolutely futile to subsidize the settlement of Jews on Russian lands that were then opening up under collectivistic plans. The issue was settled in a compromise over Agro-Joint, the agency of the (American) Joint Distribution Committee in Russia. It was promised that the Agro-Joint dollars would not be used to establish an autonomous Jewish republic within Russia, such as that later established at Biro-Bidjan, but would merely be devoted to emergency relief.[15]

In Buffalo, the leader of the movement to send money to Palestine rather than elsewhere was David Diamond, then a rising young lawyer. Local enthusiasm for overseas relief either to Palestine or to Russia had. waned by 1926, and the *Buffalo Jewish Review* lamented: "If there is one thing which characterizes post-war humanity it is the absence of any meliorative or emancipatory movement. The failure to acquire an historical perspective has left nothing but disillusion and fatigue." "The terms starvation, misery, death, have been said over and over so many times," said the editor, "that they sound in our ears like echoes from empty cans." [16] In 1926, the United Jewish Campaign attempted to raise $225,000 in Buffalo; but it met with little enthusiasm. It was not until the following year, when the Federation and the United Jewish Campaign conducted a joint drive, that the spark was ignited. Even Christian interest was aroused in 1927. A meeting was held at the Hotel Statler under the sponsorship of the American Christian Fund for Jewish Relief, marking one of the first occasions in Buffalo of Christian interest in the plight of the East-European Jew.

After four years of relief work, the United Jewish Campaign was discontinued in 1929. It had collected about $15,000,000 which had been used by J.D.C. for the rehabilitation of Jewish life in eastern Europe. But it was all in vain, for Poland and the surrounding lands were about to be destroyed as Jewish centers. Still, American Jews on the eve of the Great Depression unwittingly felt that their task was over, never dreaming of the blood-thirsty dictators who would soon make foreign relief more imperative than ever.[17]

Although the Federation had pushed local problems into the background during the war and the new prosperity had itself eliminated many of these problems, after the 1918 Armistice local needs again became pressing. With the return of peace, an accumulation of petty problems demanded attention: cases of Jews caught peddling without licenses, transients in need of temporary help, broken eyeglasses in need of repair, children in need of new shoes for Passover, an eighty-four-year-old man who wanted to peddle "for a pastime" but who either could not or would not pay the municipal fees. Things were getting back to normal at Federation headquarters on Jefferson Avenue.

Meanwhile, the funds of the Federation were slowly accumulating. In 1912, there were 496 members and a treasury of $17,407; six years later, there were 860 members and a treasury of $26,355. Growth was too slow, however, and in 1918, there was considerable debate about how to raise more funds without resorting to ticket sales and raffles. The need to broaden the base of its subscriptions was evident, for in the last year of the war only 7% of the Jews in Buffalo had made donations, and the total subscription amounted to less than $3 per capita. This city was obviously falling far behind other communities in support of its united charities. It was time for a change.[18]

The Buffalo Federation decided to revamp its structure in an effort to gain increased popular support. As part of the re-organization, but principally to reflect the growing emphasis on social service rather than on charity, the name was changed in 1919 from the Federated Jewish Charities of Buffalo to the Jewish Federation for Social Service. It was also decided at this time that the Board of Governors was too cumbersome a body for effective administration, and a small executive committee was chosen from its members.

A campaign was launched to bring a thousand new subscribers to the Federation, and for the first time modern methods, derived from fund raising campaigns of the war years, were used to put increased pressure on non-subscribers. As an inducement to the new members, the beginning of the fiscal year was shifted from September to January 1st, so that members would not be bothered with the fund raising campaign at the same time that they were required to pay up their synagogue dues before the fall High Holidays.[19]

After the 1918 Armistice, the whole idea of community service shifted from the old concept of charity dispensed as a moral obligation to social welfare and rehabilitation. Mary E. Richmond's seminal book, *Social Diagnosis* (published 1917), touched off a whole new scientific approach to the problem of relief, with the emphasis on short-run aid being replaced by long-run programs devoted to health, education, recreation, vocational guidance and physical therapy. The result of this shift in attitude was that the Federation gradually became more and more dependent on professional workers to carry out the programs planned by its lay policy makers. As early as 1915, this new departure was felt in the appointment of Mrs. Sarah Rummel as Domestic Educator with headquarters at the Jewish Community Building. In one of her reports to her employers she stated that she had found the needy to be poor shoppers who did not seem to buy the proper amount of food and who often spent their stipends on the wrong things. They had not, she reported, learned "American standards" of cleanliness, comfort and health.[20]

Meanwhile, in an attempt to widen the scope of the Federation, the Committee of Eleven was formed in 1920. One of the proposals entertained by this committee was to consolidate the Jewish Fresh Air Camp, the Jewish Mothers Club, the Talmud Torah, the Hebrew Benevolent Loan Association, the House of Shelter, the Jewish Young Men's (and Women's) Association, the Old Folks Home and the Buffalo Hebrew Orphan Asylum Association into the Federation. In order to induce some of these organizations to join, the committee was willing to guarantee observance of Orthodox customs wherever they were demanded and not to interfere with the original purposes of these institutions. Finally, the Committee of Eleven wanted the Federation to raise additional money to take care of such outside appeals as the Hebrew Immigrant Aid Society, the National Farm School and several Jewish hospitals for consumptives located in Denver.[21]

All of these farsighted plans, however, came to naught, for no progress at all was made in the directions indicated until 1925, when the Talmud

Torah came into the Federation. Despite the promises, individual institutions feared they would lose their autonomy and be forced to accept unwelcome changes. Each organization had its own bureaucracy and some office holders feared that they might lose their jobs under federation. In addition, some remnants of the East-West Side cleavage continued even after the war.

The first really modern fund raising campaign was launched in the midst of great pessimism during the sharp post-war panic of 1921-1922. This effort, however, was so successful that it set the pace for all Federation campaigns to come and it moved Buffalo from a backward place in American Jewish circles to a position of high standing. With a goal of enrolling 3,000 new subscribers and raising sights to what was then the staggering sum of $90,000, the drive was opened by Rabbi Nathan Krass of New York on November 27, 1921, with these practical, if not inspired, words: "Open your hearts and then your purses." Almost immediately $50,000 poured in as a result of the first high-pressure Federation campaign in the city. In the spirit of post-war nationalism, "red, white and blue brigades" ferreted out the gifts and brought in the new members. The drive "went over the top" for a total of $98,580, and 500 happy "warriors" celebrated a "victory dinner" at the Hotel Iroquois on December 4, 1921. Rabbi Menachem M. Eichler, who spoke at the dinner, proudly announced that the successful drive marked a new era of harmony in the community. Although his words were true in the sense that the drive had brought many people together in a concerted effort, such organizations as the Talmud Torah, the Jewish Mothers Club and the Fresh Air Camp were still outside of the union.[22]

To summarize, there were then five constituent groups in the Federation. The Sisterhood of Zion had as its main function the operation of the Jewish Community Building, but its work was to decrease as Jews moved steadily uptown. The Ladies' Sewing and Aid Society, although its weekly meetings were no longer needed, hesitated to disband even after a motion to dissolve had been passed. The old Hebrew Union Benevolent Society was also on the decline. In 1923, this organization changed its name to the Men's Benevolent Society, and seven years later, with its tasks almost eliminated, it was absorbed in a program of re-organization. The Ladies' Benevolent Society still carried on in a limited way some of its original functions. Of the five organizations then affiliated with the Federation, the old Jewish Aid Society was still active in 1921; but it, too, eventually lost its identity.

During the prosperous Coolidge Era, the Federation constantly raised funds and increased its list of subscribers. As its membership grew, so did its activities. The Federation established milk stations, patterned after the well-advertised Nathan Straus plan of New York City which had sold milk at one cent a glass. A playground, equipped by Marvin M. Marcus in memory of his wife, was enlarged, and by 1923 a nutrition clinic, a vacation school and art classes were in operation. Flora I. Dudley, a deeply religious Christian woman, was appointed Federation nurse to serve at the building in the rear of the Community Building. Under the chairmanship of Dr. Mansfield Levy, the Dispensary of the Jewish Federation for Social Service was established.

Maurice S. Tabor was the secretary-treasurer of the 1924 campaign which collected over $119,000. To whip up enthusiasm, the men were organized into regiments and battalions. As if that were not enough, the "forces" were backed up by a "Flying Squadron." These workers swooped down on potential donors armed with stacks of cards arranged according to the occupations of the intended givers. The technique apparently worked, for the drive was a success.[23] Buffalo continued, however, to be beleaguered with rival campaigns. Although the Federation had reduced a half-dozen drives to one, organizations outside of the city made many independent demands on local people. Late in 1924, the annual Federation appeal, with Harry J. Lehman as chairman, surpassed expectations to yield $135,000. The post-war recession had passed and the steady series of successful drives reflected the tinsel prosperity of the decade.[24]

The 1927 campaign for funds, as previously mentioned, was the first to combine local and outside appeals when the Federation joined with the United Jewish Campaign to raise $171,703. The slogan of this appeal was "Suppose Nobody Cared," and the general chairman was the dapper Willard W. Saperston. In order to induce the local group to participate, the United Jewish Campaign asked for only $33,000 of the total to be collected.[25]

Imbued with the majestic optimism of the day, Federation leaders were at this time predicting annual budgets of $200,000 and engaging in the popular fallacy of talk about "ending poverty in our time." Maurice S. Tabor led the 1928 drive for funds. He worked quietly, skillfully, and efficiently behind the scenes to spark the campaign to a successful conclusion. The extent of the efforts of the Federation at this time can be judged from the staggering sum of $189,430 spent in the year 1927 alone. Much of this money went to support the 297 families and 285 individuals then still receiving assistance. In those peaceful days, the overseas allotment amounted to but a fraction of the annual budget.[26]

The Silver Jubilee of the Federation was celebrated at Hotel Statler on November 25, 1928, coinciding with the opening of the annual appeal. Seated at a special "Founders' Table" were August Keiser, the original financial secretary, Miss Cecil B. Wiener, Joseph Desbecker, Theodore

Hofeller, Mrs. Julius Altman, Mrs. Julius L. Saperston, Eugene Warner, Eugene Wolff, Mrs. Gustave Benjamin, Mrs. Israel Aaron, Mrs. A. J. Elias, Mrs. Theodore Hofeller and Mrs. N. Wolff. The principal address was delivered by Aaron Sapiro, the attorney whose recent suit against Henry Ford for one million dollars had made headline news.

Dr. Lester Levyn (1886-1938) was then president of the Federation. A nephew of the merchant and political leader J. L. Davis, Levyn had been born in Buffalo where he became a prominent radiologist. Of the large donors in this Silver Jubilee campaign (which raised more than the quota of $176,868), two are of especial interest: Isaac S. Given donated $1,000 over and above his original contribution when he heard that the popular young hero, Charles A. Lindbergh, had landed safely in Mexico City after a solo flight from New York. In addition, the daughters of the recently deceased Mayer Wile set up a Federation endowment fund of $5,000 in memory of their father.[27]

The last pre-depression Federation campaign was started November 24, 1929, one month to the day after the ill-fated stock market collapse. Although the workers fell short of their appointed goal of $188,725, they did manage to raise $110,000 at the opening dinner. While this 1929 campaign proved disappointing at the time, it would be many years until the amount subscribed would again be equalled or surpassed by the Buffalo Jewish community.[28]

In the meantime, as this incessant fund raising was going on, life in the William Street area was undergoing some striking changes. The recent war, as we have seen, set in motion certain forces that were eventually to destroy the downtown Jewish neighborhood. Not the least of these changes was the liberation of the youth from his Europeanized home environment and his desire for rapid Americanization. For Jews of the William Street district, a very important agent in this change was the Jewish Community Building at 406 Jefferson Avenue. Early in the life of this center, young men like Jack Yellen and the future physical education instructor, Leo Safir, formed the Jewish Community Athletic Organization to meet the demands of the youngsters of the area who were anxious to participate in American team sports.

By 1917, Samuel Kuttner had come from the College Settlement in New York to serve as director of "old 406." He was a trained social worker, and organized many groups. It is significant of the attitude of the day, that many of these organizations often avoided Jewish names and selected, in their Yankee-Doodle enthusiasm, American-sounding names. Such clubs as the Spartans, the Hudsons, the Community Boys, the Orions, the Merry Hearts, and the Titans were located at the Community Building.

One of the oldest and most important of these young men's groups
was the Arya Association. In those days when the East Side synagogues
had no ancillary social organizations, this association provided many of
the functions that are now performed by temple-sponsored social groups.
Among other activities, the members often helped in the Federation drives,
and they sometimes joined in affairs with the Rochester and Niagara
Falls Arya "dens." They were enthusiastic Zionists, and in 1918, by means
of a vaudeville show at the Elmwood Music Hall, raised $1,000 for
Palestine. Music was a special interest of this local group. Its "club musician" was the son of Cantor Samuel Arluck, now Harold Arlen of Hollywood fame.

The fourth convention of the Arya clubs was held in Buffalo in 1923
with Louis A. Goldberg in charge. Goldberg was also founder and first
editor of the *Senior Review,* a paper published at the Jewish Community
Building. Later a well-known accountant in Buffalo, his record was to
include two terms as president and many years as secretary of Temple
Emanu-El, and one-time service as Grand Chancellor of the New York
State organization of the Knights of Pythias.[29]

The Jewish Community Building did much to spread American culture
among the neighborhood youngsters. Victrola concerts and amateur
dramatics brought the young people into the building and there they
were encouraged to join a club, to meet other young people socially
and to engage in intellectual pursuits. The Federation offered at the
Jefferson Avenue building community services on Friday nights, Hebrew
and Sunday school classes, public lectures, as well as physical, cultural
and Americanization programs. Specialized services included violin lessons, sewing classes, a salesmanship course, drama groups, discussions on
the new post-war cult of behaviorism, and even free sessions for young
ladies in its "charm school." In addition to these classes, mass activities
kept the auditorium busy almost every evening in the week. All this was
carried on with an annual budget of only $10,000, a tenth part of which
was made up by entrance fees for special events.

The most serious defects revealed by a 1922 evaluation of "Old 406,"
were in the physical building. Although it was less than ten years old,
its wooden stairs were in need of repair and the athletic equipment was
poor. There was insufficient space, and the administrative staff was forced
to find extra rooms in the annex on Mortimer Street.[30]

When Jacob I. Cohen replaced Kuttner as head of the Community
Building, he soon discovered the inadequacies of his facilities. Cohen
found only one small playground and two patches of brown grass that
passed for parks in the neighborhood; and he discovered that a sandwich
given to a hungry child, even though accompanied by a kind word,

scarcely took the place of a full meal. To supplement the athletic facilities of the Jefferson Avenue building Jewish children swam in the pools at nearby public schools and at Hutchinson Central High School.[31]

The community noted with satisfaction that many Jewish boys and girls who had been trained in the forensic clubs at 406 Jefferson Avenue met with success in high school debating and declamation contests. Among these lads were the late A. Irving Milch; the late Abraham Axlerod; Hyman J. Schachtel, long a rabbi in Houston, Texas; and Abraham Okun, Assistant Corporation Counsel of Buffalo. Others who were there trained in public speaking include: Rabbi Joseph Gitin; Joseph Brownstein, a prominent attorney; Leonard Finkelstein, long-time assistant district attorney of Erie County; Victor Einach, regional director of the New York State Committee Against Discrimination; Jacob Blinkoff, attorney of Great Neck, Long Island; Samuel Blinkoff, assistant executive director of the Buffalo Municipal Housing Authority; and Manus Roizen, one-time president of the Bureau of Jewish Education.

Recognizing this potential service to Buffalo, Miss Wiener called for a broader use of the Community Building. In farsighted fashion, she remarked on the rapidly aproaching end of the settlement house era with the termination of large scale immigration, the residential shift out of the area, and the steadily increasing standard of living. She called out courageously for a community house that would serve all elements of the population. Charles Polakoff, then president of the Federation, was, as an East Sider, more sensitive to the changing needs of the community than were some of the Old Guard. He declared that the deterioration of the Jefferson Avenue community made it unsafe after nightfall for children and young women, many of whom came downtown by trolley car from the West Side and the Humboldt districts. Despite his pleas for a move uptown, nothing happened, for too many of his associates still regarded a community center as a philanthropic rather than a public service institution.[32]

Meanwhile, "old 406" hummed with activity and, in 1927, 91,000 persons (many of whom were tallied several times) passed its counting machine at the front entrance. It was always crowded, but the stream was gradually decreasing because of neighborhood difficulties. Already three-quarters of the clientele lived outside the district and each year more and more people became affiliated with modern synagogues that served social and recreational needs as well as religious requirements. The need for Americanization classes was decreasing steadily, and the new director, Louis Shocket, reported that many Jewish boys were being attracted, despite the difficulties, to the YMCAs, principally by the opportunity to swim.

Shocket did his best to provide a suitable social atmosphere for these young people. In 1927, under the chairmanship of Leo Safir, the Community Building sponsored the first annual Jewish Field and Track Meet at the old Broadway Auditorium. Another event was the "Jewish Community Sport Nite" to which most synagogues sent representatives who competed in relay races, dashes, potato races and the usual field games. This annual Sports Night continued for several years, with trophies for various events donated by the Sisterhood of Zion and the Buffalo *Evening News*. In addition to the sports nights, an active Boy Scout movement was encouraged and a spirit of friendly rivalry grew among the various Jewish troops in the city.[33]

Despite these efforts, however, Jewish boys continued to attend non-Jewish clubs and organizations for recreational and sports activities and, in 1928, Miss Wiener queried pointedly: "Must they always be unwelcomed and unwanted members of Christian organizations?" For Miss Wiener, the temples could never hope to take the place of a really adequate community center. But many long and heated battles were to be fought before this need was ultimately fulfilled. Talk of a new building persisted while the prosperity of the boom days continued, and as late as the 1929 stock market crash, Miss Wiener was still urging the construction of a new building.[34] But there was little talk of expansion in the bitter years of the depression decade. Ultimately, as those hard-scrabble days stretched out, more and more people were unemployed. Eventually the need for a place where the economically displaced could congregate actually hastened the construction of a genuine community center.

While the Buffalo East Side was thinning out, the city was being affected in other ways by the chain reaction set into motion by the war of 1914-1918. Just as American Jews were affected in their social and economic status by this great upheaval, so the conflict aroused new interest in Zionism. Before 1914, the Zionists had a relatively small organization in the United States, but during the years that followed it really became a mass movement. The war devastated eastern Europe, the heartland of European Jewry, and Palestine became more necessary than ever before as a place of refuge and as a homeland. Then in 1917, the British-sponsored Balfour Declaration to which President Wilson gave consent and blessing seemed to promise the fulfillment of Herzl's dream. The very next year, the American Zionists re-organized in Pittsburgh, and out of the old Federation of American Zionists emerged the Zionist Organization of America (Z.O.A.). So contagious was this new nationalist fervor that from 1914 to 1920 the ranks of American Zionists increased ninefold.[35]

In general, Buffalo shared in this national enthusiasm, although some members of the older Reform group remained indifferent. Buffalo, however, soon became known as a staunch Zionist center.

In tracing the history of Zionism after 1914, one must be careful to distinguish several divisions in the movement. First there is Z.O.A. (General Zionists), a group that maintains neutrality on religious ideology but is economically devoted to free enterprise. The next group is Hadassah (the women's general Zionist group); and third is Mizrachi, the Orthodox wing of Zionism. The Poale Zion and other labor groups that were left of center in religious and economic thought make up the last Zionist grouping.

The General Zionists organized a "Zionist Council of Buffalo" during the war which was to serve as an *ad hoc* committee made up of various local groups. The president of this Council was Rabbi Nachman H. Ebin. Joseph A. Sapowitch, then a young furniture dealer and later a national leader in Jewish education, served as secretary for the organization. The local Zionist district was formed under the leadership of this Council, conforming to the changes in the national organization. In the fall of 1918, all Zionists in the area were registered and Buffalo and its environs became one of the original Z.O.A. districts in the country. The registration, postponed because of the epidemic of Spanish influenza, finally took place on November 17, 1918. The process, which lasted a week and took place at the Talmud Torah, succeeded in listing 3,200 local Zionists. Elections for officers were held on February 2, 1919, and the fact that there were four polling booths on the East Side to one at Elmwood and Utica reveals where the real Zionist strength in Buffalo lay. The *American Jewish Review* (forerunner of the present *Buffalo Jewish Review*) reported that the great strength of Zionism was concentrated in the Orthodox East Side *shuls*, and it is, therefore, significant to note that local traditionalists at first supported the cause of the General Zionists rather than that of Mizrachi.[36]

Thus, the Buffalo district of the Z.O.A. began in 1919 with the attorney, Louis Goldring, as first president. The following year the national Z.O.A. convention opened on Thanksgiving Day in Buffalo, having been brought to the city largely through the efforts of Mr. Goldring. National Hadassah met there simultaneously. Goldring (1885-1950) was born in Europe and was admitted to the New York State Bar in 1911. A law partner of Carl Sherman (1892-1957), Goldring moved to New York in 1928 where he spent the balance of his years.

On Thanksgiving Day, the first morning of the convention, Abraham Yellen (1873-1920), a pious and saintly man of the old school and a pillar of the Pine Street Shul, was shot while tending his store by three holdup men. Mr. Yellen, the father of the well-known family of song writers, physicians and lawyers, died the next day, and on the second morning of the convention, the delegates stood for a minute in silent mourning. This murder was particularly tragic, since it followed hard on the heels of the death of Mrs. Yellen just three months earlier. A large family was orphaned in a tragic catastrophe. Mrs. Yellen had been known for her countless deeds of charity in her East Side home where many unfortunates had been fed, clothed and comforted. In her honor, her son Jack wrote the famous song, *Mein Yiddishe Mamme.*[37]

The Buffalo convention of the Z.O.A. came just after Britain had been awarded the Palestinian Mandate at the San Remo conference. The delegates therefore optimistically expected the speedy implementation of the Balfour Declaration. The spirit of the day called for an *economic* Zionism to build up the reclaimed homeland, for at that time but 2% of Palestinian acreage was in Jewish hands. The hope was that the capital for its economic development would come from the United States and that the manpower to fill up the land would come from eastern Europe.

Many important people were among the 1,500 delegates that crowded into the Hotel Lafayette. The general chairman of the convention committee was the indefatigable Charles Polakoff. Among the speakers was Rabbi Abba Hillel Silver, who neatly bridged the gap between Zionism and Americanism by saying that the Jews were here in America to stay despite the help that they would give to Palestine. During the convention, Buffalonians played a prominent part in the national Zionist movement, with Louis Goldring on the nominating committee, Leon H. Miller on the budget committee, and Rabbi Ebin on the national executive committee.[38]

Soon, however, the rumblings of an international storm that was to shake American Zionism for ten years were to be heard in Buffalo. Local Zionists were destined to be deeply involved in the stir created by this conflict.

In 1919, flushed with victory over the burgeoning Z.O.A., Justice Louis D. Brandeis visited Palestine. During his sojourn there, he became convinced that Yankee ingenuity was needed to replace the lackadaisical East-European economic methods then in force in the Holy Land. Brandeis had met Dr. Chaim Weizmann in 1919 at London, and he had saluted him as head of the world Zionist movement. But soon the two men were to be violently opposed to each other. At the 1920 World Zionist Congress in London, Brandeis spoke out in favor of making America "the Great Hinterland . . . the reservoir of money and men to restore Palestine." Weizmann, on the other hand, who was then president of the World Zionist Organization and ultimately destined to become the first president of Israel, wanted emphasis on cultural Zionism, with more stress on the rejuvenation of the Jewish people than on business know-how. But Brandeis insisted that the Jews of the United States would not invest in Palestine unless up-to-date business methods were employed.

Probably the immediate cause of the rift between Brandeis and Weizmann was a 1921 proclamation that called upon the Jews of America to support Keren Hayesod (Palestine Foundation Fund), established to provide funds to enable those who settled on public lands in Palestine to purchase their home-sites. The Brandeis group opposed the plan because they felt that it confused investment with charity. Eventually the rift boiled down to a preference by the Brandeis group for development of Israel by private investments, and a preference by the Weizmann group for development through public funds.

The crisis came at the 1921 Cleveland convention of the Z.O.A. The delegates refused to give a vote of confidence to the Brandeis group, and the Weizmann block won out. Thereupon, Judge Julian W. Mack, a Brandeis supporter and president of the Z.O.A., resigned in protest, and he and his followers walked out to form their own schismatic Palestine Development Corporation.[39]

This split in Zionist ranks had strong local reverberations. Leon H. Miller, the intellectual leader of Buffalo Zionists, was ardently pro-Brandeis, as was David Diamond. The Brandeis plan was to stay formally within the Z.O.A., but to take up a stand of passive resistance. This group decided to devote itself to independent constructive work in Palestine. Thus various independent bodies sprang up within the framework of the Z.O.A. Each was devoted to some special plan or idea to develop basic industries, or to build low-cost housing, or some other similar scheme in the hope of building up a spirit of self-support among the Jews of Palestine. For example, Miller assumed the presidency in 1923 of a Palestine Development League of Buffalo, with Charles Polakoff as vice-president. The quarrelling between factions of the Z.O.A. became so bitter that Miller later wrote: "Since the Cleveland convention of 1921, there was hardly a Zionist organization in Buffalo." [40]

The pro-Brandeis group in Buffalo seems to have been stronger than the pro-Weizmann faction, not only because it was led by men like Miller, but also because the majority seemed to prefer, as the saying went, the Washington ways of Brandeis to the Pinsk methods of Weizmann.

The East Siders, however, looked on the Brandeis group as a West Side organization, and they pointed as evidence of their claim to the fact that the publicity for the cause was being printed in English instead of in Yiddish. On October 31, 1921, Leon H. Miller, Mrs. Fannie Brickman, her brother David Diamond, Louis Goldring and Rabbi Eichler all resigned from the local Zionist organization and a pro-Weizmann group led by Dr. George J. Saylin took over. Saylin, who was elected president, was of European birth and was fluent in Yiddish. Dr. Saylin spoke and wrote extensively for Weizmann's plan and charged that Justice Brandeis did not understand traditional Jewish philanthropy and wanted to deny the Palestinian Jews the benefit of it. A local branch of Keren Hayesod was promptly organized, and the pro-Weizmann group brought the arch-foe of Brandeis to Buffalo to speak at an East Side mass meeting. The Rochester-born Louis Lipsky spoke in Yiddish and lashed out against the Palestine Development Corporation of the Brandeis faction. And so the battle was joined.[41]

By 1923, the Palestine Development Corporation was selling shares at $10 each and the Buffalo quota was almost filled through the efforts of such men as the veteran Zionist and friend of Herzl, Jacob De Haas, who addressed one meeting so effectively that many shares were sold imme-diately.

When the Miller group brought the renowned Professor Felix Frank-furter of Harvard Law School to Buffalo to speak in favor of the Palestine Development Corporation, this coup forced Weizmann's supporters to bring up equally heavy oratorical guns for Keren Hayesod. They brought Weizmann himself, president of World Zionist Organization, to speak at a banquet held in the Montefiore Club. After his introduction by David Ruslander, Dr. Weizmann very shrewdly devoted part of his speech to complimenting the ladies. It was a politic move, for the Buffalo Hadassah had 600 members, while the men who had used up all their energies feud-ing had only forty-five! [42]

With the passage of time, there were increasing signs of unity. In 1925, Louis Goldring was returned to the presidency of the Buffalo Zionist District with many representatives of the dissenting groups, including Leon H. Miller, present. The Palestine Development Corporation had al-ready merged with other Palestinian financial groups and they were now united under the name of the New Palestine Investment Corporation. This newly organized group devoted itself solely to economic activities. As a result of this move by the national group, the local branch of the Palestine Development Corporation, with Miller as chairman, lost its status and ultimately decided to cooperate with the local district. Mean-while, as the pro-Brandeis group was withdrawing from its original in-flexible stand, the Keren Hayesod had raised $8,000,000 in four years and thus seemed marked for success.[43]

The union of the Jewish National Fund and Keren Hayesod was the UPA (United Palestine Appeal) which had been launched in Baltimore in 1925. In the fall of that same year, Buffalo Zionists tried to raise $75,000 as a UPA campaign under the joint auspices of Keren Hayesod (the Palestine Foundation Fund) and the Jewish National Fund, as part of this national campaign to raise $5,000,000.

This first UPA drive got off to a fairly good start locally with about one-third of the quota raised on the opening night. For a time, however, it looked as though the evening was not going to be a success, and Rabbi Stephen S. Wise, who came to Buffalo for the occasion, became so angry at the hesitancy of the crowd to contribute, that he harangued them with these words: "I am not a picayunish alms seeker. . . . I have given my life and my fortune to the cause, and I demand better treatment than this." [44] Despite these words of a self-styled martyr to the cause, only a few more pledges were brought in during the evening, for the tensions that had split the local Zionists were still working against the total cause of Palestine rebuilt.

In 1926, the Z.O.A. national convention met once more in Buffalo. Louis Goldring was again president of the local district and once more had much to do with bringing the event to this city. A whole galaxy of world Jewish leaders convened at the Hotel Statler; probably never before in the history of Buffalo had so many Jewish leaders descended on the city. Among them were Louis Lipsky; Chaim Nachman Bialik, the great Hebrew poet; Dr. Shemarya Levin; Stephen S. Wise; Abba Hillel Silver; and the prolific young writer Maurice Samuels. The chairman of the convention committee was David Diamond, then only twenty-eight years old. The delegates began pouring into the city on Friday, June 25. The morning train from New York was met by an honor guard provided by Mayor Frank X. Schwab, and then a cavalcade wound its way to City Hall where Mayor Schwab presented the keys to the city to the visiting dignitaries. After the official city reception, the guests were escorted to the Hotel Statler along streets bedecked with blue and white Zionist flags. "Mr. Statler," said a press report, "must have turned over the entire hostelry to the Jewish nation, for in every chair, in every wing, in every lobby, the occupant was a Jew or a Jewess." Other Zionist organizations met here concurrently.

Louis Goldring opened the first meeting on Sunday, June 27, at the old Elmwood Music Hall, by stating that he had been converted to Zionism by Leon H. Miller who had been the first Zionist that he had ever met. This noble beginning was given a bit of a jolt when Dr. A. T. Rubin rose to express the hope that despite the Brandeis break, "Leon will once more take an active part in the Zionist movement." Despite this rather tactless remark, the convention did not become another Donnybrook. Although the local Zionists were greatly impressed by the Hebrew speech of Dr. David Yellin, principal of the Hebrew Teachers College at Jerusalem, their basic attitudes were well summed up by the poet Bialik who said, before he departed from the city, that the American Zionists were not yet ready for their main role. They tended, he remarked, to think too much of Zionism in terms of charity; they were "holiday Zionists," most active at sumptuous banquets.[45]

Despite its early promise, Buffalo was still noticeably lagging in the Zionist cause. The UPA of 1927 opened with a kosher banquet, reflecting the traditional influence of the chairman, Emil Rubenstein. Over 350 workers ran down about 6,000 cards which were arranged according to the vocations and professions of the potential donors. Israel Goldin, the Broadway department store magnate, gave the largest contribution, $1,100, a sign that the day of the "king-sized" gift was still to come.[46]

The next year, in a campaign to restore "Buffalo to its old position as the premier city in America for Zionist effort and activity," the city once more set out to raise $50,000. But the local Zionists were still demoralized and almost hopelessly split. On the national level, however, things began to improve. Louis Lipsky withdrew from active Zionist leadership and this withdrawal paved the way for an understanding between the rival factions within the Z.O.A.

In what was destined to be the last pre-depression Palestine drive, the quota for Buffalo was reduced to $25,000. Most likely the local squabbles between factions had something to do with the reduction. A ray of light in that fateful year 1929 came at the 16th World Zionist Congress at which the Jewish Agency was formed in an effort to unite all groups in Jewry except the outright anti-Zionists. But before the Big Crash, American Jews, as always in times of quiescence, drank "the drowsy syrups of prosperity," and did not work to full capacity. They were shaken out of this lethargic state, however, in mid-summer of that year by the Hebron riots in Palestine, in which Arabs raided the Jewish quarter of that city and murdered many Talmud students including some Americans. A new sense of emergency seemed to sweep Buffalo, for even old-line Reform Jews, not hitherto interested in Zionism, pitched in to raise an emergency fund of $5,000. These riots also caused Justice Brandeis to break his long silence when, on November 24, 1929, he reiterated his faith in the movement which had suffered because of his grievance.[47] Then, at the Cleveland convention of the Z.O.A., in June 1930, the Brandeis-Mack group resumed control of the national organization after a lapse of nine years, although Brandeis, because of his judicial post, refrained from active leadership.

The withdrawal of Lipsky, the appeasement of Brandeis, the Hebron riots, the salutary effect of the creation of the Jewish Agency, and the issuance of the Passfield White Paper which further narrowed British

promises in Palestine, all helped revive Zionism in Buffalo. On Rosh
Hashana of 1930, Dr. Israel Efros, rabbi of Beth El and close friend of
Leon Miller, called for unity in Zionist ranks, and Rabbi Joseph L. Fink
of Beth Zion also made a strong plea for peace now that "sanity and perspective [are] restored." [48]

An open letter calling for the re-organization and re-vitalization of the
local district was then circulated. About 400 people attended a meeting
for which Leon H. Miller emerged from retirement to address the gathering and declare that the newest outrages might actually be a blessing in
disguise, for they might consolidate the Jewish community. "The Buffalo
Zionist District," the press reported, "came to life again Thursday evening,
November 6, 1930." Leon H. Miller was elected to the presidency by acclamation and the group was reactivated. [49]

Thus far we have related the story of men who, in Buffalo and
elsewhere, struggled for the Jewish homeland promised by the Balfour
Declaration. Meanwhile, a second, and most successful unit of Zionism
had been organized in 1912 by Miss Henrietta Szold. Within half a dozen
years, Hadassah, as this distaff branch of the movement was called, had
grown to 5,500 members.

The local Hadassah unit originated at the home of Mrs. Leon H. Miller
on November 27, 1920, while the Z.O.A. was holding its national convention here. Fourteen years later, to honor Mrs. Miller's pioneer work, Buffalo Hadassah endowed an operating room at the Hebrew University
Hospital in Jerusalem in her honor. Among the women attending this
organizational meeting at her home were the wives of board members of
the Zionist District. Mrs. Miller was elected first president and Mrs. Samuel Kavinoky vice-president. Twenty-nine of the group became charter
members of Buffalo Hadassah and established National Hadassah's 103rd
chapter. So active was this organization that membership grew rapidly
within a few months.

Hadassah promptly launched its first fund-raising campaign with a
benefit dance, the proceeds of which were to be used for training a Buffalo Hadassah nurse and for supplying medicines for Palestine. It was also
planned to establish a textbook fund for the translation of important scientific books into Hebrew. Soon the group began to sponsor an annual
linen shower. A press report describes the activities of the ladies in those
early days: "Some knit; some sew; others are procuring members, securing funds, spreading healthful propaganda—and in addition a small group
is studying Hebrew." [50]

Each year, it seemed Buffalo Hadassah surpassed its previous efforts.
In 1923, under the chairmanship of Miss Sarah Rubenstein, the idea of

the donor's campaign was launched, and the following year the local chapter was congratulated by the Palestinian Supplies Bureau for the unusually large gift of bedspreads, sheets, pillow cases and other linens that the ladies had gathered. The Buffalo women were inspired to these efforts by those who visited Palestine and returned to speak glowingly of the work of Hadassah there. "Last week was Buffalo week in our office," wrote Miss Henrietta Szold from Jerusalem to Mrs. Miller, as she described the visit of some Buffalonians to Jerusalem. "Mr. and Mrs. L. Cohen, Mr. and Mrs. Louis Maisel, Mr. and Mrs. L. Goldin, all passed through." [51] Miss Szold visited Buffalo the following year to speak to Hadassah on "The Place of Palestine in Modern Jewish Life," and roused the women to the ambitious task of raising $10,000. By 1926 the local group was given a lift when both the Z.O.A. and the Hadassah national conventions were held in Buffalo. In 1930, Hadassah again met there, and throughout the decade that followed, the organization mushroomed. It was at this time that Hadassah adopted the "Donor's Luncheon" as a fund-raising device: each member, in order to be admitted to the luncheon, raised a certain sum (originally $10). The device was an immediate success and continued in various forms for many years. Another activity of Hadassah was the Youth Aliyah movement through which victims of Hitler were sent to Palestine.

Junior Hadassah was organized in 1921 with Dinah R. Rosenblatt as president and Leya Greenberg (Mrs. Irving I. Crouse) as secretary. The younger group grew rapidly and, by 1938, when it was meeting monthly at the Hotel Statler, it boasted 125 members. Leaders in the Junior Hadassah on both a local and a national level during this period were Celia B. Slohm (Mrs. William Bernstein), who was elected national president of Junior Hadassah in 1934 and served two terms; Hannah Schiff (Mrs. Alvin J. Franklin); Miss Zella Ruslander and Janet M. Sukernek (Mrs. Selig Adler). Junior Hadassah's special project was Meier Shfeyah, a children's village in Palestine. In addition, the organization promoted citriculture in Palestine, helped JNF, and sponsored a nurses' training school in Jerusalem.

The third Zionist organization, Mizrachi, never took firm root in Buffalo. It had been organized in Europe in 1902 as an outlet for Orthodox Zionists who wanted to reconcile the nationalistic impulse with faith and tradition. American Mizrachi dates from 1914 and a chapter was formed in Buffalo shortly thereafter. Its growth was possibly impeded by the decision here of many right-wing religious leaders to cast their lot with the general Zionists. [52]

The Mizrachi group, which had lived a precarious existence in Buffalo, was re-organized in 1932 under the leadership of Rabbi Gedaliah Kaprow; and in that same year, Rabbi Meyer Berlin, president of Mizrachi World Organization, and Rabbi Wolf Gold, president of Mizrachi of America, visited Buffalo. Such activity locally brought the 16th annual convention of Mizrachi to this city on November 24, 1932, and Max M. Yellen was chairman of a large committee that acted as hosts to the delegates.

After this event, Mizrachi was active for a time with youth groups, fund-raising and other programs. Occasionally an attempt to start a local branch of Hapoel Ha-Mizrachi (Labor Mizrachi) brought life to the show, for it was in the spirit of the 1930s to reconcile tradition and non-Marxian socialism. At the end of the decade, the national president of Mizrachi, Leon Gellman of St. Louis, came to Buffalo when the Upstate New York Region met here; but the Mizrachi flame never burned brightly on the Niagara Frontier.

The Women's Mizrachi group was organized some time in the 1930s and for years was stronger than the men's group. Chief members were Mrs. Ruth Orenstein, Mrs. Morris Steinhorn and Mrs. Henry Apfelgreen. The work of this group was greatly expanded after the arrival in 1953 of Mrs. Isaac Klein, wife of the rabbi of Temple Emanu-El. Known today as the Deborah Chapter of the Mizrachi Women of America, it now has a membership of 175, made up largely of women from Conservative and Orthodox congregations who want to aid both Israel and traditional Judaism.

Poale Zion, whose origins have already been discussed, was a representative of the fourth type of Zionist organization, the left-wing segment. "Productivity, creativeness and a life of labor," became the watchword of this group which is now more frequently called the Labor Zionist Organization of America. Closely related to Poale Zion is the Farband, the fraternal order of Labor Zionism. Founded in Rochester in 1913, Farband came to Buffalo soon thereafter, and among its early leaders here were Morris Goldman, Jacob Sandler and members of the Zackheim family.

In 1915, the national convention of the order was held in this city. About 2,000 people crowded into the Broadway Auditorium to listen to some of the most famous Jewish leaders of the day, including Dr. Chaim Zhitlowsky, Dr. Isaac Hurwitz and Pinchas Rutenberg (later founder of the Palestine Electric Company). Also in attendance was David Ben-Gurion, later Prime Minister of Israel, who, according to local legend, was stricken with malaria while here and nursed back to health on a Jewish farm near Buffalo.

Unlike other Socialists, the members of Farband felt a strong sense of kinship with their brethren in eastern Europe, which, during World War I, was the cockpit of fighting, and they took up weekly collections for the sufferers. In 1917, when the famous Jewish Legion was organized under Vladimir Jabotinsky, several Buffalo members of Farband joined.

After the war, Farband, jointly with Poale Zion, founded the Palestine Workers Fund to help cooperative settlements in the Holy Land. They raised funds by holding two flower days each year in which they sold flowers on the street corners in Jewish neighborhoods.[53]

Another activity of the Farband was a house-to-house campaign to spread the gospel of Labor Zionism; but Buffalo never had a very large Jewish proletariat, and what there was here a generation ago has all but vanished. From the right, Farband and Poale Zion were under attack in those days as being too Socialistic, but from the left they were charged with being too Jewish. Gradually Poale Zion became less Marxist in tone as its members became alienated by the course of Soviet Russia, and as this took place it was accompanied by a shift of interest from Yiddish to Hebrew. Slowly but surely they moved toward a more normative type of Jewishness. As part of this philosophical shift, Poale Zion stopped sending money to Russian and German workers in 1924, and concentrated on aiding Jewish laborers in Palestine and elsewhere.[54]

During the 1920s there were two Poale Zion groups in Buffalo. In addition to the older circle, some post-1918 immigrants, fresh from the Old World, organized their own group. After maintaining separate organizations for five years, the two factions united into a single chapter.

In addition, there were two women's groups of Labor Zionists in Buffalo. In 1920, the local Farband founded the Manya Shochat Women's Club, named in honor of a Jewish woman revolutionary who fled to Palestine after throwing a bomb at a Russian official. The club named in her honor collected funds for the Kupat Holim (Palestinian health insurance and sick relief). The Pioneer Women, a parallel organization, was founded locally in 1927 and soon absorbed the Manya Shochat Women's Club. The chief purpose of the Pioneer Women is to assist the working women's council of Israel by raising money for nursery schools, centers for the care of children of working mothers and vocational schools for girls. The Pioneer Women of Buffalo in the 1950s numbered about 300 and were divided into two groups. Chapter One was made up of a Yiddish-speaking group, and Hanita (or Chapter Two) was composed of an English-speaking element.

Still another branch of Labor Zionism came to Buffalo in 1929 with the establishment of the "Dr. Shapero Chapter" of Young Poale Zion. Habonim, as this group is now called, began with eight founding members, and its strength gradually grew to thirty-five within two years. In 1931, the Young Poale Zion National Convention was held in Buffalo with seventy-five delegates and 125 visitors in attendance. The principal attraction was Manya Shochat of Palestine. The speeches at the convention reflected the *Zeitgeist* of the depression years, for there was much talk of whether Palestine should be rebuilt on the "old ideas of competition and exploitation" or according to the "social vision of the prophets." [55]

Members of the Buffalo branch of Young Poale Zion worked actively in the election year of 1932 on behalf of the Socialist candidate Norman Thomas. It was during the New Deal Era that this group was strongest in Buffalo. It held frequent joint meetings with the similar groups in Rochester and Toronto; and at the 13th annual convention of Young Poale Zion held in Buffalo in 1935, Habonim was launched. Habonim is an Americanized group with more emphasis on constructive Judaism than on Socialist ideology. A great deal of encouragement and guidance was given to the local Young Poale Zion branch by Uriah Zevi Engelman during his years in Buffalo as principal of several Hebrew schools and later as head of the Bureau of Jewish Education. Gradually, this organization declined in strength. One of the major reasons for the drop in membership was that the real leaders of the movement left Buffalo to settle in Palestine. A grand farewell was given in 1932 to the first *Halutzim* to go from Buffalo by the Pioneer Women, Poale Zion, Farband, Young Poale Zion, Junior Hadassah and the Ladies' Branch of Mizrachi. These organizations all joined to say goodbye to *Havera* Gordon and *Havera* Berkun. Later, other members of Young Poale Zion left to become settlers in Palestine.[56]

Very important nationally and locally in these years was the present National Committee for Labor Israel, better known as the Histadrut. Organized in Palestine in 1920, it gradually assumed many important functions. From 1923 to 1939, Histadrut, as a great colonizing agency, trained and assisted more than one million young settlers, besides setting up many industrial and agricultural cooperatives. Today, it is the nationally supported labor organization of the Jewish state and controls almost every facet of the Israeli economy. In America, its ideology made gradual inroads into the ranks of the anti-Zionist Arbeiter Ring, for Histadrut sympathized with and supported the cause of labor all over the world.

The Histadrut drives were called *Gewerkschaften* (labor unions) campaigns, and their purpose was to raise funds in order to put tools and machinery into the hands of the Palestinian proletariat. Histadrut's first Buffalo appeal, supported by local Poale Zion groups, opened in 1923. This initial campaign was sponsored by the National Labor Committee for Palestine in which all Jewish trade union locals were united. It is said that the *Gewerkschaften* campaigns raised about $300,000 in Buffalo in the thirty-five years that followed. In 1924, when the United Hebrew

Trades began to campaign for Histadrut nationally, many American-Jewish workers, who hitherto had thought of Zionism as a reactionary movement, were brought into the fold. The Histadrut fought the anti-Zionist Jewish Bundists (European Socialists) who wanted multinational Socialism instead of a Zion rebuilt. Gradually the Bundist idea waned and, just at the time when Reform Judaism was making its peace with Zionism, so also, on the other end of the social spectrum, Jewish labor groups were being converted to pro-Zionism.

By 1926, the *Gewerkschaften* campaign was able to bring into its circle as affiliate groups such otherwise separate organizations as the Arbeiter Ring, the Farband and the Hebrew Social Club. In that year, the Buffalo quota was $5,000 of a $250,000 national quota.[57] The recognized leader of that campaign and of many thereafter was Abraham B. Wagner (1892-1939) who had been born in Sokolovka and had prospered in Buffalo in the manufacture of boxes.

During the Great Depression, left-wing Zionism gained ground in Buffalo and elsewhere, for in those bitter years the program of these groups was particularly attractive. On April 5, 1934, the labor element, flushed with victory after having just obtained a majority in the World Zionist Congress, launched a great *Gewerkschaften* campaign. On the world scene labor groups were to dominate the Zionist movement until the independence of Israel in 1948, and even after that date, they were, under the name Mapai, to form the strongest single political party in Israel. Locally, these Socialist-Zionists were a relatively weak, but very articulate, minority. Dr. Uriah Z. Engelman, a devoted sympathizer of the movement, conceded their lack of a substantial following in Buffalo.[58]

The cultural activities of the Labor Zionists in Buffalo centered in the Poale Zion Folk Shule located at 488 Jefferson Avenue. This was one of several Yiddish-oriented afternoon schools in Buffalo. Also located in the same building, as we have seen, was the Jewish National Workers Institute. At its height, the school had an enrollment of about 150 pupils. There were four teachers and the core subjects were the Yiddish language and Jewish culture. Although students paid a modest tuition, the main source of funds was derived from concerts, said to have been played before "packed" halls. All was not sweetness and light at the school, however, for at one time the president of the Talmud Torah, Israel Swados, charged that the Yiddishists were teaching Socialism. An aroused community sent a committee to investigate the curriculum, but it reported that no dangerous doctrines were being taught. This Poale Zion school shut its doors in 1933 because Jews were leaving the East Side. Thereafter, until it, too, closed in 1954, the Arbeiter Ring conducted the only Yiddishist school in Buffalo.[59]

Labor Zionism enjoyed another boom during World War II when both the struggle against Fascism, which helped unify the community, and the *mesalliance* with the Soviets strengthened all left-wing groups. A sign of the times was the launching of the 1941 *Gewerkschaften* campaign, at Temple Emanu-El, with Dr. Joseph L. Fink delivering the opening talk. Significantly, during the war, the German-Yiddish word *Gewerkschaften* was dropped and the present name, Histadrut, was adopted in its stead.[60]

The establishment of Israel in 1948 somewhat softened ideological differences among American Zionists, for arguments diminished as the community was stirred to help the fledgling state. Meanwhile, with the new post-war prosperity, came complacency and increasing indifference to all burning ideologies. From time to time the old issues were to be raised in reaction to certain Israeli policies, but the passage of time brought increasing cooperation among the various Zionist segments.

To return to the main burden of the story, until Sarajevo the history of Jews all over the United States was marked by internal strife and division. In work and play, in synagogue and cultural pursuits, in nationalist origins and in championship of the Zionist cause, American Jews were torn asunder, mostly because of ingrained Old World prejudices. The predominant twentieth-century theme of American Jewish history is the unification of communities, once so widely split by the polyglot nature of the great folk migration of the late nineteenth century.[61]

The succession of anti-Jewish outrages that came in the wake of World War I was a strong impetus to unity. In the knowledge of slaughter and beating and pillage being meted out to helpless men and women, there was born a common concern for all the Jewish people. A new call for leadership came just as the wartime prosperity accelerated the rise to prominence of the Russian Jews. As the eastern Europeans and their children achieved economic status and enhanced secular cultural tone, their accomplishments plus their numerical superiority made them the natural leaders of American Jewry.

The gradual closing of the American haven to Europeans helped bridge the gap that once separated the downtown greenhorn from his more sophisticated uptown neighbor. As the pace of immigration slowed down, the melting pot became a pressure cooker that speeded up the process of assimilating the foreigner. American hospitality toward immigrants had begun to wane even before the war cut off the supply, and the return of peace failed to revive the cordiality once displayed toward newcomers. A series of congressional laws cut down immigration from countries with surplus Jewish population and, in 1924, the Johnson Act all but shut America's doors to them. The National Origins Act, which went into effect five years later, still further curtailed the existing quotas, and during the Great Depression, President Hoover cut these even lower. One great period of American history had come to an end.

Finally, one of the most effective forces of unification in any community, Jewish or not, is marriage; and intermarriage among the various factions, especially in Buffalo, hastened the solidification of the Jewish community. The older families were either dying out or were moving away from Buffalo, frequently to New York City or to California. They had fewer children and a high percentage of bachelors or spinsters, possibly because they could not find suitable mates. Others, more often than not, intermarried with the newer arrivals from eastern Europe. As the second and third generations grew up, went to college, joined fraternities and sororities and began to apply the American standard of the size of one's bank account in judging suitability for marriage, the old rifts and cleavages were all but forgotten.

In the final analysis, however, the community could never have become integrated had the later immigrants remained in the vicinity of William Street. As long as they lived in the crowded downtown area, the East Siders could hope for little development of social grace or refinement. As they followed the trails that led out of the old tenement area, however, they began a new life with much higher standards than they had experienced in their first years in this country.

Once the newer immigrant fled the ghetto, he did everything in his power to achieve status and erase the marks that distinguished him from his more cosmopolitan neighbors. He sent his children to more socially acceptable public schools (in Buffalo they usually transferred from Hutchinson Central High to Lafayette), and occasionally the younger children were sent to private schools like the Buffalo Seminary or the Nichols School. He attended a more up-to-date synagogue and discarded his cap for a Homburg. As he moved out of the ghetto, the man on the social climb very likely changed his job in the process of "second settlement." Finally, as he left his first home in America, the immigrant gradually cut the ties that bound him to his friends from the village or town in the Old Country; he abandoned his membership in the immigrant social organization or synagogue to which he had clung in such desperation on his arrival in the strange new land. He became, in effect, an American.

After the new Russian Jews of the heavy 1905-1914 immigration forced out some of the older settlers, the coming of the Negro to the William Street district almost finished the job of clearing the Jews from the area. It was here that southern Negroes, drawn to the North by the opportunity for wartime jobs, came to rent living quarters. The attraction of Buffalo as a Negro labor market can be seen in the phenomenal rise in the colored population from the end of the nineteenth century until the 1918 Armistice. In 1890, between 1,000 and 1,500 Negroes lived in Buffalo; in 1918, about 10,000 were there.[62]

This influx of colored people tended to depopulate the area of white inhabitants. The 7th and 6th wards were the most heavily populated Jewish wards at this time. The census figures show that during the Wilson years both population and the number of dwellings in these wards decreased. In other words, the Negro displaced more persons in these neighborhoods than his migration was able to replace.

A 1922 Jewish Welfare Board survey of Buffalo revealed that 70% of the children with obviously Jewish names attended school in the downtown neighborhood; the rest were scattered throughout the city with the heaviest concentration on the West Side. Despite these figures, it was obvious that the Jewish population in the ghetto was declining rapidly, for the percentage of Jewish children attending School No. 32 in the heart of the district dropped 20% within a few years.[63]

The editor of the *Buffalo Jewish Review,* writing two months after Congress had all but shut off immigration, predicted the end of the William Street settlement: "Without the intimate contact of fresh recruits from abroad, the Ghetto will lose its charm and distinctiveness in speech and manner." Few families, he declared, lived there any longer than necessary. "To those who have lived in the Ghetto and who understand its hardships, its struggles, its pathos, its sympathies, its loyalties, its hopes, and everything that made it human, its passing will bring a sigh of relief, a regret more inspired by reminiscence than actual sorrow." [64]

The majority of the displaced East Side inhabitants moved either to the West Side which had had a Jewish settlement dating from the 1890s, or else moved northward into the Humboldt-East Ferry region. As early as 1920, however, there was some penetration into what was later to become the most concentrated Jewish area, the North Park section. Here, the homes were relatively new and modern, for it was this neighborhood that had been developed by the building boom that preceded the Great Depression. Surveying the residential shift of the period, a competent sociologist estimated that in 1938 about a quarter of Buffalo's 20,000 Jews lived in the Humboldt section; a slightly smaller number were in North Park; a fifth of the families still lingered downtown; about the same number were on the West Side; and the remainder, just under 10%, were scattered throughout the city.[65]

In other words, within less than twenty years the William Street district had lost more than two-thirds of its Jewish population.[66] Nevertheless, this neighborhood still housed many important Jewish institutions in 1938, including the Jewish Community Building, the Jewish Welfare Society, the Mothers Club, the Gemilut Hasadim, the Hachnosat Orhim, and seven Orthodox synagogues. The only units of Jewish life that had moved out of the district prior to Pearl Harbor were the Bureau of Jewish Education, the "Y", and the Jewish Federation for Social Service. Then a new war hastened the end of the East Side as a Jewish settlement; and fifteen years after its termination, the last remaining downtown synagogue (the Jefferson Avenue Shul) closed its doors forever. All other vestiges of a once thriving Jewish neighborhood had long since disappeared.

Within the intervening decades, striking changes were taking place in the individual synagogues. When Rabbi Max Drob, an ardent traditionalist, arrived at Beth El in 1913, a scant sixty-eight members constituted a congregation beset by financial worries. During Rabbi Drob's six year ministry, the West Side grew by leaps and bounds. By the time he left Buffalo, Beth El was a solvent institution boasting a membership of 250 souls and a synagogue school that had almost quadrupled its registration in a half dozen years. The Men's Club, the Women's Club, the Boy Scouts, the Camp Fire Girls, the Athletic and Social Club were all either founded or had prospered under his leadership.

One of the reasons that Rabbi Drob left was that he could not countenance Beth El's steady drift to the left. In his farewell sermon, preached on June 28, 1919, he warned the congregation that, if they persisted in changing small things, they would eventually undermine Jewish authority. He ended his last sermon with the statement that he would always attack sin and not sinners, and stated that he was leaving because he felt that in his new synagogue in New York he could carry his message to hundreds on the Sabbath, rather than to just a handful of worshippers.[67]

The replacement for Rabbi Drob satisfied the demands of the congregation for more liberal guidance. Menachem M. Eichler, born December 27, 1872, in Hungary, came to the United States at the age of twenty. Ordained by the Jewish Theological Seminary of America in 1899, Rabbi Eichler had served in pulpits in Philadelphia and Boston. On November 21, 1920, some 500 people attended his installation as Beth El's spiritual leader. Rabbi Louis J. Kopald of Beth Zion called for unity among all Jews, and Rabbi Nachman H. Ebin spoke for the Orthodox groups. The principal speaker was the Buffalo-born Rabbi Marvin Nathan who had, some years before, served at Beth El.[68]

Rabbi Eichler's seven years at Beth El were eminently successful. A moderate and conciliatory man, he was able to reconcile the modern development of spirituality with the traditional leanings of some older members of the congregation. He was outspoken on secular problems of the day and he made his sermons lively and interesting. Among other things, for example, he talked about prohibition, denouncing it and saying that conditions under the Volstead Act would be ludicrous if they were not so tragic. The older folks in the congregation were charmed by Rabbi Eichler's biblical stories and vast rabbinical lore which he tailored to suit the Torah reading of the week. He added variety to the Sabbath services by periodically inviting guest rabbis to address the congregation. Even Eugene Warner, the ardent Reform leader, said of Rabbi Eichler that he was the man who had helped bring harmony to the community.[69]

In those halcyon days, when Beth El was located in the heart of a flourishing Jewish neighborhood, the synagogue bristled with activity. Evidence abounds that Rabbi Eichler was a good fund raiser and organizer. He gave careful, fatherly guidance to the various clubs that sprang up during his ministry. The synagogue soon had so many ancillary organizations that it was necessary to federate them into a Beth El Council to which each group elected delegates.

Suddenly, in the midst of a successful career, Rabbi Eichler died at the relatively early age of fifty-five. He was stricken on May 11, 1927, while dining at the home of his daughter. On Sunday, May 15, this warm, genial, imposing-looking man beloved by children and adults alike, was laid to rest. Among the many famous rabbis who came to eulogize him were Rabbis Solomon Goldman of Cleveland and Herman Abramowitz of Montreal.[70]

Rabbi Eichler was replaced by the foremost Jewish scholar ever to come to Beth El; but it was perhaps this very erudition that made routine parish work difficult for Israel Efros. For the first High Holidays after Rabbi Eichler's death, Dr. Efros, then dean of the Baltimore Hebrew College and Teachers Training School, preached at Beth El. Although he was reluctant to leave his academic work and was loath to take on everyday rabbinical duties, he allowed himself to be persuaded to enter the active rabbinate. He was installed as rabbi of Beth El early in 1929, just nine months before the catastrophic stock market crash.

Israel Efros had been born in the Ukraine in 1890 and had come to the United States while still a lad. By 1915, he had earned a Ph.D. at Columbia University, and in that same year was ordained rabbi at the Jewish Theological Seminary. An extremely versatile man, Efros was master of half a dozen languages. A prolific writer, he had published much of his own poetry and Hebrew dramas. In addition, he was co-author of a pioneer Anglo-Hebrew dictionary and had written several books on Jewish medieval philosophy. Hence, it was natural for him to think of himself as a teacher rather than a minister, and he told his congregation that he would view the synagogue as "a modern academy" where he would reconcile religious tradition with modern scientific thought.[71]

Despite a propitious beginning, Dr. Efros's experience as a practicing rabbi was not a happy one. When the depression struck, it became necessary for the congregation to retrench and thus some of its rabbi's educational plans were frustrated. In his intellectual approach, Dr. Efros was too far over the heads of most of his parishioners. Despite the fact that he attracted devoted and lasting intellectual followers drawn from all temples in the city, his mystical, poetic ways estranged him from the average member of his congregation. Ultimately, the breach was widened over a religious question.

For some years Beth El had contemplated the use of an organ during religious services. As we have seen, after some flirtations with Reform during its first years on Richmond Avenue, Beth El turned to the right again with Rabbi Drob. Rabbi Eichler, although much more liberal than his predecessor, never tried to force the organ issue. In 1927, however, the Marine Trust Company gave an organ to Beth El and it was accepted on condition that it be played only at weddings and not at regular Sabbath and Holiday services where the use of instrumental music is forbidden by Orthodox law and custom.[72] Three years later, Charles Polakoff temporarily retired as president and was replaced by Jacob Morrison. The new incumbent won the support of the board of trustees on the issue that the organ be played during the late Friday evening services. Rabbi Efros strongly protested the move, and for a time even refused to attend services. After a temporary rapprochement, Dr. Efros left Beth El at the end of his elected term. Subsequently, his friends throughout the city endowed a chair for him at the University. Dr. Efros headed the Semitics department thus created, until 1941, when he left to occupy a similar position at Hunter College.

Dr. Efros was replaced by Rabbi Reuben J. Magil (b.1904), who served for five years. On March 1, 1940, Rabbi H. Elihu Rickel (b.1911) became rabbi of Beth El. The most militant religious liberal in the congregation's long history, Rabbi Rickel made many changes in the ritual that pleased the advocates of modernism. It was during his incumbency that, in 1947, Beth El celebrated with great éclat its centennial anniversary. Rabbi Rickel had served as a naval chaplin during the recent war and, some years after his return from the service, he accepted an appointment as Lieutenant Commander in the United States Navy. The congregation was next led by Dr. Gershon G. Rosenstock who, in turn, was succeeded by Rabbi Milton Feierstein. Since 1950, Beth El's cantor has been a Buffalonian, Gerald De Bruin. From the early days of Rabbi Rickel in Buffalo (1942), Beth El's religious school had been under the competent supervision of Marvin H. Garfinkel. In 1957, Mr. Garfinkel abandoned a public school career in order to devote full time to synagogue affairs as the Educational and Executive Director of Buffalo's oldest synagogue. The congregation then had about 600 members, and plans were progressing to erect a school and activities building in the northern suburbs of the city, at a cost of $400,000. This one-story building, located in the Town of Tonawanda on Sheridan Drive near Eggert Road, was scheduled for completion in the fall of 1960. While Beth El planned to retain, for the time being, its Richmond Avenue Temple, the new edifice was to house the school and to contain a sanctuary where regular services could be conducted.

During the same period, Temple Beth Zion likewise witnessed growth and change. In 1917, the conference of the Central Conference of American Rabbis was held in Buffalo, with Beth Zion acting as host to the visiting delegates. Rabbi William Rosenau of Baltimore presided over the 150 rabbis who met at the Temple Centre where they were welcomed by President Herman Wile. This was a spirited convention, held just four months before the Balfour Declaration with its alluring promise of a Jewish homeland. Tempers ran high as square-jawed Rabbi Stephen S. Wise led a forlorn fight for a pro-Zionist declaration by the convention. Recalling the episode several years later, Rabbi Wise looked up at the ceiling of Beth Zion where he was guest preacher and said: "I made these rafters ring." [73]

The Union of American Hebrew Congregations, the lay Reform group, met in Buffalo in 1921, and Beth Zion played host once more. The conference began with evening services at Beth Zion on May 23 and Rabbi Kopald warmly welcomed the visitors. The main business meetings were held at Hotel Lafayette. The Buffalo lawyer, musician and wit, Simon Fleischmann, was toastmaster at the principal banquet. Beth Zion buzzed with the activities of committees: a Banquet Committee, a Hotel Committee, a Luncheon Committee, a Printing and Publicity Committee, an Entertainment Committee, a Reception Committee and, even, heaven forfend, an Automobile Committee.[74]

In this same year, almost as counter friction to reverse the wheels of progress, a sharp crisis shook the accustomed tranquility of Beth Zion. The controversy revolved around the question whether the synagogue should continue its system of assigned pews or change to a system of first-come-first-served seating. The question was a cardinal one, for if the change were made the congregation could expand and open its doors to the sons and daughters of the more recent immigrants, many of whom were ready to join a Reform Temple. Members of older families, who had long owned their own pews and who preferred a more exclusive house of worship, fought the change, whereas a more far-sighted element demanded it. Rabbi Kopald and President Wile contended that the unassigned system was more democratic and this argument bore weight in a period marked by the general decline of elitism. Moreover, there were strong economic reasons for the new departure, for only a small number of pews had been sold in recent years, and this fact complicated temple finances. The storm over free seating had been brewing for several years until it was brought to a head by community changes engendered by the first war with Germany.

The seating problem at Beth Zion eventually reached the pages of the *American Jewish Review* and an editorial warned that, if Beth Zion did not change to free seating, it would have to limit its membership, with the result that "Temple attendance will be grounded in snobbery and will deteriorate into little more than a fashionable soirée or reception." Therefore, advised the editor, the issue should be discussed in every Buffalo Jewish home "to the end that one may be as good as the next one in the house of the Lord." [75]

Following this press campaign, the Beth Zion board, in 1920, adopted the proposal of a special committee which provided, in essence, for free seating. Under the amended by-laws, however, certain pew holders who insisted on retaining their seats would be allowed to keep them. The proposal stirred up a good deal of controversy and protests poured in upon the harassed officers. [76]

The matter finally was put before the membership at large on December 19, 1920. Simon Fleischmann led the advocates of change and his brilliant leadership won the day by a vote of 73 to 29. It was resolved that the plan was to go into effect for a trial period of two years after 60% of the pew owners had given their consent in writing. The proper consent having been obtained, the new system was adopted for the fall Holidays of 1921. The rabbi and officers now had a free hand to go ahead with their favorite project. [77]

The debate over the seating problem vexed the congregation for another year, but in 1923 the unassigned system was made permanent. The congregation decided at this time to repay members who had paid for their seats. Eventually this plan was abandoned because of the Great Depression; and the vast majority of pew owners voluntarily surrendered their seats. [78]

In retrospect, time has vindicated the proponents of the change, and the unassigned system proved even more successful than its most enthusiastic supporters of a generation ago could foresee. Within one year after the change, Beth Zion gained eighty-eight members, and this initial spurt began the steady expansion of the temple to the point where it eventually became one of the largest synagogues of its kind in the land.

Another step toward liberalization of synagogue management was taken about this time when two women were elected to the board of trustees. It was, from the first, a hallmark of Reform to stress the equality of the sexes and, in most American synagogues, the first step toward liberalism had usually been to seat the women with the men at services. Nevertheless, the old nineteenth-century habit of placing managerial responsibilities in the hands of men alone continued until the war of 1917-1918 advanced the cause of women's rights in many fields of action. In 1922, the board agreed to amend the by-laws so that the board of trustees would consist of nine men and two women (either members in their own names or wives of members). Subsequently, the first two women in the history of Beth Zion selected to sit on the board were Mrs. Henry Nathan and Mrs. A. L. Warner. At the annual meeting of 1924 the problem of female rights in the synagogue was settled for good. It was then decided that wives and adult daughters of members in good standing were to be regarded as non-dues paying members with the right to vote and hold office.[79]

In the midst of the fabulous twenties the most influential rabbi in its history came to Beth Zion. Born in Springfield, Ohio, in 1895, and educated in the secondary schools in Dayton, Joseph L. Fink was to make a profound impact on the city of Buffalo. The future rabbi received his B.A. from the University of Cincinnati, and then went on the next year to earn his M.A. at the University of Chicago. Two years later, he was ordained rabbi at the Hebrew Union College.

Rabbi Fink's first pulpit was at Temple Israel in Terre Haute, Indiana, where he was installed, May 2, 1919. Here he spent an interesting five years. He arrived at the time that the mayor and all members of the City Council were about to be sent to Leavenworth for the common political crime of "boodling." An ardent civic reformer and tireless public speaker, Rabbi Fink threw himself into the work of cleaning up the town. Indiana, in the 1920s, was the most Klan-ridden state of the union, and Rabbi Fink became a favorite target of these patrioteers. The Klan did not like the idea of his being president of the Community Chest and demanded his resignation. He boldly confronted the Klan and spoke to its members. So persuasive was the young rabbi that he emerged from that meeting with a pledge from his hooded hosts for a contribution of $1,800 to the Chest.[80]

Meanwhile, in Buffalo, Rabbi Kopald, then only in his thirties, developed the dread disease that was to plague him for ten years. Although he was given a six-months leave of absence in July 1922, Rabbi Kopald returned to Buffalo for the High Holidays, at which time Rabbi Leo Mannheimer was engaged to help him. The onset of a severe winter once more drove Rabbi Kopald from his pulpit, and part of his duties fell upon young Solomon Frank. Frank (b.1900) was the son of the well-known Buffalo Hebrew teacher, Abraham Frank, who taught for many years at Temple Beth David. The younger Frank was a lawyer with a gift for preaching and writing on Jewish subjects. Later, he abandoned law for the rabbinate. He left Buffalo to accept a rabbinical post in Winnipeg and from there he moved on to Montreal.

Early in 1924, because of declining health, Rabbi Kopald was again given a leave of absence. The need for a competent assistant grew acute later in the spring, but the Hebrew Union College informed the congregation that no forthcoming graduate of that year possessed sufficient experience to assume the responsibilities of the post. By chance, Rabbi Fink had stopped over in Buffalo on his way east to take ship for graduate study in Germany, and during his brief stay in the city he had preached for Rabbi Kopald. He was subsequently invited by the board to become assistant rabbi and he cancelled his European plans in order to accept the Buffalo appointment.

Rabbi Fink began his ministry at Beth Zion on September 1, 1924, and he was tendered a reception following his first regular Friday evening sermon. His position was difficult, to say the least. Rabbi Kopald was in Asheville, North Carolina, and both he and his congregants had then every hope that he would be fully restored to health. But Rabbi Fink made the best of a trying situation and he soon won the confidence of Temple Beth Zion. He made it clear that he was anxious to work both in community affairs and in personal counselling. And work he did! Young, energetic, an easy and fluent speaker with a photographic memory that enabled him to recall just exactly the right quotation from a phenomenal range of Jewish and secular reading, this newcomer to Buffalo enraptured his audiences and soon was in incessant demand.

On June 2, 1926, less than two years after he came to Beth Zion, Rabbi Fink was unanimously elected rabbi. His predecessor was made Rabbi Emeritus, a post that Rabbi Kopald held until he accepted a smaller congregation for his declining days, at Glencoe, Illinois.

As Beth Zion's membership increased steadily under Rabbi Fink's stewardship, it became evident that the congregation needed more space than the designers of the 1915 annex had envisioned. Herman Wile, then a spry sixty-three, resumed the presidency in 1927. The membership was then over 650, and Wile, who heard that the property next door was for sale, thought the time ripe for further expansion. With the financial assistance of some influential board members, the president bought the property directly to the north of the synagogue for $55,000, confident that Beth Zion would in turn buy it for building purposes. The congregation ratified the purchase and assumed title to the property which was to house a new school building, a rabbi's study and an enlarged Temple Centre. The new addition, designed by Edward M. Plant, was completed in 1929 just prior to the collapse of the business boom that had fostered the plans for expansion.[81]

Originally, when the Delaware Avenue Temple was dedicated in 1890, the school consisted of three classrooms. With the 1929 addition, the Temple School could boast of sixteen classrooms. Meanwhile, the old problem of an effective Sunday school curriculum still plagued the congregation. Solomon Frank had been appointed teacher at Beth Zion in 1921; but this energetic young man, like the temple leaders, was puzzled by the problem of teaching Hebrew. The sophisticated students of the "jazz age" thought it dull and useless, while wiser heads realized that a Jewish religious education devoid of Hebrew was a contradiction in terms.

In an attempt to halt the drift, the chairman of the School Committee was empowered to appoint a subcommittee to investigate the school. Many of the newer members, fresh from their traditional backgrounds, were upset by the lackadaisical approach of many of the older members towards an intensive Jewish education. Part of the objection was directed toward the principal, Miss Rachel Marks, whose forte was secular rather than religious training. Shortly thereafter, Miss Marks resigned and Miss Nettie Morris became acting principal and Miss Adelle H. Land, later professor of education at the University of Buffalo, was engaged to train the Sunday school teachers in methodology.

The emphasis on teaching techniques becomes apparent in the advertisement that Beth Zion ran for "Two Hebrew teachers able to speak English fluently and able to teach Hebrew with modern methods." By the time that the new school building was opened, the synagogue had decided to pay increased attention to its school problem. A full-time educational and social director was brought to Buffalo. He was Bernard Fischlowitz of St. Louis, who remained at Beth Zion only two years. In 1931, the school was taken over by Louis T. Masson, a talented high school science teacher. Four years later, another full-time appointment was made. This time the temple chose a highly trained Jewish educator with fifteen years of experience in New York City behind him. Samuel H. Rosenberg remained at Beth Zion until 1942, and he subsequently became Director of the Bureau of Jewish Education in Atlanta. After his departure, Masson returned as principal. In 1950, he was replaced by Dr. Louis L. Gitin who, like his predecessor, combined a public school career with the supervision of the Beth Zion religious school.

With the completion of the addition to the north side of the temple in 1929, Rabbi Fink moved into a commodious study attractively furnished by the Women's Temple Society. His city-wide reputation was greatly enhanced when he began his Humanitarian Hour over station WBEN in 1930. For over two decades Buffalonians looked forward each Sunday to a sparkling discussion of religious, ethical, economic and aesthetic subjects.

Dr. Fink's regular routine at the height of his career is a prime example of the demands placed upon a modern rabbi. He had, of course, his regular synagogue duties, and his devotion to his pastoral work was always exemplary. Nevertheless, he found time to serve as president of the local B'nai B'rith lodge and was Jewish chaplain for the Buffalo Police and Fire Departments. A 33rd degree Mason, and former vice-president of the Rotary Club, he was adopted into the Bear tribe of the Tuscarora Indian Nation. In one single week he addressed the congregation of a Polish National Catholic Church, spoke to 500 Scotsmen on the birthday of Robert Burns, preached to the Methodists on Mission Sunday, lectured to a Negro assembly on public housing, and even managed to instruct a civic group on the art of being a good neighbor.[82] What a far cry from the eastern European rabbi who had been wont to seclude himself in a remote book-lined corner of his wooden synagogue!

In October 1949, Beth Zion celebrated Dr. Fink's silver anniversary as rabbi of the temple. A weekend of festivities began with a special Friday evening service and ended with a gala banquet at Hotel Statler. Rabbi Victor E. Reickert of Cincinnati preached at the temple, and President Nelson Glueck of Hebrew Union College, along with many local religious and civic dignitaries, paid tribute to him.[83] During this jubilee year, Rabbi Fink's friends gave a substantial gift in his honor to the Hebrew Union College. Three years later, Dr. Fink reached the summit of his career when he was elected president of the Central Conference of American Rabbis. During this period of renown he travelled extensively throughout the country and widened his national reputation.

In the fall of 1958, Dr. Fink ended his active ministry. He was named Rabbi Emeritus, and the former associate rabbi, Dr. Martin L. Goldberg, succeeded him. Rabbi Herbert Tarr came to Buffalo to assist Dr. Goldberg in handling a congregation that numbered over 1,500 families.

Like other Buffalo congregations, Beth Zion felt the effects of the general exodus to the suburbs, and after 1950 a demand arose that the congregation build in the area to the north of Buffalo. In the mid-fifties, Beth Zion, contemplating another addition to its Delaware Avenue Temple, appointed a Planning Committee with Sol J. Levy as chairman. The group recommended expansion on the present site, but, even though plans were already drawn up, the temple board reversed its previous action and appointed another committee to seek a suburban site. This about-face recognized that the Jewish center of gravity had shifted beyond the northern city limits. This shift was made manifest when, in 1955, a group of younger couples established, independently of Beth Zion, Temple Beth Am (formerly the Suburban Congregation for Reform Judaism) and began to hold services in space generously provided by the Amherst Community Church in Snyder. The first rabbi of the new congregation was Milton Richman, who was replaced in 1958 by Rabbi Daniel E. Kerman. Buffalo's newest synagogue already boasted 210 members. A year later, the temple moved into its own quarters on Sheridan Drive and Indian Trail Road in Amherst.

Almost simultaneously with the organization of this new Reform group, Beth Zion decided to offer its many suburban members educational facilities designed to save parents the long and often icy drive downtown. In 1955 the congregation began to acquire school space from various churches and to move part of its Religious School beyond the city limits. Later, work was begun on a $450,000 edifice located on Sweet Home Road in the town of Amherst. While the Delaware Avenue Temple still served as the nucleus of the religious and directional activities of the congregation, High Holiday services had already been shifted to Klein-hans Music Hall in order to accommodate the growing membership. Like many synagogues elsewhere, Beth Zion sought to serve its city and suburban members by maintaining both a central and an out-of-city building.[84]

While Beth Zion was growing by leaps and bounds, repeated efforts were being made to unify the Orthodox Jews of Buffalo at the other end of the ideological spectrum. Each attempt to unite them, however, proved to be abortive, and the persistent failure of these efforts explains in part the establishment and growth of new Conservative synagogues.

The first of these attempts to organize the right-wingers came in 1916 when, in imitation of the earlier *kehillah* movement in New York City, the Jewish Kehillah of Buffalo was organized. One of the principal motives that brought the coalition into being was the desire to bring some order and regulation into the chaos that ruled in the slaughter houses and kosher butcher shops in Buffalo. Furthermore, the founders wished to promote East Side harmony by selecting a "Chief Rabbi" who could settle the rivalry then existent among downtown institutions and religious leaders.

The leaders of this movement were Morris Smolev, Bernard Phillips, Jacob Rosokoff, Max Cornblum, Morris Simon, Karl Berlin and Morris Singerman. Smolev (1862-1927), who had been born in Odessa, came to the United States about 1883 and peddled after his arrival in Buffalo. He later owned a scrap metal firm on Broadway and was president of the big Hickory Street Shul for many years.[85]

In 1917, the newly formed group selected their first and only spiritual leader. He was Nachman H. Ebin (1883-1940) who had been born in Slutzk, Russia. Ordained in Europe before his arrival here, he carried on his rabbinical studies at the budding center of American Orthodoxy, the Yeshiva Rabbi Isaac Elchanan in New York. In 1907, Ebin married the American-born Sarah D. Ashinsky, daughter of a famous Pittsburgh rabbi and niece of Buffalo's Rabbi Max Drob.

Both Rabbi Ebin and his father-in-law were among the first Orthodox leaders to embrace Zionism whole-heartedly. It was natural, therefore, that after his arrival in Buffalo, Ebin became a staunch friend of L. H. Miller. At a time when traditional rabbis were usually anti-Zionist or else indifferent, Rabbi Ebin did much to popularize Herzl's program in Buffalo. His work in the Z.O.A., however, did not diminish the rabbi's interest in religious Zionism and he was a founding father of the American Mizrachi movement.

Possessed of a stately appearance, innate dignity, poise and kindliness, Rabbi Ebin contributed greatly to the unification of all right-of-center factions in Buffalo. After his arrival, he selected B'rith Israel on Hickory Street as his main synagogue. Eventually, Rabbi Ebin had eight congregations under his nominal jurisdiction, with a total membership near three thousand.[86]

Rabbi Ebin left the Buffalo community in 1921 to accept a pulpit in Bensonhurst, Brooklyn, which post he occupied until his death. After his departure, the *kehillah* movement disintegrated, although the concept of Orthodox unity was to have a persistent if unsuccessful life in Buffalo during the ensuing decades.

In 1925, another attempt to achieve Orthodox unity was made when the Buffalo Council of Jewish Congregations was incorporated, with Nathan Swerdloff as first president. This organization attempted to regulate charity to itinerant mendicants, stabilize traditional Jewish life in the city and supervise *kashrut* which had once more become a vexing problem after the departure of Rabbi Ebin. At the peak of its power, the organization boasted of representatives of a dozen congregations on its board of directors. While many other men who were technically outside of the Orthodox group lent a hand from time to time, the real impetus for unity had to come from a group of older lay leaders who, in Buffalo, were never numerous or energetic enough to solve a problem that was never really solved anywhere. By 1929 the Buffalo Council of Jewish Congregations had become dormant.[87]

In the following decade, Max M. Yellen strove heroically to revive the organization. He brought Harris S. Selig, director of the National Federation of Orthodox Jewish Congregations, to establish a branch of that movement in Buffalo. For a time Mr. Yellen's efforts achieved a certain measure of success. Following the death of Rabbi Abraham M. Franklin in 1932, the city was without an Orthodox rabbi with sufficient prestige to lead the traditionalists. To fill the need, the Council brought Rabbi Joshua S. Zambrowsky (1876-1939) to Buffalo in 1933. A learned and gentle scholar, he had been rabbi in his native city of Warsaw until he settled in Syracuse at the age of forty-eight. Patriarchal in appearance and gentle in demeanor, Rabbi Zambrowsky worked for the will-o-wisp ideal of Orthodox unity until his death. Although often referred to as "Chief Rabbi," the title was misleading for, here as elsewhere, it meant only that certain segments in the community looked to him for spiritual leadership and general supervision of *kashrut*.[88]

Since World War II, Buffalo has been honored by the presence of an outstanding talmudic authority, Rabbi Bericz Zuckerman. This European-trained scholar is known throughout the Jewish world for his writings on the Code of Maimonides and other medieval rabbinic works. "A rabbi's rabbi," he is often consulted throughout the United States on difficult questions of a *halakhic* nature.

In recent years, however, even feeble attempts to maintain an Orthodox coalition have virtually come to an end, the older generation that once supported the Council having passed from the scene and their children for the most part having long since been attracted to more liberal congregations. The eclipse of the Council was hastened by internal bickering among the remaining downtown congregations and by community changes engendered by World War II. In 1960, the traditionalists were still laboring to restore communal supervision of the kosher slaughter houses and butcher shops. Significantly, however, there was no mention of a "Chief Rabbi," for the modern Orthodox group had their own rabbis and the East Side congregations had either disappeared or had been reconstituted in different form in the North Park area of the city. To trace this development it is necessary to turn from the story of united Orthodox action to the history of individual synagogues.

In the heyday of William Street, eight synagogues, if one includes the Fillmore Avenue Shul, flourished east of Main Street. After 1920, however, both the Clinton Street and the Pine Street congregations steadily declined. For a while the Jefferson Avenue Shul showed new vigor. Cantor Hyman Schulsinger came in the 1930s, but he left for Detroit at the end of the decade. After his departure no replacement was made and the bulletin board of the *shul* still carried his name almost twenty years after he ceased serving the congregation. The two Hickory Street synagogues lasted in the old neighborhood until World War II. B'rith Israel retained 150 members as late as 1931, and Rabbi Samuel Gitin attracted many to the neighboring Anshe Emes with his eloquent Yiddish sermons. Samuel Gitin (1872-1942) had been born in Smolensk and had studied at European *Yeshivot*. An eloquent *maggid*, he came to Buffalo in 1917, after ten years in Rochester, and served first at the Pine Street Shul and then at Anshe Emes. His passing during the course of World War II helped mark the end of the Buffalo East Side as a Jewish section.[89]

While the older downtown congregations were dwindling, the Fillmore Avenue Shul enjoyed the Indian summer of its East Side existence. Ahavas Achim, to give it its official name, sprang up in the 1890s in the Fillmore-Broadway area where some Jews lived by preference and others conducted businesses. The neighborhood was predominantly Polish, and the synagogue seems to have been founded principally for the convenience of Jewish retailers who resided in the vicinity. According to tradition, the group first met for Sabbath services in the spacious kitchen of Mrs. William Laufer, wife of one of the pioneer Jewish merchants in the vicinity. Important members of the congregation at the time of its incorporation in 1897, besides Mr. Laufer, were: Samuel Davis, Joseph Elster, Aaron Kreinik, Jacob Sarnofsky, Samuel Cohen, Joseph Cohen and the ubiquitous teacher Morris Diamond. In 1912, a stately synagogue was erected on Fillmore Avenue about 1,000 feet north of Broadway.

Surviving records of the congregation indicate that its members were all men who either lived or had stores in the neighborhood. The secretary and unofficial leader of the congregation for many years was Solomon Yochelson, a neighborhood butcher, and father of Dr. Samuel Yochelson. The names of many of the early families of Ahavas Achim became well known in Buffalo's business and professional world: Harry Arbesman, father of the allergist Dr. Carl Arbesman; Charles Lederman, furniture store owner; Morris Posmantur; Herman Adler; Harry Zolte; Louis Silverstein; Louis Maisel; Samuel Liebeskind and Samuel Seeberg, and others.[90]

As a result of the flush years that followed 1914, many Jews moved away from their stores in the Fillmore area, but the synagogue continued in its original location. The Young Men's Club, which was organized in 1919, had as its prime mover Louis Gerstman (1865-1927) who was the long-time president of the congregation. Gerstman had been born in Poland and, after a period in England, came to Buffalo when he was nineteen years old. He married the Buffalo-born Sarah Cohen who joined her husband in the synagogue's manifold activities.[91]

The rabbi in the 1920s was B. N. Goldberg, a native Palestinian. Rabbi Goldberg's Hebrew and Sunday schools were at one time staffed by seven teachers, who taught 300 pupils both in the synagogue proper and in overflow classrooms in an adjacent private home. At this time, the Fillmore Avenue Shul had its own *Hevra Kadisha,* a good cemetery, a library, a Ladies' Auxiliary and a Young Women's Club. The Young Men's Club, generally scoffed at by the elders, drew youths from the whole East Side, and was very active with such enterprising young men as Paul Swados and Gordon Cohen as leaders. Ahavas Achim was one of the few congregation of its genre to make a serious effort to hold its young people.

The inevitable decline, however, soon set in. Registration in the school dropped, perhaps because of the attraction of free tuition and more progressive education at the Talmud Torah. A temporary fillip for the congregation came in 1926 when the chapel at the cemetery on Pine Ridge Road was dedicated. This chapel had been the gift of Mr. and Mrs. Herman Adler, an energetic and philanthropically-minded couple who had built up a department store at 1000 Broadway. After 1927, Louis Silverstein, a *shohet* who had prospered in the poultry business, led the synagogue activities until the *shul* left the neighborhood.[92]

Eventually, the Fillmore Avenue group joined with the Anshe Lubavitz (Pratt Street Shul) to build the present edifice on Tacoma Avenue which is known as Ahavas Achim-Lubavitz. Here the united synagogues were led by Rabbi Alvin M. Marcus and Cantor Morris Markowitz, with effective lay help from their long-time president, Samuel Benatovich.

As the William Street neighborhood gradually lost its former residents, several other areas of Jewish concentration opened up in the city. The first of these, as already noted, was the lower West Side. An interesting phenomenon, however, was the fact that, prior to 1945, only one original downtown congregation (Beth El) moved into any of the newer neighborhoods. For the most part, the people in the secondary Jewish areas of settlement founded houses of worship of their own. These became Orthodox, Conservative, Reform, and even Reconstructionist, as the accidents of population shift threw groups of Jews together in these new neighborhoods.

Even prior to the opening of the Roaring Twenties, many Jews had already penetrated the upper West Side, north of Utica Street. So popular was this district of the city among Jews that in 1921 the chorus of the B'nai B'rith minstrel show sang, "Elmwood Avenue will soon be like William Street." Beth El, the nearest congregation, was located too far down Richmond Avenue for the traditional Jews to walk to services; it was, moreover, too modern to attract the stauncher traditionalists. It was natural, therefore, that these old-timers should found an Orthodox congregation in the vicinity of their new homes. The leading man in gathering these scattered right-wing elements into one group was Joseph Rosenblatt, a pioneer baker in Buffalo. They first held services in the fall of 1919 at the Elmwood Studio, on the second floor of a building on the northeast corner of Elmwood Avenue and Auburn. The synagogue began under the name of Congregation Beth Israel, but this name was taken within a few years by some secessionists who left the main group.[93]

After the departure of the splinter group, the remaining members became incorporated under the name of Congregation Beth Abraham. In 1923, the congregation bought a house at 1045 Elmwood Avenue and converted it into a usable synagogue.[94]

This small congregation flourished in the late twenties just prior to the great stock market crash. Morris Diamond opened a daily Hebrew school at Beth Abraham, and under the leadership of such younger men as Harry Altman and Meyer Palanker, an active social program was introduced with a flourish of banquets at Hotel Statler. By 1928, the quarters of this group were so crowded that the congregation bought the house next door for High Holiday overflow services and to provide two extra classrooms. For a time the congregation even had a rabbi. But then came the Big Crash and the group atrophied. Yet, despite the hard times of the Depression Decade, the little congregation struggled on. Joseph A. Sapowitch, a prominent furniture dealer in South Buffalo, stepped in when Joseph Rosenblatt died, and lent stout assistance to the group, a support that he gave unstintingly for over a quarter of a century.

Beth Abraham never became a thriving institution despite its promising beginnings. In the late 1940s, when the Elmwood Avenue section became almost depopulated of Jews, the congregation could foresee the end of its life in that neighborhood. It finally gave up the effort to maintain an independent synagogue and merged with the former splinter group, Beth Israel, which for many years had been worshipping in a reconverted church a few doors away. The joint congregations then settled down to a hard but steady existence in the old Beth Israel synagogue at 1073 Elmwood Avenue. Despite much agitation for mild reform, the merged groups continued to worship as a strictly Orthodox congregation.

The next area to develop as an unmistakable Jewish section was the district centering east between Jefferson and Humboldt Parkway. This neighborhood grew rapidly after 1918, and eventually produced three Orthodox and one Conservative synagogues. The first of these was Temple Beth David, the second Conservative synagogue in Buffalo, which was founded in 1923. An unorganized group of Jews held services on the High Holidays of 1921, at Delta Temple Hall, located at East Utica and Fillmore Avenue. It is most likely that many of these people were among those who later founded Temple Beth David. Among the pioneer leaders of the Humboldt group was Joseph Sanes, first president of the congregation and destined to be influential in its affairs for over three decades.

By 1923, some fifty members of Beth David were worshipping in a private house at 652 Humboldt Parkway. A Ladies' Auxiliary, a Young Women's Club and a Men's Club had already been organized by the time the congregation gathered at Boreal Hall on Glenwood Avenue to usher in Rosh Hashana of 1924. In the meantime, the congregation had acquired land on the east side of Humboldt Parkway and had begun plans to erect a synagogue.[95]

With Jacob Tick as chairman of the Building Committee, strongly supported by Samuel Coplon, work on the new synagogue was promptly started. At the ceremonies for the laying of the cornerstone on November 23, 1924, Mayor Frank X. Schwab addressed an audience of 500. The principal speaker was Rabbi Eichler of Beth El, a good portent that the new congregation would be Conservative.

The new building was dedicated on August 30, 1925, under the presidency of Joseph Sanes and the vice-presidency of Solomon Brown. All the rabbis of Buffalo, participated in the dedication. Mayor Schwab once more spoke, in his inimitable Buffalo-German style, to the pleasure and amusement of his listeners.[96]

The acting rabbi of the new synagogue was the young Buffalonian, Solomon Frank, who had gained experience at Beth Zion. Rabbi Frank, however, served only on an interim basis, and the first permanent spiritual leader was elected in 1926. He was Rabbi C. David Matt, a graduate of the Jewish Theological Seminary, who had served for fourteen years in Minneapolis before accepting the call to Buffalo. Rabbi Matt had been born in Europe in 1887, but he arrived in the United States at the early age of three. He nevertheless spoke a fluent Yiddish and his occasional sermons in that language attracted the older people to Beth David. He was an excellent teacher, a gifted poet and a facile writer whose writings often made the pages of Anglo-Jewish periodicals.

Rabbi Matt's arrival in Buffalo on March 4, 1927, significantly coincided with the eightieth year of Beth El's existence. During that whole long period, only Beth El and Beth Zion had chosen rabbis who spoke idiomatic English and who could act as effective representatives of Buffalo Jewry to the Gentile community. And now to Beth David came an experienced rabbi who was destined to make his synagogue an influence in the city.

It was at an elaborate ceremony that Rabbi Matt was installed on April 8-9, 1927. Rabbi Eichler, who had actually taught the new rabbi when he was a boy in Philadelphia, delivered the Sabbath sermon. In that same year Jacob M. Judelsohn, father of the pediatrician Dr. Louis Judelsohn, was elected cantor. This genial man with a strong tenor voice officiated at Beth David for many years.

Rabbi Matt remained at Beth David only two years, but during his time the congregation prospered. It was probably impossible for Rabbi Matt to resist the call that came in 1929 to serve in the city of his childhood, at the West Philadelphia Jewish Community Center.[97]

No account of Beth David during the heyday of its Humboldt Parkway existence would be complete without some mention of Dr. and Mrs. William Stone. This Canadian couple moved into the section in the 1930s and for twenty years Buffalo's Jewish leaders gathered around their hospitable hearth to talk of local and national affairs. Dr. Stone, a physician of unquestioned integrity and known for his devotion to all good causes, died in 1954 at the age of fifty-three. Beth David and the community mourned the loss of a friend to all in distress.

After Rabbi Matt left Beth David, a veritable parade of rabbis passed through this synagogue, none of whom remained for more than a few years. First of these was Dr. Harry Silverstone, the son of a well-known Orthodox rabbi of Washington, D.C. During his days at Beth David, the school was developed under the guidance of Uriah Z. Engelman, later director of the local Bureau of Jewish Education. Rabbi Silverstone was replaced by Rabbi Judah Nadich who served from 1936 to 1940. Rabbi Nadich, fresh from the seminary and only twenty-four years old, handsome and immaculately groomed, made a lasting impression on Beth David and the Buffalo community during his brief stay. He was a strong leader, and during his time the synagogue's membership rose to 255 and the Sisterhood's to 200. The Sunday school had 250 students, and the Hebrew school had 190.[98] For a time Beth David buzzed with activity; but the young, energetic rabbi left in 1940 to become assistant to Dr. Solomon Goldman of Chicago.

In rapid succession, three rabbis then came and left Beth David. Rabbi Theodore Friedman, an exceptional scholar, served for two years. He was replaced by Rabbi Moses Lehrman, who officiated at Beth David from 1943 to 1947; then came Rabbi Sidney B. Riback who remained with the congregation until he accepted a Chicago pulpit.

After mid-century, the neighborhood began to change very rapidly as Negroes replaced Jews in the district. In 1955, Beth David gave up the struggle to remain in the vicinity and merged with Congregation Ner Israel, in the North Park area, under the name of Temple Beth David-

Ner Israel. The old synagogue building on Humboldt Parkway was sold and the congregation moved into the partially completed Ner Israel structure on Starin Avenue at Taunton. Under the leadership of Rabbi Seymour Freedman, William Berger and the veteran Joseph Sanes, the united congregations completed the erection of an imposing synagogue.

While Temple Beth David was still flourishing in the Humboldt Parkway section, several Orthodox synagogues sprang up nearby. Made up of people religiously to the right of the middle-of-the-road Beth David, Congregation Ohel Jacob, founded in 1926, located eventually at 493 East Ferry Street. The mainstay of this congregation for many years was Benjamin Meshorer (1863-1955) who had been born in Berditchev, Russia, and came to the United States in 1898. At first he had been active in B'rith Israel on Hickory Street as well as in the independent B'nai Israel Cemetery Association. He was a one-time president of Ohel Jacob and was the leading man in the acquisition of the East Ferry Street building. This congregation was to be the last remnant of the once thriving Jewish community in the Humboldt district of Buffalo.[99]

The last synagogue to be founded in the Humboldt section was the Humboldt Orthodox Center, established just before the Hitlerian War. Rabbi Gedaliah Kaprow (1907-1951) was the moving force in this organization. A native of Sokolovka, Rabbi Kaprow, who had been ordained at the Yeshiva Rabbi Isaac Elchanan, arrived in Buffalo in 1931, served several congregations and lived with his *Landsleute* on the East Side before founding the Humboldt Orthodox Center. With a nucleus made up of his former congregants, Rabbi Kaprow bought an old telephone building on Glenwood Avenue and converted it to a synagogue, and for a time this congregation thrived. A great friend of the aged at the Rosa Coplon Old Folks Home, its residents looked forward each month to Rabbi Kaprow's Yiddish talks. He was genuinely interested in Jewish education and conducted a model school. But, in 1951, at the young age of forty-four, Rabbi Kaprow died.[100] The congregation declined rapidly, and in 1955 the building was sold, and the congregation sought in vain for a site for a new synagogue or for a merger with another congregation.

The third area of Jewish concentration in Buffalo after the decline of the East Side was at the northernmost limits of the city, in the section known as North Park. Here, in an area east of Delaware Avenue, Jews began to move into the side streets that intersected Hertel Avenue to the north and south. It all began when a handful of venturesome young couples from the East Side, in the early 1920s, skipped the Elmwood and Humboldt sections and settled directly in the North Park area. Jewish real estate brokers helped develop the neighborhood, and they advertised new two-family homes for sale for $14,250 at $1,500 down and $27.50 a month. For a time Jewish families in the vicinity had no religious services and were forced to go downtown for the High Holidays; but soon the usual demand for a neighborhood *minyan* prompted the establishment of synagogues in the new location. By 1923, a kosher butcher opened a shop on Wellington Road and he soon had a competitor on Hertel Avenue.[101] The movement northward came in two waves. By 1938, North Park was said to have over 4,000 Jews, but the big rush to this area came as Jews recovered from the Great Depression and as the older areas of Jewish concentration declined rapidly during the 1940s. By the onset of the Korean War, well over half of the Jewish population of Buffalo lived in the North Park section of the city.

The first synagogue to spring up here was Temple Emanu-El, destined to become in time the city's largest Conservative congregation. The prime mover in the establishment of this synagogue was Abraham Meadows (1884-1928), a furrier who lived on Lovering Avenue. Meadows called a meeting at his home on June 15, 1924, as the first step in forming a permanent congregation. In attendance at this meeting were Morris Singer, who was to serve the temple so long and ably, Barnet Berman, and a Mr. S. Davis, who was appointed secretary for the initial meeting. On July 13 the name Temple Emanu-El was chosen, and a mass meeting was held ten days later at Hertel Avenue Hall in order to raise funds. The first officers of the new group were: Barnet Berman, president; Harry Feldman, vice-president; S. Davis, treasurer; and Morris Paltzek, secretary.[102]

Services were held for the High Holidays of that year in a hall at 1313 Hertel Avenue, with 150 in attendance. Solomon Frank preached at these services and Cantor Joseph Livingston, a tall, white-bearded gentleman, officiated. At the conclusion of Yom Kippur, the Sisterhood was organized with Mrs. S. Rubner as first president. In all probability, without these valiant efforts on the part of its women, the infant congregation would never have survived. A devoted group, which included Mrs. Alex Yenoff, Mrs. Charles S. Gudovitz, Mrs. William Malkinson, Mrs. Susman Ginsberg and the late Mrs. J. R. Morrison, raised money in ways too varied and complicated to chronicle here. In more than one early financial crisis their help saved the day.

During the course of the 1924 services, $11,000 was pledged as a result of an appeal made on *Kol Nidre* eve. With this good start, a Hebrew school was opened at 1313 Hertel Avenue. A committee was then appointed to find a site for the new synagogue. The Scalp and Blade Club, at 281-283 Parkside Avenue, was subsequently purchased, with the Erie County Savings Bank holding a mortgage for $22,000. Whether through

oversight on the part of those who selected the location, or through a
shift in the population in the new area, that lower part of Parkside Avenue
soon proved to be situated too far from the main sector of Jewish settlement. Ultimately the congregation had to abandon this building and seek
a new home.

Meanwhile, Temple Emanu-El was incorporated on December 1, 1924.
The next year, Louis A. Goldberg became a member. A rising young
communal leader who was to be twice elected president, he subsequently
served for many years officially as secretary and unofficially as "watchdog
of the Treasury." During the early part of the following year, the synagogue witnessed a phenomenal growth. The building on Parkside was
dedicated, and already very active in congregational affairs at that time
was Hyman Kahn who was destined to serve it devotedly for many years
thereafter. The first Annual Dance was held early in the spring as a fund-
raising device, and ever since, this affair has been an outstanding event.
A Young Men's Club sprang into existence and soon became a vital part
of the life of the congregation. At the end of 1925, Emanu-El was ready
to choose its second set of officers. Symon Rossen was elected president
and Hyman Kahn became treasurer. Morris Singer, a businessman, gave
of his services as principal of the Sunday school which already had sixty-
eight students, and even a Boy Scout group, Troop 156, was established.
All in all, 1925, the first full year of its existence, was a good one for
Temple Emanu-El.[103]

The next epoch in the life of the temple was marked by a series of
frustrating attempts to find a permanent site for the synagogue. It became
increasingly obvious that the Parkside location would not do, and from
1927 to 1929, the congregation celebrated the High Holidays at the Park
View Building on Hertel Avenue, although Sabbath services were still
held at Parkside Avenue. The school, however, had been moved to 1472
Hertel Avenue, where 150 students were instructed in seven classes. One
of the hindrances to the selection of a permanent site was the existence
of a rival congregation in the area, called Anshe Zedek. These two groups
almost united in 1928; but the merger failed, primarily because of a dis-
agreement about seating. Anshe Zedek, essentially made up of Hungarian
traditionalists, opposed mixed seating as it was practiced by Temple
Emanu-El.[104]

The early years of the depression found the congregation still without
a permanent home. So Temple Emanu-El, influenced by a recent canvass
of Jewish educational facilities in Buffalo, turned its attention to its school.
A communal survey had revealed that the 1,429 Jews in the North Park
section had a total of 495 children between six and fifteen years old, but
there was no adequate religious schooling available to them. This de-

plorable condition, when brought to light, prompted the synagogue to look to its own school which had never properly flourished. Israel Luskin, a high school mathematics teacher, was engaged to run the school and he was also provided with an assistant. In addition to his educational duties, Luskin was also required to preach at the Friday evening services. Emanu-El also made use of a city-wide roster of laymen who volunteered to preach each Sabbath. This group was formed at the behest of several synagogue presidents who pointed out to Mr. Emil Rubenstein that many pulpits in the city were vacant because of the depression. Rubenstein mustered a group of bright young lawyers who possessed sufficient Jewish background to enable them to prepare their talks. These men worked out a circuit system to insure that Sabbath evening and morning services in all parts of the city would be covered. The arrangement worked well for about a year, but it was discontinued when it became apparent that the newer synagogues could not exist without permanent spiritual leaders, while members of the older *shuls* seemed uninterested in English sermons devoted mainly to topics of the day.[105]

The stock market crash seemed to help the congregation make up its mind, for in 1930 the building on Parkside was sold and they rented space at Norwalk Hall, 1444 Hertel Avenue, in the building that already housed the school. Morris Singer, president from 1930 to 1933, helped promote another grand membership drive, with the depression dues set at one dollar a month.[106] It was also under Mr. Singer's leadership that the congregation engaged its first permanent rabbi. He was Joseph Gitin, son of the East Side rabbi, Samuel Gitin. It was strange that this Conservative synagogue should select as its rabbi a recent product of a Reform seminary; but some of the older members favored the choice because of the staunch traditionalism of his father. The times argued for this marriage of convenience. Temple membership had shrunk from 145 to sixty. In addition to the effects of the business panic on membership, people had lost heart for congregational affairs because, after eight years of searching, no location had been discovered for a permanent abode. At the time, the incumbent cantor was Charles S. Gudovitz who, by 1960, had served Emanu-El with devotion and dignity for twenty-nine years.

The year 1933 signaled the end of the period of wandering for Temple Emanu-El. On November 13 in that year, the congregation obtained an option to buy the North Park Baptist Church on the southeast corner of Colvin and Tacoma Avenues. This church, which had been built at the cost of $200,000, had been in financial difficulty as a result of the prevailing hard times. One of the principal negotiators in the purchase was Abe Mason, then a lumber dealer, who assisted Barnet Berman, the president of Emanu-El, in finally settling for the purchase of the building for

$75,000. (The mortgage secured at the time was at long last burned in 1958, thanks to the untiring efforts of the incumbent president, David Reifer.)

The building was remodelled at a cost of about $10,000. Over the large baptismal font in front of the church, Louis Greenstein, the architect, installed a beautiful *bimah*. When the renovations were completed, the temple was dedicated on May 27, 1934, with all the rabbis in the city on hand to speak a word of greetings and good wishes. Simon Greenbaum (1887-1953) lit the *Ner Tamid*, and the Beth Zion choral group sang.[107]

With the dedication of the new temple, a new era in the history of Emanu-El began. J. R. Morrison was installed as president in October 1934, and provided exceptional leadership. Rabbi Gitin left to accept a pulpit in a Reform synagogue in Butte, Montana, and he was replaced by Rabbi Morris Adler (b.1907), a recent graduate of the Jewish Theological Seminary. He was twenty-eight when he came to Buffalo in 1935, but he was already a seasoned orator and leader. This was altogether a most fortunate choice for Emanu-El, for Rabbi Adler's influence extended far beyond his own synagogue. He became a community leader, rising within two years to the presidency of the local Z.O.A. district.

Things began to hum under Rabbi Adler. The Men's Club came to life; membership in the Sisterhood rose to 323 in 1938; there were 178 pupils in the daily school and 120 in the Sunday school, and sixteen teachers were occupied with their instruction; and Emanu-El had in that year 310 members. The period of lethargy was definitely over. After a brief but effective tenure, Rabbi Adler left Temple Emanu-El in the summer of 1938 to go to Congregation Shaarey Zedek in Detroit, where he became one of the outstanding Conservative rabbis in the United States.[108]

Rabbi Adler's successor was Eli A. Bohnen, a Canadian-born graduate of the Jewish Theological Seminary, who came to Buffalo in 1939. This handsome, saintly, ministerial man with great depth of character soon won the hearts of his congregants.

Temple Emanu-El continued to thrive as the wartime prosperity accelerated the population drift to the North Park area. During this time, the congregation benefited from the vigorous leadership of Louis M. Bunis, who was president. An overflow service for the High Holidays was organized in 1943, and this prompted a rise in membership, for now many more could be accommodated each fall.[109]

During the war years, Rabbi Bohnen served as a chaplain in the Army, and his place was temporarily taken by Rabbi Manuel Saltzman. Rabbi Bohnen resigned in 1948 to accept the pulpit of a congregation in Providence, Rhode Island. He was replaced by Rabbi Nathan Kollin of Richmond, Virginia, who remained four years. In 1953, Rabbi Isaac Klein of

Springfield, Massachusetts, came to Temple Emanu-El. This national Jewish leader, eminent army chaplain and learned Harvard Ph.D., was elected to his pulpit for life after only two years in Buffalo. Dr. Klein's national reputation was enhanced when, in 1958, he was chosen president of the Rabbinical Assembly of America. By that year, Emanu-El had a membership of 800 and an annual budget of $131,000. After a precarious beginning, it had emerged as one of the leading congregations in the city.

Coincident with Emanu-El's rapid development, the congregation already mentioned as a rival was also putting down roots in the North Park area. In 1925, a group of Hungarian-born Jews formed a synagogue originally known as Ohev Zedek. Determined also to found a school, they induced Hyman S. Weinstein (1873-1947), who had conducted a private *heder* on the East Side since his arrival in Buffalo about fifteen years before, to move to the North Park area. The congregation bought a two-family house at 141 Crestwood, where Mr. Weinstein conducted the school and brought to the organization his long-time experience as a congregational secretary. In his home above the synagogue the secretary-teacher for many years dispensed religious articles and thus helped spread traditional Jewish practices in this newer part of the city. In 1930, the congregation changed its name to Anshe Zedek; and the following year they bought a Masonic Temple which had originally been built as a Methodist Church. In this new location, at 85 Saranac Avenue, the congregation enjoyed a measure of success.[110]

Rabbi Chaim Davidovitch, who since his recent arrival from Europe had been with the larger Hickory Street Shul, moved to North Park in 1934 and became rabbi at Anshe Zedek, a post he held for eleven years. His ultimate successor was a Buffalo man, Chaim Weinstein. Rabbi Weinstein had the congregation change its name to Ner Israel. In 1952, Ner Israel sold its Saranac Avenue building to Yeshivath Achei T'mimim Lubavitz and built a school and temporary sanctuary at Starin and Taunton Avenues where, as has already been told, this congregation united with Temple Beth David; a merger that facilitated the completion of the synagogue's building program.

The final congregation to arrive in the North Park section was the Yeshivath Achei T'mimim just mentioned. In 1940, Rabbi Joseph Isaac Schneersohn, the famous hasidic "rebbe" of Lubavitz, with followers scattered all over the world, arrived with his family in New York. Old and broken in health by his wartime experiences, the "Lubavitcher rebbe" nevertheless set out to revive Orthodox Judaism by training devoted young men whom he sent out to establish day schools which would form vital centers for the propagation of Torah-true Judaism. In 1942, Rabbi

Harry Fogelman came to Buffalo and opened a school in the old Humboldt neighborhood. Here, with varying success, he and his successors conducted a school that tried to combine both religious and secular primary education.

Drawn by the magnetic pull to the North Park area, this group bought the Saranac Avenue synagogue and utilized it as both a synagogue and a day school. The latter, known as the Hebrew Academy of Buffalo (and a separate organization from the synagogue maintained in the same building), was the only school if its kind in the city until a more progressive traditionalist element organized the Kadimah School, which opened in the fall of 1959.

To sum up, at the end of the Eisenhower Era, North Park contained six synagogues: two that were indigenous to the district, and four that were transplants in whole or in part from other neighborhoods. But a decade and a half of postwar prosperity had started another neighborhood hegira, this time into the suburbs that fringed the city on its northern limits.

Buffalo's first suburban congregation was neither Reform, Orthodox, nor Conservative, but was strongly influenced by the Reconstructionist approach of the contemporary Jewish rabbi, sage and philosopher, Dr. Mordecai M. Kaplan. The decision to found a kind of synagogue hitherto unknown to Buffalo was largely due to the efforts of Louis M. Bunis. Mr. Bunis, of department-store fame, came from Rochester where he and some of his colleagues who were to help him found the new temple had been boyhood friends of the late Rabbi Milton Steinberg, one of Dr. Kaplan's most noted disciples. It was therefore in the logic of events that when these liberals became discontented with affairs at Emanu-El they would turn to Reconstructionism as the basic guide for promoting modern Judaism in the fast-growing suburbs.

The organization meeting was held in 1952, and it was then that the decision to found Temple Sinai was made. The group purchased the Kenilworth Evangelical Church in the Town of Tonawanda, where they worshipped pending the day that they could erect a suitable structure to house the growing congregation. This day was brought closer by the selection of Sinai's first spiritual leader, Rabbi Nathan Gaynor (b.1918), who arrived in Buffalo in 1954. Trained at the Jewish Theological Seminary of America, Rabbi Gaynor brought vigorous leadership to his congregation and in less than five years Sinai moved to its new, modern synagogue located on Alberta Drive in the town of Amherst.

Meanwhile, under Rabbi Gaynor's guidance, Temple Sinai defined its religious and secular program. In a published statement, the congregation declared that it stood basically upon three freedoms: "Freedom of Jewish self-expression," "Freedom of our religious leaders to speak their minds and thus be able to fulfill their rabbinic tasks," and "Freedom to completely utilize the democratic process."

In addition to these seminal principles, Temple Sinai avowed its belief in Judaism as a practical way of life for both the individual and the group, based upon a maximal rather than a minimal amount of Jewish content in its services and school curriculum. To implement these aims, Sinai stressed the participation of women in all parts of its services, and emphasized its faith in the democratic process by subjecting all vital decisions to a congregational vote. Stating that Sinai was autonomous but not separatist, the congregation affirmed its belief in the concept of *Kelal Yisroel*, which it defined as "the all-embracing character of Judaism and the Jewish people, both in Israel and in the Diaspora." [111]

In this spirit, Sinai's synagogue practice came to rest somewhere between Reform and Conservatism. Hebrew rather than English was stressed in the prayers, but the congregation adopted the Reconstructionist *siddur* which modernized the ritual, changing some prayers, deleting others and adding many new ones. Like Reform congregations, Sinai observed only one day of other holidays; but, following the Israeli practice, retained two days of Rosh Hashana. The covering of heads during prayer, and the wearing of the *tallit* was continued as in traditional synagogues; but in embracing theistic naturalism, Reconstructionism goes farther than the classical tenets of Reform Judaism. In many ways Dr. Kaplan's philosophy bears a strong intellectual resemblance to William James's religious pragmatism.

In the fun-filled 1920s, while the younger members of Buffalo Jewry were leaving the old East Side and pushing uptown, what was happening to their ancient faith? Viewed from Jewish eyes the picture was not a happy one. The *avant-garde* of the day were told by Gertrude Stein that they were a "Lost Generation"; and the Jews among them were even more lost than their non-Jewish fellow-thinkers. The period marked, in many respects, the nadir of American Judaism. Perhaps the dominant intellectual impulse of the generation that matured after 1914 was a revolt against the Victorian order, and in Jewish circles this revolt was intensified by the social and economic adjustments that accompanied the exodus from eastern Europe. Later, Professor Marcus L. Hansen was to explain that the grandchildren of American immigrants tend to remember the values of their cultural heritage that their parents had wished to forget; but in the 1920s "Hansen's law" had not yet begun to operate. It was only with the maturation of the third generation of Jews, who felt more

secure as Americans than did their fathers, that the general tendency to
slough off Judaism as part of the immigrant cultural handicap ceased.
Moreover, after 1930, American Judaism was to be strengthened by the
increased identification that resulted from the Hitlerian fury and the
heightened pride that came with the establishment of the State of Israel.
Then, too, in recent years all established religions in the United States
have gained from the neo-Orthodox nature of contemporary theology.
But in the 1920s, all religions, and Judaism perhaps to an even greater
extent than the other faiths, suffered from an uncongenial climate of
opinion created by a mixture of Freudianism, hedonism, Bohemianism,
Marxian economics and outright intellectual nihilism.

The modernized Jews of yesterday did not see that the "Melting Pot"
had failed to melt and that American society resembled rather a huge
chopping bowl in which the various national ingredients poured into it
were still recognizable. To be sure, the contents of the bowl had undergone some changes, but the religious differences of its national groups
had been highly resistant to change. For 300 years, non-English-speaking
immigrants to these shores had given up their native tongues, their culture and their folkways; but they had, in large measure, retained their
individual religions. Hence, as religious loyalty among Jews weakened,
they became increasingly estranged from the ordinary American social
pattern. Religious division cut across American society in a tri-dimen-
sional way and the chief importance of the Jew in American life was that
he formed part of a separate religious group. But this fact, so obvious
today, was not fully realized a generation ago, for despite superficial
contrary appearances, assimilation was then in full swing among the
younger American Jews. If it appears to some old-timers of 1960 that in
their youth greater numbers of fervent Jews crowded the synagogues, it
is an illusion caused by the fact that there were then more first-generation
East-Siders alive who made it appear so. In the 1920s, says Will Herberg,
most American Jews were ready to relegate the synagogue "to the limbo
of obsolescent institutions." Time, however, was to reverse this hasty
judgment. As the twentieth century lengthened it became apparent that
Jews were something more than just another immigrant group ultimately
destined to lose their identity completely. Other nationalities, such as the
Italians and Poles, could preserve their folkways in America for a while,
but could not permanently hold back the floodwaters of assimilation. For
these people there could be no meaningful return of the third generation,
for men could not return to a way of life that had been lost in the process
of Americanization. But Judaism, which constituted a faith as well as a
culture, transcended the forces that were destroying the identity of other

immigrant groups. Judaism in America proved to be "very different from the kind of ethnic or cultural foreignness that tends to disappear."

As American Jewish life stabilized, it fitted well into the religious pattern of American life for, once the gates were shut against immigrants, it was religion rather than nationality that differentiated white Americans from one another. Slowly but surely the majority of Jews came to realize that such religious differentiation meant equality rather than inferiority; for while American society tolerated no permanent cultural or national differences within the country, it recognized and encouraged organizational separateness based on theological grounds. After 1930, it has been observed, the synagogue became the most American of all Jewish institutions.[112]

This revival of the synagogue, however, still lay in the lap of the future at a time when Jews *en masse* believed that their ancient heritage was just another piece of Old World baggage which ought to be discarded. The 1920s was a decade of roseate optimism, for the greatest brutalities of our dismal century were still to come. Despite the Ku Klux Klan and Henry Ford, it then looked as if Russian anti-Semitism had abated and no one could foretell that civilized Germany would return to barbarism within a decade. The immediate postwar period formed, as Frederick Lewis Allen has so aptly put it, "the Indian Summer of the Old Order." Jewish life reflected the Pollyanna spirit of the day and even the *Buffalo Jewish Review* greeted the year 1926 by saying that "we gaze into the future with limitless hope and unbounded enthusiasm." [113]

Meanwhile, Jews of the "Lost Generation," like the pathetic Robert Cohn of Hemingway's *The Sun Also Rises*, were busy disassociating themselves from their ancestral ties. In 1922, a young Jew who visited Buffalo on a business trip gave vent to the feelings of his generation when he said: "I am a Jew, of course. I never deny it. But I rarely have occasion to admit it. I don't look much like a Jew and so few people know it . . . In fact, I learn more every day why Gentiles hate Jews! And, in fact, you know, I really don't blame them in most cases." [114] This attitude was particularly marked among college students. On campuses throughout the country an alarming percentage of Jewish students matriculated either as Unitarians or as having no religious affiliation. So bad was the situation at the University of Illinois that a Christian Professor of Biblical Literature, Dr. Edward Chauncey Baldwin, was sufficiently shocked to draw the matter to the attention of some Jewish leaders in the state. "I am ashamed," said Professor Baldwin to a B'nai B'rith audience, "because . . . [Jewish students] know so little about the Scriptures which their own forebears created." [115] The men whom Dr. Baldwin addressed in due time established the first Hillel Foundation in an effort to stem the tide away from Judaism among college youth. The movement was sponsored by several national B'nai B'rith leaders who understood the needs of the time.

It was not, of course, only in ivy-clad college towers that this attitude prevailed, for a similar spirit pervaded all branches of Jewish life. In 1926, a group at Beth El in Buffalo could even debate the subject: "Resolved, Judaism is dying out." [116] A few years later, some Buffalo Jews sponsored a public debate which mooted the question of whether or not "assimilation is the best method of eliminating racial prejudice." Soon, however, Hitler was to begin his wholesale genocide and the fact was not lost upon the world when he failed to spare descendants of Jews whose grandparents had long since become Christians.

In many respects religious cynicism of the younger Jews merely reflected the advanced thought of the day. "People are drifting away from superstition and bunk," said Thomas A. Edison in 1928, "increase in scientific knowledge is responsible." [117] The everyday life of Americans was being transformed by rapid technological advances such as the radio, automobile and automatic refrigerator. Seldom, in those carefree days, did Americans concern themselves seriously with social and political unrest beyond the seas. Small talk revolved around flappers, bootleggers and sensational gangster murders. In such an atmosphere affairs of religion went by the board. When, in 1928, the famous actress Nora Bayes (née Dora Goldberg) was buried with Christian Science rites, the *Buffalo Jewish Review* lamented that in the confusion of the great exodus from Europe, American Jews had not found time to build the kind of synagogues and schools that would hold their native-born children. "The blame," said the editor correctly, "is on all of us." [118]

Thus, it should not have been particularly surprising to the city's Jewish leaders when some out-of-town social scientists studied the community in 1928 and revealed that upward of 90% of the youth groups in the city had no Jewish content in their program, nor, for that matter, anything of any real cultural value. To the questionnaires distributed by the survey group, only 1½% of Jewish organizations contacted replied that one of their aims was the promotion of Judaism. The survey further disclosed a paucity of effective lay leadership in Jewish organizations; and its final report deplored the fact that the city had so few professional workers who were literate in Jewish matters.[119]

The same report called attention to a rise in juvenile delinquency, particularly in the downtown Jewish neighborhood which was then rapidly deteriorating. Part of the moral decline of the day could be attributed to the wholesale failure of that "noble experiment," national prohibition. Jews, like many other immigrant groups, did not pay too much attention to the Eighteenth Amendment. Remarkably free from the curse of alcoholism, temperate by nature, it was difficult to see the utility of a law that ran counter to an age-old habit of mankind and was not sanctioned by the Bible. Moreover, many Jews of the period had grown up in the cruel czarist environment in which it had been necessary to defy governmental edicts in order to eke out a living. To such people it seemed sensible to disregard a law that did not seem reasonable.

The Volstead Act of 1919 fostered evasion of the ban on liquor by allowing the use of wine for "sacramental purposes." Some rabbis and lesser Jewish functionaries, like physicians of the dry era who prescribed spirits for all too many ailments, abused the law. Perhaps the situation was worse in Buffalo then elsewhere, for its location opposite Canada made it a natural center for bootlegging, and the heavy Catholic population in the city who also disliked prohibition helped engender outright defiance of the law.

When the situation became apparent, responsible Jewish elements in the city repeated endlessly the talmudic dictum that "the law of the country in which you live is your law." In 1921, the *Buffalo Jewish Review* implored local Jews to use grape juice for religious purposes (as Jewish law allowed) and not to buy the permitted annual allotment of fifteen gallons of sacramental wine. Emil Rubenstein spoke out fearlessly against Jews who violated the Federal law in the name of piety; and in return some bootleggers threatened his life through anonymous telephone calls.[120]

Not all of the men and women of the "Jazz Age," however, were hellward bound on a handcar, and some very worthy projects were begun in the post-Armistice decade, but were eclipsed by the more sensational events of those wild-oats days. It was an era when women had just received full political equality and, flushed with victory, they set out to prove their worth. Possibly this crusading spirit helped create some new women's service organizations and clubs. One of the most useful of these projects was the Jewish Mothers Club, incorporated in 1919. The organization sprang up in the William Street area as a means of providing working or sick mothers with daytime care for their children. The Jewish Mothers Club Nursery and Temporary Home, as it was first called, opened its doors at 252 Adams Street.

The club had been organized by a group of East Side women who were aided by the Ladies' Manhattan Auxiliary. One of the chief architects of the plan was Mrs. Sarah Rummel, a social worker. Among her associates were Mrs. Sarah Jacobs, Mrs. Henry Maisel and Mrs. Esther Lichtman Bedell (1895-1959), who served the club in many capacities for twenty-five years. By 1921, the Home was caring for Jewish children from eighteen months to twelve years of age and was staffed with five full-time employees, plus volunteer workers and an attending physician. The spirit seems to have been progressive, for both the domestic educator and the field worker visited the homes of the parents to help them solve the problems of child care. Financed in part by the people it served, fees ranged from 10 to 50 cents a day, depending upon ability to pay. These modest sums, of course, were not sufficient and additional income was derived from synagogue appeals and free gifts of food and clothing on the part of generous merchants. Even haircuts were given to the children by a kindly Jewish barber, Mr. Chodorow, whose shop stood at the corner of William and Hickory Streets.

In 1928, while Mrs. Bertha S. Serotte was president, the Mothers Club bought a larger house on Johnson Street near Broadway where it accommodated twenty children in its kosher kitchen. In theory, the Home was not supposed to accept clients whose plight was known to the Federation authorities, but in practice this understanding was not always observed. Some of the lingering immigrant suspicions of centrally organized charity are reflected by the following statement of a member of the Mothers Club: "When a mother brings in a child and asks us to care for it, we do not treat her as a 'case.' We simply take the child." This attitude was especially apparent during the depression-ridden 1930s when the demands on the Mothers Club multiplied and its annual drives received considerable response. With the returning prosperity of the following decade, however, the needs for which the Home had been founded gradually disappeared. The Johnson Street house was closed in 1954 and two years later the members of the club distributed its remaining assets to worthy institutions in the city.[121]

In the hot summer of 1921 still another group of women was planning to meet certain relief needs that would supplement the work of the Federation. Most of these young matrons had just moved out of the East Side and, like the Mothers Club circle, they liked the idea of spontaneous help for the poor without much investigation and red tape. Their newly-formed Naomi Relief Club thus set out to help indigent Jewish families who, for one reason or another, were not known to other organizations.

The membership of the Naomi group stabilized at about thirty. The club raised funds chiefly by sponsoring card parties, New Year's Eve celebrations, and public concerts. They specialized in lending emergency relief until another organization could take over a family, in giving special gifts at Passover time and other holidays and, for a time, they provided the hospitalized East Siders with kosher food. During the Great Depression, the Naomi Club paid special attention to the local Jewish junk peddlers who had been ruined by the Big Crash.

Hard times, however, brought closer cooperation with the Federation authorities. In 1934 the executive director of the Jewish Welfare Society, Miss Laura Margolis, earnestly addressed these women on the immediate need to find employment for the men roaming the streets of Buffalo in search of work. Miss Margolis urged her listeners to merge with the proposed Employment Service of the Jewish Welfare Society. Her plea was successful and the club raised funds for the Employment Service and provided woman-power to keep it in operation.

As the depression waned, a new need arose. Provision had to be made for Hitler's victims who were being hounded out of their native lands. In 1940, when the employment problem for refugee women was still important, the Federation urged the Naomi Club to establish a Refugee Exchange Bureau (Opportunity Shop) where the newcomers could use their talents and sell their wares. A city-wide committee was established with Mrs. Eugene Warner as chairman and Mrs. Joseph M. Singer, so long active in Naomi, as vice-chairman. This Refugee Division was a large undertaking, involving about 600 women, and the Naomi Club lost its identity in the merger.[122]

In contrast to the two women's associations previously mentioned, the Jewish Liberal Arts Club is still active and functioning. Organized in 1926 by a small group of women anxious for intellectual stimulation, it developed into a force for social and community service. Its leaders seemed to sense the confusion in the arts that so marked the hectic 1920s and they set out, in their own words, "to direct the energy used in this confusion into a constructive purpose." This they hoped to achieve by urging their members to consider "the utility and beauty of art as a whole." Soon the club had listed sixty names and began an annual fund-raising concert which long has been a cultural highlight of Buffalo's Jewish calendar. For over three decades the meetings of the club have included lectures and discussions on cultural and civic subjects, dramatic presentations and reviews of current books. By 1938, the Liberal Arts Club had become interested in helping worthy students complete their college education. Beginning in a modest way, the group, through its Scholarship Fund, has assisted many students at the University of Buffalo and elsewhere.[123]

Dating also from the Harding-Coolidge Era is the Montefiore Club, the latest and most successful organization of its type in Buffalo's Jewish history. We have already noticed the persistent tendency of American Jews to found clubs of their own. This tendency accelerated as the present century matured, for there were greater numbers of Jews who desired and could afford club membership, while at the same time they were ex-

cluded from many non-Jewish social organizations. Precisely at the point
of success where other immigrant groups could join the old Anglo-Saxon
élite, the Jew of prominence and wealth was excluded. A representative
club under Jewish auspices was, therefore, a virtual necessity if the Jewish community was to participate in this area of ordinary American social
life.

The Montefiore was the successor of the Standard, Phoenix, and
Apollo Clubs, all of which had been founded for similar purposes. It, in
turn, has existed longer than any of its predecessors, but it was founded
somewhat accidently. About 1920, Montefiore Lodge of B'nai B'rith had
grown to the point where its members thought that they could afford a
permanent meeting place. David Rodenberg, president of the Lodge,
heard that the old Saturn Club on Delaware Avenue and Edward Street
was for sale; but when he tried to buy, he found that the Apollo Club
had already been given an option on the Saturn property. Rodenberg then
visited August Keiser and other Apollo members and they released their
option hoping that a new all-community club would unite Buffalo Jewry.
The original idea of putting the new club under B'nai B'rith auspices
was dropped, for the chief aim of the group was to draw together, for
social purposes, all segments of the male Jewish population. So the Montefiore Club was opened to all men of good character who could afford
the dues, and for almost forty years it has been a chief center of Jewish
social activity in Buffalo.[124]

Meanwhile, the country club boom had started as newly-paved roads
invited tired businessmen to drive out of the city and forget their cares
in a more relaxing atmosphere. Spacious clubhouses, often designed
along Tudor lines, began to dot the adjacent suburbs of America's cities.
Then, too, there was the growing attraction of golf, the ideal game for
men who knew that it was not wise to reduce their middle-age spread by
more strenuous exercise. Buffalo Jewry shared, with the rest of Calvin
Coolidge's America, the urge to get "out in the open with the ozone—in
the wide green country where recreation will rule." To satisfy this urge,
some local Jews organized the Willowdale Country Club in 1919 and it
opened its doors two years later on a site on Sheridan Drive near Forest
Road. A building fund to construct a new clubhouse lasted for several
years, culminating in the collection of some $80,000. With this money the
members built an English-style country house surrounded by a nine-hole
golf course.

Both the Montefiore and Willowdale were hard hit by the depression,
for many businessmen who suffered financial reverses found it necessary
to relinquish their memberships. Impelled by reasons of economy, the
two organizations merged as the Wilmont Town and Country Club.

During the gas-shortage days of World War II, however, the country club was temporarily abandoned while the Montefiore resumed its independent existence. After the war, the old country club group bought back their original quarters, renamed it the Westwood Country Club and have flourished with the prosperity of the Frantic Fifties.[125]

While their parents were busy forming and joining clubs, Jewish boys and girls in Buffalo played an active part in scouting. The first Jewish Boy Scout Troop in the city had been established in Beth Zion in 1911, not long after the founding of the movement in the United States. Scouting in Buffalo owed much to Milton C. Guggenheimer who was the first Jewish Scoutmaster and who served many terms as president of the local district of the Boy Scouts of America. From Beth Zion, scouting spread to the Jewish Community Building on Jefferson Avenue, and eventually all of the modernized synagogues formed troops of their own. This, in time, led to a movement to find suitable quarters for summer encampment. Several Jewish troops had pitched their tents with other troops at Scouthaven near Freedom, New York, and in 1934 the Jewish Committee on Scouting was organized to solve the problem of better summer arrangements that would include more specific Jewish content. The following year this committee opened its own campsite at Scouthaven, equipped with a kosher kitchen and facilities for Jewish worship. All other activities, however, were carried on in cooperation with the non-Jewish troops at the summer rendezvous. Old-time scouters helped set up a scholarship fund to make it possible for needy Jewish scouts to go to summer camp. The Boy Scout movement was paralleled by various types of similar activities for girls.[126]

An important new development was the decision of the Jewish Committee on Scouting to purchase 200 acres of beautifully wooded land near Warsaw, New York. Withdrawal from Scouthaven was chiefly motivated by mounting difficulties arising from the maintenance of a separate kosher mess hall. Camp Jecosi, designed to accommodate several hundred campers, was formally dedicated on July 19, 1959. It was opened on a non-sectarian basis.

Another bond of union among Buffalo Jewry was forged with the advent of the city's first Anglo-Jewish newspaper. For many years such papers and magazines, published in metropolitan centers, had serviced Buffalo subscribers; but the time had now come for the Queen City to have its own Jewish chronicle.

The *American Jewish Review's* first monthly issue was published on November 9, 1917. The enterprise was backed by Albert Hershkowitz, who had run a similar newspaper in Atlanta. However, the going was hard and after a few months of struggle Hershkowitz sold the Buffalo paper to Philip and George W. Cohen. The Cohens were specialists in setting up or rejuvenating such papers and had originally come to Buffalo to revamp Hershkowitz's advertising policy. After the ownership changed hands, the new editors urged rabbis in the vicinity to write for the paper in the hope of achieving a more authentic local flavor. Rabbi Kopald of Beth Zion was a leading contributor, and for a time the *Review* seems to have mirrored largely his reactions to Jewish problems.[127]

Hence, Buffalo's first Jewish newspaper, in sharp contrast to its long-lived successor, reflected a Reform, elitist, mildly anti-Zionist point of view. Its pages were closer to the interests of the older families of German descent than to the point of view of the newer immigrants, many of whom still relied upon New York's Yiddish press for their information on Jewish affairs. In 1919, the *Review* rejected the idea of a Jewish State then about to be pressed upon delegates to the Versailles Peace Conference. The editors felt that the Jews ought to remain dispersed throughout the world until all mankind shall come "to know the Jew and respect him for his high moral sense and his value." Zionism, the paper felt, was a "distraction" rather than an "answer," and it reasoned that Jews themselves ought to put a brake on the movement before it did more mischief.[128] In addition to this attitude, so repugnant to the rising generation of Jewish leaders, the Cohens put too much trivia in their paper and frequently failed to assess current problems of Jewish interest from a world-wide point of view.

In 1921 the paper became a weekly and its name was changed to the *Buffalo Jewish Review*. In August of that year the publishers sold out to Elias Rex Jacobs and Myer B. Teplitz. Mr. Jacobs, then just under thirty, was a graduate of the City College of New York and Columbia Law School. Understanding the psychology and longings of the Jewish masses throughout the world, and unflinching in his Zionist outlook, Mr. Jacobs soon made his paper palatable to the great majority of his readers. In the coverage of local news, he limited his focus to the Niagara Frontier and built the circulation of the paper from 2,500 to 11,000.

The *Buffalo Jewish Review* has long enjoyed nation-wide esteem. Mr. Jacobs' success has been due to a number of factors. To begin with, the staff included the many-faceted talents of his wife, Ida; and secondly, "The Jacobs" wisely took advantage of centralizing agencies for the dissemination of Jewish news. Shortly before they came to Buffalo, the Jewish Correspondence Bureau (later the Jewish Telegraphic Agency) was established at The Hague as a globe-wide clearing house for Jewish news and matters of related interest. It did for the Jewish press what the Associated Press had done for ordinary newspapers in the nineteenth century, making possible authentic and immediate coverage of important events throughout the world. But the *Review* never forgot its obligations to Buffalo and it became a community organ stressing Jewish life and activity in the local area, which also included readable items on important national and world developments. The paper did much to bring order into Jewish life in Buffalo at a time when too many organizations were often trying to do too many things at the same time. As Jewish life became increasingly complicated, the *Review* tried earnestly, if not always successfully, to direct the community's energies and activities.[129]

As the Anglo-Jewish press was providing a service entirely designed for Jewish use, other new forms of exclusively Jewish enterprises came to the city. One of the first of these services to cater to the growing population was the funeral home. Prior to 1914, the various *Hevrot Kadisha* prepared the Orthodox dead for burial, while the actual funerals were conducted by non-Jewish undertakers. The first Jewish mortician in Buffalo was William Sultz who, in 1921, was part of the firm of Cutler and Sultz. In 1935, Mr. Sultz sold his Linwood Avenue building and equipment to Charles Etkin who had previously founded a rival establishment. Meanwhile, a former business associate of Etkin, Nathan Mesnekoff, had gone into business for himself. After Mr. Sultz's retirement, Buffalo Jewry was served exclusively by members of the Etkin and Mesnekoff families. The use of Christian undertakers has become increasingly infrequent.[130]

Strangely enough, Buffalo Jewry was more successful in caring for the deceased than for the ailing. The move to found a local Jewish hospital failed. Such institutions had long existed in many American cities, and Buffalo had always been anxious to follow suit. It was pointed out that in a Jewish hospital needy Jews would be better cared for, and the aged sick who usually observed the laws of *kashrut* would encounter neither food nor language problems. Moreover, the move would benefit Jewish physicians in the area who at the time felt that some hospitals discriminated against them. The *Buffalo Jewish Review* thought the proposed hospital a splendid opportunity to turn the other cheek. "It will," predicted an editorial, "present the concrete answer of thousands of Jews to the spirit of Fordian anti-Semitism when our people open the doors of their hospital to Gentiles as well as Jews."[131]

Meanwhile, the Jewish Hospital Association had been incorporated, with such leading physicians as Drs. Julius Ullman, Sigmund Goldberg, Marcel Hartwig, Bernard Cohen, Abram L. Weil, Nathan Kavinoky and

Isaac Sernoffsky signing as petitioners.[132] The project was revived in 1920 when the association chose Dr. Ullman as president, with an able list of fellow officers. The East Side-West Side composition of the elected slate demonstrated the new spirit of togetherness that was rapidly welding Buffalo Jewry.

Nevertheless, the building campaign made but fitful progress despite the energetic leadership of the chairman, Arthur Victor, Sr. Early in 1921 about 2,000 people assembled at the old Statler Hotel to report progress and to solicit additional gifts. Solomon Jacobson, the movie magnate, led the list of donors with a contribution of $10,000, which was earmarked for the purchase of a suitable site. Morris Altman, speaking for the local produce dealers, promised free food for one year and pledged to supply the hospital kitchen thereafter at cost. The speeches, including a fine address by the superintendent of Cincinnati's Jewish hospital, were roundly applauded, and a committee was chosen to search for a convenient location. A year later, a second annual meeting was held with Dr. Sigmund S. Goldwater, director of New York's Mt. Sinai Hospital, as the speaker of the evening. The world-famous Buffalo obstetrician, Dr. I. W. Potter, also spoke, as did Mr. J. L. Davis; but it was obvious that plans were still in the blueprint stage. The workers were not dismayed, however, and by 1925, $550,000 had been pledged and a site of seventy acres was purchased on Niagara Falls Boulevard, one mile west of Main Street. This ephemeral success was due to many generous gifts, especially those of Isaac S. Given and Joseph and D. H. Coplon. Much of the enthusiasm for the project was generated by the personal dynamism of the twenty-three year old attorney, Harold B. Ehrlich, who was secretary of the Hospital Association.[133]

However, it was soon apparent that still more money was needed, and the group tried to raise another $100,000, using the slogan "Give While You Live." Mr. Given pledged an additional $21,000 in the hope of giving the campaign a lift; and eventually it was reported that the grand total had reached $640,000. Soon the committee realized that it would cost at least a million dollars to open the hospital's doors. Meanwhile, the community wearied of the long delay and membership in the Hospital Association had dropped sharply. This waning enthusiasm came just as a new survey of the community reported that there was no urgent need in the city for increased hospital facilities and that the money could be spent to better advantage in other ways.* What hope remained to the Jewish

---

* An important factor in the decision against a Jewish hospital was the increasingly liberal attitude of existing hospitals in putting Jewish physicians on their staffs. In other words, during the long debate over the need for the hospital, conditions changed to remove one aspect of the need for it.

Hospital Association after this blow was killed by the ensuing business panic.[134]

Although plans for a Jewish hospital in Buffalo never materialized, the strenuous efforts devoted to the proposal indicated enlivened interest in matters relating to the Jewish community. Buffalo was pulling itself out of its nineteenth-century doldrums and much of the new spirit came from boys bred on the East Side who, after 1920, began making their mark in politics and the professions. Like the country in general prior to the New Deal Era, Buffalo Jews were more prone to be affiliated Republican than Democratic. As late as 1927, a Hebrew-American Republican Club flourished in the William Street neighborhood and here many rising young lawyers had their first taste of grass-roots politics.[135] Among the younger group who were later active in G.O.P. ranks were Philip Halpern, Jacob Tick, Harold B. Ehrlich, Maurice Frey, Frank E. Freedman and George M. Raikin. But Buffalo Jewry was by no means solidly Republican and such ambitious young leaders as David Diamond and Samuel C. Markel were devoted Al Smith Democrats. For many years, local politics had been the monopoly of the old Anglo-Saxon group, the Irish and the Germans. Now, however, the children of the newer immigrants were eagerly entering the mainstream of American life. In this respect, the Jews were a generation ahead of other immigrants of the period. Usually they had been the first of their national groups to come to the New World, and Buffalo Jews whose parents had been born in Poland were well Americanized at a time when the non-Jewish Poles were still living in cultural isolation. Moreover, the doors of the universities, so long closed to Jews in Europe, were now open to them in the United States. Prepared by an American education, they soon ventured into the exciting game of politics.

As an increasing number of Buffalo Jews were admitted to the bar, they, like their non-Jewish colleagues, found that the law was often the handmaiden to politics. Nevertheless, one of the most successful Buffalo Jewish politicos of his generation was a merchant rather than a lawyer. He was Jacob L. Davis (known familiarly as "J.L.") who had been born in Cleveland in 1867, but who had been brought to Buffalo as an infant. Mr. Davis began his business career with a department store at 1888 Niagara Street which he conducted in partnership with a brother. Later the firm opened another retail store on another site and for many years this establishment was a landmark in the Grant-West Ferry Street shopping center.

Prior to embarking on a political career, "J.L." had been long active in Beth Zion, the Federation and many Jewish and municipal undertakings.

At sixty-one, he was elected councilman-at-large on the Republican ticket and he served in this position until 1932. Although he appealed for Jewish votes with Yiddish slogans in certain sectors of the city, he ran strongly in Hungarian neighborhoods because of his Black Rock business connections. It was partially due to his efforts that Riverside Park became a reality and bustling Niagara Street was widened to relieve traffic congestion. Mr. Davis failed in his bid to become president of the Common Council and, on his retirement from that body, he was appointed by the mayor as chairman of the Board of Assessors. Thereafter, until his passing in 1937, Mr. Davis devoted much of his time to city and Jewish affairs. Temple Beth Zion, in particular, benefited from his wise counsel and at the time of his death he was its vice-president.[136]

Other local Jews who achieved prominence in politics in those years included George M. Raikin (1894-1950), who was appointed councilman-at-large by a Republican mayor and was subsequently elected to that position. Big, burly Samuel Sapowitch was made public administrator by the surrogate of Erie County in 1940. He served efficiently for a number of years and his zeal in tracking down the heirs of some particularly complicated estates made front-page news.

Buffalo Jewry, during this period, became especially associated in the public mind with one branch of the state judiciary. When the popular Judge Louis W. Marcus died in 1923, he was replaced in the Eighth Judicial District of the Supreme Court by Samuel J. Harris (b.1877), who was twice re-elected to his office. In 1940, Governor Herbert H. Lehman assigned him to the Appellate Division, Fourth Department, and he was renamed to this position by Governor Thomas E. Dewey for the final three years of his term. In the fall of 1947, Philip Halpern (b.1902) was elected on the Republican ticket to succeed Judge Harris. The new judge had had a brilliant legal career which had brought him, at an unusually early age, state-wide prominence. Graduated at twenty from the University of Buffalo Law School, Mr. Halpern worked for a time in New York with the Brooklyn-Manhattan Transit Corporation. He soon returned to his native Buffalo and, at twenty-three, began to teach at his alma mater, rising in time to become dean of its Law School. In 1943 he became chief counsel of the Public Service Commission of the State of New York, also serving as a member of the Enemy Alien Hearing Board during World War II. Five years after Judge Halpern's election to the bench, Governor Dewey appointed him to the Appellate Division, Third District—a distinct honor since it was unusual for a judge to serve outside of his own district. But judicial work did not consume all of the judge's fabulous energy. Always interested in the cause of international organization, Judge Halpern in 1953 became principal adviser to the United Nations Commission on Human Rights. After he had served three years, the Commission appointed him sole United States member of the U.N.'s Sub-Commission on the Prevention of Discrimination and Protection of Minorities.[137]

Another eminent graduate of the local law school, David Diamond (b.1898), entered politics at twenty-seven, when he ran for the position of Judge of the City Court. Despite a seven-nights-a-week campaign which startled the local politicians, Mr. Diamond was defeated, for he was a Democrat in a period of G.O.P. ascendancy. His interest in public service continued, however, and in 1937 Mayor Thomas L. Holling appointed him Corporation Counsel. He served this reform-minded administration faithfully until January 1, 1941, when Governor Lehman named him to fill a vacancy on the bench of the Eighth Judicial District of the Supreme Court. But even a man of Judge Diamond's caliber could not keep his seat in this hide-bound Republican district and, at the conclusion of his appointed term, he retired from politics. Since then he has achieved distinction as a practicing lawyer, as mentor in Zionist causes, and as mainstay of the United Jewish Federation of Buffalo whose president he became in 1959.[138]

Not until 1959 was Buffalo to have two Jews elected to the bench of the Eighth Judicial District. In that year, Jacob Tick (b.1895) won election as the candidate for Supreme Court Justice on the Republican and Liberal tickets. A native son, Justice Tick had been graduated from Master Park High School, distinguishing himself in both baseball and debating. His early interest in Jewish education has already been mentioned; he maintained this interest throughout his long public career. In 1943 Mr. Tick gave up the private practice of law to serve as Comptroller of Erie County—a post he held for sixteen years. Seldom before had western New York profited from the service of such an efficient administrator. In a period of rising costs, Comptroller Tick reduced the county debt from $44 to $1.2 million, and his reputation for economy and integrity helped him win the hard-fought judicial election of 1959.

Another attorney who often made the front pages of the local newspapers was William J. Brock (1898-1952). Born in Buffalo and educated locally, Mr. Brock specialized in New York negligence law and became one of the city's most able trial lawyers. An ardent internationalist, he was active in a number of groups that after Pearl Harbor pressed for global political unity.

Since so many of Buffalo's Jewish professional men received their training at the University of Buffalo, it was natural that they and their families hailed its rapid development in the post-war years. Although the university dated from 1846, until the establishment of the College of Arts and Sciences in 1913 it was merely a collection of loosely federated professional schools. Just prior to the outbreak of World War I, however, a group of civic-minded men and women determined that the time had come to establish a genuine seat of learning on the Niagara Frontier. Members of Buffalo's uptown Jewish families gave leadership and money to the cause, while downtown immigrant parents pinched pennies so that their sons and daughters might receive a higher education. To such families the university's growth was a boon, for few of them could afford the luxury of sending their children to out-of-town colleges. The University of Buffalo was a godsend to poverty-stricken immigrant children of all nationalities who could now complete their education while supplementing the family budget with after-school earnings.

During the long tenure of Chancellor Samuel P. Capen, who served the University of Buffalo from 1922 to 1950, it became apparent that in this institution there would be no discrimination against minorities on either the student or faculty level. This was particularly noteworthy in the 1920s, for it was a period when many colleges were openly or secretly limiting the number of Jewish students who knocked at their doors. Chancellor Capen, a liberal-minded and level-headed Yankee educator, refused to follow the national tendency to limit Jewish admissions, or keep down to a bare minimum Jewish faculty appointments. These wise policies were continued by Dr. Capen's successors and for the past forty years Buffalo Jewry has taken great pride in the university and has ever been responsive to its growing needs.

A signal instance of Jewish interest in the university came in 1925 when, on the approach of his sixtieth birthday, Emanuel Boasberg established the chair in American history that bore his name. "I have selected American history as the subject for this gift," Mr. Boasberg wrote to the university authorities, "because I believe that the study of the history of our country will tend to inspire the youth of this community with a devotion to the duties and privileges of American citizenship." To fulfill his purpose, Mr. Boasberg pledged $100,000 to be paid to the university in twenty equal installments. Over half of the pledge had been paid when Mr. Boasberg died, but the inroads of the depression made it necessary for his heirs to discontinue the Boasberg chair. Nevertheless, the original gift proved to be of inestimable value to the college, for it brought to Buffalo one of the country's outstanding historians, Julius W. Pratt (b.1888), who inspired countless students during the thirty-two years that he taught American history on the Main Street campus. In these three decades Professor Pratt brought national recognition to the university for his writings on American expansionism and foreign policy.[139]

The Buffalo Jewish community continued its interests in university affairs and, in 1946, due in large measure to the untiring efforts of Arthur

I. Goldberg, Montefiore Lodge No. 70 of B'nai B'rith and the United Jewish Federation of Buffalo secured the establishment of a branch of Hillel Foundation on the campus. A dozen years later, there were some 700 Jewish students at the university served by Hillel's director, Dr. Justin Hofmann. Moreover, a number of special-purpose funds at the university have been endowed in memory of Jewish men and women.

As the universities here and elsewhere attracted greater number of Jewish students, certain professions appealed particularly to the generation that came of age after the 1918 Armistice. This was especially true of callings, in addition to medicine, that sought to alleviate human suffering. The pioneer Jewish podiatrist in Buffalo was the Spanish-American War veteran, Joseph Cohen. He was followed by many younger men, some of whom have been professionally active on a state-wide level. Dr. Reuben Cohen served two terms as president of The Podiatry Society of the State of New York.

Pharmacy also attracted many Jewish lads because of the convenient location of the University of Buffalo and because this course required fewer years than medicine. Many of the local graduates opened their own stores and the Jewish druggist, once a rarity in the city, became a commonplace.

For many years Jews seemed to shy away from architecture, although the firms of Dankmar Adler in Chicago and Albert Kahn in Detroit had long been nationally known. Heavy industry in Buffalo and elsewhere did not welcome Jewish professional assistance and this fact may account for the reluctance of Jewish boys to enter an occupation so closely related to Big Business. As the general situation improved and as an architect could count on an increasing number of Jewish clients for business, communal and residential work, a few venturesome souls began to matriculate in out-of-the-city schools of architecture. The first of these pioneers in Buffalo was Eli W. Goldstein (1886-1945) who completed his work at Cornell University when he was twenty-five. During his many years of practice in Buffalo, Mr. Goldstein designed the North Court and Sherwood Apartments. In Jewish circles he is remembered as the architect of the gate that guards the entrance of the Ahavas Achim cemetery on Pine Ridge Road.

Even better known in the field was Louis Greenstein who trained at Columbia and set up his practice in Buffalo in 1914. In the course of his long professional career, Mr. Greenstein designed the Medical Arts Building, supervised the renovation of Beth El's interior, planned the original Temple Beth David on Humboldt Parkway and the 1959 construction of Temple Beth David-Ner Israel. Mr. Greenstein was also responsible for the stately chapel and gates that beautify Beth El's Pine Hill Cemetery. Twice in his career he won signal awards—in 1924 for the design of the official seal of the City of Buffalo, and in the following year for the design of the seal of Erie County.

The promising architectural career of Edward M. Plant (1901-1935) was cut short by his premature death. His early professional experience came in Miami; but he returned to Buffalo in 1927. In the eight short years that remained to him he planned the imposing addition to Temple Beth Zion in 1929, supervised the construction of the Elk Street Market, and designed numerous private residences in the Kensington district of Buffalo.

Graduated as a civil engineer from Cornell, Jacob Fruchtbaum (b.1896) received the Wasson Medal of the American Concrete Institute for his work on the General Mills Building in Buffalo. Later, he pioneered in a promising new field and served as architect-engineer for the nuclear reactors of the Massachusetts Institute of Technology and the University of Buffalo.

Melvin Morris, Jack Kushin, and Milton Milstein represent the younger generation of Buffalo Jewish architects. Mr. Morris prepared at the Carnegie Institute and won in competition the first award of the American Academy of Rome. Mr. Kushin designed the Tacoma Avenue synagogue of Congregation Ahavas Achim Lubavitz. Mr. Milstein, who studied architecture at Syracuse University, specialized in the designing of schools. He was so successful in this line of endeavor that his designs have been adopted for the projected elementary school building program of the local Board of Education. It was Milstein, too, who planned the Jewish Center of Buffalo. For this project, Mr. Milstein received an award from the New York State Association of Architects.

No account of Buffalo Jewish architects would be complete without mention of Gordon Bunshaft (b.1909) whose work has become internationally famous. Mr. Bunshaft was born in Buffalo and, after graduating from Lafayette High School, pursued his professional education at the Massachusetts Institute of Technology. He rose to become senior partner of Skidmore, Owings and Merrill of New York and Chicago, reputed to be the largest architectural firm in the United States. Bunshaft planned Lever House, the first all-glass building to be erected in New York City. His design of the building for the Connecticut General Life Insurance Company in Hartford, Connecticut, attracted national attention during the building boom of the 1950s.[140]

While many of the younger Jewish men in Buffalo were entering the professions, others were gaining additional prominence in the business fields. Isaac S. Given, as we have already seen, was important in Main Street retail circles, as was his brother-in-law, Louis L. Berger. Still another department-store magnate was Isaac Kantrowitz (1870-1930). Born in Boston, Mr. Kantrowitz came to Buffalo early in the century, representing a national dry-goods organization which controlled Oppenheim Collins & Co., and it was with this store that Mr. Kantrowitz was associated. He was an ardent community worker and achieved prominence in the Liberty Loan campaigns and in numerous civic charity drives.[141]

Because so many Jewish immigrants had been furriers in ice-clad Russia, it was natural for many of them to continue their calling on this side of the water. The best known of this group in Buffalo was a World War I veteran, Nathan L. Kaplan (1893-1958), who came here shortly after being discharged from the service and established the thriving firm that bears his name. The older members of the Palanker family brought their skill in preparing pelts with them from the old country and their name, too, became associated in the Buffalo mind with the retail fur business.

Mention should also be made of other Buffalo Jewish merchants of the more recent period. In wearing apparel and department-store work there was Joseph R. Morrison, associated with the stores that bear the same name, Harold M. Hecht, formerly director of the William Hengerer Co., and the Bunis family, headed by Louis M. Bunis, who established the Sample stores. In other lines of endeavor there were Ignatz Eckstein of the Whitney Seed Co. Inc.; Harry J. and Myron G. Lehman, whose Wildroot products associated Buffalo with hair tonic; Joseph Markel of Markel Electric Products; and Daniel Roblin and Samuel Greenfield in the housewrecking and scrap metals industries respectively. The Angert family of the automobile parts business represented Buffalo Jewry in that area and at one time they could advertise their concern as "The World's Largest Auto Wreckers."

Because of the location in Buffalo and nearby Jamestown of furniture manufacturers, it was natural for enterprising men to establish retail furniture stores. Moreover, in a period of constant urban growth, Jewish merchants tended to concentrate on supplying city-dwellers with many commodities, and furniture was always a necessity for young couples about to set up their own homes. Some of these families wished to pay for their heavy goods from their future earnings. One of the first Jewish men in the city to recognize the utility of installment buying in furniture wares was Louis Maisel (1874-1946). Mr. Maisel came to the United States at the age of sixteen and began his business career in Buffalo with a picture-framing shop located in a small nook at 967 Broadway. It was a fortunate choice of location, for it was in the center of

Buffalo's rapidly growing Polish district that was to develop into a great shopping center. In time, the little shop grew into one of the area's leading furniture marts, with a branch located in downtown Buffalo. Mr. Maisel, who also prospered by wise real estate investments, was among the first East Side Jews to be drawn into Federation work, and throughout his life he supported liberally many worthwhile Jewish and non-Jewish causes. In addition to his interest in organized national and local movements, Mr. Maisel retained the Old World tradition of private charity and made a hobby of helping worthy young men establish themselves in various industries, including agriculture. Mr. Maisel brought many families from his own little town to Buffalo, many of whom have become leading Jewish citizens of the city.[142]

Besides several branches of the Maisels, certain other Jewish families achieved success in the retail furniture line. There was the older Spangenthal family, the Victors, the Coplons, several of the Sapowitch family, including Joseph Anthone, who was related to them by marriage, and Charles Lederman and his son, Israel R. It has often been noted by general historians that Jews provided the raiment that all but wiped out class distinction in dress; but their contribution in improving living conditions in American homes was almost as great.

As already noted in previous chapters, Buffalo Jews early turned their interest to various aspects of the jewelry trade. As business interests broadened in the twentieth century, this concentration became less noticeable, but one later development demands consideration. Mr. Arthur J. Block (b.1885) was graduated from Cornell University and for a time was engaged in the clothing business. Later, in conjunction with his brother Edgar, he bought control of the retail jewelry firm of T. C. Tanke, Inc., reputed to be one of the largest stores of its kind in the country.[143]

It is perhaps significant that in one generation this branch of the Block family of Ihringen left the field of banking for retail marketing. In contrast to some other cities where Jews are to be found in large numbers in banking and other forms of Big Business, locally their economic importance has been in the distribution of goods rather than in finance or heavy industry. Despite the fact that the present head of the New York Central System is of their faith, Jews of the Niagara Frontier occupied no positions of importance in the development of Buffalo as a major rail center. They have not been intimately connected with shipbuilding on the Great Lakes, with the large-scale distribution of coal, with the grain industry, the production of steel, or the manufacture of car wheels —all primary industries for which the area has long been noted. Neither have local Jews engaged in drop-forging that gives employment to so many here, nor in the manufacture of automobiles in the days when Buffalo was known for its Pierce Arrow cars. The Niagara Frontier is one of the nation's greatest chemical centers, and many airplanes are built in the area. Buffalo's harbor, the busiest fresh water port in the world, is dotted with some of the largest grain elevators in operation. Yet in all these wealth-producing activities Jews have played a relatively minor part. Unlike neighboring Rochester, a garment center in which Jews have led in one of the major occupations of the city, Buffalo Jews have gained indirectly rather than directly from the primary occupations of western New York. They are, more often than not, employed as attorneys, sales representatives, and sometimes even as managers of these industries, but they have neither owned nor controlled them. It therefore seems sensible to believe that while Jews here have prospered as a whole, their per capita wealth is less than in some other cities of comparable size.

On the other hand, the Jewish immigrant habit of investing savings in real property continued apace. In 1923 a group of East Siders formed the Jewish-American Real Estate Association, beginning with a capital stock of $25,000. This was an attempt to combine the old fraternal features of the *Landsmanschaften* societies with opportunities for speculation in property. The experiment, however, was not a success and it was liquidated with a clear record of no losses to investors.[144]

There were, however, some other real estate ventures that prospered to the point where they left indelible imprints on the city's growth. In crowded New York and Chicago, Jews had pioneered in the development of new areas and in the construction of apartment houses, because they recognized the residential needs of families anxious to leave congested areas for more pleasant surroundings. The building impetus reached Buffalo in the 1920s and the Elliott Apartments were constructed on a part-ownership cooperative plan. The entrepreneur in this case was Isydor Lasser who, backed by partners, also put up the Sherwood, Gates Circle, Windsor and Mayflower Apartments.

Another important real estate developer of the period was Bernard N. Hyman whose forebears had been so active in nineteenth-century Beth El affairs. Mr. Hyman understood the importance of the growth of the University of Buffalo to property on northern Main Street, and he did much to build up the area located opposite the university and running to the city line at Kenmore Avenue.[145]

Turning from matters of economics to cultural developments of the period, Buffalo Jews did their share in fostering the theater, music and the fine arts. The last legitimate stage house in the city opened its doors on Labor Day, 1927, as the Erlanger Theater. It was originally built by Abraham Erlanger, a nationally famous theater man with Buffalo family connections. Although Mr. Erlanger did not reside in the city, his sister, Mrs. Lina Bergman (1861-1956), lived here for seven decades. Her son, Leonard, was associated with his uncle in the firm of Klaw and Erlanger, and it was through this connection that Mr. Erlanger sought to provide Buffalo with a legitimate theater. It was a source of regret to many citizens when, in the late 1950s, the theater closed its doors, unable to compete with more popular forms of entertainment of the television era.

Jack Yellen, the lyricist (b.1892), is Buffalo Jewry's most famous contemporary musical representative. We have earlier noted the origins of this talented family, which migrated to Buffalo shortly before the turn of the century. For many years, Jack, the eldest son, commuted from Tin Pan Alley to Buffalo, interrupting this routine with frequent trips to Hollywood. In the 1920s he wrote lyrics for the hit "Rain or Shine," and his "Happy Days Are Here Again" was the Roosevelt theme song in the landslide Democratic victory of 1932. Among Mr. Yellen's many other contributions that were written in English, perhaps the best known are "Lovin' Sam," "I Wonder What Became of Sally," "Ain't She Sweet," "Forgive Me" and "Dream Kiss." [146]

Important on the local musical scene was D. Bernard Simon (1906-1953), a practicing lawyer who left his profession to devote the last dozen years of his life to pursue his artistic interests. While still a law partner of his brother-in-law, Edward H. Kavinoky, Mr. Simon played in various orchestras and made music his hobby. A turning point in his career came in 1939 when he produced *This Is So Sudden,* a musical comedy, for a Temple Beth Zion benefit performance. After this great Buffalo success, Mr. Simon became involved in the New York theatrical world. During this creative phase of his musical career, he directed and produced, writing the book, lyrics and music for five productions as well as two local pageants of a religious nature. His best known published songs are "My Mind's On You," "I'll Be Back," "More Than Yesterday" and "Someone Said." [147]

In contrast to Mr. Simon who left the law for music, Dr. Lesser Kauffman (1877-1939) combined psychiatry with musical activities. In 1922 he was one of the founders of the Buffalo Symphony Society and was for many years chairman of its executive committee. A learned amateur, he made himself an authority on chamber music and was responsible for bringing some well-trained quartets to Buffalo. A man of rare versatility, Dr. Kauffman was a patron of the Buffalo Society of Natural Sciences and interested in the local Historical Society.[148]

One son of Buffalo found fame as a Hollywood magnate. Mr. Charles

Boasberg was graduated from Cornell and early became affiliated with RKO pictures. Rising from manager of the western New York branch to general sales manager, he succeeded in 1957 to one of the most important offices in the motion picture industry—president of Warner Brothers Distributing Corporation.

Meanwhile, in the world of opera, Buffalo Jewry was represented by Thelma Altman (Mrs. Robert Fixler), youngest daughter of the active communal leader, Morris Altman. Miss Altman, after her graduation from the Eastman School of Music in Rochester, sang as a mezzo-soprano for the New York Opera Company and the Schenectady Choral Society. In 1943 she was invited to join the Metropolitan Opera Company. After a half dozen years with this celebrated group, she retired to do occasional opera work in various parts of the country.

Perhaps Buffalo Jewry's foremost contribution to the field of visual arts is Lewis W. Rubenstein. Professor Rubenstein of Vassar College was born in 1908, son of Mr. and Mrs. Emil Rubenstein. The younger Rubenstein did several murals in various buildings located on the Harvard campus, and many of his easel creations have since been hailed by competent critics. Mr. Rubenstein developed an unusual art form which he calls "time painting." These are continuous ink scroll paintings, shown in a specially constructed viewing frame designed to produce a sequential narrative or an unfolding landscape. Locally, Rubenstein's major contribution is the mural that decorates the main entrance to the Jewish Center—a remarkable piece of work in which the artist included an Israeli motif.[149]

Finally, in the world of art, Alexander O. Levy (1881-1947) must receive notice. He prepared for his life's work in Cincinnati and New York, and in 1911 began to exhibit his paintings with the Buffalo Society of Artists. For many years Levy was art director of the famous Buffalo mail-order house, the Larkin Company. His work was exhibited in many American cities and he won numerous national and local prizes. Levy's sketch class was a popular gathering place of budding amateurs, and in art circles he is still remembered as the first president of the Arts Club of Buffalo.

These were some of the manifold activities of Buffalo Jewry during the colorful years that followed the war with Hohenzollern Germany. Meanwhile, a natural leader had entered on the scene, a man who was destined to dominate many facets of organized Jewish life. Eugene Warner had been born in Buffalo on January 7, 1876, the son of Edward and Matilda Warner. After his graduation from Harvard in 1898, young Warner returned home and prepared for a legal career at the University of Buffalo Law School. While still a student, he became managing clerk of the law firm of Shire and Jellinek, where Moses Shire made him his special protégé. For a while after his admission to the bar, Mr. Warner remained with Shire and his partner, but eventually he set up an office of his own, specializing in cases involving bankruptcy. On February 19, 1907, he married Miss Nellie Bendheim, stepdaughter of one of the community's foremost leaders, Theodore Hofeller.

The law, however, was not sufficient outlet for an ambitious and articulate young man with the keen interest in public affairs that so marked the generation that came of age during the Progressive Era. Mr. Warner inherited an intense interest in synagogue affairs from his father. His mother, too, had long served the cause of Reform Judaism in Buffalo, singing in the choir when it was still volunteer work and later serving as first president of the Women's Temple Society. Little wonder then, that their son Eugene was long active on the school board of Beth Zion, served on its board of trustees and, in later years, made an annual hit with the congregation as he read favorite portions of the Yom Kippur Day service.

It was in the rapidly developing field of social service, however, that "Gene" Warner made his most lasting impact on the history of the Jewish community. He was, as we have earlier related, a prime mover in organizing the Federation. It was in the nature of things that he should become its president and he served in this office longer than any other man has, or probably ever will serve. First elected in 1919, he returned to office in 1931 and, after a lapse of one year, came back to serve until declining health forced his retirement in 1942.

Gene Warner's remarkable organizational ability was first fully acknowledged during the stirring years of World War I, when he directed the Buffalo drive of the Joint Distribution Committee. This experience made him an expert in securing able co-workers, keeping an eye on minute details, prodding the unwilling and the ungenerous, and maintaining campaign morale by timely and forceful statements from headquarters. He had, moreover, a lively ingenuity which he used to set up campaigns, borrowing military terms when martial thinking was in vogue or using other gimmicks in less heroic-minded decades. Of course he was repeatedly called upon to head these annual drives; his leadership soon came to be taken for granted.[150]

Mr. Warner realized that he lived in an age of transition, when old-fashioned charity was becoming professionalized social work. Although it must have caused him some inward uneasiness, he tried to adjust his thinking to the inescapable facts of the twentieth century. An insight into the man may be gained by the fact that his favorite piece of Jewish literature was Maimonides' peerless description of the eight degrees of charity. To the ever-growing majority who demanded that additional community funds be earmarked for Palestine and for communal projects not designed for the under-privileged, he gave reluctant ground. He compromised enough to head off serious revolt during his lifetime, but he must have surmised that, right or wrong, a new orientation towards Jewish life was in the making. In secular affairs his innate conservatism was moderated by acquaintance with labor problems made through his participation in the New York State Mediation Service.

Active though he was in the affairs of Buffalo Jewry, Mr. Warner had sufficient energy left to lead in civic and state movements. He headed the Buffalo Council of Social Agencies for two years, and he was a one-time president of the New York State Conference on Social Work. The city called on his experience during the Great Depression, and he served on the Mayor's Committee on Unemployment and the Erie County Emergency Relief Bureau. He freely gave of his talents during the critical months which followed Pearl Harbor, and he helped bring both the Federation and the United Jewish Appeal into an all-community drive, the United War and Community Fund.

What sort of a person was this multifaceted man, Eugene Warner? It is as difficult to think of him divorced from community leadership as it is to picture General Robert E. Lee without an army or Dr. William Osler without a stethescope. At first glance Warner could have been mistaken for a poet, for he was bald and he wore his side hair long. His natural air of dignity was enhanced by his eyeglasses, which often dangled from his side on a long black cord. Like Theodore Roosevelt, whom he so ardently admired and whose picture hung in his office, "Gene" Warner believed in the strenuous life. At the age of fourteen he won the bicycle championship of Buffalo on a high-wheeled velocipede and he rode on the bicycle team at Harvard. As an adult, his favorite outdoor hobby was fishing and he was particularly at home in the cool waters of Georgian Bay.[151]

Eugene Warner's last years coincided with the crucial days of World War II when the values of the European Enlightenment which he so admired were threatened with extinction by Axis barbarism. It is fitting to close this chapter with an account of Mr. Warner, for his life, in a sense, was a symbol of what had happened to the Jewish people during his own span. When he came to manhood, American Jewish leaders were usually prime optimists, believing that light had dawned everywhere but in darkest Russia. The events of 1914 set in motion a chain reaction which eventually changed that optimism to profound pessimism. Eugene Warner died December 30, 1943, at a time when it was still too soon to know for certain that the free world and the Jewish people would survive. The conflict then raging, like the earlier one a generation before, was to alter the whole course of history. To view these changes in proper context, we must review in detail certain economic and social trends which were accelerated by this "War For Survival."

CHAPTER

———◦⧫◦———

NINE

"Out of the Depths . . ."

IN THE YEARS immediately preceding the Great Depression, the Buffalo Jewish community basked contentedly in the sunshine of an unprecedented prosperity. After 1924, with the virtual cessation of immigration, Old World cultural remnants in most cities waned rapidly and consequently immigrant institutions began to wither. The Americanization process, which had hitherto been so important, shifted its focus. Many communities now aimed to make literate and understanding Jews out of Americans, whereas the former stress had been on Americanizing the immigrants as quickly as possible. A corresponding change in emphasis from charity to service occurred. The old division between German and East-European Jews prolonged this process of change, and it was marked occasionally with bitter disputes. Locally, the former group wished to maintain the Federation as a charity agency directed by a few philanthropically-minded laymen, whereas the latter refused complete integration of their own institutions into the Federation until a professional, modern point of view was adopted toward social service. Eventually the views of the East-European majority triumphed.

By 1928, Beth El and Beth Zion could no longer live in private little worlds. The whole trend of American culture was, by this time, pitted against such concepts of separation. Improvements in modern transportation, revolutions in the media of mass communication, and the leadership of such papers as the *Buffalo Jewish Review* combined to break up the little isolated pockets of congregational groups. If Jews were to survive as Jews amidst the all-enveloping secular American milieu, they had to be knit together tightly, and the most feasible means toward this unity was the Federation. In the next twenty years, two forces were to accelerate this process of unification: business depression at home and the Hitlerian terror abroad.

Samuel Lubell has pointed out that America's new immigrants came of age with the advent of the New Deal. Slovak, Jew, Pole, Italian, Czech, Hungarian—all these immigrant groups that had hitherto remained unassimilated entered the mainstream of American life as a result of Roosevelt's policy of incorporating them as full citizens in the broadest sense of the term. In this general trend, Jews held special advantages because they were used to an urban culture from the Old World, and because they had a high occupational and class mobility that demonstrated itself in many ways. Although most of them moved quickly out of the proletariat into the professional, business and managerial ranks, even those who remained in the factories benefited from the new emphasis on unionization.

Simultaneously, however, Jews were threatened by problems that arose with the Big Crash. During the 1930s, while a rabid form of isolationism was rampant in America, Jews were in real danger of a growing anti-Semitism. Nevertheless, this was eventually counteracted by the Nazi persecutions of European Jewry, which evoked sympathy in America, and by active work on the part of a half-dozen organizations of which the Anti-Defamation League, the American Jewish Committee and the American Jewish Congress were the most important. A further ironic result of the Hitler period was the fact that in the face of wholesale persecution abroad, local differences in the Jewish communities in America were patched up and forgotten.

All in all, therefore, because of these two forces, as Jews became more and more Americanized externally—in their dress, recreation and occupation—sociologically they became an integral part of an urbanized and industrialized America. Consequently, as Dr. Uriah Z. Engelman has pointed out, by Pearl Harbor, most Buffalo Jews were well rooted, stable citizens. Almost half of them had been born in Buffalo, and only a tiny fraction had failed to become naturalized.[1]

But this is to get ahead of the story. What was the Buffalo Jewish community like on that fateful day in 1929 when the prosperity bubble burst? The community was described by a professional New York social worker as: "Old, well established in communal life. Usual multiplicity of interests, exaggerated conflicts of personalities. Well developed sense of communal responsibility and obligations. Comparatively liberal in giving." [2] The old East Side community was fairly well abandoned by this time, and the upper West Side and Humboldt Parkway areas were at the height of their popularity. It was a period of relative economic stability in which most of the recent immigrants had been absorbed and were living in well-kept, neat and comfortable homes. Their children were enjoying the recreational and educational facilities of the public school system and the older ones were eagerly preparing themselves for careers. Business was brisk, times were prosperous, the Federation fund-raising campaign of 1928 went over the top with a thumping $187,827 pledged—and then the bottom fell out.[3]

On "Black Thursday" October 24, 1929, the New York stock market collapsed. In a single day, stocks fell an average of forty points and over 16,000,000 shares were dumped on the New York Stock Exchange. At first, industrialists, bankers and business leaders, as well as President Hoover, mistakenly thought that this was just a momentary halt in the march of economic progress. Some even went so far as to state that it was a salutary event that removed the inflation from Wall Street. Ultimately, it turned out, however, that over-speculation was merely the symptom of a cancerous condition in the nation's economy. Production had far outrun consumption and it was now evident that the Coolidge-Mellon plan of fostering perpetual prosperity by favoring Big Business had just not worked. Gradually but inexorably the disease spread. The depression that followed the crash encompassed the United States and, by 1931, hard times had leaped across the oceans and had stricken most of the world.

Generally speaking, the local pattern reflected the national picture. The effects of the business panic increased gradually through 1930; things got worse the following year. Each summer seemed better than the harsh winter that it had preceded. At least in the summer nature did not seem to be in league with the forces against which the people struggled. Worst of all was the bitter winter of 1932-1933. With the coming of the New Deal, gradual improvement was noticed; but then the sharp recession of 1937-1938 set the people back on their heels once more. Genuine recovery lagged until World War II really primed the economic pump.

The first impact of the slump was felt in the drive of late fall in 1929. For the first time in Federation history, the campaign failed to reach its goal; it fell short by $17,000. Reflecting the early optimism of the nation before the full realization of the extent of the economic upset, the Federation President, Dr. Lester I. Levyn, stated: "Considering the severity of the Wall Street upheaval which shook the very foundation of the financial structure of the nation, I would classify our failure as a success." [4]

While this campaign was under way, the Bureau of Jewish Social Research of New York was evaluating the structural organization and everyday activities of the Buffalo Federation. Such a survey had been mooted since 1915, but the city leaders had been hesitant about spending philanthropic funds for it. There is evidence that certain Federation leaders opposed the study, for they clung to their nineteenth-century prejudices and looked with suspicion on "the scientific accuracy of surveys and statistics." [5] But more progressive counsel prevailed and, to assist the survey team, a Citizens Committee of several hundred men and women was formed under the chairmanship of Eugene Warner. For about a year, the professionals probed and pried and studied, and finally on April 23, 1930, the recommendations were laid before the Board of Governors by Dr. Samuel A. Goldsmith, Director of the Bureau of Jewish Social Research. This report urged that the Federation be re-organized into five departments: a Jewish Welfare Society, a Jewish Child Care Association, a Jewish Committee on Recreational and Educational Activities, a Jewish Committee on Medical Service, and a Bureau of Jewish Education. Other suggestions included the absorption into the Federation family of the Naomi Club, the Jewish Mothers Club, the Rosa Coplon Jewish Old Folks Home, the Jewish Fresh Air Camp and the Hebrew Benevolent Loan Association. [6]

Some of these recommendations were ignored and some were subsequently followed. In possible anticipation of the report, the Federation had drastically revised its constitution a month before the full verdict was known. A more democratic way of voting for the Board of Governors had thus already been instituted. In addition, a Jewish Welfare Society (later called the Jewish Community Service Society) was created by merging the Ladies' Hebrew Benevolent Society, the Jewish Aid Society, the Men's Hebrew Benevolent Society and the Ladies' Sewing and Aid Societies, all of which now lost their separate identities. To explain these changes to the community, Eugene Warner described how the old idea of individual organizational autonomy had painlessly yielded to the concept of cooperative organization. Prior to the change, Warner said, the majority of the members of the Board of Governors of the Federation had also served on the boards of the various constituent societies. "This resulted," he went on to say, "in the obliteration of the activities of the Men's and Women's Benevolent Societies and the Jewish Aid Society, and to some extent the Board of Governors did the work of the other organizations. In other words, the Federation became an amalgamation instead of a Federation." Warner was merely recognizing that, by 1930, the Jewish Welfare Society was actually a *fait accompli* that was simply waiting for formal recognition.

After announcing these fundamental changes, Eugene Warner, almost as though in warning, instructed the Jewish community of Buffalo in the functions and duties of the Federation. The central body, he stated, did more than just raise subscriptions; it supervised, directed and represented the community in seeing how these funds were handled. The Federation, he announced, through its Board of Governors, set the policy and saw to it that the community needs were met by directing the expansion or curtailment of services as needs arose or disappeared.[7] It seems as though, having yielded to the reforms, he was making sure that the general public clearly understood where ultimate control was to lie.

While this survey was being made and the changes implemented, plans for the fall campaign of 1930 were being worked out in the face of unprecedented economic prostration. All resources were used up, and the Federation called on the workers and contributors at the opening of the drive to reach the goal of $141,148 in spite of all obstacles. To launch the campaign, Lieutenant Governor Herbert H. Lehman came to Buffalo, and so great was the response to his address that $92,000 was raised the opening night. As a result of the indefatigable work of Warner, assisted by the venerable August Keiser and many other volunteers, the quota was exceeded before the end of the campaign.[8]

In 1931, however, the economic situation deteriorated. Layoffs and severe cuts in salaries and wages were felt throughout the country. The banking systems of Austria and Germany collapsed and the depression became global in scope. World trade was greatly reduced, and the United States, which President Hoover insisted was beginning to fight its way out of the quicksand of the depression, was sucked back under the surface when Europe went down.

Meanwhile, real emergency measures had to be taken by the Federation, for relief was still a private affair in those pre-WPA days. Not only was there no Federal relief of any real sort available, but the Jewish tradition of private aid was very strong. It had persisted in America since 1654, when, as the story went, despite the opposition of Peter Stuyvesant, the Dutch West India Company had allowed Jews to remain in New Amsterdam provided that they took care of their own needy and did not become a burden to others.[9] Many old-timers were dedicated to this hoary concept and did everything possible to handle Jewish relief needs privately, although, like so many other noble ideas, this one too ultimately had to be abandoned.

In this black year of 1931, the Federation circulated a flyer throughout the Buffalo community that announced that relief cases among Jewish families had increased 43% beyond normal. It called for voluntary gifts of food to keep families from starvation during the long winter ahead.[10]

These were the days when the breadlines stretched depressingly along the streets and when adults stood for hours in line outside soup kitchens so that they might preserve what little food they had at home for their children. Then it was that sad-eyed men and women sat shivering on street corners behind pathetic little mounds of apples that they sold for 5 cents a piece. Locally, the mayor advocated a plan whereby each block would employ a man to tend the lawns or shovel snow and look after furnaces. His salary was to be made up by a payment of one dollar each week by each family on the block. But often even a dollar a week to help a neighbor was too much. As another effort to relieve some of the suffering, the Federation asked its members to place "mite boxes" on their tables. If they were fortunate enough to have food for themselves, they might drop a small coin at meals for those who were destitute. "Minute Men" from the various organizations in the Federation circulated through the city in search of waste material, old clothing and anything salvageable to be returned to the newly established Salvage Shop located at 107 Broadway.[11]

By this time Eugene Warner had abandoned all his other interests to devote his abundant energies to social work exclusively. He single-handedly mapped out the Federation campaign for 1931 and set the goal at $160,600. President Hoover had established a national committee for welfare and relief mobilization, and Warner declared the campaign of the Buffalo Federation that year to be part of the White House effort to stimulate local giving. No campaign ever directed by this indefatigable leader had failed, and he worked heroically to make this one a success too. He printed and distributed a pamphlet in the shape of a heart with the legend: "An Appeal to your Jewish Heart." But the opening night brought pledges of only $80,000 which was $12,000 below the initial subscription for the previous year. The depression had taken its toll.[12]

Soon, however, slight changes were beginning to be apparent in the local attitude toward the acceptance of outside help in handling relief. Warner, for example, became a member of the principal committee of the National Appeals Information Service for Jewish Federations (a part of the newly-formed Council of Jewish Federations and Welfare Funds). Although Warner was active in its decisions, there remained a reluctance on the part of certain Federation officials to accept any outside guidance. In fact, George W. Rabinoff, a field worker for the Council, visited Buffalo in 1932 and reported that the Federation was controlled by the old German group with too many "philanthropic paternalistic motives, with little capacity or willingness to community organization which would involve a division of responsibility with other groups and modifications of programs. These leaders speak in terms of established practices and traditions as immutable." [13]

Meanwhile, on the national scene pressure was being brought by more liberal elements to have the state take over the relief tasks. Morris D. Waldman of the American Jewish Committee was the national leader of this movement. Blessed with broader vision than others of his generation, Waldman sensed that, with the decline of immigration, relief and Americanization efforts would become minor problems. He argued that, since eventually the state must care for all the destitute, the municipal agencies should concentrate on setting up a community-wide system of conserving specific Jewish values. [14]

In the fall campaign of 1932, sights were realistically lowered to a goal of $140,000, the amount pledged but not collected in the previous year. In this campaign, the Federation seized upon Franklin Delano Roosevelt's recent campaign slogan of the "Forgotten Man" and proposed to make him the "Most Remembered Man." In a last minute effort to stimulate extra giving, parallel lists were distributed:

Givers	Takers
Frozen Assets	Frozen Hearts
Cannot Buy a New Car	Have no Carfare
Shrunken Incomes	Shrunken Bodies
Resigned from Club	Dispossessed from House
No Cocktails	No Food
Taxes are Too High	The Welfare Allowance is Too Small

Now more than ever—Give!

Despite all these gimmicks, the initial pledges slipped still farther below the preceding year. It was only after heroic efforts in the course of a prolonged campaign that a total of $114,496 was raised, and this was considerably short of a whittled-down goal. [15]

By the following year, things could not have looked blacker than they did in Buffalo. June 22, 1933, was "the longest day in the year, and one of the darkest." The Jewish Federation for Social Service had a mere $38 in its treasury and it faced immediate debts of almost $10,000. Warner issued a handbill that called attention to this unprecedented emergency. "To give wide publicity to the extent of unemployment, the misery and suffering and distress would not be desirable," he wrote; ". . . to publish all that is known of dissatisfaction, want and despair would be dangerous." He suggested, in imitation of wartime practice, meatless days during each week to help people to honor their pledges. He cited a total of $128,000 in unpaid pledges over the previous three years. "Either the Jewish community is willing to sacrifice a little and help a great deal," he concluded, "or we must throw up our hands and say, 'We Are Through.' " [16]

The minute books of almost all synagogues in the city show that they could hardly keep going in those dark years. Membership shrank and income from dues and cemetery plots became a trickle. "Organized religious life," said the *Buffalo Jewish Review*, "is experiencing the most trying year to an extent never before known." [17]

In the fourth year of the depression the physical effects began to show up in the children and in the aged. The Federation's Nutritional Clinic reported in 1933 that it had never been faced with so many cases of hunger and sickness. The clinic cared for 659 children that year, and over 2,000 people were examined and treated by its volunteer doctors. It is ironic but a fact, that after being regularly treated at the clinic, some children of relief families were in better shape than those of parents who tried valiantly to keep up the struggle on their own without resort to help from others.[18]

By this time the initial efforts of Franklin Delano Roosevelt to set up such devices as the NRA in an attempt to give the economy a gigantic boost began to put heart in the people. The 1933 campaign opened with the presentation of a play, *Dark Windows*. Although the final result fell short of the goal by almost $25,000, the net result was about $5,000 higher than that of the previous year. Thus, by the end of that critical year, the Federation proudly reported that it could still handle almost all of the welfare cases, although it had curtailed its activities and had allowed its physical plant to fall into disrepair.[19]

Depression-born was the Hospital Visiting Committee that brought cheer to thousands of patients. The local rate of Jewish suicides rose during these years probably at the same pace as the national. Illegitimate pregnancies increased as economic conditions postponed weddings. One of the Hospital Visiting Committee reported: "Time forbids enumerating details of many interesting cases of attempted suicides, dope fiends, unwed mothers, cripples and incurables." Relief expenditures alone in this dark year of 1934 reached over $66,000.[20]

The campaign for that year lagged and bogged down. There just simply wasn't enough money available in Buffalo to supply the quota, and the Federation issued this pathetic statement: "For the first time in the history of the Jews of Buffalo, the organization will be compelled to refuse relief and to turn relief cases over to the Public Welfare Department. Do you realize what this means?" The community, however, seemed unmoved at the prospect, for at the end of the campaign for that year, they were still $25,000 short of the goal.[21]

Light finally began to break through the black clouds of the depression in 1934. In that year, for the first time, a professional person, Laura L. Margolis, became Executive Director of the Jewish Welfare Society. She faced a situation in which the relief case load had increased over 50% within one year, but the campaign for 1935 raised 94% of its quota, the greatest improvement of any drive since the fateful campaign of 1929. [22]

This trend continued until hopes were dashed once more when this gradual upturn was halted by the sharp recession that hit the country in mid-summer 1937. It was in this year that the Federation conducted the first joint campaign with the United Jewish Appeal since 1931. The going was naturally hard and the formal end of the campaign, found both the Federation and the United Jewish Appeal short of their goals, the former having raised $164,000 and the latter, $41,000.[23]

By now the European war clouds were gathering ominously. The year 1938 was the year of the futile appeasement at Munich. That memorable fall, in another joint campaign, the Buffalo Jewish community set out to raise the largest total sum hitherto attempted in the history of the city. The campaign was opened by James G. MacDonald, the great and good advocate of the Jewish case before the League of Nations. His appeal was greatly helped by the coincidence that on November 8, 1938, Hitler burned the synagogues in the Reich and closed the vise on the German Jews. The sense of crisis created by these outrages spurred the people on so that in twelve days all but a small fraction of the quota was raised. At the brink of World War II, Buffalo Jews had shifted their focus sharply from home problems to those of their suffering brethren beyond the waters.[24]

The dual responsibility of sending relief to Jews in distress throughout the world while caring simultaneously for victims of oppression who fled to these shores was not a new one. During the long decades of the Russian pogroms, Buffalo Jews were quite familiar with such problems and their solution. During the Wilson Era, the community measured up once more to the task of relocating and caring for dispossessed members of their people.

Ten years after the 1918 armistice, however, Europe had reached a point of relative stability and the need for overseas relief, apart from the challenge to re-settle Palestine, had dwindled to the point where organizations like the Joint Distribution Committee were almost on the verge of disbanding. Then Germany ran amuck.

After laying hands on the German Jews, Hitler in turn devoured Austria and the Sudeten part of Czechoslovakia. By the spring of 1939, he had gulped down the rump of that unfortunate country. Then in rapid succession with the outbreak of World War II, Poland fell, and the Nazis goose-stepped into France, the Lowlands, Hungary, Yugoslavia and Roumania. The greatest genocide in modern history, ultimately to cost the lives of some six million Jews, had begun in earnest.

American Jewry now faced up to a gigantic challenge. Never before had one community been required to take on single-handedly the relief burdens of world Jewry. For the first time the fate of the entire Jewish people was placed in the hands of the New World. It was not only a question of material survival, but of moral and political survival as well. And it was not to stop with the defeat of Hitler, for after 1945, the American-Jewish community had also to care for the survivors of the concentration camps. Moreover, American Jewry supported Israel in the War of Independence, and then provided for refugees from the Arab states which expelled or oppressed their Jewish citizens in retaliation for the military victory of Israel.

When Hitler seized power in January 1933, Jews in America, like many other civilized beings, underestimated him. They could not believe that anything quite so horrible could happen in twentieth-century Germany and they looked for the early overthrow of this maniacal dictator. Pollyannas argued that the responsibilities of office would temper Hitler's madness. How wrong they were! In June 1934, he liquidated his domestic political enemies in the famous blood purge. Shortly thereafter, President Paul Von Hindenburg died, and the one-time corporal became *Reichsfuehrer*. Less than two years later, Hitler defied the Treaty of Versailles by marching his troops into the Rhineland; and he now began to make it perfectly clear that, by severe racial laws, he would liquidate the 600,-000 Jews of the Reich.

Very shortly after Hitler took his first steps against the German Jews, their American brethren reacted in protest. Buffalo Jewry held a protest meeting on April 3, 1933 at the Elmwood Music Hall. Here, the Right Reverend Cameron D. Davis, Episcopal Bishop of the Diocese of Western New York, Reverend Albert C. Butzer of Westminster Presbyterian Church, and the nationally prominent John Lord O'Brian decried the actions of Hitler.[25] A month later, headlines in the Jewish press blazoned: "Millions Parade in New York—Protest Against Nazi Acts." Rabbi Jonah B. Wise, who was in Germany on a visit, accurately predicted that the relief problem caused by Nazi brutality would surpass anything hitherto known in the annals of civilized nations.[26]

The situation in Germany was graphically brought home to Buffalonians in the middle of 1933, when Mr. and Mrs. Louis Maisel made a hurried trip to Germany to fetch their daughter Florence (later Mrs. David Popper) home from the university at which she was spending her junior year. Mr. Maisel's letter to his family in Buffalo was printed in the *Review*. "All that you read in the paper," he wrote, "does not tell 100th part of what is going on in Germany." He went on to predict that the Brown Shirts would surely try to enslave the world once they had the power to do so. What he saw abroad, Mr. Maisel said, made him glad that he had invested in Palestinian heavy industry, for now this land must become the chief place of refuge for those hounded out of Germany.[27]

During the worst year of the depression, at a time when many American Jews were barely able to make ends meet, they were called upon to make heroic sacrifices to offset the new streamlined savagery. The United Jewish Emergency Appeal was called into being in 1933, and the goal for Buffalo was set at $28,000. The distribution of these funds shows that it was not yet apparent that the Nazi paranoiac was truly dangerous.[28]

It was not until three years later that any really effective attempts were made to provide for foreign relief. By that time the depression had temporarily lifted and people were able to look to the welfare of others. Furthermore, as the government of Poland stepped up its anti-Semitic campaign by segregating Jews in universities, local Buffalonians became more alert to the global problem, for this hit nearer home than the German situation. Louis Silverstein, the local poultry dealer, was a member of the National Committee of Polish Jews in America that now turned its attention to the European situation.[29]

In the meantime, under the chairmanship of Alfred M. Saperston, the United Jewish Campaign set out to raise $50,000. The local rabbis issued a joint appeal to the people in 1936 to prepare them for the campaign; it appeared in the *Review* under the headline: "Jews of Buffalo, Awake!— Arise!" At the opening banquet, attended by almost 500 people, $20,000 was raised and responsible spokesmen promised to continue the appeal until every family in the city had been canvassed. It was now apparent that the community was responding to the danger that threatened world Jewry.[30]

From this time onward the local Jewish community became continuously more generous in the annual campaigns for foreign relief. Under the leadership of such men as Emanuel Boasberg, Jr., Charles Dautch, Stanley G. Falk, Edward H. Kavinoky, Alfred M. Saperston and, of course, Eugene Warner, there was a trend toward ever increasing consolidation of the various appeals in order to eliminate duplication. Eventually, the United Jewish Appeal, supported throughout the country by numerous welfare funds, joined all the individual relief campaigns into one. In Buffalo, the first president of the U.J.F. was David Diamond, an ardent

Zionist, who helped persuade the various Zionist groups in the city to accept this united fund.[31]

More important than the amount of money raised in these overseas relief campaigns of the Hitlerian years were the people who came to America, and especially to Buffalo, and the problems which their arrival posed. Because of the severe economic situation in the years immediately prior to the Nazi crisis, more people were leaving the United States than were coming in. As the national income plunged downward, for every three aliens that arrived on these shores, five decided to return to the old country in search of the economic stability that they had failed to find in the Land of Opportunity.[32] When the first German refugees began to straggle into this country after 1933, the problems raised by such people and the solution for them had been almost forgotten.

We do not know exactly how many Jewish refugees came to Buffalo during those dreary days. In 1941, Dr. Uriah Z. Engelman estimated that about 450 had come to Buffalo in the preceding eight years. The overwhelming majority of these people were mature, married folk.[33] This influx was, therefore, quite unlike that of the czarist displacement in which the people were usually young and strong. In the worst days of the Romanov pogroms some preferred to remain in the Pale. Hitler's more efficient tactics allowed no choice. All had to go.

Some of these uprooted came to Buffalo under a quota set by the National Refugee Service in New York. Many, however, came because they had kinsmen, often very distant, who had been here for generations. These relatives signed affidavits required by law to guarantee that the newcomers would not become public charges.* Or sometimes, a stranger assumed the responsibility for hundreds of families. Outstanding in this respect was Max M. Yellen, who was subsequently awarded the Seventy-fifth Anniversary United HIAS Service Award "for years of service in helping immigrants." He was selected for his efforts during the Hitlerian fury "when he was instrumental in helping to rescue thousands of Jews and bringing them to the United States." No one will ever know how many of these affidavits Mr. Yellen signed himself or persuaded his friends to sign.

Because the earliest refugees arrived while we were still in the throes of the depression, some of them found it extremely difficult to be absorbed into the labor-glutted economy. Engelman estimated that over half of the local German refugees came with vocational training that could be used

---

* Nearly every synagogue in Buffalo entered into a contractual agreement with some displaced rabbi or other religious functionary, and thereby saved numerous families from destruction.

in their adopted country.[34] The profession in which it was most easy to make the transition to American ways was medicine. Thus physicians usually took the New York State Boards (some were required to serve an American internship) and then began their practice. Dr. Heinz Lichtenstein, a Heidelberg M.D., who became one of the leading psychiatrists in Buffalo, was one of the more notable who made the adjustment. Another example was the world-famous immunologist, Dr. Ernest Witebsky, who eventually served as Dean of the School of Medicine at the University of Buffalo.

For attorneys, the problem of retraining was much more difficult than it was for doctors. The human body is the same whether it speaks German or English, but the body of the law varies from country to country. The transition, therefore, from the European civil law to the English common law was not simple. The refugee lawyer had to be largely re-educated. One learned barrister who came to Buffalo was forced to earn his living by delivering milk; many entered other occupations. Arthur Lenhoff was one, however, who was brilliant and vigorous enough in his middle years to make the transition. He had held high judicial office in his native Austria before fleeing to this country where he rose to become Distinguished Professor of Law at the University of Buffalo.

It was also difficult for some teachers to make the adjustment to the American educational system and many of the less fortunate were forced into other occupations. The University of Buffalo, however, gained the services of Dr. Fritz Kaufmann (1892-1958) who was Associate Professor of Philosophy at Buffalo for about a dozen years.

To help this newest set of refugees adjust to American life, several organizations sprang up in Buffalo. The earliest of these, the Buffalo Jewish Club, was later called Haven Club. Unlike the eastern Europeans who had come here a generation before, these Germans did not have the common bond of Yiddish to unite them with the immigrants who had preceded them. At first they felt at home with neither their Americanized relatives in Beth Zion nor with the more recently arrived East-European Jews who made up the bulk of the Jewish population of the city. Consequently, it was natural that a circle should be formed where they could continue their own cultural atmosphere and where they could learn the English language and American customs.

For the pre-Pearl Harbor refugees, the paramount problem was to find employment. Here help was forthcoming from the Federation's German Refugee Committee, headed by Stanley G. Falk, with much of the counselling done by a placement worker from the Jewish Welfare Society. This committee evolved into the Buffalo Refugee Service when the Naomi Club, B'nai B'rith, plus Jewish medical and dental societies agreed to help the Federation meet a mounting problem. This combined group serviced newcomers in many small towns in the vicinity and had lent a hand to about 600 individuals prior to active American participation in the war.[35]

During the 1940s the nature of the refugee problem changed. With the economy at full blast, job placement was no longer a factor. For a few years the stream of new arrivals dwindled, for few could cross the most war-torn seas in all history. As General Eisenhower's soldiers made their way into Hitler's chambers of horror, popularly called concentration camps, the extent of the Nazi massacre slowly penetrated the American mind. Most of the survivors of European Jewry eventually were smuggled into British Palestine or, after 1948, were welcomed by the fledgling Israeli state. Some, however, came westward under slightly relaxed American immigration quotas and their arrival posed a new set of problems. The German refugees of the 1930s had arrived dispirited, but usually sound in body. But a decade later it was necessary to rehabilitate men, women and children whose bodies and minds had been seared in the wartime Hell designed by Hitler. Buffalo received its share of these unhappy DPs. By 1947, a skilled migration worker, employed by the Jewish Welfare Society, was handling a case load of almost 300 concentration camp victims. Because it was generally the youngest and most fit who had managed to survive, these newcomers were speedily absorbed into the rapidly expanding economy of the day. Most of these later immigrants were eastern Europeans, for those German Jews destined to escape the gas chambers had made their getaway before the war. Those who came after the war, however, were almost invariably men and women who somehow had managed to remain alive in bondage, or else natives of countries where the Nazi Juggernaut had penetrated too late in the war to kill *all* the Jews in its path.

This fresh wave of immigrants added a new element to Jewish life in Buffalo. One of them, for example, Mrs. Gerda Klein, published a book, *All But My Life*, in which she told the story of her captivity and liberation by an American soldier, Kurt Klein, whom she subsequently married. In the Eisenhower Era it became commonplace to meet Jews on the streets of Buffalo who differed in no way from their neighbors, except for the blue concentration camp number tatooed on their arms, which told the grim story more eloquently than any words that they could muster.

While their complacent world was being shaken in the New Deal years, first by the Great Depression and second by the march of Fascism,

Jews of America became more intensely interested in their identification as Jews and in the restoration and re-emphasis of those elements in their cultural heritage which were specifically Jewish. One of the immediate results of this re-awakening was a fresh concern with the perennial problem of Jewish education.

The Buffalo Bureau of Jewish Education had its origins in the last years of the Roaring Twenties. By then, several generations of Buffalo parents had been reared in the American public schools without benefit of any intensive Jewish training. Often these mothers and fathers were schizoid about Jewish education for their children: they vaguely wanted to transmit their faith to them and to explain to them what Judaism was, but they did not know how, for they could not give to others what they themselves did not possess. Out of a Jewish population of approximately 20,000, only about 1,500 children were enrolled in the local Hebrew schools. At least half of the Jewish children in the city were receiving no Jewish education at all.[36]

Prior to the founding of the Bureau, a few sporadic attempts had been made to remedy this serious situation. But the situation in the city was not to be improved by isolated efforts, for a definite organized attempt to cope with the over-all problem was clearly indicated. In his Rosh Hashana message for 1927, Rabbi Fink, prompted by Herman Wile and Sundel J. Holender, labelled the Jewish educational conditions in Buffalo as "utterly deplorable" and called for a representative city-wide committee to study the problem. The *Buffalo Jewish Review* seconded this sermon in a strong editorial and, following the national pattern, established the month of Tishri as Jewish Education Month.[37]

As a result of these actions and other expressions of serious concern, two studies of the Jewish population of Buffalo were authorized. One, as we have already seen, was conducted by the Bureau of Jewish Social Research of New York City, whereas the other was a local affair planned and implemented by laymen.

The "do-it-yourself" project, sponsored by Herman Wile, began in the fall of 1928. Mr. Wile was nominally in charge, with Sol J. Levy as executive director and Maurice S. Tabor as his chief assistant. With about a thousand volunteer workers, they divided the city into six regions, each with five subdivisions made up of ten districts. The *Buffalo Jewish Review* hailed the effort as "the biggest and most worth-while project that has ever been undertaken in Buffalo and its success must be assured." At a gigantic pep meeting held at Beth El, all rabbis of the city urged united action to insure the success of the surveys.[38]

The final reports of both groups revealed that, of the estimated 4,000 children between the ages of five and fourteen, only a little more than half were getting any sort of Jewish education. Of those enrolled in Jewish religious schools, only one-third were getting daily training; the rest were going to Sunday school only.[39]

The professional survey team issued a report at the end of its work in which it recommended the establishment of a Bureau of Jewish Education with an annual budget of $55,426. It called for the affiliation of all schools in the city with the Bureau to supply the curriculum. It urged the erection of two new buildings, one in the Hertel district and one in the Humboldt area, for educational purposes, and it recommended the renovation of the Buffalo Hebrew School on Hickory Street. In order to finance these projects, the report suggested that standard tuition fees be charged in all schools.[40]

Following the digestion of both surveys, the Bureau of Jewish Education was ready for operation in the fall of 1930, almost a year after the stock market crash. It was founded to set forth three objectives: first, "to promote the idea of, and the necessity for, a Jewish background on the part of the Jew so that he may intelligently understand his relation to the Jewish group, and in turn the relation of the Jewish group to the general American environment"; secondly, "to make it possible for the largest number of Jews, children and adults, in this city to receive an effective and positive Jewish education;" finally, "to raise the standard of Jewish education on all levels through the advisory and supervisory facilities of the Bureau." [41]

The first director of the Bureau of Jewish Education was Ben M. Edidin (1900-1948) who arrived in Buffalo on July 1, 1930. Edidin had formerly worked with Alexander M. Dushkin in re-organizing the Chicago Board of Jewish Education and ultimately became Supervisor of Schools and Director of the Extension Department of the Board of Jewish Education in that city. A graduate of the University of Wisconsin, Edidin had been to Palestine where he studied at the Hebrew University in Jerusalem. In Buffalo, after doing graduate work in the School of Education at the University of Buffalo, he received the first Doctorate of Education awarded by that institution.[42]

After his arrival, Edidin threw himself with zeal into the work of establishing the Bureau and implementing its policies. One of his immediate aims was to make the Buffalo Hebrew School a model of its kind. Fortunately, at this time, Adolph Winters left $10,000 in his will to remodel the outmoded Hickory Street building, and the new director was able to launch his new program in a relatively attractive plant. A contemporary described the spirit of unity that pervaded the dedication ceremonies: "There was the old-fashioned Orthodox rabbi with covered head and bearded face and saintly eyes. There was the confirmed Hebraist whose soul was consecrated to the program of the cultural and national rebirth of his people. There was the president of the most liberal and Reform congregation in the city. Not a word of bitterness or hostility passed the lips of any one of these speakers, no light jesting or corrosive cynicism. . . . From the caverns of years of neglect and disregard springs this Bureau." [43]

Early in his career in Buffalo, Edidin pledged himself to provide in-service growth for the seventy-five Sunday school teachers in the community. To accomplish this goal, he worked with a subcommittee in order to enlarge the existing courses for Sunday school teachers and to have them meet weekly throughout the season. He saw to it that there were courses in both method and content for teachers in service and prospective members of the profession. In 1933, he organized a conference of Sunday and week day teachers to which he invited experts from outside the city to lead the discussions. His example was followed by his successors in the Bureau who sponsored each spring a meeting of the local Sunday and daily religious school teachers.

Dr. Edidin was an expert in motivating city-wide adult-education classes. The public was eager in those hard-scrabble years to find some inexpensive ways of occupying the evening hours, for it was a time when such games as monopoly and jigsaw puzzles provided cheap entertainment for the impoverished. In similar fashion, night school relieved the tedium of the depression and also satisfied the spirit of self-improvement that filled the air. He organized Tarbut College, deriving the name from the Hebrew word for culture. In this College, Edidin combined offerings for teachers with classes for intellectually curious adults. He recruited some of the best teaching talent in the city to offer courses in introductory, intermediate and advanced Hebrew, all periods of Hebrew literature and Jewish history, and various problems relating to community organization.

Through the medium of Tarbut College, the Buffalo Jewish community made the acquaintance of an outstanding newcomer to the city. Harry J. Brevis, a Detroit lawyer, who entered the rabbinate after he lost his sight, came to Buffalo in 1932 following his marriage to Miss Anna Bear (see *supra* p. 265). Rabbi Brevis achieved national distinction when he developed an International Hebrew Braille Code that was ultimately adopted throughout the world. After making his Buffalo teaching debut at Tarbut, Rabbi Brevis offered courses at the local university, wrote distinguished articles for leading journals of opinion, ministered to Temple Beth-El in neighboring Batavia, and, in his capacity as chaplain, did outstanding work in several public institutions in western New York. In 1959, the local Z.O.A. district named him "Man of the Year" and the Hebrew Union College-Jewish Institute of Religion conferred upon him the degree of Doctor of Divinity.[44]

To return to the story of Tarbut College, this thriving institution of the 1930s found its quarters where best it could. It continued in various downtown locations until World War II drew most of its students into the armed services. After 1945, the advent of television and the dispersion of the Jewish community into the suburbs depleted its registration until it finally disappeared.

One of the concomitant contributions to Jewish education that Edidin made to Buffalo was his sponsorship of the Buffalo Jewish Choral Society, a new organization that he found on his arrival in the city. This group, led by Samuel Luskin, first met in the violin studio of Julius Singer, the son of the well-known *Hazzan* Singer. The Choral Society presented programs of Palestinian, Hebrew, liturgical, Yiddish folk and secular music. Among those who participated in its programs over the years were Cantors Jacob Judelsohn, Harry Hart Kaufman, Charles S. Gudovitz, William Nissenson, and Mrs. Irving I. Crouse and Melville Ehrlich. In recent years it was located at the Jewish Center of Buffalo where it was led by Bernard Mandelkern, Morris K. Poummit and Professor Irving Cheyette.[45] But Edidin's stay here was not a happy one. When he left in 1935, he was regarded as a failure, although history was to prove that most of what he accomplished or attempted was right.

A complex of reasons explains Dr. Edidin's predicament. He did not realize that the community's establishment of the Bureau of Jewish Education was in the spirit of lip service rather than of firm conviction that such an agency was necessary or desirable. Individual rabbis and community leaders were reluctant to delegate power to a centralized agency no matter how efficiently it might work. Nor did Edidin comprehend that his community approach, his emphasis on Hebrew as a spoken tongue, and his uncompromising Zionism were not the convictions of the majority of the Federation leaders of his day.[46] It was, moreover, his misfortune to arrive just as the pall of the depression spread over the nation, including Buffalo and its Jewish community. The Bureau, with its need for money, was established just at a time when the Federation needed every penny it could lay its hands on for relief; and its Board of Governors was not inclined to divert shrinking relief funds into ambitious educational projects.

Despite these handicaps, Edidin was able to report, seven months after his arrival, that 500 additional Jewish children were getting some form of instruction as a result of the establishment of the Bureau. In addition, Tarbut College had thirty students enrolled, most of whom were not Sunday school teachers, but interested adults.[47]

The Bureau's troubles increased during 1931. No additional synagogues affiliated their schools with it. As the depression deepened, school enrollment suffered as children were required to help their parents at home or in the store. Moreover, congregations had begun to dismiss teachers whose salaries they could no longer afford. Despite vigorous pupil enrollment campaigns, no significant changes in registration were forthcoming in the worst years of the long business slump. Dr. Edidin finally gave up the struggle and left Buffalo in 1935 to accept a post in the educational system of Palestine. Before he left, however, he made the rounds to various community leaders begging them not to allow the institutions that he had founded here to perish.

His successor, who served only from 1935 to 1937, was Paul A. Veret. Determined to make Buffalo an "Encyclopedic Center," Veret began publishing a series of pamphlets and brochures, principally for distribution elsewhere. This costly enterprise brought some criticism and in 1937 Mr. Veret left to accept a position in Omaha.

For a time after Veret's departure, it looked very much as if Buffalo would abandon its Bureau of Jewish Education. It was saved only by hard work against the forthright opposition of some laymen who never cared for it and some rabbis who thought it an inconvenient burden. In 1938, however, Uriah Z. Engelman, who was then principal of Beth David, was appointed director, a post which he occupied for six years. He expressed his philosophy and general attitude toward the Bureau in a report that he made to its Board a few months before he was actually awarded the post. In this statement of purpose, he frankly termed the relationship between the Bureau and the community "very disappointing." He pointed out that local teachers did not like the Bureau and proposed as a remedy less centralization and more teacher participation in cardinal decisions, a practice that he and his successors have followed. He also called for a campaign of education in order to enlighten the lay leaders on the aims of the Bureau. Finally, charging that the classroom teacher had been reduced to a "routine worker" instead of being a missionary with a definite attitude, he called for a Professional Council made up of rabbis, teachers and principals to formulate policy.[48]

Uriah Engelman, a serious person with scholarly demeanor, subsequently earned a Ph.D. in Sociology at the University of Buffalo and became a talented statistician and demographer whose writings have won him national recognition. With such a capable statistician in office, it was natural to expect another survey of the community. Following the approach of Robert and Helen Lynd in their epoch-making sociological study, *Middletown*, he used Buffalo as an example of a typical medium-sized American-Jewish community. He synthesized the results of his survey in a series of articles entitled "Medurbia" which drew national attention following publication in the *Contemporary Jewish Record*.[49]

The most lasting monument that Dr. Engelman left in Buffalo was the High School of Jewish Studies. Beginning with a modest enrollment of fifteen students, it grew steadily until registration stabilized at about 130 at the end of the 1950s. This secondary school attracted a surprising number of girls and helped overcome the perennial teacher shortage by stimulating young people to go into the profession.

Meanwhile, Engelman could also point out in 1940 that five congregational schools and the Workmen's Circle Shule had come under his supervision, making a total of about 1,000 students matriculated in institutions subsidized partially or wholly by the Bureau. He reported other activities of his agency besides the improvement of instruction: it functioned as a clearing house for textbooks and visual aids; its music and reference libraries were in constant use; its Book Shop served as a central purchasing agency to distribute books of Jewish interest. The Professional Council of teachers was functioning, and the Bureau had established an Inter-School Education Evening as well as an Information Service. The Bureau also functioned as the central mimeographing service for many organizations in the city. Just before the entrance of the United States into the war against the Axis, the Bureau of Jewish Education seemed to be coming into its own.[50]

In 1943, Herman Wile, who had been president of the Bureau since its inception, retired. He was succeeded by Jacob Morrison (1881-1952). One of the fairly rare Roumanian Jews in the city, Mr. Morrison had come to Buffalo in 1903. Through experience in sheet-metal work with the Ford Motor Company and the E. R. Thomas Company, he acquired the knowledge to establish his own firm, Morrison Steel Products Inc. Possessed of good common sense and executive ability, Mr. Morrison had a strong sense of community leadership. He was humorous and could influence an audience in his rough, blunt, but good-humored way.[51]

Shortly after Mr. Morrison became president, Dr. Engelman resigned his position to become Director of the Research Department of the American Association for Jewish Education. He was replaced by Mark M. Krug, a suave young man who had spent most of his formative years in Israel. When Krug arrived in Buffalo in 1945, he found a budget of $21,711, and he was to prove himself very adept at getting more money from the Federation, a feat made easier by the war-born Cadillac prosperity and Jacob Morrison's backing and influence.

Krug's regime was marked by an expansion of activities and services such as the kindergarten, Beth Hayeled Moriah, and by a growing uniformity in curricula and texts. His most significant contribution to the educational system of Buffalo, however, was the establishment of a College of Jewish Studies in the fall of 1946, which has since been merged administratively with the high school.

Other innovations introduced during these postwar years include a model *seder* (later televised) and other holiday shows through the High School of Jewish Studies, and a Jewish Book Fair.[52]

Before the Jewish Center was built, Krug entered into an agreement with Herman A. Eigen, who was the Center's Executive Director, to provide for the sharing of quarters in the new building. This widely-advertised "Buffalo Plan" provided that the Bureau was to occupy the south wing and was to have first option on the use of rooms in that section of the building. It was also agreed that both groups were to promote cultural activities of a Jewish nature in the Center.[53]

When Mr. Krug left Buffalo in 1949 to accept a similar position in Chicago, the community was fortunate in securing as his successor Dr. Elazar Goelman. Dr. Goelman, a veteran of the recent war, was a product of the Jewish day schools of New York City, and had also attended Western Reserve University and Dropsie College. During his decade of service, he endeared himself to Buffalo by virtue of hard work, enlightened leadership, and a winning personality which sparkled with wit and good humor. In 1959, to the profound regret of all, he resigned to become Dean of Gratz College and Director of Jewish Education in the Quaker City. The Bureau then chose as its sixth director, Mr. Reuben Resnik, Educational Director of the well-known Chicago congregation, Anshe Emet.

As stabilized by Dr. Goelman, the Bureau committed itself to many worthwhile functions. First of all, it conducted the High School and College of Jewish Studies which centralized secondary Jewish education throughout the city. Secondly, the Bureau stimulated attendance at summer camps. This practice proved to be very effective in supplying deficiencies in religious education by placing children in a completely Jewish environment during the vacation months where learning was coordinated with a full program of outdoor recreation. By the end of the 1950s, over sixty children each summer were either attending Hebrew-speaking camps or else making student tours to Israel.

Through Bureau initiative, classes in modern Hebrew were introduced in the regular day session of Bennett and Riverside High Schools, at Kenmore Evening High School, and at the University of Buffalo. For adults, the Bureau conducted an annual Book Review Workshop for lay leaders, helped in planning study groups, and sponsored a Hebrew-speaking circle. It also published educational material, such as the *Dictionary of Jewish Life* and a *Song Leaders Manual.*

Community-wide projects for pupils included the annual Tu Bishvat rally, prize contests for Hebrew and English essays, a Hebrew Spelling Bee and the promotion of Jewish arts and crafts. With the Jewish Center, the Bureau sponsored the Jewish Cultural Series and the Yiddish Cultural Forum. It ran the Jewish Book Shop and the Jewish Community Library. At the end of thirty years of service, the Bureau was the recognized agency for Jewish education in the city, despite the fact that it never achieved the all-inclusive aims set by its first director.[54]

Paralleling the development of the Bureau of Jewish Education was the growth of the Buffalo "Y" and the eventual establishment of the Jewish Center, quarters in which the Bureau was to share. Although the history of the "Y" dates back to 1858, as we have seen, it had been allowed to go dormant during the late 1920s. With the onset of hard times, however, a growing demand for inexpensive recreational facilities revived interest in the movement. A secondary factor was the arrival of refugees from the Hitlerian frenzy, for a Center could be of great help in integrating these harried people.

At the same time that these factors worked for a revitalization of the old "Y", obstacles were placed in the path of such re-establishment. Certain community leaders, clinging to the "settlement house" notions of a by-gone day, proposed expansion of the facilities of the Jewish Community Building on the East Side. In opposition, stood such energetic, rising young professional men as Samuel B. Darlich, David Diamond and Max M. Yellen, who took a community view of the situation and called for the establishment of a Center for the great majority rather than a glorified settlement house for a small underprivileged minority.

Consequently, in 1935, a group met at the Statler Hotel to press its plan. They elected Mr. Darlich as temporary chairman and organized a membership drive. For two years this group did yeomen work, gathering a building fund in the face of many odds pitted against it. In 1937, it announced the purchase of a rambling old-fashioned house at 277 Linwood Avenue which it was to remodel in order to accommodate 250 members. Most actively engaged in this project were Samuel Darlich, Max M. Yellen and the rising young attorney Ralph Saft. When the building opened its doors, Mr. Darlich, in a public letter, described the project as "an indispensable means in this community of reaching the generation of tomorrow." He also pointed out that Buffalo was the only city of its size in the United States that lacked such a Center.[55]

Although considerable unsolicited funds had been received, the "Y" needed still more. The drive was aided by the astute circulation of a congratulatory letter from John W. Pontius, director of the Buffalo YMCA, to Darlich on the purchase of the new building. Mr. Pontius, after offering his good wishes, went on to say that, although his organization did not try to proselytize, "the YMCA is a Christian institution nevertheless. While many of the Hebrew faith find themselves happy in its atmosphere of Christian service to people of all faiths, it is also very apparent to us that there are many of more conservative Jewish convictions who come into the YMCA only for its physical privileges . . . . I think they are entitled to their convictions; and that they should not, because of lack of facilities under the direction of their own faith, be forced to find the benefits they deserve under auspices with which they cannot fully identify themselves." [56] This prick to the conscience of the community stimulated donations to the "Y" effort.

It was an age of surveys. Another one conducted by the Jewish Welfare Board, in 1938, revealed what must have been clear to everyone, including even the die-hards who refused to do anything about it. Many young people were drifting away from Judaism because they had no place to meet. It was obvious, said the J.W.B. report, that Buffalo needed a Jewish Center that would consolidate the "Y" and the old Jewish Community Building. Evidently the community agreed, for the "Y" had one thousand members when, in 1938, it appointed its first Director of Activities, S. Saul Elgart. One of the first things that Elgart did was to establish Camp Avodah, a day camp for children, in the yard behind his building. It was a wise move, for it helped to advertise his organization. In this same year the Jewish Young Women's Association at long last merged with the men's group. [57]

When Harry Bluestone was appointed Executive Director of the "Y" in 1940, the tide seemed to turn. Bluestone was the son of the famous Zionist of New York, Dr. Joseph Bluestone. The younger Bluestone had a strong Hebrew background which, combined with good professional training in social work, made him especially effective in stressing the Jewish cultural aspects of Center work.

An honest and an indefatigable worker, Bluestone built on what he found, and soon he had about sixty-six groups functioning at 277 Linwood Avenue. A strong Zionist himself, Bluestone provided a home for all varieties of pro-Palestine expression. He arranged for stimulating classes, lectures and forums, and with severely limited facilities did his best to provide a physical and recreational program. [58]

With the involvement of the United States in World War II, came a rapid growth in "Y" membership and a corresponding expansion of activities. Bluestone in these days worked wonders. He cooperated with the

Federation Employment Agency on job problems, housed Hadassah's education classes, worked with the Bureau of Jewish Education on a series entitled "Orientation to Jewish Life." He also organized musicales, a photography club, and even a riding club. He helped refugees who fled in the face of the advancing Axis Juggernaut and sponsored soldier relief work. New problems arose with dateless girls whose morale was low, as well as with mothers on the swing shift of local aircraft plants whose children needed nursery schools and kindergartens.[59] After several years of good work in the face of countless obstacles, Bluestone resigned in 1943, ironically enough just on the eve of the formal incorporation of the "Y" into the Federation family. The first step in merging the "Y" and the Jewish Community Building into a community-wide Center had been taken.

Then came an act of God which precipitated action. Three minutes after the bells announced the New Year of 1945, the Linwood Avenue house burned to the ground. This apparent catastrophe ultimately turned out to be for the good, for it thoroughly aroused the community. Preliminary meetings were held and a coordinating committee was set up to investigate the formation of a Jewish Center. Finally on July 9, 1945, a special meeting was called at which representatives of the Jewish Community Building, the "Y", and the Jewish Community Center (formed in 1938 by a merger of the Sisterhood of Zion and the Daughters of the Star) elected officers of the new Jewish Center of Buffalo. Joseph Markel (a strong "Y" man) became president; Mrs. Barney B. Lazarus and Harold Horowitz became vice-presidents; Jacob Tick and Arthur Victor, Jr., were to serve as co-treasurers. A few days later, after a quiet but effective private appeal, it was announced that 119 generous people had pledged $139,185 for a new building.[60]

The energetic director of the new Jewish Center was Herman A. Eigen who busied himself with eliminating duplicate activities in the merged groups and coordinating and strengthening existing programs. To carry out a temporary program pending the construction of a building, Mr. Eigen rented space from four synagogues and two public schools. He operated from headquarters located in the Root Building, where he was assisted by Robert H. Weiner and a part-time staff.[61]

In 1946, the Center purchased land at the northeast corner of Delaware Avenue and Summer Street. This site was selected, rather than the North Park area, because the neighborhood was considered so stable that it would not deteriorate. Furthermore, it was near Beth Zion and Beth El and convenient to business and professional centers of the city. A special Committee on Facilities, under the chairmanship of Max Gross, consulted with the Building Bureau of the Jewish Welfare Board in New York City before drawing up plans for the proposed Center. The local architects for the $764,000 building were James W. Kideney and Milton Milstein.

As the building progressed, a Study Commission headed by Edward H. Kavinoky and Mrs. Hyman L. Levin, and acting in consultation with the National Jewish Welfare Board, worked out a stimulating social, educational, and recreational program for the new building. To insure that the wishes of the community would be duly regarded, the Commission took counsel with about 250 lay leaders. The Study Commission also consulted with joint inter-agency committees, with the Bureau of Jewish Education, with Camp Lakeland, with leading synagogues and with Zionist groups before making its final report.

Programs were thus arranged, before the new building was formally dedicated, for all age groups ranging from toddling nursery school youngsters to gray-haired "golden-agers." In the second category, the Center realized that current tendencies toward increasing longevity and earlier retirement left a good many lonely, older people who would use its facilities to good advantage. Other programs envisaged seminars on world affairs and intercultural relations, the promotion of athletics, hobby clubs and aesthetic interests such as art, music and drama.[62]

After doing a superlative job in putting this ambitious blueprint into operation, Mr. Eigen resigned in 1954 to head the Center system in Cleveland. His successor was David M. Kleinstein, a law school graduate who had switched his interests to social work. Under his vigorous leadership, the Center housed about seventy groups and began to lay plans for an expansion of its activities into the nearer suburbs.

It was also during the challenging years now under review that B'nai B'rith made great advances on the Niagara Frontier, paralleling its phenomenal strides throughout the country. Following the 1918 Armistice, this order enjoyed a new spurt of activity as its Anti-Defamation League (dating from 1913) busied itself in an attempt to counteract the Ku Klux Klan and the Fordian type of anti-Semitism. Its greatest work, however, came during the 1930s against the German Bundists and the home-grown variety of Fascists who plagued Franklin D. Roosevelt's America.

Locally, Montefiore Lodge of yesteryear was blessed with magnificent leadership. In addition to Emil Rubenstein, Benjamin D. Reisman, David Ruslander and Israel Rumizen (popularly dubbed the four "R's"), there was a coterie of outstanding younger men. Among them were Emil L. Cohen, Samuel Blinkoff, Maurice Frey, Lewis H. Ruslander and Arthur I. Goldberg, (1912-1953). Mr. Goldberg's passing at an early age was a heavy blow, for he was one of the most energetic leaders of his generation. A life-long journalist of unquestioned talent, he was chief rewrite man for the Buffalo *Evening News* and simultaneously headed the Information Services of the University of Buffalo. For many years Mr. Goldberg arranged the University's popular Round Table of the Air, and in 1945 was awarded the Gold Key by the Junior Chamber of Commerce for outstanding service to the community.

Montefiore Lodge's heyday began in 1931, when Emil Rubenstein returned to the presidency. Under his stewardship monthly meetings began to sparkle as discussions of the current Jewish crisis formed part of the regular agenda. Ben Edidin, Director of the Bureau of Jewish Education, commanded the interest of all with his brief but pointed summaries of current happenings. The hall buzzed with excitement as outstanding speakers were brought to town during the winter season. This interest was stepped up when, in 1933, Hitler came to power and began to put into effect the evil policies he had so long promised at Brown-Shirt rallies. "If the Gentiles will spend money to join the Nazi movement," said Mr. Rubenstein in an enthusiastic moment, "why should not Jews spend to join B'nai B'rith which is the only organization equipped to combat it?" [63] Even level-headed non-Jews were sometimes unbalanced in the face of the wave of anti-Semitism that swept over the world in the 1930s. It was frequently said that Adolph Hitler was the most effective membership chairman in ninety years of B'nai B'rith history. Consequently, interest in Anti-Defamation work was the fashion of the day in Buffalo where a small part of the German element openly defended the Third Reich. To Jews who preferred a do-nothing policy, B'nai B'rith leaders explained that German Jewry was being systematically destroyed because it had remained silent at a time when it was still possible to answer its maligners.

Once the Anti-Defamation League became popular, the enthusiasm for it at times got out of control. Dr. Israel Efros, the scholarly and usually cautious rabbi of Beth El, helped persuade the Board of Education to ban the *Merchant of Venice* as required reading in high-school English classes. This action was rash enough to draw fire from the New York *Times*, and locally Professor Willard H. Bonner supplied a corrective when he publicly complained that if one should apply this reasoning to literary offerings, *Macbeth* would not be read because it might offend the Scots; *Othello* would surely outrage the Negroes; and the Catholics might reasonably demand the elimination of Chaucer, Spenser and Milton from the local curricula.[64]

In the period of excitement over the spread of Fascism, Montefiore Lodge became so large that the meetings sometimes became unwieldy. After the collapse of the Axis, however, enthusiasm waned as the Jewish problem became less pressing and as the attractions of television and suburban living kept members home on lodge nights. The time had come to decentralize B'nai B'rith, in order to encourage larger participation. While Montefiore remained the strongest B'nai B'rith unit in Buffalo, Balfour, Humanity and Frontier Lodges sprang into existence in the postwar decade.

Any account of B'nai B'rith would be incomplete without some mention of the work done by the wives and daughters of its members. The political emancipation of women that came with the 19th Amendment spurred women all over the country on to greater participation in community life. B'nai B'rith was influenced by this general trend and, in 1922, ninety-three Buffalo women met to form an auxiliary chapter. The first president of Montefiore Chapter No. 34 was Mrs. Adele R. (Mrs. Israel) Rumizen who was followed by Mrs. David Ruslander.

At the start, Montefiore Chapter stressed Americanization work. At one time, its members even provided baby-sitters so that immigrant mothers could go to night schools to prepare for naturalization examinations. In addition, the ladies looked after the needy and even bought graduation dresses for East Side children. Two decades later, the chapter helped greatly in establishing a Hillel Foundation at the University of Buffalo and often sent volunteers with refreshments to serve at school affairs. Especially prominent in this and other work of the auxiliary were Mrs. Morris Steinhorn and Mrs. Arthur I. Goldberg. The B'nai B'rith women of recent years have been particularly active in fund raising, A.D.L. work, and in bringing cheer and comfort to former servicemen confined to the Veterans Hospital.[65]

While hard times were intensifying interest in B'nai B'rith, the depression psyche had an equally stimulating effect on contrasting ideological groups within the Buffalo community. As we have noted previously, many Jews, as members of an oppressed group in czarist Russia, were attracted towards Socialism in somewhat greater numbers than other segments of the New Immigration. The outright radicals, almost invariably anti-religious and anti-Zionist, must be differentiated from the thinkers and workingmen who tried to fuse Jewish nationalism with Socialist theory. This former tight-knit group, always relatively small in number, followed the American Communists when the latter broke with the Debs Socialists and accepted the supremacy of Moscow. Those Jews who followed the party-line without deviation were influenced by the "Yevsekzie," the militant anti-religious clique of Jewish Communists within the Soviet Union.

In the Buffalo of the 1920s, the radical situation was thoroughly confused, but it seems sensible to believe that only a handful here were ingrained Communists. It is probable, however, that Jews here, as elsewhere, had more than their share of non-card-carrying fellow travellers because they had, prior to the 1939 Nazi-Soviet Pact, always thought of bolshevism as an effective counter-agent to anti-Semitism. Moreover, in the early revolutionary days, many Jews and Jewish sympathizers occupied seats of power in the Communist hierarchy. Michael Kalinin (1875-1936), for example, was chairman of the Communist Party's Central Executive Committee for the final dozen years of his life, and he was known to be pro-Jewish. Kalinin released, for world publication, copies of his speeches which almost invariably recalled the religious intolerance of the Romanovs and pointed out that the Soviet Union had been the first nation to outlaw anti-Semitism.[66] Although it was generally recognized that Judaism as a religion had been all but blotted out, many American Jews naively believed that their Russian kinsmen fared no worse than other citizens of the U.S.S.R.

Meanwhile, many non-radical American-Jewish organizations hailed Soviet attempts to settle Russian Jews *en masse* in the Ukraine and in the Crimea. Funds for such projects came from eminently conservative sources such as the Warburg family of banking fame and Julius Rosenwald of Sears Roebuck and Company. The principal agency for helping the Soviet Union resettle its Jews was Agro-Joint, a subsidiary of the American Joint Distribution Committee which sent millions of dollars to Russia.

When Dr. Joseph A. Rosen, head of Agro-Joint, visited the United States in 1925, he breathed optimism concerning the ultimate future of Jewish life under the Communists. He reported that the government was keeping faith in helping Jews resettle on land set aside in the Odessa region, the Ukraine, White Russia and the Crimea. He found a persisting Jewish spirit in Russia, and reported that books on Jewish subjects were coming into the country from Poland and that some Yiddish literature was even being privately printed under Soviet imprimatur.[67]

Less enthusiastic than Dr. Rosen, but nevertheless not really pessimistic, was Z. Wendroff, a brilliant Yiddish writer who had toured Jewish settlements in the Ukraine, Crimea and White Russia. His report, which was transmitted through the pages of the *Buffalo Jewish Review*, described how Sovietization had impoverished the Jews who had been in business and how they had moved to the new settlements because they could not exist otherwise and were not permitted to migrate to the United States or Palestine. Some Jewish Communists in Russia, Wendroff said, seemed more than satisfied, but on the whole they did not paint a happy picture of life there.[68]

One must recall that, a generation ago, not all American Jews had by any means become converted to Zionism. Although many of them supported Soviet land settlements merely in the hope of saving Jewish lives, still others thought that this type of wholesale removal was a better solution to the Jewish problem than that offered in capitalistic and British-controlled Palestine. To illustrate: the following question was debated before the Beth Zion's Men's Club: "Resolved, that the colonization of the Jews in Crimea be preferred to the colonization in Palestine." The affimative won! To indicate how clouded were the international issues of that time, the very next meeting of the same group was addressed by Count Felix von Luckner who spoke of his U-boat exploits during the Kaiser War.[69]

After Stalin had come to power, the Kremlin concentrated on the creation of an autonomous Jewish republic within the U.S.S.R. Biro-Bidjan, as it was named, is a 36,000 square mile area in the Amur-Ussuri district of Siberia, near the border of Manchuria. The scheme was first announced in 1928 and was developed during the following decade. This was one more of the Russian resettlement plans to discredit Zionism and draw funds from the United States. The official language for Biro-Bidjan was to be Yiddish and it consequently attracted many American sympathizers, many of whom were militant secularists. Even a Yiddish newspaper was established there, although it was devoid of Jewish content and merely echoed the familiar party-line.

The high point in Biro-Bidjan's history came when it was declared an autonomous region. Comrade Kalinin proclaimed: "After an interim of hundreds of years, the Jews will again become a nation with their own state." [70] Some misguided men of the period, discouraged with the lack of progress in British Palestine, welcomed Biro-Bidjan as a good substitute. It was said to be able to absorb 25,000,000 people and, because at that time Russia was the archenemy of the Third Reich, many looked at Communism with less critical eyes than they would today. The depression Zeitgeist, moreover, did its work in making men tolerant of radical ideologies.

A branch of the Jewish Colonization Organization for Russia (ICOR), with headquarters on William Street, celebrated the political inauguration of Biro-Bidjan, the "First free Jewish state" since the destruction of the Second Temple. It is charitable, in view of later developments, not to dwell upon the arguments advanced by the group; but they met twice a month at the Jewish Community Building, and some Buffalonians were even on ICOR's national board.[71]

The Popular Front, as the union of all non-Fascist elements was called, reached its height in 1936 as Moscow sent out word to party units in the

United States and other democratic countries to cooperate in a friendly fashion. In addition to these tactics for winning friends, the Russians adopted that same year a "democratic" constitution that deceived many people. Locally, Temple Emanu-El played host when S. Almazoff, General Secretary of ICOR, debated the merits of Biro-Bidjan with Rabbi Reuben J. Magil of Beth El.[72]

By 1939, enthusiasm for the Siberian project was already on the wane. The Moscow blood purges caused much disillusionment and it was recognized that the dictator of the Kremlin never really intended to help anyone but Russia in Biro-Bidjan. Even the Yiddishist part of the scheme was recognized as a palpaple fraud. Finally, Stalin's 1939 pact with Hitler swept away the last support for the Moscovites among American Jews. A brief revival of sympathy was felt during World War II, while Russia was our ally against Germany, but Stalin's subsequent actions against Israel and renewed Russian anti-Semitism all but wiped out pro-Soviet feeling in American Jewry. Erstwhile Biro-Bidjanites in time became quite conventional Jews.

Another left-of-center Jewish segment quite active in former days was composed of various labor groups. These moderate radicals were Yiddishists rather than Zionists. The Jewish Labor Lyceum League of Buffalo, N. Y., was formed in 1919 and campaigned to raise funds to purchase a centrally located meeting hall. Well known East Side labor leaders were among the incorporators of this organization. They included Benjamin Etkin, Dr. Theodore N. Alpert, Samuel Obletz, Morris Gevirtzman, Harry Serotte, Sol Kissin and Dr. Meyer Kremer. They acquired the Temple Theater on William Street near Jefferson for $37,000 and converted it into the Jewish Labor Lyceum. It functioned for only a few years, but while it existed it was the nucleus of Yiddishist culture in the city. Although financed primarily by the Arbeiter Ring, the Lyceum's quarters were rented freely to other groups, and many opposing ideologies were voiced within its walls.[73]

In the meantime, the Arbeiter Ring had moderated its extreme radicalism when the outright revolutionaries departed to join the recently formed Communist Party of America. Influenced greatly by Dr. Chaim Zhitlowsky, those who remained in the Workmen's Circle sought to establish a truly Yiddish culture group in America on a secular basis. All, however, who belonged to the Ring were not anti-religious; many of them were synagogue-going Jews who happened to be proletarians. Politically, they were usually Debs Socialists who fought off Communist infiltration. There was, of course, a small segment of extreme leftists, locally dubbed "Die Linke," planted there to convert the rest. But even this group moved out to become overtly Communist. Old-timers insist that the Buffalo Workmen's Circle was composed mostly of non-Communists. This contention is strengthened by the fact that in 1924, they supported the Progressive candidate Robert M. LaFollette for President and that they consistently opposed the writings of the American Yiddish Communist organ, *Die Freiheit.*

The struggle over Communism in Jewish and other labor circles was very bitter in the 1920s, and when it was over these groups had changed almost beyond recognition. In the course of the great debate over Moscow, much of the emphasis shifted from economic to cultural subjects.[74] For example, no sooner had the local Erlanger Theater opened its doors in 1928, than they brought the great Yiddish actor Jacob Ben Ami to Buffalo in the play *Diplomacy.* This interest in the stage had existed for some time in Buffalo. Morris D. Waxman had been operating a Yiddish theater on William Street, and *The Blind Painter* played at Shubert's Teck in 1927. A group called the Jewish Literary Society was interested in Yiddish drama, and presented a one-act comedy in 1931 at the Jewish Community Building. For a time the Yiddish Radio Players even conducted a program on station WEBR.[75]

With the general depopulation of the East Side, the Jewish labor group moved its headquarters to the Humboldt neighborhood. Samuel Brody who had operated a candy store at William and Pratt Streets, later located at 416 East Ferry Street, where he continued to sell tickets for all types of Yiddish cultural events. Wherever Brody lived, that place automatically became the unofficial center of Yiddish culturalists.

A temporary fillip to the Jewish labor movement came as the protracted depression evoked a momentary lack of faith in the merits of the free enterprise system. Then, too, the pervasive New Deal spirit was congenial to the goals of organized labor. In 1937, the local Workmen's Circle intensified its propaganda program, assisted by funds from its National Youth Committee. The minute books for the Roosevelt decade reveal that its members were dedicated Socialists who met each Sunday in a Debs Club. They were intensely anti-Franco in the Spanish Civil War then raging, and they definitely preferred the CIO to the AFL.[76]

The 1938 survey of the Jewish Welfare Board gives a good indication of the strength of the Jewish labor movement in Buffalo a generation ago. There were then four branches of the Arbeiter Ring with a total membership of 205 men. There was also a Youth Circle with two dozen members, and a Workmen's Circle Ladies' Branch with sixty-eight on its rolls. The J. L. Peretz Shule taught thirty-five pupils who attended four afternoons a week and on Sunday.[77]

Despite the efforts of such men as Sam Brody, Matthew Rosen and

David Bridger, the talented teacher of the Peretz school, it was difficult to transmit the Yiddish secular heritage to American boys and girls. In the beginning, as we have seen, members of the Arbeiter Ring were assimilationists who retained their mother tongue because they did not know any other language. It was under the influence of Dr. Zhitlowsky that they began to regard Yiddish culture as a value in itself. In the 1930s, however, this point of view began to lose popularity. Militant secularism was becoming outmoded as it became apparent that in the United States the basis of division was religious rather than ethnic. The Yiddishists became reluctantly aware that the values that they had espoused, such as an alien language and culture, were far more likely to be overwhelmed in the American milieu than was the synagogue. Moreover, the steady progress of Zionism popularized Hebrew rather than Yiddish as a possible second language for American Jews.

Undoubtedly, the de-proletarianization of the Jew hastened the abandonment of the Yiddishist outlook. Along with other Americans, Jews were constantly striving toward middle-class status, and this tendency all the Yiddish schools in the world could not combat. Even those who remained workers became Americanized and adopted the vernacular in the course of lively union-hall debates.

Along with national leaders like Sidney Hillman and David Dubinsky, Jewish workers gradually modified their zealous Socialism and replaced it with ordinary American party affiliations. Their outlook became more and more conventionally American Jewish. All these forces were hastened by Hitler, who inadvertently united all Jews, and by the fact that, after 1933, Zionism was no longer an abstract theory. World War II was a great Americanizing force, and the disillusionment with Russia after 1945 caused the complete collapse of the old, dogmatic, internationalist outlook of the ingrained Marxists. By the middle of the twentieth century the onetime radicals and their children were hardly distinguishable from Jews of Reform or Orthodox background.[78]

In the 1950s there were still several branches of the Arbeiter Ring in Buffalo, but well has it been said that there is *nicht ein arbeiter in dem ganzen Ring*. By mid-century, Italians, Negroes and Poles were the workers in Buffalo, while Jews were generally employers or professional men who took a different view of labor from that which once they held. About 200 men, however, kept up membership in the Circle for the sake of old times. Their children were active in temples, Zionism, and such typically bourgeois organizations as B'nai B'rith. Politically they were no more radical than other Stevenson Democrats, and some even looked askance at the mild Socialism of Israel. They had succumbed to the American curse of conformity of thought; the melting process of the Jewish community had been successful; and the "drowsy syrups of prosperity" had speeded the process. It was the unusual man indeed who continued to dream of a Socialist Utopia at a time when every schoolboy understood the difference in human and spiritual values between the Iron Curtain countries and those of the free world.

The final groups to be accounted for during the years that separated the two great wars of our time are the various Zionist organizations. In 1933, there were in Buffalo the General Zionists (Z.O.A.), Hadassah, the small but militant Labor Zionist groups, and a struggling Mizrachi outfit.

When Hitler struck, the non-Zionists were simply bowled over, for there seemed no other humanitarian or practical answer to the problem of refugees than Palestine. Fascist terrorism coincided with the abatement of Reform opposition as the older liberal rabbis were being replaced by younger men usually recruited from traditional homes. A great many non-Zionists joined the older nationalists in these years, although some of the converts attempted to stress only "philanthropic Zionism," a factor which would later divide Zionist ranks. "Today all Jews are Zionists," said a Buffalo rabbi. "That is as true as any statement so brief can be in so controversial a field as Jewish life." [79] In the urgency of the moment, long-standing ideological feuds were forgotten. Weizmann and Brandeis Zionists smoothed over old differences; Orthodox, Conservative and Reform, Labor and General Zionists all cooperated as never before. Membership drives under such men as Harry A. Rachlin and Rabbi Morris Adler of Emanu-El were pre-eminently successful.

The Palestinian cause was greatly strengthened by the arrival in Buffalo of Mr. and Mrs. Ernest S. Freudenheim who did so much both on the local and national levels for the Zionist Youth Commission.

In the tense days just before Hitler's invasion of Poland, interest in the cause was fanned by the attitude of Great Britain. To keep the Arabs in line in the face of impending war with Germany, London placed crippling limitations on immigration into Palestine. Had the White Paper of 1939 been rigidly enforced, it would have insured an Arab majority in Palestine. Protest meetings were called in Buffalo, and animosity toward England reached alarming proportions until it was halted by the outbreak of the war against the Axis. "The enemy of my enemy" says an old Arab proverb, "is my friend." Despite lack of cooperation from London, the Palestinian *Yishuv* was soon fighting valiantly with the British against a common foe as Rommel's Afrika Corps raced across North Africa toward the Suez Canal.

All over the free world, Zionist units developed war programs. In

Palestine, Hadassah trained nurses and technicians, while the women of all Buffalo Zionist groups united to form a "Save a Child Campaign." [80] By 1944, local excitement reached fever pitch, for the White Paper of 1939 was scheduled to go into effect in March of that year. David Diamond was chairman of a Buffalo Emergency Committee for Palestine which held a rally at Kleinhans Music Hall under the slogan "You Can Help Kill the White Paper." Another group organized a local branch of the American Palestine Committee with prominent non-Jews serving as officers.[81]

Meanwhile, a national non-Zionist group had long since emerged. This was the American Jewish Committee that had been founded in 1906 in order to unite the voice of American Jewry. As its program developed, the American Jewish Committee fought against racial and religious prejudice and defended the civil, religious and economic rights of Jews and non-Jews alike. Gradually A.J.C. came to look on Palestine as a practical answer to the Jewish problem; but it did not support it as a political state. Even after the emergence of Israel, the Committee expressed conservative views: "Within the framework of American interests, we shall aid in the upbuilding of Israel as a vital spiritual and cultural center and in the development of its capacity to provide a free and dignified life for those who desire to make it their home." At another time the group expressed its views as follows: "The Committee is convinced that in America, Jews, drawing their cultural and spiritual substance from both American and Jewish sources, will take their place as normal, secure members of society." [82]

Because this organization sought to do its work without publicity or fanfare, it was bound to collide, from time to time, with the Zionist forces that used endless publicity, petitions and pressure politics to further their aims. A local chapter of the American Jewish Committee was formed here in 1945, after Judge Samuel J. Harris had met in New York City with national officials. The first officers were Judge Harris, chairman; Sol J. Levy, vice-chairman; Haskell Stovroff, secretary; and Arthur I. Goldberg, treasurer. Eventually, the Niagara Frontier Chapter, open to anyone of good character, stabilized its membership at about 200. In recent years, its members have scarcely differed in ideology from other segments of the community.

In the meantime, to counteract the accepted conservatism of the American Jewish Committee, a rival national organization had been formed during World War I under the leadership of the dynamic rabbi of the Free Synagogue in New York, Stephen S. Wise. This American Jewish Congress was especially designed to bolster a vital, democratic, ardently pro-Zionist leadership at the forthcoming Versailles Peace Conference.

At that conclave, the American Jewish Committee stressed the minority rights of Jews in Poland and other succession states, whereas the American Jewish Congress was much more interested in implementing the true intent of the Balfour Declaration. In Paris, however, the two groups reached an understanding and worked in unity for the common cause of the Jewish people.

Locally active in the American Jewish Congress were such men as Harry Harriton, Jacob I. Cohen, Edward Schwartz, Rabbi M. M. Eichler, Charles Dautch, Sol Jacobson and Dr. Hiram S. Yellen. In the early 1920s, this central group, which united about thirty organizations in Buffalo, was primarily interested in fighting the National Origins Act, which severely limited immigration to the United States, and in protecting the rights of Jews under the League of Nations Covenant.

A long-brewing conflict between these two outfits came to a head in 1943 at a meeting at Hotel Statler to select Buffalo delegates for an American Jewish Conference, proposed by the national president of B'nai B'rith, Henry Monsky. A bitter contest broke out between those who urged caution and those who, stirred by stories of Jewish massacres in Europe and British intransigence in Palestine, wanted immediate action. After an acrimonious election, Emil Rubenstein and David Diamond were sent by Buffalo to the conference which opened September 2, 1943, at the Hotel Biltmore in New York City.

The delegates to this assembly were weary of makeshift compromises and by acclamation affirmed the now-famous Biltmore Resolutions which demanded commonwealth status for Palestine, the end of the 1939 White Paper, and a Jewish Army to defend the *Yishuv* from the Axis. On their return, Diamond and Rubenstein reported to a public meeting on the conference, and Buffalo Jewry overwhelmingly approved the Biltmore platform.[83]

Here and elsewhere, this conference marked the beginning of the end of opposition to political Zionism. There was heightened pride in the events that culminated in the 1948 Israeli declaration of independence. The only vocal anti-Zionist faction henceforth was the American Council for Judaism, but, although a handful of Buffalonians joined, no organized group existed here. On the question of Israel, the local Jewish community had become almost unanimous.

As its constituents became more and more involved in the incessant international crises of our time, the Federation found that forces stronger than any that it had faced in the past were coming to bear on it and changing it beyond recognition. This was the period when American-Jewish life underwent the transition from nineteenth-century concepts of charity to modern social-service orientation. Among the old-timers in the organization there still lingered the belief that its prime duty was an eleemosynary concern for the unfortunate. Only by degrees did its veteran leaders accept responsibility for the general welfare of the Jewish community in the broadest sense of the term.

The final years of the Depression Decade were filled with the stresses and strains that usually accompany drastic changes. George Wolfe, a field worker for the Council of Jewish Federations and Welfare Funds, reported to New York in 1938 that, headed by Rabbi Morris Adler of Temple Emanu-El, a group was organizing to oppose the Warner regime. According to this observer, the insurgents were demanding an overhaul of the Federation's voting structure, increased allocations for overseas relief, and a freer hand for the professional workers who were in charge of the Federation's program of social service.[84]

This crisis passed, but, in 1940, in an apparent last ditch stand against the invasion by professional workers, the Board of Governors issued a statement of policy: "This union is similar to that of the various states of the United States who retain certain local rights but have given up to the National Government certain powers for the common good." In an effort to strengthen the lines of authority, the document outlined the responsibility of the various constituent elements and agencies. The Board of Governors would guide the general policy making of the constituent groups. The Federation had the right to examine and approve the budgets of its constituent agencies, but the agencies were restricted from raising additional funds or expanding activities without permission. The Federation could scrutinize hours of work, salaries, and operations of its affiliated bodies and make recommendations. The agencies in turn were required to make monthly reports on finance and to explain any deviations from the budget.

Despite these efforts to strengthen the lines of control, the older generation could not possibly stay the tide of modernism that was engulfing it. Wolfe came to Buffalo once more after this 1940 manifesto had been issued, and his report to his home office revealed the rivalry, tension and confusion that existed beneath the surface. He observed that Benjamin B. Goldman, newly appointed head of the Jewish Welfare Society in Buffalo, wanted to transfer relief cases to the county once and for all. Goldman was opposed, however, by the Old Guardists, who feared that future campaigns would fail without the traditional appeal for refugee relief. Wolfe relayed Goldman's opinion that it was the attitude of a few intransigents that kept such organizations as the Rosa Coplon Old Folks Home and the Jewish Mothers Club out of the Federation, that impeded the work of the Bureau of Jewish Education, and opposed the rapidly developing Jewish Center.[85]

Nevertheless, the handwriting on the wall signalled the end of an order, for the final pre-Pearl Harbor drives were conducted without the usual strong emphasis on the need for relief funds. This démarche proved successful, for the campaign launched in October 1941, went over the top for the first time since the Big Crash. The Federation, long geared to the primary focus of alms-giving, now had to find a new *raison d'être,* for it was apparent that henceforth the indigent would be looked after by the state rather than private charity. Significantly, in the allocations for 1942, less than half of the funds were earmarked for the Jewish Welfare Society. It was still the lion's share, but from this point on financial assistance would get increasingly smaller portions of the budget pie. The campaign for 1943 proved to be another landmark, for it was destined to be the last Buffalo drive designed primarily for local relief needs.[86] In those stirring days when the Russians were turning back the Nazi invaders at Stalingrad and the Americans were invading North Africa, Buffalo as well as the nation reached the end of an era.

The year 1943, a crucial one for both the Grand Alliance and Buffalo Jewry, was marked by two important local changes. First of all, the Federation abandoned its longtime headquarters on Jefferson Avenue, for the well-worn establishment there was to give way to a housing project. Instead of making the move directly to the center of the city, however, the Federation purchased a three-story factory at Monroe and Genesee Streets. Perhaps it was difficult to find suitable downtown quarters in wartime, but it was whispered that the irreconcilables still could not conceive of the Federation as anything but a charitable agency and so they chose to keep it in an area where some poor Jews still resided. Secondly, that self-same year marked the first joint drive for funds collected for the benefit of about 100 Jewish and non-Jewish groups in Buffalo. Hitherto, both the Federation and the United Jewish Fund campaigns had been separately conducted. Now they were consolidated with other annual city-wide appeals into one huge United War and Community Fund. This War Chest, which was created as a result of pressure from Washington, combined such organizations as the USO, YMCA, the Buffalo and Erie County Joint Charities, the AFL and CIO, and overseas relief for our many stricken allies. The clarion call was sounded for "fighting dollars." [87]

By "D Day," in 1944, Eugene Warner, who had influenced Federation policies for four decades, was gone. To provide for the future, a Plan and Scope Committee, headed by Judge Harris, contemplated the appointment of a professionally-trained director for the Federation. A representative of the Council of Jewish Federations and Welfare Funds reported to headquarters: "Buffalo seems engaged in a process of self-study, from which effective and fundamental community organization may come about."[88]

Then came the axial year of 1945, marked by victory in Europe and Asia, and the ushering in of the Atomic Age. In the midst of the noise of the peace celebrations, a note of unrest was heard as Russia seemed indisposed to settle down, and the vacuums created by the collapse of the Axis nations were menaced by the awful bulk of the Soviet bear. At home, a saddened nation saw Franklin D. Roosevelt replaced by Harry S. Truman, and three months later the British electorate chose the colorless Clement Attlee to succeed the masterful Winston Churchill. The United Nations was created in April 1945, and then promptly hamstrung by Russian intransigence, a turn for the worse that would vex the dearly-bought peace for many years.

This epoch-making global shake-up was paralleled in miniature on the Buffalo Jewish scene, although the overtones here were to be increasing unity rather than division. Eugene Warner, who had surrendered his unique Federation position at the summons of death, was replaced by Maurice S. Tabor as acting president. The immediate postwar period was also marked by the rise of some younger community leaders, most important of whom was the brilliant and versatile attorney, Edward H. Kavinoky. A 1926 graduate of Harvard Law School, Mr. Kavinoky returned to practice in his native Buffalo and his position in legal circles was secure long before he reached his fortieth birthday. Few men in the history of the city were influential on so many varied fronts. Kavinoky, at one time or another, played a leading role in Red Cross affairs, headed the Council of Social Agencies of Buffalo, the Harvard Club, the Buffalo Philharmonic Society, and the Buffalo Council on World Affairs.

Meanwhile, Ed Kavinoky had occupied so many positions of importance in the Jewish community, that he became an elder statesman at the early age of fifty. His first significant Jewish assignment was the Jewish Welfare Society which he headed for six years. Shortly after the war he was elected president of the Federation and, following his term of office, he continued to wield much influence by virtue of his superlative ability and eminent position in the community at large. It has often been noted that Mr. Kavinoky bore a strong intellectual resemblance to Eugene Warner; but the younger man was more closely in touch with the newer elements in the community, for he sprang from their ranks and understood their point of view. If, initially, he was somewhat cautious on Zionist matters, in time he became one of the most effective voices for Israeli causes on the Niagara Frontier.[89]

To return to the events of 1945, a new age for the Federation dawned with the arrival of Arthur S. Rosichan who had just been appointed Executive Director. Mr. Rosichan, a brilliant and intellectually-curious young man in his late thirties, was a native of Cleveland who had worked his way up the ladder to executive leadership in his home city and in Pittsburgh. A graduate of Western Reserve University School of Applied Social Science, Rosichan had gained practical experience with the United States Transit Bureau and as a field representative for the Council of Jewish Federations and Welfare Funds. He enjoyed an excellent reputation as a skilled trouble-shooter and resourceful fund raiser.

Art Rosichan arrived in Buffalo precisely at a moment when a temporary lacuna in lay leadership, the accumulated experience of wartime unity, and a booming prosperity, all gave him the opportunity to act; and act he did! Promptly, he defined the main areas of community interest in their order of importance: Health, Welfare, Recreation, Jewish Education, Public Relations, and Fund Raising. (Obviously, such a system of values which placed "Recreation" before "Jewish Education" would be subsequently challenged by those who did not share his angle of vision.) Rosichan went on to state: "The purpose of centralized community organization is to plan, develop and co-ordinate programs in these areas." The new executive expressed the hope that Buffalo would become "community organization minded." He promised to erase divisions that had invited duplication of effort in the past; and set as his goal the promotion of the greatest good of the greatest number.[90]

One of the principal changes that took place under Rosichan's direction was the conversion of the old Jewish Welfare Society into the new Jewish Community Service Society. Significantly, the word *Welfare* was replaced by the phrase *Community Service* to reflect the shift in emphasis from Victorian to modern ideals. The principal functions of the Society were redefined as 1) family service, counselling, refugees, transients, 2) child care, 3) vocational guidance and placement, 4) job retraining, 5) student training. The concept of relief was significantly absent.

At Rosichan's suggestion, the Eugene Warner Medical Clinic and the Guggenheimer Dental Clinic were abandoned, for it was felt that these health services could be met adequately by non-Jewish agencies. The philosophy, generally, was that the Federation or its agencies ought not to offer those services that could be obtained elsewhere, unless a particularly Jewish problem was involved in the process. On the other hand, counselling was emphasized, for "the Jewish client who needs help with his personal plans for self-dependence wants to share his personal problems and plans with an agency of his own group, just as a child turns to his parents." [91]

Henceforth, what little relief was necessary amidst the unprecedented prosperity, was usually turned over to Erie County. The concept of the Jewish community taking exclusive care of its own indigent was recognized as outmoded; at long last the ghost of Peter Stuyvesant had been laid. To the exceptional client who refused to turn to an outside agency, the community still extended a helping hand and it continued to give temporary assistance to needy wayfarers. On the other hand, child problems were of particular concern to the Jewish Community Service Society and it still handled adoptions and foster-home placements. The bulk of its work, however, came in the areas of pyschological counselling, vocational guidance and job placement. In 1958, as an integral part of its Family Service program, it set up its own Psychiatric Clinic, open to all on a non-sectarian basis. The new establishment was headed by Dr. Samuel Yochelson who enjoyed a fine professional reputation in the field. Meanwhile, J.C.S.S. had been cooperating with the School of Social Work at the University of Buffalo, using university students in apprentice work, and providing a convenient laboratory and field training center. "The Jewish Community Service Society," stated a brochure, "is a multiple service casework agency with the broad objective of promoting and conserving a wholesome individual and family life in the Jewish community." [92]

Following the termination of the wartime emergency, there was a real danger that Buffalo would revert to the familiar practice of numerous sectarian campaigns for funds earmarked for local use. This reaction was averted by the timely intervention of Maurice S. Tabor, president of the Federation, who was stoutly assisted in his efforts by David Diamond, Edward H. Kavinoky and Charles Dautch, then president of the United Jewish Fund. These men were largely responsible for having Jewish needs included in the 1946 Community Chest which was a peacetime carry-over from the joint wartime drives. Buffalo Jewry thus became almost unique in the country in that henceforth, with the exception of capital expenditures, all purely local needs would be met by funds allocated from the Community Chest. [93] *

In the interim, following the last joint war drive, the United Jewish

---

* In 1960, the Community Chest became the United Fund of Buffalo and Erie County. It is hoped that this re-organization, under the directorship of Harris N. Snyder, will result in the inclusion of additional agencies and the elimination of duplicating county-wide appeals.

Fund had resumed an independent annual campaign. With unprecedented demands for aid to displaced persons abroad and to the new State of Israel, the Buffalo community raised undreamed of amounts. In the spring of 1946, the United Jewish Fund launched its initial king-sized drive. Almost immediately the goal of half a million was over-subscribed and ultimately the total donated was $732,000. The age of big giving had arrived, brought into being by limitless needs which chanced to coincide with the most enduring boom in American economic history. In the following year, skillful leaders guided by the resourceful Rosichan headed a group of dedicated workers who raised $1,032,000. This wave of generosity crested in 1948 when Buffalo's UJF total reached an astonishing $1,466,000.[94]

Then, in 1949, the Jewish Federation for Social Service merged with the United Jewish Fund. Both organizations had been unofficially connected, since the war, with the UJF headquarters located in the Federation offices. Such a union without the benefit of parchment and seals was unrealistic. Moreover, the Federation needed more money than it was getting from its annual share of the Community Chest. Some provision had to be made for specific Jewish objectives that transcended the scope of a community-wide inter-faith appeal.

This consolidation was completed with Howard T. Saperston acting for the Jewish Federation for Social Service and Victor Wagner for the United Jewish Fund. The new organization was called the United Jewish Federation of Buffalo, Inc., and Mr. Saperston became its first president. As a result of the merger, the Federation now had representation from every Jewish organization in the city with a membership of two hundred or over.

After a decade of devoted service, Mr. Rosichan resigned to accept a similar position in the Canadian metropolis of Montreal. His successor was Sydney S. Abzug, a fellow Clevelander, who had formerly been Executive Director of the Albany Jewish Community Council. Under Mr. Abzug's quiet but efficient direction, the United Jewish Federation enjoyed an all-time popularity among its immediate constituents and an enhanced prestige in the city at large.

While the war was effecting many changes in community structure, it also sparked Jewish activity at home and on the various military fronts. Unlike certain other conflicts when Jews, as other groups, were sometimes dubious about the merits of the fight, circumstances removed all questions in their minds about this "War For Survival." They could not have been more unanimous in their support of the national cause, and they could scarcely have given more to insure the victory of the Grand Alliance.

Attorney Benjamin D. Reisman, president of B'nai B'rith Grand Lodge No. 1, pointed up this situation in a speech in which he stressed the stake of all Jews in the outcome of the war. Reform, Conservative, Orthodox; believing and non-believing; the informed and the uninformed; Zionists, non-Zionists and anti-Zionists—all were as one in facing the common foe. But Mr. Reisman called for even greater unity and effort: "Petty strife, lack of understanding and selfish wasteful insistence upon the minute preservation . . . of the autonomy of overlapping fraternal, religious and other Jewish organizations must cease. Centralized authoritative direction and responsibility must be established." [95]

All Jewish organizations did yeoman work on the home front. Especially active were the women of B'nai B'rith who furnished recreation rooms for members of the armed forces at the local Coast Guard Station and at the Marine Hospital on Main Street. They also conducted a canteen at the University of Buffalo which at first was converted to a school for ground training for Air Force officers and later became part of the Army Specialized Training Program. Privately, and on an organizational basis, they became blood donors and sent packages to soldiers in stateside training camps and in units overseas. They also joined the Red Cross to serve as nurses aides and as Gray Ladies. Members of Montefiore Chapter worked with Civilian Defense, collected scrap and made up kit bags for departing soldiers and for the Bundles for America campaign. They set out to sell a million dollars in bonds in the Third War Loan Drive and, thanks to extraordinary effort, went over the top by almost one-third of their goal. [96]

Not a single synagogue in Buffalo failed to engage in some sort of war work. In many ways the conflict fostered a revival of interest in religion and drew denominations together. The first public Inter-faith Service in Buffalo was held in Kleinhans Music Hall on Armistice Day, 1942, to hear Father William A. Maguire, a naval chaplain who had been at Pearl Harbor. A "Day of Mourning" was held the following month at Temple Beth El for the Jews who had already perished in Europe. At this service were Mayor Joseph A. Kelly and representatives from every major church in the city. Such meetings were held more frequently as people learned the horrifying news of what was happening while Hitler's armies swept through the Jewish heartland in eastern Europe. On Memorial Day, 1943, Reform, Conservative and Orthodox congregations united for a Memorial Service for the victims of Hitler. By this time the story of the heroic resistance of the remnant of the Warsaw ghetto was known in Buffalo. Six weeks before, the people of the Warsaw ghetto had perished to the last child as they courageously held off the attacking Nazis of whom they took their toll.[97] No greater monument to human dignity exists.

In addition to spiritual work, the synagogues also released their rabbis who were of military age and suitable for chaplaincy. The first to join the Armed Forces was Rabbi H. Elihu Rickel of Beth El. In July 1943, he entered the United States Navy as a lieutenant j.g. After preliminary training at the Naval Training School for Chaplains at Williamsburg, Virginia, he was sent to the Marine Corps Barracks at Parris Island. Later he saw a great deal of action in the Pacific and was decorated for courage shown in action at Iwo Jima.[98]

Rabbi Eli A. Bohnen of Temple Emanu-El was second to go. He reported to the Army Chaplain School at Harvard University late in 1943, after almost the entire community said good-bye to him at a reception held in his own synagogue. When he finished his training, he went to Camp Gruber, Oklahoma, to serve with the famous 42nd Rainbow Division. He was with this outfit when it formed part of General Eisenhower's "crusade" to liberate Europe. With the war in Europe almost over, Rabbi Bohnen conducted *seder* services on Passover, 1945, in a German city at No. 29 Adolph Hitler Strasse. He was awarded the Bronze Star by Major General Harry J. Collins at Salzburg, Austria.[99]

Meanwhile, Buffalo Jewish boys in the services overseas were meeting two chaplains who had once ministered to Buffalo synagogues. Rabbi Morris Adler, formerly of Temple Emanu-El was one. Another was Rabbi Judah Nadich who had been at Beth David. Before "D Day," Rabbi Nadich had been the first Jewish chaplain in England and reports drifted back home of his renewing acquaintance with Buffalo men and women in service.

It was overseas, too, that many Buffalo boys met a fatherly and devoted chaplain who was to come to their city in later years. Chaplain Isaac Klein had entered the army from Springfield, Massachusetts, early in the war. After serving for a time at Mitchell Field, Long Island, Rabbi Klein went with the 9th Bomber Division to Europe. Buffalonians of the 1950s were never to forget the first-hand account of Dr. Klein's incredible wartime experiences. He arranged a *seder* in a devastated French town with the native chef preparing "fish à la Yid." He comforted liberated DPs in many languages, and he built up lasting friendships with GIs who after the war were to visit and write to him with clocklike regularity. Little wonder, then, that in 1949 Dr. Klein was given the simulated rank of Brigadier-General and sent by President Truman to advise General Lucius D. Clay concerning Jewish religious life in the American zone of Occupied Germany.

The Jewish "Y" at Linwood Avenue threw itself wholeheartedly into the war effort. The projects that were conducted by this organization almost defy enumeration. A local Army and Navy Service Committee provided services for such servicemen as were visiting or passing through the city, saw to it that they were invited to Jewish homes for Passover eve, gave them *matzot,* and provided all suitable embellishment for the festival season. The "Y" promoted the sale of war stamps and bonds, cooperated with the Hanita Pioneer Women to raise money for the Red Cross and the USO, collected scrap and recruited blood donors. It shared in the Buffalo Public Library program of collecting reading matter for servicemen, and provided entertainment for soldiers passing through the crossroads of Buffalo. As Harry Bluestone, its director, reported in 1942, the house on Linwood Avenue had been turned into "a service organization with an extra-mural program of service on the civilian-military front." In his capacity as representative of the Army and Navy Service Committee of the Jewish Welfare Board, Bluestone coordinated all local groups in their wartime social, recreational and religious service activities.[100]

Shortly after the disastrous fire at the Linwood "Y" in 1945, the Servicemen's Lounge was re-opened at Temple Beth Zion with a gala dance, floor show and buffet supper. Here the lounge was operated by a committee of the Women's Division of the "Y". It was noted that with so many young men withdrawn from the local pool of eligibles, Buffalo Jewish girls were more than anxious to help visiting soldiers and sailors make their leisure hours sociable.[101]

Most of this activity was purely Jewish, but a great deal more war work was done in cooperation with local or national non-Jewish agencies. Participating in the President's Committee on War Relief Agencies were the Joint Distribution Committee, the United Palestine Appeal and the National Refugee Service. It was apparent to all that an enlargement of these specific Jewish agencies would speed the day of victory.

Locally, Edward H. Kavinoky was president of the Buffalo Council of Social Agencies and Victor Einach was assistant executive secretary. In 1941, shortly before Pearl Harbor, this agency published a mimeographed study, *Channels of Defense,* a detailed manual of what welfare agencies could do for the health and welfare of the community and for civil defense in the event of war. It was widely sold here and for a time was used as a text at the University of Buffalo School of Social Work. When war did break out, it influenced thinking on such topics as the most economical use of labor, municipal care, organization of nursing services and adequate nutrition in the face of food shortages.

Another organization that drew Jewish support was the Buffalo War

Council. On its advisory committee was Edward H. Kavinoky; and D. Sloan Hurwitz served on its salvage committee. Many Buffalo Jewish women served on its Coordinating Committee on Emergency Volunteer Services. Especially prominent was Mrs. Meyer H. Riwchun, an organizer of this committee and secretary of its Volunteer Service Bureau.

So intensely was this war felt that even the Buffalo Junk Peddlers' Association, composed of older and less Americanized Jews, did its bit. At the suggestion of Isadore Fineberg, these determined men blitzkrieged the city for one whole day in 200 vehicles of all sorts, collected 300 tons of scrap, and turned $4,000 over to funds devoted to public purposes.[102]

When we turn our attention to those who valiantly served and to those who "gave the last full measure of devotion," we find the task of the historian very difficult indeed. Mordecai Myers was a lone figure on the Niagara Frontier in 1812; Marcus Flintrowitz was the only Buffalo Jew in the Mexican War. In the Civil and Spanish American Wars, the number of Jewish participants was relatively small and all could be accounted for. Even in 1917-1918, the number of Buffalo Jews who participated was manageable. But in World War II, the numbers who participated were so great that individual attention even to those with exceptional service records cannot always be given. Despite the utmost care, many an unsung hero whose name did not come to light will be unintentionally slighted. All in all, over half a million American Jewish men and women rallied to the colors. All casualties—dead, wounded, captured, lost in action—amounted to 35,157, and citations for valor went to more than 36,000. We have no exact figures for participation by Buffalo Jews, but we do know that by May, 1944, 2,182 Buffalo Jewish men and women were in service, and sixteen had already been killed or lost.[103]

Of the many physicians who answered the call of their country, some achieved outstanding records. Dr. Hiram S. Yellen, who had received his medical degree just in time to see 1918 service as a first lieutenant, was recalled in 1940. For a time he was chief of surgical services at Fort Hancock. Shortly before that fateful December 7, 1941, he was sent to Kodiak, Alaska, where he helped establish the base hospital at Fort Greeley. When the casualties were brought in from the Attu campaign, Dr. Yellen had his hospital ready to treat them. By 1943, Dr. Yellen was a full colonel and was a veteran of the Kiska campaign of the Aleutians. He subsequently was shipped to southern England where he was in charge of the 103rd General Hospital, the largest of its kind in that area. General Eisenhower decorated him with the Legion of Merit and later Governor Dewey conferred the State Distinguished Service Cross on him.

One doctor who did not come to this area until after the war had a most interesting service record. Dr. Theodore Bronk, head pathologist at Mount St. Mary's Hospital, Niagara Falls, was a first lieutenant at Camp McKinley in the Philippines on December 7, 1941. He was captured on April 12, 1941, and survived the horrible Death March from Bataan. Held prisoner in the Philippines until 1944, he was rarely allowed to give the medical aid so sorely needed by his fellow prisoners. Dr. Bronk was taken to Camp 17 near Mogi, Japan, located just across the bay from Nagasaki. There he witnessed the dropping of the second atomic bomb in August 1945.[104]

Dr. John J. Maisel, a local internist, entered the army as a major in 1942. In Europe, he served with the forces that liberated some concentration camp victims. He reported that many Jews died despite immediate medical treatment, so bad was their condition. Dr. Maisel kept a prayer book in his pocket and frequently went from treatment of the sick to read the burial service at mass graves, for there was no rabbi with his unit. Dr. Allen S. Morris, the well-known Buffalo practitioner, died of natural causes in a southern army camp. Other Buffalo Jewish physicians whose military service demands special mention include Dr. Benjamin E. Obletz, one of the city's leading orthopedists, and Dr. Irving Hyman, a distinguished neurologist.

It is almost impossible to ascertain the number of Jewish youths of Buffalo that fell from 1941 to 1945. The synagogue plaques provide a partial clue. Beth Zion's marker carries the names of 340 men and women.

Private Morris M. Strauss, son of Mr. and Mrs. Hyman Strauss, fell on Washington's Birthday, 1943, as Eisenhower's troops tried to wipe out enemy resistance in Tunisia. The following year, as the scene of activity was transferred to Europe, Lieutenant Joseph Pugash lost his life in the amphibious operations that preceded D Day.

John Guggenheimer and Joseph Bernhardt of Beth Zion died in service. Sergeant Bruce Malkinson of Temple Emanu-El was shot down over the South Pacific and Philip Bunis was killed while on bivouac duty. Air Force Lieutenant August L. Goldenberg was reported missing in action in the Sicilian campaign of 1943. Lieutenant Milton I. Fineberg, formerly with the Buffalo *Evening News,* was killed at Luzon on June 16, 1943. His wife, Beatrice, subsequently married the erudite Buffalo-born historian Richard Hofstadter. Private Albert Alt, aged 21, fell during the Battle of the Bulge, December 19, 1944, and Private Louis Leifer was killed in France a few months thereafter. In May 1945, came the sad news that Lieutenant Hyman Markel, son of the aged, infirm and saintly rabbi of the Pine Street Shul, died of wounds received in the Italian campaign. It was only after the war that the family of Private Harry F. Markson was notified that he had fallen in the Italian fighting. Corporal Louis

Garborsky also lost his life in Italy. Private Edward Kasnachey was killed in action, and Private Robert J. Feinberg died in service on July 18, 1945. Albert Konikoff and Norman Goldberg fell in battle. Private Morris H. Barstein, who had previously been twice decorated, was killed on Leyte, November 8, 1944. Morris, the only son of Mr. and Mrs. Max Barstein, fell while attending the wounded as a member of a Medical Corps attached to General Douglas MacArthur's invading army.

Each Friday, the community followed the service careers of its men in the weekly *Review* column, "With Buffalo Jewish Boys in the Service." There they read of the wounds received by Privates Hyman Finkelstein and Harry S. Taub in Germany. They learned, too, how Private Kurt Klein (no relative of the lieutenant of the same name of *All But My Life* fame) was wounded in the Marshall Islands and recovered to receive two additional wounds in the furious fighting which took place around Leyte. The *Review* also reported that Corporal David M. Garelick, son of Reverend Samuel Garelick, was wounded at Anzio and that Sergeant Jerome H. Shapiro was among those hospitalized during the final Nazi lunge in the last days of the European war.[106]

It was in this crucial Battle of the Bulge that the Nazis captured and shot Staff Sergeant Kurt R. Jacobs of the Intelligence Division of the American army. Jacobs, born in Berlin, had come to Buffalo after his flight from Hitler's Germany. His body was subsequently recovered by the Yanks as they hurled the enemy eastward into Germany. Somewhat similar to the Jacobs case, was that of Flight Navigator Merle S. Wood, one of nine Air Force men whose B-29 was shot down over Kiel, Germany. All the men, including Lieutenant Wood, bailed out successfully. His eight non-Jewish comrades became P.O.W.s and were eventually liberated; Wood was never heard from again.[107]

These were the Jewish lads who made sacrifices, great and small, to return human freedom and dignity to a world that had seen such concepts taunted, abused and destroyed. Those who suffered and died in the invasion of "Fortress Europa" were especially ironic symbols, for they poured their blood back upon the very soil from which their ancestors had fled to the congenial shores of the United States. It was almost as if these American Jews, in making these costly sacrifices, were assuring their six million slain brethren that, though the slaughter had been frightful, Hitler had not reached his ultimate goal, for there was hope in the future of our world for the remnant of the people that he had set out to destroy.

The decoration and awards earned by Jewish soldiers from Buffalo are almost countless. At best we can merely sketch the circumstances of some of them. Sergeant Daniel J. Cohen, a veteran of fifty Air Force missions, received the Distinguished Flying Cross. Sergeant Eugene Schultz's work as a medical corps man in Burma was brought to the attention of his superiors, and Private Julius Kramer was decorated for bravery in General MacArthur's celebrated "return" to the Philippines. The Soldier's Medal for heroic action outside the field of combat went to Sergeant Harvey W. Morrison; and Sergeant Robert N. Rosen, already previously decorated, received an Oak Leaf Cluster. The Purple Heart, given to servicemen wounded in battle, was bestowed upon Sergeant Raymond L. Wolffe; and Private Daniel Bookbinder made the *Review's* headlines when he survived the rigors of a Nazi prison camp. The Bronze Star Medal for meritorious or heroic achievement was given to a number of Buffalo Jewish soldiers, including Private Irving N. Rosen who helped capture a German general. Silver Star medals, for gallantry in action, were pinned upon Charles R. Sanders and Robert Elpert.[108] Perhaps the most decorated warriors of our group were Harrison G. Swados and Sanford M. Satuloff. Sergeant Swados received the Purple Heart, a Bronze Star with Oak Leaf Cluster and eventually a Silver Star. Lieutenant Satuloff of the 441st Anti-Aircraft Battalion, attached to the 3rd Infantry, paralleled this record except for the award for wounds. Satuloff's battalion won distinction in the fierce battle for Colmar Pocket, a point in France that, under Hitler's orders, was to be held at all costs by a special detachment of S.S. men. When it was taken, Satuloff and his comrades were awarded the Presidential Unit Citation and the French government conferred on these men the red Fourragère.

If space permitted, the list could be embroidered. Lieutenant Colonel Howard F. Beir was said to have been the only American to have had five different sets of flight wings.[109] Major William H. Hartzberg, a seasoned attorney who had served the Naval Intelligence in the first war against Germany, was with the Army Air Force in a similar capacity in the second conflict. Early in 1945, the news reached Buffalo that Bernard Dobosen of the 33rd Armored Division, along with two other United States soldiers, was reported to have been among the first three Americans to penetrate the borders of Germany proper. Later came the welcome news that Sergeant Samuel Fagin, son of the communal leader Max Fagin, was released from a Nazi P.O.W. camp by advancing American soldiers.[110]

Buffalo's Jewish women also did their bit in the armed forces. Sergeant Jeanette E. Garfinkel, who enlisted in 1942, is said to have been the first Buffalo WAC; certain it is that she was the first of her faith from this region of the country.[111] Sara Carrel was a corporal in the Women Marines, and Betty Snyder, of an Emanu-El family, was also in the service. Buffalonians read with interest and concern how Laura Margolis, formerly Executive Director of the Jewish Welfare Society, had been captured by the Japanese while on a mission of mercy for the Joint Distribution Committee. Released by the Tokyo authorities in 1943, Miss Margolis was repatriated with some other non-combatants aboard the Swedish liner "Gripsholm." After a period of rest, her next assignment was to care for the homeless Jews who found a temporary asylum in Franco's Spain.[112]

Every so often the news had a romantic touch. In 1944, Lieutenant Alfred Schwab, serving with the Military Intelligence in Morocco, met and married Helene Ifrah, daughter of the Rabbi and Chief Judge of Casablanca. The new Mrs. Schwab was but one of many Jewish war brides from various parts of the world who added a touch of variety to the unvarying composition of Buffalo Jewry.

Many other more anonymous members of the local Jewish community helped their country parry the Axis thrust. Their deeds of valor and interesting experiences, however, escaped the attention of contemporary journalists and chroniclers, and history can not relate their exploits.

When the guns lay silent and the last troopship had docked, the GIs who returned pinned the ruptured duck in their buttonholes, wore army shirts and chinos mixed with brand new civilian clothes as they took up the threads of life in a greatly changed world. Many of them had left jobs paying $20 or $25 a week and returned to find a booming prosperity. Many others seized the opportunity of the GI Bill of Rights to get an education that they never otherwise would have had; and, thanks to Uncle Sam, many others were able to establish a business or buy a home that would have been beyond their reach. Almost with frenzy, these erstwhile warriors, sick to death of the camp and the field, settled down to American communal living, married the girl next door or the one they found in their wartime travels, and began raising families. They either sought out their old jobs guaranteed to be held for them by law or entered new fields of endeavor. They joined the American Legion, the Veterans of Foreign Wars, the AMVETS, the Catholic War Veterans or the Jewish War Veterans posts. They retired as quickly as possible into a comfortable, secure and contented civilian routine of life.

In Buffalo, there was a local Jewish War Veterans post waiting to welcome the returning soldiers. So many came back that for a brief time there were two local posts, but in the 1950s the rival groups merged as Buffalo Frontier Post #25 of the Jewish War Veterans. As the memories of the war faded, the post dropped to about 275 members with a Ladies' Auxiliary of about 140.[113]

Many recently married GIs had broken the ties with the old neighborhoods and either preferred to settle in the suburbs or were forced to buy homes there, for there had been no new construction in the city during the war and very little of it in the preceding depression decade. Moreover, to many returning veterans, the old familiar streets looked shabby. The postwar tendency toward larger families was also responsible for the move out of the city, for parents with children wanted them to have room to play. With the movement toward the country, business interests, always sensitive to population shifts, were quick to build shopping plazas in suburban areas. Soon, arterial highways were constructed to link the outlying communities with the heart of the city where most husbands worked.*

Locally, many of the younger Jewish people who moved to the suburbs were newcomers, drawn here by war industry and its post-1945 growth. These newer folk never had any emotional roots in the city itself and were somewhat more willing than the natives to cut themselves off from the community proper. For many old residents who had lived in the North Park or East Side area, the temptation was great to break out of the second floor flat and buy a spanking new ranch home in the country. A Federation official characterized this group as men who "in their youth never knew the handle of a lawn mower from the blade, and who are now lavishing hours of tender loving devotion in order to grow a rich verdant lawn in their own back yard." [114] Hence, from various motives, postwar Buffalo sensed a strong movement out of the city in a general northeasterly direction, but it was a multi-faceted spread that failed to concentrate in any single suburb. This fact vexed many farsighted leaders who wished to expand Jewish facilities, for action was often paralyzed because not one of the outlying towns or villages developed a heavy Jewish population. To be sure, high-powered automobiles and express highways linked Kenmore, Tonawanda, Eggertsville, Amherst, Williamsville and Cheektowaga, and a synagogue or Center in one could be used by residents of all. But, said budget-minded opponents of expansion, these same highways also led more quickly and conveniently to present facilities in Buffalo. It was a problem that had never faced Buffalo Jewry before, because all previous shifts had centralized in one direction.

Less than a decade after VJ Day, the Jewish population in suburban Buffalo had grown to such an extent that thirty families petitioned the Federation to study the needs of outlying communities and the proper

---

* Some idea of the suburban growth of Buffalo in the 1950s can be gathered from the following statistics: In 1950, Buffalo was the fifteenth largest city in the nation, with a population of 580,132. Ten years later, because the city limits had not been enlarged, Buffalo was the twentieth largest city, with a population of only 528,387. (New York *Times,* July 31, 1960.) Nevertheless, Erie County grew in the same decade from 899,238 to 1,058,636. According to the Buffalo Chamber of Commerce, the county's growth was mainly the result of a shift in population from Buffalo to its nearer suburbs.

means of meeting them. The Board of Governors responded by setting up a Suburban Needs Committee which promptly began an investigation. It revealed that about 1,400 families, roughly one-fifth of the Jewish population, were residing outside of the city limits. The report pointed out, what everyone knew to be a fact, namely that there was no concentration in any one point, but that a new Jewish section was developing "in a belt stretching like an arc over the northern and eastern part of the city. The area of settlement is eight miles across and several miles deep." [115] To indicate the speed of the shift, the report stated that about one-third of the families studied had been in their new homes for less than a year. The older neighborhoods were rapidly breaking up, but where could forward-looking synagogues locate in the sprawling suburban communities and still be conveniently located to more than a handful of families? This problem was less troublesome for such congregations as Sinai and Beth Am which originated outside of the city and chose central suburban locations, but the older institutions were not willing to risk the loss of membership by failing, in time-honored fashion, to follow their congregants. It was suggested that all the synagogues band together to erect one civic, religious and cultural center with suitable quarters for all; but there was considerable opposition to such a "shopping center" approach to Judaism. Another idea often mooted was the erection of a consolidated suburban religious school; but opposing ideologies and rival congregational interests gave pause to advocates of the plan.

In summing up its report, the Suburban Needs Committee stated its unanimous opinion "that the facts presented call for a prompt and total community approach in order to avoid unnecessary competition and duplication of planning and facilities." [116] The report aroused great interest in the community and resulted in the establishment of a Planning Committee, representing a cross-section of the community. It was felt that action could not be delayed, for although many suburban youngsters were at the time under school age, they would soon be in need of Jewish schooling. After several meetings, the Planning Committee temporarily shelved a proposal for a unified religious school. It was decided, however, that the Federation should provide increased recreational facilities for its suburban constituents, for almost half of the families queried had expressed a strong interest in an annex for the Jewish Center. In 1955, the Center was granted a modest sum in order to experiment with a suburban extension program, and its success resulted in the decision to erect a branch outside of the city limits.[117]

Three years later, the Federation purchased a tract of ground at North Bailey Avenue and Sheridan Drive for the construction of a branch recreational building for the Jewish Center. Meanwhile, some of the older synagogues were also on the move and were anticipating the removal of at least part of their activities to the suburbs. As already noted, Beth Zion constructed a school building on Sweet Home Road, and Beth El built on Sheridan Drive near Eggert Road, while at the same time almost every Emanu-El board meeting had on its agenda the consideration of a new suburban site. By the end of the Eisenhower Era, the shift to the suburbs was virtually a *fait accompli* and Buffalo Jewry was busily engaged in meeting the problems that arose from this trek.

All this ferment was a portent for the good. For several millenia of Jewish history, an inter-play existed between vigorous communal institutions and the creation of a dynamic, purposeful Jewish way of life. The relation between these two forces was reciprocal, for Jews with a strong instinct for survival had, throughout the centuries, forged institutions to insure the perpetuation of their heritage. In due time, these synagogues, schools and communal societies repaid their founders by refreshing the well-springs of Jewish life.

This rule-of-the-thumb pattern for survival, which had worked so long and so well in the Old World, encountered major obstacles when it was carried across the seas. The first of these impediments involved the *time* factor in American-Jewish history. The pioneer Jews to inland America arrived during a century of emancipation and enlightenment. It was an age when, in the Western world, Judaism was being crowded out of men's lives by a new personal freedom that promised so much to so many, and by the competing pressures of a rapidly advancing technologial civilization. Nowhere else in modern Jewish history did the secular ways and learning of the Gentiles have the magnetic pull that they had here in the United States. Moreover, it was an era when the under-pinnings of all faiths were sapped by the nineteenth-century upheaval in scientific and religious thought. Hitherto, the skeptics had been a cloistered minority; henceforth, evolution, Bible criticism and the intricacies of comparative religion were to be encountered on every intellectual front. American Jewry, unlike its older counterparts, could no longer operate merely with the autonomous demand of "Thus saith the Lord." All religions had to adjust to new and unprecedented circumstances; all had to find new rationalizations to justify their existence. The American-Jewish community, however, was doubly handicapped, for the adjustment was impeded by its isolation from older and more mature Jewish centers.

Hence, the second obstacle has to do with *space*. The evanescent New World community was very much separated from Europe until modern liners made an express highway of the Atlantic. The ocean moat was wide and deep and it long isolated America from the European founts of Jewish culture and Jewish learning. We had to go it alone precisely at a time when the challenge to all religions was tremendous and when our own spiritual resources were most meager.[118]

This paucity of adequate leadership, lay and clerical, involves still another factor. For many years there was a sifting process with the more learned and the more pious elements preferring to remain in Europe. It was, generally speaking, the more worldly and the less intensely Jewish who migrated westward. And once in the New World there was another selective process under way, for the more conservative immigrants chose to remain in the settled seaboard area because they did not wish to risk the Jewish future of their children on the cutting edge of the frontier.

Despite all these obstacles, Jewish hinterland communities made fitful but steady progress toward stability and maturity. The first step in Buffalo came on that spring Sunday afternoon in 1847, when a handful of men founded Beth El in a roughly finished room at the Western Hotel. Out of this little acorn, many sturdy oaks grew and flourished. Two decades later, the titanic migration from the Russian Pale threatened, for a spell, community solidarity. In time, however, the newcomers were absorbed and their vibrant energy helped Buffalo Jewry weather the shocks of our turbulent century. Over-optimism would be unjustified in view of present threats to global peace, but it can be confidently said that American communities have, in time-honored fashion, risen to the challenge created by a world-shaking upheaval. If the Cold War can but be kept from becoming hot, tomorrow will witness an even greater day for the Jewish people in Buffalo and elsewhere.

DOCUMENTATION
GLOSSARY
BIBLIOGRAPHY

Documentation

1. Photostat of a sermon delivered by the Reverend Gershom Mendes Seixas, 1814. The original is in the collection of Captain N. Taylor Phillips and the photostat was secured through the courtesy of the American Jewish Historical Society.
2. *Loc. cit.*
3. Quoted in *Publications of the American Jewish Historical Society*, XXVII, 396-397 (1920).
4. *Loc. cit.*
5. Morris U. Schappes (ed.), *A Documentary History of the Jews in the United States, 1654-1875* (New York, 1950), 128.
6. *Ibid.*, 591-592.
   Leon Hühner, "Jews in the War of 1812," *Publications of the American Jewish Historical Society*, XXVI, 173-200 (1918).
7. Lewis F. Allen, "Founding of the City of Ararat on Grand Island—by Mordecai M. Noah," in *Publications of the Buffalo Historical Society*, I, 305-328 (1879).
8. *Loc. cit.*
9. John T. Horton, "Old Erie—The Growth of an American Community," vol. I of John T. Horton *et al.*, *History of Northwestern New York* (New York, 1947), 62.
10. Allen, *loc. cit.*

413

11. Noah's speech is printed in *Publications of the American Jewish Historical Society*, XXI, 229-252 (1913).
12. Buffalo *Emporium*, Sept. 17, 1825.
13. *Ibid.*, Jan. 28, 1826.
14. Allen, *loc. cit.*
15. Edward Hungerford, *Pathway of Empire* (New York, 1935), 189 ff.
16. Samson Falk, "A History of the Israelites of Buffalo," *Publications of the Buffalo Historical Society*, I, 289-304 (1879).
17. *Loc. cit.*
18. From the somewhat scanty statistics cited in Chapter Two, it would seem that the shortage of Jewish women in the early days of the Buffalo community was not as serious as might be expected. It seems sensible to believe, however, that in Buffalo, as elsewhere, the very paucity of numbers made it difficult to find suitable Jewish mates.
19. Horton, *op. cit.*, 147.
20. For information on the growth of Buffalo as a railroad hub, see *ibid.*, 100.
21. *Ibid.*, 143.
22. Thomas S. Cutting, (compiler), *Buffalo City Directory, 1848-1849* (Buffalo, 1848), preface.
23. James S. Buckingham, *America, Historical, Statistic and Descriptive*, (3 vols. London, 1841), III, 13.
24. *Ibid.*, III, 39.
25. Horton, *op. cit.*, 104.
26. *Ibid.*, 84.
27. *Ibid.*, 106, 151.
   Julia F. Snow, *Early Recollections of Buffalo* (Buffalo, 1908), 137. Samuel M. Welch, *Home History. Recollections of Buffalo* (Buffalo, 1891), 44.
28. Horton, *op. cit.*, 115.
29. Roy W. Nagle, *Romance of Buffalo* (Buffalo, 1939), 8.
30. Cadmus M. Wilcox, *History of the Mexican War* (Washington, 1892), 622.
31. Information on Flintrowitz is based on photostats of his enlistment record and documents concerning his pension and that of his widow. These photostats were furnished by the General Services Administration, National Archives and Records Service, Washington, D.C. Some information was also obtained from the state census records of 1860 and 1870, preserved in the office of the clerk of the County of Erie, Buffalo, N. Y.
32. Case 31698, Surrogate's Court of the County of Erie, Erie County Hall, Buffalo. N. Y.

CHAPTER II

ROOTS AND BRANCHES

1. For background on the early German-Jewish emigration to the United States see Mark Wischnitzer, *To Dwell In Safety* (Philadelphia, 1948), 5 ff.; Marcus L. Hansen, *The Atlantic Migration, 1607-1860* (Cambridge, 1941), 139 ff.; Bernard D. Weinryb, "Jewish Immigration and Accommodation to America: Research, Trends, Problems" in Moshe Davis and Isidore S.

Meyer (eds.), *The Writing of American Jewish History* (New York, 1957), 366-403. In his *Adventure in Freedom* (New York, 1954), 46 ff., Professor Oscar Handlin makes the point that conditions in eighteenth-century divided Germany were even worse than later, yet no mass emigration resulted. Handlin therefore believes that the salient factor in this German-Jewish upheaval after 1815 was the coming of the Industrial Revolution which, by loosening the underpinnings of the old agrarian economy, made the Jewish economic position untenable and forced many to leave the villages in which they and their ancestors had lived so long.

2. Hansen, *Atlantic Migration,* 139.
3. *Ibid.*, 150.
4. Wischnitzer, *op. cit.*, 5-6.
5. *Ibid.*, 7.
6. Marcus L. Hansen, *The Immigrant in American History* (Cambridge, 1940), 131.
7. *Ibid.*, 45.
8. *Ibid.*, 50, 52.
9. United States Department of Commerce, *Statistical Abstract of the United States, 1957* (Washington, 1957), 92.
10. *Occident,* II, 373 (October, 1853).
11. Inquiries to the Yivo Institute for Jewish Research, New York, N. Y., on the precise meaning of "Hoch-Polish" have not proven fruitful. However, older Jewish residents of Buffalo still use the word on occasion. As far as the authors have been able to determine, families thus designated came from central-western Poland as this region would have been delineated on a nineteenth-century map. The focal point seems to have been near the Prussian-Polish border.
12. Wischnitzer, *op. cit.*, 28.
13. *Ibid.*, 35, 40.
14. This problem is discussed by the late distinguished sociologist, Louis Wirth, in *The Ghetto* (Chicago, 1928), 146-148.
15. Lee M. Friedman, *Pilgrims in a New Land* (Philadelphia, 1948), 280-288.
16. *Ibid.*, 288.
17. Statement of Mayer Klein, a Chicago Jewish pioneer, quoted in Wirth, *op. cit.*, 154-155.
18. Isaac M. Wise, *Reminiscences* (Cincinnati, 1901), 38.
19. For material on Kohn, and extracts from his diary, see Abram V. Goodman, "An American Jewish Peddler's Diary," *American Jewish Archives,* III, 81-111 (June, 1951).
20. See Salo W. and Jeannette M. Baron, "Palestinian Messengers in America, 1849-1879," *Jewish Social Studies,* V, 115-162; 225-292 (April; July, 1943).
21. This story was told to Selig Adler by his grandmother, Mrs. Catherine Rubenstein, who arrived in Buffalo in 1871. It is confirmed by Mrs. Rubenstein's daughter, Mrs. Joseph G. Adler, who still recalls her mother's frequent mention of the episode.
22. The facts and deductions cited above are based on a study of the 1860 state census records preserved in the office of the clerk of the County of Erie, Buffalo, N. Y.
23. The background of Jewish penetration into the clothing field is told in Lee M. Friedman, *Jewish Pioneers and Patriots* (Philadelphia, 1942), 325 ff.

We have also drawn, for background, on Stuart E. Rosenberg, *The Jewish Community in Rochester, 1843-1925* (New York, 1954), 6-7, 10, 13, 120-123.

24. Friedman, *Jewish Pioneers*, 336.

25. This fact is borne out by listings in *The Commercial Advertiser Directory for the City of Buffalo* (Buffalo, 1855). The clothiers are listed in the appendix under "Business Directory." See also Buffalo *Commercial Advertiser,* September 24, 1860, where an article speaks of the growth of the industry and of the unrest of the local journeymen tailors, then working 84 hours a week for wages ranging from three to four dollars per week.

26. Based on extended conversations with the late Mr. Herman Wile of Buffalo, who came here in the early eighties and was engaged in the men's clothing industry until he retired at an advanced age.

27. We are indebted to Dr. S. Joshua Kohn of Trenton, N. J. and historian of the Jewish Community in Utica, N. Y. for information on the Warner family during their Utica days. Culling his information from Utica city directories of the period, Dr. Kohn finds that Leopold Warner arrived certainly as early as 1850 and about two years later was joined by his brothers, Joseph and John. They were capmakers at 30 Bleecker St., although Leopold was also listed, at times, as a clothing merchant. In the oldest Jewish cemetery in Utica there lies buried a Hanna Warner, an unmarried young woman of 21, who died April 5, 1851. The inscription on the tombstone, copied for us by Dr. Kohn, suggests that she was a sister of Leopold, Joseph and John. Other information on the Warners is derived from Buffalo census records, city directories, and a sketch of Joseph Warner in Mark S. Hubbell (ed.), *Our Police and Our City* (Buffalo, 1893), 547.

28. The Torah presented to Henry Brock when he left Dunkirk was, in 1954, in the possession of a direct descendant, Mr. Joseph L. Brock of Buffalo. Evidently there were other Brocks here at the time, about whom we have little information. On October 25, 1957, Rabbi Elihu Schagrin of Binghamton, N. Y., wrote the authors that he has, in his possession, a festival prayer book printed in Diernfurt in 1780. The flyleaf bears the inscription: "Found in the home of Abraham Brock, Buffalo, July 23, 1856." This book, according to Rabbi Schagrin, came into the possession of a religious functionary in Syracuse who carried it on his travels to Chicago and McGregor, Iowa. This man died in Detroit en route back to Syracuse in 1874 and the book was returned to his survivors whose descendants now live in Binghamton.

29. Isaac A. Wile, *The Jews of Rochester* (Rochester, 1912), 20.

30. These facts and deductions come from a close study of the state census records for 1860. Miss Renate Kaufmann, who made this study while working on the present project, found 239 unmistakable Jewish listings, and broke the figures down according to the following age groups:

Age	Males	Females	Total
Under 14	—	—	106
14-19	19	18	37
20-39	26	31	57
40-59	25	12	37
Over 60	1	1	2
			Total 239

Miss Kaufmann was able to determine place of birth in 90 cases. This sampling, taken for what it is worth, reveals that their countries of birth were:

Germany	38	Russia	3
Poland	29	France	2
United States	8	England	1
Holland	5	Denmark	1
Austria	3		

CHAPTER III
A COMMUNITY EMERGES

1. For a penetrating account of Jewish adjustment to the nineteenth-century American milieu see Hyman B. Grinstein, *The Rise of the Jewish Community of New York, 1654-1860* (Philadelphia, 1945), 4-6.
2. Henry S. Commager, *The American Mind* (New Haven, 1950), 5.
3. Marcus L. Hansen, *The Immigrant in American History* (Cambridge 1940), 5.
4. Grinstein, *op. cit.*, 5. For a good comparison with contemporary Protestant practices, see C. Allyn Russell, *A History of the Fredonia Baptist Church* (Dunkirk, 1955), *passim*.
5. Beth El Minute Book, November 25, 1849. These Minute Books, excluding some volumes for the 1880s, 1890s and the period prior to 1910 which apparently have been lost, are to be found at Temple Beth El, 151 Richmond Avenue, Buffalo, N. Y.
6. *Ibid.*, Dec. 13, 1856.
   Grinstein, *op. cit.*, 227, has some cogent observations on the problems that beset early American congregations in maintaining adequate congregational schools.
7. Beth El Minute Book, August 3, 1856; April 1, 1860.
8. Grinstein, *op. cit.*, 15.
9. *Ibid.*, 465.
10. The above account is based largely on advertisements appearing in the 1850s in various Anglo-Jewish periodicals such as *The Asmonean* (N.Y.); *The Jewish Messenger* (N.Y.); and *The (American) Israelite* (Cincinnati).
11. Beth El Minute Book, May 9, 1847; April 23, 1848; August 12, 1849. Samson Falk, "A History of the Israelites of Buffalo," in *Publications of the Buffalo Historical Society*, I, 289-304 (1879).
12. For information on Noah we have relied on a letter of Eugene D. Hofeller to Martha Morris, March 12, 1952, in the files of the United Jewish Federation of Buffalo, Inc.; on some unidentified newspaper clippings preserved in the Scrapbook of Joseph Desbecker, now in the possession of his daughter, Mrs. Mildred Desbecker Shire, of Buffalo; on Case 16391 Surrogate's Court of the County of Erie in the Erie County Hall; on Falk, *loc. cit.*; and on the Buffalo *Evening News*, November 6, 1932. In addition, we have examined the Noah family Bible which contains some contem-

porary notations and which is also in the possession of Mrs. Shire who is descended from Michael W. Noah.

13. A good account of these and other early community problems is in Jeremiah J. Berman, "The Trend in Jewish Religious Observance in Mid-Nineteenth Century America," in *Publications of the American Jewish Historical Society,* XXXVII, 31-53 (1947).

14. Jeremiah J. Berman, *Shehitah* (New York, 1941), 359-362. The points made by Rabbi Berman are amply illustrated in the early Minute Books of Beth El.

15. Information on the procurement of and prices for various articles used on the different festivals is in the Beth El Minute Books for January 20, 1850; March 5, 1854; November 6, 1864; October 3, 1865.

16. Louis Wirth, *The Ghetto* (Chicago, 1928), 140.
    For information on early American-Jewish burial practices see Grinstein, *op. cit.,* 317.

17. William Hodge, "Buffalo Cemeteries," in *Publications of the Buffalo Historical Society,* I, 49-5 (1879).

18. Buffalo *Evening News,* January 15, 1947.

19. Mr. Leon I. Schulgasser, a local attorney, was kind enough to use his professional knowledge to prepare a brief for us untangling the records of these transactions from the Libers of Deeds in the office of the clerk of the County of Erie, Buffalo, N. Y.

20. Beth El Minute Book, April 27, 1851.

21. *Ibid.,* September 27, 1853.

22. The Jacobsohn cemetery, after the dissolution of the society of that name, was turned over to Congregation Beth Zion (later Temple Beth Zion). According to the Beth Zion Minute Book of June 7, 1868, part of the land was leased for ten years to Henry Weil provided that he fence in the graves. In 1887, Beth Zion began the move to rebury the remains in the old cemetery in Beth Zion's Pine Ridge Road cemetery. This was done in April, 1893, and the land was sold for $5,250 to Abraham Oppenheimer and Theodore Hofeller. In petitioning for the court's permission to sell the parcel of land, Beth Zion's attorneys described it as being on the east side of Fillmore Ave., 72 feet south of Fillmore and Sycamore, running south along the east line of Fillmore about 50 feet and then east in a line parallel with the north line of Broadway to the west line of Mills St. (Corporation Box 14330 in the office of the clerk of the County of Erie, Buffalo, N. Y.) Beth El held on to its original cemetery until 1907. On July 7 of that year, Attorney Emil Rubenstein petitioned the court that Beth El be allowed to "sell all of its irregular lot on Stanislaus Street, now known as the Jaconson [*sic*] Cemetery." (Corporation Box 4078 in the office of the clerk of the County of Erie, Buffalo, N. Y.) Even to the final disposition of the Beth El cemetery, some confusion about these two pieces of land existed.

23. Falk, *loc. cit.*
    Grinstein, *op. cit.,* 103 ff. has good background material on the nature and origins of these early mutual-benefit societies.

24. *The Occident,* IX, 382 (October, 1851).

25. Buffalo *Express,* January 22, 1916; unidentified newspaper clippings from the Scrapbook of Joseph Desbecker.

26. Corporation Box 9511 in the office of the clerk of the County of Erie, Buffalo, N. Y.
    Further information on the Jacobsohn Society was obtained from unidentified newspaper clippings in the Scrapbook of Matilda Brock, in 1954 in the possession of the late Miss Bertha M. Brock of Buffalo. The date of the incorporation of the Jacobsohn Society was April 19, 1851, but it had already been in existence almost 4 years.
27. Corporation Box 6779 in the office of the clerk of the County of Erie, Buffalo, N. Y.
28. Buffalo *Evening News,* September 6, 1910; Buffalo *Express,* June 3, 1867; for the will of Rachel Van Baalen Boasberg, which begins "In the Name of God, Amen," see Case 27638, Surrogate's Court of the County of Erie in Erie County Hall, Buffalo, N. Y.
29. Corporation Box 11780 in the office of the clerk of the County of Erie, Buffalo, N. Y.
30. Falk, *loc. cit.;* Beth El Minute Book, May 9, 1847; April 23, 1848; *The Occident,* V, 275 (August, 1947); Buffalo *Evening News,* January 15, 1947; Reuben J. Magil, "History of Temple Beth El," in *Official Souvenir History,* published in connection with Temple Beth El Ball (Buffalo, February 27, 1935), 6-9; *Temple Beth El's First Century: Centennial Souvenir Book* (Buffalo, 1947), 11-13.
31. Beth El Minute Book, December 8, 1850; the records of the state census of 1850 in the office of the clerk of the County of Erie, Buffalo, give Slatsky's birth place as Germany and the date of his birth as 1795; Montefiore Lodge #70, Minute Book, February 22, 1875; Beth Zion Minute Book, January 9, 1876; Buffalo *Commercial Advertiser,* December 18, 1875. Slatsky's story is so confused in the records that it is not clear if he was called Isaac Moses or Moses Isaac Slatsky.
32. Falk, *loc. cit.*
33. Beth El Minute Book, April 23, 1848; Salo W. and Jeannette M. Baron, "Palestinian Messengers in America 1849-1879," *Jewish Social Studies,* V, 115-162; 225-292 (April; July, 1943).
34. Beth El Minute Book, July 23, 1848.
35. *Ibid.,* July 22, 1847.
36. *Ibid.,* September 3, 1848; September 10, 1848.
37. *Ibid.,* February 18, 1849; unidentified newspaper clipping in the Scrapbook of Matilda Brock; Magil, *loc. cit.,* 6; *The Occident,* IX, 383 (September, 1851).
38. Beth El Minute Book, December 31, 1848; February 6, 1849; February 6, 1850; November 13, 1850; August 31, 1862.
39. *Ibid.,* July 29, 1850; Mark Moritz to Millard Fillmore, July 19, 1850. Millard Fillmore Papers, V, 152, Buffalo Historical Society.
40. Beth El Minute Book, July 21, 1850; July 29, 1850; *The Asmonean,* II, 108 (July 26, 1850); Buffalo *Commercial Advertiser,* July 27, 1850; *The Occident,* VIII, 259 (August, 1850).
41. Beth El Minute Book, January 20, 1850.
42. *Ibid.,* July 15, 1850.
43. What little we know of the origins of Congregation Beth Zion in 1850 comes from Falk, *loc. cit.,* and an unidentified newspaper clipping, dated January 3, 1925, in the Scrapbook of Joseph Desbecker.

44. *Ibid.;* See also *American Jewish Review,* September 10, 1920; H. Perry Smith (ed.), *History of the City of Buffalo and Erie County* (2 vols., Syracuse, 1884), II, 307.

45. Falk, *loc. cit.*

46. In 1954, Miss Miriam Rosenau, daughter of Sol Rosenau, a member of Congregation Beth Zion and later a founder of Temple Beth Zion, allowed Selig Adler to examine this prayer book which is in her possession.

47. Falk, *loc. cit.;* Jacques J. Lyon and Abraham De Sola, *A Jewish Calendar for Fifty Years* (Montreal, 1854), 154.

48. *The Occident,* IX, 382-383 (September, 1851).

49. Beth El Minute Book, August 27, 1860.

50. Falk, *loc. cit.*

51. These by-laws are dated May 1, 1853, but presumably the decision to have them drawn up was taken on February 13th.

52. A full set of these by-laws is in the Beth El Minute Book in the space following the proceedings of the meeting of February 13, 1853. Twenty-two members signed these by-laws, evidently on May 1st. All were able to attach their signatures in English, except one Abraham Levy who made his mark.

53. Beth El Minute Book, October 5, 1853.

54. *Ibid.,* August 28, 1853.

55. *The Occident,* XIII, 407 (November, 1855).

56. Quoted in Max J. Kohler, "Judah Touro, Merchant and Philanthropist," in *Publications of the American Jewish Historical Society,* XIII, 93-111 (1905).

57. These tablets evidently were placed on the wall of the Pearl St. synagogue and removed, in 1874, to Beth El's new building on Elm Street. For many years after Beth El moved to its present site on Richmond Ave., they were forgotten. In the 1930s, however, they were refurbished and placed in a prominent place at the main entrance to the sanctuary.

58. Beth El Minute Book, April 5, 1854.

59. *Ibid.,* May 26, 1856.

60. *Ibid.,* June 10, 1856.

61. *Ibid.,* April 4, 1858. The proceedings are so confused that it is impossible to determine Altman's motives in withholding the money. The rest of the legacy, $388, was used to pay outstanding debts of the congregation.

62. Benjamin Rabinowitz, "The Young Men's Hebrew Associations, 1854-1913," in *Publications of the American Jewish Historical Society,* No. 37, 221-326 (1947).

63. *The Occident,* XVI, 454 (December, 1858). For personal recollections of Mr. Bergman we have relied on the memories of the late Judge Cecil B. Wiener and Miss Bertha M. Brock of Buffalo.

64. *The Occident,* XVI, 454 (December, 1858).

65. Falk, *loc. cit.*

66. Beth El Minute Book, April 17, 1862.

67. *Ibid.,* September 24, 1862.

CHAPTER IV

WAR, PROSPERITY, AND REFORM

1. John T. Horton, "Old Erie—The Growth of an American Community,"
   vol. I of John T. Horton et al., *History of Northwestern New York* (New
   York, 1947), 180-181; 188-193.
2. James G. Randall, *The Civil War and Reconstruction* (Boston, 1937), 411.
3. Horton, *op. cit.*, 177-178.
4. Photostat of Marcus's "Declaration For Invalid Pension," dated May 5,
   1904, furnished by the General Services Administration, National Archives
   and Records Service, Washington, D.C.
5. *Ibid.*
6. For information on Marcus we have relied upon, in addition to photostats
   concerning his military record and pension history, an unidentified newspaper clipping in the possession of Mrs. Hiram Marcus of Buffalo; an interview between the late Miss Bertha M. Brock and Selig Adler; and
   records of the state census of 1870 preserved in the office of the clerk of
   the County of Erie, Buffalo, N.Y.
7. The story of Oppenheimer's war record is based on conversations between
   Selig Adler and Nathan Oppenheimer, Jr., of Buffalo. There is no documentary evidence to buttress the family's statement, but there is also no
   good reason to deny the statements of all his surviving grandchildren. We
   found additional information on Oppenheimer, but nothing on his war
   record, in the *Hebrew Standard,* Nov. 16, 1906; in his will, Case 52996
   Surrogate's Court of the County of Erie in Erie County Hall, Buffalo; in
   a letter from Marjorie C. Frost of Nunda, N.Y. to Pierson L. Cohen, October 28, 1954.
8. Frederick D. Bidwell (comp.), *History of the Forty-ninth New York Volunteers* (Albany, 1916), 283.
   Information on Rosenau is from material in the Scrapbook of Miss Anne
   Rodell, Buffalo. For the Noah story we found information in the Scrapbook
   of Mrs. Mildred Desbecker Shire of Buffalo.
9. We have pieced this information together from records of a local census of
   1865 preserved in the office of the clerk of the County of Erie, Buffalo;
   from the Scrapbook of Stuart J. Goldberg of Buffalo who previously had
   run down information on Simon Jacobs; from a conversation between the
   late Daniel W. Barmon of Buffalo and Selig Adler, August 26, 1954, about
   George Rosenberg; from a study of Jewish names in the original muster
   rolls of various regiments recruited in Buffalo. This latter study was made
   by Miss Renate Kaufmann with the help of the Buffalo Historical Society.
10. Records of the local census of 1865 for Ward 5, District 1, p. 119, pre-
    served in the office of the clerk of the County of Erie, Buffalo.
11. Buffalo *Times,* January 27, 1911.
12. *Buffalo Jewish Review,* April 28, 1933, April 26, 1935, April 24, 1936;
    Buffalo *Courier-Express,* April 19, 1936.
13. See Horton, *op. cit.*, 185-186.
14. Income tax lists for 1863 are to be found in the Buffalo *Courier,* February

18, 1865; information on the Altman fire is from the Buffalo *Commercial Advertiser,* January 20, 1866.

15. H. Perry Smith (ed.), *History of the City of Buffalo and Erie County* (2 vols. Syracuse, 1884), II, 253-254.

16. Buffalo *Courier,* February 18, 1865; Buffalo *Times,* April 20, 1910.

17. Samson Falk, "A History of the Israelites of Buffalo," in *Publications of the Buffalo Historical Society,* I, 289-304 (1879).

18. Stuart E. Rosenberg, *The Jewish Community in Rochester 1843-1925* (New York, 1954), 16-17.

19. Buffalo *Commercial Advertiser,* April 18, 1865; April 20, 1865; April 28, 1865.

20. Hyman B. Grinstein, *The Rise of the Jewish Community of New York, 1654-1860* (Philadelphia, 1945), 352-358; Rosenberg, *op. cit.,* 26 ff.

21. Grinstein, *op. cit.,* 369.

22. *The (American) Israelite,* VIII (April 11, 1862), 324.

23. *The Occident,* XII (January, 1855), 525.

24. *The (American) Israelite,* X (June 24, 1864), 413.

25. *Ibid.,* VIII (June 20, 1862), 406.

26. *Ibid.,* VII (July 27, 1860), 30; (April 12, 1861), 322.

27. *Ibid.,* VII (July 27, 1860), 30.

28. Marcus L. Hansen, *The Atlantic Migration,* 1607-1860 (Cambridge, 1941), 306.

29. Salo W. and Jeannette M. Baron, "Palestinian Messengers in America, 1849-1879," *Jewish Social Studies,* V (April; July, 1943), 115-162; 225-292.

30. Most of our knowledge of this ghost congregation comes from a study of its cemetery transactions in the Liber of Deeds, 210, p. 215, in the office of the clerk of the County of Erie, Buffalo.

31. *The (American) Israelite,* VIII (January 17, 1862), 231; (June 20, 1862), 406.

32. See Falk, *loc. cit.*

33. Buffalo *Express,* December 16, 1900; records of the state censuses of 1860 and 1870 and Levyn's will, Case 37635 Surrogate's Court of the County of Erie in Erie County Hall, Buffalo; interview between Selig Adler and Judge Cecil B. Wiener of Buffalo, June 24, 1954; Scrapbook of Mrs. Mildred Desbecker Shire of Buffalo, a granddaughter of Mr. Levyn.
There are records of some other children: Dorina Evelyn, who changed her name to Lewyn; Michael William Levyn, who probably died in childhood; Bertha Levyn Meltzer. The youngest child, Sadie Levyn Morse, died in 1943 at the age of 65.

34. Beth Zion Minute Book, January 1, 1911; *Buffalo Jewish Review,* July 6, 1928. Keiser's first wife, Augusta, died June 29, 1858, at the age of 21. Evidently her remains were subsequently removed to the Beth Zion cemetery on Pine Ridge Road and her resting place is marked by a stone erected by her son, August Keiser. Leopold Warner remarried in the 1860s. His second wife, Jette Haber (1832-1897) was born in Baden.

35. Beth Zion Minute Book, September 7, 1863. Buffalo *Times,* January 22, 1911.

36. Buffalo *Express,* January 19, 1923, January 20, 1923; interview between Selig Adler and Sol Rosenau's daughter, Miss Miriam Rosenau of Buffalo,

July 29, 1954; Beth Zion Minute Book, October 4, 1903; September 9, 1920; state census of 1860, *loc. cit.*

37. Beth Zion Minute Book, September 1863. The day of the month is not indicated, but internal evidence would lead one to believe that it was held shortly before Rosh Hashana, September 14-15, 1863.

38. *The (American) Israelite,* X (October 2, 1863), 106.
Buffalo *Comercial Advertiser,* September 2, 1863.

39. *The (American) Israelite,* X (October 9, 1863), describes the local situation in Buffalo in detail.

40. *Ibid.;* Falk, *loc. cit.;* Buffalo *Commercial Advertiser,* April 18, 1865.

41. *The (American) Israelite,* X (April 15, 1864), 334.

42. The essential connection between Congregation Beth Zion and Temple Beth Zion is apparent from a close reading of Rabbi Falk's account cited above. This continuity is also apparent from a letter of Louis M. Brock to Rabbi Isaac M. Wise, published in *The (American) Israelite,* XI (December 16, 1864), 197. To be sure, Temple Beth Zion decided, November 6, 1864, to seek new incorporation (see Corporation Box 14330 in the office of the clerk of the County of Erie, Buffalo), but such practice was common for all congregations undergoing major and sometimes even minor structural changes.

43. Frances M. Wolcott, *Heritage of Years; Kaleidoscopic Memories* (New York, 1902), 13.

44. Buffalo *Commercial Advertiser,* May 27, 1865.

45. Quoted in *The (American) Israelite,* XI (December 16, 1864), 197.

46. Corporation Box 967; volumes of Liber of Deeds, 241: 434; 347: 474 in the office of the clerk of the County of Erie, Buffalo; Beth Zion Minute Book, August 18, 1874, September 6, 1874; Falk, *loc. cit.;* Buffalo *Evening News,* September 12, 1890.
In 1857, the Jacobsohn Society deeded its cemetery to the Orthodox Congregation Beth Zion. In 1862 this congregation bought some land on Pine Ridge Road from George and Maria Freund and later in this year it acquired the adjacent cemetery lands of the abortive Shearith Israel United Congregation. In 1865, these combined parcels of land were divided between the Reform Beth Zion and the group calling itself Anshe Emes Beth Zion. At the same time, title to the Jacobsohn cemetery in the Fillmore-Broadway area was transferred to Temple Beth Zion. The surviving members of Anshe Emes Beth Zion who deeded the congregation's cemetery lands to Temple Beth Zion in 1874 were Aaron and Simon Weil, Henry Wertheimer and William Southeimer.

47. Buffalo *Commercial Advertiser,* May 26, 1865; Buffalo *Courier,* May 27, 1865. The Buffalo Public Library has a copy of the program of the day which was printed in both German and English.

48. Buffalo *Courier,* May 27, 1865; *The (American) Israelite,* XI (February 17, 1865), 27; (June 9, 1865), 397.

49. United States Department of Commerce, *Statistical Abstract of the United States, 1957* (Washington, 1957), 92.

50. Quoted in *The (American) Israelite,* X (August 21, 1863), 59.

51. Buffalo *Times,* January 29, 1911.
Interview between Selig Adler and the late Daniel W. Barmon of Buffalo (Nicholas Hyman's grandson), August 26, 1954.

Nicholas Hyman's son, Abraham N. (1855-1921), was born in Buffalo. He married Rebecca, daughter of Samuel Bennett who died in Buffalo in 1865. Eventually A. N. Hyman went into business with his father under the firm-name of N. Hyman & Co.

52. Beth El Minute Book, March 7, 1865; April 16, 1865. Brock had been elected president of Beth El, April 24, 1864, and many synagogue meetings are recorded as having been held in his place of business.

53. Warrensky's granddaughter, Mrs. Roland May of Buffalo, gave this information to Selig Adler in an interview, June 18, 1954. Much of our information on Warrensky is based on this interview.

54. Beth El Minute Book, August 4, 1864; March 7, 1865.

55. To reconstruct the important, but forgotten story of Warrensky, we have relied on various items in the Beth El Minute Books for the years he served the congregation; on the interview with his granddaughter cited above; on the Buffalo *Times,* January 10, 1911; for a general account of the Fenian incident, see Merton M. Wilner, *Niagara Frontier* (4 vols. Chicago, 1931), I, 461 ff.

56. Buffalo *Express,* January 26, 1865; Buffalo *Commercial Advertiser,* February 7, 1865; unidentified newspaper clippings in the Scrapbook of Miss Anne Rodell, Buffalo.

57. Beth El Minute Book, February 5, 1865; February 6, 1865; March 12, 1865; April 16, 1865.

58. *Ibid.,* May 17, 1864.

59. *Ibid.,* May 5, 1864.

60. Baron and Baron, "Palestinian Messengers in America," *loc. cit.* For light on Greenberg, who seems to have been an important man in the community, we found some information in the Buffalo *Times,* February 9, 1911; there is some information of a personal nature in the state census records of 1860, *loc. cit.,* Buffalo; and the Minute Book of Beth El has occasional helpful information.

61. Falk, *loc. cit.*

62. Buffalo *Times,* February 9, 1911.

63. Much of our information on the early days of B'rith Sholem comes from a dictated statement, evidently prepared by Israel I. Friedlander, who came to Buffalo in 1870 and died in 1925. We are indebted to Mr. Max M. Yellen of Buffalo for the discovery of this valuable source.

64. Baron and Baron, "Palestinian Messengers in America," *loc. cit.*

65. See fn. 63, above.

66. Beth Zion Minute Book, July 4, 1875.

CHAPTER V

THE GILDED AGE

1. This application book, in the custody of the Secretary of Montefiore Lodge #70, Buffalo, runs from 1866 to 1910. In these 44 years, 223 applications were filed.

2. Samson Falk, "A History of the Israelites of Buffalo," in *Publications of the*

Buffalo Historical Society, I, 289-304 (1879); Buffalo *Times,* April 18, 1910; interview between Selig Adler and the late Mr. Herman Wile of Buffalo, August 5, 1954.

3. Quoted in Lee M. Friedman, *Pilgrims in a New Land* (Philadelphia, 1948), 291.

4. Oscar Handlin, *Adventure in Freedom* (New York, 1954), 87.

5. H. Perry Smith (ed.), *History of the City of Buffalo and Erie County* (2 vols., Syracuse, 1884), II, 253 ff.

6. Falk, *loc. cit.;* Buffalo *Express,* Nov. 12, 1881; Buffalo *Courier,* Nov. 12, 1881; state census of 1870, preserved in the office of the clerk of the County of Erie, Buffalo; Stuart E. Rosenberg, *The Jewish Community in Rochester 1843-1925* (New York, 1954), 5; 246, fn. 14; 249, fn. 3.

7. Buffalo *Commercial Advertiser,* April 17, 1871; state censuses of 1860 and 1870, *loc. cit.;* Montefiore Lodge #70 Minute Book, April 17, 1871; Beth Zion Minute Book, April 16, 1871.

8. Cases 10392, 10397, 10410, Surrogate's Court of the County of Erie, Erie County Hall, Buffalo; interview between Selig Adler and Joseph Rothschild of Buffalo, August 5, 1954. The prayer book mentioned was acquired by Selig Adler from Temple Beth Zion in 1938.

9. Interview between Selig Adler and Herman Wile, August 5, 1954; George M. Bailey, *Illustrated Buffalo: The Queen City of the Lakes* (New York, 1890), 111.

10. Buffalo *Express, The City of Buffalo: Its History and Institutions with Illustrated Sketches of its Industries and Commerce and some of its Citizens* (Buffalo, 1888), *passim.*

11. Buffalo *Times,* February 8, 1911; Alfred F. Cohen to Selig Adler, August 20, 1957. According to Mr. Alfred F. Cohen, his grandfather erected the Abraham F. Cohen block on Seneca St. near Louisiana. The latter's oldest son, Ovid, was a pioneer here in the jewelry business in a store called the Emporium which stood on the present site of the Marine Trust Company's bank at Main and Seneca.

12. Buffalo *Times,* May 31, 1909; interview between Selig Adler and the late Daniel W. Barmon of Buffalo, August 26, 1954. Originally the concern, now Barmon Bros. Co., Inc., was called the Electric Wrapper Co.

13. Irving A. Mandel, "Attitude of the American Jewish Community Toward East-European Immigration," *American Jewish Archives,* III, 11-36 (June, 1950).

14. See *The (American) Israelite* (May 19, 1882), 370.

15. Quoted in Mandel, *loc. cit.*

16. Montefiore Lodge #70 Minute Book, July 1, 1872; January 13, 1873; May 2, 1875; April 17, 1877; March 8, 1880.

17. *The (American) Israelite* (December 19, 1879), 2.

18. Quoted in Hyman B. Grinstein, *The Rise of the Jewish Community of New York, 1654-1860* (Philadelphia, 1945), 109.

19. Printed material distributed by District #1, B'nai B'rith, and attached to the Minute Book of Montefiore Lodge #70 for the year 1884. The dispute started when the eighth council of the Union of American Hebrew Congregations asked various lodges for aid.

20. Application book of Montefiore Lodge #70; *The (American) Israelite,* XII (March 2, 1866), 277.

21. Montefiore Lodge #70 Minute Book, October 9, 1871.
22. *Ibid.*, May 4, 1874.
23. *Ibid.*, November 13, 1876.
24. *Ibid.*, February 9, 1875.
25. *Report of the Executive Committee of the Constitution Grand Lodge, I.O.B.B., 1891-1892* (New York, 1892), 5-8.
    The 1911 situation is discussed in a similar report of the Grand Lodge for 1911-1912, p. 11.
26. Based upon material distributed by District #1 in 1915, found with the old Minute Books.
27. Montefiore Lodge #70 Minute Book, February 23, 1880; Buffalo *Express*, November 13, 1894; interview between Selig Adler and Miss Cecil B. Wiener of Buffalo, August 16, 1954.
28. Our efforts to uncover the intimate history of these lesser known orders in Buffalo have been largely fruitless. We have had to depend upon scattered references to their existence in the synagogue Minute Books and in the records of Montefiore Lodge #70. *The American Jewish Year Book 1900-1901* (Philadelphia, 1900), 113-163, has been helpful in giving us information about these organizations' activities in Buffalo at the turn of the present century.
29. Falk, *loc. cit.*
30. *American Hebrew*, II, 135 (May 7, 1880).
31. *The (American) Israelite* (January 16, 1880), 3.
32. *Ibid.*, (November 19, 1880), 163.
33. *Ibid.*, (May 19, 1882), 370.
34. Rosenberg, *op. cit.*, 200.
35. Mark S. Hubbell (ed.), *Our Police and Our City* (Buffalo, 1893), 192.
36. John T. Horton, "Old Erie—The Growth of an American Community," vol. I of John T. Horton *et al.*, *History of Northwestern New York* (New York, 1947). 62.
37. Rosenberg, *op. cit.*, 109.
38. Inasmuch as the records, if any were kept, of these clubs have been lost, we know very little about them. Such information as has survived comes from occasional Buffalo items in *The (American) Israelite*, a few social scrapbooks that have survived, and the memories of some survivors now in their nineties such as Miss Miriam Rosenau. Falk records that in 1876 the Standard (Social) Club had 52 members.
39. Our information on this wedding is based on unidentified newspaper clippings, and other material preserved in the Scrapbook of Miss Anne Rodell of Buffalo.
40. We also owe this information to Miss Rodell's Scrapbook. This valuable source on the society of the 1880s was preserved by Miss Rodell's aunt, Miss Miriam Rosenau, who was a bridesmaid at the Marcus wedding in 1886 where the ditty quoted was sung.
41. Buffalo *Express*, January 23, 1890.
42. *Proceedings at the Sixth Annual Meeting of the Charity Organization Society of Buffalo embracing Reports of the Council, 1884,* 21. We are indebted to Miss Cecil B. Wiener for a small handbook entitled: *Laws and Regulations of The Hebrew Board of Charities,* printed by Matthews, Northrup & Co. in Buffalo about 1891. Evidently this Board of Charities,

a predecessor of the later city-wide federation of Jewish charities, was formed sometime in the late 1880s.

43. *American Jewish Year Book 1900-1901*, 337; *Buffalo Jewish Review*, May 1, 1925.

The Ladies' Hebrew Benevolent Society, also dating from the 1860s, continued to be active, spending a little over half of the amount annually disbursed by the men's group. In 1883 the older women's division was apparently replaced by the Ladies' Hebrew Charity Association (later known by several other names and finally as the Women's Jewish Benevolent Society). Four of the founders, Mrs. Rebecca Friedman, Mrs. Bertha Levy, Mrs. Paula S. Kaufmann, and Mrs. Aaron Fybush were present when this association celebrated its 42nd anniversary at Beth Zion in 1925.

44. Beth Zion Minute Book, November 4, 1866; April 17, 1870; March 3, 1872.

45. *Ibid.*, September 15, 1867. According to this source the boy was adopted by Henry Brock.

46. *The (American) Israelite* (January 2, 1880), 2; Rosenberg, *op. cit.*, 133 ff.

47. Handbill in the Scrapbook of Matilda Brock, examined while in the possession of the late Miss Bertha M. Brock of Buffalo; *The (American) Israelite* (May 16, 1879), 6; (January 2, 1880), 2.

48. *The (American) Israelite* (May 5, 1882), 358; (October 27, 1882), 148; *American Hebrew*, IX, 91 (January 6, 1882); Rosenberg, *op. cit.*, 134-135.

49. Federated Jewish Charities of Buffalo *Minute Book*, April 17, 1910; Federated Jewish Charities of Buffalo *Year Book, 1914-1915*, 45-46; Rosenberg, *op. cit.*, 223-224.

50. *Buffalo Jewish Review*, November 7, 1924; August 3, 1928.

51. *Proceedings at the Fifth Annual Meeting of the Charity Organization Society of Buffalo embracing Reports of the Council, 1883*, 5.

52. Horton, *op. cit.*, 252.

53. Interview between Selig Adler and Mr. Rosenau's sister, Miriam, July 29, 1954; unidentified newspaper clippings in the Scrapbook of Miss Anne Rodell; Hubbell, *op. cit.*, 767.

54. Beth Zion Minute Book, December 22, 1894; December 14, 1896. In 1895, C.O.S. inaugurated the Church District Plan by which each participating institution was assigned a section of the city to administer non-denominational relief. This system was soon superseded by district committees and volunteers. By 1914 the relief problem had become so complex that C.O.S. was already advocating government assistance to supplement private relief.

55. Horton, *op. cit.*, 252.

56. Beth Zion Minute Book, November 10, 1867.

57. *Ibid.*, June 2, 1872; April 4, 1875; June 6, 1875.

58. Lars G. Sellstedt, *Art in Buffalo* (Buffalo, 1910), 23-25.

59. Interview between Selig Adler and Mr. Roblin, August 26, 1954.

60. *Jewish Messenger*, XXIII, (June 5, 1868), ed. page.

61. *The (American) Israelite*, XIII (Dec. 28, 1866), 6; (May 31, 1867), 6; (March 17, 1882), 298; (May 19, 1882), 370.

62. Falk, *loc. cit.*

63. Frederick Ullman, *Incidents and Events* (n.p., 1939), *passim*.

64. *Hazefirah*, No. 83 (1887), p. 3.

65. Buffalo *Express,* May 17, 1869, September 6, 1880; unidentified newspaper clippings in the possession of the late Miss Bertha M. Brock of Buffalo.

66. For the above mentioned disputes over ritual see Beth Zion Minute Book, April 6, 1867; August 4, 1867; August 30, 1868; October 4, 1868; May 2, 1869.

67. The first absolute indication of the dropping of the second days of the Holidays comes from the Buffalo *Express,* September 30, 1867. From the context one would gather that it had been the practice for some time.

For an enlightening account of reform changes of this period, see Jerome W. Grollman, "The Emergence of Reform Judaism," *American Jewish Archives,* II, 3-14 (January, 1950).

One would gather from the Beth Zion Minute Book, September 17, 1882, that all men must worship there with uncovered heads. Whether or not this was ever enforced is problematical. In the last few decades there has certainly been no objection to the wearing of a skullcap by the occasional visitor who prefers to do so.

68. *The (American) Israelite,* XIII (June 28, 1867), 5.

69. Buffalo *Commercial Advertiser,* Dec. 27, 1886; Buffalo *Express,* December 28, 1886; Beth Zion Minute Book, December 25, 1886.

70. See Grollman, *loc. cit.*

71. A copy of this constitution, adopted October 4, 1868, is in the Beth Zion Minute Book for that date.

72. Beth Zion Minute Book, March 20, 1879; September 1, 1880; March 6, 1881.

73. *Ibid.,* January 5, 1873.

74. Buffalo *Express,* September 3, 1911; Beth Zion Minute Book, October 12, 1896; September 25, 1911.

75. Telephone interview between Selig Adler and the late Rudolph Warner, August 16, 1954; Beth Zion Minute Book, January 4, 1875; *Buffalo Jewish Review,* July 19, 1929.

76. Falk, *loc. cit.;* interviews between Selig Adler and the late Miss Cecil B. Wiener and Miss Bertha M. Brock, July 4, 1954.

77. Buffalo *Evening News,* February 26, 1943.

78. Ullman, *op. cit.,* 20; Montefiore Lodge #70 Minute Book, April 9, 1877, August 11, 1884; Beth Zion Minute Book, October 24, 1886; December 19, 1890; March 2, 1891; September 24, 1891.

79. Beth Zion Minute Book, July 6, 1873; September 14, 1873; June 10, 1874; June 23, 1874; December 6, 1874.

80. Buffalo *Commercial Advertiser,* July 13, 1875; Buffalo *Courier,* July 14, 1875; Buffalo *Express,* July 14, 1875; Montefiore Lodge #70 Minute Book, June 26, 1875.

81. Beth Zion Minute Book, December 2, 1866; September 20, 1873.

82. *Ibid.,* November 14, 1869.

83. This notebook and other material throwing light on the Beth Zion school of the early eighties is in the possession of Dr. S. Albert Levitan of Buffalo. Rabbi Hecht's book was published in Cincinnati in 1882.

84. I. B. Berkson, quoted in Louis L. Gitin, "The Development of a Reform Religious School, Buffalo, New York, 1864-1953" (unpublished Ed.D. dissertation, University of Buffalo, 1954), 59.

85. The information here documented was culled from the Beth Zion School Board Minute Book for the period November 5, 1890-December 2, 1895.
86. Beth Zion Minute Book, February 19, 1871; May 11, 1871.
87. Interview between Selig Adler and Miss Cecil B. Wiener, July 4, 1954.
88. Rosenberg, *op. cit.*, 104.
89. James Parton, "Our Israelitish Brethren," *Atlantic Monthly*, XXVI, 385-403 (1870).
90. Buffalo *Express*, April 9, 1874; August 11, 1874.
    Details of construction of the new synagogue are in the Beth El Minute Book, February 21, 1875; January 1, 1875.
91. Buffalo *Express*, August 15, 1874; Buffalo *Commercial Advertiser*, August 15, 1874; Buffalo *Times*, January 31, 1911.
92. Beth El Minute Book, July 26, 1874.
93. Buffalo *Times*, February 11, 1911; *Buffalo Jewish Review*, January 27, 1922; Buffalo *Evening News*, January 15, 1947.
94. Beth El Minute Book, June 27, 1880.
95. *Ibid.*, October 27, 1878.
96. *Ibid.*, January 17, 1866.
97. In the 1860s, the present Beth El cemetery on Pine Ridge Road was bought to replace the old burial ground near Fillmore and Broadway. The Minute Books for this decade and those that followed it are filled with problems pertaining to both the old and new cemeteries, for both were out of the city and constantly subject to acts of vandalism. Although Jewish law is reluctant to allow disinterment, by 1874 some families began to re-move their dead for reburial in Pine Ridge cemetery. Beth El continued to hold the old cemetery, however, until after 1900, and tried in vain to keep it in some state of good repair.
98. Beth El Minute Book, April 10, 1882, April 16, 1882, September 23, 1882, October 1, 1882; interview between Selig Adler and the late Daniel W. Barmon of Buffalo, August 26, 1954; *Hebrew Standard*, XLIX (November 16, 1906), 9; Buffalo *Times*, February 17, 1911; Buffalo *Express*, January 27, 1926.
99. Beth Zion Minute Book, February 18, 1895.

CHAPTER VI

THE NEW EXODUS

1. Bernard D. Weinryb, "Jewish Immigration and Accommodation to America: Research, Trends, Problems," in Moshe Davis and Isidore S. Meyer (eds.), *The Writing of American Jewish History* (New York, 1957), 366-403; Stuart E. Rosenberg, *The Jewish Community in Rochester 1843-1925* (New York, 1954), 63 ff.
2. Oscar Handlin, *Adventure in Freedom* (New York, 1954), 47.
3. *Ibid.*, 81-82.
4. Cf. Simon Dubnow, *A History of the Jews in Russia and Poland*, III (Phila., 1920), 10.
5. For general background we have drawn heavily upon Mark Wischnitzer,

To Dwell In Safety (Philadelphia, 1948), 37-39, 67-68; and Zosa Szajkowski, "How the Mass Migration to America Began," *Jewish Social
Studies*, IV, 291-310 (October, 1942).

6. Samuel Joseph, *History of the Baron de Hirsch Fund* (pamphlet, n.p.,
   1935), 1-10.
7. *Hazefirah*, No. 83 (1887), p. 3.
8. Rosenberg, *op. cit.*, 64.
9. Nathan Goldberg, "Dynamics of the Economic Structure of the Jews in
   the United States," in *The Writing of American Jewish History*, 233-256.
10. *Ha-Maggid he-Hadash*, No. 3, p. 274 (1894).
11. See Irving A. Mandel, "Attitude of the American Jewish Community To-
    ward Eastern European Immigration," *American Jewish Archives*, III,
    11-36 (June, 1950); and Zosa Szajkowski, "The Attitude of American
    Jews to East-European Jewish Immigration, 1881-1893," in *Publications
    of the American Jewish Historical Society*, XL, 221-280 (1951).
12. Quoted in Mandel, *loc. cit.*
13. *Ibid.*
14. *Ibid.*; Wischnitzer, *op. cit.*, 73.
15. See Szajkowski, "The Attitude of American Jews," *loc. cit.*
16. Mandel, *loc. cit.*
17. John Higham, "Anti-Semitism in the Gilded Age: A Reinterpretation,"
    Mississippi Valley Historical Review, XLIII, 559-578 (March, 1957).
18. Jacob L. Hollander, "Forces and Tendencies of Jewish Charity," speech
    delivered May 17, 1910, in St. Louis, in *Proceedings of the Fifth Con-
    ference of Jewish Charities* (Baltimore, 1910), 50-55.
19. Mark S. Hubbell (ed.), *Our Police and Our City* (Buffalo, 1893), 295.
20. *Ibid.*, 303; Frank S. Presbrey, *The City of Buffalo* (pamphlet, New York,
    1895), *passim*.
21. George M. Bailey, *Ten Years in Buffalo* (pamphlet, Buffalo, 1890), 3 ff.
22. Hubbell, *op. cit.*, 297; Buffalo *Express*, January 12, 1890; New York
    Tribune, February 7, 1892; Buffalo *Courier*, July 1, 1894.
23. *Greater Buffalo*, April 15, 1897. In 1880 the population of the city was
    155,134; in 1890 it was 255,647.
24. New York *Tribune*, February 7, 1892; Buffalo *Courier*, April 10, 1904.
25. *Hazefirah*, No. 83 (1887), p. 2.
26. John T. Horton, "Old Erie—The Growth of An American Community,"
    Vol. I of John T. Horton *et al.*, *History of Northwestern New York* (New
    York, 1947), 359.
    The population of Buffalo, according to the census of 1910, was 423,715.
    In that year Buffalo had 62,586 foreign-born Poles, 19,247 citizens born
    in Italy, and 6,547 foreign-born Jews.
27. H. Perry Smith (ed.), *History of the City of Buffalo and Erie County* (2
    vols., Syracuse, 1884), II, 308.
28. Montefiore Lodge #70 Minute Book, November 14, 1881; June 27, 1887.
29. *The (American) Israelite*, XXVIII (June 9, 1882), 394.
30. *Ibid.*; *Ha-Maggid*, XXXVI, 350-351 (1882).
31. *The (American) Israelite*, XXVIII (June 23, 1882), 411.
32. Buffalo *Courier*, September 22, 1891; Beth Zion Minute Book, November
    2, 1891.
33. For instance, in 1911, Max, Albert and Morris Siegel went into the whole-

sale millinery business, the first Jews in this locality to venture into this end of the trade. Later they expanded into the retail business. Ultimately some of their employees went into the trade independently and now operate the Chic Maid Manufacturing Company which is controlled by Lester and Max Gross.

34. Harry and Dan Roblin, sons of the kosher butcher Rabolinsky, founded the Buffalo Housewrecking Company. Eventually this firm turned largely into a retail supply house. The Roblin brothers became active in local politics at the same time that they continued their business interests in two concerns known as Daniel A. Roblin Scrap Metals and Roblin Incorporated. Among other large local concerns that grew out of this interest in waste materials is Morrison & Risman Co. Inc., and the Samuel Greenfield Co. Inc.

35. David Cohen was a policeman for many years in the First Precinct and was still living in 1960 in Binghamton, N. Y. The Jewish fireman was Benjamin Kempner. These facts and figures were carefully compiled for the authors by Miss Renate Kaufmann who used various local sources.

36. Rosenberg, *op. cit.*, 105.

37. Bailey, *op. cit.*, 4, 14; Hubbell, *op. cit.*, 306-308.

38. We know much more about Frederick Ullman than most of his contemporaries because late in life he privately published his memoirs, *Incidents and Events*, (n.p., 1939). See especially pp. 8, 31, 65-66, 76.

39. Buffalo *Courier-Express*, May 6, 1946.

40. Hubbell, *op. cit.*, 811-815.

41. Buffalo *Evening News*, January 5, 1924; *Buffalo Jewish Review*, May 29, 1931; Truman C. White (ed.), *Our County and its People* (2 vols., Boston, 1898), II, 100.
    Another branch of this family operates the present day Seidenberg & Co. tobacco firm in New York City.

42. Interviews between Selig Adler and the late Mr. Herman Wile of Buffalo, August 5, 1954; and Mr. Joseph Rothschild of Buffalo, July 26, 1954.

43. *Buffalo Jewish Review*, January 9, 1925; Buffalo *Courier-Express*, August 16, 1927; September 8, 1940; interview between Selig Adler and Joseph Rothschild, July 26, 1954.

44. Buffalo *Courier-Express*, April 18, 1942; *American Jewish Review*, January 3, 1919.

45. Buffalo *Courier-Express*, October 30, 1949.

46. *Ibid.*, April 24, 1948.

47. Buffalo *Evening News*, April 3, 1931.

48. Merton M. Wilner, *Niagara Frontier* (4 vols., Chicago, 1931), III, 542-544.

49. *Buffalo Jewish Review*, July 15, 1927; August 21, 1931.

50. The Wildroot Co., which was one of the largest firms of its kind until it recently became part of Colgate-Palmolive, was founded in 1912 by Jay Greentree, Harry J. Lehman and Hoyt Sheehan. Harry J. Lehman (1883-1959) was a member of one of Buffalo's oldest families, his grandfather, Meyer, having settled here before the Civil War. Mr. Lehman had a long and distinguished record of service to the city of Buffalo and its Jewish community. Born in Bradford, Pa., he died in Buffalo on October 29, 1959.

51. Ullman, *op. cit.*, 38-42, 66; *Hebrew Standard*, XLIX, November 16, 1906.
52. *Albany Law Journal* (supplement on the University of Buffalo Law School and the Erie County Bar), January 7, 1899; *Political Blue Book* (Buffalo, 1905), 232; *Hebrew Standard*, XLIX, November 16, 1906.
    Henry L. Schwartz (1859-1904) was another early Jewish lawyer of the firm Baker, Schwartz and Dake. He met a sensational end when he was shot in his office by a disgruntled client who killed himself after his crime. See Buffalo *Express*, February 27, 1904.
53. Buffalo *Express*, January 3, 1913; Buffalo *Courier-Express*, May 21, 1943; Buffalo *Evening News*, July 29, 1954. Interviews between Selig Adler and Herman Wile, August 5, 1954, and Joseph Rothschild, July 26, 1954.
54. *American Jewish Review*, December 5, 1919; Buffalo *Evening News*, August 18, 1923; White, *op. cit.*, II, 13-14.
    Eugene L. Falk, (1866-1929), another son of Rabbi Falk, was also a prominent attorney of this age. In addition to his legal practice that continued in the firm of Falk, Twelvetrees, Johnston and Siemer, he had wide and profitable business interests. Although he died in New York, he maintained his father's old home at 76 W. Tupper Street as his official residence. See *Buffalo Jewish Review*, October 4, 1929.
55. Buffalo *Evening News*, *A History of the City of Buffalo*, (Buffalo, 1908), 230-231; Buffalo *Evening News*, December 26, 1932.
56. *Hebrew Standard*, XLIX, November 16, 1906; Buffalo *Evening News*, September 2, 1930; interview between Selig Adler and Mr. Justice Fleischmann of Buffalo, October 3, 1954. We are indebted to Judge Samuel J. Harris of Buffalo for many interesting sidelights on Mr. Fleischmann's legal career. Mr. Simon Fleischmann, who married Laura Justice in 1898, was survived by six sons, the most famous of whom, Manly, became nationally known for his service to the administration of President Harry S. Truman.
57. Most of our information here comes from a pamphlet written by Bianca Fleischmann, entitled *My Autobiography*. It was privately published in 1953.
58. *Hebrew Standard*, XLIX, November 16, 1906; *American Jewish Review*, September 10, 1920.
    Dr. Alois Jokl was trained at the University of Vienna and began to practice in Buffalo in 1894 in the heart of the William Street district. Dr. Joseph Spangenthal (1870-1941) was graduated from the University of Louisville Medical School and came to Buffalo in 1895. He specialized in and taught dermatology.
59. Most of our information on Dr. Schroeter was furnished by his daughter, Mrs. Ernst Levi of Buffalo.
60. *Buffalo Jewish Review*, July 15, 1921; interview between Selig Adler and Dr. S. Albert Levitan of Buffalo, April 9, 1954.
61. Buffalo *Evening News*, July 15, 1941; *Buffalo Jewish Review*, July 18, 1941.
62. Buffalo *Evening News*, November 8, 1897; *Buffalo Jewish Review*, November 15, 1929.
63. *The (American) Israelite* (January 9, 1896), 4; *Hebrew Standard*, XLIX, November 16, 1906; Buffalo *Evening News*, February 23, 1933. We are

indebted to Mr. Stuart J. Goldberg for permission to examine his father's Scrapbook and remaining manuscripts.

64. *American Jewish Review,* October 8, 1920; *Buffalo Jewish Review,* February 5, 1926. We are indebted to Mrs. Herbert L. Heymann of Buffalo for information about her father, Dr. Ullman, and other members of the Ullman family.

65. Buffalo *Evening News,* July 6, 1942; *Buffalo Jewish Review,* July 10, 1942. At his death, Dr. Weil cancelled all outstanding bills, and left a great deal of money to various charitable organizations in the city.

66. Buffalo *Evening News,* January 24, 1943; Wilner, *op. cit.,* III, 505. Dr. Kavinoky was the father of one of Buffalo's outstanding attorneys, Edward H. Kavinoky; Mrs. D. Bernard Simon; and Mrs. William J. Isaacson, a successful novelist who publishes under her maiden name, Bernice Kavinoky.

67. Buffalo *Courier-Express,* May 6, 1945.
In 1927, the Gilead Dental Society, which did for dentists what the Maimonides Club did for physicians, was founded. It is actually the graduate chapter of Alpha Omega Fraternity, an international Jewish dental fraternity. The chief local organizers were Dr. Harry H. Goldberg (1892-1944), and the long-time dean of Jewish dentists, Dr. Myer D. Wolfsohn.

68. In the Buffalo *Courier-Express,* February 11, 1934, an elderly resident by the name of Mrs. William Skolnik, recalled that it was the attraction of the store fronts that sent so many Jews to the East Side. We are also indebted to Miss Cecil B. Wiener for her recollections on the subject, given to Selig Adler in an interview, July 4, 1954.

69. The sociologist, Louis Wirth, in *The Ghetto* (Chicago, 1928), p. 4, pointed out that in the American sense, in contrast to the European, the word *ghetto* means a voluntary clustering in a neighborhood and the word applies particularly "to those areas where the poorest and most awkward group of Jewish population . . . resides." It is used by the present authors not in any pejorative sense, but merely as a convenient term to designate this neighborhood.

70. *Buffalo Jewish Review,* September 29, 1933; interviews between Selig Adler and Mrs. Bertha Shapiro, October 14, 1954, and Mrs. T. Rieger, March 19, 1955.

71. Statement of Mr. Munter's daughter, Mrs. Joseph Zisser of Buffalo, October 18, 1954.

72. Henry W. Hill (comp.), *Municipality of Buffalo, New York: A History, 1720-1923* (4 vols., New York, 1923), II, 518-519.
The local school system was greatly improved by reforms instituted by Superintendent Henry P. Emerson, who took office in 1893. Nevertheless, the schools in this part of the city remained overcrowded during the years of maximum Jewish immigration.

73. Corporation Box 9668 in the office of the clerk of the County of Erie, Buffalo. Among the founders of the Ladies' Hebrew Association were Rachel Davis, Emma Brenner, Rebecca Freedman, Carrie Bloomfield and Charlotte Goldberg. The chief spirit behind the Ladies of Loyalty (which flourished for about 25 years after 1915) was Mrs. Bertha Levy. The Lady Dreyfus Lodge was a social and sick benefit group that disbanded in the 1940s.

74. Buffalo *Times,* February 12, 1911; *Buffalo Jewish Review,* January 9, 1925, March 6, 1925, March 22, 1940; *American Jewish Year Book 1900-1901* (Philadelphia, 1900), 336; Mrs. Stella Engel to Mrs. Carl Pratter, September 1, 1954.

At the time of its founding, each member of the Manhattan Society paid $1.25 on joining and an annual dues of five dollars. Active in the early years of the organization were Charles Polakoff, Sol Jacobson and Dr. Jacob Goldberg. The society had 480 members in 1911. It slowly declined after World War I and, its purposes having been fulfilled, it dissolved shortly after 1945. Its affiliate, the Manhattan Ladies' Auxilary, was founded in 1896, had a peak membership of some 200 women at one time, and folded up sometime in the early 1920s. Mrs. Stella Engel was for many years active in the ladies' branch of the society.

75. The Queen City Social and Benefit Society was founded on the East Side in 1891, later moved uptown, and survived until after 1945. Another similar group was the Unterstützung Verein. (Help Society). There was also the Ladies' Montefiore Benevolent Society which existed from 1886 to 1901, and the International Social and Benefit Society.

76. *Buffalo Jewish Review,* January 2, 1925; October 23, 1925.

77. Buffalo *Express,* May 9, 1909; *Buffalo Jewish Review,* November 21, 1924, March 21, 1927, January 17, 1930, April 14, 1933; interview between Selig Adler and Mr. Meyer Shapiro of Buffalo, August 25, 1954.

Some of the vitality of B'rith Abraham is traceable to Rabbi Stephen S. Wise who was a member and friend of the organization. Through him, the order had close ties with the American Jewish Congress. In turn, B'rith Abraham was connected with the World Jewish Congress which dates from 1936.

The Independent Order of B'rith Sholem came to Buffalo in 1905 and its twenty-fifth Anniversary Congress was held here in 1930. This organization, like B'rith Abraham, was strongly Zionist and active in the American Jewish Congress.

78. Buffalo *Times,* June 1, 1938.

The 1882 re-incorporation of the synagogue mentions the names of Samuel Apenheim, Louis Starsky, Harris Cohen, Anshel Bergman, Nathan Harris and Samuel Eldridge as trustees. Corporation Box 4103 in the office of the clerk of the County of Erie, Buffalo.

79. The writer was the mysterious Yehuda ha-Cohen Vistinazky, in *Ha-Maggid he-Hadash,* I, 6 (1892).

80. We are indebted to Mr. Max M. Yellen for allowing us to examine a copy of this constitution in his possession. Written in Yiddish, it was printed by S. Knebel, 96 William Street, Buffalo, and is dated 1894.

81. Buffalo *Times,* September 8, 1926. Paltrovich, who seems to have started out as a *shohet,* came to the United States from Poland in 1872. His previous service was in Chicago, Boston and Cleveland, and he spent the last 12 years of his life in New York.

82. Buffalo *Express,* January 5, 1925; *Buffalo Jewish Review,* January 9, 1925; interview between Selig Adler and Mr. Morris Singer of Buffalo, July 25, 1954. Rabbi Jacob Singer of Chicago is one of *Hazzan* Singer's surviving children.

83. Corporation Box 972 in the office of the clerk of the County of Erie, Buf-

falo. Jacob H. Mayerberg (1823-1886) had been born in Sinje, Lithuania, and came to the United States in 1867. Louis W. Rubenstein came from Kalet, province of Suwalki. In 1872, he married Mayerberg's eldest daughter, Catherine (1850-1940). The last survivor of their nine children is Della R. Adler (b. 1876), mother of one of the authors of this history.

84. Buffalo *Commercial Advertiser,* July 1, 1889; September 23, 1889. Beth Jacob's cemetery, which dates from 1882, is not near the other Jewish burial grounds on Pine Ridge Road, but is in a secluded parcel of land at Doat and Genesee Streets.

85. *Ha-Maggid he-Hadash,* I, 6, 16 (1892).

86. The Beth Jacob Minute Books for the years indicated are in the possession of Mr. Arthur E. Schulgasser of Buffalo. We are indebted to him for permission to examine them.

87. *Ha-Maggid he-Hadash,* I, 6 (1892). Vistinazky was reported in 1894 to have left Buffalo for New York. He seems to have been a non-practicing rabbi who prayed at Beth Jacob and was probably related to one of its important families.

88. Corporation Box 4092, in the office of the clerk of the County of Erie, Buffalo.

89. *Idem.*

90. Corporation Box 571, *loc. cit.*

91. Unidentified newspaper clippings in the possession of Mr. Rosokoff's daughter, Mrs. Harry Schwartz of North Tonawanda, N. Y.

92. Corporation Box 10550 in the office of the clerk of the County of Erie, Buffalo.

93. Corporation Box 571, *loc. cit.; Buffalo Jewish Review,* December 26, 1924, January 16, 1925, November 4, 1942. There is also a plaque in memory of Mr. Bergman on the front outside wall of the present B'rith Israel-Anshe Emes Synagogue.

94. Buffalo *Evening News,* November 4, 1932.

95. Interview between Selig Adler and Mr. Charles Dautch of Buffalo, October 15, 1957.

96. Ahavas Sholem Minute Book, November 12, 1895; February 9, 1896; March 31, 1896; April 6, 1896.

97. *Ibid.,* April 6, 1896; April 18, 1896; August 1, 1897; December 4, 1898.

98. Corporation Box 4089, in the office of the clerk of the County of Erie, Buffalo.

99. For background information here, we are indebted to Mr. Louis Ablove of Buffalo who carefully prepared a detailed statement for us. Other parts of the Sokolovka story are based upon an interview between Selig Adler and Mr. Bernard Berkun of Buffalo, January 5, 1955.

100. Corporation Box 579 in the office of the clerk of the County of Erie, Buffalo; interview between Selig Adler and Mr. Sam Dozoretz of Buffalo, January 2, 1958.

101. *The (American) Israelite* (November 14, 1895), 2; *American Jewish Review,* September 10, 1920.

102. Buffalo *Express,* August 30, 1897; Buffalo *Commercial,* August 30, 1897.

103. Unidentified newspaper clipping in Mrs. Shire's Scrapbook.

104. Higham, *loc. cit.*

105. Beth Zion Minute Book, May 19, 1888, June 12, 1888, September 25,

1890, August 15, 1894, December 15, 1894; Buffalo *Courier-Express*, January 5, 1940.

106. Quoted in *Review of Reviews*, I (1890), 299.

107. Buffalo *Commercial Advertiser*, January 19, 1889; Buffalo *Commercial*, April 26, 1911; Hubbell, *op. cit.*, 694 ff.; White, *op. cit.*, II, 379-380.

108. Buffalo *Courier*, August 28, 1898, June 4, 1905, May 27, 1906, March 27, 1908; Buffalo *Express*, March 3, 1905, October 31, 1906, November 1, 1907; *American Jewish Review*, September 12, 1919; *Buffalo Jewish Review*, June 12, 1936.

109. Because all records have apparently been lost, we have had to reconstruct the history of these clubs from various indirect sources. In the main, we have relied upon the Buffalo *Commercial*, May 21, 1890; Liber of Deeds, 650:582 in the office of the clerk of the County of Erie, Buffalo; *American Jewish Year Book 1900-1901*, 337; *Hebrew Standard*, XLIX, November 16, 1906; Ullman, *op. cit.*, 43; interview between Selig Adler and Miss Miriam Rosenau of Buffalo, August 1, 1954.

110. Wischnitzer, *op. cit.*, 123; Mildred G. Welt, "The National Council of Jewish Women," in *American Jewish Year Book 1944-1945* (Philadelphia, 1944), XLVI, 55-72; Mrs. Emile Levy to Mrs. Henry S. Cohen of Buffalo, April 26, 1950; old programs in the Scrapbook of Mrs. Rena F. Jellinek of Buffalo; interviews between Miss Renate Kaufmann and Miss Cecil B. Wiener, August 18, 1954 and Mrs. Henry S. Cohen, September 7, 1954; Buffalo *Times*, October 26, 1902.

In the 1930s, a junior group of the National Council of Jewish Women was formed in Buffalo after the organization had been defunct here for many years. A senior section was formed in the next decade, dissolved, but re-constituted in 1953 with a membership that stabilized at about 400. Its main activities are community service on a non-sectarian basis and educational activities of both a Jewish and non-Jewish nature. We are grateful to Mrs. Robert Tobin, Mrs. Sidney Abrams and Miss Sophie Hadida for information on the latest activities of the group.

111. *Hebrew Standard*, XLIX, November 16, 1906; White, *op. cit.*, II, 460 ff.

112. Beth Zion Minute Book, January 25, 1887, February 28, 1887, March 5, 1889; interview between Selig Adler and Mr. Herman Wile, August 5, 1954.

113. David S. Philipson, *My Life As An American Jew* (Cincinnati, 1941), 22; Buffalo *Commercial*, May 31, 1897.

114. Beth Zion Minute Book, November 3, 1901; May 4, 1902.

115. *Ibid.*, July 5, 1907, December 6, 1908, March 15, 1909; interview between Selig Adler and Mr. Herman Wile, August 5, 1954.

116. Buffalo *Commercial Advertiser*, January 19, 1889.

117. Quoted in *The (American) Israelite* (January 23, 1896), 1.

118. Israel Aaron, "The Reintroduction of Congregational Singing," *C.C.A.R. Yearbook*, XXII, 333-339 (1912).

119. Beth Zion Minute Book, June 12, 1893.

120. *Ibid.*, November 1, 1897; November 14, 1898; October 3, 1904; November 6, 1904; June 6, 1909; October 9, 1909. It is impossible to say for certain whether or not Beth Zion actually ever held Sunday morning services. Survivors of the period are unanimous in denying it, yet the Beth Zion Minute Book, October 9, 1909, ordered that the choir be employed

henceforth for both Saturday and Sunday mornings. Quite possibly this decision was reversed; certainly Sunday morning services did not last long enough to make an impression on the community or to leave any traces that can be verified.

121. Interviews between Selig Adler and Miss Cecil B. Wiener, July 4, 1954, and Mr. Herman Wile, August 5, 1954.
122. Beth Zion Minute Book, September 19, 1909.
123. *Ibid.*, April 7, 1912, May 10. 1912, May 12, 1912, May 20, 1912; Buffalo *Evening News*, May 15, 1912; Buffalo *Enquirer*, May 15, 1912; *The (American) Israelite* (May 16, 1912), 7.
124. Benjamin Rabinowitz, "The Young Men's Hebrew Associations, 1854-1913," in *Publications of the American Jewish Historical Society*, No. 37, 221-326 (1947).
125. Corporation Box 11373 in the office of the clerk of the County of Erie, Buffalo.
126. *Loc. cit.*, Buffalo *Express*, May 5, 1902; Buffalo *Times*, October 26, 1902. The first board of trustees were Mrs. Henry Altman, Mrs. Israel Aaron, Mrs. Benjamin Desbecker, Mrs. Marcus Spiegel, Mrs. Daniel Desbecker, Clara Desbecker Weill, Belle Jellinek, Amalie Fischer, Theresa Rosenberg, and Miriam Rosenau.
127. Buffalo *Express*, May 5, 1902, September 19, 1902; Buffalo *Courier*, September 19, 1902.
128. *Annual Report of the Charity Organization Society of Buffalo, N. Y., 1903* (Buffalo, 1903), 63-64.
129. Buffalo *Express*, August 26, 1907, October 10, 1907; *Hebrew Standard*, XLIX, November 16, 1906.
Another charitable organization of the period was the Daughters of the Star, originally a study group that early joined the Sisterhood of Zion's Americanization work. The Daughters of the Star were Beth Zion women, led by Mrs. Henry Altman who met for educational and philanthropic purposes, and were especially interested in helping needy maternity cases.
130. Beth Zion Minute Book, October 3, 1888; October 19, 1888; December 2, 1888. Edward Warner replaced Julius Altman on the committee.
131. *Ibid.*, October 8, 1889; October 20, 1889; October 25, 1889.
132. *Ibid.*, August 24, 1890, September 1, 1890; Buffalo *Evening News*, September 12, 1890. To finance the construction, Beth Zion borrowed $40,000 from the Albany Savings Bank.
133. Buffalo *Commercial*, September 6, 1890, September 13, 1890; Buffalo *Evening News*, September 12, 1890; Buffalo *Express*, September 14, 1890.

CHAPTER VII

PROGRESS AND POVERTY

1. George H. Schodde, "The Zionite Movement," *Harper's Weekly*, XL, 620 (June 20, 1896).
2. Jessie E. Sampter, "Zionism in America Before the British Mandate," in Jessie E. Sampter (ed.), *Modern Palestine* (New York, 1933), 35-51.
3. *Maccabaean*, December, 1901, 134-135; February, 1902, 95; October, 1908, 170.
4. Mrs. Leon H. Miller to Selig Adler, July 9, 1954.
5. Unidentified newspaper clipping, 1902, Leon H. Miller Scrapbook, in the Zionist Archives and Library of Palestine Foundation Fund, New York, N. Y.
6. Mrs. Leon H. Miller to Selig Adler, July 9, 1954.
7. *Maccabaean*, May, 1903, 291; July, 1904, 55; September, 1904, 159. Buffalo *Express*, June 30, 1905.
8. This information is based on the local Poale Zion Minute Books, placed in our hands by Mr. Isadore Wolk of Buffalo and translated from the Yiddish for us by Dr. Shia Moser of the University of Buffalo.
9. Melvin Weinman, "The Attitude of Isaac Mayer Wise toward Zionism and Palestine," *American Jewish Archives*, III, 3-23 (January, 1951).
10. Quoted in Naomi W. Cohen, "The Reaction of Reform Judaism in America to Political Zionism, 1897-1922," in *Publications of the American Jewish Historical Society*, No. 40, 361-394 (1951).
11. For instance, Rabbi Abraham J. Karp of Rochester, N. Y. has in his possession a political leaflet of a Rochester Jewish Republican organization which urged Jews to vote for the McKinley-Roosevelt ticket in 1900 because Colonel Roosevelt had helped humble anti-Jewish Spain.
12. John T. Horton, "Old Erie—The Growth of an American Community," vol. I of John T. Horton *et al.*, *History of Northwestern New York* (New York, 1947), 339-340.
13. Buffalo *Times*, January 27, January 29, 1911; interviews between Selig Adler and David Rodenberg of Buffalo, August 24, 1954, and with the late Daniel W. Barmon of Buffalo, August 26, 1954.
14. Bernard D. Weinryb, "Jewish Immigration and Accommodation to America: Research, Trends, Problems," in Moshe Davis and Isidore S. Meyer (eds.), *The Writing of American Jewish History* (New York, 1957), 366-403; Peter Roberts, *The Foreign Population Problem in Buffalo* (pamphlet, Buffalo, 1908), *passim*.
15. Buffalo *Express*, May 18, 1903.
16. *Loc. cit.*; Cyrus Adler, *The Voice of America on Kishineff* (Philadelphia, 1904), 51-53.
17. Buffalo *Express*, May 18, 1903.
18. *Ibid.*, May 25, 1903.
19. For background here, we have drawn heavily on Mark Wischnitzer, *To Dwell In Safety* (Philadelphia, 1948), 98 ff.
20. Federated Jewish Charities of Buffalo, *Hand Book, 1905*, 11-12; *ibid., 1906*, 14; Federated Jewish Charities of Buffalo, *Year Book, 1913*, 23-24.

For many years about 115 immigrants a year arrived in Buffalo under the sponsorship of IRO. This number gradually increased, reaching 194 in 1913. In that year the New York office sent $1,221.96 to cover the cost of settling the newcomers.

21. Buffalo *Express*, June 29, 1900; March 4, 1902; March 2, March 6, 1904.
22. Federated Jewish Charities of Buffalo, *Year Book, 1910,* 8, 19.
23. Wischnitzer, *op. cit.,* 123.
24. Federated Jewish Charities of Buffalo, *Year Book, 1914-1915,* 18.
25. Printed handbill found in the Beth El Minute Book for 1900.
26. Federated Jewish Charities of Buffalo, *Year Book, 1914-1915,* 17.
27. *Ibid., 1911,* 11.
28. *Ibid., 1910,* 12-13.
29. Buffalo *Express*, May 16, 1909, May 3, 1926; Buffalo *Courier-Express,* October 22, 1927; Jewish Welfare Board, Report on Buffalo, 1923, 38; Jewish Welfare Board, Report on Buffalo, 1938, 62. (These reports are in the files of the National Jewish Welfare Board, 145 E. 32nd St., New York, N. Y.)
    In 1921, the mission on Hickory Street was molested by Jewish boys. *The Senior Review,* May, 1921, I, No. 4, (official publication of the Jewish Community Building) strongly protested this vandalism.
30. Jewish Welfare Board, Report on Buffalo, 1938, 35-36, 60.
    As late as 1938, about 30 Jewish children a week used the facilities of Westminster House (Presbyterian), at 421 Monroe Street. However, there was an agreement with the Jewish Community Building to try to steer Jewish children to 406 Jefferson Avenue, while the Jews did their best to direct Protestant children to Westminster House.
31. Federated Jewish Charities of Buffalo, *Year Book, 1910,* 5.
32. Often men apprehended in Buffalo for wife desertion were simply too poor to help their families; sometimes the deserters thought that abandonment was a kindness, for they reasoned that the Jewish charities would care for their children. In 1911, Miss Wiener called the desertion problem a "national menace." By this time, the National Conference of Jewish Charities had set up a National Desertion Bureau that published pictures, names and other data about missing husbands. Buffalo cooperated in this effort. *Ibid., 1911,* 9.
33. *Ibid., 1914-1915,* 18.
34. Irving A. Mandel, "Attitude of the American Jewish Community Toward Eastern European Immigration," *American Jewish Archives,* III, 11-36 (June, 1950); *American Jewish Year Book 1900-1901* (Philadelphia, 1900), 137.
35. See his *Three Centuries of Growth* (pamphlet, published by the Labor Zionist Organization of America, New York, 1954).
36. *American Jewish Year Book 1900-1901,* 137-139.
37. Annette F. Arywitz, "A Short History of the Jewish Community Service of Buffalo" (Master of Social Science thesis, University of Buffalo, 1948), 11-13.
38. *Buffalo Jewish Review,* February 11, 1938; unidentified memo in the 1928 files of the [Buffalo] Jewish Federation for Social Service; interview between Selig Adler and Miss Cecil B. Wiener of Buffalo, July 4, 1954.
39. Arywitz, *loc. cit.,* 13 ff.

40. Buffalo *Evening News,* July 20, 1909; *Hebrew Standard,* XLIX, November 16, 1906; Mrs. Myra S. Morrison to Selig Adler, September 17, 1954.
41. Unidentified memo in the 1928 files of the Jewish Federation for Social Service.
42. Federated Jewish Charities of Buffalo, *Hand Book, 1905,* 14.
43. *Hebrew Standard,* XLIX, November 16, 1906.
44. Buffalo *Evening News,* January 16, 1929; Buffalo *Courier-Express,* January 16, 1929; *Buffalo Jewish Review,* January 18, February 8, 1929; Jewish Federation for Social Service, *Year Book, 1928-1929,* 9, 34.
45. Federated Jewish Charities of Buffalo Minute Book, February 2, February 23, March 23, 1909; interview between Selig Adler and Miss Cecil B. Wiener, July 6, 1954.
46. Solomon Morrison (1864-1938), who participated in this early merger, came to Buffalo as a youth from Russia. At his death, he was president of Morrison & Risman Co., Inc., dealers in iron and steel scrap, and president of the Morrison Railway Supply Corporation. Isaac Hoenig (1859-1920), who arrived here in 1880, prospered in the clothing business. At his death, he left a fund known as the Isaac Hoenig Memorial Fund, to be lent to students pursuing higher education. The loans were to bear no interest and no pressure to repay was made until the borrower was well established.
47. Buffalo *Evening News,* February 21, 1941; Buffalo *Courier-Express,* February 22, 1941; *Buffalo Jewish Review,* March 6, 1931, February 28, 1941. For 25 years, Mr. Given operated Given's Inc. Selling his store in 1930, he was forced to take it back during the ensuing depression. He was active in many downtown businessmen's associations, and his other interests included a directorship in the Liberty Bank and promotion of the I.S. Given Realty Corporation. A Republican in politics, he was one-time chairman of the Buffalo Planning Board and a member of the Zoning Board of Appeals. He was active in many Jewish and non-Jewish charities, especially the Buffalo Eye and Ear Hospital and Wettlaufer Clinic.
48. Federated Jewish Charities of Buffalo, *Year Books, 1911,* 5-6; *1914-1915,* 8.
   In 1912, Dr. Jerome Hilton Waterman died and left $20,000 to establish the Herman and Malvina Waterman Fund. The interest from this fund was divided between the Sisterhood of Zion and the Federated Charities. Two years later, Mr. and Mrs. Eugene Warner gave $1,500 for a dispensary, and about the same time the first non-Jewish bequest was received from Edward H. Butler of the Buffalo *Evening News.* By 1914, subscriptions had substantially increased. In that year, a touching Yom Kippur Eve appeal, made by Rabbi Louis J. Kopald of Beth Zion, yielded $14,000 in a few minutes.
49. *Hebrew Standard,* XLIX, November 16, 1906. Mrs. Elkus subsequently became Mrs. Roland Crangle and continued to live in Buffalo.
50. *Ibid.;* Jewish Welfare Board Report on Buffalo, 1938, 82; Arywitz, *loc. cit.,* 17; Buffalo *Courier-Express,* February 3, 1959.
51. *Buffalo Jewish Review,* November 19, 1926; interview between Selig Adler and Miss Wiener, July 6, 1954.
52. Mr. Lurie left Buffalo for Detroit. Later, he became Superintendent of the Jewish Social Service Bureau of Chicago, Director of the Bureau of Jew-

ish Social Research in New York, and eventually, Executive Director of the Council of Jewish Federations and Welfare Funds.

53. In 1908, out of 1,417 families on public relief, only 52 were Jewish, while three years later, of 6408 families of all nationalities reported by the Overseer of the Poor, only six were Jewish. Louis J. Kenngott (comp.), *Annual Reports of the Overseer of the Poor to the Common Council, 1908, 1911* (Buffalo, 1908, 1911), *passim.*

54. Unsigned report, January 1, 1911, in the files of the Federation.

55. In 1906, a "Federation Supply Store" was established at Zion House to sell articles repaired by pensioners. This project proved ephemeral. In those days the Federation purchased its coal for the poor from Charles S. Jacobowitz (1878-1950). After a widely varied career, Charles Jacobowitz established the corporation that bears his name and manufactures brewing machinery.

56. Federated Jewish Charities of Buffalo, *Year Book, 1914*, 12, 16.

57. *Buffalo Jewish Review,* September 30, 1921.

58. Report of S.J. Harris in Federated Jewish Charities of Buffalo, *Year Book, 1910*, 25-28.

59. *Ibid., 1914-1915*, 34-48. When Leopold Keiser died in 1912, he affirmed his life-long devotion to Jewish education by bequeathing the school $1,000.

60. Judge Harris was succeeded as principal of the school in 1927 by the future Comptroller, and later Justice, Jacob Tick. Next came Abraham Axlerod, a product of the school, and later principal of Lafayette High School. In 1928, with its entire budget derived from the Federation, the school had in addition to Principal Tick, two supervisors and 19 teachers. When the building on Jefferson Avenue was abandoned during World War II, the school was closed. Since then, the High School of Jewish Studies, conducted by the Bureau of Jewish Education, has taken its place in the field of secondary education, while the individual synagogues attend to primary education.

61. Oscar Handlin, *Adventure in Freedom* (New York, 1954), 155.

62. Buffalo *Courier,* March 21, 1898; Buffalo *Enquirer,* March 22, 1898.

63. Federated Jewish Charities of Buffalo, *Year Book, 1909,* 22-23.

64. *The Buffalo Directory 1920* (Buffalo, 1920), 86-89.
    Other agencies sprang up to promote Americanization, particularly the Buffalo Chapter of the North American Civic League for Immigrants. Active on its steering committee was Solomon Ginsberg (1869-1928). Born in Columbus, Indiana, Ginsberg had served as a page in the United States Senate. He came to Buffalo in 1891 to establish a branch for a Detroit railroad supply firm. Later, he was president of the New York Car Wheel Company and interested in real estate ventures.

65. Federated Jewish Charities of Buffalo, *Year Book, 1913,* 24-25.

66. David Block to Selig Adler, July 25, 1954. Rabbi Bloch could find no synagogue traditional enough to suit him, and after 1919, maintained a *minyan* for Sabbath observers in his Clinton Street home.

67. Buffalo *Courier-Express,* November 15, 1944.

68. Ahavas Sholem Minute Book, May 9, May 30, November 14, 1897; *Hebrew Standard,* XLIX, November 16, 1906.

69. *Buffalo Jewish Review,* October 5, 1923, May 12, 1939; Mrs. Lillian Hirsch to Cecil B. Wiener, April 29, 1955.

70. *Hebrew Standard,* XLIX, November 16, 1906.

71. Buffalo *Express,* June 13, 1909.
   To raise money for the maintenance of the school, tickets were sold for High Holiday services conducted there, and about 1915, it was agreed that for every fowl slaughtered a two-cent tax would be paid for its support. Additional funds were raised by the sale of *matzot,* distributed through David Jacobson's wholesale food house. In addition, funds were raised through bazaars, synagogue appeals, and through the efforts of an auxiliary called the Ladies of Judea.

72. Paul Swados to Cecil B. Wiener, December 10, 1954.

73. Jewish Welfare Board, Report on Buffalo, 1923, 31; *Buffalo Jewish Review,* November 2, 1923.

74. Federated Jewish Charities of Buffalo, *Hand Book, 1906,* 11.

75. At the time of its 1914 organization, the trustees of the Fund were Eli D. Hofeller, Adolph Spangenthal, August Keiser, Gustave Benjamin, Cecil B. Wiener, Irma Altman, Sarah Rubenstein, Fanny Harris and Emma M. Exstein.

76. In 1945, an additional 120 acres of land was purchased by the Federation from Mr. Henry Wendt whose price was the equivalent of a $20,000 gift to the cause. In later years, the camp was converted from the dormitory system to the cabin system in order to permit both sexes to attend simultaneously. This expansion was greatly aided by the late Abraham Axlerod, director of the camp for many years. By the mid-1950s the camp was able to handle 558 children in three summer shifts, and in the off seasons the grounds were used by various organizations for weekend educational meetings. The present director is Morris Siegel and the office work is handled in the Jewish Center by the Executive Secretary, Mrs. Camille M. Plant. We are grateful to Mrs. Plant for much information about the camp. We have also drawn on scattered information about the Jewish Fresh Air Camp preserved in the Federation's files.

77. Benjamin Rabinowitz, "The Young Men's Hebrew Associations, 1854-1913," in *Publications of the American Jewish Historical Society,* No. 37, 221-326 (1947).

78. Buffalo *Express,* November 12, December 16, 1900; *American Jewish Year Book 1900-1901,* 538.

79. Beth Zion Minute Book, March 7, 1915. In 1915 the Jewish Community Athletic Association was incorporated, the directors being J. Selig (Jack) Yellen, David Rosenblatt, Julius L. Rosenblatt, Benjamin Sherris, Samuel Wilner, Benjamin Brock and Harry Altman. This seems to have been one of the various names that the group composing the "Y" adopted for the time being. (Corporation Box 7895 in the office of the clerk of the County of Erie, Buffalo, N. Y.)

80. *American Jewish Review,* May 2, 1919.

81. *Ibid.,* February 11, 1921.

82. *Buffalo Jewish Review,* December 2, December 16, 1921; August 25, 1922.

83. Jewish Welfare Board, Report on Buffalo, 1923, 33 ff.

84. *Buffalo Jewish Review,* April 25, 1924.

85. *Ibid.*, November 21, 1924; February 13, December 4, 1925.
86. Will Herberg, "The Jewish Labor Movement in the United States," in *American Jewish Year Book 1952* (Philadelphia, 1952), 3-74.
87. We have been greatly influenced in our understanding of American Jewish labor problems by the insights shown in C. Bezalel Sherman's *Three Centuries of Growth.*
88. *Loc. cit.*; Herberg, "The Jewish Labor Movement."
89. *Arbeiter Zeitung*, February 13, November 13, 1891; February 3, February 17, June 2, 1893.
90. Our information on the Reinsteins is based on several telephone interviews between Selig Adler and Dr. Victor Reinstein of Buffalo.
91. *Arbeiter Zeitung*, June 30, July 28, November 24, 1893; March 30, May 25, 1894.
92. We have gained insight into the problems of the Arbeiter Ring and have been allowed to examine much material concerning it through the courtesy of Mr. Isadore Wolk.
93. This information is based upon the Minute Books of the local branch of the Arbeiter Ring, translated and summarized for us by Mr. Isadore Wolk. In 1954 he had the Minute Books in his possession, having found them among the possessions of a deceased leader of the organization.
94. *Ibid.*, Buffalo *Express*, February 21, 1908.
95. Oscar I. Janowsky, *The Jews and Minority Rights 1898 to 1919* (New York, 1933), 145-146.
96. *American Jewish Year Book 1911* (Philadelphia, 1911), 231.
97. Arbeiter Ring Branch #29 Minute Books; Herberg, "The Jewish Labor Movement."
98. This information is based upon a brief prepared for us by Mr. and Mrs. Isadore Wolk, based on original Yiddish sources in their possession.
99. *Ibid.*
100. Corporation Box 13404 in the office of the clerk of the County of Erie, Buffalo.
101. *American Jewish Year Book 1900-1901*, 336; *Hebrew Standard*, XLIX November 16, 1906; interviews between Selig Adler and Mr. Meyer Shapiro of Buffalo, August 18, 1954 and with Mrs. Melvin Greene of Buffalo, March 15, 1958.
102. Corporation Box 6772 in the office of the clerk of the County of Erie; *Hebrew Standard*, XLIX, November 16, 1906; *Hebrew Benevolent Loan Association, Buffalo, N. Y., 1897-1947* (pamphlet, Fiftieth Anniversary Dinner, Buffalo, 1947), *passim.*
103. This information is based on a series of interviews between Selig Adler and Mr. Meyer Shapiro and on an examination of various audits of the Hebrew Benevolent Loan Association's books placed in our hands by Mr. Shapiro.
104. Buffalo *Courier-Express*, February 3, 1952.
105. *Buffalo Jewish Review*, January 23, 1925; February 4, 1927.
106. Corporation Box 19044 in the office of the clerk of the County of Erie.
107. Corporation Boxes 1879, 6785, *loc. cit.*
108. *Hebrew Standard*, XLIX, November 16, 1906.
109. Chevra Kadisha Anshe Lubavitz Minute Book, December 19, 1910. (This

book is in the possession of the present congregation Ahavas Achim-Lubavitz.)

110. Erland Gjessing, "Ghetto in Miniature," a series of articles in the Buffalo *Express*, May 9, May 16, May 19, 1909.

111. William A. Douglas and William Lansing, "Housing Conditions in Buffalo," in Robert W. De Forest and Lawrence Veiller (eds.), *The Tenement House Problem* (2 vols., New York, 1903), I, 119-128.

112. U.S. Immigration Commission, *Immigrants in Cities* (Senate Document 338, 61 Cong. 2 Sess., 2 vols., Washington, 1911), I, 615, 619, 675; II, 69-101.

113. Harry L. Lurie in Federated Jewish Charities of Buffalo, *Year Book, 1914,* 29-30.

114. Horton, *op. cit.,* 238.

115. David Soibelman, "Razing of Mortimer Street Evokes Memories," unidentified newspaper clipping in the Scrapbook of Paul Drozen, Buffalo.

116. Buffalo *Courier-Express,* December 20, 1936.

117. Leo J. Rosen to Selig Adler, August 15, 1957.

118. Interview between Selig Adler and Dr. Charles Simon of Buffalo, September 17, 1954.

119. Although it has been repeatedly denied that Buffalo had a Jewish paper in the 1890s, it is listed in Frank H. Severance, "The Periodical Press of Buffalo, 1811-1915," in *Publications of the Buffalo Historical Society,* XIX, 179-280 (1915).

120. Buffalo *Express,* June 14, 1909.

121. Corporation Box 3739 in the office of the clerk of the County of Erie.

122. "Official History of the Rosa Coplon Jewish Old Folks Home, Buffalo, New York," typescript sent to the authors by Samuel Roberts, executive director of the Rosa Coplon Jewish Home and Infirmary; *Buffalo Jewish Review,* February 23, 1945.

123. "Official History of the Rosa Coplon Jewish Old Folks Home"; *Buffalo Jewish Review,* May 30, 1924; Buffalo *Express,* May 26, 1924.

124. *Buffalo Jewish Review,* October 8, October 15, October 22, October 29, 1926.

125. *Ibid.,* December 22, 1933.

126. *Ibid.,* September 24, October 22, 1937.

127. Rabinowitz, "The Young Men's Hebrew Associations," *loc. cit.*

128. Mr. Joseph's colleagues on the Building Committee were Emanuel Boasberg, Eli D. Hofeller, Louis Weill, August Keiser, Isaac E. Harris and Adolph Spangenthal.

129. Unidentified newspaper clippings in the Scrapbook of Marvin Davis, Buffalo; Federated Jewish Charities of Buffalo, *Year Book, 1913,* 56-57; *Buffalo Jewish Review,* February 11, 1938.

130. *American Jewish Review,* January 3, 1919; Buffalo *Courier,* July 5, 1923; Buffalo *Evening News,* November 28, 1923.

131. Buffalo *Evening News,* December 6, 1943.

132. *Hebrew Standard,* XLIX, November 16, 1906; interview between Miss Renate Kaufmann and Miss Sophie C. Hadida of Buffalo, August 18, 1954; Elizabeth Hirshfield, *Concerning Women Suffrage* (pamphlet published by the Buffalo Political Equality Club, Buffalo, n.d.), *passim.*

133. *Buffalo Jewish Review,* April 10, 1931.

134. *Ibid.*, November 15, 1929; Rabbi Harry J. Brevis to Selig Adler, April 15, 1958.

135. A breakdown of Beth El addresses from a 1915 list of members, reveals that 41 families were still living on the East Side, 68 had already moved to the West Side, while 10 were scattered in non-Jewish neighborhoods throughout the city.

136. *American Jewish Year Book 1900-1901,* 140.

137. From 1895 to 1899, Rabbi David Wittenberg served the congregation. In 1899, Rabbi Ettlinger came and five years later he was succeeded by a Reverend S. Cooper who, in the fashion of an earlier day, served as cantor, preacher and teacher. Following his 1906 ordination at the Jewish Theological Seminary, Rabbi Arthur Gintzler came to Beth El; but he did not remain long. This information has been pieced together from scraps in the Beth El files, left by previous researchers who may have seen the lost Minute Books.

138. *Buffalo Jewish Review,* April 18, 1924; interview between Selig Adler and Mr. Samuel Slick of Buffalo, June 15, 1954. Cantor Slick later served at the Fillmore Avenue and Pine Street Shuls.

139. *Buffalo Jewish Review,* September 2, 1921, August 2, 1925, June 15, 1928; Buffalo *Evening News,* March 12, 1940.
Mr. Polakoff subsequently married Bessie Bernstein who survived him. He retired as president of Beth El in 1929, but was returned to office two years later and it was under his leadership that the congregation weathered the depression.

140. Beth El Minute Book, May 8, 1910.

141. Buffalo *Express,* May 10, 1909.

142. *Temple Beth El's First Century: Centennial Souvenir Book* (pamphlet, Buffalo, 1947), 19.

143. Other members of the building committee were: J. L. Davis, Frank L. Cohen, Pincus Cohen, Joseph Coplon, A. N. Hyman, Louis Sukernek.

144. Buffalo *Evening News,* October 26, 1936.

145. Buffalo *Commercial,* March 23, July 25, 1910; Buffalo *Express,* July 24, 1910.

146. The Fair was opened by Mayor Louis P. Fuhrman and each night of the week's celebration was devoted to some social, fraternal, or benefit society. Music was supplied by an orchestra, and there were a grocery booth, a candy booth, a Liliputian booth, an arts and crafts booth, and a crystal booth. A program of the occasion is preserved in the Beth El Minute Book for 1910.

147. This history, with suitable illustrations, was published in Grace Carew Sheldon's column, "Buffalo of the Olden Time," in the Buffalo *Times* during the period from December 28, 1910, to February 19, 1911.

148. Beth El Minute Book, April 3, April 17, May 8, 1910.
The dissenters were handed deeds to lots in the cemetery and given the option of rejoining the synagogue within two years. To protect the East Siders even further, it was agreed that dues at Richmond Avenue were not to be more than $30 a year, unless the individual member agreed to pay more. They were also promised that the pews were to be in the same location as those occupied on Elm Street.

149. Buffalo *Commercial,* September 11, 1911; a copy of the program has been preserved in the Beth El files.

150. Buffalo *Times,* January 1, 1911; unidentified newspaper clippings in the Scrapbook of Marvin Davis; Jacob H. Landau, *Service Manual of Temple Beth El* (pamphlet, Buffalo, 1911).
    The new cantor was Samuel Arluck who went with Beth El from the East Side, but who returned downtown in 1913. Arluck was long remembered in Buffalo for his beautiful voice and remarkable selection of music. In the 1920s he went to Syracuse, where he spent the remainder of his life. His son is Harold Arlen, the famous Hollywood song writer.

151. Buffalo *Evening News,* April 20, 1931; *Buffalo Jewish Review,* April 24, 1931. His eldest son is Rabbi Hyman J. Schachtel of Houston, Texas.

152. Report of President Charles Polakoff, April 16, 1911, Beth El files.

153. Report of Polakoff, April 27, 1913; Franklin W. H. Becker to Polakoff, May 17, 1913, *loc. cit.*

154. Beth El Minute Book, April 4, 1915; April 26, 1916.
    During these years and those that followed, the Beth El cemetery on Pine Ridge Road was improved and enlarged. From 1906 to 1915, the congregation spent about $10,000 in improving the land. Ultimately, the cost was to reach $80,000, with Israel Goldin, a successful retail merchant, contributing $7,500. Also helpful were Max Grossman (1866-1938) and his wife who for many years were mainstays of the temple's religious services. Eventually, a beautiful fence of natural stone was built around the cemetery to end the vandalism that had plagued the place since Civil War days. In addition, an imposing gate and a fine chapel were built on the grounds and the improved cemetery was dedicated in 1926. See Buffalo *Courier-Express,* September 13, 1926; *Buffalo Jewish Review,* September 3, September 17, 1926.

155. Copies of the programs for these productions and various sources of information about them are in the Beth El files for 1916-1917.

156. In addition to his clothing interests, as early as 1894 Mr. Wile had a pioneer motion picture house on the present site of the Ellicott Square Building. A founder of the Wholesale Merchants Association, which later merged with the local Chamber of Commerce, he was also a founder of the Wholesale Clothing Manufacturers Association, and sat on its board for 27 years. Buffalo *Evening News,* December 29, 1958.

157. His terms of office were: 1902-1904; 1908-1921; 1927-1948. As early as 1925, he was made Life Honorary President. Although he had refused to accept re-nomination in 1921, he returned to office six years later and led Beth Zion for another 21 years.

158. This sketch of Mr. Wile is based on a number of interviews with him held in the summer of 1954. We have also relied upon an unpublished biographical essay of Mr. Wile, prepared by Dr. Milton Plesur.

159. Kopald to Leon H. Miller, October 2, 1923, L. H. Miller Scrapbook; *Buffalo Jewish Review,* June 7, October 12, 1923.

160. *American Jewish Review,* April 11, 1919; *Buffalo Jewish Review,* April 29, 1921.

161. During Rabbi Kopald's years at Beth Zion, the temple prospered partly as a result of his efforts and partly from the affluence that came with the

war. In the three fiscal years following 1916-1917, the budget rose from $20,000 to $27,000.

162. *Buffalo Jewish Review,* November 4, 1927; Buffalo *Evening News,* February 5, 1931; interview between Selig Adler and Mr. Herman Wile, August 5, 1954.

163. Buffalo *Express,* September 19, 1915; Buffalo *Commercial,* September 25, 1915. An Historical Committee headed by Eugene Warner prepared a brief history of the temple, using the 1864 date of organization. It is entitled *Fifieth Anniversary First Temple Beth Zion 1865-1915; Twenty-Fifth Anniversary Present Temple 1890-1915; Dedication The Temple Centre 1915* (Buffalo, 1915).

164. Beth Zion Minute Book, December 22, December 29, 1912; June 23, June 28, October 5, October 12, 1913; February 1, 1914; January 10, 1915; *Fiftieth Anniversary Temple Beth Zion,* 14 ff.; Corporation Box 14330 in the office of the clerk of the County of Erie.

165. Buffalo *Commercial,* September 25, 1915.

CHAPTER VIII

WAR, PROSPERITY, AND UNITY

1. John T. Horton, "Old Erie—The Growth of an American Community," vol. I of John T. Horton *et al., History of Northwestern New York* (New York, 1947), 377-378.

2. Milton H. Petzold to Camille B. Michel (Mrs. Edward M. Plant), February 18, 1920. Mrs. Plant allowed us to examine this letter concerning her late brother, and also supplied additional information.

3. Henry W. Hill (comp.), *Municipality of Buffalo, N. Y.; A History, 1720-1923,* (4 vols., New York, 1923), II, 876-877.
    Daniel J. Sweeney (ed.), *History of Buffalo and Erie County, 1914-1919* (Buffalo, 1920), 495 ff.

4. Frederick Ullman, *Incidents and Events* (n.p., 1939), 59-62.
    American Jewish Review, September 12, 1919.

5. Sweeney, *op. cit.,* 183.

6. This list was compiled for the authors by Miss Renate Kaufmann who drew heavily upon a printed list of Lafayette High School graduates who served in World War I. She also interviewed a number of survivors, and studied various listings in municipal and county histories.

7. Rubenstein's wartime letters were examined through the courtesy of his sister, Mrs. Rhea Fass of Buffalo.

8. Beth Zion Minute Book, August 10, 1917.

9. *Ibid.,* December 2, 1917, August 4, 1918; Beth El Minute Book, October 2, 1917, February 13, 1918, April 10, 1918, December 1, 1918.

10. Federated Jewish Charities of Buffalo *Year Book, 1917-1918,* 5, 9 ff.

11. For a fuller discussion, see Solomon Grayzel, *A History of the Jews* (Philadelphia, 1955), 713-714. According to Dr. Grayzel, it is possible that from 1919 to 1921 there were over 1,200 pogroms in the Ukraine **alone.**

12. *American Jewish Review,* January 9, 1920, July 23, 1920, September 10, 1920; Buffalo *Express,* July 12, 1920; Buffalo *Commercial,* July 12, 1920; *Buffalo Jewish Review,* September 30, 1921, July 6, 1945.
A "Bernard Cantor Fellowship" was established at the Jewish Institute of Religion in New York and its first recipient was Nathaniel Cantor who left H.U.C. to accept it.

13. *Buffalo Jewish Review,* January 20, 1922; January 27, 1922; February 3, 1922; February 10, 1922; February 17, 1922.

14. *Ibid.,* August 1, 1924.

15. *Ibid.,* September 18, 1925.

16. *Ibid.,* June 18, 1926; October 15, 1926.

17. *Ibid.,* March 18, 1927; December 20, 1929.

18. Federated Jewish Charities of Buffalo *Minute Book,* January 21, 1918; Federated Jewish Charities of Buffalo *Year Book, 1917-1918,* 7-9.

19. Annette F. Arywitz, "A Short History of the Jewish Community Service of Buffalo" (unpublished thesis for the degree of Master of Social Science, University of Buffalo, 1948), 24 ff.; Jewish Federation for Social Service *Year Book, 1918-1919,* 5 ff.

20. An undated report of Mrs. Rummel to the Board of Governors was found in the Federation's files. After 1923, the work that Mrs. Rummel started was carried on by some public health nurses under the supervision of volunteer doctors and dentists. Graduates of the University of Buffalo were employed as case workers, and after the establishment of the School of Social Work at the University in 1935, trained case workers became locally available. Even before that time, Leah Gleichman had worked in the field of child welfare. The first purely professional case worker was Bernice Milch. By 1935, the modern case work system was fully in force. Arywitz, *loc. cit.,* 59 ff.

21. Arywitz, *loc. cit.,* 24-25.

22. *Buffalo Jewish Review,* November 4, 1921; November 25, 1921; December 2, 1921; December 9, 1921.

23. *Ibid.,* November 16, 1923; November 23, 1923; November 30, 1923.

24. *Ibid.,* October 31, 1924; November 21, 1924; December 5, 1924; December 12, 1924.

25. *Ibid.,* November 26, 1926; December 3, 1926; December 10, 1926; December 24, 1926.

26. *Ibid.,* November 4, 1927; November 11, 1927; December 9, 1927. The disbursements cited are taken from a letter to the Buffalo Chamber of Commerce, April 3, 1928, found in the Federation's files.

27. *Buffalo Jewish Review,* November 23, 1928; November 30, 1928; December 7, 1928; July 1, 1938.

28. *Ibid.,* November 8, 1929; November 22, 1929.

29. Federated Charities of Buffalo *Year Book, 1917-1918,* 15 ff.; *Buffalo Jewish Review,* April 15, 1921, May 6, 1921, December 16, 1921, June 9, 1922, June 16, 1922, September 8, 1922, January 4, 1924.
Organized about 1915, the Deborah Club for girls also met at the Jewish Community Building. It flourished for a time but dissolved when it lost too many members through matrimony.

30. Jewish Welfare Board, Report on Buffalo, 1923, 13 ff. In the files of the National Jewish Welfare Board, 145 E. 32nd St., New York, N. Y.

31. *Ibid.*, 40; *Buffalo Jewish Review*, June 4, 1926.
32. Jewish Federation For Social Service *Year Book, 1926-1927*, 11-13, 29; *ibid., 1927-1928*, 28-29.

    In 1926, Louis Shocket, a recent graduate of the Jewish School of Social Work in New York, replaced Mr. Cohen as director of the Jewish Community Building. He remained in Buffalo until 1945 and then served in similar capacities in several southern cities until his death in 1957.
33. Report of Louis Shocket to Board of Governors, January 1, 1927, in Federation files; Jewish Federation for Social Service *Year Book, 1927-1928*, 30 ff.; *Buffalo Jewish Review*, January 21, 1927, January 3, 1930.
34. *Buffalo Jewish Review*, November 29, 1929.

    In 1929 the Community Building program was enriched by the employment of Morris Selib (b. 1905) as Assistant Director. A devoted and learned Jew, later to gain prominence as an attorney, Mr. Selib helped put Jewish content of a more traditional nature into the program just at a time when new conditions made such a step mandatory.
35. For a detailed account, see Selig Adler, "Backgrounds of American Policy Toward Zion" in Moshe Davis (ed.), *Israel: Its Role in Civilization* (New York, 1956), 251-283.
36. *American Jewish Review*, October 4, 1918; November 1, 1918; December 6, 1918; March 7, 1919.
37. *Ibid.*, September 10, 1920; December 10, 1920.
38. *Ibid.*, December 10, 1920; minutes of the 1920 Buffalo convention preserved in the Zionist Archives and Library of Palestine Foundation Fund, New York, N. Y.; *Buffalo Commercial*, November 23, 1920.
39. Brandeis' London statement of July 14, 1920, was incorporated into the minutes of the Buffalo convention; Jacob De Haas, *Louis D. Brandeis* (New York, 1929), 139-145; Alpheus T. Mason, *Brandeis: A Free Man's Life* (New York, 1946), 460-464.
40. L. H. Miller to Emanuel Newman, November 20, 1930, Scrapbook of L. H. Miller, Zionist Archives and Library.
41. *Buffalo Jewish Review*, October 21, 1921, December 16, 1921; interview between Selig Adler and the late Dr. A. Morris Gilden of Buffalo, November 16, 1954.
42. *Buffalo Jewish Review*, September 21, 1923; November 30, 1923; February 22, 1924; February 29, 1924; April 11, 1924; May 23, 1924; May 30, 1924; June 6, 1924.
43. *Ibid.*, May 1, 1925; May 15, 1925; May 22, 1925.
44. *Ibid.*, October 30, 1925; November 13, 1925; December 4, 1925; December 11, 1925; unidentified Buffalo daily newspaper clippings in the Scrapbook of Mrs. Leon H. Miller, Buffalo.

    The Palestine Foundation Fund was designed to facilitate the emigration of Jews to Palestine, and the Jewish National Fund (Keren Kayemet l'Yisrael) bought land from Arabs in order to get it into Jewish hands either by rental or by sale. This latter organization survives today as an Israeli semi-governmental agrarian agency. UPA continued until 1929 and then, for the time being, the two drives were again separated. UPA was again reconstituted in 1935, and retained this name for four years until it became part of the United Jewish Appeal (UJA).

45. *Buffalo Jewish Review,* June 18, 1926; June 25, 1926; July 2, 1926; July 16, 1926.
46. *Ibid.,* March 18, 1927; May 6, 1927; May 13, 1927.
47. *Ibid.,* May 17, 1929; August 16, 1929; September 6, 1929; September 27, 1929; November 29, 1929; December 27, 1929.
48. *Ibid.,* September 19, 1930; October 17, 1930.
49. *Ibid.,* October 31, 1930; November 14, 1930.
50. *Ibid.,* February 11, 1921; Buffalo *Courier-Express,* April 13, 1941.
51. Quoted in Buffalo *Courier,* May 16, 1924.
52. Beth Jacob Minute Book, July 1, 1917, October 31, 1920; statement of Samuel Schanzer to Selig Adler, November 11, 1954. According to Mr. Schanzer, a Mizrachi unit was organized here in 1915 under the leadership of Sigmund Schanzer, Joseph Gross and Harry Harriton. It did not have continuous existence, however, and prior to 1932 functioned mostly within the Z.O.A. district.
53. This information is based upon Minute Books and other material formerly in the possession of Mr. Isadore Wolk of Buffalo and now preserved at the Yivo Institute in New York. These Yiddish sources were translated for the authors by their colleague, Dr. Shia Moser.
54. *Buffalo Jewish Review,* April 18, 1924.
55. *Ibid.,* July 3, 1931; September 4, 1931; September 18, 1931.
56. *Ibid.,* September 9, 1932. During the 1920s all Labor Zionist groups met at the Jewish Workers Institute while it existed at 488 Jefferson Avenue. Later, they met at the Labor Zionist Center located further uptown on the same street, and for a time there was a Poale Zion Center at 467 Broadway.
57. *Ibid.,* March 12, 1926. Much of our information on the left-of-center Zionist groups is based upon interviews between Selig Adler and Mr. Nathe Dozoretz of Buffalo. Because the Buffalo Jewish proletariat was always relatively small, the going was hard for the small coalition that actively supported these *Gewerkschaften* campaigns. These campaigns, in the 1930s, yielded about $4,000 a year.
58. See Uriah Z. Engelman, "Medurbia," *Contemporary Jewish Record,* IV, No. 4 (August, 1941), 339-348; No. 5 (October, 1941), 511-521.
59. Based upon material cited in fn. 53 of this chapter.
60. *Buffalo Jewish Review,* January 29, 1941.
61. See Mr. Sherman's pamphlet, *Three Centuries of Growth* (New York, 1954).
62. Federated Jewish Charities of Buffalo *Year Book, 1917-1918,* 11-12.
63. Report of the Jewish Welfare Board on Buffalo, 1923, *loc. cit.*
64. *Buffalo Jewish Review,* July 25, 1924.
65. Uriah Z. Engelman, *A Study of the Size of Families in the Jewish Population of Buffalo* (University of Buffalo Studies, XVI, No. 1, November, 1938).
66. The 1922 survey of the Jewish Welfare Board (released 1923) found that 70.6% of Buffalo's Jews lived on the East Side; 16 years later, Dr. Engelman estimated that only 19.9% still lived there. As to the total Jewish population of the city, it was estimated in 1920 to be 18,000; six years later it was said to be 20,000. While accurate figures for 1960 are lack-

ing, it is estimated to be at present about 28,000. This figure would, of course, include the immediate suburbs.

67. *American Jewish Review,* July 4, 1919.
68. *Ibid.,* July 23, 1920, December 10, 1920; Buffalo *Commercial,* July 8, 1920; Buffalo *Courier-Express,* May 12, 1927.
69. *Buffalo Jewish Review,* November 23, 1923.
70. *Ibid.,* May 13, 1927; May 20, 1927.
71. Buffalo *Courier-Express,* January 28, 1929; *Buffalo Jewish Review,* February 1, 1929; unidentified newspaper clippings in the Scrapbook of Mrs. Leon H. Miller.
72. Beth El Minute Book, July 19, 1922; April 26, 1927.
73. Buffalo *Express,* June 29, 1917, July 4, 1917; Buffalo *Commercial,* June 29, 1917.
74. A Scrapbook containing information on this convention, including some unidentified newspaper clippings, is in the Beth Zion Minute Book for May, 1921.
75. *American Jewish Review,* June 25, 1920.
   There is good reason to believe that Rabbi Kopald prodded the editor of the *Review* to keep pressing the issue. It reprinted an article by Rabbi Max C. Currick of Erie (August 20, 1920) which asserted that the old reserved system was un-Jewish and told of the success of free seating in his own synagogue.
76. Beth Zion Minute Book, November 7, 1920.
77. *Ibid.,* December 19, 1920; May 1, 1921.
   The two-year trial period was a stormy one, for the new by-laws provided that temple dues were to be assessed by the board's decision as to what a member could afford to pay. It was a period of business recession and there were considerable protests to this arrangement until it was abandoned.
78. Dr. Joseph L. Fink to Selig Adler, November 21, 1957.
79. Beth Zion Minute Book, September 16, 1923, October 5, 1924.
80. This material on Dr. Fink's career is based in large part upon a souvenir pamphlet of his life prepared in 1949 by the late Arthur I. Goldberg and distributed at the time of Dr. Fink's twenty-fifth anniversary as rabbi of Beth Zion.
81. This information is based upon a speech made by the late Mr. Herman Wile in 1939 and is in the Beth Zion files for that year.
82. For these intimate details we have drawn heavily upon A. I. Goldberg, (comp.), *In Honor of Dr. Joseph L. Fink on his Twenty-fifth Anniversary as Rabbi of Temple Beth Zion* (pamphlet, Buffalo, 1949).
83. Buffalo *Evening News,* October 24, 1949.
84. Dr. Joseph L. Fink to Selig Adler, November 21, 1957.
85. Corporation Box 7899 in the office of the clerk of the County of Erie, Buffalo, N. Y.; interview between Selig Adler and Mr. Meyer Shapiro of Buffalo, August 18, 1954; information on Mr. Smolev was furnished the authors by his daughter, Mrs. Morris Steinhorn of Buffalo.
86. *American Jewish Review,* March 5, 1920; September 10, 1920.
87. A photostat of the papers of incorporation has been furnished the authors through the kindness of Mr. Max M. Yellen of Buffalo. Evidently it evolved from a committee representing all "Orthodox Jewish Synagogues" and

Temple Beth David that was functioning at least as early as 1924. See *Buffalo Jewish Review*, February 8, 1924; July 10, 1925; September 4, 1925; September 11, 1925; May 24, 1929. The organization achieved a certain ephemeral success in its earlier years in pooling the amount of money sent out of the city to Orthodox institutions and regulating its allocation.

88. Buffalo *Evening News*, May 2, 1933, August 26, 1939; *Buffalo Jewish Review*, April 22, 1932, July 1, 1932, July 22, 1932, January 27, 1933, March 10, 1933, May 5, 1933, January 6, 1939.

89. Buffalo *Times*, June 13, 1931, July 8, 1931; interview with Dr. Louis L. Gitin, August 5, 1954.
In 1951, the Pine Street Shul opened a branch on Hertel Avenue near Delaware; the downtown *shul* was demolished in 1960.

90. Corporation Box 155 in the office of the clerk of the County of Erie, Buffalo. After worshipping in the Laufer home, but prior to the erection of a permanent synagogue, the congregation used a converted private house on Fillmore Avenue.

91. *Buffalo Jewish Review*, February 18, 1927. Additional information on Mr. Gerstman was supplied the authors by several members of his large and prominent family of children.

92. *Buffalo Jewish Review*, June 17, 1921, September 30, 1921, November 26, 1926, July 5, 1929, December 11, 1931; Buffalo *Courier-Express*, September 7, 1926.

93. *Buffalo Jewish Review*, April 29, 1921; August 26, 1921; September 9, 1921; September 30, 1921. The first site of worship proved too small for the group and in 1920, it moved elsewhere and eventually to St. Andrew's Scottish Club at 509 Lafayette Avenue, where they worshipped on Holidays. During this period, the congregation prayed on Sabbaths in the home of Abraham Luxemberg on Forest Avenue.

94. Corporation Box 4177 in the office of the clerk of the County of Erie, Buffalo; *Buffalo Jewish Review*, September 7, 1923. In the year of the opening of the new synagogue at 1045 Elmwood Avenue, Joseph Rosenblatt became president, an office which he held until his death in 1934. Other important members at the time were Ellis Simon, Hyman J. Fogel (1890-1950, for many years the secretary), Jacob Rivkin, the Ravnitsky brothers who were all kosher butchers, Emil Rubenstein, and members of the Lansky and Yellen families.

95. Corporation Box 13904 in the office of the clerk of the County of Erie; Report of the Jewish Welfare Board on Buffalo, 1923, 30; *Buffalo Jewish Review*, September 16, 1921, December 21, 1923, August 29, 1924.

96. *Buffalo Jewish Review*, June 6, 1924, September 26, 1924, November 28, 1924, August 28, 1925; Buffalo *Express*, November 24, 1924.

97. *Buffalo Jewish Review*, October 15, 1926; February 25, 1927; April 8, 1927; April 15, 1927; August 30, 1929.

98. Jewish Welfare Board, Report on Buffalo, 1938, 40. In the files of the National Jewish Welfare Board, *loc. cit.*

99. Corporation Box 18690 in the office of the clerk of the County of Erie; Buffalo *Evening News*, December 14, 1955; *Buffalo Jewish Review*, September 27, 1929. In addition to Ohel Jacob, Rabbi Rubin Weinstein,

a native Palestinian who came to Buffalo in 1923, founded and conducted a synagogue in his own home in 1934. First located on Roehrer Avenue, Congregation Tifereth Zion later moved to Woodlawn Avenue. It went out of existence, due to the decline of the neighborhood, in the late 1940s.

100. *Buffalo Jewish Review*, December 4, 1931; October 5, 1945.
101. *Ibid.*, October 12, 1923, September 26, 1924; interview between Selig Adler and Mr. Morris Singer of Buffalo, July 25, 1954.
102. *Buffalo Jewish Review*, June 13, 1924, July 11, 1924, July 18, 1924; *Silver Anniversary Bulletin of Temple Emanu-El* (pamphlet, Buffalo, 1950), *passim*.
103. *Buffalo Jewish Review*, February 27, 1925; April 3, 1925; October 23, 1925; December 11, 1925.
104. Emanu-El Minute Book, September 26, 1928; September 27, 1928.
105. *Ibid.*, September 11, 1929, October 16, 1929, November 13, 1929, November 20, 1929, December 18, 1929; interview between Selig Adler and Mr. Samuel Sapowitch, August 16, 1959.
106. *Buffalo Jewish Review*, January 9, 1931; February 27, 1931.
107. Emanu-El Minute Book, November 13, 1933; Buffalo *Courier-Express*, December 23, 1933, May 28, 1934; Buffalo *Evening News*, December 23, 1933, January 8, 1934, January 13, 1934; *Buffalo Jewish Review*, January 12, 1934, May 18, 1934, December 29, 1934. An appeal to the entire community was made in January, 1934, and a dinner attended by 1,000 was held to raise funds for the new building. In this fashion, over $15,000 was raised, the principal workers being J. R. Morrison, Hyman Kahn, Susman Ginsberg, Morris Singer, and Lester Gross.
108. Report of the Jewish Welfare Board on Buffalo, 1938, 41, *loc. cit.*; *Buffalo Jewish Review*, April 1, 1938, July 15, 1938.
     In 1938, Emanu-El acquired its own cemetery, purchasing part of Elmlawn Cemetery at Brighton Road and Delaware Avenue in Tonawanda. William Rosenthal headed the committee at the time. The most active member in this phase of the congregation's activities has been Mr. William Malkinson.
109. *Buffalo Jewish Review*, July 16, 1943. It was at this time that the congregation began a campaign to raise $50,000 for a building fund which ultimately raised only about 50% of the goal and was set aside for future use.
110. Corporation Box 8930 in the office of the clerk of the County of Erie, Buffalo; *Buffalo Jewish Review*, September 11, 1925, October 30, 1925, October 1, 1926, May 2, 1930, August 28, 1931; Buffalo *Evening News*, August 29, 1931.
     In part, this success was the result of efforts outside of the group. Max Grossman of Beth El lent assistance and Nathan Swerdloff (1862-1937) gave the congregation good lay leadership. Also active in the congregation at this time were Joseph Berger, David Bisgeier and Henry C. Price, an energetic and popular attorney who died in 1941. We are indebted to Mrs. Joseph Woldman for information about her father, Hyman S. Weinstein.
111. This information on Temple Sinai is based largely upon typed informa-

tion which we were allowed to examine through the kindness of Rabbi Nathan Gaynor.

112. See Will Herberg, "Religious Trends in American Jewry," *Judaism*, III, 229-240 (1954).

113. *Buffalo Jewish Review*, January 8, 1926.

114. *Ibid.*, August 25, 1922.

115. *Hillel* (pamphlet published by B'nai B'rith Hillel Foundations in American Universities, n.d., n.p.), 9.

116. *Buffalo Jewish Review*, January 1, 1926.

117. Quoted *ibid.*, February 24, 1928.

118. *Ibid.*, March 30, 1928.

119. Bureau of Jewish Social Research, Survey of the Buffalo Jewish Community, 1929, 78. Files of the United Jewish Federation of Buffalo.

120. *Buffalo Jewish Review*, April 29, 1921; Horton, *op. cit.*, 390; Mr. Rubenstein often spoke of these threats to his nephew, one of the authors of this book.

121. Corporation Box 7907 in the office of the clerk of the County of Erie, Buffalo; *Buffalo Jewish Review*, May 20, 1921, April 26, 1929, May 24, 1929, June 14, 1929, February 21, 1930; Engelman, "Medurbia," *loc. cit.*; interview between Dr. Milton Plesur and Mrs. Jack Siegel of Buffalo, August 31, 1954. The evidence would indicate that the Mothers Club grew out of an informal association of women who had been performing similar service for some four years prior to their decision to incorporate.

122. *Buffalo Jewish Review*, December 4, 1931, June 16, 1933, March 23, 1934, December 4, 1936, October 11, 1937; Report on Buffalo of Jewish Welfare Board, 1938, 35; interview between Selig Adler and Mrs. Morris Singer of Buffalo, July 25, 1954; detailed history of the club prepared for the authors in 1955 by one of its longtime members and officers, Mrs. Joseph M. Singer of Buffalo.

123. *Buffalo Jewish Review*, January 7, 1927, January 14, 1927, February 18, 1927; Report on Buffalo of Jewish Welfare Board, 1938, 33; various interviews between members and Miss Renate Kaufmann.

124. *Buffalo Jewish Review*, April 29, 1921, April 25, 1924, October 16, 1925, October 30, 1925; interview between Selig Adler and Mr. David Rodenberg of Buffalo, December 2, 1954; digest of information in the Scrapbook of the Montefiore Club, prepared for the authors by Miss Renate Kaufmann.

125. *Buffalo Jewish Review*, July 15, 1921, September 21, 1923, March 25, 1927, June 11, 1937; interview between Dr. Milton Plesur and Mr. D. Sloan Hurwitz of Buffalo, September 1, 1954.

126. *Buffalo Jewish Review*, October 21, 1921. Much of the information on the Jewish scouting movement in Buffalo was obtained from a brief prepared for the authors by Mr. Isadore Morrison of Buffalo.

127. "Periodical Press of Buffalo," in *Publications of the Buffalo Historical Society*, XXIV, 383-386 (1920); *American Jewish Review*, September 6, 1918; interview between Selig Adler and Mr. Philip Cohen of Buffalo, October 3, 1954.

128. *American Jewish Review*, March 17, 1919; April 11, 1919.

129. Interview between Selig Adler and Mr. Elias Rex Jacobs of Buffalo,

August 1, 1955; *Buffalo Jewish Review*, December 18, 1925, January 27, 1928.

130. *Buffalo Jewish Review*, September 9, 1921, February 27, 1931; interview between Selig Adler and Mr. William Sultz of Buffalo, November 14, 1954.

131. *American Jewish Review*, October 8, 1920, November 12, 1920; *Buffalo Jewish Review*, February 11, 1921.

132. Corporation Box 7900 in the office of the clerk of the County of Erie, Buffalo. The incorporation date was 1916.

133. *Buffalo Jewish Review*, February 11, 1921, January 6, 1922, January 27, 1922, February 3, 1922, June 5, 1922, August 14, 1925, September 25, 1925, October 23, 1925; Arywitz, *loc. cit.*, 24.

134. *Buffalo Jewish Review*, March 19, 1926, April 30, 1926, May 7, 1926, May 14, 1926, May 21, 1926, October 22, 1926, April 1, 1927, March 2, 1928, March 22, 1929; Buffalo Communal Survey, 1929, Summary, 6, *loc. cit.*; Montefiore Lodge #70 Minute Book, January 19, 1933.

135. *Buffalo Jewish Review*, October 14, 1927.

136. *Ibid.*, March 3, 1933; Buffalo *Evening News*, Spetember 16, 1937. Much information concerning Mr. Davis was obtained from his Scrapbook, now in the possession of his son, Mr. Marvin Davis of Buffalo.

137. *Buffalo Jewish Review*, October 3, 1924, October 9, 1925; interviews between Selig Adler and Judges Harris and Halpern.

138. *Buffalo Jewish Review*, October 30, 1925, April 24, 1925; interviews between Selig Adler and Judge Diamond.

139. *Buffalo Jewish Review*, July 10, 1925; interview between Selig Adler and Mr. Emanuel Boasberg, Jr., of Buffalo, April 18, 1959.

140. This information on Buffalo Jewish architects is based on information supplied the authors by Mr. Louis Greenstein, Mr. Jacob Fruchtbaum, Mrs. Edward M. Plant, Mr. Milton Milstein and Mrs. Harry Blum, all of Buffalo.

141. Buffalo *Evening News*, July 19, 1930.

142. *Ibid.*, August 26, 1946; interview between Selig Adler and Mr. Sidney B. Maisel of Buffalo, April 18, 1959.

143. Buffalo *Courier-Express*, September 8, 1940.

144. Corporation Box 13613 in the office of the clerk of the County of Erie, Buffalo; *Buffalo Jewish Review*, January 30, 1925, March 11, 1927; interview between Selig Adler and Mr. Meyer Shapiro of Buffalo, August 1, 1954.

145. *Buffalo Jewish Review*, April 23, 1926; May 7, 1926.

146. *Ibid.*, January 27, 1928.

147. Information on Mr. Simon's career was furnished the authors by Mrs. D. Bernard Simon of Buffalo.

148. Buffalo *Courier-Express*, March 13, 1939.

149. Interview between Selig Adler and Mrs. Jonah D. Margulis of Buffalo, April 18, 1959.

150. Buffalo *Times*, January 6, 1936; Buffalo *Evening News*, December 30, 1943; *Buffalo Jewish Review*, February 2, 1934, January 3, 1936, January 10, 1936; Arywitz, *loc. cit.*, 42, fn. 2.

151. Buffalo *Times*, January 6, 1936.

CHAPTER IX
"OUT OF THE DEPTHS . . ."

1. Uriah Z. Engelman, "Medurbia," *Contemporary Jewish Record,* IV, No. 4 (August, 1941), 339-348.
2. Field Report of George W. Rabinoff to the Council of Jewish Federations and Welfare Funds, March 5, 1932. In the files of the C.J.F.W.F., 729 Seventh Avenue, New York, N. Y.
3. Jewish Federation for Social Service *Year Book, 1928-1929,* 2.
4. *Ibid., 1929-1930,* 20.
5. *Ibid.,* 22. Here Miss Cecil B. Wiener states that she originally suggested the survey in 1915.
6. *Buffalo Jewish Review,* May 2, 1930.
7. Eugene Warner, "Federation Evolution," in Jewish Federation for Social Service *Year Book, 1929-1930,* 13-17.
8. *Buffalo Jewish Review,* November 28, 1930; December 5, 1930; December 12, 1930.
9. Oscar Handlin, *Adventure in Freedom* (New York, 1954), 6.
10. Flyer in the 1931 files of the Buffalo Bureau of Jewish Education.
11. *Buffalo Jewish Review,* March 20, 1936.
12. *Ibid.,* October 30, 1931; November 6, 1931; November 20, 1931.
13. Rabinoff's report of April 13, 1932, *loc. cit.*
14. *Buffalo Jewish Review,* May 27, 1932.
15. *Ibid.,* December 16, 1932; December 30, 1932; January 6, 1933; January 13, 1933.
16. Handbill in the 1933 files of the United Jewish Federation of Buffalo.
17. *Buffalo Jewish Review,* January 1, 1932.
18. Flora I. Dudley's annual report on "The Roof Clinic," 1933, in the files of the United Jewish Federation of Buffalo.
19. *Buffalo Jewish Review,* October 27, 1933; November 10, 1933; November 24, 1933; December 1, 1933. See also Jewish Federation for Social Service *Year Book, 1933,* 2-3.
20. Report of Lillian A. Hirshberg, January 17, 1934, for the Hospital Visiting Committee in the files of the United Jewish Federation of Buffalo. Mrs. Hirshberg gave much of the credit for the success of this committee to Mrs. Charles Bock. The figures on relief sums are from the Jewish Federation for Social Service *Year Book, 1935,* 20.
21. *Buffalo Jewish Review,* October 19, 1934; November 2, 1934; November 16, 1934; November 23, 1934. The quota for this campaign was set at a little over $150,000, which was $21,620 more than was raised in the preceding drive of 1933.
22. *Ibid.,* October 18, 1935, November 1, 1935, November 15, 1935, November 22, 1935; Jewish Federation for Social Service *Year Book, 1936,* 3.
23. *Buffalo Jewish Review,* October 29, 1935, October 15, 1937, November 19, 1937, November 26, 1937; Jewish Federation for Social Service *Year Book, 1938,* 1. The figures given are in round numbers.
24. *Buffalo Jewish Review,* October 7, 1938; October 21, 1938; November 12, 1938; November 25, 1938. Stanley G. Falk headed this United Jewish Campaign of 1938.

25. *Ibid.*, March 24, 1933; March 31, 1933; April 3, 1933.
26. Wise to Eugene Warner, May 18, 1933, files of the United Jewish Federation of Buffalo.
27. *Buffalo Jewish Review,* July 14, 1933.
28. *Ibid.*, May 19, 1933; June 1, 1933. Eugene Warner was chairman, Louis Maisel treasurer, and Samuel B. Darlich secretary. Until this drive was combined with the Federation drive in 1937, the Federation ran its annual campaign in the fall and the overseas drive was held in the spring.
29. There was no United Jewish Appeal drive in Buffalo in 1934, but the following year, Stanley G. Falk headed a campaign that resembled the 1933 effort. It was part of a national effort to raise $5,000,000, arranged by JDC and the American Palestine Campaign. Buffalo's quota was set at $27,500. *Ibid.*, January 18, 1935; February 15, 1935; February 22, 1935; March 1, 1935.
30. *Ibid.*, May 15, 1936; May 22, 1936; May 29, 1936; June 5, 1936; June 12, 1936.
31. In the spring of 1939, Warner headed a united appeal to raise $75,000 in Buffalo. This joint drive for $20,000,000 in the country was sponsored by JDC and UPA. The following year, Warner, who was the regional director of JDC, pressed for local action to aid a country-wide campaign for $23,000,000 that would also include the National Refugee Service. Harold B. Ehrlich headed the local drive which, due to the wartime emergency, set its sights for $149,205. Late in 1940, however, the union of UPA, JDC and the National Refugee Service was dissolved. After a period of much bickering over the allocation of funds, the local United Jewish Fund was formed on March 25, 1941, to unite all local overseas appeals. The 1941 Buffalo quota was set at $150,000, but the going was hard and the campaign had to be lengthened. Only with returning prosperity and popular realization of the needs of world Jewry was there to be the phenomenal fund-raising of the late 1940s.
Ibid., May 19, 1939; April 19, 1940; May 17, 1940; June 7, 1940; March 14, 1941; March 21, 1941; March 28, 1941; May 2, 1941; May 9, 1941.
32. *Ibid.*, July 31, 1931.
33. "Medurbia (II)," *Contemporary Jewish Record,* IV, No. 5 (October, 1941), 511-521.
34. *Loc. cit.*
35. Reports of George Wolfe to the Council of Jewish Federations and Welfare Funds, November 4, 1937; April 24, 1940; August 6, 1940: *loc. cit.*
36. Jewish Welfare Board, Report on Buffalo, 1923, 32. In the files of the National Jewish Welfare Board, 145 E. 32nd St. New York, N. Y.
37. *Buffalo Jewish Review,* September 23, 1927; September 30, 1927.
38. *Ibid.*, July 13, 1928; July 20, 1928; August 10, 1928; August 24, 1928; August 31, 1928; September 14, 1928; September 21, 1928. Regional directors were: Jerome L. Schwartz, Jacob Tick, Frank E. Freedman, Harry J. Lehman, Joseph Markel and Samuel Schanzer. According to the *Buffalo Jewish Review,* January 29, 1943, Mr. Tick originally called Mr. Wile's attention to the situation in 1926. This survey was privately financed; of the $1,650 expenses incurred, Mr. Levy paid $500 and Mr. Wile paid the balance out of his own pocket.
39. Part of the community's difficulty with Jewish education stemmed from insufficient funds. Prior to the establishment of the Bureau, about $45,000

a year had been spent for religious education. The Federation allotted for the Jewish Community Building Sunday School and the Talmud Torah $14,000 a year; various congregations spent $16,000, while miscellaneous expenditures accounted for the rest.

40. Survey of the Buffalo Jewish Community: Jewish Education Section, 1929, 1 ff. A copy of this survey by the Bureau of Jewish Social Research is in the files of the United Jewish Federation of Buffalo. Section V, on Jewish Education, was prepared by Louis Hurwich of Boston.

41. From a note in the files of the Buffalo Bureau of Jewish Education. It would seem that these aims, as here stated, were placed in their concrete form at a later date by Dr. Elazar Goelman, director of the Bureau, 1949-1959. They express, however, the intentions of the founders.

42. Alexander M. Dushkin, "Ben M. Edidin," *Jewish Education,* XX (Fall, 1948). Edidin had originally prepared for an agricultural career in Palestine, but later decided to remain in this country in the field of Jewish education.

43. Rabbi Joseph L. Fink in *Buffalo Jewish Review,* September 19, 1930.

44. Rabbi Harry J. Brevis to Selig Adler, April 15, 1958.

45. Brief prepared for the authors by Mrs. Irving I. Crouse, October 28, 1954; Buffalo *Evening News,* January 29, 1940.

46. For instance, see Eugene Warner's statement in the Jewish Federation for Social Service *Year Book, 1930,* 15. Here he spelled out that the principal work of the Bureau was to be in fostering the Jewish religion, rather than the Hebrew language.

47. This report of Edidin to the Board of Governors of the Federation, made January 26, 1931, is quoted extensively in the *Buffalo Jewish Review,* February 6, 1931.

48. This report of April 18, 1938, is in the files of the American Association for Jewish Education, 1261 Broadway, New York, N. Y.

49. This survey was sponsored jointly by the Conference on Jewish Relations and the Federation. Dr. Engelman, as his part of this study, concentrated on the school situation, studying 4,400 family units. Its findings indicated, contrary to Edidin's reports, that the percentage of Jewish children receiving some kind of Jewish training had increased only slightly since the founding of the Bureau in 1930. *Buffalo Jewish Review,* August 26, 1938, September 9, 1938; Field report of George Wolfe to the Council of Jewish Federations and Welfare Funds, February 28, 1938, *loc. cit.* Dr. Engelman's "Medurbia" articles are cited elsewhere in the documentation for this chapter.

50. Summary of Dr. Engelman's annual report of 1940-1941 to the Executive Committee of the Buffalo Bureau of Jewish Education, in the files of the Bureau. The High School of Jewish Studies began to function in 1943.

51. Henry W. Hill (comp.), *Municipality of Buffalo, N. Y.* (4 vols., New York, 1923), IV, 270-271.

52. Annual reports of Krug to the Executive Committee of the Buffalo Bureau of Jewish Education, 1946, 1947, in the files of the American Association for Jewish Education, *loc. cit.* By the fiscal year of 1948-1949, the Bureau's budget had climbed to $45,905.

53. This agreement, dated July 1, 1948, is in the files of the Bureau. From January to April, 1949, a joint inter-agency committee ironed out the

details and drew up a suggested "pattern of cooperation" between the Bureau and the Center.

54. Based upon a memorandum in the Bureau's files for 1954 and an interview between Selig Adler and Dr. Elazar Goelman, July 15, 1959. Another study of Jewish Education in Buffalo was undertaken in 1955 by the American Association for Jewish Education. It was conducted by Dr. U. Z. Engelman and Mrs. Shashana Ginsberg, assisted by a local committee headed by Jacob Lansky. It found 2,718 pupils enrolled in all schools, an increase of some 600 since the 1938 study. A 29-page summary of the full report, containing many interesting details on Jewish education in Buffalo, may be found in the files of the United Jewish Federation of Buffalo.

55. *Buffalo Jewish Review,* May 24, 1935, July 30, 1937; Mr. Darlich's letter is quoted in Jewish Welfare Board, Report on Buffalo, 1938, 70. The report is in the files of the National Jewish Welfare Board, New York, N. Y. Dr. Charles Bernheimer was in charge of this survey, made at the request of the Buffalo "Y" groups.

56. This letter is quoted in the 1938 JWB Report, cited above.

57. Field Report of George Wolfe to the Council of Jewish Federations and Welfare Funds, February 28, 1938, *loc. cit.* According to Wolfe's report of August 6, 1940, the Federation gave the "Y" a subsidy of $5,000. This was the result of the work of a joint committee which insisted upon it. It was given for one calendar year, subject to the understanding that the "Y" would not conduct an independent campaign. See also *Buffalo Jewish Review,* November 3, 1939.

58. Max M. Yellen to Eugene Warner, December 16, 1940. Files of the United Jewish Federation of Buffalo.
In 1940, an abortive effort was made to buy the Elks Club on Delaware Avenue. Five years later, still another effort to acquire the property failed; but the community did then pledge $200,000 for the anticipated purchase and this money later became the nucleus of a building fund for the present Jewish Center.

59. Annual Report of Harry Bluestone, May 13, 1942. In the possession of Mr. Max M. Yellen of Buffalo.

60. *Buffalo Jewish Review,* July 13, 1945, July 20, 1945; Corporation Box 11373 in the office of the clerk of the County of Erie, Buffalo.

61. Eigen succeeded Sidney Nelson who had been executive director after Bluestone's resignation. Information on how the Center operated in those migratory days is in "A Report on the Jewish Center of Buffalo to the Jewish Federation for Social Service, October, 1947," in the files of the United Jewish Federation of Buffalo.

62. A report of this "Study Commission," dated June 1, 1949, is in the Federation's files. Interview between Selig Adler and Mrs. Hyman L. Levin, July 15, 1959.

63. Montefiore Lodge #70 Minute Book, September 11, 1933.

64. John T. Horton, "Old Erie—The Growth of an American Community," vol. I of John T. Horton *et al., History of Northwestern New York* (New York, 1947), 404.

65. Statement prepared for the authors by Mrs. Morris Steinhorn, July 1, 1954.

66. *Buffalo Jewish Review,* August 6, 1926; October 9, 1931.
67. *Ibid.,* October 2, 1925; October 8, 1926.
68. *Ibid.,* September 18, 1925.
69. *Ibid.,* October 26, 1928.
70. *Ibid.,* February 26, 1932.
71. *Ibid.,* August 1, 1930; December 7, 1934; March 8, 1935; August 26, 1935.
72. *Ibid.,* March 20, 1936. There was also "The American Committee for the Settlement of Jews in Birobidjan" which was active here and elsewhere.
73. Corporation Box 7908 in the office of the clerk of the County of Erie, Buffalo.
74. The Minute Books of the local Workmen's Circle Branch, which we examined while they were still in the possession of Mr. Isadore Wolk of Buffalo, bear out the general trends portrayed by Will Herberg in "The Jewish Labor Movement in the United States," *American Jewish Year Book 1952* (Philadelphia, 1952), 3-74.
75. *Buffalo Jewish Review,* October 14, 1927; October 21, 1927; February 27, 1931.
76. The minutes of the Youth Committee in Buffalo, dating from January 7, 1937, were examined while they were still in Mr. Wolk's possession. They are now in the custody of Yivo in New York.
77. Jewish Welfare Board, Report on Buffalo, 1938, 33, *loc. cit.* Until 1933 there was an Independent Workmen's Circle, with headquarters in Boston. In 1933, this organization merged with the New York outfit and, its Buffalo branch followed suit locally.
78. See Herberg, *loc. cit.*
79. Dr. Joseph L. Fink in *Buffalo Jewish Review,* January 17, 1936.
80. *Ibid.,* January 16, 1942; July 3, 1942.
81. *Ibid.,* January 7, 1944; January 28, 1944.
82. Pamphlet examined in the Library of the American Jewish Committee, New York, N. Y. It is dated 1949.
   A.J.C. was active on a small scale in Buffalo almost from the time of its origin, although no regular chapter seems to have existed here until 1945. Among those who belonged when membership was still an invitation affair were Judge Louis W. Marcus, Simon Fleischmann, Herman Wile, Eugene Warner, Frederick Ullman and Rabbi Louis J. Kopald. Rabbi Fink joined after his arrival in Buffalo and often defended the A.J.C. point of view. See *Buffalo Jewish Review,* November 15, 1929.
83. *Buffalo Jewish Review,* July 2, 1943; September 3, 1943; October 29, 1943.
84. Field reports of George Wolfe, February 28, 1938; June 11-12, 1938, *loc. cit.*
   Part of this crisis was caused by the resignation of Miss Laura Margolis as Executive Director of the Jewish Welfare Society. Wolfe reported that this resignation came, in part, because of interference by Federation officials in the conduct of Miss Margolis' duties.
85. This statement of policy is in the files of the United Jewish Federation of Buffalo; Field Report of George Wolfe to the Council of Jewish Federations and Welfare Funds, August 17, 1940, *loc. cit.*

86. Annette F. Arywitz, "A Short History of the Jewish Community Service of Buffalo" (unpublished thesis for the degree of Master of Social Science, University of Buffalo, 1948), 164.
The Federation drive for 1941 set its goal at $166,000. This was the last campaign destined to be headed by Eugene Warner. The 1942 drive, headed by Joseph Markel, set its goal at $164,063. It went over the top for the first time since the onset of the depression. The 1943 campaign, headed by Willard W. Saperston, set its goal at only $145,755. This reduction probably came because of decreasing relief needs at home and increasing overseas demands that were then handled by a separate campaign. *Buffalo Jewish Review,* October 25, 1940; November 15, 1940; October 31, 1941; November 7, 1941; November 14, 1941; October 23, 1942; November 13, 1942.

87. Field Report of Samuel Weingarten to the Council of Jewish Federations and Welfare Funds, April 23, 1943, *loc. cit. Buffalo Jewish Review,* February 26, 1943; March 19, 1943; April 30, 1943; May 7, 1943; May 14, 1943; May 21, 1943; June 11, 1943; June 18, 1943. The War Chest attempted to raise $3,280,000, of which $385,000 was to go to Jewish causes. Despite the unprecedented emergency the going was hard and it is probable that the goal was not reached.

88. Field Report of R. Fitterman to the Council of Jewish Federations and Welfare Funds, July 27, 1944, *loc. cit.*

89. Biographical material on Edward H. Kavinoky, as of October, 1958, furnished the authors by Mr. Kavinoky.

90. *Buffalo Jewish Review,* February 9, 1945, March 23, 1945; Arywitz, *loc. cit.,* 165 ff.

91. "A Report on the Jewish Community Service Society submitted to the Jewish Federation for Social Service, October, 1947." Files of the United Jewish Federation of Buffalo.

92. *Ibid.;* interview between Selig Adler and Mr. Sydney S. Abzug, Executive Director of the United Jewish Federation of Buffalo, July 15, 1959.

93. Sketch of the Federation's history, dated December 10, 1952, in the files of the United Jewish Federation of Buffalo.

94. These statistics were furnished to the authors by Mr. Sydney S. Abzug, July 15, 1959.

95. Benjamin D. Reisman, "The Jew Faces the World," address delivered before B'nai B'rith Victory Lodge #1481, April 10, 1944. A printed copy of this speech is in the Minute Book of Montefiore Lodge #70 for 1944.

96. Buffalo *Courier-Express,* November 21, 1944; statement prepared for the authors by Mrs. Morris Steinhorn, July 1, 1954.

97. Buffalo *Courier-Express,* November 12, 1942; December 28, 1942; May 31, 1943.

98. *Buffalo Jewish Review,* September 24, 1943; October 12, 1945.

99. *Ibid.,* October 29, 1943; December 14, 1943; April 13, 1945; November 23, 1945.

100. Annual Report of Harry Bluestone, May 13, 1942. *Loc. cit.*

101. Buffalo *Courier-Express,* March 4, 1945.

102. Unidentified newspaper clippings from the Scrapbook of Paul Drozen, Buffalo.

103. Note in Montefiore Lodge #70 Minute Book, May, 1944.

104. Interview between Selig Adler and Dr. Yellen, August 6, 1958; interview between Selig Adler and Dr. Bronk, July 15, 1958; Dr. Heyman Smolev to Selig Adler, November 4, 1957.
105. Buffalo *Evening News,* January 15, 1947.
106. This information has been culled from the wartime columns of the *Buffalo Jewish Review,* and has been implemented by numerous interviews with survivors or, in other cases, with members of their families. The information is too detailed for the usual type of annotation.
107. Mrs. Jerry Blanke to Selig Adler, July 13, 1959; interview between Selig Adler and Mrs. Milton M. Bron, July 31, 1959.
108. This information is based primarily upon a reading of the *Buffalo Jewish Review's* column, "With Buffalo Jewish Boys in the Service," for the years indicated.
109. Interviews between Selig Adler and Mr. Swados and Mr. Satuloff, July 30, 1959; Howard F. Beir to Mrs. Elwood G. Becker, August 4, 1959. Lieutenant Colonel Beir was in the service from 1940 to 1946, wore American Air Force, American paratroopers, British paratroopers, R.A.F., and Royal Yugoslavian Air Force flight wings.
110. *Buffalo Jewish Review,* January 12, 1945.
111. *Ibid.,* April 14, 1944.
112. *Ibid.,* August 27, 1943; November 19, 1943.
113. The local branch of the Jewish War Veterans was organized in 1927 by Sol Feldman. It received its charter two years later, and was then called Louis Marshall Post #25. In 1932, William Sultz of Buffalo, who had served in the cavalry during World War I, became Senior Vice-Commander of New York State. Prior to the "Y" 's acquisition of 277 Linwood Avenue, this was the home of the Jewish War Veterans. In 1935, the post acquired its own cemetery plot in the Beth El cemetery, apparently helped in this effort by Erie County. In 1941, the National Encampment was held in Buffalo and here, the Buffalo-born Benjamin Kaufman was elected National Commander. In 1951, the post was located at a building on Grant and West Ferry Streets, but later located at 576 Taunton. *Ibid.,* November 25, 1927, December 16, 1927, October 4, 1929, November 8, 1929, July 29, 1932, September 5, 1941; Buffalo *Courier-Express,* May 30, 1935.
114. Martin M. Cohn and Marvin G. Lerner, *The Growth of Suburban Communities* (mimeographed pamphlet published by the Council of Jewish Federations and Welfare Funds, New York, 1955), Part II, 1. Mr. Lerner, then Assistant Director of the United Jewish Federation of Buffalo, had delivered his part of this published material which deals with Buffalo, before the National Conference of Jewish Communal Service, Atlantic City, May 24, 1955.
115. *Ibid.,* Part II, 2-3.
116. *Ibid.,* Part II, 4.
117. *Ibid.,* Part II, 6.
118. We have drawn heavily here on Selig Adler, "The Challenge of Survival," *Hadassah Newsletter,* Vol. 36, No. 3, 4 ff. (November, 1955). We are also indebted to the insights of Professor Jakob J. Petuchowski as presented in his article, "The Limits of 'People-Centered' Judaism," *Commentary,* vol. 27, 387-394 (May, 1959).

Glossary

Aliyah (aliyot): Literally, "going up." The honor of being called up to the reading of the Torah at divine services.

Ashkenazi (Ashkenazim): Originally, Jews of German origin; later applied to Jews elsewhere who followed the conventional Ashkenazic ritual.

Ba'al Koreh: Reader of the Torah at synagogue services.

Bar Mitzvah: Literally, the "son of the commandment." A Jewish boy who has reached the age of thirteen, or the celebration at a boy's thirteenth birthday.

Ben B'rith: Literally, "son of the Covenant." A Jew; term often applied to individual members of B'nai B'rith.

Beth Din: Literally, "house of judgment." A Jewish court of arbitration.

Bimah: Platform in a synagogue from which reading is done.

Cheder: See Heder.

Chevra Bikur Cholim: Society for visiting the sick.

Deutchuks: Literally, "Germans." Name often applied to the earlier German-Jewish settlers by the East-European immigrants.

Elul: Sixth month of the Hebrew year, roughly corresponding to August.

Ethrog (ethrogim): Citron used as part of the religious celebration of Succot.

Folk Shule: Literally, "people's school." Name usually applied to the secularly-oriented Yiddishist schools.

Gemilut Hasadim: Literally, "performance of deeds of kindness." An organization which grants non-interest bearing loans.

Gemütlichkeit: Cozy; comfortable; pleasant.

Goyim (sing. Goy): Literally, "nations." Non-Jews.

Guberna: Russian province of imperial days.

463

Hachnosat Orhim: Literally, "hospitality to guests." Name given to the Jewish communal institution that served the physical needs of Jewish transients.

Hadas: Myrtle. One of the four plants used as part of the religious celebration of Succot.

Haggadah: Narrative text of the Home Service on the first two nights of Passover.

Halakhic: Legal.

Hallah: Twisted loaves of bread used at the Sabbath and festival table.

Hanukkah: The Feast of Lights, a mid-winter minor festival celebrating the victory of the Maccabees over the Syrian Hellenists.

Halutz (halutzim): Literally, "pioneers." Builders of the modern Israeli state.

Hasid (hasidim): Member of a school of pietistic Jewish thought founded in the eighteenth century by Reb Israel Ba'al Shem Tov (Master of the Good Name).

Haskalah: The Enlightenment.

Haver (havera): Comrade.

Hazzan (hazzanim): The cantor, whose function it is to chant the Hebrew liturgy at the synagogue service.

Heder (hedarim): Jewish religious school.

HEP, HEP: Anti-Semitic slogan or cry, originating in the Middle Ages. Its exact origin is unknown.

Hevra (sometimes Chevra): Group; society.

Hevra (hevrot) Kadisha (sometimes also Chevra Kadisha): Literally, "holy association." A society the members of which perform the sacred rites associated with burying the Jewish dead.

Hevra Tehillim: Adult group dedicated to the daily reading of the Psalms.

High Holidays: Rosh Hashana and Yom Kippur.

Hol (sometimes Chol) Hamoed: Intervening workdays between the first and last days of Passover and Succot (Tabernacles).

Hoshana Rabba: Seventh day of the festival of Succot.

Hovevei Zion: Literally, "lovers of Zion." Early Zionist societies.

Jahrzeits: Death anniversaries.

Kaddish: Literally, "sanctification." The doxology recited especially in memory of the departed.

Kashrut: The state of being kosher; observance of the Jewish dietary laws.

Kehillah (kehillot): The Jewish community, sometimes applied to an individual congregation.

Kiddush: Literally, sanctification. The benediction chanted over the cup of wine on the Sabbath and festivals, declaring the sanctification of these holy days.

Kislev: Ninth month of the Jewish year, roughly corresponding to December.

Kol Nidre: Prayer chanted at the beginning of the Yom Kippur Eve service.

Kosher (kasher): Food that is ritually acceptable in accordance with Jewish religious practice.

Lag baOmer: The thirty-third day of the (Omer) period between Passover and Shavuot. A minor holiday, sometimes called the Scholars' Festival.

Landsman (Landsleute): Fellow countrymen; immigrants originating from the same town or region in Europe.

Landsmanschaften: Societies in which immigrants banded together according to European places of origin.

Litvaks: Jews who migrated from Lithuania and its adjacent provinces.

Maggid: A preacher.

Maskilim: Adherents of the Haskalah.

Matzot: Unleavened bread eaten on Passover.

Megillah: Literally, "scroll." Usually used to signify the Book of Esther, read on Purim.

Mehuttan: The father-in-law of one's son or daughter.

Menorah: Candelabrum.

Meshulahim: Literally, "messengers." Colloquially, collectors for various Jewish institutions.

Mikvah: Ritual bath maintained by observant Jews for purification purposes.

Minha: Daily afternoon prayers.

Minhag: Religious custom.

Minyan: Literally, "number." A minyan or quorum of ten males above the age of thirteen is required for public Jewish worship.

Mitnaged (mitnagdim): Name applied to the European Jews who opposed the eighteenth-century hasidic movement.

Mitzvah: Literally, "a commandment." A good deed.

Mohel (mohelim): One who performs the rite of circumcision. A mohel must be qualified by both piety and experience.

Musaf: Latter part of the Sabbath and holiday morning services.

Ner Tamid: Eternal Light, placed near the Ark of a synagogue.

Nicht ein arbeiter in dem ganzen Ring: "Not a single laborer in the entire Circle."

Nichts für Ungut: Literally, "Nothing for unworthy purposes." In present-day German the idiom of the phrase has changed, but it was probably used here in its literal sense.

Orah: Stranger; wayfarer; guest at a family table.

Parnas: Community leader; in the United States usually a synagogue president.

Piyyutim: Hymns.

Polterabend: Literally, "evening of noise." Colloquially, a night of merry-making held shortly before a wedding.

Purim: Literally, "lots." The minor festival whose history is recorded in the Book of Esther.

Rebbetzin: Rabbi's wife.

Rosh Hashana: Jewish New Year.

Rosh Hodesh: A minor festival, consisting of one or two days, occurring at the beginning of each Jewish month except Tishri. The advent of this seventh month is marked by Rosh Hashana.

Schnorrer: Beggar.

Seder: Literally, "order." Usually used in reference to the evening meal and Home Service on the first two nights of Passover.

Sephardi (Sephardim): Jews of Spanish or Portuguese origin.

Sephardic: Of Spanish or Portuguese origin or custom. The same term was later applied to the ritual of the East-European hasidic Jews.

Shabbes: The Sabbath.

Shammash (Shames): Sexton.

Shastening: Derived originally from the Hebrew infinitive, lishtot, "to drink," it was used by German Jews to mean heavy drinking or imbibing.

Shavuot: Literally, "weeks." The Feast of Pentecost or Feast of Weeks. Occurs seven weeks after the second day of Passover.

Shohet (shohetim): One who slaughters animals or fowl according to Jewish ritual. Must be an observant Jew and must be certified by a rabbi as proficient in the knowledge of laws pertaining to ritual slaughter.

Shofar: Ram's horn sounded in the synagogue during the Rosh Hashana services and at the termination of Yom Kippur.

Shtetl: European home town.

Shul: A synagogue.

Shule: A school.

Siddur: Prayer book.

Sofer: A scribe; a copyist of Holy Texts.

Succot: The Feast of Tabernacles or Feast of Booths.

Tallit: Prayer shawl.

Talmud: The body of Jewish civil and canonical law, consisting of the Mishnah, or text, and Gemara, or commentary; also restrictedly, the Gemara alone.

Talmud Torah: An elementary school for Jewish religious education.

Tammuz: Fourth month of the Jewish year, roughly corresponding to July.

Tishri: Seventh month of the Jewish year, roughly corresponding to September.

Torah: In a limited sense, the Pentateuch. More broadly, Torah refers to all Jewish learning and culture, both biblical and rabbinic.

Trefa: Forbidden food; unkosher.

Tu Bishvat: An ancient minor festival occurring on the fifteenth day of the eleventh month of the Jewish year. In recent times, it has been celebrated as Jewish Arbor Day.

Yehudim: Literally, "Jews." In the United States of the *circa* 1900, it was often used to describe the German Jews who used the Hebrew word "Yehudim" in contrast to the East-European colloquial term, "Yüden."

Yeshiva (Yeshivot): A school of advanced talmudical studies.

Yishuv: The modern Jewish settlement in Palestine or Israel.

Yom Kippur: The Day of Atonement.

Yom Tov: Literally, "a good day." Refers to a Jewish holiday.

Yüden: Jews.

Bibliography

I. MANUSCRIPT MATERIAL: MINUTE BOOKS AND MISCELLANEOUS DOCUMENTS

Arbeiter Ring, Branch #29. Minute Book, 1903-1920. Formerly in the possession of Mr. Isadore Wolk of Buffalo, these books have been deposited with the Yivo Institute for Jewish Research, 1048 Fifth Avenue, New York, N. Y.

B'nai B'rith Montefiore Lodge #70. Minute Book, 1870-1910; 1921-1945. In the custody of the lodge secretary, Herman Strauss, Buffalo, N. Y.

Chevra Kadisha Anshe Lubavitz. Minute Book, 1910-1911. In the possession of Ahavas Achim-Lubavitz Synagogue, Buffalo.

Congregation Ahavas Sholem. Minute Book, 1895-1920. Examined while in the possession of Arthur Plesur, formerly of Buffalo.

Congregation Beth Jacob. Minute Book, 1916-1929. In the possession of Arthur E. Schulgasser, Buffalo.

Farband Labor Zionist Order (Jewish National Workers Alliance). Minute Book, Dr. Syrkin Branch #48, 1913-1920. Formerly in the possession of Mr. Isadore Wolk of Buffalo, now deposited with the Yivo Institute for Jewish Research.

Millard Fillmore Papers, Buffalo Historical Society.

Poale Zion (Labor Zionist Organization of America). Minute Book, Buffalo branch, 1905-1920. Formerly in the possession of Mr. Isadore Wolk of Buffalo, now deposited with the Yivo Institute for Jewish Research.

Seixas, Gershom Mendes. Photostat of a sermon delivered in 1814, describing the ravages of the War of 1812 on the Niagara Frontier, and appealing for help for the destitute. The original is in the Captain N. Taylor Phillips Col-

467

lection; the photostat was obtained through the courtesy of Rabbi Isidore S. Meyer of the American Jewish Historical Society.

Temple Beth El. Minute Book, 1847-1885; 1910-1924. In the Archives of Temple Beth El, Buffalo.

Temple Beth Zion. Minute Book, 1864-1924; School Board Minute Book, November 5, 1890-December 2, 1895. In the Archives of Temple Beth Zion, Buffalo.

Temple Emanu-El. Minute Book, 1928-1933. In the Archives of Temple Emanu-El, Buffalo.

United Jewish Federation of Buffalo, Inc. (Formerly Federated Jewish Charities of Buffalo and Jewish Federation for Social Service). Minute Book of the Board of Governors, 1909; 1910; 1918. In the Archives of the United Jewish Federation of Buffalo.

Youth Committee of Arbeiter Ring, Branch #29. Minute Book, 1937-1939. Formerly in the possession of Mr. Isadore Wolk, now deposited with the Yivo Institute for Jewish Research.

Zionist Organization of America. Minutes of the 1920 Buffalo convention. In the Zionist Archives and Library of Palestine Foundation Fund, 515 Park Avenue, New York, N. Y.

II. OTHER MANUSCRIPT SOURCES AND MISCELLANEOUS UNPUBLISHED MATERIAL

Ablove, Louis, "How the Jews of Sokolovka Came to Buffalo." Specially prepared brief for the authors.

American Association for Jewish Education, 1261 Broadway, New York, N. Y. Archives.

Annual Report of Uriah Z. Engelman to the board of the Buffalo Bureau of Jewish Education, April 18, 1938.

Annual Reports of Mark M. Krug to the executive committee of the Buffalo Bureau of Jewish Education, 1946; 1947.

Arywitz, Annette F., "A Short History of the Jewish Community Service of Buffalo." (Master of Social Science thesis, University of Buffalo, 1948).

Bluestone, Harry, Annual Report to the Board of Directors, YM-YWHA, May 13, 1942. Copy in the possession of Max M. Yellen, Buffalo.

Buffalo Council of Jewish Congregations. Photostat of papers of incorporation, 1925, furnished the authors by Max M. Yellen.

Buffalo Bureau of Jewish Education. Archives.

Agreement between Herman A. Eigen and Mark M. Krug, July 1, 1948, concerning the joint use of the Jewish Center.

Engelman, Uriah Z., Summary of annual report to the executive committee of the Bureau for the academic year 1940-1941.

Goelman, Elazar, Undated statement summarizing the aims of the Bureau.

———, Memorandum, 1954, on the future plans and aims of the Bureau.

Report of a joint inter-agency committee on the use of the Jewish Center, April, 1949.

Council of Jewish Federations and Welfare Funds, 729 Seventh Avenue, New York, N. Y. Archives.

Field Reports from Buffalo:

R. Fitterman, July 27, 1944.

George W. Rabinoff, March 5, 1932; April 13, 1932.

George Wolfe, November 4, 1937; February 28, 1938; June 11-12, 1938; April 24, 1940; August 6, 1940; August 17, 1940.

Samuel Weingarten, April 23, 1943.

Crouse, Mrs. Irving I., "History of the Buffalo Jewish Choral Society." Specially prepared brief for the authors.

Gitin, Louis L., "The Development of a Reform Religious School: Buffalo, New York, 1864-1953." (Ed. D. dissertation, University of Buffalo, 1954).

"History of Congregation B'rith Sholem, Buffalo." Dictated statement, evidently made by Israel I. Friedlander who resided in Buffalo from 1870 until his death in 1925. In the possession of Max M. Yellen, Buffalo.

Letters of information to the authors and their collaborators concerning the history of Buffalo Jewry:

Howard F. Beir to Mrs. Elwood G. Becker, August 4, 1959, telling of his military career in World War II.

Mrs. Jerry Blanke to Selig Adler,* July 13, 1959; describing the capture and death of Kurt Jacobs in World War II.

David Block to S.A., July 25, 1954; outlining the career of his father, Rabbi Aaron Joseph Bloch.

Rabbi Harry J. Brevis to S.A., April 15, 1958; biographical information about himself and his wife.

Alfred M. Cohen to S.A., August 20, 1957; career of his grandfather, Abraham F. Cohen.

Mrs. Stella Engel to Mrs. Carl Pratter, September 1, 1954; story of the Manhattan Ladies' Auxiliary.

Dr. Joseph L. Fink to S.A., November 21, 1957; recent history of Temple Beth Zion.

Marjorie D. Frost to Pierson L. Cohen, October 28, 1954; information on Abraham Oppenheimer during his residence in Nunda, N. Y.

Mrs. Harold Hirsch to Cecil B. Wiener, April 29, 1955; light on career of Harry Harriton.

Mrs. Emile Levy to Mrs. Henry S. Cohen, April 26, 1950; early history of the National Council of Jewish Women.

Mrs. Leon H. Miller to S.A., July 9, 1954; biographical material on L. H. Miller.

Mrs. Myra S. Morrison to S.A., September 17, 1954; biographical information on Julius L. Saperston.

Milton H. Petzold to Camille B. Michel (Mrs. Edward M. Plant), February 18, 1920; concerning the death of Jerome Michel in World War I.

Leo J. Rosen to S.A., August 15, 1957; biographical material on Isaac Rosen.

Rabbi Elihu Schagrin to S.A., October 25, 1957; concerning information found in the flyleaf of an old prayer book in Binghamton, N. Y.

Dr. Heyman Smolev to S.A., October 14, 1957; October 29, 1957; describing the military careers of Buffalo Jewish physicians in recent wars.

Paul Swados to Cecil B. Wiener, December 10, 1954; biographical information on Israel Swados.

Morrison, Isadore, "The Jewish Boy Scouts of Buffalo," specially prepared brief for the authors.

---

* Hereafter S.A.

National Jewish Welfare Board, 145 E. 32nd Street, New York, N. Y. Archives.
Report on Buffalo, 1923.
Report on Buffalo, 1938; prepared by Dr. Charles Bernheimer.
"Official History of the Rosa Coplon Jewish Old Folks Home, Buffalo, N. Y.",
typescript copy furnished the author by the Home's executive director,
Samuel Roberts.
Plesur, Milton, "Herman Wile," unpublished biographical sketch in the pos-
session of Dr. Plesur, Buffalo.
Simon, Dr. Charles, "Biography of Dr. Ferdinand Simon," specially prepared
brief for the authors.
Singer, Mrs. Joseph M., "History of the Naomi Club," specially prepared brief
for the authors.
Snyder, Stanley, "Mrs. Mayme Ruben Kahn," specially prepared brief for the
authors.
Steinhorn, Mrs. Morris, "In Retrospect: B'nai B'rith Montefiore Chapter #34,"
specially prepared brief for the authors.
Temple Beth El. Archives.
Reports of the president, Charles Polakoff, April 16, 1911; April 27, 1913.
Franklin W. H. Becker to Charles Polakoff, May 17, 1913.
Temple Sinai, Buffalo. Typed information concerning the aims and program
of Temple Sinai, 1953-1958. In the possession of Rabbi Nathan Gaynor,
Buffalo.
United Jewish Federation of Buffalo, Inc. Archives.
"A Report on the Jewish Center of Buffalo to the Jewish Federation for
Social Service, October, 1947."
"A Report on the Jewish Community Service Society submitted to the Jew-
ish Federation for Social Service, October, 1947."
Annual Report of Flora I. Dudley, R.N., on "The Roof Clinic," 1933.
Annual Report of Ben M. Edidin, director of the Bureau of Jewish Educa-
tion, January 17, 1934.
Eugene D. Hofeller to Martha Morris, March 12, 1952.
Jewish Federation for Social Service to Buffalo Chamber of Commerce,
April 3, 1928.
Kavinoky, Edward H., and Levin, Mrs. Hyman L., "Report of the 'Study
Commission' for the Jewish Center, June 1, 1949."
Report of Mrs. Lillian Hirshberg for the Hospital Visiting Committee, Janu-
ary 17, 1934.
Report of Mrs. Sarah Rummel, Domestic Educator, [n.d.].
Report of Louis Shocket, director of the Jewish Community Building to the
Board of Governors, January 1, 1927.
Sketch of facts and figures concerning the early history of the Federation,
1928.
Sketch of the Federation's history, dated December 10, 1928.
Statement of aims and policies of the Board of Governors, June 5, 1940.
Summary of report of Dr. Uriah Z. Engelman and Mrs. Shashana Ginsberg
on Jewish Education in Buffalo, made under the auspices of the American
Association for Jewish Education, 1955.
Survey of the Buffalo Jewish Community, September, 1929. Submitted by
the Bureau of Jewish Social Research, New York, N. Y. (Section V on
Jewish Education, was prepared by Louis Hurwich, director of the Boston

Bureau of Jewish Education and principal of the Hebrew Teachers College in that city).

Unsigned report, January 1, 1911, concerning Federation relief work and expenditures for 1910.

Rabbi Jonah B. Wise to Eugene Warner, May 18, 1933.

Max M. Yellen to Eugene Warner, December 16, 1940.

III. SCRAPBOOKS AND MISCELLANEOUS FAMILY MATERIAL

Brock, Bertha M. Scrapbook. Examined while in the possession of the late Miss Brock of Buffalo, contains unidentified newspaper clippings.

Brock, Matilda. Scrapbook. Formerly in the possession of Miss Bertha M. Brock; contains programs of nineteenth-century Buffalo social events and similar items.

Davis, Jacob L. Scrapbook. In the possession of Marvin Davis, Buffalo. Contains material relating to the business and political career of J. L. Davis.

Desbecker, Joseph. Scrapbook. In the possession of Mrs. Mildred Desbecker Shire of Buffalo. Contains many items of interest about the Desbecker, Noah, and Levyn families. Mrs. Shire also has the family Bible of Michael W. Noah, which has important genealogical information inscribed on the flyleaf.

Drozen, Paul. Scrapbook. Unidentified newspaper articles dealing with Jewish life on the Buffalo East Side and Jewish contributions to the World War II war effort. In the possession of Mr. Drozen, Buffalo.

Fass, Mrs. Rhea. Scrapbook. Filled with material relating to the military career of her brother, Harry J. Rubenstein. In the possession of Mrs. Fass, Buffalo.

Goldberg, Stuart J. Scrapbook. Contains information on the careers of Simon Jacobs and Dr. Jacob Goldberg. Includes some letters and documents of historical interest. In the possession of Stuart J. Goldberg, Buffalo.

Jellinek, Mrs. Irwin H. Collection of printed items relating to nineteenth-century Jewish social life.

Miller, Leon H. Scrapbook. In the possession of the Zionist Archives and Library of Palestine Foundation, New York, N. Y. Includes correspondence and unidentified newspaper clippings relative to Mr. Miller's long and active participation in Zionist affairs. Items date from the turn-of-the-century to the 1930s.

Montefiore Club. Scrapbook. In the possession of the Montefiore Club, Buffalo. Contains items dealing with the club's history and activities.

Rodell, Anne. Scrapbook. In the possession of Miss Rodell, Buffalo. Contains valuable items relating to Buffalo Jewish life in the latter half of the nineteenth century; some documents of the Civil War period; unidentified newspaper clippings relating to various members of the Rosenau family. Miss Rodell also owns a prayer book, published in New York in 1860, which was used in Buffalo before Temple Beth Zion adopted a Reform prayer book. The flyleaf of this book contains valuable genealogical information.

Schwartz, Mrs. Harry. Scrapbook. Unidentified newspaper clippings relating to the career of Jacob Rosokoff. In the possession of Mrs. Schwartz, North Tonawanda, N. Y.

Temple Beth Zion. Scrapbook. Contains programs, unidentified newspaper clippings, and other material relative to the 1921 Buffalo convention of the

Union of American Hebrew Congregations. In the Temple Beth Zion Archives.

Weil, Isaac, Confirmation Note Book. Valuable for information on Beth Zion's Religious School, *circa* 1883. In the possession of Dr. S. Albert Levitan, Buffalo.

IV. OFFICIAL UNITED STATES DOCUMENTS AND PUBLICATIONS

Military record of Marcus Flintrowitz, a soldier in the Mexican War. Photostatic copies of enlistment and pension claims furnished by General Services Administration, National Archives and Records Service, Washington, D. C.

Military record of Leopold Marcus, a soldier in the Civil War. Various records, including "Declaration for Invalid Pension, May 5, 1904." Photostats furnished by General Services Administration.

Military record of Mordecai Myers, a soldier in the War of 1812. Typed record of military service furnished by General Services Administration.

United States Department of Commerce, *Statistical Abstract of the United States, 1957* (Washington, 1957).

United States Immigration Commission, *Immigrants in Cities*, 2 vols. (Senate Document 338, 61 Cong., 2 sess., Washington, 1911).

V. PUBLIC RECORDS OF ERIE COUNTY

A—Corporate Records: Office of the clerk of the County of Erie.

Corporation Box   4078—Temple Beth El (1848).
    "   "   9511—Jacobsohn Society (1851).
    "   "   4075—Congregation Beth Zion (1851).
    "   "   6779—Hebrew Benevolent Society of the City of Buffalo (1854).
    "   "   11780—Young Men's Hebrew Benevolent Association of Buffalo (1861).
    "   "   14330—Temple Beth Zion (1864).
    "   "   972—Congregation Beth Jacob (1881).
    "   "   4103—Congregation B'rith Sholem [previously incorporated (1866) as Chevra B'rith Sholem] (1882).
    "   "   9668—Ladies Hebrew Association (1886).
    "   "   4092—Congregation B'rith Israel (1887).
    "   "   10550—Congregation Anshe Lubavitz (1890).
    "   "   4089—Congregation Ahavas Sholem (1892).
    "   "   11373—Sisterhood of Zion (1893).
    "   "   155—Congregation Ahavas Achim (1897).
    "   "   6772—Hebrew Benevolent Loan Association (1899).
    "   "   571—Congregation Anshe Emes (1908).
    "   "   6882—Holy Order of the Living [Cemetery Association] (1912).
    "   "   1879—Buffalo Hebrew Social Club (1914).
    "   "   579—Congregation Anshe Sokolovka (1915).
    "   "   7895—Jewish Community Athletic Association (1915).
    "   "   7900—Jewish Hospital Association (1916).

Corporation Box 19044—First Austrian and Galician Association of Buffalo (1916).
"   "   6785—Hebrew Progressive Club of Buffalo (1916).
"   "   3739—Daughters of Israel Jewish Old Folks Home (1916).
"   "   7899—Jewish Kehillah of Buffalo (1916).
"   "   13404—Workmen's Circle Cemetery of Buffalo (1918).
"   "   7907—Jewish Mothers Club (1919).
"   "   7908—Jewish Labor Lyceum League of Buffalo (1919).
"   "   4177—Congregation Beth Abraham (1922).
"   "   13613—Jewish-American Real Estate Association (1923).
"   "   13904—Temple Beth David (1923).
"   "   4904—Temple Emanu-El (1924).
"   "   8930—Congregation Anshe Zedek [First Hungarian Congregation Anshe Zedek] (1925).
"   "   18690—Congregation Ohel Jacob (1930).
"   "   11373—Jewish Center of Buffalo (1945).
B—Records of Deeds: Office of the clerk of the County of Erie.
   Liber 210, p. 215.
   Liber 241, p. 434.
   Liber 347, p. 474.
   Liber 650, p. 582.
C—Surrogate's Court records: Erie County Hall.
   Cases 10392; 10397; 10410; 16391; 27638; 31698; 37635; 52996.
D—State Census Records: Office of the clerk of the County of Erie.
   1850; 1860; 1865; 1870.

VI. PAMPHLETS

Bailey, George M., "Ten Years in Buffalo" (Buffalo: Buffalo *Express,* 1890).

Buffalo *Evening News,* "A History of the City of Buffalo" (Buffalo: Buffalo *Evening News,* 1908).

Cohn, Martin M., and Lerner, Marvin G., *The Growth of Suburban Communities* (New York: Council of Jewish Federations and Welfare Funds, mimeographed pamphlet, 1955).

Engelman, Uriah Z., *A Study of the Size of Families in the Jewish Population of Buffalo* (Buffalo: University of Buffalo Studies, XVI, No. 1, November, 1938).

Goldberg, Arthur I. (comp.), *In Honor of Dr. Joseph L. Fink on his Twenty-fifth Anniversary as Rabbi of Temple Beth Zion* (Buffalo: Temple Beth Zion, October 22, 1949).

Hebrew Benevolent Loan Association, Buffalo, N. Y., 1897-1947 (Buffalo: Fiftieth Anniversary Dinner, December 7, 1947).

Hillel, B'nai B'rith Hillel Foundations in American Universities, ([n.p.], [n.d.]).

Hirshfield, Elizabeth, *Concerning Women Suffrage* (Buffalo: The Political Equality Club, [n.d.]).

Joseph, Samuel, *History of the Baron de Hirsch Fund* ([n.p.], 1935).

Landau, Jacob H. (comp.), *Service-Manual of Temple Beth El* (Buffalo, 1911).

Laws and Regulations of the Hebrew Board of Charities (Buffalo: Matthews, Northrup & Company, 1891).

Lyons, Jacques L., and De Sola, Abraham, *A Jewish Calendar for Fifty Years* (Montreal, 1854).

Magil, Reuben J., "History of Temple Beth El," in *Official Souvenir History* (Buffalo, Temple Beth El, February 27, 1935).

Nagle, Roy W., *Romance of Buffalo* (Buffalo: The Manufacturers and Traders Trust Company, 1939).

Presbrey, Frank S., *The City of Buffalo* (New York: Forum Publishing Company, 1895).

Roberts, Peter, *The Foreign Population of Buffalo* (Buffalo, 1908).

Sherman, C. Bezalel, *Three Centuries of Growth* (New York: Labor Zionist Organization of America-Poale Zion, 1954).

Silver Anniversary Bulletin of Temple Emanu-El (Buffalo: Temple Emanu-El, 1950).

Temple Beth El's First Century: Centennial Souvenir Book (Buffalo: Temple Beth El, 1947).

Warner, Eugene, *et al.*, *Fiftieth Anniversary First Temple Beth Zion 1865-1915; Twenty-fifth Anniversary Present Temple 1890-1915; Dedication The Temple Centre 1915* (Buffalo: Temple Beth Zion, 1915).

VII. MISCELLANEOUS PRINTED MATERIAL

Annual Report of the Charity Organization Society of Buffalo, N. Y. (Buffalo, 1903).

The Buffalo Directory 1920 (Buffalo: J. W. Clement & Company, 1920).

The Commercial Advertiser Directory for the City of Buffalo (Buffalo: Thomas & Lathrop, Publishers, 1855).

Congregation B'rith Sholem, Buffalo. Constitution of 1894 (Buffalo: S. Knebel, 96 William Street, 1894). In the possession of Max M. Yellen, Buffalo.

Cutting, Thomas S. (comp.), *Buffalo City Directory, 1848-1849* (Buffalo: G. Reese & Company, 1848).

Harrison, William S. (comp.), *The Political Blue Book: An Official Manual of Buffalo and Erie County, N. Y.* (Buffalo: The Dau Publishing Company, 1905).

Kengott, Louis J. (comp.), *Annual Reports of the Overseer of the Common Council, 1908; 1911* (Buffalo, 1908; 1911).

Political handbill of a Rochester, N. Y., Jewish-Republican organization, urging Jews to vote the McKinley-Roosevelt ticket of 1900, on the grounds that Colonel Roosevelt had helped humble anti-Semitic Spain in the recent Spanish-American War. In the possession of Rabbi Abraham J. Karp, Rochester, N. Y.

Proceedings at the Fifth Annual Meeting of the Charity Organization Society of Buffalo embracing Reports of the Council, 1883 (Buffalo, 1883).

Proceedings at the Sixth Annual Meeting of the Charity Organization Society of Buffalo embracing Reports of the Council, 1884 (Buffalo, 1884).

Reisman, Benjamin D., "The Jew Faces the World," printed copy of an address delivered before B'nai B'rith Victory Lodge #1481, April 10, 1944. Attached to Montefiore Lodge #70 Minute Book for 1944. In the possession of the lodge secretary.

Report of the Executive Committee of the Constitution Grand Lodge, I.O.B.B., 1891-1892 (New York, 1892).

Report of the Executive Committee of Grand Lodge #1, I.O.B.B., 1911-1912 (New York, 1912).

United Jewish Federation of Buffalo, Inc. (Formerly Federated Jewish Charities of Buffalo; Jewish Federation for Social Service).

Hand Book of The Federated Jewish Charities of Buffalo for the Year 1905 (Buffalo, 1905).

Year Books of the Federated Jewish Charities of Buffalo, N. Y., 1909; 1910; 1911; 1912; 1913; 1914; 1914-1915. (Buffalo, 1909-1915).

Year Book 1917-1918: Federated Jewish Charities of Buffalo, N. Y. (Buffalo, 1918).

Year Books 1918-1919; 1926-1927; 1927-1928; 1928-1929; 1929-1930: Jewish Federation for Social Service (Buffalo, 1919-1930).

Year Books 1930; 1933; 1935; 1936; 1948: Jewish Federation for Social Service (Buffalo, 1930; 1933; 1935; 1936; 1938).

VIII. NEWSPAPERS AND PERIODICALS

A—Local Newspapers

Buffalo *Commercial,* 1890; 1897; 1910; 1911; 1915; 1917; 1920.

Buffalo *Commercial Advertiser,* 1850; 1860; 1863; 1865; 1866; 1871; 1874; 1875; 1886; 1889.

Buffalo *Courier,* 1865; 1875; 1881; 1891; 1894; 1898; 1902; 1904-1906; 1908; 1923.

Buffalo *Courier-Express,* 1926; 1927; 1929; 1932; 1934-1936; 1939-1946; 1948; 1949; 1952.

Buffalo *Emporium,* September 17, 1825; January 28, 1826.

Buffalo *Enquirer,* March 22, 1898; May 15, 1912.

Buffalo *Evening News,* 1890; 1897; 1909; 1910; 1912; 1923; 1924; 1929-1934; 1936; 1937; 1939-1943; 1947; 1949; 1955; 1958.

Buffalo *Express,* 1865; 1867; 1869; 1874; 1875; 1880; 1886; Extra Souvenir number, September 1888; 1890; 1894; 1897; 1900; 1902-1908; Erland Gjessing, "Ghetto in Miniature," in May 9, May 16, May 19, 1909 issues; 1910; 1911; 1913; 1915-1917; 1923; May 3, 1926.

Buffalo *Times,* 1902; 1909; Grace Carew Sheldon, "Buffalo of the Olden Time," a series of articles running from December 28, 1910 to February 19, 1911, dealing with the history of Temple Beth El; 1911; 1926; 1931; 1936-1938.

B—Out-of-town Newspapers

New York *Times,* July 31, 1960.

New York *Tribune,* February 7, 1892.

C—Jewish Newspapers and Periodicals: Local and out-of-town.

American Hebrew, New York, May 7, 1880; January 6, 1892.

American Jewish Review, Buffalo, September 6, 1918-February 11, 1921.

Arbeiter Zeitung, New York, 1891; 1893; 1894.

The Asmonean, New York, July 26, 1850.

Buffalo Jewish Review, April 8, 1921-August 14, 1959.

Ha-Maggid, Lyck, East Prussia, 1882.

Ha-Maggid he-Hadash, Berlin, Cracow, 1892; 1894.

Hazefirah, Warsaw, No. 83, 1887.

Hebrew Standard, New York, November 16, 1906.

The Israelite [or *The (American) Israelite*], Cincinnati, 1860; 1862-1867; 1879; 1880; 1882; 1895; 1896; 1912.

The Jewish Messenger, New York, June 5, 1868.

The Maccabean, New York, 1901-1904; 1908.

The Occident, Philadelphia, 1847; 1850; 1851; 1853; 1855; 1858.

The Senior Review, Buffalo, May, 1921.

D—General Periodicals

Albany Law Journal, supplement on the University of Buffalo and the Erie County Bar, January 7, 1899.

Greater Buffalo, April 15, 1897.

Review of Reviews, New York, 1890.

IX. GENERAL LITERATURE

A—Biographies and Memoirs

De Haas, Jacob, *Louis D. Brandeis* (New York: Bloch Publishing Company, 1929).

Fleischmann, Bianca, *My Autobiography* ([n.p.], privately printed, 1953).

Mason, Alpheus T., *Brandeis: A Free Man's Life* (New York: The Viking Press, 1946).

Philipson, David S., *My Life as an American Jew* (Cincinnati: J. G. Kidd & Son, 1941).

Snow, Julia F., *Early Recollections of Buffalo* (Buffalo: The Matthews-Northrup Works, 1908).

Ullman, Frederick, *Incidents and Events* ([n.p.], privately printed, 1939).

Welch, Samuel M., *Home History. Recollections of Buffalo during the decade from 1830 to 1840, or fifty years since.* (Buffalo: P. Paul & Brothers, 1891).

Wise, Isaac M., *Reminiscences* (Edited by David S. Philipson, Cincinnati: L. Wise & Company, 1901).

Wolcott, Frances M., *Heritage of Years: Kaleidoscopic Memories* (New York: Minton, Balch & Company, 1902).

B—General Works

Adler, Cyrus (ed.), *The Voice of America on Kishineff* (Philadelphia: The Jewish Publication Society of America, 1904).

The American Jewish Year Book 1900-1901 (Philadelphia: The Jewish Publication Society of America, 1900).

The American Jewish Year Book 1911 (Philadelphia: The Jewish Publication Society of America, 1911).

Bailey, George M., *Illustrated Buffalo: The Queen City of the Lakes* (New York: Acme Publishing and Engraving Company, 1890).

Berman, Jeremiah J., *Shehitah* (New York: Bloch Publishing Company, 1941).

Bidwell, Frederick D. (comp.), *History of the Forty-ninth New York Volunteers* (Albany: J. B. Lyons Company, 1916).

Buckingham, James S., *America, Historical, Statistic and Descriptive*, 3 vols. (London: Fisher, Son, & Company, 1841).

Commager, Henry S., *The American Mind* (New Haven: Yale University Press, 1950).

Dubnow, Simon, *History of the Jews in Russia and Poland*, 3 vols. (Philadelphia: The Jewish Publication Society of America, 1916-1920).

Friedman, Lee M., *Jewish Pioneers and Patriots* (Philadelphia: The Jewish Publication Society of America, 1942).

——, *Pilgrims in a New Land* (Philadelphia: The Jewish Publication Society of America, 1948).

Grayzel, Solomon, *A History of the Jews* (Philadelphia: The Jewish Publication Society of America, 1955).

Grinstein, Hyman B., *The Rise of the Jewish Community of New York, 1654-1860* (Philadelphia: The Jewish Publication Society of America, 1945).

Handlin, Oscar, *Adventure in Freedom* (New York: McGraw-Hill Book Company, 1954).

Hansen, Marcus L., *The Atlantic Migration, 1607-1860* (Cambridge: Harvard University Press, 1940).

——, *The Immigrant in American History* (Cambridge: Harvard University Press, 1940).

Hecht, Sigmund, *Epitome of Post-Biblical History* (Cincinnati, 1882).

Hill, Henry W. (comp.), *Municipality of Buffalo, New York: A History, 1720-1923*, 4 vols. (New York: Lewis Historical Publishing Company, 1923).

Horton, John T., Williams, Edward T., and Douglass, Harry S., *History of Northwestern New York*, 3 vols. (New York: Lewis Historical Publishing Company, 1947).

Hubbell, Mark S. (ed.), *Our Police and Our City* (Buffalo: Bensler & Wesley, 1893).

Hungerford, Edward, *Pathway of Empire* (New York: R. M. McBride & Company, 1935).

Janowsky, Oscar I., *The Jews and Minority Rights 1898 to 1919* (New York: Columbia University Press, 1933).

Randall, James G., *The Civil War and Reconstruction* (Boston: D. C. Heath & Company, 1937).

Rosenberg, Stuart E., *The Jewish Community in Rochester 1843-1925* (New York: Columbia University Press, 1954).

Russell, C. Allyn, *A History of the Fredonia Baptist Church* (Dunkirk: McClenathan Printery, 1955).

Schappes, Morris U. (ed.), *A Documentary History of the Jews in the United States, 1654-1875* (New York: Citadel Press, 1950).

Sellstedt, Lars G., *Art in Buffalo* (Buffalo: The Matthews-Northrup Works, 1910).

Smith, H. Perry (ed.), *History of the City of Buffalo and Erie County*, 2 vols. (Syracuse: D. Mason & Company, 1884).

Sweeney, Daniel J. (comp.), *History of Buffalo and Erie County, 1914-1919* (Buffalo: The Committee of One Hundred, 1920).

White, Truman C. (ed.), *Our County and its People*, 2 vols. (Boston: The Boston History Company, 1898).

Wilcox, Cadmus M., *History of the Mexican War* (Washington: Church News Publishing Company, 1892).

Wile, Isaac A., *The Jews of Rochester* (Rochester: Historical Review Society, 1912).

Wilner, Merton M., *Niagara Frontier,* 4 vols. (Chicago: S. J. Clarke Publishing Company, 1931).

Wirth, Louis, *The Ghetto* (Chicago: University of Chicago Press, 1928).

Wischnitzer, Mark, *To Dwell In Safety* (Philadelphia: The Jewish Publication Society of America, 1948).

X. ARTICLES

Aaron, Israel, "The Reintroduction of Congregational Singing," *C.C.A.R. Yearbook,* XXII, 333-339 (1912).

"Address by Mordecai M. Noah," American Jewish Historical Society, *Publications,* XXI, 229-252 (1913).

Adler, Selig, "Backgrounds of American Policy Toward Zion," in Davis, Moshe (ed.), *Israel: Its Role in Civilization* (New York: Seminary Israel Institute of the Jewish Theological Seminary of America, distributed by Harper & Brothers, 1956), 251-283.

——, "The Buffalo Project: Writing the History of a Medium-Sized Community," in Davis, Moshe, and Meyer, Isidore S. (eds.), *The Writing of American Jewish History* (New York: American Jewish Historical Society, 1957), 158-169.

——, "The Challenge of Survival," *Hadassah Newsletter,* XXXVI, 4 ff. (November, 1955).

Allen, Lewis F., "Founding of the City of Ararat on Grand Island—by Mordecai M. Noah," *Publications of the Buffalo Historical Society,* I, 305-328 (1879).

Baron, Salo W., and Baron, Jeannette M., "Palestinian Messengers in America, 1849-1879," *Jewish Social Studies,* V, No. 2, 115-162; No. 3, 225-292 (April; July, 1943).

Berman, Jeremiah J., "The Trend in Jewish Religious Observances in Mid-Nineteenth Century America," American Jewish Historical Society, *Publications,* XXXVII, 31-53 (1947).

Cohen, Naomi W., "The Reaction of Reform Judaism in America to Political Zionism, 1897-1922," *ibid.,* No. 40, 361-394 (June, 1951).

Douglas, William A., and Lansing, William, "Housing Conditions in Buffalo," in De Forest, Robert W., and Veiller, Lawrence, (eds.), *The Tenement House Problem,* 2 vols. (New York: The Macmillan Company, 1903), I, 119-128.

Dushkin, Alexander M., "Ben M. Edidin," *Jewish Education,* XX, (Fall, 1948).

Engelman, Uriah Z., "Medurbia," *Contemporary Jewish Record,* IV, No. 4, 339-348; No. 5, 511-521 (August; October, 1941).

Falk, Samson, "A History of the Israelites in Buffalo," *Publications of the Buffalo Historical Society,* I, 289-304 (1879).

Goodman, Abram V., "An American Jewish Peddler's Diary," *American Jewish Archives,* III, 81-111 (June, 1951).

Goldberg, Nathan, "Dynamics of the Economic Structure of the Jews in the United States," in Davis and Meyer, *op. cit.,* 233-256.

Grollman, Jerome W., "The Emergence of Reform Judaism," *American Jewish Archives,* II, 3-14 (January, 1950).

Herberg, Will, "Religious Trends in American Jewry," *Judaism,* III, 229-240 (1954).

——, "The Jewish Labor Movement in the United States," in *The American Jewish Year Book 1952* (Philadelphia: The Jewish Publication Society of America, 1952), 3-74.

Higham, John, "Anti-Semitism in the Gilded Age: A Reinterpretation," *Mississippi Valley Historical Review*, XLIII, 559-578 (March, 1957).

Hodge, William, "Buffalo Cemeteries," *Publications of the Buffalo Historical Society*, I, 49-75 (1879).

Hollander, Jacob L., "Forces and Tendencies of Jewish Charity," speech delivered May 17, 1910, in St. Louis, in *Proceedings of the Fifth Conference of Jewish Charities* (Baltimore, 1910), 50-55.

Hühner, Leon, "Jews in the War of 1812," American Jewish Historical Society, *Publications*, XXVI, 173-200 (1918).

Kohler, Max J., "Judah Touro, Merchant and Philanthropist," *ibid.*, XIII, 93-111 (1905).

Mandel, Irving A., "Attitude of the American Jewish Community Toward East-European Immigration," *American Jewish Archives*, III, 11-36 (June, 1950).

"Miscellaneous Items Relating to Jews in New York," American Jewish Historical Society, *Publications*, XXVII, 379-403 (1920).

Parton, James, "Our Israelitish Brethren," *Atlantic Monthly*, XXVI, 385-403 (1870).

Petuchowski, Jakob J., "The Limits of 'People-Centered' Judaism," *Commentary*, XXVII, 384-387 (May, 1959).

Rabinowitz, Benjamin, "The Young Men's Hebrew Associations, 1854-1913," American Jewish Historical Society, *Publications*, No. 37, 221-326 (1947).

Sampter, Jessie E., "Zionism in America Before the British Mandate," in Sampter, Jessie E. (ed.), *Modern Palestine* (New York: Hadassah, 1933), 35-51.

Schodde, George H., "The Zionite Movement," *Harper's Weekly*, XL, 620 (June 20, 1896).

Severance, Frank H., "The Periodical Press of Buffalo, 1811-1915," *Publications of the Buffalo Historical Society*, XIX, 179-280 (1915).

Szajkowski, Zosa, "The Attitude of American Jews to East-European Jewish Immigration, 1881-1893," American Jewish Historical Society, *Publications*, XL, 221-280 (1951).

——, "How the Mass Migration to America Began," *Jewish Social Studies*, IV, No. 4, 291-310 (October, 1942).

Weinman, Melvin, "The Attitude of Isaac Mayer Wise Toward Zionism and Palestine," *American Jewish Archives*, III, 3-23 (January, 1951).

Weinryb, Bernard D., "Jewish Immigration and Accommodation to America: Research, Trends, Problems," in Davis and Meyer, *op. cit.*, 366-403.

Welt, Mildred G., "The National Council of Jewish Women," in *The American Jewish Year Book 1944-1945* (Philadelphia: The Jewish Publication Society of America, 1944), 55-72.

Index

481